CHAHAR   JEHOL

Sui-yüan

Chang-chia-kou

Ta-t'ung   Nan-k'ou
Peking
Lukaochiao   Hsia-tien

Fu-ku   Ping-hsing Pass
Shen-mu   Paoting   Tientsin

Tsang-chow

-yao-pao

T'ai-yüan   CHIHLI
(HOPEH)

SHANSI

Tai-hang Shan   Huang Ho   Tsi-nan

u County   SHANTUNG

Lo-yang

HONAN   K'ai-feng

Tou-fu-tien
Tan-feng
Man-ch'uan Pass   Hsü-ch'ang   Wu-chia-chi
Ching-tzu Pass

ch'uan   Hsin-chi
Huang-ch'uan   Shang-ch'eng   KIANGSU
Kuang-shan   Ku-shih   Peng-pu
Teng-hsien   Lo-shan   Cheng-yang Pass
Hsin-yeh   Hsin-yang   Ho-ch'iu
Wang-chia-tien   Liu-an   Ho-fei
Sha-wo   Chin-chia-chai   Yangtze
Hsuan-hua-tien   San-ho-chien   Huo-shan
Ch'i-li-p'ing   Ma-ch'eng   Ma-pu   Shanghai
E   H   Lo-yang-tien   Sung-fou   Li-chia-chi   Su-chia-pu
An-lu   Hankow   Ying-shan
Huang-pei   Yi-shui   ANWHEI
Yun-meng   Huang-kang
Ho-k'ou
Huang-an   Kuang-chi   Huang-mei   Ning-po
Hung-hu Lake   Kao-ch'iao   Kiu-kiang
Wu-hsueh   Lu-shan (Ku-ling)
Ma-hui-ling   CHEKIANG
Ping-chiang   Nanchang   Mu-lan Mountain
Changsha   Li-chia-tu
Liu-yang   Chin-hsien
Ch'ang-sha   Chang-shu   Fu-chou
N   Yung-feng-Lung-kang
Chi-an   Ning-tu   Ch'ang-ti
Fu-t'ien
Ching-kang-shan   FUKIEN
Kan-chou   Ch'ang-t'ing
Hui-ch'ang   Jui-chin
Chun-men-ling   Wu-p'ing County
Hsun-wu   Shang-hang
Sung-k'ou   San-ho-pa
Mei-hsien   Ta-p'u   Chang-chou
-wei   Ch'ao-chou
Canton   P'u-ning   Swatow
-ch'ao-ch'ing   Liu-sha   T'ang-k'eng
Tungkuan   Lu-feng   Chia-tzu Harbor
Lo-ting   Hai-feng
Hu-men
Kuan-chung   Hong Kong   Pearl River

YELLOW SEA   Dairen

EAST CHINA SEA

TAIWAN

KIANGSI

T'ung   T'ing   Kan

THE RISE OF THE
CHINESE COMMUNIST PARTY
1928-1938

Volume Two of the Autobiography of Chang Kuo-t'ao

THE RISE OF THE CHINESE COMMUNIST PARTY 1928-1938

*Volume Two of
the Autobiography of Chang Kuo-t'ao*

by Chang Kuo-t'ao

THE UNIVERSITY PRESS OF KANSAS
Lawrence, Manhattan, Wichita

© 1972 by the University Press of Kansas
Library of Congress Catalog Card Number 76-141997
Standard Book Number 7006-0088-4
Printed in the United States of America

Designed by Fritz Reiber

CONTENTS

v

ABBREVIATIONS

CC: Central Committee
CCP: Chinese Communist Party
CEC: Central Executive Committee
CPSU: Communist Party of the Soviet Union
CSC: Central Standing Committee
CYC: Communist Youth Corps
ECCI: Executive Committee of the Communist International
KMT: Kuomintang (The Nationalist Party of China)
SYC: Socialist Youth Corps
The shortened form Comintern is used for the Communist International

FROM OPPORTUNISM
TO ADVENTURISM

CHAPTER

Volume one of my autobiography dealt with the rise of the Chinese Communist Party (hereafter CCP) from 1919 to 1927—from its roots in the May Fourth Movement until its break with the Kuomintang (hereafter KMT) during the period of the Wuhan government—at which time the CCP was on the verge of collapse. The question then was where the CCP should go. It is worth our mentioning that the CCP presumed to enter a period of sovietization after the Nanchang Uprising, that neither the concept of sovietization nor its practice met the needs of the Chinese revolution, and that the CCP has since gone astray and become leftist.

Summing up the lessons that we learned during the period of KMT-CCP cooperation, I may say that the National revolution was indeed imperative to the Chinese revolution, being its primary mission, and that KMT-CCP cooperation was absolutely necessary because the KMT represented the aspiration of the Chinese people for a strong and independent country, while the CCP, biased towards the interests of the peasants and the workers, was the left wing of that revolutionary force. However, the policy concerning KMT-CCP cooperation was wrong. The CCP disregarded the resolution of its Second National Congress, no longer wanting to remain a minority party, and decided to speculate and infiltrate the

1

KMT in an attempt to control it. Therefore, we may say that the CCP's policy of joining the KMT was one of opportunism.

The missions of the National revolution did not end in spite of the KMT-CCP split. The National revolution was still in the early stages of development when the Wuhan government was about to terminate in the summer of 1927. At that time the Northern Expedition had not yet been completed, the warlords and other reactionary forces were still active, and China was still a long way from being unified. In addition, since the unequal treaties had not yet been abrogated, the big powers not only possessed their Concessions in Shanghai, violating the territorial rights of China and controlling her economy, but also were able to use their armed forces and gunboats to interfere with the internal affairs of China and to oppose the Chinese revolution. The more the Chinese revolution advanced toward North China, the greater was the opposition that it encountered from the Japanese forces of aggression. In spite of the facts that Chiang Kai-shek had enforced a purge of Chinese Communists within the KMT and that Wang Ching-wei had then broken with the CCP, the KMT was still fighting against the warlords of the Fengtien clique and did not collude with the big powers such as Japan. The CCP's biggest mistake was its failure to realize this point and that the National revolution had not yet succeeded, even though the KMT and CCP had split and a lot of CCP members had been killed by the KMT. The modern history of China would have been different had the CCP at that time continued to call upon the people to make joint efforts for the sake of the National revolution, to fight against their primary enemies—the imperialists and the warlords—and to oppose the KMT's reactionary act of purging Chinese Communists and breaking with the CCP.

The unchangeable policy of the Communist International (hereafter Comintern) impaired the CCP and the Chinese revolution. The policy was that due to the KMT-CCP split, sovietization should ensue; the agrarian revolution should replace the frustrated national liberation movement; and the leadership of the proletariat should ensue, because Chiang Kai-shek's reactionary acts implied the end of the bourgeois revolution. These concepts made the Chinese Communists deceive themselves as well as others. By means of so-called dialectics, they emphasized their opposition to the Chiang Kai-shek regime. They considered these their most important tasks in order to oppose the imperialists. They simply did not realize that this shift in the purpose of the revolution from opposing foreign countries to opposing the Nationalist government helped the Japanese forces of aggression and almost destroyed the CCP.

They did not give up the Soviet movement until they were in great difficulties and were forced to ask Chiang Kai-shek to allow them to participate in a joint movement of resistance against Japan. The second KMT-CCP cooperation to resist the Japanese put an end to the Soviet movement. I will give a detailed account of this later.

Now, let me start with the Nanchang Uprising. The August 1 Nanchang Uprising was a CCP armed rebellion against the KMT after the KMT-CCP split. Nominally it was a joint KMT-CCP action, but actually it was led entirely by the CCP's Front Committee. As far as CCP policy changes were concerned, this uprising was a transitional stage, because the CCP entered the new era of sovietization soon after the failure of this uprising. This event actually spearheaded the CCP's uprising policy, and it was full of adventures. Subsequent uprisings, such as the Autumn Crop Uprising and the Canton Uprising, contained even greater degrees of adventurism. The official record of the CCP indicated that this was a shift between two extremes—from rightist opportunism to leftist adventurism. But I would like to revise this phraseology. The CCP's policy of joining the KMT was radical rightist opportunism, but neither the Comintern nor the CCP admitted this, making only a few criticisms regarding some errors in executing this policy. The policy of sovietization was radical adventurism, but the Comintern and the CCP would not admit this either, only criticizing a few obviously hasty moves.

I believe these criticisms of mine are fair and impartial, because they are not intended to show off my foresight, but are based on my bitter experience. I was very unhappy as I left Hankow for Kiukiang by boat on the evening of July 26, 1927. The deaths of a great many CCP members aroused my indignation. I was in a dilemma because I wanted to rise in revolt, but I did not think that we had any hope of success in the Nanchang Uprising. I resented the leadership of the Comintern, but I could not break away from it. Although I fully realized that it was a big mistake for CCP members to join the KMT, I could not imagine what our future would be like after we changed this policy. I was further disturbed by the facts that the Comintern was trying to stop the Nanchang Uprising, that Lominadze was an all-out leftist adventurist, and that Ch'ü Ch'iu-pai was gambling. In short, I was troubled by indignation, a desire to revolt, vexation, bewilderment, and worry about the serious consequences of the uprising in case it should fail. Only General Galen's sincere suggestion was something of a comfort to me. I was of the opinion that it would be more feasible for both the CCP's military force and Chang Fa-k'uei's Fourth Front Army to return to Kwangtung and that I should talk them into doing this.

I arrived in Kiukiang on the morning of the twenty-seventh. It was very crowded at the waterfront, as a large number of Communists and KMT leftists had come to this port from Wuhan. Most of them were waiting for transportation to Nanchang, and some of them were trying to sneak to cities on the lower reaches of the Yangtze, such as Shanghai. They discussed the current situation, and CCP leaders took advantage of that opportunity to ingratiate themselves with KMT leftists in an attempt to increase the influence and force of the Nanchang Uprising. This was also a port for military transshipment. The Fourth Army was being transferred from Wuhan to Nanchang via Kiukiang. At Kiukiang, I soon located Ho Ch'ang, a member of the CC of the CCP; Kao Yu-han, a political instructor at Wuhan Military Academy; Yün Tai-ying, a member of the CCP Front Committee; Liao Ch'ien-wu, director of the Political Department of the Fourth Army; and Kuan Hsiang-ying, a member of the CC of the CCP; and we held a meeting. I told them briefly about the resolution of the July 26 session of the Central Standing Committee (hereafter CSC), but they were unanimous in saying that the plan for the Nanchang Uprising had to be executed and that it was too late to make changes in it. Yün Tai-ying, especially, was extremely radical in his view.

I asked Yün why we could not reconsider the plan; and he said that it had been decided upon before my arrival and that they had not thought it necessary to wait for me. In addition, he accused the Comintern and the leaders of the CCP of thwarting the Chinese revolution and of causing thousands upon thousands of our comrades to be killed, and he said that their leadership had collapsed completely. He said that everything was set for the uprising and that he would rather die than obey this "international instruction" requesting them to withhold their action. He emphasized that they should act according to their plan despite the Comintern and the leaders of the CCP, and he also threatened to expel me if I continued to demoralize them.

I was shocked by his resentment. He was an honest and polite man, and he had always been friendly to me. He was nicknamed Gandhi in the CCP, because he had no enemies and no desire to compete with others. My feelings after he finished speaking were very complex. He insisted on the uprising, and it was obvious that he had stored up his resentment for a long time and had not had an opportunity to express it until then. I admired him for his resoluteness, and was ashamed of myself for my inability to cope with Lominadze with such resoluteness as his. I also felt that I myself and the leaders of the CCP had lost our prestige in leadership. I was very sorry and I made no further comments except to suggest, in a low voice, postponement of our discussion until after our arrival in Nanchang.

I had a two-day stopover at Kiukiang while I waited for a train, so I did not leave for Nanchang until the twenty-ninth, accompanied by Yün Tai-ying. At that time the Nanchang-Kiukiang Railroad was in very poor shape, with very few cars running on it, most of which were being used for military transportation. Although there were no regularly scheduled passenger or freight trains on this railroad, we had to be patient and wait for a train, since this was the only transportation available. In those two days Yün Tai-ying and I worked very hard on such matters as dispatching a few men to Shanghai in secret to organize a propaganda campaign and action against Wang Ching-wei for his break with the Communists and also to organize clandestine operations there. All those matters were based on the assumption that the Nanchang Uprising would take place as scheduled.

Soon after my arrival in Nanchang on the morning of July 30, I had a meeting with Chou En-lai, Li Li-san, P'eng P'ai, Yün Tai-ying, T'an P'ing-shan, Yeh T'ing, Chou I-ch'un, and several others. I started the meeting with a very detailed account of the July 26 session of the CSC, and requested that they familiarize me with the situation in Nanchang. The main points of my account were that the primary concern of the Comintern and its representative in Hankow was whether the Nanchang Uprising could succeed; that we could not expect any assistance from the Soviet military advisers, nor could we expect any financial support from the Comintern; that the directive from the Comintern was obviously intended to stop the uprising; that General Galen's proposal to move our forces and those of General Chang Fa-k'uei back to Canton together was worth our attention; and that I had been sent to investigate actual conditions there and to discuss the problem with them again.

The conference room was filled with a tense atmosphere. Some of the participants had to leave in a hurry to meet Ho Lung and others at a special committee meeting, while the rest of them had urgent business to take care of. They were too tense and anxious to discuss such things as chances of success and alteration of the plan, and they would be angry with anyone who made a discouraging remark.

Soon after I finished speaking, Li Li-san said hastily and briefly, "It's all been arranged. Ha! Ha! Why should we reconsider it?" Except for me, Yeh T'ing was the only one who held an opposing view. He was of the opinion that it would not be easy for the Nanchang Uprising to succeed, that it would be more advisable for the CCP forces to return to Kwangtung in conjunction with Chang Fa-k'uei's forces, and that CCP members would be safer if they would hide in the Fourth Army. Yeh T'ing and Ho Lung always disagreed somewhat. Therefore, Yeh T'ing said calmly, immediately after Li Li-san, "Perhaps it is better for us to postpone our action until later." As Yeh was a troop commander, his words worried T'an P'ing-shan a great deal. So T'an said in a threatening manner, "If our comrades in the Army should fail to act now, it would be very hard to convince ourselves that all of our previous military operations were the military operations of our Party." Chou En-lai backed him up and said hastily, "We'd better act now."

In spite of the strange atmosphere, I reiterated my ignorance of the local situation, the concern of the Comintern over the chances of success of the uprising, and the basis for General Galen's attempt to postpone that action. My remarks irritated Chou En-lai. As he did not like lengthy discussions, he said angrily, "This is not in agreement with what the leaders of the CCP sent me here for. I will have to resign my position, and I will not attend today's special committee meeting if we do not act now."

Chou En-lai's anger was the culmination of that tense meeting. It was very obvious that except for Yeh T'ing and myself, none of the participants wanted to alter their decision. It seemed that they had already "mounted the tiger," so it was too late to change their minds. What I actually wanted was only to reopen the discussion. As I had no intention of insisting on changing the plan, I did not want to go too far. So I did nothing more than say just a few words in criticism of Chou En-lai's attempt to threaten us with his resignation. Then they changed the subject and began to discuss some urgent matters, while I interviewed some of the comrades individually in order to find out about local conditions.

The first one that I talked to was Li Li-san, who insisted that the uprising was all set and that it was too late to make any changes in it. His two primary reasons for not being able to stop the uprising were first, that they should not violate the secret agreement between the CCP and Ho Lung, and second, that if the plan for the uprising was to be changed, then they would not be able to keep their plan for the uprising secret. Li Li-san, like other CCP leaders, was not willing to discuss the chances for success, as if this subject were a devil that might hamper their actions. Nor did he especially emphasize the need to rise in revolt, as if the uprising would still not be enough to stop everything. Therefore, he reiterated the phrase "It's too late to stop it and too late to make any changes." Moreover, there were other comrades who shared his view.

Li Li-san gave me a detailed account of the relationship between the CCP and Ho Lung. He explained, "Ho Lung used to be a bandit. In the past the relationship between him and the CCP was not very close. Now that he is determined to follow the CCP, we should not let him down. We and Ho have sworn to act together, have gotten into a position from which there is no retreat, and have determined to go ahead, no matter what the consequences may be. Any change now will cause a serious misunderstanding." Li also warned us, saying, "Ho is a discontented and suspicious person who is displeased with Chang Fa-k'uei. He thinks that his history and background would prevent him from becoming somebody in the National Revolutionary Army and that he would be disarmed sooner or later. If we change our plan and cooperate with Chang Fa-k'uei, he may consider us to be double-crossers and perhaps will try to make the first move and inform Chang of our plan in order to defend himself and lay all the blame on us." In order to supplement Li Li-san's explanation, Chou En-lai said, "Ho Lung has decided to take part in the uprising and has secretly obtained the unanimous consent of all division commanders under his command. They all think that this is the only way for them to rise to higher positions. As they have all been informed of the entire plan, together with the launching time of the uprising, it would be inadvisable to make any changes." Then, T'an P'ing-shan, who was the first person to talk Ho Lung into participating in the uprising, also said to me, "In addition to his fears, Ho Lung has the ambition of taking Chang Fa-k'uei's place. We should take advantage of his ambition and make him commander-in-chief. Any contact that we have with Chang Fa-k'uei will make Ho suspicious of us."

Li Li-san also gave me a detailed account of the fact that the secret plan for the uprising would soon become known to the enemy because too many people already knew about it; moreover, it was not hard for people to sense it due to the movement of our personnel, the wording of our propaganda, and the attitudes of some of our comrades. He warned me, "The present situation has made it impossible for us to cooperate with Chang Fa-k'uei or to return to Kwangtung together with his forces to set up a new base for the National revolution there even if he is sincerely willing to do so, because he will not remain friendly to us once he arrives in Nanchang and begins to realize that we had plotted an uprising against him." Then Chou En-lai joined us in this discussion. We tried to find out how great the possibility was that the secret would be divulged. Those who already knew the secret plan exceeded one hundred, including important CCP cadres, more than ten KMT leftists such as Chang Shu-shih, and senior officers of Ho Lung's forces. In addition, we were communicating with many places at that time. Correspondence, telegrams, and personal contacts were exchanged daily between Nanchang, Kiukiang, and Hankow. We also had to communicate with Chu Teh, commander of the Training Regiment of the Third Army at Fu-chou, and Yu Sa-tu, the leader of the Workers' and Peasants' Army at P'ing-chiang, Hunan, requesting them to act according to schedule. Therefore, our conclusion was that it was impossible for us to keep this secret or cover it up, and that it was too late to cancel some of those actions.

On the basis of this conclusion, I expressed my support of the decision of the Front Committee and declared that the uprising plan could not be changed. I told them that I would take full responsibility for our inability to comply with the Comintern's directive and for how to reply to the leaders of the CCP. Yeh T'ing also expressed his willingness to act no matter what might happen. I am a responsible man. I felt that I must strictly carry out the mission assigned to me by the leaders of the CCP, but that it was more important that I should try to seek some hope of success for the Nanchang Uprising. Therefore I did not pay too much attention to the actions of those comrades who opposed me at Kiukiang and Nanchang. They did not fully understand me even when I reiterated that I did not radically oppose the uprising and then expressed my support of it.

We did not discuss anything concerning alteration of the plan at an emergency session of the CCP Front Committee on the morning of the thirty-first; instead we decided to carry out the plan according to schedule. All participants in the meeting then knew that Chang Fa-k'uei, Wang Ching-wei, and Sun Fu had arrived at Lu-shan and were convening a meeting there; there were some indications that they were trying to cope with the Nanchang situation. In view of such an act on their part, we had to have some discussion about the steps that we should take. At first the Nanchang Uprising was scheduled to start on the morning of the thirty-first, but at my request it was postponed until the morning of August 1. Based on this decision, all of us were assigned some emergency work and were sent away to do it individually. The Nanchang Uprising of August 1, 1927, finally took place and became one of the major events in the CCP's history of struggle.

In order to understand the development of the Nanchang Uprising, we must first of all understand something about the leadership of the CCP. It seemed that incompetence and disorderliness on the part of the leaders of the CCP predestined the Nanchang Uprising to failure. In order to explain this, let me first tell you something about T'an P'ing-shan. He began to act in the Nanchang-Kiukiang area without having the consent of the leaders of the CCP. He said that he would create a new situation in Nanchang, implying that he would plan an uprising in Nanchang and actually lead it, disregarding the authority of the Comintern and the CC of the CCP until he could achieve some success.

T'an's ambition was not compatible with his ability. During the period of KMT-CCP cooperation and the KMT's subsequent reorganization, he had held important positions. He had had an important role in the CCP from the very beginning; at the same time he was a member of the CC and concurrently head of the Organization Department of the KMT. Those high positions made him very conceited. He loved to boast that he had formerly been a member of the T'ung-meng Hui and that he had widespread connections with KMT leftists. Furthermore, he was one of the few senior members and leaders of the CCP, and he was liked by Stalin. Therefore, it seemed that he was the best representative of the leftist revolutionary forces. However, the fact was that neither the KMT leftists nor CCP members had much confidence in him. Perhaps he was not fully aware of this fact.

During the late period of the Wuhan government, the Comintern and the leaders of the CCP were displeased with T'an and blamed him for being too weak when he tendered his resignation to the National government from his position as head of the Department of Agricultural Affairs. Perhaps it was this criticism that fired up his determination to act on his own. On the eve of the Nanchang Uprising he showed his hatred for the Comintern and the leaders of the CCP in both his words and his attitude. He vented his spleen on me because he thought that I was an orthodox member of the CCP leadership. When someone proposed that the Declaration of the Uprising that he had submitted be given to me for revision, he objected to that proposal and angrily accused me of attempting to monopolize everything. However, his objection was not supported by the other comrades; on the contrary, it disgusted many of them.

After the outbreak of the Nanchang Uprising, T'an was made chairman of the KMT Revolutionary Committee. He was the man who had helped Ho Lung rise to power, and it looked as though he could also lead the CCP Front Committee, by means of which he could exercise his command over such important military commanders as Yeh T'ing. Everything seemed to be what he had dreamed of. Therefore he put on airs and acted as if he were a big shot. Nevertheless, others treated him with indifference, and nobody was willing to support him. Then he began to realize his problem and to understand that he should not openly oppose the CCP leadership. He therefore tried to improve relations between himself and others, including me, and he tried to show more respect for others; but his efforts did not succeed, because none of the important cadres believed that T'an could become the central figure inside or outside the Party.

Undoubtedly at that time the armies of Yeh T'ing and Ho Lung needed a political banner. They needed solidarity in order to boost their morale, and they also needed a forceful call for support. I mentioned this fact to my comrades, but I did not know what to do about it. Our failure to provide an influential spokesman during the Nanchang Uprising greatly weakened the CCP leadership.

Chou En-lai, chairman of the Front Committee, was capable of guiding the political affairs, but he did not want to do so. He did not talk much about politics, and he seldom called a committee meeting. When a meeting was held, important policies were never discussed. As Chou then served concurrently as director of the Staff Group of the Revolutionary Committee, he concentrated his attention on military affairs. Perhaps he was of the opinion that military victory was first in importance because it would enable the rebel forces to get a foothold in the Tung Chiang (East River) area of Kwangtung. Perhaps he thought that military victory was a prerequisite to everything else, and premature talk about political leadership would be either empty talk or asking for trouble. Most of the important figures of the CCP such as Li Li-san were of the same opinion as Chou En-lai. They emphasized the need for uprisings and thought that anyone who doubted or opposed this policy was unreliable and irresolute. Such disregard was the basis for adventurism.

I was in quite an awkward situation at that time, but I could not do anything about it. I should have returned to Hankow to give my report to Central Headquarters, but interrupted communications prevented me from doing so. I had to follow the movement of the troops. I was not only opposed by T'an P'ing-shan, but was also misunderstood by such comrades as Li Li-san, Chou En-lai, Yün Tai-ying, and others. They thought that I was irresolute in my attitude towards the uprising, and that I was engaging in wishful thinking with regard to Chang Fa-k'uei. I knew that my leadership and prestige had suffered damage. Though I attended the meetings of the Front Committee as usual and did what I could, I was unable to save the CCP leadership from confusion and disorderliness.

On the eve of the uprising, all participating troops moved rapidly towards Nanchang from all directions, and the CCP personnel from the Kiukiang area also poured into Nanchang. It seemed that Chang Fa-k'uei had already found out something about the forthcoming uprising. On July 31, Chang left Kiukiang for Nanchang via the Nanchang-Kiukiang Railroad, but he was interrupted in the vicinity of the Ma-hui-ling station. Nieh Jung-chen, who was to direct the uprising activities there, reported that when Chang Fa-k'uei arrived at Ma-hui-ling, the railroad was no longer open. He alighted and asked the troops who were on the move, "Where are you going? By whose order?" Then he continued, "I am Commander-in-Chief Chang, and I command you to halt." For fear that Chang might influence the troops' decision, Nieh Jung-chen had someone set up a machine gun and fire a few warning shots, which compelled Chang to be quiet. Nieh therefore began to direct his troops to destroy the railroad, and he moved his troops from along the railroad beyond Ma-hui-ling towards the Niu-hsing station and the vicinity of Nanchang, posting security sentries there.

The Nanchang Uprising was scheduled to start at three o'clock on the morning of August 1. The first step was to disarm the government troops in the city who did not participate in the uprising. By July 31 the troops of Yeh T'ing and Ho Lung had been deployed to strategic locations in the city of Nanchang and its suburbs. Yeh T'ing was in command of all these troops. That evening I stayed in Yeh's divisional headquarters. It was not yet three o'clock when I heard shots. Pretty soon about three thousand government troops under Chu P'ei-te that had been stationed in the city were disarmed without violent resistance. Soon after the uprising started, Yeh T'ing had several telephone calls from his subordinates telling him that the encircled government troops had expressed their willingness to surrender and to participate in the uprising. He answered those calls in a resolute manner with, "Let's disarm them first." All of the government institutions in Nanchang were captured before daybreak. During the morning of August 1 all of Nanchang was occupied.

Our immediate problem then was to establish a new government and work out an appropriate military strategy.

When we discussed the problem of the type of government we were going to set up, what T'an P'ing-shan, myself, and others contemplated was either a formal national government or a provisional government; none of us proposed a Soviet regime. Most of us were of the opinion that a formal government needed a secure territory, which could be obtained by additional military victories. We also knew that the Comintern favored a powerful national government and opposed Trotsky's proposal to set up a Soviet regime. Therefore, we decided to organize a provisional government which would be called the Revolutionary Committee of the Chinese Nationalist Party (KMT).

The primary missions of the Revolutionary Committee of the Chinese Nationalist Party were: (1) To call upon the people to support Dr. Sun Yat-sen's Three Principles of the People and his Three Policies; and (2) to convene the KMT's national congress, reorganize the KMT, set up a National government at the opportune moment, and then launch a punitive expedition against the rebels in the Wuhan and Nanking areas. As a matter of fact, the declaration that we made at Nanchang was based on these two points.

The Revolutionary Committee was composed of twenty-five persons including T'an P'ing-shan, Soong Ch'ing-ling, Wu Yu-chang, Teng Yen-ta, Ho Hsiang-ning, Yün Tai-ying, Chang Shu-shih, Kuo Mo-jo, Chou En-lai, myself, Li Li-san, Chang Fa-k'uei, Ho Lung, P'eng P'ai, Lin Chu-han, and Chu Teh. This slate was decided upon by the CCP Front Committee, proposed by T'an P'ing-shan at a meeting, and accepted. That meeting was also attended by KMT leftists. The newly appointed committee members were immediately sworn in, and they elected T'an P'ing-shan chairman and Wu Yu-chang secretary general. Of those KMT leftists, Chang Shu-shih was the only one present; the others, such as Soong Ch'ing-ling, Ho Hsiang-ning, and Teng Yen-ta, did not show up. We placed their names on the list in order to take advantage of the name KMT. As to Chang Fa-k'uei, he actually opposed the uprising, but the CCP also placed his name on the list in order to win him over and please the troops of the Fourth Army. KMT leftists who actually participated in the Nanchang Uprising were Chang Shu-shih, Chiang Chi-huan, Hsiao Ping-chang, and some middle and junior cadres of the KMT. Therefore, although the Revolutionary Committee used the name of the KMT, it was completely controlled by the CCP.

In addition, the formulation of a proper military strategy was an even more urgent problem. A portion of the Second Front Army under Chang Fa-k'uei's command was approaching Nanchang from Kiukiang on a so-called punitive expedition against the "rebels." Chu P'ei-te was rallying his troops at Chi-an and Chang-shu in preparation for a counterattack on Nanchang. It was easy for both Nanking and Wuhan to send their troops to Kiangsi to reinforce Chang and Chu. Under these circumstances, we concluded that Nanchang was suffering enemy threats from every direction and was obviously not a good foothold. There were two opinions about what course of action we should take. Some of us favored moving south to take the Tung Chiang (East River) area of Kwangtung, using the Ch'ao-chou, Swatow area as a base for unifying all of Kwangtung Province and then launching a northward expedition.[1] Some advocated moving west to invade Hunan in order to occupy a certain amount of land in conjunction with the Hunan Peasant Army and then use that area as a base for further expansion.[2] Ho Lung was very interested in the latter proposal, because he had formerly operated in the area of western Hunan. However, the majority voted for the southward movement on the grounds that the Tung Chiang area was poorly defended and an easy place to capture, that we would not suffer enemy threats from every direction there, that it would be easier for us to make a strong expansion there because we had laid a good foundation of the peasant movement in that area, and that our occupation of Swatow, a seaport, would make it possible to receive aid from Russia. Moreover, most of the people were not willing to go to Hunan. At that time they questioned such policies as sovietization, guerrilla warfare, the agrarian revolution, and so forth. In fact, Mao Tse-tung ran a great risk in voluntarily going to Hunan. At first he even attempted to lead the Peasant Army to Nanchang to participate in the uprising, but he was unable to do so due to lack of time.

How to expand our military strength was another difficult problem. The Twentieth Army under Ho Lung was weak in combat strength. Its First Division, under the command of Ho Ching-tsai, and its Second Division, under the command of Ch'in Hsien-yuan, had three regiments each, which were under strength and whose weapons were very old. Its Third Division, under the command of Chou I-ch'un, had only one regiment. Therefore it was an imperative task to strengthen the Twentieth Army. The Twenty-fourth Division, under the command of Yeh T'ing, and the Seventy-third Regiment, an independent regiment under the command of Chou Shih-ti, were the main forces used in the Nanchang Uprising. The CCP then resolved to activate another regiment so that it could join that independent regiment to form the Twenty-fifth Division. The CCP was trying to unite the Twenty-fourth Division, the Twenty-fifth Division, and the Tenth Division, under Ts'ai T'ing-chieh, to form the Eleventh Army, making Yeh T'ing and Ts'ai T'ing-chieh its commander and deputy commander respectively. Ts'ai T'ing-chieh, who succeeded Ch'en Ming-shu as commander of the Tenth Division, which was stationed in the vicinity of Nanchang, had assumed a neutral attitude towards the Nanchang Uprising and did not express his support of it until after strenuous persuasion by the CCP. Chu Teh had formerly been the party representative of the KMT in Yang Sen's forces. When Yang forsook the Wuhan government, Chu Teh left Yang and joined his friend Chu P'ei-te, and the latter made Chu Teh commander of his Training Regiment. Later Chu P'ei-te deported the CCP members who were in his forces, but he kept Chu Teh in spite of the fact that Chu Teh was also a CCP member. He did this because he and Chu Teh had been friends since they had served with the Yunnan forces. Therefore, the CCP then granted Chu Teh a special favor and made him commander of the Ninth Army in the hope that he could influence Chu P'ei-te's army and convert it into a new military power.

After these political and military arrangements had been made, the Revolutionary Committee finally took shape. Chairman T'an P'ing-shan was the leader, handling both internal and external affairs. Wu Yu-chang, in his capacity as secretary general, activated a Secretariat, which was the administrative arm of the Revolutionary Committee. Within the committee, the Staff Group was set up, with Chou En-lai as its director, Liu Po-ch'eng as its chief-of-staff, Ho Lung as Front Commander, Yeh T'ing as Deputy Front Commander, and Kuo Mo-jo as director of its Political Department. The Staff Group corresponded to the National Military Council of the Nationalist government. Within the Revolutionary Committee there were also the Peasants' and Workers' Committee, with me as chairman and Li Li-san, Kuo Liang, P'eng P'ai, Ch'en Yin-lin, and several others as members, which was responsible for leading the peasant and labor movements and for establishing local governments; the Party Affairs Committee, with Chang Shu-shih as chairman, which was responsible for leading the KMT's organizational work; the Propaganda Committee with Yün Tai-ying as chairman; the Finance Committee, with Lin Chu-han as chairman; and the Political Defense Bureau, which was added to the Revolutionary Committee later, with Li Li-san as director. These units were simultaneously party, political, and military in nature. They inherited some characteristics of the

Nationalist government of the KMT, but they also had some CCP peculiarities.

The platform of the Revolutionary Committee was very much like that of the KMT during the early stages of the Northern Expedition. The most extraordinary aspect of it was the decree that a landlord's land should be confiscated and redistributed among poor peasants if its total area exceeded 200 mou (a Chinese acre). This was the first announcement of the CCP's land-confiscation policy, although it was announced under the guise of being Dr. Sun Yat-sen's policy of "land to the tiller." It also decreed that village administrative bodies should be set up through elections. As a result of the elections, worker and peasant organizations would of course be the framework of those administrative bodies. Our platform was not too different from the earlier KMT platform on such points as opposition to imperialism and warlordism, abolition of unnecessary taxes and levies, reduction of land rental and interest rates, and so forth.

Because of the military situation, the Revolutionary Committee had to leave Nanchang before it could establish operations and get its propaganda campaign into full swing. The southward movement of CCP forces caused a great deal of uneasiness both within and outside the Party. Many people felt that the CCP troops were trying to evade the government forces. CCP Central Headquarters at Wuhan had instructed those regional branches and the worker and peasant organization to stop responding to the Nanchang Uprising. Therefore, the Front Committee could no longer expect any action from the workers and peasants in Hunan and Hupeh. The committee also realized that it was too late to rush Yu Sa-tu's troops, which had organized an uprising at P'ing-chiang, to Nanchang to link up with the main forces. Therefore, Yu was instructed to remain there and act at his own discretion. Later on, Yu's forces became the skeleton of the Workers' and Peasants' Red Army of Hunan, which was organized by Mao Tse-tung.

On August 5, the forces of the uprising, escorting the huge Revolutionary Committee, moved towards the Ch'ao-chou, Swatow area of Kwangtung through Fu-chou and Jui-chin in eastern Kiangsi. Except for displaying the banner of the Revolutionary Committee, this army was no different from other units of the National Revolutionary Army, although its morale was even worse than that of those units during the early stages of the Northern Expedition. It was summer, and the baggage train was heavy and required a great deal of civilian labor. Many civilian baggage bearers who had been pressed into service deserted, as did many soldiers.

It was then that the CCP cadres first learned something about military movements.

The march on the first day was very disorderly, and it was only ninety li in length. By the time that they reached Li-chia-tu, where they spent the night, many of the troops had blisters on their feet. The VIP's tried to ride in sedan chairs, but they could not find bearers. Walking seemed to be the most difficult thing in the world. When they started on their journey, most of the people tried to carry with them as many personal belongings as possible, but during the march those things became very heavy burdens. One's favorite small article, which weighed only a few ounces, became as detestable as anything else. Therefore they decided to get rid of these burdens, as the majority of them requested. On a river bank at Li-chia-tu, fancy clothes and other articles were piled up like a colorful hill and were destroyed by fire in order to show the determination of those cadres. This determination might be regarded as the first step by CCP members towards becoming members of the proletariat. However, some of them could not help asking themselves with a sigh, "Why were we so stupid? Why didn't we give those things to local civilians?" At that time CCP members would act on the impulse of the moment. This story proves that we always learned how to be smart when we were making mistakes.

Chou En-lai waited for me on the roadside somewhere between Li-chia-tu and Fu-chou, wanting to discuss an important matter with me. He told me in a sad voice, "According to an escapee, the Tenth Division under the command of Ts'ai T'ing-chieh defected to the enemy side and fled eastward when it reached Chin-hsien. Pretending that he wanted to address the officers, Ts'ai assembled them and arrested and killed Fan Meng-sheng, commander of the Thirtieth Regiment, and about thirty CCP members.[3] Only one of our comrades escaped and returned safely, while several dozen others are missing. Therefore our assets in the Tenth Division have been completely destroyed."

Then Chou continued, "It was my fault, and I should take all the blame." He had a special reason for saying this. When Chang Fa-k'uei's Second Front Army was moving towards Nanchang, Yeh T'ing's division was in the vanguard, with Ts'ai T'ing-chieh's division following it. On the eve of the Nanchang Uprising, Ts'ai's troops were stationed in the vicinity of Nanchang. Ts'ai himself did not arrive in Nanchang from Kiukiang until August 1. At Yeh T'ing's divisional headquarters, it was Chou En-lai, Yeh T'ing, and I who had negotiated with Ts'ai regarding his cooperation. Ts'ai looked uneasy when he arrived at Yeh T'ing's headquarters, probably because he did not take part in planning the uprising. I did not talk very much, because I did not know Ts'ai very well. Chou En-lai talked a lot with Ts'ai to explain the need for the uprising. At the same time Yeh T'ing, as Ts'ai's old friend, urged him by saying, "Buddy! let's say it's a deal, O.K.?" Ts'ai thought a moment and then said that he was willing to take orders from us. Because of Ts'ai's irresolute attitude, most of the members of the Revolutionary Committee and the Staff Group somewhat distrusted him and suggested that some powerful men be sent to bring the Tenth Division under control. But Chou En-lai thought Ts'ai should not be distrusted. Chou made Ts'ai a member of the Staff Group, deputy commander of the Eleventh Army and concurrently commander-in-chief of the left wing, and ordered Ts'ai to move his forces south alone through Chin-hsien. Moreover, Chou told the CCP members in the Tenth Division, such as Fan Meng-sheng, to obey Ts'ai, but he did not caution them against possible dangers. Now that Ts'ai had defected and Fan Meng-sheng and some other CCP members had been killed, it was only natural for Chou to have a guilty conscience because he had failed to take preventive measures.

After Chou finished his report, I felt so sad that I did not comment for a while. I said to him, "This is an irreplaceable loss. Judging from the fact that Ts'ai has moved his forces eastward, I assume that he has no intention of opposing us. It would have been worse if he had stayed with us and defected at a more critical moment after our arrival in the Tung Chiang area. We were too careless in handling this affair, and we should use it as a lesson. This incident, if it becomes known, will affect our morale; we had better keep it secret. Don't be dejected at such a critical moment, and don't say you are to blame and wish to resign. You must face it, no matter what happens." He seemed to be greatly moved and said that he would face it and make the best of it. It was too bad that we lost our most powerful division.

After Ts'ai's defection our strength, including the Revolutionary Committee, totaled about twenty-five thousand men with about thirteen thousand small arms. We marched through the eastern Kiangsi area, where the CCP's influence was slight. At that time we did not have enough cash to procure food and other necessities. We were unable to start mass movements and establish local governments in that area, because all of the personnel of the former local government had fled by Chu P'ei-te's order, and most of the civilians had gone into hiding to avoid the hazards of war. We had to commandeer food all along the way from rich people, and our morale was gradually eroded. Instances of stragglers and cases of malaria were increasing among the troops. These were problems of ours which could not be solved overnight.

The Ninth Army under Chu Teh's command was a very peculiar force. Chu served concurrently as chief of the Public Security Bureau of Nanchang for some time after the Nanchang Uprising. The Ninth Army had about one thousand men when it left Nanchang, including some troops of the Training Regiment, some policemen from Nanchang, a few armed and unarmed personnel from local government units in Nanchang, and a bunch of transport bearers. All of our units participating in the march would request Chu Teh to provide transport bearers, because he knew the local areas in Kiangsi better than they did. Therefore the Ninth Army was frequently assigned such chores as making arrangements for the arrival of the main body of troops, commandeering food, and obtaining civilian labor. The Ninth Army had so many cases of desertion that only three or four hundred troops remained when it arrived at Fu-chou, and its total strength had further decreased to a little over one hundred men by the time that it reached Jui-chin. Several days later these men were transferred to other units, and the designation Ninth Army thus came to an end. At that time I saw Chu Teh frequently. He was very unhappy about the demise of the Ninth Army and said that it could not be helped.

On about August 20 we had a violent battle at Hui-ch'ang with an enemy force under Ch'ien Ta-chun. We defeated and forced it to retreat to Chun-men-ling. As a matter of fact, we encountered Ch'ien's advance unit when we reached Jen-t'ien-shih near Jui-chin. So we occupied the city of Jui-chin to prepare for combat. Our intelligence indicated that Ch'ien Ta-chun's division was located at Hui-ch'ang, ninety li south of Jui-chin, while the enemy force under Huang Shao-hsiung was still in the Hsun-wu area, a considerable distance from Hui-ch'ang. They both had the same task of preventing our forces from moving south. Therefore we decided to defeat them decisively, going after Ch'ien first.

This battle was planned by Liu Po-ch'eng, our chief-of-staff. For the first time Liu, who was rumored to be Liu Po-wen (a renowned ancient militarist), was able to demonstrate that he was a "military genius." According to his operational plan, the Twentieth Army under the command of Ho Lung was to make a frontal attack, while the Eleventh Army under the command of Yeh T'ing was to outflank the enemy on the right. But Liu made a mistake in calculating times and distances. According to to his estimate, the distance between Jui-chin and Hui-ch'ang was ninety li by the highway along the front, and one hundred and ten li by the small trail on the right flank, but actually that small trail was more than one hundred and fifty li. Therefore the outflanking force had not yet reached its attack position when Chou I-ch'un's division of Ho Lung's force was defeated at the front, and Ho had to use his general reserves, the First and Second divisions, as reinforcements. The defeat of Ho Lung's troops enabled the enemy to use part of its frontal strength to reinforce its left flank. Therefore Yeh T'ing's force had to fight a very hard battle before it was finally able to defeat Ch'ien's forces in the vicinity of Hui-ch'ang and then capture the city of Hui-ch'ang. Ch'ien's forces retreated in disorder to Chun-men-ling, ninety li south of Hui-ch'ang. We had to stop our pursuit due to extremely heavy casualties.

Ch'en Keng, who was then a staff officer with the Staff Group, took part in that battle; and he told me something about its course. He said that the fighting between Ch'ien Ta-chun's forces and Yeh T'ing's Eleventh Army was the most violent action he had ever experienced. It was more violent than that of the two T'ung-chiang battles in which Ch'en took part. The hand-to-hand fighting near the city wall of Hui-ch'ang was especially terrible, as most of the middle-grade and junior officers on both sides were schoolmates of Whampoa. They knew each other; some of them had been good friends since childhood; some were classmates at Whampoa; some had served in the same battalion or company. Even though they cursed each other during the battle, they still called each other by their pet names or nicknames. Some shouted, "Why are you Communists revolting?" And others shouted back, "Why are you willing to be the bloodhounds of the counterrevolutionaries?" There were some people on both sides who were in tears while they fought like mad dogs. Ch'en Keng was greatly moved when he witnessed that impressive situation; but he had to refrain himself and urge his men to attack the enemy.

After telling his story, Ch'en Keng made the following comments: "It seems to me that political struggle is so cruel that it can make many old comrades and friends fight with one another. The Whampoa alumni in Ch'ien's forces showed such resoluteness on the battlefield that they must have been deeply indoctrinated by the counterrevolutionaries. Therefore it will not be easy to eliminate the prejudice that exists between the KMT and the CCP. It is not enough to rely only on hard fighting if we want to win." His description and comments gave us a realistic picture of the first battle between the KMT and the CCP.

Ho Lung was formally sworn in as a CCP member soon after the Battle of Hui-ch'ang. His cooperation with the CCP was beyond questioning, but he was not like a Communist in his way of living. He had a huge staff at his army's headquarters. He rode in a sedan chair which required four men to carry it, so he had to keep a dozen chair-bearers. In addition, he had cooks that prepared both Chinese and Western food. Every time that they stopped the march for the night, he would feast himself. There was not much friendship between him and the VIP's of the Revolutionary Committee, including Yeh T'ing. Ho Ching-tsai, commander of the First Division of Ho Lung's forces, was his brother, and Ch'in Kuan-yuan, commander of the Second Division, was a relative of his. They had also been subordinates of Ho Lung's when he was a bandit leader. His troops, acting somewhat like bandits, were poorly disciplined. They did not get along well with troops of the Eleventh Army under Yeh T'ing's command, and Yeh's men called them bandits behind their backs.

Therefore the VIP's of the CCP expressed their admiration for Ho's cooperation, on the one hand, and feared, on the other hand, that the cooperation might fail and something might happen. Someone even said, "We had better watch out. When the situation becomes unfavorable to him, Ho Lung can lead his troops away and return to his former career." For this reason, the VIP's of the CCP frequented Ho's headquarters, enjoyed the exceptionally good food, and chatted with him in order to influence him and promote his friendship. I was one of those who frequented his headquarters and ate and chatted there.

On one occasion Ho Lung told his guests something about his life when he was a bandit. He said triumphantly, "To be a bandit, one must be very clever, and, most important of all, one must be vigilant." He carried his gun with him at all times, putting it beside the pillow while he slept. It had become a habit with him that when he heard something while he was in bed, he automatically reached for his gun. When he was with his troops on the move, he acted like a god and did not appear too often, in order to prevent someone from assassinating him. His cooperation with other forces was for his own benefit, and he used every precaution to prevent loss. He operated many years in the border areas of Szechwan, Kweichow, Hunan, and Hupeh. He cooperated with whoever was powerful there. Should anything go wrong, he would run away or double-cross his partner. He had done this sort of thing many times. His story shocked all of his listeners.

At that time Ho Lung also admired the CCP for its way of doing things. He thought that the CCP's methods were much better than his own had been when he was a bandit. He said that his best idea when he was a bandit was nothing but a simple concept of robbing the rich and aiding the poor, and of taking up the cudgel for the poor; while it was obvious that the CCP had a complete system for doing things, because it had principles, a platform, and the ability to organize the workers and peasants. Ho Lung's philosophy was the then-prevailing bandit-warlordism, or the brigandism which had prevailed during the peasant uprisings in Chinese history. Mao Tse-tung, who used to be a soldier, knew all about "brigandism." In fact, his guerrilla tactics were based on it.

After the Battle of Hui-ch'ang, Chou En-lai and Chou I-ch'un recommended that Ho Lung be admitted to the Party. Their justifications for their recommendation were that Ho showed an attitude of sincere cooperation during the period from the Nanchang Uprising to the Battle of Hui-ch'ang, that he himself had made such a request, and that failure to respond to his request would make him unhappy. Their recommendation was unanimously approved by the Front Committee. However, in the eyes of the average CCP member, Ho Lung was a special member who had been admitted to the Party for the sake of both military and political necessity.

A ceremony for swearing Ho Lung into the Party was held at Jui-chin while we were resting near there after the Hui-ch'ang victory. I officiated at that ceremony. In my capacity as a representative of CCP Central Headquarters, I made a speech advising him to abide by communism, execute the Party's policy, and obey disciplinary regulations. He swore that he was willing to be a faithful CCP member and to do what I advised. Then T'an P'ing-shan, Chou En-lai, Li Li-san, Yün Tai-ying, and several others congratulated him and welcomed the new member. Ho looked tense during the ceremony. He seemed not to know what restrictions he would have to accept. We had a cordial talk after the ceremony. He said that it was less difficult to be admitted into the CCP than to a bandit group or the Brotherhood Association. I pointed out that the internal solidarity of a bandit group or the Brotherhood Association depended entirely on strict discipline; while the CCP depended on the willingness of its members to abide by principles and carry out the Party's policy, in other words, it depended primarily on one's belief and secondarily on discipline. I told him that the disciplinary regulations of the CCP were simple, but that they had to be strictly observed. Later on, when Ho Lung escaped to Shanghai after the complete failure of the Nanchang Uprising, the CCP treated him very well and had someone indoctrinate him with communism everyday. That indoctrination gradually Bolshevized him. This is how we converted a famous bandit leader into a CCP member.

Military movements are decided according to various factors including some unimportant ones. After the Hui-ch'ang victory, we contemplated the following three courses of action: 1. To exploit the victory, attack the survivors of Ch'ien Ta-chun's forces at Chun-men-ling, and then advance through Hsun-wu to capture the Mei-hsien area. 2. To use the Jui-chin, Ch'ang-t'ing area as a base and send a portion of our forces to capture the Ch'ao-chou, Swatow area (Tung Chiang area). 3. To advance through Ch'ang-ting, Shang-hang, and Ta-p'u and attack Ch'ao-chou and Swatow.

However, we were carrying on litters some four hundred soldiers who had been wounded in the Battle of Hui-ch'ang, and we did not want to abandon them. Due to the flight of local people, it was very hard to obtain transport bearers in Kiangsi. However, our troops operating in the Ch'ang-ting area informed us that procurement of transport bearers was not a problem in Fukien, that the wounded and sick soldiers could be shipped to Ch'ao-chou and Swatow in junks on the Han River, and that they had already impressed more than a thousand "big-footed" women (with unbound feet) to serve as litter-bearers. The subsequent arrival of those women at Jui-chin made us very happy. Therefore, we decided to follow the third course of action. Our troops stayed at Jui-chin for about two weeks, then we all crossed the Kiangsi-Fukien border and advanced towards the Ch'ang-ting area.

In the early stages of the CCP, its military movements were rather immature. Its intelligence operations were not good enough to enable it to get information about enemy locations and movements. The organization of troop units, coordination between them, and political work were not good either. CCP military commanders complained that the Revolutionary Committee was a burden that slowed up the march. Therefore, the movement from Jui-chin towards Ch'ao-chou and Swatow through Ch'ang-ting and Shang-hang was made in three successive groups. The first group was the main combat force, which hurried toward the region of Ch'ao-chou and Swatow in order to seize it while its defenses were poor. The second group comprised units of the Revolutionary Committee. The third group was composed of those wounded and sick soldiers who were being transported under the charge of Li Li-san, chief of the Political Defense Bureau, and of a battalion led by Chou Shih-ti which served as the rear guard. Thus the entire force formed a very long procession line. When the advance unit reached Ch'ao-chou and Swatow, the rear guard was still in the area of Ch'ang-ting and Shang-hang.

A lot of things that happened during the march are worth mentioning, and I would like to cite a few of them to help describe that march. Although it was not a rapid march, it exhausted the troops, especially the gentlemanlike intellectuals, and made them look depressed. Under such conditions, we could not conduct political and propaganda work to boost our morale. Yün Tai-ying, who was in charge of this work, often complained and said, "The march has made the officers very exhausted. How can they spare any energy to 'peddle the medical plaster' (propagandize)? As we are occupying civilian houses, impressing civilian labor, and commandeering food during this march, we have frightened all of the civilians away. In this situation, what effect can our propaganda produce? Our political personnel themselves are depressed. How can they boost the morale of the troops?" So he decided to set himself up as an example. He walked in the hot sun bareheaded and barefooted. He lost all of his changes of clothing; the dirty and ragged uniform that he wore was the only one that he had left. On his shoulder was a piece of cloth that served as an all-purpose towel. All of us called him "Gandhi," because he was dark and skinny and his skin was peeling due to too much sun. Then quite a few people followed suit, which greatly moved the soldiers, who would say, "Those VIP's can endure greater hardships than we can." This was an example of our political work at that time.

The Workers' and Peasants' Committee led by me was composed of about forty men. During the march we were busy billeting ourselves, posting security sentries, and trying to find out about local conditions; we had no time to hold meetings, make plans, organize the local workers and peasants, or set up local governments. After we arrived at a village near Ning-tu, the Workers' and Peasants' Committee was billeted on the farm of a wealthy landlord. In the farmyard, P'eng P'ai sighted a suspicious-looking young fellow, and talked to him skillfully in order to find out the truth about him. That young man fell into P'eng's trap and led P'eng to a wood on a small hill to meet his four colleagues. One of them, who was more cautious, said that they belonged to the A-B League,[4] and he began to ask P'eng questions. All of a sudden P'eng drew his gun, taking them by surprise, and disarmed them. At first they planned to gather twenty or thirty men to raid us at night, but we frustrated their plan. This event can give the readers a general idea of the conflict between the KMT and the CCP in the early years. From then on, the name A-B League became something real in our minds.

We left Ch'ang-ting for Shang-hang by boat, but we did not commandeer local boatmen, nor did we collect local hydrographic information. Since several of the committee members had boating experience, we hired two boats and steered them downstream ourselves. We had not traveled far before we encountered very strong currents in a section of the river that was dotted with many big rocks. We fought our way forward, and our paddles and poles were destroyed one after another. Many of those who were steering the boats fell overboard; they were lucky that the water was shallow so that they did not drown. The climax of our danger was when our best poler fell overboard. We traveled about sixty li, then we could not proceed any farther and had to abandon the boats. After we disembarked, we walked into a deserted tract of land.

This tired and hungry team followed a mountain trail. By the time that it was totally dark, we had not yet seen a populated place. At about 10 P.M. we met several passers-by. They told us in southern Fukien dialect that there was a small town of Wu-p'ing County ahead, that Wu-p'ing County and the town were both occupied by bandits, and that they were refugees from there. Their dialect had to be translated before we could understand it. Fortunately there was someone in our group who understood that dialect. Then we began to understand that we were heading for a bandit hangout. They told us that the bandits were very fierce and that it was already too late for us to try to evade them. They also told us that in that town there lived three or four hundred bandits who at that moment were watching a stage show, and that the businessmen of the town were with the bandits.

We pretended to be calm to hide our fear and said to them, "It's all right. We are looking for those bandits. Our army will be here soon." After the passers-by left, we decided to run the risk and go to the town anyhow. We rearranged our team to look like an advance unit, with myself as commander and other committee members disguised as soldiers. Following a trail, we entered the town and billeted ourselves in an uptown bean-curd shop. Kuo Liang, who was short and was acting as my bodyguard, played his part very well. He shouted all kinds of commands and said to the shopkeeper, "By order of our commander, go tell their leader to carry on with their show. This advance unit will stay uptown instead of downtown to avoid any misunderstanding." The bandits stopped their show and took precautions against us, but they did not start any conflict.

We had a hearty meal in that shop. I asked the shopkeeper and his two assistants, who seemed to be spies for the bandit group, "Have you heard the news that our army defeated Ch'ien Ta-chun's forces at Hui-ch'ang?" They said that they had. Then I continued, "Our army intends to take big cities and the entire country. We don't want any trouble with the leader of this town. Go tell the leader of the bandits to come to see me, and perhaps we can appoint him to some position." Then one of the three told me that their big boss was not in town and only a detachment commander was available, that they would pass my words on to him, but that they could not assure us that their big boss would be present. So we went to bed.

When we were leaving there the next morning, the bandits sent a guide to lead us across the mountain and to a small town by a river. We found out that the river was called the Ting River, the one on which we had encountered danger. During the trip, the guide told us that his commander was a very hospitable man who kept his word and did not want any trouble with the Communist Army, that he had ordered his subordinates to take good care of our stragglers, if any, and that maybe he would like to call on Commander-in-Chief Ho Lung someday. Thus we moved out of that bandit base. We hired two boats at the town and left for Shang-hang. Even though the river was as treacherous as before, we had a nice trip this time, because we had experienced local boatmen with us. We saw quite a few wrecked boats in the river; we also saw many wounded and sick soldiers and some Revolutionary Committee personnel on both banks, waiting for transportation.

Li Li-san, who was responsible for the river transportation, arrived at Shang-hang before we did. I told him about our dangerous trip, and neither of us could help laughing. He said that he had also done a foolish thing. At Ch'ang-ting he had commandeered about one hundred boats together with about four hundred boatmen in order to ship all those under his command to Shang-hang. He had not tried to find out the hydrographic conditions of the river, nor had he let the boatmen steer their own boats. Instead he made a reallocation of the men. As he thought the young and able-bodied boatmen more capable than the old ones, he let them handle the boats carrying important cadres and wounded and sick officers, and he let the older men handle the boats carrying less important personnel along with wounded and sick soldiers. He had made a big mistake. The older boatmen were more experienced, and all the boats that they steered arrived at Shang-hang safely, while most of the boats handled by the young boatmen were damaged or destroyed. Many cadres fell overboard and encountered danger. They were still waiting for transportation along the banks, and Li had to send some boats back to pick them up. In addition, he had to compensate the boat owners for their losses.

Those foolish actions not only made good stories to laugh over but also good lessons. However, it is not easy for people, including Li Li-san and myself, to obtain lessons from their own mistakes.

We stayed for two days at Shang-hang, and then proceeded on foot towards Ta-pu in Kwangtung. As T'an P'ing-shan had already left, along with the advance unit, the responsibility for leading the Revolutionary Committee units then fell on my shoulders. They were very disorderly units, especially the Secretariat and the Finance Committee, whose members insisted on riding in sedan chairs. For instance, Chiang Chi-huan, the secretary general, was so fat that it required eight chair-bearers to take turns carrying him. My group was composed of a little over three hundred men, but the total number rose to about one thousand when one included chair-bearers and the transport labor. Li Li-san's Political Defense Bureau was a big organization which consisted of about four hundred men including a company of troops. As they were taking care of about five hundred wounded and sick personnel, the total number in that group exceeded two thousand men, including the transport labor. Li had to stay to take care of some unfinished business and could not proceed until a couple of days later. The battalion that served as the rear guard under the command of Chou Shih-ti was still on its way from Ch'ang-ting to Shang-hang by land.

I led the Revolutionary Committee units from Shang-hang to Ta-pu. As we moved along the Ting River on the Kwangtung-Fukien border, I was able to appreciate the grandiose scenery of gorges, rapid currents, and roaring rivers. After we arrived at Ta-pu, we stayed overnight at the village of Tsou Lu, an important personage of the Hsi-shan Conference clique. When we departed from there, we left him a letter of thanks to show our politeness, even though he was our enemy. We transferred to bigger junks at Ta-pu and moved downstream on the Ting River towards San-ho-pa. Our advance force did not prepare any defense at San-ho-pa, although it was an important location for our march. Therefore we suffered enemy threats from almost every direction soon after our arrival. One enemy regiment of Huang Shao-hsiung's forces assumed a defensive posture against us at Sung-k'ou, which was thirty li from San-ho-pa. In addition, a militia force with fifty small arms was hiding inside the town of San-ho-pa in an attempt to raid us from within and thus assist Huang Shao-hsiung's force.

In view of such a critical situation, I immediately held a meeting with Chu Teh and P'eng P'ai in order to make a joint decision with regard to appropriate actions. At that time Chu was no longer commander of the Ninth Army, and P'eng was nicknamed "King of Peasants in the T'ung-chiang Area"; they were both traveling with the Revolutionary Committee. We gathered some twenty riflemen from among the Revolutionary Committee units, and let Chu Teh, under the name of commander of the Ninth Army and concurrently Guard Commander of the Revolutionary Committee, lead them to guard against the enemy from the Sung-k'ou area. P'eng P'ai, together with ten-odd men, armed with pistols, was responsible for disarming the militia force in that town. I myself stayed in a big house, entertaining the gentry of the town and pretending to be calm in front of them. Most of the other personnel of the Revolutionary Committee remained on board the boats. At that time the main force of our army was in the Ch'ao-chou, Swatow area, about three hundred li away. The troops led by Li Li-san and Chou Shih-ti were still in the Shang-hang area and would not arrive until two or three days later. While we were having a very anxious time waiting for reinforcements, we had to mask our fears in order to fool the enemy.

Quite unexpectedly, we succeeded in tiding ourselves over our difficulty. At first P'eng P'ai successfully disarmed the militia force in town because he knew the local environment very well. In addition, he detected some ten enemies carrying pistols, including, of course, some of Huang Shao-hsiung's spies. In two or three hours we brought the entire town under control and obtained more small arms. Many of the town's celebrities came to me to express their welcome. The platoon led by Chu Teh engaged the advance unit of Huang Shao-hsiung's force at a place eight li from San-ho-pa. The enemy, ignorant of our actual situation, immediately retreated towards Sung-k'ou. Chu Teh therefore detailed eight soldiers to make a feigned pursuit, while he himself hustled back and forth between San-ho-pa and the front in order to put on airs like a real army commander in front of the countryfolks.

Thus we held out, and two days later Li Li-san's and Chou Shih-ti's troops arrived one after the other. Then the Revolutionary Committee units, led by myself, Li Li-san, and P'eng P'ai and escorted by a company of troops from the Political Defense Bureau, moved on along the Han River in two groups, one by land and the other by water, towards Ch'ao-chou and Swatow. At the same time Chu Teh and Chou Shih-ti, along with the rear-guard battalion, remained in San-ho-pa, to exercise surveillance over the enemy in the Mei-hsien area and to take care of the wounded and sick soldiers that were left there. Later on, Chu and Chou were isolated there by the enemy when our main force suffered a defeat at T'ang-k'eng and started to flee towards the area of Liu-sha, P'u-ning, Hai-feng, and Lu-feng. Completely isolated, they were compelled to lead their troops and the slightly wounded soldiers towards the Kwangtung-Kiangsi border, and they started a guerrilla movement there with a force that totaled some one thousand men. Chu Teh's troops suffered a great many hardships and finally linked up with Mao Tse-tung's men at Ching-kang-shan. Their forces together formed the main body of the Workers' and Peasants' Red Army.

According to our plan, Swatow was going to be our provisional capital, and we wanted to do a lot of things there for the sake of our development. Chou En-lai, who arrived there before we did, knew the locale better, because he had once been the Administrative Commissioner of the Tung Chiang, Swatow area in 1925. Therefore we had to listen to him. At his suggestion, Li Li-san was appointed chief of the Public Security Bureau of Swatow and was made responsible for keeping law and order there. The CCP underground organization in Swatow was small and powerless; the local people assumed an attitude of indifference, of wait-and-see, towards us; enemy agents were so active there that the enemy plain-clothes team once raided the Public Security Bureau of Swatow.

Enemy forces under the command of Hsü Ching-t'ang, Huang Shao-hsiung, and Wu T'ing-yang had occupied strategic positions near T'ang-k'eng to the west of Ch'-ao-chou and Swatow in an attempt to attack us from those heights. We, too, were assembling our forces and deploying them to the T'eng-k'eng area to prepare for a decisive battle. We thought that this battle would decide our fate, and everyone of us was bustling about to supply the front. This battle would also decide the future of the Revolutionary Committee.

Two days later Chang T'ai-lei stole from Hong Kong to Swatow to convey an order from the leaders of the CCP. At first he was regarded as a savior from overseas, but then we were disappointed when we discovered his purpose. He wanted us to conform to the new policies of the central authorities, converting the Revolutionary Committee into a Soviet and dropping the title of "Chinese Nationalist Party (or KMT)," abandoning Ch'ao-chou and Swatow, transferring our forces to Hai-feng and Lu-feng, and then combining them with local peasants to form the Workers' and Peasants' Red Army. Such a change would be something that would affect our future movements. We were using the title of "The Revolutionary Committee of the Chinese Nationalist Party" and had a platform that fitted this title; our forces were confronting the enemy and a violent battle was imminent. At such a critical moment it would take a lot of thought to decide how we could change our title and platform, and how we could disengage our forces from those of the enemy. Even Chang T'ai-lei, who was representing the central authorities, was not able to solve this problem either.

Chang T'ai-lei mentioned something about the CCP's August Seventh Meeting and the situation thereafter. He told us that the CCP's Central Headquarters, led by Ch'ü Ch'iu-pai, had already been moved back to Shanghai; that he had been made a member of the Politburo of the CC and concurrently secretary of the Kwangtung Regional Committee and had been given full power by the central authorities to direct our work; that all such leaders of the Nanchang Uprising as us had lost their former positions as leaders, T'an P'ing-shan and Li Li-san were no longer members of the Politburo, and Chou En-lai and I were demoted to alternate members of the Politburo. Chang did not say that we had been accused of being opportunists; but from the punishment imposed on us, it was not hard to infer the attitude of Central Headquarters, led by Ch'ü Ch'iu-pai, towards us.

Therefore, we unanimously requested Chang T'ai-lei to be our leader there, but he declined. He would not accept the position of secretary of the Front Committee, nor would he agree to lead us even without a specific title, because he had to leave for Canton in a hurry to assume the office of secretary of the Kwangtung Regional Committee. He told those who were in charge of local CCP organizations in Ch'ao-chou and Swatow to stay underground in order not to suffer losses after the departure of our forces. Passing on an order of Central Headquarters, he also said, "Chang Kuo-t'ao and Li Li-san should leave for Shanghai immediately to discuss with the central authorities our future policies, Chou En-lai should assume responsibility for taking care of all matters here, and T'an P'ing-shan should also leave here after the chairmanship of the Revolutionary Committee is cancelled." I asked him, "Aren't you demanding that we leave the troops and disband?" He answered, "The order of Central Headquarters after the August Seventh Meeting must be enforced." This made us feel that the leaders of the CCP were no longer expecting any success from the Nanchang Uprising, and that the so-called Russian aid was impossible.

Knowing that it would be difficult to solve this problem, Chou En-lai soon left for the front to direct operations there on the pretext that the situation there had become tense. Prior to his departure Chou said to

Chang T'ai-lei that these things must be done step by step, that we must first of all defeat the enemy force at T'ang-k'eng before we would move our forces to Hai-feng and Lu-feng, and that the proposed changes should not be made until after the battle. In view of the situation, Chang T'ai-lei was obliged to agree.

I had a cordial talk with Chang T'ai-lei. In a somewhat indirect manner, I told him of the lesson that I had learned from what happened to me on the eve of the Nanchang Uprising, when Lominadze, who paid attention to nothing but opposing opportunism, had asked me to comply with the directive of the Comintern to stop the uprising, but my proposal had met with unanimous objection at Nanchang. I also told him that he was not facing reality either and that perhaps his main theme was also "antiopportunism"; that it would be a great loss if we did not aim our guns at the enemy, and thus lost our assets because we opposed opportunism; that the change from Revolutionary Committee of the KMT to Soviet could not be made overnight, and we might as well undertake a gradual change; that a radical change in the thick of battle was like having an actor dismantle his own stage.

Although we could not calculate exactly how much our morale was affected and how much the outcome of that battle was the result of such discouragement from Central Headquarters under Ch'ü Ch'iu-pai, as imposed on us by Chang T'ai-lei, at least we were sure that it disturbed us so much that we could not devote all of our efforts to the battle. This was indeed regrettable. I was then of the opinion that the central authorities should help us wholeheartedly to win the Nanchang Uprising and should not perform such a foolish act, and that the central authorities should neither hastily change the name of the Revolutionary Committee of the KMT nor dismiss T'an P'ing-shan from the office of chairman because he was the "insignia" of that uprising.

Our military defeat ended our internal dispute. As the enemy force was defending the heights near T'ang-k'eng with the aid of fortifications, our force was finally defeated due to extremely heavy casualties. The defeat at T'ang-k'eng on October 3 decided the total failure of that uprising.

Having heard the news of our defeat, the Revolutionary Committee units that were in Swatow immediately fled towards the P'u-ning area. Disorder and fear soon spread among our men. During the retreat, I met Nieh Jung-chen who was coming back from the front. He said to me dejectedly, "This defeat was caused entirely by improper leadership. The Staff Group failed to collect information concerning the enemy situation and the terrain. They did not know how to do anything except send troops to the front to fight hard battles. Comrade Yeh T'ing was a fierce general, all right, but even he knew nothing more than how to attack. He fought fearlessly like a mad man, but afterwards he was so exhausted that he could not even make an orderly retreat. This tragic defeat has taught us a lesson which we must remember if we want to fight again in the future."

Chang T'ai-lei stayed with us for about a week in Swatow. During the retreat we were also together for part of our journey. Then he turned around and departed for Canton in disguise by way of Swatow. When we were parting company, he said to me, "The failure of the uprising was exactly as Central Headquarters predicted. Now we can do nothing but carry out the instructions of Central Headquarters." I said, "I have to discuss this with the comrades from the front. Perhaps I won't return to Shanghai soon if the situation is not too serious."

On the afternoon of October 4 we linked up at Liu-sha with our troops who were retreating from T'ang-k'eng. I stopped over at a small, neat roadside temple. Some of the personnel of the Workers' and Peasants' Committee were assigned to keep law and order during the trip, but some of them lost contact with me, so only a few of my men were near me. I met Li Li-san there. His Political Defense Bureau was also in great disorder and was out of control. Then Chang Shu-shih, Kuo Mo-jo, Lin Tsu-han, and Chiang Chi-huan arrived in succession; T'an P'ing-shan and Yün Tai-ying had gone ahead of us. It seemed that the troops retreating from T'ang-k'eng were more frightened than the personnel from Swatow, the rear area. While they were running along, they kept yelling, "Run! The enemy is coming!"

The important members of the Revolutionary Committee gathered in that small temple at Liu-sha, waiting for Chou En-lai, Ho Lung, and Yeh T'ing, in order to hold an emergency meeting to decide on our course of action. Soon Chou En-lai, lying on a litter, was carried there. He looked sick and dejected. (In fact, Ho Lung and Yeh T'ing had already preceded us, and Chou was bringing up the rear.) He got out of the litter, walked into the crowded temple, and then announced loudly, "Why haven't you left, gentlemen? We have had orders from Central Headquarters that from now on we Communists will not take advantage of the banner of the KMT any more, and, instead of that, we will fight alone under the banner of the Soviet. The Revolutionary Committee of the KMT no longer exists. If you gentlemen want to leave us, let's part here." Chang Shu-shih immediately said in reply, "All right!

Let's do it this way." Chou made this announcement in dejection and anger. It was obvious that his announcement was based on the order of Central Headquarters that had been conveyed to us by Chang T'ai-lei a few days earlier, and that he had decided to announce it in his capacity as secretary of the Front Committee because the military defeat had been too sudden to enable him to discuss it with us. His decision finally terminated the cooperation between the CCP and the KMT leftists, and it initiated the period of the CCP's displaying the banner of the Soviet. It also indicated that the revolutionary movement led by the CCP was going further astray.

When our men were about to leave in order to evade the enemy, Chou En-lai wanted to have an emergency talk with me and Li Li-san. He said, "You two must leave the troops immediately and steal back to Shanghai. I will stay with the troops and will take whatever actions are appropriate according to circumstances during the march. All personnel will be sent to Hong Kong or Shanghai except those who must stay." Then I asked him, "Are you feeling any better? You should leave the troops first, because you are sick. Let me stay in your place. How is the situation at the front?" He answered me immediately, "My illness is no problem; I think I can hold on. I cannot leave the troops, because I am going to the Hai-feng, Lu-feng area to raise the banner of the Soviet. We should not carry on our discussion any longer. You'd better go quickly before it is too late. The situation at the front was very bad, and at this moment I don't know how many of our troops can survive." Thus we parted company at that small temple.

By the roadside near the temple, Li Li-san and I made the necessary arrangements for dispatching our men. We told our men to hire some guides and leave that dangerous war zone for the Hai-k'ou area. Then I left there and followed a footpath across the fields, along with Li Li-san, Ho Ch'ang, who was a member of the Standing Committee of the CYC who was returning to Shanghai, a field-grade officer, and a guide.

I did not know what my travel companions were thinking. As for myself, I looked over my shoulder many times at that disorderly group, and many thoughts crowded in upon me. We walked about one li, then we could hear that the shooting in the Liu-sha Highway area was becoming intensified. The troops on the highway were in great disorder, and we could see from a distance that some of them were resisting but some were running at random. We tried to turn to boost their morale and encourage them to fight resolutely in order to turn the enemy attack; but our guide, a capable peasant assigned to us by the CCP County

Committee of P'u-ning, objected to our doing so. He knew the area very well, so he quickly led us out of the shooting area.

Soon we reached a village with peel towers as it was getting dark. The shooting in the Liu-sha area ceased. In order to make us feel better, the guide said, "I knew that the enemy fire would not harm our forces because it was getting dark." He quietly led us into his house through the back door, stepped out for a while, and then returned with a bundle of civilian clothes. So we took off our uniforms and put on the civilian clothing. We were very hungry, and he prepared a very nice dinner for us.

In this village there were two landlords who opposed the Peasant Association, but most of the rest of the villagers were members of that association. Our guide was an especially active member, and it seemed to us that his family was quite well-off. We hid there and kept quiet in order to avoid attracting the attention of the landlords. After dinner we gave our pistols to the guide and asked him to put them away for later use in peasant uprisings. He was very happy and hid them carefully. Then he led us out the back door, and we followed a mountain trail that led towards the coast.

The four of us, following the guide, walked all night on an uninhabited mountain, but we were as calm and leisurely as if we were on an excursion. We asked the guide a lot of questions, but he, like a supreme commander, always smiled and did not answer. He would not tell us how far we were going to walk, nor would he tell us what our destination was or when we would arrive. We stopped only two or three times during the trip to drink some spring water and eat a few cookies. He did not let us rest even though we were tired and hungry; he walked ahead of us and hurried us up. He did not stop until we could see a harbor in front of us at noon the next day. He said, "That is Chia-tzu-kang over there. We must walk there separately, pretending that we do not know each other. When we reach downtown, I will walk into a shop that I know, and you should also enter it one by one, without saying anything. Just leave everything to me, and you will be taken care of for sure. We have walked more than one hundred li via the mountain trail since last night, and we are lucky to have arrived safely. We must be more cautious in town." We all said smilingly, "We'll follow your orders."

We entered Chia-tzu-kang, one at a time and unhurriedly, pretending that we were ordinary travelers. It was a fishing harbor, and the entire market in town was full of marine products. Many fishing boats of various sizes were anchored in the harbor, and fishing nets of all types were spread out on the beach. The local people used such things as shells to decorate their homes; the women in town also wore them as ornaments. There were neither militia nor police in the town. Except that the local market was controlled by some big fishmongers, the town itself was like a utopia without rulers. As total strangers, the four of us stepped into a shop on the beach in accordance with the guide's instructions. We sat on a long bench like ordinary customers, watching our guide's face as he talked with the shopkeeper. Then our guide led us upstairs behind the shop, and said to us, "You may rest here. This shopkeeper is chicken-hearted; he does not want you to stay overnight here, but he will bring you some food. Don't leave this room. I am going to hire a boat, and you will embark on the boat as soon as I get one."

The four of us did not follow his advice completely. We took walks in the street separately after lunch. We saw our guide drinking tea and talking with some fishermen on a boat, and we also saw him whispering with other fishermen on the beach. He came back towards evening and said that he had hired a boat for a hundred silver dollars and that it would leave for Hong Kong at midnight. He also said that he did not know the fishermen well, and he would try to find out more about them. We were so anxious to get out of there that without any hesitation we sent one of our group, along with the guide, to see the boat owner, pay him one hundred silver dollars, and urge him to make prompt preparations for the voyage.

After it was dark, the four of us, feeling very carefree, took a stroll on the beach. Then our guide came up to us with an anxious look and said, "I hired the wrong boat. That was a pirate boat. The boat owner has already found out that you are ranking officers, and he will murder you if he thinks that you have any valuables with you. I did not know this before. You must not sail on that boat." Then he pointed his finger at the boats in the harbor and whispered to us, "Look! These are fishing boats, while those few are pirate boats."

We immediately asked him to hire another boat for us, and he did so in a moment. He insisted on getting the money back from the pirate boat, but we stopped him. We wanted him to speed up the other boat so that we could make an earlier departure; at the same time we wanted him to tell the owner of the pirate boat that we would leave the next evening instead of that evening, so that the pirates would not know about our actual movements. In addition, we advised our guide to leave town the next morning for the sake of his own safety, and told him to forget about the one hundred dollars. At about 10 P.M. we embarked on the second boat and sailed for Hong Kong.

Other comrades escaped in a way that was somewhat similar to ours. Many of them escaped to Hong Kong via Chia-tzu-kang, and then proceeded elsewhere. Due to enemy interceptions and pursuits, Ho Lung's troops were totally disarmed, and only a few survivors of Yeh T'ing's forces fled to Hai-feng and Lu-feng to link up with the Peasant Army there. Chou En-lai, T'an P'ing-shan, Ho Lung, Yeh T'ing, Liu Po-ch'eng, Kuo Mo-jo, Yün Tai-ying, Lin Tsu-han, and some others also left the troops during those two days and fled by sea to Hong Kong or Shanghai. The Nanchang Uprising thus came to a tragic end. As I have mentioned before, Chu Teh's troops were isolated at San-ho-pa and were still fighting there. We might say that his force was the only unextinguished spark left over from the Nanchang Uprising.

Eight Months in Hiding

After I returned to Shanghai, I spent eight months in hiding—from October, 1927, to May, 1928. That was a sad period, during which I felt sorry about the CCP's setbacks and held a grievance against the punishment inflicted on me. I was one of the founders of the CCP, and I loved it more than anybody else did. Therefore I had to oppose Ch'ü Ch'iu-pai's policy of adventurism. In addition, I was in an anxious mood and led an uneasy life, because I had to avoid the police constantly and so my movements were restricted. That state of mind and life did not change until late May, 1928, when I took a trip to Moscow to attend the CCP's Sixth Congress.

On the night of October 5, 1927, we were on board a fishing boat sailing along the coast of Kwangtung towards Hong Kong. The sea was calm and the voyage was peaceful. The owner and helmsman of the boat was a kind old man, and the two honest young men who were his assistants were his nephews. They were very attentive, waiting on us. Whenever they sighted any suspicious boat at a distance, the boat owner wuold advise us to lie down in the cabin to avoid being seen by others.

The boat was very small. There was no furniture in the cabin, and we had to sleep on the coarse planks of the deck. The cabin was only three-feet high from deck to ceiling, so that we might hit our heads against the ceiling if we sat up carelessly. Though I was exhausted, my confused mind and the noise of the sea striking against the hull pre-

vented me from sleeping well. Therefore I would not regard the trip
as having been comfortable.

On board the boat we discussed such problems as how to escape to
safety, what to do in Hong Kong, what to do in Shanghai, and so forth.
We sighed over our predicament. The saying "Whoever wins will be
called king, while whoever loses will be called bandit" was not applicable
to our situation then. We could not be called king, but we could not be
called bandit either, because we had left our troops. As we had lost
everything, we were very much like the "dog that has lost its home."

On the morning of the third day, our boat entered T'ung-lo-wan
(Bay) of Hong Kong through Li-yu-men, and we landed there. In the
eyes of the people in Hong Kong we must have looked like monsters. We
had not shaved for several days. We were still dressed in the coarse
clothing, now spotted with traces of mud, that we had obtained at Liu-
sha, along with worn and dirty straw hats and old cloth shoes; but we
walked arrogantly. We bought a lot of newspapers, which we had not
had access to for more than two months, and we read them while we
walked. Our actions and appearance attracted the attention of many
people who must have guessed that we were officers of the forces defeated in Swatow.

We entered the famous Ta Tung Hotel and selected a big room.
We looked like countryfolks or beggars, but we behaved very haughtily.
The hotel boy did not say anything except that he asked us with a smile
to pay the rent. We didn't have much left in our pockets, because we
had paid double boat fare at Chia-tzu-kang and also other travel expenses. So the four of us pooled our money and paid our two-dollar
rent; the balance was barely enough for bus fare, but not enough for
even one day's food. Therefore we left in the room our straw hats,
newspapers, and personal belongings, which were almost nothing, and
went out to seek assistance.

Ho Ch'ang and the officer went to look for the CCP's secret contact
in Hong Kong, who had to be reached in a roundabout way. Li Li-san
and I went to look for P'eng Tse-min, an overseas Chinese who used to
be the chief of the KMT's Department of Overseas Affairs. P'eng, a KMT
leftist who was friendly to us, had sneaked back to Hong Kong and resumed his merchantile career when the KMT leftists at Wuhan parted
company with the CCP. We found him in a pretty big store at Chung-
huan while he was talking business with two customers who wore
Western suits and looked like overseas Chinese. He was a little surprised
by our appearance and did not know what to say to start our conversation.

So we stayed a little while and then left. He followed us out of the store, asked where we were living, promised to help us get away from Hong Kong, and gave us all the money that he had in his pocket, a little more than ten Hong Kong dollars. We accepted his money with delight, because it was the thing we needed most then, and then we parted company with him.

Due to the fact that we had embarrassed P'eng Tse-min, we decided not to call on anyone else. As a matter of fact, very few of our friends there were reliable. We walked the streets, bought some inexpensive clothing, shoes, and socks, had hair cuts, and took baths in order to minimize the vulgar appearance that we had acquired in Swatow. Ho Ch'ang and the officer had also got in touch with the CCP contact, but they had to wait at the hotel for the liaison personnel. They also got some money, bought some clothes, and changed their appearances.

While we were waiting for assistance, we went to bed at about 9 P.M. in order to enjoy a good sleep which we had not had for many days. At midnight someone knocked at the door and woke us up. It was the CCP contact in Hong Kong. He said to us hastily, "Leave here without any delay. According to reliable information from Canton, the Nationalists there have already discovered your identity and this address. Wu T'ieh-ch'eng, chief of the Public Security Bureau, will come over to Hong Kong along with his men to negotiate for your arrest and extradition with the police authority here." We immediately packed our things and followed him out of that hotel. I said to myself, "Let Wu T'ieh-ch'eng arrest those ragged clothes and worn straw hats."

He led us as we walked for a while down the street, making quite a few turns to make sure that no one was shadowing us. Then he led us to an upstairs room in a building on a hillside street. This one room in the building housed the CCP reception station, while the other rooms were ordinary residences. When we walked into the room, several others were already there; some of them were also from Swatow. Our arrival made the room more crowded. The contact told us to be quiet and said that a gambling game might provide a good cover.

Then he explained to us in a low voice why he had not come to see us sooner and said that he had not wasted any time. He criticized us for getting a room at the Ta Tung Hotel when we looked so awful. He said that we would have been in big trouble for sure that night had he not warned us in time. He told us that everything had changed, that it was no longer the Wuhan period, that one should avoid his former friends and comrades in the street, because they were not necessarily as trustworthy as before, and that a careless hello might risk one's being sold out.

This young contact's admonition made Li Li-san and me smile at one another, because we thought that we were being admonished by a novice. He was about twenty, a new member since the August Seventh Meeting, and as arrogant as Ho Ch'ang due to their youth. We stayed overnight in that crowded room, some sitting up and some lying on the floor.

The next morning we silently parted company according to the contact's plan. He got a little room for me in a small hotel and bought me some necessary articles and a boat ticket to Shanghai. Among the articles was a bag which was so large that I had to buy a cotton quilt in order to fill it up. In the afternoon I walked out of that small hotel as inconspicuously as possible and embarked for Shanghai. I did not know about the movements of my three companions.

In the steerage cabin of the ship I heard a familiar voice, so I had to be very cautious. I climbed into the top one of three berths to avoid notice. When the ship was under way, I found that the familiar voice came from Chu Pao-t'ing, an old friend of mine. He was a native of Ning-po, an old seaman who was nicknamed "Harelip Chu" because of his harelip. He had many friends, including most of the sailors on this ship; he drank a lot and liked to chat loudly with others. Although this time he was a passenger in the steerage cabin, a lot of people came to chat with him.

Chu was a reliable CCP member and one of the leaders of the Seamen's Union. However, the way he talked then made me question his reliability. I was afraid that even if Chu had not changed, it might attract the attention of other seamen who knew us if I conversed with him. I was also afraid that Chu might reveal my identity if he got drunk, so I decided not to let him see me. It was not easy to do this, because we shared the same cabin. Therefore, I pretended to be seasick and did not get out of my berth unless Harelip Chu was either asleep or absent. Thus I experienced the suffering of pretending to be sick; and since I had to stay in bed all day, I was buried in deep meditation and anxiety. I spent three days this way on board and then arrived in Shanghai without being seen by Harelip Chu. As a matter of fact, Chu at that time was still a faithful CCP member, and all of my worries and suffering during that voyage were unnecessary.

Soon after my arrival in Shanghai I got hold of CCP Central Headquarters and began to experience the terror that existed in Shanghai after the KMT's April 12 purge. Li Li-san had also arrived in Shanghai, but I do not know whether he came by the same boat. He disguised himself as a wealthy businessman, looking somewhat like a playboy, apparently disguised as a richer man than I. At the residence of Li Wei-han, chief of the Organizational Department of the CCP's Central Headquarters, which was headed by Ch'ü Ch'iu-pai, I saw Li Li-san again and discussed our lodging problem with him. Li Wei-han gave us another briefing on security precautions.

Li Wei-han told us that Central Headquarters had rented a flat for us in a small alley on Chungking Road in the British Concession and that we should move into that house in the guise of travelers, because the lessee told the landlord that he was renting the house for friends of his from out of town. Therefore, we immediately discussed with each other the best ways of disguising ourselves. As I looked pale, I disguised myself as a sick school teacher who had come to Shanghai to see doctors. Li Li-san disguised himself as my younger brother, a senior bank clerk who had accompanied me to Shanghai and at the same time was taking care of some business. Li Wei-han commented, "Wonderful!"

So we moved into the CCP hostel for senior personnel. It was a two-story house. The landlord lived downstairs, and we occupied the upstairs. It was a spacious six-room flat which had already been equipped with some rented furniture. We acted our parts very well. Li Li-san asked me every day, "Brother, how are you feeling today?" The comrades who visited with us would also say something about my illness, as if they were relatives or friends of ours coming to wish me well. Perhaps our landlord thought that I was a T.B. patient. Li Li-san was a restless person who went out every day no matter how much risk he had to take. Sometimes he went to a movie alone. Thus he looked very much like a busy businessman.

Li Li-san and I lived there without having anything to do. I felt as if we were convicted opportunists waiting for punishment. Chü Ch'iu-pai did not want to see us. Other Politburo members did not discuss Party policy with us, nor did they want to listen to our report of the Nanchang Uprising. They did not pay any attention to taking care of the escapees from Liu-sha until we asked them to do so. What Central Headquarters assigned us to read primarily was "A Letter from the August Seventh Meeting to All CCP Members."[5] We read that document over and over, and it made us think about a lot of things.

Li Li-san told me that until he read that document he had not understood why Chang T'ai-lei wanted us to leave the troops in Swatow for

Shanghai and why Chang had not wanted to keep T'an P'ing-shan as chairman of the committee, and that he began to understand that we had both been found guilty of committing the big mistake of opportunism and were going to be ideologically reformed. He pointed out that the document was quite provocative and that it was arbitrary in many respects. He said that he had never seen the "Resolution of the Eighth Enlarged Plenum of the Comintern," and he asked me whether or not I had seen it, because according to the document, we had violated that resolution. I answered, "No," and said that we should try to find a copy of the resolution and read it.

"A Letter from the August Seventh Meeting to All CCP Members" did not clearly propose the establishment of a Soviet regime, but it did introduce the CCP's subsequent sovietization movement and it sowed the seeds of the CCP's incorrect policy of adventurism. Definitely the CCP was too biased towards the united front of the National revolution during the period of KMT-CCP cooperation; it still wanted to preserve the united front, and therefore it had to make repeated concessions even after the famous Ma-jih, or Equine Day, Incident of May 21, 1927, when the Hunanese army successfully suppressed the sizeable Communist-led labor and peasant organizations in Changsha. The Comintern had also given instructions to try to stop the Nanchang Uprising in order to avoid the total collapse of that united front. However, the letter upheld the opposite view. It stated that "it was incorrect to regard the National revolution as being contradictory to the class struggle and the social revolution."[6] Such a false statement denies the contradictory nature of national revolution and class struggle. It further said, "The destruction of feudalism is a fatal blow to imperialist rule over China. . . . The class struggle against the bourgeoisie in China can destroy the prop that the imperialists use to support their oppression."[7] In this manner it emphasized the class struggle, on the one hand, and neglected any concrete anti-imperialist tasks for the Chinese revolution, on the other hand. Therefore, it did not pay any attention to the national united front from then on.

In fact, Chiang Kai-shek's victory did not change the semicolonial status of China and could not keep China from the danger of being totally colonized. Therefore, the abolition of unequal treaties, the expulsion of foreign powers from China, and the fight for independence and liberty remained the primary tasks of the Chinese revolution. After the Sian Incident in 1936, the CCP had to announce that it had abolished the Soviets and the Red Army, had stopped its agrarian revolution, and was going to cooperate with the KMT for a second time in order to complete those unfinished revolutionary tasks of 1927. Those acts were a relentless irony against the Comintern's unalterable formula of revolution.

It was indeed necessary then to review the CCP's policies and to reorganize its Central Headquarters, but the letter was a ridiculous article that would satisfy the needs of the Comintern (that is, it purposely put the blame for the defeat on the leaders of the CCP and ignored the Comintern's own errors). That article, which condemned opportunism, was written by Lominadze, who was invested with full authority. He was a hidden Trotskyite, and would always smuggle some Trotskyism into his writing. His article implied that CCP members carried out a series of revolutionary works, while CCP Central Headquarters was not revolutionary or was even counterrevolutionary. That of course violated logic. He had a bias towards the "left" deviationist line, and did not think that a young political party such as the CCP would make bold "left" moves. Therefore he praised the left moves especially, and his praise encouraged the policy of adventurism. It was strange, however, that such an important document did not contain a word about the historically significant Nanchang Uprising, which had just started at that time. Perhaps he thought that any word about the uprising would affect the view held in that document and thus make it unsuitable for use in attacking opportunism. As a matter of fact, in accusing the central leadership of the CCP without regard to the consequences, he considered neither the future of the CCP nor the benefit of the Comintern, because his accusations exactly fit the mistakes of the Comintern.

The Letter quoted the resolution of the Comintern's Eighth Plenum: "In view of the present situation, it is impossible for the CCP, a political party of the working class, to secure leadership of the proletariat in China by staying outside the KMT."[8] I do not want to comment on whether it was correct to try to secure leadership by staying within the KMT. By the end of May, 1927, it had become obvious that the attempt to secure leadership inside the KMT was impossible. However, after Borodin initiated an anti-Chiang movement in early 1927, especially after Chiang's purge of Communists in April, Borodin complied with Stalin's wish and requested the CCP to make as many concessions as possible in order to maintain the Wuhan government of the KMT leftists. He thought that the Wuhan government was at least like a log floating on the ocean— the Communists who fell overboard could use it for a life buoy. For this reason Borodin, who was well informed about the situation, wanted us to make concessions and did not let the CCP withdraw from the KMT until the very last moment in order to avoid making more mistakes of opportunism. No wonder that Ch'en Tu-hsiu, in his letter to all CCP members, wrote, "Numerous other mistakes will ensue as a matter of course since the Party has committed such a radical mistake as the aforesaid [the mistake of staying in the KMT in accordance with the instruction of the Comintern, or the mistake of opportunistic policy]."

Comrades who had inside information concerning the August Seventh Meeting told me something about it. The August Seventh Emergency Meeting was hastily convened with a few participants including Ch'ü Ch'iu-pai, Jen Pi-shih, Chang T'ai-lei, and Li Wei-han. The so-called Letter to All CCP Members was prepared beforehand by the representative of the Comintern, translated into Chinese by Ch'ü Ch'iu-pai, and accepted after being read once in front of the meeting. Soon afterwards, the CCP called a meeting of the Hupeh cadres and transmitted the resolution of the August Seventh Meeting. A lot of comrades questioned the central leadership about its attitude towards the Nanchang Uprising, why it had dealt a heavy blow at those comrades who led the Nanchang Uprising, and why it had dismissed Li Li-san, Ts'ai Ho-sen, Chou En-lai, and me from the Politburo.

Ch'ü Ch'iu-pai explained the reason for the punishment imposed on these important Politburo members. He pointed out that Ch'en Tu-hsiu and T'an P'ing-shan deserved severe punishment because they were condemned as opportunists by the resolution of the August Seventh Meeting —T'an P'ing-shan could be dismissed from the Party, while Ch'en Tu-hsiu might retain his Party membership, while they both had actually been dismissed from the CC; and that I, Li Li-san, Chou En-lai, and Ts'ai Ho-sen had also been punished because I had expressed opposition to the Comintern and had defended opportunists in the past, Li Li-san had been held responsible for the mistaken leadership of the General Labor Union of Hupeh, Chou En-lai had been held accountable for disbanding the labor pickets, Ts'ai Ho-sen had made mistakes of opportunism in the text of propaganda materials that he had prepared. He said that the absurd instructions of the National Peasant Association, mentioned in the Letter of the August Seventh Meeting, originated with Mao Tse-tung, that Mao should be held responsible for them, and that Mao should also take the correlative responsibility for incorrect policies of opportunism because after the Equine Day Incident he had told the CCP's Hunan Provincial Committee to cancel the peasants' Ch'ang-sha Invasion Plan.

Jen Pi-shih was a hero at the August Seventh Meeting because the CYC's Central Headquarters, which he headed, had long opposed Ch'en Tu-hsiu's policy of opportunism. Li Wei-han, who had formerly been secretary of the Hunan Provincial Committee of the CCP, succeeded in evading the blame for lacking vigilance prior to the Equine Day Incident and became a "hero of the Hunanese peasant movement." Chang T'ai-lei, who was familiar with the Comintern, of course supported it. Chü Ch'iu-pai found it very difficult to explain his own responsibility for the past. He reiterated that he had long since opposed Ch'en Tu-hsiu's policy of opportunism; that he had been able to accept all of the Comintern's instructions, had avoided mistakes of opportunism, and had fought resolutely against opportunism; and that he thought it his duty to lead the CCP.

The seven members of the Politburo, which was reorganized after the August Seventh Meeting, were Chü Ch'iu-pai, Su Chao-cheng, Li Wei-han, Chang T'ai-lei, Hsiang Ying, Hsiang Chung-fa, and Lu Fu-t'an. Four of them were regarded as members of the working class in order to conform with a policy of a higher percentage of workers. Hsiang Ying had been a worker in Wuhan for a short period of time; Hsiang Chung-fa, who had been chairman of the General Labor Union of Hupeh, had started his career as a barge worker; Su Chao-cheng was a famous seaman; Lu Fu-t'an was a Cantonese worker who formerly had been an important person on the Kwangtung and Hong Kong Strike Committee. In addition, Jen Pi-shih and Lo Chueh frequently attended meetings of the Politburo in their capacities of secretary of the CC of the CYC and secretary of the Shanghai Regional Committee of the CCP respectively. Su Chao-cheng was secretary of the CC of the CCP for a period of time; Ch'ü Ch'iu-pai did not formally hold that position until Su died of illness a short time later.

On November 11 the CC of the CCP held an enlarged meeting, but I was excluded from it. That meeting was designed to reach a conclusion about the unsuccessful Nanchang Uprising and to set forth clear guiding principles for our future operations because the August Seventh Meeting had not clarified such principles. The November 11 meeting formally decided to establish a "Soviet regime of the workers' and peasants' democratic dictatorship" and to carry out the agrarian revolution by organizing uprisings from the lowest level up to higher levels. From then on, the slogan of sovietization, which had long since been proposed, became a definite program. In addition, that meeting thought the environment for the Chinese revolution was becoming more and more favorable, therefore it brought forward a Trotskyite concept of "unceasing revolution." Such a concept exposed Lominadze's scheme. Later on, the CCP's Sixth Congress criticized that meeting a little for its mistake in using the phrase "unceasing revolution." It seemed that it was this phrase which had encouraged adventurism.

That meeting negated the meaning of the Nanchang Uprising, saying that the use of KMT's banner in that uprising was an indication of opportunism, which should take the blame for the failure of that uprising. That was the reason why T'an P'ing-shan was dismissed from the CCP. By then T'an had escaped to Shanghai from the Ch'ao-chou, Swatow area. The CCP expelled him from all of its units and did not give him any chance to defend himself. Soon afterwards T'an published a statement in the *Shen Pao* (Shanghai Daily), announcing his apostasy from the CCP and saying that the policies of the CCP were unsuited to the present Chinese revolution.

At that enlarged meeting, I was tried *in absentia* and dismissed from membership on the CC. Several others were also punished.[9] I was charged with "falsifying the orders of higher authorities." This charge was based on Chang T'ai-lei's report in which Chang said that I failed to follow the instruction of Central Headquarters to lead the Nanchang Uprising resolutely and that I tried to stop the Nanchang Uprising with a falsified order from the central authorities. Such a distortion of facts made me feel that the central authorities then were very dishonest. Many comrades took up the cudgel for me. They asked the central authorities why I was not permitted to attend the meeting to defend myself, and why the facts had been distorted. I wrote a long letter to the enlarged meeting to explain my innocence. Some of the comrades requested Ch'ü Ch'iu-pai to give me a responsible position on the grounds that I was still a CCP member and should be given fair treatment in spite of being dismissed from the CC.

Under pressure from those comrades, Ch'ü Ch'iu-pai had to come to see me. He looked embarrassed and did not say a single word about the enlarged meeting or my dismissal from the CC. He said to me that all of the resolutions of the CC were based on instructions from the Comintern and its representatives. He was passing the buck and implying that the punishment imposed on me was Lominadze's idea. I responded to his explanation with nothing but a smile. He also said that perhaps the leadership of Central Headquarters was not good enough at that time, but that it had made some progress in the field of Bolshevization; that some comrades were of the opinion that the Central authorities were making moves that were "left" and "bold," but that they thought "left" better than "right." He thought it better not to assign me any practical task in order to keep me free from danger, because I was an "important criminal" wanted by the reactionary government. Therefore he hoped that I would be available at all times to provide the central authorities with advisory recommendations based on my experience.

Then I said to Ch'ü, "Now that our revolution has suffered such a great setback and many comrades have given their lives, how can one be justified in seeking personal interests? I hope that the central authorities can do their job well, and in that case, it will be a great blessing in spite of our setbacks. I want to know more about the actual situation so that I can make timely recommendations to the central authorities." He expressed his appreciation for my promise; but the fact was that he did not let me participate in Party affairs, and regarded my occasional recommendations as opportunistic ones.

Chou En-lai was the luckiest. Soon after his return to Shanghai, he expressed his full support of the CC that was reorganized after the August Seventh Meeting, his obedience to the instructions of the Comintern, and opposition to opportunism. At the same time his position in the CCP was elevated due to the Nanchang Uprising. He luckily escaped responsibility for the defeat of the Nanchang Uprising, and was authorized to make arrangements for many of the comrades who escaped to Shanghai after the defeat of the Nanchang Uprising. Therefore he not only escaped punishment at that enlarged meeting but also became again a member of the Politburo in charge of military and secret-service affairs. However, Li Li-san was not so lucky, being still shelved there pending a new assignment.

Chou En-lai was a realist, clever and diplomatic. He and I endured difficulties together during the later period of the Wuhan government and the Nanchang Uprising. Perhaps he was sorry that the outcome for me should have been so different from that for him. He asked me to direct the assignment of tasks to those who had escaped from the Ch'ao-chou, Swatow area. I promised to help him because I could not decline his request. I did not know that the secret reception center for those escapees was under the direction of a Russia-schooled man by the name of Ho Chia-hsing until I got there. He was married to Ho Chih-hua, Chu Teh's divorcee who had visited Germany with Chu. When she returned to Wuhan from Germany via Moscow, such comrades as Teng Yen-ta and Chang Po-chun had told me something about her untrustworthiness, and I believed them. Therefore I said to Chou En-lai, "That reception center is not trustworthy, because I saw Ho Chih-hua there, and she is a dangerous woman." Chou did not listen to me, probably because he was influenced by the concept of "getting rid of opportunism and boldly using new cadres." So I quit going to it after I had worked there a couple of mornings. That was the only work I did for the CCP Central Headquarters under Ch'ü Ch'iu-pai.

I was not willing to work for Ch'ü because I thought his policy regarding uprisings wrong and harmful. In principle, I did not object to resorting to uprisings, but I was of the opinion that an uprising must be well prepared and founded on the people's struggles rather than be carried out hastily by a few men. Unfortunately Ch'ü Ch'iu-pai's Central Headquarters, under Lominadze's direction, treated uprisings as everyday routine, and regarded any actions other than uprisings as actions of opportunism. Thus the so-called uprising policy led to spur-of-the-moment uprisings, forced uprisings, and uprisings on command. It did not succeed in overthrowing the reactionary government; instead it jeopardized us and helped the enemy. It was not an exaggeration to say that such uprisings were "suicide."

Ch'ü Ch'iu-pai's uprising policy made its debut in the 1927 Autumn Crop Uprising. In Ch'ü's opinion, that was a genuine agrarian revolution, entirely different from the Nanchang Uprising, which was somewhat opportunistic. At that time violent retaliation was made by the landlords and local gentry in Hunan, Hupeh, Kiangsi, and Kwangtung in the wake of the peasant movements there. They used terroristic methods to collect land rent or debts from the peasants. The peasants often lost their property, their homes, and even their lives just because they failed to obey the landlords. In places where the Peasant Associations continued to be influential, the peasants were brewing rebellions in order to prevent the loss of all of their autumn harvest to the landlords. Therefore, local CCP organizations in Hunan and Hupeh proposed autumn crop struggles, and CCP Central Headquarters attempted to develop those struggles into an autumn crop uprising in order to realize the agrarian revolution.

During the Autumn Crop Uprising, the central authorities of the CCP thought that only "Red Terror" could cope with "White Terror," and it brought forth a "burn and kill" policy, requesting the peasants to kill all of the landlords and burn all of their houses. In practice, this policy was not effective; it only dragged the CCP into terrorism and made the landlords and local gentry resort to more violent means against the peasants. By that time the KMT regime was no longer concerned about the interests of the peasants; it was actually encouraging the land-lords and local gentry to persecute the peasants. This gave the CCP a good opportunity to act in the rural areas. However, it was not an opportune time for organizing the peasants to make large-scale uprisings, because it had not been long since their sufferings had ceased. More-over, the influence of the Peasant Associations and the willingness of the peasants to struggle against the landlords varied from place to place; even a local uprising was not always possible at any place. Such an incorrect uprising policy not only prevented the revival of the peasant movement, but also caused the Peasant Associations in many places to suffer additional heavy blows.

Ch'ü Ch'iu-pai's uprising plan, which he dreamed up in an attic in Shanghai, was really ridiculous. He presumed that all people were revolutionaries; that the more they suffered pressure, the more they would react against it; and that an uprising could be made as soon as a CCP member started it boldly. He completely disregarded the strength of the enemy. According to his way of thinking, once a CCP member secretly set fire, with a single match, to a landlord's house and then shouted the slogan "Kill all the landlords and confiscate their land," tens of thousands of peasants would rise in revolt in response to his action. Having gained control of the rural areas, those peasants would then proceed to take the cities; having occupied many cities, they would proceed to take the provincial capital; having taken many provinces, they would go on to capture the national capital; and a Soviet regime could finally be set up as a result of the uprisings.

Why could such obvious adventurism become prevalent then? The will of Lominadze was one of the primary reasons. He did not under-stand conditions in China and thought that Bolshevik magic could pro-duce miracles. At the same time Ch'ü Ch'iu-pai, who was under a nervous strain, thought that everything of the past was opportunistic and therefore wanted to make everything then as "left" as possible. He thought that some more uprisings would not only wash out the dirty stains of opportunism in the past but would also build up the prestige of his new leadership. A lot of our comrades were indignant over the oppression that they were suffering and were anxious for revenge. Those comrades helped to spread the influence of that policy. For instance, Ho Ch'ang, who parted with me at Hong Kong, told me that he was dis-satisfied with our moderate actions during the Nanchang Uprising, and that he himself would act without any restraint.

The harm caused by that policy was obvious. Many local CCP

organizations that blindly followed that policy without regard to their own strength suffered heavy losses, while some of the CCP local organizations that had wise leaders and did not thoroughly implement the policy were able to preserve some of their strength, and this constituted the foundation of the subsequent Soviet zones that were scattered in the outlying areas.

Mao Tse-tung's troops in eastern Hunan were the main forces of the Autumn Crop Uprising. He was able to preserve some strength and later to become a hero at Ching-kang-shan because he was wise enough to know his own environment and did not make hasty moves. As his men, mostly armed peasants, failed to link up in time with the main force of the Nanchang Uprising, they turned towards the mountain area on the Hunan-Hupeh border and operated alone. When his men suffered great defeats in their attacks on such cities as P'ing-chiang and Liu-yang, he was criticized for being a military adventurist who relied solely on rifles; in order words, he was regarded as an opportunist who did not want to rouse the people to action. When he was compelled to retreat towards Ching-kang-shan, he was criticized for being an escapee who ignored the lives of the people. Due to those criticisms, he was repeatedly punished. However, he did not fall victim to "adventurism," because he could firmly control his force of about one thousand men, establish the Ching-kang-shan base, and cope with the blame laid on him by the central authorities of the CCP.

The CCP central authorities also demonstrated their hasty and bold moves in Shanghai. Though Ch'ü Ch'iu-pai and his colleagues did not plan to capture Shanghai by means of an uprising, they deliberately made some risky moves in order to demonstrate the CCP's strength in Shanghai. The CCP's organization in Shanghai had suffered extremely heavy losses during the KMT's April 12 purge, and it was in need of a careful and fine organizational effort in order to recover its lost strength. However, Ch'ü Ch'iu-pai and his colleagues were too impatient to do such basic tasks as organizing secret cells within the labor unions, strengthening the organization of CCP branch headquarters, and so forth. They slighted the efforts that had been made in these fields by the CCP in previous years, because they thought those efforts were opportunistic. They called upon the CCP members and CCP organizations in various factories and districts to run extreme risks. They thought that it was worthwhile to do so even if the members had to sacrifice their lives, because that was the way to intimidate the enemy and increase the influence of the revolution.

Very often the central authorities sent a few or perhaps a dozen members to hide among the workers of a certain factory while those workers were going to work or leaving for home, and they would shout such slogans as "Armed Uprising!" "Down with the Kuomintang!" "Support the Soviets!" and so forth. Frequently these members were arrested and killed by Concession policemen or other secret-service personnel. Many CCP members lost their lives in Shanghai because the central authorities forced them to run such risks as circulating leaflets, mounting wall posters, holding risky meetings, and so forth. Some couriers were needlessly killed because they were ordered by the central authorities to run the police check point. Those actions encouraged useless risks and gave members the mistaken idea that security precautions were cowardly measures.

Ch'ü Ch'iu-pai and his colleagues thought that some poison of opportunism still remained in the minds of those comrades who had formerly shouldered important duties, and therefore a risky assignment was a good test of their Bolshevization. Such a thought gave rise to unfair treatment of and improper job assignments for our comrades. Some senior members lost their lives due to such risky assignments. Some junior members who were selected to fill important posts lowered the working efficiency, increased the loss of lives, and even betrayed the Party.

Comrade Hsü Pai-hao, who was killed in one of those risky actions, was a good example. He was a respectable CCP member who had been a laborer. The important positions that he had held, such as member of the Hupeh Provincial Committee of the CCP, member of the National General Labor Union, secretary general of the Provincial General Labor Union of Hupeh, and so forth, made him as important in the Party as Hsiang Ying and Liu Shao-ch'i. He and his wife, Ch'in I-chun, had arrived in Shanghai from Hankow in October and lived in the same hostel as I did. Ch'ü Ch'iu-pai turned down Hsiang Ying's proposal to assign Hsü an important leader's job and instead assigned him to do difficult low-level work in order to cleanse himself of his past mistakes of opportunism. Soon afterwards Hsü, who was very well known, was arrested along with several others in a small street gathering of only about a dozen workers and was subsequently killed.

Soon after Hsü's arrest, Ch'ü Ch'iu-pai sent someone to inform me that Hsü was an opportunist who might have revealed our address, and he therefore advised me to move out of that hostel right away. I resented Ch'ü's words, which aggravated the sorrow of Hsü's wife. I hated

Ch'ü for his hasty moves and for his prejudice against Hsü Pai-hao. I thought that perhaps the fact that Hsü lived in the same hostel as I did aggravated Ch'ü Ch'iu-pai's suspicions against him and thus caused such a tragic consequence. I said to the messenger in indignation, "Go tell Ch'ü Ch'iu-pai that it is he who has killed Hsü Pai-hao. He has needlessly sacrificed the life of an important member. It is contemptible that he should slander this man as an opportunist. I trust that Hsü did not betray us, so I will stay here. Tell him not to worry about me." Facts proved later that Comrade Hsü had fully demonstrated his noble character and had not divulged any secret in spite of the tortures that he was forced to suffer before he was put to death.

The banner of the Soviet made its first appearance during the December 11, 1927, Canton Uprising, which was the most important action taken by the CCP's central authorities under Ch'ü Ch'iu-pai's leadership. When news of that uprising reached Shanghai, Ch'ü was very happy, imagining that the uprising would succeed. I told them that it would be very difficult for our force to stay in Canton and that it should be promptly transferred to the Hai-feng, Lu-feng area where we had laid a good foundation with our peasant movements. However, my recommendation, though practical, was regarded as one of "escapism," designed to discourage the mutineers. Li Li-san was optimistic about the uprising. He told the central authorities that he was willing to do anything for the uprising in case they needed him. Three days later news reached Shanghai that the Canton Uprising had failed and that Chang T'ai-lei, then secretary of the CCP's Kwangtung Provincial Committee, had been killed in action; so Li Li-san was immediately sent to head operations in the Kwangtung region. From then on, that young fellow followed in Ch'ü Ch'iu-pai's footsteps; later he surpassed Ch'ü by creating the so-called "Li Li-san Policy Line."

On about December 20, Comrade Wang I-chih—Mme. Chang T'ai-lei—escaped to Shanghai from Canton with her one-year-old daughter. She was assigned to the room in my residence that Li Li-san had previously occupied. Her arrival made all those living in the house feel sad. She had been a pretty woman, but after her arrival there she became a weeping woman with disheveled hair and a grimy face. She had restrained her grief while she was traveling in order to conceal her true identity; but soon after her arrival, she could withhold her grief no longer and burst into tears. I expressed my condolences to her and said, "Grieving is of no use. We might say that T'ai-lei has died a good death because he was a hero in the Canton Uprising. We may soon die, too, and perhaps our deaths will be worse."

Comrade Wang I-chih herself took part in that uprising, so she knew all about it and gave me a detailed account of it. What follows is a brief account of her story.

At about 3:00 A.M. on December 11, shots were heard in Canton City. The main force of the uprising was the Training Regiment, under the command of Comrade Yeh Chien-ying of the Fourth Corps. There were many CCP members hidden in this regiment. First of all they brought the reactionary officers in that regiment under control; then they began to attack and disarm the Artillery Regiment and the Security Regiment of the Fourth Corps; and then they occupied all of the government organizations in the city. Not too many members of the Workers' Red Defense Team took part in that uprising; therefore, the strength of the uprising force of about two thousand men actually was frail when scattered in the big city of Canton. The area on the south bank of the river was still under the control of government forces under Li Fu-lin. The mutineers were not even able to capture the liaison station of the Fourth Corps in Canton. Moreover, the peasants in the suburbs did not respond to the mutineers' action.

At noon on the eleventh in Canton City a people's rally was held and a Soviet regime was proclaimed. The gathering had a small attendance, which was composed primarily of CCP members and a few pro-Communist workers. The uprising came as a surprise to the citizens of Canton, who avoided the uprising because they did not think it would succeed. Even the union workers assumed a wait-and-see attitude and did not engage in any action such as a general strike. The Machine Workers' Union actually opposed it. The mutineers advanced many slogans before the rally, such as "Down with Imperialism," "Down with the Warlords," "Rice for the Workers," "Land for the Peasants," "All Political Powers Belong to the Soviet of Workers, Peasants, and Soldiers," and so forth. Then they announced the founding of the Soviet government of Canton with Su Chao-cheng as chairman; Chang T'ai-lei as chairman of the People's Committee and concurrently the member of the People's Committee in charge of Navy and Army affairs; Chou Wen-jung as committee member in charge of labor; P'eng P'ai, the member for land; Yang Yin, the member for eliminating reactionaries; Ho Lai, the member for economy; Ch'en Yü, the member for the judiciary; Yün Tai-ying as secretary general; Yeh T'ing and Chang T'ai-lei as commanders-in-chief; and Hsü Kuang-ying as chief-of-staff. Thus the Soviet government was formally proclaimed. Chang T'ai-lei was hustling about, directing military operations, and had no time to take care of the business of the new government. So everything was laid on Chang T'ai-lei's shoulders, because most of the high-ranking people such as Su Chao-cheng and Yeh T'ing were not in Canton at the time.

Chang T'ai-lei had been planning that uprising since his return to Canton in the middle of November from the enlarged meeting of CCP Central Headquarters which was held in Shanghai. He had many secret meetings with Neumann, a German who was a representative of the Comintern.[10] Chang told his wife that Neumann was even more fierce than Lominadze, although Neumann was the latter's assistant, and that both Neumann and Lominadze were frivolous fellows, not as wise as Borodin. He also told her about the enlarged meeting's resolution to punish me. He said that that resolution was based on his report, but that it was those two frivolous fellows who had insisted on his making it. Then he told her with a sigh that it was easy to be a leader and that a little carelessness could result in punishment like that which I was suffering. Since T'ai-lei was dead, she wanted me to know that her husband had held no prejudice against me.

While the Nanchang Uprising was going on, Chang Fa-k'uei led his forces back to Kwangtung. As the Canton area was occupied by Li Chi-shen's forces, Chang fought with Li over territorial matters, and the conflict between them became more violent after the Nanchang Uprising ended. On November 17, Chang drove Li and Huang Shao-hsiung out of Canton under the pretext of protecting the KMT; and a war soon ensued.[11] Chang's troops were subsequently transferred to the front in the T'ung River, Hsi River, and Pei River areas; and the defense of Canton City was greatly weakened. Neumann thought that it was the best time for an uprising because the unit that was left to defend Canton happened to be the Training Regiment. After the twentieth of November, Chang T'ai-lei and they began to step up their preparations for an uprising. Every day they discussed how to gather strength for the uprising, how to prepare the platform, and how to organize the Soviet regime.

Chang T'ai-lei and they decided to schedule the uprisings on December 11, because Chang Fa-k'uei's forces and Li Chi-shen's forces were in the thick of war during the early part of December. Most of our comrades there were not optimistic about the future of the uprising, because the strength of the workers and peasants there had repeatedly suffered damage, but those comrades had to act in accordance with the order. Some of them proposed not to stay stubbornly in Canton City, but Neumann objected to their proposal. He was of the opinion that it would be internationally significant if the Soviet regime could stay in Canton for ten days. My narrator, Wang I-chih, did not think that it was worth exchanging the lives of thousands of our comrades and the foundation that we had laid in Kwangtung over the past years just for the existence of the Soviet in Canton for ten days. She could not find any justification for Neumann's decision except that he was trying to win the commendation of the Comintern at the expense of the lives of those Chinese Communists including Chang T'ai-lei.

Less than three days after the outbreak of the uprising, Chang Fa-k'uei's forces moved back to the outskirts of Canton and attacked the mutineers. Li Fu-lin's forces, under cover from foreign warships, crossed the Pearl River to attack the Ch'ang-ti area.[12] The Machine Workers' Union led the reactionary workers to raid us here and there. We were suffering attacks from every direction. Quite a few comrades proposed a retreat towards the Tung Chiang area, but Neumann ordered that defense fortifications be constructed along the streets to prepare for street fighting. At noon on the thirteenth, Chang T'ai-lei was killed in an attack by the converging enemy. The mutineers were put to disorderly flight, and the uprising thus failed. Only a few comrades led some troops in a retreat towards the suburbs. Canton City soon became a city of terror. The Wen-te Road and Hsi-kuan areas were ablaze, shots were heard everywhere, and bodies were piled up in the streets. A lot of people were killed by mistake. When Wang I-chih stole out of Canton by the Canton–Hong Kong ferry on the evening of the fifteenth, the city was still in great disorder, and the government forces were searching the city for Communists under martial law.

After she finished her story of the uprising, Wang I-chih said that she had been completely dejected since that tragic event. She regretted that Chang T'ai-lei had been foolishly obedient, and said that the defeat would not have been so disastrous if he had not fought stubbornly in the city of Canton in compliance with Neumann's instructions. She resented Ch'ü Ch'iu-pai's spur-of-the-moment uprisings and his disregard for the safety of the cadres. Ch'ü's hailing her as a "heroine" was not enough to make up for the sorrow of the bereaved wife and child. Soon afterwards, she apostatized and led a life of seclusion.

The disastrous defeat of the Canton Uprising shocked the entire CCP. Even though the central authorities under Ch'ü Ch'iu-pai boasted that the Canton Uprising was a great act on the part of the Bolsheviks, quite a few comrades thought it an opportunistic military venture which ruined the foundation laid by the CCP in Canton over the past years. Later on, Stalin had to say that the Canton Uprising was a battle of retreat. At that time I not only resented the harm done by adventurism, but also protested against the slogan "Kill all landlords and local gentry," which was contained in the platform of the uprising force.

After the Canton Uprising was defeated, Ch'ü Ch'iu-pai and his colleagues continued to make hasty moves. They underestimated the CCP's losses under the uprising policy and the disappointment and fear among our men that were caused by the defeats. They insisted that the more the CCP fought, the stronger it would become; that the people's willingness to make revolution was constantly increasing; and that the tide of revolution was rising. They garbled information and distorted facts about the uprisings in their propaganda. Staying at Central Headquarters, they made and enforced uprising plans for wherever there was a little foundation of CCP local organization. The most famous one of those plans was the so-called Hunan-Hupeh Uprising Plan. In Shanghai, they continued to assign impossible and risky tasks to CCP members, and whoever raised any objection was dubbed an "opportunist" and punished. All of these things compelled me to oppose the central authorities headed by Ch'ü Ch'iu-pai.

What I saw and heard about during that period of time was a succession of hasty moves made by Ch'ü Ch'iu-pai and his followers. I felt that the CCP, which had endured for seven hard years, would thus be destroyed. I was tortured by the bad news concerning the detection of our clandestine organizations, the arrest and death of our comrades, and our setbacks here and there. In spite of the fact that I was leading a very insecure life because I had to keep running to escape police detection, I made every attempt to seek a way to save the CCP from its crisis.

In the eyes of Ch'ü Ch'iu-pai and his colleagues, I was the leader of those who opposed the central authorities. My residence was regarded as a club for opportunists. Those who also lived in that hostel one after another included Li Li-san, Hsü Pai-hao, Mme. Hsü, Wang I-chih, Liu Shao-ch'i, and Liu's wife. Liu Shao-ch'i and his wife arrived in Shanghai from Wuhan not long before the Canton Uprising. They were also regarded as opportunists of the Wuhan period. Perhaps that was the reason why they were also lodged in the same hostel as I was. During that period of time, we had many visitors. For instance, Lin Po-ch'ü, who was wanted by the Nanking government and was hiding in Shanghai, often came, along with his wife and niece, to see us. In our house we and our guests could talk about anything we pleased with regard to our Party, and we could express our complaints. Some of them joined me in criticizing Ch'ü Ch'iu-pai's "antiopportunism," "hasty moves," "irrational orders," and "unjust punishment." These, of course, were detested by Ch'ü Ch'iu-pai.

After a conclusion on the causes for the disastrous defeat of the Canton Uprising had been reached some time after the twentieth of December, I recommended to Ch'ü Ch'iu-pai that he change his policy. I pointed out that this was not the time to continue to stage uprisings, but the time to preserve our remaining strength; that Central Headquarters should prohibit our units in various places from staging unauthorized uprisings or any actions that risked the lives of our comrades; that emphasis should be placed on secretly organizing the peasants, permitting the peasants' army to rest in outlying areas, security measures for units in the cities, reforming the Party's branch headquarters, and organizing secret cells among the workers and students; and that the preservation of these assets would enable us to stage a successful uprising in the future.

My proposals conflicted with the policy of the central authorities, but Ch'ü Ch'iu-pai could not find sufficient reasons for contradicting my views. At the same time, some of the department heads, such as Hsiang Ying, who used to be a worker, did not want to continue to make hasty moves, because such moves had caused terrible losses. Ch'ü Ch'iu-pai told me that I would be allowed to make recommendations and to take part in some of their work provided that I would willingly admit my past mistakes of opportunism, accept the resolutions of the August Seventh Meeting and the November enlarged meeting, and completely agree to the uprising policy. Such unreasonable conditions were unacceptable to me, therefore Ch'ü and I could not arrive at an understanding.

In late February, 1928, Ch'ü and I had an important conversation, at which time we both put our cards on the table. Ch'ü said resolutely that no matter how many lives it might cost, Central Headquarters would insist on the uprising policy and oppose any slander about so-called hasty moves. I told him that I would organize a workers' and peasants' party to save the CCP from its present crisis should he fail to stop immediately the uprising policy which was endangering the life of the CCP. Ch'ü left in anger as soon as I had finished speaking. However, this plan of mine was not implemented for various reasons. Ch'ü Ch'iu-pai said later at the CCP's Sixth National Congress that he had never attempted to organize anything like a workers' and peasants' party, though he had made mistakes. When he said this, he was aiming at me. In addition to our differences of opinion on policy matters, the decreasing frequency of our meetings with each other, which was a safety precaution against danger, further aggravated the misunderstanding between Ch'ü Ch'iu-pai and me.

At that time a slight act of carelessness could cause us Communists to be arrested and secretly executed without trial. Yang Hu and Ch'en Ch'un, two notorious "executioners," were enforcing in Shanghai a terroristic policy of "it is better to kill a thousand innocent ones than allow one guilty one to get away." Ordinary people in Shanghai were living in fear of being suspected of being Communists. In our house such events as the sudden disappearance of Hsü Pai-hao, the sobbing of Wang I-chih, the visits of different types of people, and so forth were likely to arouse the suspicions of our landlord.

The unsuccessful suicide attempt of Liu Shao-chi's wife, Ho Pao-chen, at the beginning of 1928 put us in an especially awkward situation. Liu Shao-chi and Wang I-chih had been good friends before either of them married. Now that Wang I-chih was grieving over the death of her husband and was living in the same house, Liu Shao-ch'i felt obliged to console her. Ho Pao-chen was a jealous and narrow-minded woman. Perhaps our repeated setbacks made her more pessimistic. One day a maid found that she had poisoned herself in her room. Liu Shao-ch'i had to run extremely great risks to send her to a private hospital immediately. A few days later she returned home safely from the hospital. Soon after that suicide attempt, Wang I-chih moved out of the house. Liu Shao-ch'i told the doctor and the landlord that it was a little matter of jealousy and asked them to keep it under their hats; thus he avoided police investigation.

I had long been of the opinion that it was wrong for the central authorities to keep such an important cadre as Liu Shao-ch'i idle in that hostel. Then Ho Pao-chen's unusual act made it imperative for us to move away from there. Therefore, I went to see Li Wei-han, chief of the Central Organizational Department, and requested him to assign some tasks to Liu Shao-ch'i and his wife and to arrange a new secret residence for us. Li was friendly to me and was concerned about our situation. On about January 20, a few days before the Chinese New Year, another incident happened when I was visiting Li Wei-han, again to discuss our residence problem.

It was twilight and I was chatting at Li Wei-han's residence with Li and Kung Yin-ping, who was treasurer of Central Headquarters. Ho

Shu-heng dashed in and stammered out that he and several others had been arrested by the police while they were conducting some street activity. He was soon set free because the police thought he was an old pedant, which he had acted like in front of the police detective who was questioning him; so he had hurried back to ask Li Wei-han to rescue those who were still under arrest. We immediately realized that the police had deliberately set Ho free in order to locate his colleagues. At that time Ho had not ascertained whether or not he was being followed. Therefore, Li and Kung immediately burned all of the documents that were there, and we left, one by one, in less than five minutes.

I walked out of the alley, jumped into a rickshaw, and directed the rickshaw puller to run fast and make a lot of turns. With the aid of a street lamp, I saw that I was being followed by a man in another rickshaw. I knew that he could not arrest me without permission from police headquarters, but knew that I would eventually be arrested and killed if I could not shake him. So I jumped off the rickshaw downtown and walked into the crowd. For the next few hours I alternated between walking fast by myself and riding a rickshaw in order to get rid of that shadower.

At about 11 P.M. I thought that I had gotten rid of him. For the sake of my own safety, I went to the Kuang-t'ai-lai Hotel at San-yang-ching bridge instead of returning to my residence. As soon as I walked into the room that I had picked out, the desk manager came and asked me to sign the register. I found a suspicious-looking man standing beside the desk manager, so I knew that I was still being followed. In a calm and composed manner I signed the register, paid the rent, took off my coat and hat, and told the bellboy to go fetch some water. Soon after the man and the desk manager went downstairs, I also walked downstairs by another stairway. I was without my coat and hat, pretending that I was going to the rest room. When I passed the front desk, the man was faced toward the wall, making a telephone call. I dashed through the doorway, passed through a few small alleys, and jumped into a rickshaw. The street was quiet at night, and the rickshaw puller ran rapidly. I looked around and made sure that I had gotten rid of the shadower this time.

I heaved a sigh of relief and said to myself, "What a shame! But at least I am safe for the time being." I decided not to return to my residence, because I did not know what had happened to Li Wei-han and the others or whether my residence was still safe. I went to Lin Chu-han's house, which only a few comrades knew about. At that time Lin was in Moscow. It was midnight when I knocked at his door and awakened Mrs. Lin from her sleep. In order to prevent their neighbors from becoming suspicious, I said that I had come from Nanking and that my pocketbook had been stolen by a pickpocket. Mrs. Lin, who was a highbred woman and was experienced in revolutionary activities, immediately knew what was going on. She let me stay and cooked some food for me.

I told her everything and asked her niece, a CYC member, to collect information for me the next day. Mrs. Lin congratulated me on my escape from danger, and said with amusement, "That fellow wasted a whole evening and lost a bounty which was almost in his hands."[13] On the afternoon of the next day Miss Lin found out that Li Wei-han and the others were safe and that there was no problem about my residence. Therefore I went back to it in the twilight.

I thought that the central authorities were foolish to let Ho Shu-heng continue his street activities. As a matter of fact, the unnecessary danger that we encountered this time was caused by such a foolish act. Li and Kung did not fall into an enemy trap either, but I was told that they also had many close shaves. Li had to give up his house, along with everything inside it, and arrange a new residence. After that, I could not reach him because I did not know his new address. This dangerous experience scared Kung Yin-ping so much that he finally apostatized; it was reported that he escaped to Tientsin and entered into business. Ho Shu-heng also escaped to some other place. Citing this event as an example, I recommended to the central authorities that they pay more attention to directing the members' clandestine operations, which were safer and more effective.

In early February that hostel for senior cadres was finally abandoned. At the time that I left Wuhan for Nanchang, my wife and I had parted and she had returned to her native town with our son to escape persecution by the Wuhan government after it split with the Communists. She now committed our son into her mother's care and came to Shanghai alone to stay with me. We found a new house and decided to live alone. Liu Shao-ch'i and his wife were assigned to the hinterlands. From that time until almost ten years later I did not know about their whereabouts. By the time that I saw Liu again at Yen-an in 1937, he had become a leader of CCP clandestine operations in the White area, and one of the few of my friends who had won distinction. However, his wife, Ho Pao-chen, was killed by the Nationalists soon after we parted in Shanghai. Ch'in I-chun, Mme. Hsü Pai-hao, was also assigned to the interior after

she had stayed in my house for a short period of time. She was so unhappy that she apostatized later. The small group thus broke up and
left that hostel.

My wife and I moved to a house in a business district near Peking
Road. This was a safer district, because very few people with political
interests lived there, and it was some distance away from CCP units.
Only one of the couriers of Central Headquarters knew about my place,
and he was the only contact between the central authorities and me.
Hsiang Ying, who was an intimate friend of mine, visited me very often.
Between Hsiang and me there was a "mutual assistance pact," obliging
each of us to inform or rescue the other promptly in case of danger. My
wife and I liked that house very much, and I was ready to settle down
as an attic author.

We had lived there only about three weeks when we were compelled to move again because of another incident. At about 2 P.M. one
day Hsiang Ying hurried to my house to tell me that Lo Chueh, secretary
of the Shanghai Regional Committee of the CCP had been arrested at his
secret office two hours earlier, and that all of the central units might be
in danger because Lo had probably been sold out by traitors. In spite
of the fact that only one courier knew about my place, the enemy would
find out about it if that courier was caught, because he was a greenhorn.
Fortunately Hsiang Ying had rented a new house, which nobody else
knew about, and he asked us to hide there for the time being. Soon after
we arrived there, Hsiang went out to collect information.

He came back at night and said to us, "It is true that Lo was sold
out by traitors, and many of our men are in danger. According to information from Police Headquarters, a pretty woman who could speak
German and English had gone to see the chief of the Political Department of Police Headquarters that morning. She said that she had a roster
containing the names and addresses of some 350 CCP members, most of
whom were participants in the Nanchang Uprising, which she was willing
to surrender to the police if the police would give her $50,000 U.S. to-
gether with a passport, let her go to a country of her choice, and keep
the whole thing a secret. Before they made the deal, she would give
Lo Chueh's address first in order to prove the reliability of what she
said. Thus the police caught Lo Chueh."

Hsiang Ying also said that whenever the police took action to arrest
CCP members, our Central Headquarters always got a tip half an hour
ahead of time and could thus avoid loss. This time central authorties
knew nothing beforehand, but they had found out that Ho Chih-hua

was the traitor. Central Headquarters was trying to get the roster back from Ho, and then it would kill this stool pigeon. After Hsiang finished his shocking report, I told him with a sigh a story of the Wuhan period about the suspicions that comrades such as Teng Yen-ta and Chang Po-chun had had concerning Ho Chih-hua's loyalty, and their attempt to put her to death on a charge of being a spy for Chang Tso-lin. It was regrettable that Chou En-lai had failed to accept my advice and that his continued trust in Ho Chia-hsing and Ho Chih-hua had led to such a disaster.

Hsiang Ying and I had a long, all-night talk on this subject, and he told me about a lot of things that I had not quite understood. He pointed out that Central Headquarters was not very successful in its clandestine operations and that it was not paying enough attention to security measures. The CCP agencies were too numerous and too big, and their meetings were too many and too long, so that sometimes a dozen people had to stay together at a meeting for more than half a day. Documents had greatly increased in number, and their transmission had become very complicated. The CCP operation then was not like one of a clandestine organization but like one of a bureaucracy. He also pointed out that it was an unprecedented mistake to let such an unimportant person as Ho Chih-hua handle a roster containing the names of more than 350 members; that in the past even such important leaders as Ch'en Tu-hsiu had not been authorized to know so many names and addresses. It had been discovered, in addition to the fact that Ho Chih-hua was a traitor, that many new members were allowed to participate in confidential business without having their loyalty tested.

Hsiang Ying thought that the CCP had fortunately been able to escape greater loss because of Chou En-lai's successful intelligence operations as well as the enemy's ineffectiveness. He gave me a detailed account of Chou En-lai's intelligence operations. After the KMT's purge of April 12, 1927, some of our comrades, in the guise of anti-Communists, infiltrated the KMT's secret-service agency led by Ch'en Ko-fu. Three of them held important positions such as secretary and section chief in that agency, and Li K'e-nung was one of the three. Therefore we were able to find out ahead of time about the actions that Ch'en Ko-fu would take to arrest our comrades. Gradually Ch'en's suspicions had been aroused, and he began to purge the spies in his unit. Our comrades in his unit were forced to escape, and then we no longer had any agents in the KMT's secret-service agencies.

After the Nanchang Uprising, Chou En-lai returned to Central

Headquarters and headed the intelligence department again. His primary work was to direct Ku Shun-chang's secret-service men in infiltrating the police headquarters of the Foreign Concessions. Ku Shun-chang was an active member of the Ching Pang (Green Gang), and he was able to hire informants in various police units and to buy information from them half an hour or an hour before the police took action to arrest CCP members. However, there was a big failure in intelligence this time when Ku did not know beforehand about the police action concerning the arrest of Lo Chueh.

Hsiang Ying felt that the secret-service men of the Foreign Concessions and of the Nationalist government were treating the arrest of CCP members as a source of income. Perhaps they thought that arresting all of the CCP members at one time would be like destroying their source of income, and that it was better to make the arrests one at a time in order to have a perpetual source of income. Those "bad dogs" were not ideologically anti-Communist; they simply did not have any feelings about their country. They were hired by the foreigners or the Nationalists, but they acted entirely on their own behalf. It appeared that they were not trying to eradicate all of the CCP members in Shanghai; it was this delicate situation that enabled us to survive.

Hsiang Ying had a number of complaints about this type of intelligence operation. He pointed out that Ku Shun-chang was spending too much money in this area and that the intelligence organization was becoming bigger and bigger and was developing into a special system. Central Headquarters had to slacken its operation in other fields because it was spending the majority of its limited funds in the intelligence field. This type of intelligence operation was preventive in nature, while efforts to organize the workers and peasants were aggressive in nature. The slackening of aggressive types of work would change the nature of the Party, or, in other words, the CCP would change from a party of the people to a party away from the people in order to risk and speculate. He thought that the best way to avoid losses was to improve the infiltration-proof quality of the Party organization, to pay attention to security measures, and to conceal the Party organization and members in the midst of the people. He felt that intelligence work could only supplement these works rather than replace them.

After finishing his narration Hsiang suggested that I move as soon as possible and that I not let any couriers from Central Headquarters know my address. He was of the opinion that we would be in great danger if we were not able to get the roster back from Ho Chih-hua. I agreed with him, because I had also lost confidence in Central Head-quarters' security measures. I decided to look for a safer place to live.

Early on the morning of the next day Hsiang Ying went out, and I stayed in his house, waiting for information. He came back soon and told me in delight, "We've got Ho Chia-hsing and Ho Chih-hua. Ku Shun-chang and several of his men broke into their house this morning while they were still asleep. At gunpoint they surrendered the roster. Then Ku and his men shot them to death while one of the men set off a string of firecrackers outside the door, and then Ku and his men returned safely."

Hsiang Ying assumed that the police did not have a copy of the roster, and he thought that the retrieval of the roster and the death of the two traitors had greatly reduced the danger confronting us. (As a matter of fact, Ho Chih-hua was only badly wounded and was sent to a hospital by the police. Since without the roster she was no longer important, she returned to her native town in Szechwan after her wound healed.) He could not say definitely that we were completely out of danger, therefore he suggested that I move to a new place as previously planned.

I lost direct contact with the central authorities after I moved to an old alley near La-chi bridge. My landlady was a sick, old woman whose only son was serving on an ocean-going ship and was only at home once every several months. Pretending that I was a convalescent, my wife and I lived upstairs in that woman's house, and we got along very well with her. None of the couriers of Central Headquarters knew my address, so of course I did not receive any letters or documents. At the same time most of the other comrades also moved, and therefore I could not reach them either. During that period of time Hsiang Ying was the only person who knew my address. Teng Chung-hsia, an old friend of mine, knew my address later and visited once in a while.

An important aspect of my life during that period of time was my contact with Ch'en Tu-hsiu. He had not participated in the August Seventh Meeting. After he sneaked to Shanghai from Hankow, he led an extremely secret and solitary life which was not disturbed by the police actions. After the Canton Uprising failed, we felt that it was necessary for us to exchange views. Therefore I was led to his residence by a liaison man. He lived in an alley on Lao-pa-tzu Road on the border between the Foreign Concessions and the Chinese district. Perhaps he chose to live there because that was a district to which neither the foreigners nor the Nationalists would pay much attention.

We met again after a short absence from each other, but neither of us was happy. I condoled with him over the deaths of his two sons. (Ch'en Yen-nien, who had been secretary of the Kwangtung Provincial Committee of the CCP, and Ch'en Ch'iao-nien, who had been secretary of the CCP Northern Regional Committee, were killed one after the other in Shanghai during the KMT's purge that started on April 12.) We expressed our regrets over the misfortunes of many comrades, especially Li Ta-chao and Chao Shih-yen. Then we stopped talking about the past and began to discuss the current political situation.

In spite of his solitary life, Ch'en Tu-hsiu's attention to the political situation had never slackened. He talked about the union of the Nanking government with the Wuhan government, the resignation of Chiang Kai-shek on August 15, 1927, the dispute caused by the Special Committee, the punitive expedition against T'ang Sheng-chih, the party-protection movement organized by Wang Ching-wei, and so forth. He knew the inside information about all of these internal disputes of the KMT.

We promised to see each other more often, about once every two weeks, in order to discuss the political situation. For the sake of safety, I had to go to his residence early in the morning and stay there until it got dark in order to escape the notice of the police detective and other people. Living in solitude, Ch'en regarded my visits as important events, and he prepared everything for them beforehand. Only Hsiang Ying occasionally joined us in our subsequent conversations. Due to those frequent contacts, Ch'ü Ch'iu-pai accused us of being the opportunistic antagonists in the Party.

Gradually we discussed many intra-Party problems. As I have mentioned before, there had been misunderstandings between Ch'en and me. I disliked his assumption of a negative attitude during the latter part of the Wuhan period. He said that he was sorry about it, and that he was afraid he could not change the resolution of the August Seventh Meeting even though he had not made that mistake himself. Through a misunderstanding, he thought that it had been my idea and my mistake to try to stop the Nanchang Uprising. I told him that, on the contrary, I myself favored the uprising, but that I had had to try to stop it in order to comply with the directive from the Comintern. Therefore he began to understand the truth about the situation and to consider the resolution of the CCP's enlarged meeting of November concerning my punishment to be a distortion of the facts. Our explanations to each other made both of us understand the facts and thus eliminated most of the misunderstanding between us.

He made a lot of comments on Chiang Kai-shek's resumption of the office of commander-in-chief on January 4, 1928. It was his opinion that Chiang's resumption of that office would not enable the Nanking government to make any remarkable improvements; the struggles among various factions of the KMT and the struggles among KMT troop commanders would continue; contradictions would continue to exist between the Nanking government and the world powers; instead of improving the people's livelihood and stabilizing the society, the Nanking government would continue to squeeze money from the people, connive at the brutality of rascals and secret-service men, conduct cruel search-and-destroy operations in the rural area, and oppress the peasants. He concluded that the CCP would be able to rise to power if it had a correct policy for leading the struggle of the people.

He agreed completely with me in opposing Ch'ü Ch'iu-pai's uprising policy. He thought that those spur-of-the-moment uprisings were not in agreement with scientific Marxism and were in violation of Lenin's instructions concerning uprisings. In fact, all of those uprisings suffered disastrous defeats. He repeatedly advised the central authorities to change their uprising policy, but to no avail.[14] Therefore, he said that he would love to join me in trying to correct the mistakes of Central Headquarters under the direction of Ch'ü Ch'iu-pai.

I reminded him that our previous proposals to the central authorities had been regarded as opportunistic views and had not been accepted. Therefore, for the sake of a bright future, I made a serious proposal to organize a workers' and peasants' party in order to effectively save the CCP and eliminate disputes. Said party should develop on the basis of CCP membership, and the principal points of its platform should continue to be opposition to imperialism and realization of the agrarian revolution, but that party should no longer be a branch of the Comintern. Ch'ü Ch'iu-pai and his colleagues were taking advantage of the Comintern's instructions to justify their stubborn and hasty moves. Comintern representatives such as Lominadze were not familiar with the situation in China, and their foolish acts caused disasters. If the new organization, under the name of the Workers' and Peasants' Party, was a friend to rather than a branch of the Comintern so that it could make its own decisions according to the will of the majority, perhaps we could minimize our mistakes and walk out of the darkness towards a bright future.

Ch'en was greatly interested in my proposal, and thought it a reasonable way to improve the present situation of the Party. However, the previous setbacks had deprived him of his courage to shoulder such a great and difficult mission, so he said that it would be very difficult to implement. In his opinion, the Comintern would relentlessly try to frustrate our plan instead of giving it fair and just consideration; the Communists and Socialists in Western European countries would not give us their strong support because they did not pay any attention to the Orient; as for ourselves, even if our proposal were accepted with unanimous approval, it would be difficult to solve the problem of finances.

In early March the arrest of Lo Chueh caused great confusion in CCP Central Headquarters. Ch'en said to me, "The present situation indicates that it has become impossible for Ch'ü Ch'iu-pai and the others to make any more foolish moves, even if they are still crying for uprisings, because the central units are undergoing reorganization for the sake of their own safety, and most of the CCP's local units in various places have been destroyed. Now we can delay organizing the Workers' and Peasants' Party, reserving it for our last resort. Perhaps we can find other means to improve the present situation." Due to Ch'en's prudence, I canceled any plans I had to organize the Workers' and Peasants' Party, even though I mentioned it once to Ch'ü Ch'iu-pai.

On May 3, 1928, Japanese troops, under the pretext of protecting their people in Tsinan, massacred several thousand Chinese people and murdered Ts'ai Kung-shih, a Chinese envoy, there. The Japanese brutality touched off anti-Japanese movements throughout the country. Ch'ü Ch'iu-pai and his colleagues treated it with indifference. They thought that the tasks of the CCP were to stage uprisings and to oppose the Nationalist Regime, and that it would be the same as helping Chiang Kai-shek if the CCP participated in the anti-Japanese movement, because the Japanese action was aimed at the Nationalists. Such an absurd viewpoint made us angry. Ch'en Tu-hsiu and I were in favor of an all-out effort to lead the anti-Japanese movement in order both to unmask Chiang Kai-shek's compromising with foreign countries and at the same time to win the support of the people. It was a downright crime to remain outside that anti-imperialist movement. Under the influence of Hsiang Ying, who succeeded to the post of secretary of the Shanghai Regional Committee after Lo Chueh was arrested, most of the CCP members in Shanghai supported our view.

In mid-May, Teng Chung-hsia came to see me and told me that in accordance with a directive from the Comintern, the CCP had decided that in June it would convene its Sixth National Congress in Moscow to review present policies and seek internal solidarity for the Party. The Comintern was directly inviting me, Ch'en Tu-hsiu, Ts'ai Ho-sen, Lo

Chang-lung, and himself to attend that congress, and CCP Central Head-quarters had sent him to inform me that I should begin to prepare for the journey if I wished to accept the invitation. Teng Chung-hsia did not like the policy of Ch'ü Ch'iu-pai and his cohorts either, but his op-position was not as violent as ours. He, too, knew that there was a serious crisis within the Party. Therefore, he told me that he did not want to see any division in the Party, and he talked me into accepting the invitation.

Then Hsiang Ying came to see me and told me some news about the Party. He told me that Lominadze and Neumann had been trans-ferred back to Moscow and reportedly had been criticized by the Com-intern. The Comintern had recently instructed CCP Central Headquar-ters not to stage hasty uprisings, and through CCP Central Headquarters the Comintern had in turn been informed of our views in opposition to the uprising policy. In view of the CCP crisis, the Comintern had de-cided to by-pass CCP Central Headquarters and directly extend invita-tions to the five of us to attend the congress. He thought that it could be a turning point in the history of the CCP, and therefore it had be-come unnecessary to antagonize Central Headquarters directly.

I had not seen Ts'ai Ho-sen and Lo Chang-lung for a long time, and I did not know their addresses and situations. Therefore, I went to see Ch'en, to discuss with him whether we should accept the invitation. He said that he himself did not want to attend the congress, but he encouraged the remaining four of us to accept the inivitation and go. He anticipated that the Sixth National Congress would correct the ob-vious mistake of Ch'ü Ch'iu-pai's hasty moves. Therefore, he thought it would be inadvisable for us to make written recommendations or to show an attitude of noncooperation instead of participating in the congress.

One after the other, Hsiang Ying and I tried to talk Ch'en into ac-cepting the invitation and going along with us. I even said such things as, "If you don't go, a break in the relationship between you and the Comin-tern or CCP Central Headquarters will be a matter of time." He said, "The harsh criticism against me contained in the resolution of the August Sev-enth Meeting has indicated the Comintern's intention to get rid of me. Be-cause of this, my attendance will do me no good." He added that he was determined not to attend the Sixth National Congress. He had written essays for Central Headquarters publications before and would like to write some more for them in the future; but he was not willing to join the CCP's leading group and would not try to defend himself nor to criticize others. Furthermore, he said that he would not antagonize the

Comintern and CCP Central Headquarters if the Sixth Congress was successful and that he was willing to consider a proposal to let him live in Moscow as a political refugee.

Thus I informed the Central Headquarters through Teng Chung-hsia that I accepted the invitation, and asked Teng to prepare for my travel. Teng was an enthusiastic man and an old friend of mine. He was happy that I accepted the invitation, but he regretted that Ch'en Tu-hsiu did not want to go. He wanted me to make another attempt to persuade Ch'en, but I failed to do so. After the Sixth Congress, the Comintern did not again invite Ch'en to visit Soviet Russia.

My eight months of life in hiding in Shanghai thus came to an end. Then I took another trip to the distant "Red Capital"—Moscow.

IN MOSCOW

CHAPTER

The Sixth Congress of the Chinese Communist Party

In the latter part of May, 1928, I traveled through Dairen and Harbin and entered Soviet Russia by slipping across the border at Manchouli. I completed the necessary travel procedures at the frontier reception station set up by the Comintern. It took me about two weeks to complete the entire journey from Shanghai to Moscow. I stayed on in Moscow for two and one-half years, until early 1931, when the Comintern sent me back to China in connection with the rectification of the erroneous Li Li-san line of the CCP. Here I will relate some of the major events that I experienced during my sojourn in Moscow.

I did not stop over in the city of Moscow after my arrival there, but was sent to an old-fashioned manor house on its outskirts. I do not remember the name or location of this place, except that it was near a relatively secluded village situated somewhat off the main communication routes. The Comintern had probably chosen this village as the venue of the Sixth Congress of the CCP to ensure secrecy. In the past this manor house had belonged to an aristocratic landlord. Although already dilapidated, it still had some traces of splendor and dignity. Nearby was a state-operated farm with some scattered farmhouses and overgrown pathways through the fields, which presented an early summer landscape typical of Moscow's environs.

The quarters at our conference site were extremely poor, like army barracks. There was no library, nor were there any facilities for recreation. Only a simple clinic was set up for physical examinations. The doctor who examined me said that my body was strong, which pleased me tremendously, because in spite of my hard life during the past few years, I now knew that I was none the worse physically. This was indeed gratifying. The quality of our food was particularly good. Our special treatment reflected the considerable progress made by the New Economic Policy, a recovery period that the Soviet Union was passing through.

I got there relatively early. Later, delegates arrived every day, including the members of Ch'ü Ch'iu-pai's CC, who came one after the other. With the approach of the date of the congress, everybody got busy making preparations. A few nights before the opening, Nikolai I. Bukharin, chairman of the Comintern, leading a group of more than ten persons composed of Pavel Mif, head of the Comintern's China Bureau, and students of Sun Yat-sen University, suddenly showed up. Bukharin asked that a preliminary meeting be held in order to hear the opinions of us delegates. So the twenty-odd delegates present and Bukharin and his party assembled in a small conference room. In it there was only a long table surrounded by a row of chairs and benches. We squeezed ourselves in, some sitting while others stood or leaned against the wall.

To begin with, Bukharin announced that those who opposed the Comintern should speak up first. This proposal was seconded by Ch'ü Ch'iu-pai and Ch'en Shao-yü, who added, "In that case, let Comrade Chang Kuo-t'ao be the first speaker!" All present agreed unanimously and urged me to speak. Peking's delegate, Wang Chung-yi, approved of the idea that I speak up to criticize the policies of the CCP, but he objected to having anyone at will label me as anti-Comintern. So I stood up to speak out my mind, and I talked for about three hours, including translation time. The preliminary meeting was adjourned without Bukharin asking a second man to express an opinion, and there was never another session of it.

Of course I cannot recall my speech in its entirety, but I still remember the main points vividly. I started out from the point of view of my opposition to the Comintern, never denying my dissatisfaction with its leadership. Moreover, in my opinion, the mistake of the CCP leadership was not that it was anti-Comintern or that it violated Comintern directives. On the contrary, it was that the CCP was relying too much on the

Comintern. Needless to say, the leaders of the young CCP lacked experience, so obeying instructions of the Comintern was the proper obligation of these subordinates toward their superiors. We believed in the
Comintern, acknowledging the fact that the old revolutionaries of the
Comintern were more wordly-wise than we were. Whenever our views
differed with the directives of the Comintern, we invariably regarded
ourselves as a group of pupils who dared not show any confidence in
their own judgment. Consequently, we sacrificed our own convictions
in order to accommodate the Comintern directives. We even looked
upon any instruction given by the Comintern representative as Holy
Writ which had to be followed blindly. In brief, the situation had reached
the level of superstitious faith in the Comintern—which was a sad fact.

Continuing, I cited examples to prove my point. On the basis of the
Comintern directive to the effect that the main task of the Chinese revolution was the national revolution, the Comintern representative Maring
(Hendricus Sneevliet) came up with these conclusions in June, 1923:
All work should be handed over to the KMT, and all CCP members
should also join the KMT and work actively in that party; the working
class must first possess national consciousness before developing class
consciousness; in addition Maring prophesied that it would be at least
five years before China could produce a genuine Communist Party. At
that time I and other comrades differed with him and hoped that the
CCP could develop independently. At one time I was considered anti-
Comintern, and I received severe punishment from the CC of the CCP.
Yet only four years after Maring made these remarks, another Comintern
representative named Besso Lominadze told us in July, 1927, that the
CC of the CCP had committed the serious blunder of opportunism. The
main reason, in Lominadze's opinion, was that the CCP had abandoned
the leadership in winning over the proletariat in the overall revolution.
His views were diametrically opposed to Maring's, giving the impression
that the CCP had already reached a strong position and that had it not
made the error of opportunism, the Chinese revolution could have
achieved victory under the CCP's leadership. Besides, as we had no
opportunity to set forth our own opinions, we were adjudged guilty of
the crime of opposing the Comintern, and were reprimanded and
punished. Thus we had two extremely differing views before us, so
what was really the crux of the matter? Could we not discover contradictions in them? Was all this characteristic of the correct directives of
the Comintern?

I proceeded to narrate the circumstances prevailing during the period of collaboration between the KMT and the CCP. I did not point out bluntly the fundamental mistake of the policy of joining the KMT, but I did explain at length that nothing good would come out of it. I pointed out that by combining the CCP and the KMT in one organizational unit, controversies between the two parties were bound to increase day by day. Members of the CCP worked hard, even doing manual labor, and yet they were regarded as a bunch of people who were dissatisfied with their lot. The CCP had no army units of its own, so it held no strategic position to speak of. During the anti–Chiang Kai-shek period in Wuhan, we were constantly surrounded by reactionary forces both domestic and foreign. The Chinese Communists were in an inferior position, always making concessions, striving to prevent the collapse and dissolution of the anti-Chiang alliance and to stabilize Wuhan's so-called leftist authority. The most obvious fact was that the CCP did not have enough power, or at least that it did not know its own capacity, so that, though ambitious and resolute, it eventually crumbled under heavy burdens and responsibilities.

Bukharin interrupted at this juncture, saying, "We're all familiar with all these matters, so why do you waste so much time bringing them up?" I paused and reflected that since I had not put the blame directly on the basic mistake of joining the KMT, I might as well not be outspoken about the erroneous judgment of the Comintern. I continued by saying that the "Letter to Party Members at the August 7 [1927] Conference" failed to mention the relative strengths of our side and the enemy during the Wuhan period. It struck me that the error of opportunism on the part of the CC of the CCP had been held entirely responsible for the failure of our present revolution. Was such criticism fair? I went on to say that I did not deny that the error of opportunism had been committed by the CC of the CCP during the Wuhan period. Furthermore, this error ought to have been rectified; however, an improper rectification might have incited still another error of extreme leftism.

I went on to review the problem of the Nanchang Uprising, pointing out that this serious issue indicated that our policy had changed from the discontinuation of our concessions toward the end of the Wuhan period to active resistance. At that time Lominadze, on the basis of a telegraphic order from the Comintern signed by Bukharin, wanted me personally to go to Nanchang to forestall this uprising. For the sake of abiding by Party discipline, I relayed the views of the Comintern in full. Events later proved that there was no way to stop the Nanchang Uprising, which subsequently broke out. After the failure of the uprising, however, the CC of Ch'ü Ch'iu-pai had the gall to ignore facts by accusing me of not having led the Nanchang Uprising firmly and of falsifying an official edict and blocking the insurrection. This was indeed a strange situation. Continuing, I interpolated solemnly, "Let me now ask Comrade Bukharin, Did you or did you not send the telegram to prevent the Nanchang Uprising? Also, let me ask Comrade Ch'ü Ch'iu-pai, who is present here, After my arrival in Nanchang, why did you twist the facts by saying that I had relayed the official decree incorrectly?"

Backed up by facts, I criticized the CC of Ch'ü Ch'iu-pai for having toyed with the insurrection and for having blindly labeled everything in the past as opportunism in order to explain away all sorts of ridiculous behavior; Ch'ü even bragged that the present CC was the revolutionary headquarters of the Bolsheviks. Therefore, I ridiculed Ch'ü Ch'iu-pai's CC by asserting that this was by no means a headquarters of insurgents but merely a stupid "insurrectionary editorial department."

Continuing, I spelled out my views regarding the policies of the CC of the CCP, pointing out that we should not rebel at random without first making adequate preparations, such as winning over the masses and increasing our own strength. At present the White terror was quite serious, and we should consolidate our strength instead of casually making an adventurous move. But the policy of the CC was exactly the opposite. Instead of concentrating its revolutionary strength, it merely schemed for quick successes and continuous uprisings. Even after the dismal failure of the Canton Insurrection, the CC still claimed that the revolutionary tide was rising relentlessly, and it mapped out the insurrection in Hunan and Hupeh and firmly continued with the rebellion. In brief, all these actions were equivalent to suicide.

I held that there were many chances to win over the masses. I stressed that the Tsinan Massacre, which broke out on May 3, 1927, aroused a nationwide anti-Japanese tide. Ch'ü Ch'iu-pai's CC was of the opinion that this anti-Japanese movement could benefit the KMT and Chiang Kai-shek, so he adopted a passive attitude. Although I and our comrades in Shanghai differed with this opinion and requested the CC to lead the anti-Japanese mass movement, the CC continued to pay no heed. This was a downright sacrifice of the opportunity to win over the masses. The CC apparently thought that the revolution to carry out land reform was the main task, and it refused to take anti-Japanese, anti-imperialist principles seriously. But, I asked, since when had we abandoned this basic anti-imperialist task? In my opinion, being anti-Japanese by no means helped Chiang Kai-shek; on the contrary, not only could the masses rally around the anti-imperialist banner of the CCP, but they could also strike a blow at Chiang Kai-shek, the represser of the anti-imperialist campaign.

As I reached this point, Bukharin knitted his eyebrows, shook his head, and spoke up excitedly, "So that's how it happened! You'd better start elaborating from this point." I said that there were still many stories to be told, but I could only give a general outline. The alliance between the workers' economic struggle and the political struggle was originally a principle that we had applied for a long time, but that Ch'ü Ch'iu-pai's CC negated the importance of the workers' economic struggle and daily organizational work. It was the same in the peasant movement. He merely hoped that the peasants would arm themselves, attack the cities and strategic areas, and win initial victories in one or more provinces, while he neglected peasant organizations and their economic demands at various levels. As to the CCP, it had sunk and had split itself down the middle. Not only were we physically molested by the enemy, but we were also trampled by the erroneous policies of the CC. Now, in order to carry out its erroneous policies, it resorted to the method of forced orders and punishment, which nurtured a centrifugal tendency within the Party. Democracy no longer existed within the Party.

After relating these opinions, I pointed out frankly that Ch'ü Ch'iu-pai's CC had committed the grave error of putschism. Repeatedly I had suggested that this be rectified, but my suggestions were invariably rejected by Ch'ü Ch'iu-pai. For this reason, at one time I became so furious that I intended to take action in order to oppose this deviation. It was only after the Comintern directly invited me to attend this congress that I had decided to suspend my opposition and come here to air my views. It was not that I meant to settle old accounts, but I merely hoped that the error could be rectified and that a guideline for the future could be drawn up. I remember that in concluding my speech, I said, "This, then, is my honest opinion, the opinion of a person who has been labeled anti-Comintern."

Although I did not prepare my speech in advance, I said all that I wanted to say in this one speech. All present, whether agreeing with me or not, regarded it as representing the opposition within the CCP. Bukharin later admitted that he learned a great deal from my speech; therefore, he decided that it was no longer necessary for him to solicit other dissenting views. A Russian comrade who had worked in China told me after reading the transcript of my speech that it was a great oration which depicted the true situation of the CCP. Its only shortcoming, he commented, was that I did not set forth my positive views more explicitly, and he hoped that I would make up for this in my formal speech during the forthcoming congress.

More than thirty delegates attended the Sixth Congress of the CCP, which formally opened in the latter part of June. More than ten of the Chinese Communist students who were then studying in Moscow were present as observers. After the opening ceremony the congress heard Bukharin deliver the keynote speech, which was entitled "The Situation of World Revolution and the Tasks of the Chinese Communist Party." In his long report he spent a great deal of time replying to the points I had raised. His report later became the basis for the political resolution made during this congress. His performance made a deep impression on me and other comrades, all of whom agreed that he possessed an honest and outspoken style.

Speaking about the relations between the CCP and the Comintern, he avoided mentioning the Comintern's errors in policy and he did not assert that the Comintern's directives to the CCP were all correct. Nor did he state that the errors of the CC of the Ch'en Tu-hsiu period were due to violations of Comintern directives. On the other hand, he frankly admitted that it was an indisputable fact that Comintern representatives sent to China had made many serious errors. On the basis of this judgment, he expressed the regrets of the Comintern with regard to the Chinese revolution.

Referring to the period of cooperation between the KMT and the CCP, particularly the events during the Wuhan period, Bukharin held that the failure of the revolution was due to the superior strength of the enemy and to the fact that at that time the international revolutionary forces were not in a position to give effective support to the Chinese revolution. This in turn was because of the fact that while the Chinese revolution was reaching a high tide, the revolutionary movement in Western Europe was suffering great harassment. At the same time, the CC of the CCP lacked the correct understanding of the characteristics of the Chinese revolution and the role of the United Front. At a critical moment the CCP failed to break through the enemy encirclement, thus committing the error of opportunism.

On the question of the Nanchang Uprising, he declared sonorously, "It is true that the Comintern sent a telegram to forestall the insurrection." While he did not go on to comment on whether or not it was a correct move or on the reason behind the telegram, he declared that the Nanchang Uprising was a military action against the Chinese Nationalist

Party (KMT) that, basically, was a correct move. That it was not possible to coordinate the Nanchang Uprising and the Autumn Harvest Uprising was regarded as the most serious miscalculation.

Bukharin sternly criticized the error of putschism, and demanded that the present congress rectify this. But in the long run he did not wish the CCP to suffer further shake-ups, and he adopted the spirit of the mediator by calling on all CCP members to unite along the correct line of the Comintern.

He spared no effort in explaining the significance of anti-imperialism. He thought that Japan had ambitions of dividing China and, moreover, that a major war would break out in the Pacific among imperialists eager to carve up China. Consequently, the main task of the Chinese revolutionaries was to hold on to China's independence. Starting from this premise, he thought that the CCP would in the future form an anti-imperialist alliance with the massive petty bourgeoisie. He even predicted the likelihood of responsibility-sharing between the CCP and the petty-bourgeois elements of the type of T'an P'ing-shan. He was against opposing rich landlords too vehemently. Though his views on this matter were far-sighted, they were later criticized by the Stalin group as rightist opportunism.

After Bukharin spoke, it was Ch'ü Ch'iu-pai's turn to give a political report. He used up the greater part of his time relating stories concerning the period of KMT-CCP cooperation. He criticized Ch'en Tu-hsiu who, while agreeing to the CCP policy of joining the KMT, forfeited the chance to grasp the right to leadership, becoming an appendage of the KMT instead. Also, he pointed out that my consistent policy of opposing the CCP's joining the KMT showed that I dared not contend with the KMT for revolutionary leadership and that such a policy was likewise right opportunism. He claimed that he himself could abide by the Comintern directive correctly only by agreeing to join the KMT in order to fight actively for the right to leadership in the Chinese national revolution. His arguments, however, even though quoting a few of Lenin's words, failed to enumerate a number of clear historical facts to prove the one-hundred-percent correctness of his stand. Besides, he did not stress how to rectify the error of putschism, and he did not spell out the policies that should be adopted by the CCP in the future. For this reason many delegates were dissatisfied with his report.

Before the congress concluded its discussion of these reports, Ch'ü Ch'iu-pai introduced a slate of candidates to sit on various committees which would be charged with the tasks of examining various reports and proposals and of drafting the resolutions for final approval by the congress. As many delegates were not pleased with the proposed slate, which excluded comrades of the opposition, a fierce debate ensued. Finally, the slate was turned down by the congress. This, in turn, was interpreted by Ch'ü Ch'iu-pai as a vote of no confidence, so he walked out from the conference hall and appealed to the Comintern for help. As a result, the Comintern sent four experienced officials who, partly by pressure and partly by mediation, eventually managed to have the slate amended acceptably and approved by the congress.

There were differences of opinion among the delegates. Ch'ü Ch'iu-pai and his handful of followers maintained that the line followed by the CC after the August 7 Conference was correct. Wang Jo-fei and Wang Tse-k'ai, who were closely associated with Ch'en Tu-hsiu, were extremely critical and said that whatever Ch'ü Ch'iu-pai wrote and did was totally wrong. Between these two opposing opinions stood Chou En-lai, Li Li-san, and Teng Chung-hsia, who were in favor of maintaining the leadership of the Ch'ü Ch'iu-pai CC provided that the error was rectified. Ts'ai Ho-sen, Hsiang Ying, Lo Chang-lung, Wang Chung-yi, and I contended that Ch'ü Ch'iu-pai should rectify his errors completely before carrying on with his work in the CC.

This congress, however, was held under the direct supervision of the Comintern. Though Bukharin seldom took part in the discussions, Mif, director of the China Bureau, was present at each and every session, leading his men, including the land-problem expert Volen. Mif even went so far as to exert pressure on the congress in the name of the Comintern. Once he invited me for a serious talk, during which he frankly said to me, "It is the hope of the Comintern that you and Ch'ü Ch'iu-pai will be able to bury all your differences and cooperate with each other." I told him that if Ch'ü Ch'iu-pai would make amends, cooperation would be no problem. He sounded me out as to whether such cooperation would be constrained. In reply, I pointed my finger at a porcelain teacup lying on the table and said, "Well, it's just like that broken cup. Though it can be mended, the result can never look as good as a new teacup, and I do hope that nobody will ever break it again in the future." Mif replied, "But the organization of a Communist Party cannot be likened to a teacup, because a party is something organic. The Comintern is confident that it has the strength to lead the Chinese comrades, set their errors right, and make them united and able to cooperate with one another. With your approval, I will report to the Comintern to the effect that we have reached an understanding amongst us." I sensed that his words smacked of coercion, so I told him that I would respect the Comintern's decision. He apparently had said the same thing to Ch'ü Ch'iu-pai and had elicited the same response from him.

Mif's overbearing interference was really excessive, and it made the situation worse. Ch'ü Ch'iu-pai's opinions varied greatly from mine, yet after arguing them out, each of us admitted his shortcomings and mistakes and agreed to follow the majority. Things could have been solved more smoothly, but Mif apparently felt that opportunism, putschism, and the Comintern (or its agents) were all wrong, or else certain Chinese Communist leaders were in the wrong. The whole problem was not easy to clear up, and the only way out was a decision of a coercive nature by the Comintern. It was evident that the controversy could not be solved satisfactorily in this manner. Everybody felt wronged and bore grudges against Mif for meddling. Consequently, Ch'ü Ch'iu-pai and I felt during the congress that Mif was sticking his nose in too deeply, harboring an ambition to manipulate the CCP.

The activities of Ch'en Shao-yü, Shen-Tse-min, and their group during the congress did not work to Mif's advantage either. These Sun Yat-sen University students, who belonged to the Mif clique, acted as interpreters during the congress. They were relatively new comrades who primarily took pride in being extraordinary. After hearing the mud-slinging arguments among several delegates, they invariably assumed a derogatory attitude toward those senior leaders. After listening to Ch'ü Ch'iu-pai's half-baked interpretation of Marxism-Leninism, they often ridiculed him behind his back, believing that they knew much more than their elders. Other delegates who could not express themselves properly were criticized as lacking in theoretical knowledge. They were equally opposed to Ch'ü Ch'iu-pai's putschism and my opportunism, which gave the impression that in the future they should shoulder the main tasks of the Party. All this was generally regarded as a move by Mif to train and cultivate new cadres in order to attack us, the original leaders of the Party.

During the congress the activities of Hsiang Chung-fa, who had been chairman of the Hupei Provincial General Trade Union during the Wuhan period, also caused people to look askance at him. After the Wuhan split in 1927, he came to Moscow as the CCP's representative to the Comintern, where he was regarded as the prototype of the Chinese proletariat. He also followed Mif's maneuverings in all respects. Thus his status was enhanced with the passing of time, while he learned a few platitudes about Marxism-Leninism. During the congress, Mif and Ch'en

Shao-yü used him as their trump card in denouncing our errors. Hsiang Chung-fa boldly claimed that he was the successor to Ch'en Tu-hsiu. He assumed an even more patriarchal attitude than Ch'en Tu-hsiu, often rebuking certain comrades during the congress and invoking his pet phrase, "This is the correct line of the Comintern." As a matter of fact, he was by no means a man worthy of respect, but was somewhat like a rogue. Both Li Li-san and Hsiang Ying, who had had contacts with him, knew his background and often ridiculed his behavior on the sly. Most of us believed that he could not shoulder the heavy responsibilities of a leader, and we resented his "Miffy airs." However, as the CCP lacked the leadership core and the appropriate person to take his place, we had to endure him for the time being.

Though the congress was full of discordant elements, it was after all held under the forceful leadership of the Comintern, and so it was deemed essential to produce results of some sort that could be handed over properly to the Party successors. Consequently we made grandiose resolutions, which resulted in the congress being publicized as the most successful of all CCP congresses. Scrutiny, however, reveals that the contents of the resolutions were vague and inconsistent on many points, even containing hidden rocks.

In the first place, the congress defined the nature, motive power, and tasks of the Chinese revolution. After the KMT-CCP split, one of the crucial problems to be solved in earnest concerned the fundamental policies of the CCP. Based on Bukharin's report, the congress ruled that "at the present stage the Chinese revolution is a bourgeois democratic revolution" charged with two major tasks: "First, to drive out the imperialists in order to accomplish the real unification of China; second, to carry out the agrarian revolution by overthrowing completely and popularly the private land-ownership system of the landlord class."[1] The congress held that "although the two above-mentioned tasks do not yet exceed the scope of the capitalist mode of production, yet they must be accomplished by the proletariat by leading the great revolutionary power of the broad masses of workers and peasants, opposing the national bourgeoisie, overthrowing the imperialist domination and the landlord-warlord-bourgeois KMT regime through the revolutionary method of armed insurrection, setting up a workers' and peasants' Soviet democratic dictatorship, and blazing the trail of the Chinese revolution toward non-capitalism [that is, socialism]."[2] This formula later became the blueprint of Mao Tse-tung's so-called New Democracy.

The congress denounced opportunism and putschism, and pointed out that "at present there is no such thing as a revolutionary high tide in China, so the Party's general line is to win over the masses."[3] The congress held: In the cities we should mainly carry on organizational work among the laboring masses and lead the anti-imperialist movement; in the rural areas we should make good use of the existing Soviet bases, while the small number in the worker-peasant Red Army, on the basis of development of revolutionary conditions, should wrest initial victories in one or more provinces. Therefore, the congress formulated the "Resolution Regarding the Soviet Regime" and the "Resolution on Peasant Land" which concerned the confiscation of land from the landlords for distribution among poor peasants.

The most ambiguous resolution of the congress was the concept—or the formula—for the Chinese Soviets, that is, the democratic dictatorship of workers and peasants. For instance, the political resolution asserted that "The Canton Insurrection opened the way for the third stage of the Chinese revolution—the Soviet period," and at the same time it said that the Canton Insurrection was a "rearguard battle." Obviously, the two statements were contradictory. In his speech to the congress, Bukharin stressed that Japan was resorting to violence and aggression by sending troops to Tsinan and that China was facing the threat of being partitioned or of having an imperialist war break out in the Pacific. In the coming fierce struggle against imperialism, it was possible that the CCP might share power equally with the petty bourgeoisie of the T'an P'ing-shan type. This concept of "coalition government," which was obviously different from "the workers' and peasants' dictatorship," was excluded from the resolution of the congress, and yet no one ever questioned this. The complete disregard of this important statement constituted the greatest failure of that congress, and furthermore it caused the bad result of having Stalin oppose Bukharin's rightism. The resolution continued arbitrarily: "China's national bourgeois elements turn their backs on the resolution and move to the antirevolutionary camp of imperialists and rich landlords. Previously, before the spring of 1927, they had the power to weaken and undermine the warlord system, but now they have become a source of power for the consolidation and unification of imperialism and the warlord system." Such a view was extremely absurd and was completely disproved by the subsequent Anti-Japanese War of Resistance. Trotsky's idea that the CCP should not install a Soviet regime but should ask to convene a national assembly instead was never discussed. Thus the resolution of the congress failed to prove that the

CCP should henceforth take the Soviet road, besides it neglected to outline in detail the future development of the CCP.

Since the Soviet formula apparently had become a fact, the failure of the Nanchang Uprising brought an end to the hope for a left-wing KMT regime, which had been the goal of the political struggle. Furthermore, the Autumn Harvest and Canton insurrections established the Soviet banner. Nobody was prepared or willing to come out and erase this fait accompli or to push for reconsideration of the issue. As a result the central point of the discussions was diverted to the prospects of "preliminary victories in one or more provinces." That is to say, the main focus of the congress was on how to maintain the existing rural Soviets and whether this system could be further developed, and if so, how.

In commenting on the significance of the existence of Chinese rural Soviets, Stalin had some interesting ideas. On the eve of this national congress, Stalin reportedly pointed out that it was well and good that under the extremely serious situation of the White terror many CCP members had fled to remote villages in order to organize rural Soviet bases and arm the peasants, for in this manner our strength and a portion of our cadres could be preserved more easily. Later Stalin added that since China was not united and communications were extremely underdeveloped, the Soviets and the Red Army could carry on in remote places. He said that an example of this was Liu Ts'un-hou of Szechwan, a holdover from the Imperial system, who had been able to make a stronghold out of a pacified area in Szechwan for more than ten years up till that moment. It could be deduced from Stalin's words that he lacked confidence in the Chinese Soviet movement; he was even pessimistic about it. He dared not bring up the example of Sun Yat-sen, who had once occupied a corner of Kwangtung to resist Peking, or other examples of separatists. Of all things, he picked as an example the most reactionary separatist regime of Liu Ts'un-hou in the farthest outpost, which was very interesting indeed.

The slogan "preliminary victories in one or more provinces" apparently worked as a panacea, because this new term could be used first to block accusations against "warlordism," "reactionary local regimes," and "separatism," and, secondly, to explain away and facilitate the irregular activities of putschists and Stalin's disciples—the Mif clique—in order to achieve quick successes. This slogan was discussed many times during the congress. Ch'ü Ch'iu-pai once made use of this slogan to cover up his putschism in thinking that he could set up the Soviet system in the rural areas merely by taking advantage of the internal chaos in the KMT and of wars between warlords, completely disregarding whether or not there was a revolutionary high tide. In his view, joining together all the Soviets scattered in the countryside in order to encircle the big cities would usher in initial victories in one or more provinces. Although outwardly Mif and his disciples did not say much, in their hearts they always believed that under the Chinese agrarian revolution lay hidden a terriffic mystical power, on the basis of which a shortcut to the Chinese revolution could be found. Such thinking was evidenced by their strengthening of the Soviet bases and by their active organizing of the Chinese People's Soviet Republic. I was most critical of the aforementioned outlook, firmly maintaining that an agrarian revolution must be synchronized with anti-imperialism, and that without a nationwide high tide of revolutionary conditions and a resurgence of urban workers, it would be impossible to realize initial victories in one or more provinces.

Although the resolution of the congress made favorable mention of the Soviet regime and of the small workers' and peasants' revolutionary forces as a peasant struggle, still these were not to be regarded as a revolutionary regime. A warning was even made against overestimating them, because their strength was still puny. But the resolution declared that "the degree of consolidation of the reactionary domination in various areas was uneven; therefore, under a new general high tide, the revolution will achieve preliminary successes in one province or a number of important provinces." Based on this premise, the resolution proceeded: "All power depends on how the propaganda slogans of the National Assembly of Workers, Peasants, and Soldiers can be transformed into direct action." These assertions later became the foundations for the entire Soviet movement. Since Mif, Ch'ü Ch'iu-pai, and others handled the drafting of the resolution, the congress stuck to its tendency to ignore anti-imperialism. It especially underestimated the danger of Japanese aggression, ignored the KMT's political power in its resistance against Japanese aggression and its positive function for the Nationalist faction, boasted about the function of agrarian revolution, and erroneously transplanted the Soviet formula of political power. All this fomented one dispute after another within the Party, to wit, Li Li-san's putschist line, the Soviet line pursued by Mif and Wang Ming, Mao Tse-tung's guerrillaism, and my own opposition to the Party CC.

Apart from the loopholes in policy described above, another act put on by the congress concerned its promotion for Party solidarity, though this was carried out superficially. Unanimously, we elected the slate of the new CEC, except for Ch'en Tu-hsiu, who was not elected due to his absence. Members of the CEC were Hsiang Chung-fa, Ch'ü Ch'iu-pai, myself, Chou En-lai, Li Li-san, Ts'ai Ho-sen, Hsiang Ying, Ku Shun-chang, Teng Chung-hsia, Lo Chang-lung, Mao Tse-tung, Jen Pi-shih, Lu Fu-t'an, Ch'en T'an-ch'iu, P'eng P'ai, Ts'ai Ch'ang, and Wang Chung-yi. The alternates included Li Wei-han, Lo Teng-hsien, Wang Jo-fei, Teng Ying-ch'ao, Yü Fei, and others.

After the conclusion of the congress, the new CEC held its first plenary session to elect the new Politburo. Bukharin and Mif, taking it for a major event, personally attending the meeting. While the proposal to organize a Politburo was being tabled, a member stood up and said, "We should discard the incumbent members of the Politburo and elect new faces." His argument was that all of the old members had committed serious errors, and besides they could not get along well with each other. Bukharin responded that those comrades who had committed mistakes were the best members the Party had. He added that apart from those who were best left alone due to their absence (alluding to Ch'en Tu-hsiu), all the rest possessed the qualifications to take part in the Politburo. Moreover, he earnestly believed that without the participation of the original members of the Politburo or of those persons who formerly opposed the CC, it would be impossible to form a powerful Politburo. Without further explanation he produced a list containing the names of seven persons—Hsiang Chung-fa, Ch'ü Ch'iu-pai, myself, Chou En-lai, Ts'ai Ho-sen, Li Li-san, and Hsiang Ying. The list was adopted without any objection by all the members, who, under the prevailing circumstances, did not wish to set off new debates.

Mif continued by saying that nominations for members of the new Politburo had been carefully considered by the Comintern. The Comintern was highly gratified that the list was now approved. According to the practice of the CC of the CCP, nomination for membership in the Politburo should be submitted by the preceding Politburo. The fact that this time the nominations were made directly by the Comintern inferred a vote against the Ch'ü Ch'iu-pai CC. Mif, seeing that the meeting proceeded smoothly, proposed further that in the opinion of the Comintern it would be best for Comrade Hsiang Chung-fa to serve as secretary, for Comrade Ch'ü Ch'iu-pai and me to remain in Moscow to act as the CCP's representatives to the Comintern, and for Comrade Li Li-san to handle organization; Comrade Ts'ai Ho-sen, propaganda; Comrade Chou En-lai, military affairs; and Comrade Hsiang Ying, the labor movement. This multiple proposal of Mif's was also accepted speedily and unanimously.

The Sixth Congress of the Comintern was to be held shortly after the closing of the CCP congress. About half of the delegates to the CCP congress stayed on in Moscow to attend the Sixth Congress of the Comintern as China's delegates. Hsiang Chung-fa, Li Li-san, and Ts'ai Ho-sen led the other delegates to the CCP congress in returning to China one after another, to devote themselves to work in the new CC. After this congress of the CCP, it was believed that the disputes within the CC had been resolved. As the person whom the CCP considered to be the leader of the rightist opposition, I was henceforth labeled the leader of the minority by the Comintern. By so doing, the Comintern hoped to create the general impression that the intra-Party dispute, which had become public knowledge already, merely involved a quarrel between a "majority faction" and a "minority faction" without shedding any light at all on the significance of these two terms.

The Comintern congress was convened under the shadow of disputes within the CPSU between the Stalin faction and the Bukharin faction. At the time the controversy between Stalin and Bukharin had not broken into the open, and we were ignorant of its background. It was Ch'en Shao-yü who first mentioned privately that Bukharin was rightist and by no means qualified to represent the views of Stalin, the CPSU, or the Comintern. Taking advantage of this item of news, Ch'ü Ch'iu-pai claimed that Bukharin supported me—a case of a rightist backing a rightist. Moreover, Ch'ü charged that Bukharin's excessive criticism of the CC of the CCP after the August 7 Conference was his personal opinion and was not shared by Stalin.

With this news making the rounds in the congress, a situation advantageous to Ch'ü Ch'iu-pai materialized. Some delegates thought that since Bukharin was labeled a rightist and since his report advocating the sharing of political power with the petty bourgeoisie was likely to be disapproved by Stalin in the future, the CC of the CCP would unavoidably suffer some repercussions. In this atmosphere, Mif not only neglected to refute these rumors, he even let it be known that he supported Stalin. He also more or less turned against Bukharin's idea of sharing political power and of collaborating with the rich peasantry. This foul air diminished the effect of Bukharin's remarks, which indirectly meant that Ch'ü Ch'iu-pai won an unanticipated respite from criticism.

Li Li-san also spoke out on this score. He once told me to support Stalin, not Bukharin. He felt that the main thing about the Comintern was that it was antirightist, and since Bukharin was an important rightist figure, his report could not be counted on. He added that it would be better for the future policies of the CC of the CCP to be leftist rather than rightist. Li Li-san's mannerism was always ostentatious, and he loved issuing arbitrary orders; he had great self-confidence because he felt that Stalin's style of work happened to be similar to his own. So, after all, the Sixth Congress of the CCP could not completely curb putschism, which later developed into the famous "Li Li-san line."

Ferment at Sun Yat-sen University

Aided by the Soviet Russian government, the Comintern planned to train cadres of Communist parties of various countries, an assignment it regarded as important, particularly the training of Chinese Communist cadres. During the early period of the Comintern, Moscow had already established the Oriental University (Communist University for Toilers of the Far East) to train students from various Asian countries and national minority groups within Soviet Russian territory. In 1920 the Oriental University set up a Chinese class composed of CCP or CYC members selected by the CCP. The first students were Liu Shao-ch'i, P'eng Shu-chih, Lo Chiao, Po Shih-ch'i, Yuan Ta-shih, Jen Pi-shih, Pao P'u, and Liao Hua-p'ing—eight persons in all. Later, the number of Chinese students in the university steadily increased to more than sixty. During the period of Soviet support to the KMT, there was a suggestion that KMT cadres also be trained. In 1925, in memory of Sun Yat-sen, who died that year, Soviet Russia established Sun Yat-sen University, which admitted students who were members of the KMT, including Chinese Communists who had defected. During the year of its establishment its student body reached more than one thousand persons, and it became the gathering point for Chinese students in Russia. Due to the turmoil in Chinese politics, this university immediately became the main arena for debating the China problem.

When I arrived in Moscow in the summer of 1928, the relationship between the KMT and the CCP had already broken up completely, and the Comintern and the CCP were busy pursuing their anti-KMT policies. As a corollary, Sun Yat-sen University was transformed from an institution to train KMT members into a training ground for CCP cadres. Originally most of its students were sent there by various units of the KMT and most of them were loyal KMT members, although some others were defectors from the CCP. Therefore, except for those who were close to the CCP, a number of the loyal KMT members were sent packing home, while others were escorted to Siberia to do hard labor. The remainder, together with the hundreds of CCP members selected by the CC to study in Russia after the Wuhan split, came to a total of about one thousand persons. Most of them were already members of the CCP or the CYC, while the rest were Communist sympathizers. In addition to those at Sun Yat-sen University, classes for Chinese students were set up in Moscow's Infantry Academy, Artillery Academy, Engineering Troops' Academy, and the Military and Political University, the number of students in each class ranging from twenty to about fifty. Feng Yü-hsiang once sent three hundred junior officers to Russia to study in these institutions, and even in 1928 a number of them were still scattered about there. In addition, Lenin Academy had more than ten Chinese Communist students enrolled in Russian or English classes.

Karl Radek, the noted Trotskyite, was the first president of Sun Yat-sen University. Mif, who regarded himself as a Stalinist, was vice-president, establishing himself firmly on the campus in order to hamper Radek's activities. Radek once regarded the university as his base of operations for unfolding his campaign against Stalin. His theory was that although historically China had passed through the same feudal period as all European countries, she had organized her own political power, so that her historical development possessed characteristics different from those of European history. This, he argued, was due to the development of business capital and occasional political triumphs of the peasantry. Especially after the Ch'in and Han dynasties, there already was free buying and selling of land, which, with the additional factor of the encroachment of foreign capital after the nineteenth century, caused China's economic structure to move far away from the historical feudal system and to become a business and usury capitalist system. From this point of departure, he opposed Stalin's theory that there should be an alliance between the four classes—that is, worker, peasant, petty bourgeoisie, and bourgeoisie—to oppose feudalism. He held that from the start the Chinese revolution should be antibourgeois and should concentrate on the development of noncapitalism.[4] This theory was evidently Trotsky's basis for advocating that the Chinese establish Soviets during the Wuhan period. Stalin once visited Sun Yat-sen University to deliver a speech in which he stressed the anti-imperialist and antifeudal nature of the Chinese revolution and favored cooperation between the CCP and the national bourgeoisie in order to carry out jointly the anti-imperialist and antifeudal revolution.[5] These two opinions constituted the main point of disagreement at Sun Yat-sen University.

As a result of the controversy between the Trotsky and Stalin factions, the Trotskyites suffered a severe blow and Radek was relieved of his post. In the spring of 1927 Mif succeeded him as president of Sun Yat-sen University. From then on, the university was completely in Mif's hands. Within the CPSU, Mif, a Russian Communist comrade about thirty-odd years of age, was in no sense a cadre of the Stalin clique, and his education and experience were mediocre. He was a very ambitious person, however, and adept in the technique of Stalin's strategy. Unscrupulous and opportunistic, he was catapulted from being only president of Sun Yat-sen University to becoming also director of the China Bureau under the Oriental Department of the Comintern. By the time that the Sixth Congress of the CCP convened, he apparently was the Comintern's sole authority on the China problem.

Another reason for Mif's being able to influence the China problem was because his predecessors had fallen along with the failure of the Chinese revolution. Gregory Voitinsky, after returning home from China, was rebuked and reassigned by the CPSU to work with cooperatives, and was never again to discuss China's problems. Mikhail Borodin was ignored by Stalin after he returned from China. His report to the Old Bolshevik Association about his experiences in China was thoroughly denounced by Mif and others. At that time he was idle in Moscow and feeling down in the dumps. Besso Lominadze and Heinz Neumann, important Comintern figures though they still were, came under fire on account of their reckless behavior in China and, to say the least, dared not openly interfere in Chinese affairs. As to the Dutchman Maring and the Indian M. N. Roy, nobody knew where they had gone after their departure from China. In Moscow I heard no news at all about them.

Mif's management of the faction-riddled Sun Yat-sen University created a great deal of reaction there. During the Sixth Congress of the CCP, Hsiang Chung-fa and Ch'en Shao-yü would tell anybody who cared to listen, "Sun Yat-sen University is full of big problems. There is a small Kiang-Che Fraternal Association with a membership of more than one hundred and fifty persons operating on the university campus." They believed it important to get rid of these elements. When Hsiang Chung-fa returned to China, he seriously asked Ch'ü Ch'iu-pai and me to watch this matter closely.

According to Hsiang, the background of the so-called Kiang-Che Fraternal Association was something like this: When the KMT and CCP broke up in 1927, a movement developed in Sun Yat-sen University to expel KMT elements. During the period of opposition to Ch'en Tu-hsiu's opportunism, a movement of opposition to Ch'en Tu-hsiu also developed in the university. These KMT elements and followers of Ch'en Tu-hsiu had allegedly formed an alliance with the Trotskyite faction, and they relied on Radek's theses for support. In addition, there were many students who were dissatisfied with the leadership of Mif and the Party Committee of the university, and they often obstructed the university's work. The Kiang-Che Fraternal Association was the alliance of these anti-Party elements. It was called the Kiang-Che Fraternal Association because more than half of its members were natives of Kiangsu and Chekiang provinces. Ku Ku-yi, who once had been the leader of the Shanghai students, was the principal leader of this small organization; Chiang Ching-kuo was another leader. The leading group invariably got together once a week to enjoy a sumptuous dinner in a small Chinese restaurant located in a slum district of Moscow. Ostensibly these play-boys, carrying fat wallets, wanted to eat Chinese food and enjoy themselves; but in fact they went there to carry out an anti-Party plot in collusion with overseas Chinese and related members of the Chinese diplomatic mission.

We turned this matter over to Chou En-lai for disposition. As a result of his investigation, Chou En-lai believed that there was no such thing as the Kiang-Che Fraternal Association, so the case of this tiny organization vanished into thin air. At the same time, the well-known anti-Mif elements in Sun Yat-sen University were sent one after another to other schools. For example, Yü Hsiu-sung, Chou Ta-wen, and Tung Yi-hsiang were transferred early to Lenin Academy; Chu Wu-shan, Tso Ch'üan, and Chiang Ching-kuo were transferred to the Military and Political University in Leningrad. Even so, the anti-Mif activities within Sun Yat-sen University continued unabated.

The students at Sun Yat-sen University relentlessly criticized the incompetent leadership of the university authorities. As a matter of fact, everything in this young institution was simple and austere. Also, Mif and his group lacked experience in running a university. The students reproved Mif for being unable to improve the conditions and for only knowing how to suppress self-criticism and for repeatedly labeling his critics anti-Party or pro-KMT. These disgruntled students often criticized Mif in front of the Comintern and the Supervisory Committee of the CPSU. Most of them described Ch'en Shao-yü as "Mif's running dog," who drew a high salary as a mere interpreter and who, relying on Mif's power, specialized in writing brief reports attacking the students.

The events unfolding at Sun Yat-sen University quickly developed into a major dispute between Mif and the CCP delegation. After the Sixth Congress of the Comintern, Teng Chung-hsia and Yü Fei were stationed at the Red Workers International as representatives of the Chinese Trade Union, while Wang Jo-fei represented the Chinese Agricultural Union based at the Peasant International. These were in addition to Ch'ü Ch'iu-pai and myself, who became CCP representatives to the Comintern. Altogether, these five persons made up the CCP delegation headquartered in Moscow. This delegation expressed disapproval of Mif's handling of Sun Yat-sen University. As Mif saw it, the internal affairs of Sun Yat-sen University should be handled by himself as president of the university, and the CCP delegation should not meddle in them. On the other hand, the CCP delegation believed that the university authorities should only be responsible for the educational aspects, while appraisal of the students' capacity for learning and work assignments for repatriated students should be handled by the Chinese delegation.

Many organizations had a hand in the administration of Sun Yat-sen University. From the aspect of educational regulation, the university was governed by the Soviet Ministry of Education; from the standpoint of Party organization, the university's Party cell belonged to the jurisdiction of a subcommittee of the Moscow Municipal Party Committee. And since it was formed for the CCP, the university was also under the guidance of the Comintern. At the same time, most of its students were not members of the CPSU, but were members of the CCP, so the Comintern and Mif could not prevent the Chinese delegation in Moscow from making inquiries into the university's affairs.

Ch'ü Ch'iu-pai, Wang Jo-fei, and I did not want to interfere with the university directly, and in order to avoid being dragged into the whirlpool of dispute, we seldom visited the campus. However, Teng Chung-hsia and Yü Fei had many arguments with the university authorities, mainly about problems involving the evaluation of students. For instance, Li Ch'ien-ju and Yü Tu-san, who were of working-class origin, once led a great part of the student body in opposing the policies of the school's Party Cell Committee. In the opinion of Teng Chung-hsia and Yü Fei, those students were good comrades, but the university authorities regarded them as anti-Party elements. The wall newspapers on the campus often carried articles criticizing the CCP leadership. Such improper conduct, according to Teng Chung-hsia and Yü Fei, was detrimental to the prestige of the CCP leadership, while the university authorities took it as appropriate self-criticism. The students also often spread our delegation's remarks voicing disapproval against the school authorities, which produced a disturbing effect. These happenings caused Mif a great many headaches.

During September, Otto Kuusinen, head of the Comintern's Oriental Department, apparently got wind of some news involving the university and had a talk with me about problems concerning the CCP and Sun Yat-sen University in general. I told him that it was improper for the directorship of the Comintern's China Bureau and the presidency of Sun Yat-sen University to be held concurrently by the same person, namely, Mif. I reasoned that it would be best if the person responsible for guiding Chinese Communist affairs kept aloof from the internal disputes of the CCP, but that the president of Sun Yat-sen University could not avoid such involvement. Consequently, more than a few Chinese students charged Mif with having transgressed his rights by meddling in CCP affairs. After listening to my words, Kuusinen asked my opinion as to who would be the best person to take charge of the China Bureau. I replied that I really had not thought about this problem.

During this period Ch'ü Ch'iu-pai never discussed with me the question of replacing Mif, nor was he aware of my talk with Kuusinen. He also broached this matter with Kuusinen; but when he was asked about who should succeed Mif as head of the China Bureau, Ch'ü recommended Borodin. Mif later got wind of these developments. His lieutenants often jeered at the relationship between Ch'ü Ch'iu-pai and Borodin, saying that Ch'ü's recommendation of Borodin was basically in violation of the Comintern line. At the same time, both of us were dissatisfied with Mif's accusation, which widened the gap between Mif and the Chinese delegation.

Although Mif and his men were displeased with us, they felt that I had relatively great influence among the Chinese students. At that time the Chinese students in various schools were somewhat restless, often asking for improvement in study conditions or for repatriation and work in their own country. Sometimes Mif had to ask me to talk to the students. I accepted his offer gladly, because I regarded it as a worthwhile task to make the students study assiduously. In the evening I was often escorted to some military school on the outskirts to give a lecture before the Chinese students. I had no chance to ask in detail about their conditions, and all that I could do was to encourage them to study diligently.

As an example, Mif once assembled quite a number of women students to organize a nurses' training class and arranged for their practical training with an army hospital. But this class could not be kept up, because the students would not pursue learning, preferring to be repatriated instead. When I went to the training class to have an informal discussion with the forty-odd students, they poured their hearts out in a confused manner, the gist being that it was simply impossible to study due to lack of teachers and interpreters, and that what they did day after day was the work of maidservants—cleansing patients' wounds and washing spittoons. I knew that several of these students came from families of important KMT members or were people accustomed to an easy and comfortable life back home. I laughed at their girlish temperaments, thoroughly explained the importance of nursing work, and expressed the hope that they would continue to study hard. My speech quieted them down, and finally they unanimously agreed to withdraw their complaint in order to carry on with their studies. This incident was regarded by the Russians as something of a miracle, one which could be performed only by CCP members, never by the Russians.

As a result of its intercession for Chinese students in Russia, the Chinese delegation's relationship with Mif became delicate. Starting out from an authoritarian viewpoint, Mif resented any interference in student affairs by the Chinese delegation; but when the problems became unsolvable, the Chinese delegation's mediation apparently helped him considerably. Yet never once did he show any intention of adjusting our relationship.

In November, 1928, the Supervisory Committee of the CPSU set up a committee to investigate the trouble in Sun Yat-sen University, because it had received a number of complaints from the students. The investigation that was held in a small conference room was attended by four or five senior members of the Supervisory Committee of the CPSU. Mif, Poyakin, secretary of the university's Party Cell Committee, and I appeared as witnesses (Ch'ü Ch'iu-pai had left for a holiday in southern Russia). The chairman of the Investigating Committee produced a thick file of documents, announced that these papers contained accusations against the school authorities submitted by students, and explained that the purpose of the meeting was to find a modus vivendi.

Poyakin was the first to speak up in defense of the school authorities, presenting a report of the events that had transpired at Sun Yat-sen

University. In general, he considered that the principal reasons for the difficulty in running the school were the complicated backgrounds of the students and the numerous errors of the CCP. He pointed out that the student body included many intellectuals, more than a few of whom had at one time been KMT members that had crossed over to the CCP after the KMT-CCP split. The students were allegedly influenced by the ideas of the Trotsky faction, Ch'en Tu-hsiu-ism, and putschism and were petty bourgeoisie of various hues. It was therefore correct and proper for the school authorities to battle against these non-Bolshevik ideas. It had been that way in the past, and it would remain so in the future. It was a class struggle of sorts, that is, a struggle between the proletariat and the nonproletariat, which could also explain why, although trouble-makers at Sun Yat-sen University had been removed, there were still many students dissatisfied with the leadership of the university. Consequently, there was no alternative other than to carry on with the class struggle. Mif followed Poyakin by giving a brief speech, expressing his complete support of Poyakin.

I immediately spoke up to voice dissent. First of all, I commented on the so-called class struggle, saying that if the class struggle were to be applied extensively at Sun Yat-sen University, the function of education would be destroyed. A resolution of the Comintern had pointed out that even among the bourgeois intelligentsia there were some who held progressive, revolutionary ideas and should be won over. Was it not at all possible to use educational methods to win them over in this Red capital of Moscow? If they were not to be regarded as our very own, then the majority of the students would have to be expelled; and wouldn't that be a failure for education?

Continuing, I explained the true situation. I said that it was possible that the school had a few "outsiders," but the majority of the students were dissatisfied with the university administration. I cited the following reasons: First, the school had been established only recently, and its facilities were inadequate. The school had few Chinese books, fewer students who understood Russian, and even fewer interpreters, while the professors who won the students' respect were not numerous, either. Second, the secretary in charge of the Party organization in the school was a Russian comrade who, due to the language barrier, found it difficult to understand the views of Chinese comrades. More than half of the student comrades whom the Party Cell Committee trusted were those who were able to speak Russian or those who supported the Comintern and the CPSU's political line. But, generally speaking, the students had different outlooks. To them, the most important criterion was whether a person had or had not performed well while engaged in hard work in China. Often they reasoned thus: Somebody had worked hard, doing many praiseworthy jobs in China, but now he was branded as an anti-Party element because he showed a little displeasure at the school authorities. Third, the bad habits of Chinese students were related to China's backward conditions, such as being slovenly, disorderly, wasteful, petty, disrespectful to workers and employees, and so forth. These shortcomings could be rectified by patient educational methods. Fourth, the Cell Committee apparently never paid any attention to school conditions or the Chinese students' living conditions in carrying out its guidance and education. Instead, it overemphasized struggle, which made it impossible to reach an understanding with the students.

The members of the Supervisory Committee praised my views warmly. On the basis of available material, they asked a few pointed questions and expressed the same views as mine. This greatly embarrassed both Mif and Poyakin. No conclusion was reached at the meeting, which was adjourned by the chairman till a later date.

Two weeks later the Supervisory Committee of the CPSU convened the second meeting. Mif was absent, but Poyakin brought another member of the Party Cell Committee, Ch'in Pang-hsien, to the session. As soon as the meeting was called to order, Ch'in Pang-hsien began to speak in Russian. His long-winded speech had been well prepared in advance, and he delivered it rather fluently. He counterattacked the Chinese delegation's interference in the affairs of Sun Yat-sen University, singling me out in particular. Due to poor translation, I could not possibly know the entire contents of his speech. But what I understood was that he reprimanded me severely as an opportunist and that he maintained the theory that what transpired in Sun Yat-sen University was a class struggle. In his view, my opportunism had hindered the development of the open class struggle which the university should undergo. His speech caused some members of the Supervisory Committee to shake their heads.

I simply became livid with rage listening to his speech. I announced that what was being discussed was what kind of policy should be adopted for leading Sun Yat-sen University, and not the purging of the CCP delegation or me personally. Not only did Ch'in Pang-hsien divert the purpose of the meeting, but what he said was unfounded slander. This was a typical example of the bad taste of some power factions prevailing in the CPSU. Mif's and Poyakin's positions apparently had been deeply affected by my criticism of them during the previous meeting. So they refrained from making a direct rebuttal and, instead, got hold of the Chinese student Ch'in Pang-hsien to attack me. The members of the Supervisory Committee who took part in the meeting apparently were of the opinion that the meeting was not proceeding as it should; therefore they cut it short and declared it closed. Later, without further ado, the members of the Supervisory Committee made a decision on their own, criticizing the errors of the leadership of Sun Yat-sen University. Although the committee's decision had little power to restrain, it was tantamount to a hard slap in the face for Mif. As a consequence of this incident, my relations with Mif became even worse.

In spite of the widening gap between Mif and the Chinese delegation on account of the Sun Yat-sen University problem, both sides continued to exchange views on how to handle the students. Once Mif invited some members of the Chinese delegation to the Comintern's China Bureau for a discussion. During the meeting Mif produced a list of more than ten students who were to be sent down for hard labor in an outpost in Siberia. I immediately lodged a protest, arguing that it would not do much good to exile them to Siberia. What kind of impression would their friends and relatives in China get if the whereabouts of the students were not known? Why not send the students back to China and let them make good in their own country? If they were loyal to the Chinese revolution, well and good; and even if they defected, a few more reactionary elements under the serious White terror would not hurt the CCP.

Though noncommittal, Mif apparently felt irritated by my speech, and he never brought up the question again. Perhaps the brains in the Comintern, reluctant to cause Soviet Russia to make many enemies, decided to support our viewpoint. Later a great many of the students were repatriated one by one, and there were fewer cases of banishment to Siberia. Mif's policy of banishing students to Siberia to do hard labor caused considerable terror among the Chinese student body. Ch'ü Wu, son-in-law of Yü Yu-jen, who was then studying in a military academy, was so frightened by the atmosphere surrounding this kind of struggle that he had a nervous breakdown. Once he ran away from school and jumped aboard a trans-Siberian train for a clandestine trip home. But he was caught on the way and charged with desertion, which, according to Soviet Russian military regulations, made him liable to execution by a firing squad. The Chinese delegation interceded in Ch'ü Wu's behalf with the Moscow military authorities, pleading leniency on the grounds that his escape attempt was caused by his fear of the class struggle. Subsequently, Ch'ü Wu was imprisoned for many years until the Sino-Japanese

War period, when he was deported from the country. Eventually, he became an important official of the Chinese Communist government.

In spite of Mif's oppressive policy—banishing some students to Siberia, sending others packing home, and assigning still others to work in factories—those students who remained on the campus continued to oppose the leadership of the school authorities and the Party Cell Committee. There was no end to the struggle. Students who really backed Mif were limited to the so-called 28 Bolsheviks, including Ch'en Shao-yü.[6] The others, totaling more than one thousand, stood on the opposite side. Among the members of the Chinese delegation, opinions regarding various Chinese Communist problems differed greatly. But when dealing with Mif and the administration at Sun Yat-sen University, they were united in action, perhaps reflecting how abominable Mif was. When Sun Yat-sen University students held a year-end summing-up meeting in the summer of 1929, another big struggle between the delegation and Mif flared up.

Ch'ü Ch'iu-pai was invited to deliver a speech at this student meeting, where, under the fiery atmosphere caused by the students' opposition to the Party Cell Committee, he also attacked the Cell Committee's leadership. The meeting dragged on for three days without reaching any solution. Ch'ü waxed impatient. He invited members of the Chinese delegation to a conference at which he begged the delegation to adopt a united attitude and asked me to speak before the students' gathering in a similar vein. I agreed to his views and those of the delegation members. At the invitation of the students of Sun Yat-sen University, I attended the meeting to give a speech.

In it I rebuked the Party Cell's leadership for not having respected the decisions of the Sixth Congress of the CCP. As a result, in their struggle against opportunism and putschism, the cell leaders neglected intra-Party solidarity, which was vital. In the absence of any essential understanding between the Party Cell Committee and the Chinese delegation, it was only proper that many students had informed the delegation about their displeasure with the school. The Cell Committee should adopt a policy that would unify the majority of the students, instead of suppressing self-criticism and creating a schism among Party members. Everybody applauded my speech, except the 28 Bolsheviks. The atmosphere of the meeting became charged with excitement. They demanded a reorganization of the Party Cell Committee, and passed a resolution criticizing the errors of the committee's policies in the past.

The student meeting gave Mif and Poyakin a big headache. The top leaders of the Comintern apparently thought that both the Chinese delegation and the Mif faction were equally in the wrong, so they adopted a laissez-faire attitude. But the crafty Mif and Poyakin were both still full of tricks. Suddenly, they invited the secretary of the Party subcommittee of the Moscow Municipal Party Committee to attend the meeting. He was a rowdy cadre of the country-bumpkin type, ignorant of conditions of Communist parties in foreign countries and personifying the chauvinism and power outlook of the CPSU.

He started off by saying that the Chinese delegation's interference in the affairs of Sun Yat-sen University was a violation of authority. At the top of his voice he censured the past errors of the CCP, asserting that in assisting to bolshevize the CCP and train Chinese youths, the CPSU could not possibly follow the wishes of the Chinese Communist delegation. The CCP delegation simply should not have delivered speeches before the student gathering. He backed the Cell Committee's policies and interpreted the dissatisfaction of the majority of the students as an anti-Party act. Singling me out, he said bluntly that I had been adjudged a member of the rightist compromise faction by the Comintern. He said that the students simply should not have believed what I had told them. His own speech caused quite an uproar among the students.

Faced with this challenge, I became furious and stood up to make a rebuttal. I explained that the Comintern had not called me a rightist compromiser, and yet the secretary of the subcommittee arbitrarily put this label on my head. Our delegation's united stand regarding the Sun Yat-sen University affair was not to be ignored. Also I sized him up as a bureaucrat through and through who did not know how to lead Party work in such a big institution as Sun Yat-sen University. I added that when the problem arose, he ignored the Chinese delegation's views and invariably suppressed self-criticism. Thus a major stalemate developed, and the meeting was adjourned forthwith.

Ch'ü Ch'iu-pai became rather panicky when he saw this development of events. Therefore, he went out to see the subcommittee secretary to recapitulate what actually had transpired in the Sun Yat-sen University incident. He pointed out that a subcommittee secretary of the CPSU ought not to have opposed the Chinese Communist delegation. The secretary apparently felt that his speech might have been too reckless. Ch'ü Ch'iu-pai and he finally reached a compromise, and they issued a joint statement addressed to the student association. In it they explained that a misunderstanding had cropped up as a result of the language barrier, that, in fact, there had been no conflict at all, and that, moreover,

both of them were much concerned about the proper development of
Sun Yat-sen University. The joint statement was read by Ch'ü Ch'iu-pai
at the meeting, which then adopted a resolution of a perfunctory nature
to smooth the political ripples at the university.

In the meantime I had reported to the Comintern secretary general,
Piatnitski, about the speech of that subcommittee secretary and had objected to his slanderous remarks about me. Piatnitski shrugged his
shoulders and shook his head, but kept silent. I was unhappy about the
suave way that Ch'ü Ch'iu-pai handled the affair, but at the same time
I realized there was nothing the Chinese Communist delegation could do
to deal with that kind of power and bureaucracy. Also, I was then preparing for a vacation to the Ukraine, so I reluctantly agreed. Although
Ch'ü Ch'iu-pai and the secretary of the subcommittee, through their joint
statement, succeeded in formulating a policy that temporarily smoothed
over the trouble, I told Ch'ü and the others that from then on I did not
wish to inquire into the Sun Yat-sen incident again.

I stayed in Moscow for a year, during which I spent most of my
time in reading. Moscow's Chinese-language publications were mainly
the textbooks at Sun Yat-sen University, all of which I read through. I
got a monthly subsidy of 250 rubles, which at that time was regarded
as the highest salary in a Russian government office. Toward the end of
1928 my wife arrived at Moscow and went through special training at
Sun Yat-sen University. My wife and I lived thriftily. Moscow was then
so short of consumer goods that there was nothing to buy even if we had
the money. For three whole months we had nothing but fish for our
meals, and I finally got disgusted with that. So we used our savings to
buy books. I bought practically all of the English-language political
books and magazines available in Moscow. Although I could not speak
Russian, I had a smattering of knowledge of certain Russian publications
and bought quite a number of them. During the summer holiday of 1929,
I planned to enroll at Lenin Academy as an auditor to further my studies
and avoid getting involved in the Comintern's meetings and bickerings.

Revealing my plan to audit at Lenin Academy to no one, I went
directly to see Zinosanova, president of the academy. She was the wife of
Dimitry Manuilsky, chairman of the Supervisory Committee of the CC
of the CPSU. She was an old Bolshevik, a kind-hearted middle-aged
woman. I asked her permission to allow me to join the English course
of the academy, attending the classes like the other students. I explained, however, that as a member of the Chinese delegation to the
Comintern, I did not wish to take an active part in the work of the

Party Cell Committee in the academy. She gladly granted my request. At the time, regular students of Lenin Academy not only had to study their lessons but also had to enroll in the Cell Committee to undergo special training by the Party. So I could be regarded merely as an auditor, or a part-time student.

I still stayed at the Hotel Lux, a guest house for members of the Comintern. Tung Pi-wu and I were classmates at Lenin Academy, occupying neighboring seats at the school. We read Marx's *Das Kapital*. By then I was no longer drawing any salary from the Comintern. Like other students, I took my meals at the academy's dining hall. I got twenty rubles of pocket money per month, but I was supposed to pay forty-odd rubles for my room rent at the Hotel Lux, which I could not afford, of course. When I explained to the hotel administrator about my inability to pay the hotel bill, he ignored me. But after I had failed to pay the bill for three months, he simply sued me in the Moscow local court for being in arrears with my payments. I was not sure whether he was seriously trying to drive me out or whether it was merely red tape, a case of useless official formality.

I wrote to Piatnitski, explaining my predicament briefly and enclosing the court summons. Upon investigation, he learned that I had long since voluntarily sacrificed the Comintern salary and that I had been studying at Lenin Academy. He praised my determination in continuing to serve with the Chinese Communist delegation and simultaneous studying at the academy. So he convoked a meeting of the Comintern secretariat and passed a resolution confirming my right to stay at the Hotel Lux and exempting me from paying the room rent. The court case against me was thus withdrawn, while my studies at Lenin Academy automatically won the Comintern's tacit approval.

Lenin Academy was a senior Party school that was under the direct supervision of the Comintern. At the time, it had a student body numbering about three hundred persons, all sent by Communist parties of various countries. Among them were ten or more Chinese students. The class in which I enrolled was taught in English and consisted of more than ten foreign students from England, America, Australia, New Zealand, Japan, Korea, and China. The curriculum included political science, economics, dialectical materialism, history of Russian Communism, Leninism, Party-building, and military affairs. The method of education was mainly for the students to study by themselves according to a study plan. The students attended classes not more than ten hours per week, at which times they brought up their study reports and received some guidance from the professors.

The situation at Lenin Academy was altogether different from that at Sun Yat-sen University. The relationship between the academy authorities and the students in general was normal. No major disputes occurred at Party Cell Committee meetings, which were brief and not very frequent, or at caucuses of Party members. Most of the students did their studying in the library. The school leaders and the students learned and lived together harmoniously, without any of the disturbances and controversies that were found at Sun Yat-sen.

Toward the end of 1929 Stalin, with a view to consolidating his leadership, launched a big purge of the Party, which shook all of Soviet Russia. Not only did it make a great stir at Sun Yat-sen University, but it also shattered the serenity of Lenin Academy. The Party purge, launched after the collectivization of agriculture and the liquidation of kulaks, was directed against Trotskyites, Bukharin rightists, and the Industrial Party. The purification drive was like a plague, endangering everybody by its contagiousness. Even those Party members who normally claimed to belong to the Stalinist clique were not free of fright. According to Comintern and CPSU regulations, members of the Comintern and the CC of the CPSU should not have been affected by the purge, because their success in getting elected to these organizations was tantamount to having passed a meticulous security clearance. On this basis, I, a member of the CC of the CCP and an alternate member of the presidium of the Comintern, naturally had no cause for worry.

The purge at Lenin Academy was conducted by the Party Purification Committee appointed by the Comintern. Zinosanova, president of the academy, was the first to be purged at the investigative meeting. She recounted to the audience her entire political life, particularly all the errors that she had committed in the realm of politics. In the course of her hour-long confession, she even made mention of her private life during her younger days, which astonished foreign Communist Party members. Next to be removed were other responsible persons of the academy and members of the Party Cell Committee, followed by teachers and some students. If the statements of a person under fire sounded vague or doubtful, he would be cross-examined thoroughly. A Polish student, formerly an army man, who had fought in the anti-Soviet war, was arrested on the spot by Soviet secret agents, because he neglected to mention this episode in his report. A Chinese student surnamed Ma was also discovered missing during the purge campaign, because he allegedly took part in Trotskyite activities. The campaign went on continuously, day and night, and all classes were practically suspended. The drive was concluded nearly two months later, after several persons had been removed.

At Sun Yat-sen University the purge campaign was especially tense. The Purification Committee was made up of three members appointed by the Comintern, under the chairmanship of Pochin, an army man. The other two were a member of the Comintern's Supervisory Committee and Voitinsky, one-time representative of the Comintern based in China. These three members could be considered experienced and honest, not the fault-finding type. But members of the school's Party Committee were as fierce as a pack of hunting dogs who, with secret-service men, searched high and low for evidence of students' anti-Party crimes. An official announcement said that a student named Li committed suicide during the purge period. The official reason given was that as a member of the Trotskyite secret organization, Li allegedly had supplied a secret list of names of more than one hundred persons who were taking part in the Trotskyite organization, but felt conscience-stricken afterwards, and so he finally committed suicide. What the truth was, however, nobody knew. The students in general were so deeply frightened by the whole thing that they dared not inquire into the matter. From this instance, it could be surmised that the purge at Sun Yat-sen University was carried out in an atmosphere of terror.

Ch'ü Ch'iu-pai and I felt that we had no way of interfering in the purge incidents in the university, so we refrained from making any inquiry. At the time, Wang Jo-fei was also studying at Lenin Academy. He himself was suspected of being a Trotskyite, so he could not very well say anything with impunity. Teng Chung-hsia and Yü Fei, in the name of the Chinese delegation, went along to make a statement to the university authorities with regard to the investigation of Chinese students, but to no avail. Moreover, during the early stage of the purge, the so-called 28 Bolsheviks passed the test easily, and thereafter they could criticize other students without qualms.

While the purge at Sun Yat-sen University was proceeding apace, Piatnitski came to have a talk with me. He said, "You've been dragged into the purge campaign at the university. As you already know, a student has committed suicide. One of the Trotskyite elements mentioned on the blacklist has revealed that Liu Jen-ching, leader of the Trotskyite secret organization, once showed you a Trotskyite secret document and that you reportedly expressed your approval of the said paper. Is that true? I hope you'll make a good self-defense." Piatnitski was an elderly personage of the Comintern who had worked with Lenin and had done underground publishing work over a long period. His attitude was stern and his words were frank, but his heart was kind. Usually he treated me well, so it was evidently with good intentions that he confided in me regarding the above rumor. When I denied the incident and asked him whether he was in doubt about me, he replied to the following effect, "I believe you're an honest comrade, for I have always taken you as a frank and outspoken man. I have no doubts about you, but you'll have to attend the investigation at Sun Yat-sen University in order to absolve yourself." A few years later this straightforward old man was also liquidated by Stalin, and my thoughts turned to him as I recalled this incident.

I attended the investigation at Sun Yat-sen University and gave a speech. First of all, I explained that I always disapproved of Trotsky's viewpoints, and I refuted the charges of my collusion in the Trotskyite document. I explained that I had always felt dissatisfied with the leadership of the university, and I reaffirmed my antiopportunism and antiputschism stand in the CC of the CCP. Finally, I challenged anyone at the meeting who knew of any error or misconduct that I had committed to speak up without any hesitation, and said that I would be prepared to give an answer forthwith. Nobody questioned me after I finished my speech, and the matter was considered closed.

Not until a few years later did I learn the real truth about the so-called affair involving my private knowledge of the Trotskyite document. It turned out that during the Sixth Congress of the Comintern, the secretariat translated a pamphlet of some one hundred pages concerning Trotsky's views on the China problem into a number of Western languages for general distribution among all members. I got hold of an English version. At that time Liu Jen-ching was a student of Lenin Academy and was doing translations for the Chinese Communist delegation. He translated a section of this document and showed his work to me, saying that Ch'ü Ch'iu-pai had already read his translation with favorable comment. Now he showed it to me to see whether the translation contained any defects. As I happened to be busy with other matters, I told Liu that I was confident about his ability to translate, adding that it would not be necessary for me to go over it. Little did I realize that through this commonplace event, Trotskyite elements could have spread false reports alleging that I had become privy to a Trotsky document.

One can see from this incident how the purge campaign could produce fantastic chain reactions.

The Party purification work among the Chinese students dragged on for three months. Toward the end of the drive Ch'ü Ch'iu-pai suffered a heavier blow than I. A secret meeting was held in Piatnitski's office, which was attended by a few persons including Ch'ü Ch'iu-pai and me. To begin with, the member of the Comintern's Supervisory Committee who conducted the purge at Sun Yat-sen University reported on the results of the campaign there. According to the information that was available, a small, secret Trotskyite organization had allegedly been in existence for a long time among the Chinese student body and allegedly the Chinese delegation had adopted a tolerant attitude toward this. The Comintern man chided Ch'ü Ch'iu-pai for having let Liu Jen-ching, a Trotskyite leader, go back to China by way of Turkey. While in Turkey, Liu reportedly met Trotsky to ask for advice concerning a line of action for him to follow in carrying out Trotskyite activities in China. The Supervisory Committee member pointed out that some other Trotskyite elements were sent back home at Ch'ü Ch'iu-pai's suggestion. He charged that evidence proved that unreliable elements among the Chinese students had close contacts with Ch'ü Ch'iu-pai but few dealings with other members of the Chinese delegation. Ch'ü was quite embarrassed by these accusations and unable to refute them. Zinosanova and Mif, who also attended the meeting, succeeded in vindicating themselves in their brief speeches, which made Ch'ü feel all the more distressed.

Under such circumstances, I took up the cudgel against injustice. I defended Ch'ü Ch'iu-pai by asserting that Comrade Ch'ü was without doubt a loyal man who supported the Comintern line. If he had wide contacts and handled many problems, it was due to his position as the head of the Chinese Communist delegation. Before the small Trotskyite organization was exposed, who could have distinguished between those who were Trotskyites and those who were not among the Chinese students? He could not be blamed for having come in close contact with the students. My defense gave Ch'ü Ch'iu-pai a feeling of relief, but it did not help him much. The meeting was adjourned without any conclusion being reached. Thenceforth, Ch'ü Ch'iu-pai was known as the principal person responsible for the Trotskyite affair at Sun Yat-sen University.

The purge at the university was a complete victory for Mif. The Party Purification Committee held that the leadership of Mif and the university's Party Committee was correct, and the so-called 28 Bolsheviks were formally accepted as Bolshevik elements. A part of the student body that was regarded at Trotskyite was purged, while other students who opposed the Cell Committee were held in suspicion. My wife, for instance, was given a verdict to the effect that after her repatriation she must prove her loyalty through her Party work in China, and that in the meantime she was banished to a factory to work under observation. This resolution against my wife was really a symbol of punishment for me. Ch'ü Ch'iu-pai's wife, Yang Chih-hua, and most of the other students also received the same criticism and punishment as my wife.

A few days after the meeting held in Piatnitski's office, Mif invited Ch'ü Ch'iu-pai, Teng Chung-hsia, Yü Fei, and me over to his office for a meeting. (Wang Jo-fei was no longer taking part in the work of the Chinese delegation, and had passed the test of the purge campaign at Lenin Academy.) Looking unprecedently pleased, Mif assumed an arrogant expression and read a Comintern secret resolution reproving the Chinese delegation. The gist of this short resolution was as follows: The Comintern rebuked the Chinese Communist delegation for having taken steps to abet the strife among the students of Sun Yat-sen University and for having hindered the normal work being carried out by the Party organization in the university. All this was regarded as evil, schismatic activity that nurtured the development of the small Trotskyite organization and other anti-Party tendencies. The majority in the Chinese delegation, including Ch'ü Ch'iu-pai, constantly and firmly supported such activity without showing any repentance. The minority in the delegation, such as Chang Kuo-t'ao, had committed similar errors of active participation until recently, but even so they had never opposed such divisiveness.

In our minds, Ch'ü Ch'iu-pai and I understood perfectly that this resolution was decided upon jointly by a few top leaders of the Comintern and the Comintern's Supervisory Committee during that secret conference held in Piatnitski's office, but behind our backs after we had left the conference site. Mif had merely been entrusted to relay the message to us. Evidently there was no way for the conference to revise this decision, and it would be futile for us to argue about it. But Teng Chung-hsia and Yü Fei were not then aware of what had transpired, so Teng stood up to protest and oppose this resolution, adding that he would appeal to the presidium of the Comintern. Yü Fei was all excited and almost driven to tears, explaining that during his almost two years' sojourn in Moscow he had sacrificed his studies mainly to involve himself in investigative work concerning Chinese students. He added that he had reported the results of his investigations to the Party Cell Committee of Sun Yat-sen University, which had helped the Party purification drive a great deal. But now, unexpectedly, he was charged with the crime of having engaged in schismatic activities, and he just could not stand it.

Whereupon Mif gave him a bit of instruction, saying, "Comrade Yü Fei, you're a young worker, and theoretically you should concentrate on learning instead of doing what you should not be doing. It would be of no use for you to appeal to the superiors." Ch'ü Ch'iu-pai, after hearing these words, felt disappointed and said, "Let's forget it! As I see it, this resolution can't be changed, and there's nothing we can do but acquiesce!" I looked at Ch'ü Ch'iu-pai's facial expression and could only nod my head in silent approval. Both Teng and Yü looked our way, apparently helpless. So, after Ch'ü Ch'iu-pai indicated our collective approval to Mif in Russian, the meeting was closed.

This rebuke was equivalent to a special kind of purge against the Chinese Communist delegation. It was a heavy blow to the members of the delegation. In effect, it was a repressive action symbolizing Mif's bureaucratism within the CPSU against the naïve Chinese delegation. It was also tantamount to Mif's victory song. From then on, Mif could do whatever he pleased, while the Chinese delegation could do nothing but follow his decisions, being no longer in a position to speak its mind.

Riding on the crest of success, Mif went on planning to seize all the leadership of the CCP. In the summer of 1930 he was dispatched to China by the Comintern to act as its international representative and to guide the work of the CC of the CCP. Most of the so-called 28 Bolsheviks were one after another assigned back to the CC of the CCP. At the time the Comintern was already dissatisfied with Li Li-san's leadership of the Party CC. Mif immediately prepared to replace Li Li-san with the "Bolsheviks" under his command.

Confused and insecure, Ch'ü Ch'iu-pai, Teng Chung-hsia, and Yü Fei asked to be sent home. The Comintern, finding no valid reason to detain them, permitted them to return home one by one. Before their departure this fellow Yü Fei said to me, "The battlefield in this struggle has now moved to our country. In Moscow we couldn't beat Mif, but let's see what kind of bigger tricks he has up his sleeves in China." Otto Kuusinen, head of the Comintern's Far Eastern Department, apparently was aware of the angry mood of some of the Chinese delegates, for he especially spoke comforting words to Ch'ü Ch'iu-pai before the latter's departure from Moscow. He was convinced that Ch'ü had always supported the Comintern and that after his return he would continue to cooperate closely with the Comintern delegate based in China. Ch'ü did not reciprocate his sentiment, for at that time he was only eager to get away from the bitter life of Moscow. I was the only one to remain in Moscow. According to one report, the brains in the Comintern thought that I was still dissatisfied with the Comintern and they were somewhat worried about letting me go back. So I just continued to live quietly in Moscow without filing an application to return home.

I repaired to Yalta on the coast of the Black Sea for a summer holiday, adopting a passive attitude toward the work that should be done by the Comintern and the Chinese Communist delegation. When I returned to Moscow in August, however, I detected some traces of change. After his arrival in China, Mif apparently met with resistance from Li Li-san. The Bolshevik elements that he took along were all new hands, and as such they could not accomplish much in their underground work in China. Mif reported this situation to his Party disciples in Moscow, which caused them to change their attitude markedly toward me. In the past they had ignored me, afraid to have any dealings with me, but now they treated me kindly. The Comintern executive offices also accorded me due respect. They wanted me to resume drawing my salary from the Comintern. Although I was still studying at Lenin Academy, they said that they would give me the salary as usual. Moreover, they issued a purchasing coupon entitling me to buy any goods I wanted from the state-operated stores. In the Moscow of those days only a few very important persons and foreign ambassadors enjoyed such a privilege.

I continued to study hard at the library, and I did not visit the administrative building unless officially invited by the Comintern. Finally, one of Mif's men among the 28 Bolsheviks confided in me about some things that were actually happening. Apparently he had a great deal of inside information. He told me that he had once seen the Comintern's secret resolution rebuking the Chinese delegation.

According to him, there was a lot of material about the Chinese delegation during the Party purification campaign, but relatively little about me personally. He said that the person who informed on my becoming privy to a certain Trotsky document actually could not specify either the time of the event or the particular document that I was supposed to have seen. All that the informant could report was that I had said, "Very good." Except for him, there was no Trotskyite element who said that I had a close connection, or any connection at all, with the Trotskyites. In my dealings with the students, whatever opinions I expressed were the same as those that I expressed publicly, so it was reported that the Party Purification Committee did not believe the accusations about my association with the Trotskyite faction. Besides, the committee felt that I did not have a double-dealing manner. That was why, significantly, the Comintern's censure of me was very light compared with that of Ch'ü Ch'iu-pai. At the moment, apart from the Comintern view that I still nursed a grievance against it, there was no other misunderstanding.

Continuing, this "Bolshevik" told me that Ch'ü Ch'iu-pai's situation was altogether different, for he was in league with Borodin in opposing Mif and he was engaged in factional activities at Sun Yat-sen University. Ch'ü also advocated collaboration with the rich peasants, which was contrary to the Comintern resolution calling for opposition to the rich peasantry during the Chinese revolution.

During the purge, all evidence proved that many of the views expressed publicly by Ch'ü Ch'iu-pai were at variance with those he expressed to the students in private. Consequently, the Comintern suspected that he had purposely let Liu Jen-ching go. Again, from secondary sources it was discovered that Ch'ü Ch'iu-pai once had a three-hour-long secret talk with a rightist leader in Germany, during which Ch'ü showed his anti-Comintern tendencies. Perhaps he knew nothing about this yet, but in Moscow whatever a man did could not be kept secret very long.

After hearing his account, I became somewhat horror-stricken. It seemed that all representatives of foreign Communist parties were under surveillance. He also told me that after arriving in China, Mif had discovered that Li Li-san was by no means pursuing the Comintern line and was in fact rejecting the "Bolsheviks" sent by Moscow.

He quoted Mif's letter as saying that some of his students were doing a fine job at Sun Yat-sen University, but that they lacked experience in practical work vis-à-vis China. They should form an alliance with those comrades who had had work experience in the past in order to establish the correct leadership of the CC of the CCP. He mentioned that if I could actively support the Comintern line, I would be sent home by the Comintern in the future.

After learning of this inside information, I became convinced more than ever of what I had been thinking all along—that everything Mif said and did was part of the game of power. Mif apparently regarded Ch'ü Ch'iu-pai and Li Li-san as his principal opponents for the present, and in fighting against them, he wanted to cooperate with me temporarily in order to beat them one at a time. I maintained an indifferent attitude on this matter and continued to study *Das Kapital* at the library.

The above is an outline of what transpired in the struggle between the Chinese Communist delegation and Mif. Mif apparently reached the peak of his success after having completed his stint in China. According to one report, he, too, lost his power a few years later, and Stalin liquidated him in his customary manner.

Stalin and the Li Li-san Line

As a result of Stalin's mounting dictatorial powers, the Comintern was completely transformed into an organization for his personal use. This was particularly mainfest around the period of the Sixth Congress of the Comintern. The ideals of the early Comintern days faded away. Influenced by the demands of Soviet Russia, the leadership it furnished to the CCP was eroded by Moscow's political climate. The reckless behavior of Besso Lominadze and Heinz Neumann in China, which I have already described in the preceding pages, and Mif's iron-handed tactics in controlling Sun Yat-sen University were not incidental cases but were part and parcel of Stalinism. Even the ensuing Li Li-san line, which was opposed by Stalin, was in fact motivated by Stalin's ruthless behavior.

The Sixth Congress of the Comintern was opened in Moscow's Trade Union Building on July 17, 1928. The main items on the agenda were: (1) The world situation and the tasks of the Comintern; (2) the problem of colonies; and (3) the constitution of the Comintern. The congress was presided over by Bukharin, who had been upbraided as a rightist. He was charged with the task of making a report concerning the first item on the agenda, and of drafting a constitution for the Comintern. Kuusinen, head of the Far Eastern Department, gave a report on the problem of colonies. Stalin never appeared at the sessions of the congress, but he controlled everything from behind the scenes.

I was one of the members of the Chinese Communist delegation who attended the Comintern's Sixth Congress. After it was over, I moved out to live in a small guesthouse located in the city of Moscow. Chinese students of Sun Yat-sen University and other institutions streamed in to call on us delegates, and there was a mutually intimate feeling during our encounters. Some of them were my comrades-in-distress. Sometimes we had eight people squeezed into my room. Though it was rather inconvenient to converse freely, they did their best to let me in on what was actually going on in Moscow.

One of the friends said that times had changed in Moscow. Everything was under Stalin's control, and if anyone said something that conflicted even slightly with Stalin's word, it was regarded as heresy. Another said that for the present the Comintern was mainly antirightist and that Bukharin, who was regarded as a rightist, had lost power. It was rumored that I had once backed Bukharin and that consequently I was being labeled a rightist of the Bukharin faction. Some friend even asked me to keep quiet during the current congress in order to avoid trouble.

These students asserted that on no account should we get embroiled in Trotskyism. On November 7, 1927—the tenth anniversary of the October Revolution—Trotskyites secretly distributed pamphlets in Moscow opposing the leadership of the CC of the CPSU. This action was decreed antirevolutionary by the said CC. From then on, Trotskyites were no longer recognized as a faction within the Party, but as a counterrevolutionary group. Trotsky was personally exiled to Siberia, while many who were suspected of being Trotskyites were rounded up. The Trotskyites had used the China problem to attack the allegedly erroneous leadership of the CC of the CPSU and the Comintern. Anybody who charged that the failure of the great Chinese revolution of 1927 was related to the Comintern leadership would find it difficult to escape the suspicion of being a Trotskyite.

Another Chinese comrade familiar with the situation in the German Communist Party told me that the Comintern's activities in Europe had been a failure. The German Communist Party suffered more oppressive punishment from the Comintern than the CCP did. Old Party members who set up the "Sparticus League" under the leadership of Karl Liebknecht suffered reprimands, while the current Party secretary, Ernst Thälmann, whose leadership was weak, could do no more than follow Stalin's orders. Heinz Neumann, who had led the Canton Insurrection in China, was the Party's sole spirit and was also well known as Stalin's henchman. Although he was despised by old comrades of the German Communist Party, Neumann wanted to play his role in the current congress. That's why my friend took me as an opponent of Neumann and warned me to be wary of his attacks.

I was astonished by what my friends told me. I suspected that outwardly everyone was supporting Stalin's leadership, but surreptitiously many were dissatisfied with him. Was it really possible that the Comintern had changed its color? Were these clandestine opinions the result of the system of dictatorship or merely manifestations of personal prejudice? After playing it by ear for a few days during the congress, I came to the conclusion that what my friends told me was basically a realistic sketch of the situation. I highly treasured the sincere counsel that my comrades had given me in the spirit of genuine friendship.

I attended the sessions of the congress regularly, listening attentively to the translations of lengthy speeches. The conference hall would be filled to capacity if and when an important figure came to give a speech; otherwise, attendance would be very small. The majority of the delegates often left their seats to saunter about in groups of three to five in the broad corridors and lounges around the conference hall, chatting in low voices or discussing problems freely. Sometimes I found myself among them there.

Honestly, the disorderly proceedings of the congress were something I had rarely seen. What a difference in atmosphere inside and outside the conference! While the plenary session was in progress, there were also many small meetings being held outside of the main hall. As these small gatherings were manipulated by Stalinist forces, they tended to be more important than the formal plenum. In the big hall Bukharin, in his capacity as chief delegate of the CPSU, delivered a moving speech which won loud applause from the audience; but ouside of the plenary session Lominadze and Neumann—one representing the CPSU and the other the German Communist Party—were waving Stalin's banner and denouncing Bukharin's activities.

Representing the general opinion of the CPSU, Bukharin told the congress that the world had already entered the third stage. The so-called three stages were delineated as follows: The first stage alluded to the period of revolutionary upsurge after the First World War. The second stage covered the period between the failure of the revolutionary movements in Western European countries and the economic recovery in various Western European countries, which was characterized by the temporary stabilization gained by international capitalism. The passing of this period of stability now was interpreted as the beginning of the third stage; in other words, the present time marked the period of total crisis for capitalism.

As a matter of fact, the so-called total crisis of capitalism, the deepening contradictions in various capitalist countries, the mounting fierceness of the class struggle, and the increasing international importance of the Soviet Union—all these were exaggerations born out of Stalin's illusions. Starting out from this wildly imaginative position, Stalin dragged the Comintern and the CPSU along a path that took a sharp turn toward the Left, a fact borne out by developments in the next few years. At the time, Bukharin seemed to disagree completely with this kind of bombast, but he was compelled to make an affirmative report as a token of respect to Stalin and the majority opinion of the CPSU. Speaking candidly, I would say that people should no longer find fault with Bukharin, and yet he was unable to avoid being liquidated eventually.

The so-called third stage was also known as the period between revolution and war. Stalin was apprehensive of the possibility that capitalist countries, led by Great Britain, might be preparing for war against the Soviet Union, so the Comintern called upon Communist parties in various countries to support the Soviet Union, to resist any anti-Soviet attacks, and also to turn the possible war against the Soviet Union into a revolution to overthrow capitalist regimes. Bukharin, while he approved of the idea of taking serious precautionary measures against a possible capitalist offensive, also proposed that the Soviet Union take the initiative in easing the tense international situation. However, Stalin was not impressed by this view. He held that an attack could only be resisted by an attack. While displaying his iron hand within the Soviet Union, Stalin internationally intensified his opposition to the Social Democratic parties in various countries, which he described as "the most dangerous enemies" and "social fascists." Within the various Communist parties, the opposition to rightism became more insane, thus ignoring the actual conditions in those countries. Apparently only those who submitted completely to Stalin were regarded as genuine Communists.

Although Bukharin never openly expressed his dissent against Stalin and generally still accommodated Stalin, yet he was still subjected to the mounting criticisms of Lominadze and Neumann. They often spread allegations among delegates criticizing Bukharin's pronouncements or behavior as rightist and even said that if the delegates wanted to be antirightist, they had to be anti-Bukharin, too. They created rifts between various delegates, discerning which delegate was a loyal comrade and which was a Bukharinite. They stressed that Stalin's powers were uppermost and that any disrespect toward Stalin was a crime. Such maneuvers were simply unlawful and destructive in nature, indicating an aloofness to communism's respect for power.

Because I was aware of the reckless activities of Lominadze and Neumann in China, I felt displeased with Stalin. The fact that these two stooges could serve as Stalin's close aides proved to me that he had no capable lieutenants. I resented the way Stalin played around with power, doing whatever he damned well pleased. I lamented that the drive for power would destroy everything, especially the ideals of communism and the morals of Communists—even democratic principles within the Party were trampled completely.

However, I realized that I had no power to propitiate a ruler or restore national prestige. Moreover, I was too vulnerable to attacks myself, so I could only adopt a passive, defensive attitude. During the first few days of the congress I used this tactic in blocking Neumann's attack on me. Neumann, who regarded me as "China's Bukharin," once looked me up to sound out my opinions. After perfunctorily expressing his regret that he had not had an opportunity to meet me while in China, he asked me whether I would be willing to cooperate with Ch'ü Ch'iu-pai in jointly opposing rightism. I begged off by saying that I was not clear about the conditions in the Comintern and the Communist parties in various countries. As to the internal problems of the CCP, I said that they had already been resolved during the Sixth Congress of the CCP, which opposed opportunism and putschism. I supported the resolutions of that congress, and I would be likely to challenge whoever opposed those resolutions. I added that although I would not initiate a challenge myself, I would accept one if it were made. Neumann understood my meaning, and he refrained from making a speech attacking me at the congress.

The activities of Lominadze and Neumann made people look askance at them. Most delegates of other countries, including the other delegates of the CPSU, remained calm, discussing or doing things in a businesslike manner, but not spreading falsehoods. One delegate from another country, whom I did not know personally, told me, smiling, "Those two good-for-nothing fellows are members of Stalin's goon squad who specialize in fabricating trouble." Perhaps because the notes that their behavior struck were too discordant, these two cronies were later discarded by Stalin, one after the other.

The resolutions of the congress were made on the basis of its fundamental outlook toward the third stage. Internationally, disasters caused by Communist movements in various countries were more serious than those caused by Ch'ü Ch'iu-pai's putschism in China. This was particularly evident with regard to the problem of Germany. At that time, Ernst Thälmann, secretary of the German Communist Party, while attending a meeting of the Chinese delegation, gave a lengthy speech in an attempt to explain the correctness of the political line of the Comintern and of the German Communist Party. He pointed out that Germany was the focal point for the contradictions of capitalism and that there was a fierce conflict between the bourgeoisie and the proletariat within the country. In international relations there also existed many contradictions between the war's victors and its vanquished. Consequently, he considered that Germany already possessed the requisites for a proletarian revolution. But the development of the revolution was being hampered by the German Social Democratic Party. If the German Communist Party rose up and actively opposed the Social Democratic Party and the compromising tendencies of some elements in the German Communist Party toward the Social Democratic Party, then the German revolution would achieve victory rapidly.

I questioned Thälmann's views, pointing out that he had not appraised the strength of the German Communist Party. Nor had he proved that in case the regime of the German Social Democratic Party was overthrown, this would automatically mean a victory for the German Communist Party. Thälmann could not give me detailed answers to these problems, but stared at me in astonishment. Perhaps he felt that I held the same views as Bukharin.

As a matter of fact, I had not exchanged views in advance with Bukharin concerning the German problem. My doubts were based only on my intuition, but later events proved that Thälmann's viewpoints were mistaken. The policies of the German Communist Party against the social fascists were tantamount to paving the way for Hitler's control over Germany. After his ascension to power, Hitler carried out anti-Communist, anti-Russian policies. Obviously this was proof of the failure of policies adopted during the Sixth Congress of the Comintern. Later, in its Seventh Congress held in 1935, the Comintern had to revise its policies and adopt an antifascist "Popular Front" strategy. This was a song of mourning for Stalin's blind-actionism.

Unhappy about Bukharin's criticism of his blind-actionism, Ch'ü Ch'iu-pai availed himself of the opportunity to reopen the case during the Sixth Congress of the Comintern. The Chinese Communist problem had originally been settled during its own Sixth Party Congress, and the settlement had already been reported to the Comintern in an official document. In his speech at the Comintern congress, Bukharin said that under the new situation of the third stage, all Communist parties were mainly antirightist. He added that the CCP was the only exception and that it should continue to overcome its error of left putschism. This was challenged by Ch'ü Ch'iu-pai, who argued that the CCP's putschism was by no means serious and that it had been curbed. He explained that under the current White terror in China, some comrades dared not fight resolutely against the Chiang Kai-shek regime, and that this constituted the present rightist peril. That was why it was also necessary to stress antirightism in China.

Needless to say, Lominadze and Neumann supported Ch'ü Ch'iu-pai's interpretation. Besides, quite a number of Stalin's followers apparently thought that under the rising tide of antirightism, its was anticlimactic to have an exception. Some people even believed that the resolutions of the Sixth Congress of the CCP, made under the guidance of Bukharin, possibly contained some rightist stuff. They felt that although the resolutions had been approved by the Comintern, they still should hand over the CCP problem to its Eastern Department for further reexamination.

After the end of the Comintern congress, its Eastern Department constantly held meetings to discuss the problem of the CCP. As one of the principal branches of the Comintern in the Orient, the CCP was naturally highly regarded by the Comintern's Eastern Department. This department and the Western Europe Bureau represented two important bodies in the Comintern, each responsible for drafting the policies of various subbranches under its respective jurisdiction. The policies would then be referred to the Comintern presidium or secretariat for appraisal and decision.

Of course by then the Eastern Department was under Stalinist control and had been cleared of Bukharin followers. Its head, a Finn named Otto Kuusinen, was a major ideologist of the Comintern. He had at one time backed the views of Bukharin and was now busy trying to exonerate himself, and therefore he was afraid to make any decision on important matters. Kuusinen's chief adviser, Safarov, was originally a confidant of B. E. Zinoviev and had formerly been head of the Eastern Department. The reason why Safarov could stage a comeback successfully in the Eastern Department apparently was that Stalin thought this leftist opponent, who had once been rebuked during the anti-Bukharin-rightism period, could still be utilized. Another adviser was a Hungarian theorist named L. Magyar who had written a book entitled *China's Peasant Problems* and once had stressed that Karl Marx's theory on Asia's mode of production was at variance with the official version on the matter. But none of them wished to get involved in the controversy. As to Mif, who was head of the China Bureau under the Eastern Department, he strictly followed Stalin's position, afraid to express any opinion of his own. We viewed this as "bureaucracy." As a matter of fact, under the system of dictatorship, even a genius could not express himself.

Ch'ü Ch'iu-pai and I were Chinese representatives to the Comintern. During the Sixth Congress of the Comintern, Ch'ü was elected a member of its presidium and concurrently a secretary in its secretariat. I was elected as an alternate member and an alternate secretary. We were permitted to attend the regular meetings of its Eastern Department, and we had to be present especially when the China problem was under discussion.

Ch'ü Ch'iu-pai was the first person to submit a written proposal to the Eastern Department concerning problems of Chinese communism. In it he said that as a new upsurge of the Chinese revolution was forthcoming, the CCP should make active preparations for an armed insurrection to overthrow the KMT regime. He also said that like other branches of the Comintern organization, the CCP should also pay special attention to the principal danger of rightism.

It was my conviction that I should defend the resolutions of the Sixth Congress of the CCP and not allow putschism to rear its head again. Therefore I brought up a counterproposal that was diametrically opposed to Ch'ü Ch'iu-pai's. I explained that there were no immediate signs of the advent of a rising tide in the Chinese revolution; on the contrary, as the CCP had suffered extremely heavy losses, the new revolutionary upsurge was being delayed and we should, in accordance with the decisions of the Sixth Congress of the CCP, actively win over the masses and oppose the impetuosity of the petty bourgeoisie. We must absolutely not permit the resurrection of putschism.

In addition, Wang Jo-fei, the Chinese representative to the Peasant International, wrote a paper opposing Ch'ü Ch'iu-pai with regard to the agrarian land problem. Besides urging the CCP to continue to block tendencies of putschism, he pointed out that with regard to the peasant problem, these putschists not only failed to understand the significance of opposing the rich peasantry, but even committed the rightist error of cooperating with the rich peasants. Wang Jo-fei's views were clearly more advanced than mine, since he tried to dump all the blame of leftist and rightist errors into Ch'ü Ch'iu-pai's lap—which caused Ch'ü a lot of headaches.

We had heated debates and arguments about these differences of opinion. Ch'ü Ch'iu-pai accused me of being rightist—a fact that was proven, he said, by my remark to the effect that the new upsurge of the

Chinese revolution was still far off. I replied calmly that I defended the resolutions of the Sixth Congress of the CCP, which should not be revised at will without any reason whatsoever. We had first of all to find out what the theory had been based on that claimed the imminent approach of a new upsurge in the Chinese revolution.

For two months this controversy was discussed continually in the weekly meetings of the Eastern Department. The leaders in the department more or less admitted that there was insufficient reason for revising the resolutions of the Sixth Congress of the CCP, but at the same time they were reluctant to disclaim bluntly Ch'ü Ch'iu-pai's opinion. While Ch'ü was expounding his antirightist theory, Kuusinen remarked sarcastically, "It seems to me that everyone among the Chinese comrades holds both leftist and rightist tendencies." At the time, I felt perhaps his remark was appropriate for describing others besides the Chinese comrades. Generally speaking, the important figures in the Eastern Department refused to get themselves entangled in the problem involving leftists and rightists. Most of them preferred to be engaged in theoretical study and research on the problems concerning the prospects of the Nanking government after its occupation of Peking,[7] Asia's mode of production, commercial capital, usury capital, and the rich peasantry.

During the final discussion of this problem in the Eastern Department, Kuusinen announced, "Stalin himself is the highest authority on the problem of China, and he is interested in the question of how the Comintern should at the present time give additional directives to the CC of the CCP." Continuing, he suggested the formation of a three-man commission to handle the China problem, composed of Stalin himself, Mif, and Stalin's trustworthy secretary in charge of the China problem. This commission would draft a set of directives for the CC of the CCP and would also be responsible for all of the minutes of relevant discussions recorded during the Eastern Department meetings. In making this suggestion, Kuusinen evidently was trying to clear himself of the responsibilities in the Eastern Department, shoving them onto Stalin for his personal handling. Perhaps Kuusinen was nursing some pangs of conscience. From then on, the Eastern Department seldom held a meeting, and its guidance to various committees was dispensed separately by the departments concerned. This change in the system apparently was prompted by the troubles encountered during the discussions of the China problem.

In early November, two weeks after the establishment of this three-man commission on the China problem, Stalin invited Ch'ü Ch'iu-pai and me for a discussion, the first time we ever discussed the China problem directly with Stalin. On that particular day, at 9 P.M., we were seated opposite Stalin, who was sitting behind a large desk in his austere office. Puffing at his pipe incessantly, he started off by asking about our lives in Moscow. He treated us in a friendly manner, reflecting his worldliness.

Stalin asked us whether people like Soong Ch'ing-ling would call a policeman to arrest a Communist if she should meet one on the street of a big Chinese city. It turned out that after leaving Wuhan and arriving in Moscow, Soong Ch'ing-ling found that an anti-KMT drive was in progress at Sun Yat-sen University. Attending several of the student meetings, she learned that some students criticized Sun Yat-sen's views and work methods, which displeased her. So she protested openly. That was the background of Stalin's poser.

I replied frankly, "I don't think so." I explained that Soong Ch'ing-ling was not just the widow of Sun Yat-sen, but was indeed also a keen supporter of his views. She faithfully adhered to the policy of alliance with Soviet Russia and communism, which was personally drafted by Sun Yat-sen. She hated those Nanking warlords and politicians who openly rebelled against Sun's ideals and views.[8] Although in Moscow she once expressed her dissatisfaction toward us, she would not go to the extreme length of opposing communism. On second thought, she had been immersed in the Confucian moral outlook and certainly would not arrest Communists in the street at random.

Stalin asked again whether Ch'en Tu-hsiu would be able to acquire the necessary funds and the other requisites for operating a newspaper. This question indicated concern that after his expulsion from the CC of the CCP by the Sixth Congress of the CCP, Ch'en Tu-hsiu might adopt an anti-Comintern attitude. What Stalin was worried about was whether Ch'en Tu-hsiu would be able to publish a newspaper or organize a political party.

I said to him, "Ch'en Tu-hsiu will not be able to publish an influential newspaper." On the basis of what I knew, I told Stalin that before the Sixth Congress of the CCP, Ch'en Tu-hsiu was hoping that he could improve his relations with the Comintern and the CC of the CCP. His absence from the Party congress in Moscow by no means indicated a renunciation, but I would not know what his recent reactions might be. In the past, he had had the ability to run a passable newspaper, but after being a prominent Chinese Communist leader all these years, he had completely lost contact with society. It appeared that nobody would dare support him in starting a newspaper now. In my opinion, he probably would not obey the Comintern again, but he was still generally accepted as a distinguished Communist. Consequently, it was obvious that he could not publicly engage in political activities. As to whether or not he was planning to form a new politcial party, this was still doubtful. My talk with Stalin was interpreted by Ch'ü Ch'iu-pai, who kept his own counsel. Whereupon Stalin turned to ask Ch'ü whether he had any objection to the answers to these two questions and whether he had anything to add. Ch'ü agreed with my ideas in general. Judging by his expression, Stalin apparently was pleased with my views, perhaps thinking that these two problems might have an important bearing on future CCP policies. The thing was that the answer to the first question indicated that the CCP could still hope to have allies among non-Communists, while the answer to the second question showed that Ch'en Tu-hsiu was not in the position to engage in vigorous anti-Comintern activities in China. Here probably lay the reasoning behind why Stalin did not disclaim Bukharin's theory to the effect that the CCP must share power equally with the petty bourgeoisie in the future and why Stalin did not issue orders to the CCP to intensify its antirightist activities.

Changing the topic of conversation, Ch'ü Ch'iu-pai reported to Stalin the main points of recent discussions on the China problem by the Eastern Department, clarifying his own views and asking for Stalin's advice. Unexpectedly, Stalin replied coolly, "I think the resolutions of the Sixth Congress of the CCP were adequate; I have no new ideas." This terse remark could not but disparage Ch'ü Ch'iu-pai's antirightist moves.

Thereupon Stalin turned to the bolshevization of the CCP which, he said, should be attained by first studying Marxism-Leninism. Delightedly, he narrated some life vignettes about his youth, to which Ch'ü Ch'iu-pai listened so raptly that he forgot to translate them for my benefit at the time. Later he told me that, in general, Stalin had said that during his youth he had led a hard life in a poor, barren village. It was not until he reached thirty-two years of age that he had acquired the first volume of Marx's *Das Kapital*. He told how he had surreptitiously read this "Bible" in an environment surrounded by police detectives, and how he had later gone to all lengths to find the second and third volumes of *Das Kapital* and some other works of Marx and Engels. He had spent a number of years studying these books before he really understood a little about Marxism.

After a three-hour-long talk, I felt that Stalin was after all a realist with a sense of humor, and not so hideous and dreadful as generally imagined. But he had a sinister deductive logic. Any person who expressed a little dissatisfaction against communism became, in Stalin's opinion, an anti-Communist who would probably arrest Communists in the street at random. Such deductions were also applied without exception to Stalin's old comrades who had gone through thick and thin with him. Even such an old comrade as Ch'en Tu-hsiu, if he showed any displeasure, might be regarded as taking an antirevolutionary road. Perhaps this was a perversion or a kind of inferiority complex on Stalin's part.

A few days later, Stalin's three-member commission on the China problem proposed to the Comintern a directive addressed to the CC of the CCP. Its contents asserted that the Chinese revolution now found itself at ebb tide between two upsurges, and the CCP must not be too optimistic about the speedy arrival of a new upsurge. For this reason the Party CC should continue to implement all points of the resolutions made by the Sixth Congress of the CCP. On the basis of the gist of this instruction, the Eastern Department, in accordance with the economic problems prevailing in the Chinese Soviet areas, made separate decisions and instructions vis-à-vis the treatment of war prisoners and bandits. Regarding economic matters, the resolution opposed the fixing of prices of goods by force, but favored appropriate adjustment of them based on market price fluctuations in the Soviet areas. It called for the adoption of special treatment for war prisoners and of a policy of winning over local bandits. All these were the combined brainwork of Mif and the Chinese delegation, and they helped in the future development of the Chinese Soviet movement.

Although Stalin was still able to maintain a reserved attitude toward the China problem, he tended to act arbitrarily with regard to Russia's internal problems. At a time when the goal of the CPSU was to build "socialism in one country," he zealously tried to develop heavy industry without paying any attention to the limitations of the conditions that actually prevailed, in the hope that within a short period the Soviet Union would be transformed from a poor, backward country into a powerful industrial-agricultural nation. At a time when the anti-Trotskyism and anti-Bukharin-rightism movement was in progress, he established supreme dictatorial power. His brutal way of doing things forcefully was followed by Communist parties of various countries.

From the viewpoint of Russia's domestic problems, Stalin, rather than Trotsky, not only was the rightful head of the CPSU, but his policies, regarded then as necessary, won relatively popular support. His victory was built up from his anti-Trotskyite struggle. From then on, the central power of the CPSU was greatly strengthened, and Stalin could do as he pleased. In November, 1927, Trotsky and Grigory Zinoviev were expelled from Party membership. The small secret Trotskyite body was declared an extraneous antirevolutionary organization, and in September, 1928, Trotsky, who had already been banished to Siberia, was expelled from the country. In the course of the anti-Trotskyite struggle, a wild drive developed within the CPSU to oppress the opponents, which was intensified during the anti-Bukharin-rightism period.

Truth did not necessarily stand on Stalin's side in the course of the Stalin-Bukharin controversy. At the time, Bukharin and his associates apparently got no opportunity to air their views publicly. Even judging by the few bulletins issued by the CC of the CPSU, it could not be verified that Bukharin had committed any specific errors.

According to a proclamation of the CC of the CPSU, three of its Politburo members, namely, N. I. Bukharin, A. I. Rykov, and M. P. Tomskii, threatened to resign in the spring of 1928 in connection with the problem of grain purchasing. Their move was viewed as an unpardonable crime by the CC of the CPSU. The year 1928 was the beginning of the first Five-Year Plan of the Soviet Union. Due to lack of capital, shortage of food, and other factors, the CC of the CPSU adopted emergency measures for the purchase of grain, mainly by forced collection of grain from the peasants at low prices. At the same time, poor-peasants' committees were formed in the contryside to confiscate grain belonging to rich peasants. This measure caused a great stir in rural villages, and many people interpreted it as a rebirth of military communism. But Stalin held that this policy had to be carried out for the construction of socialism. Bukharin, Rykov and Tomskii thought, however, that this measure hindered reconstruction work, and so they resigned in protest.

During the second half of 1928, the struggle against Bukharin rightists intensified day by day. Bukharin never appeared in public after the Sixth Congress of the Comintern, and his works were banned from publication. The anti-Bukharin sound waves reverberated throughout Moscow, but no voice of rebuttal was heard at all. Originally, according to Russian Communist traditions, the opposition was permitted to make a public defense, even to make accusations before the Comintern against the majority faction of the CC of the CPSU, but this right was taken away by Stalin. Bukharin got no opportunity to fight back.

In early 1929 I attended an enlarged session of the CC of the CPSU, which was quite an experience. V. M. Molotov, representing the CC of the CPSU, gave a speech in which he asserted that all rightists must be eliminated without mercy. From merely opposing rightists to eradicating them—that was quite an awesome development. For some unfathomable reasons, Bukharin and Tomskii were absent from this meeting, leaving only Rykov to give a speech meekly acknowledging respect for Stalin's leadership. He and his cohorts were merely trying to temper some of the prejudices against them. Nevertheless, Bukharin and his faction still had to endure severe punishments, and later lost their lives.

Bukharin's rightist opinions, as proclaimed by the CC of the CPSU, advocated the following main points: (1) Reduce the rate of development of heavy industry and accelerate the development of light industry; (2) improve relations with capitalist countries and lessen the threats of war; (3) ease the class struggle within the Soviet Union, instead of intensifying it day by day.

Stalin held exactly the opposite views, saying that reduction in the speed of developing heavy industry would mean that the Soviet Union, which was under the threat of war, would be waiting for its own demise —and this would be absolutely intolerable. He maintained that the Soviet Union must spare no effort in speeding up the development of heavy industry. He demanded that the Russian people tighten their belts and not daydream about getting more consumer goods from the production of light industries. He did not believe that the relationship between the Soviet Union and capitalist countries could be improved. He would not even take any measures to improve foreign trade relations. He agreed that the class struggle within the Soviet Union was indeed intensifying day by day; therefore, he was in favor of using stern political methods to oppose kulaks and, within the Party, to carry out a fierce struggle on the two fronts.

Stalin's policies brought the Soviet Union close to collapse. He forced through the implementation of agricultural collectivization, and he escalated the policy of opposing kulaks to a policy of inhumanly liquidating them, thereby crippling Soviet agriculture for the last thirty years. He launched one purge after another, not only assassinating old Party comrades, but also ruining Soviet national power. If Hitler had not dug his own grave by antagonizing the whole world, Soviet Russia's destiny during the Second World War would have been more grievous.

At that time Moscow's political atmosphere was indeed stifling. Stalin stressed that the struggle on two fronts—against both left and right deviations—should be cruel and merciless. Not only did he want to attack his political foes, but also to liquidate his opponents completely. He also vehemently opposed compromise with either leftists or rightists. Anyone who was careless in word or deed was liable to be branded a member of the compromise faction. He said he was also against hypocritical double-dealers and plotters. Any loyal Party member or law-abiding citizen might at any time be labeled a double-dealer or a plotter. All of Soviet Russia was shrouded in terror, with Stalin-directed secret-service agents holding unlimited powers. Thus everybody always had to search Stalin's works as the basis for what he said in public, or else he would be in danger. The saying "Whispering costs death by execution!" reappeared in the Soviet Russia of the twentieth century.

It was under this work-style of Stalin's that the strife and the purification campaign at Sun Yat-sen University, which I described above, took place. After I attended the trials of the Industrial Party, I came to the conclusion that at least a few engineers had been sentenced and executed for dereliction of duty. I went to the countryside to visit collective agricultural farms and to investigate at close hand the antikulak and antireligious struggles. I recalled that during the Wuhan period we had also committed some excessive acts against the peasantry, but those had been, by comparison, mere child's play.

Fighting against rightist deviation became the Comintern's most important task after its Sixth Congress. In the course of the antirightist drive, much time was taken up in battling the rightist moderates of the German Communist Party and the majority faction of the CC of the U.S. Communist Party. In addition, during an enlarged session of the Comintern, Kuusinen confessed that due to his inadequate understanding of the Russian situation, he had erroneously approved in the summer of 1928 the views of the Bukharin rightists vis-à-vis Russia. He announced that henceforth, no matter how poor his understanding of any situation, he would unflinchingly and absolutely support the correct views of the CC of the CPSU and Stalin. Perhaps there was no alternative for Kuusinen. However, I felt at the time that Kuusinen's willingness to follow blindly was simply absurd. I also thought that his statement signified the loss of the Comintern's independent character.

Encouraged by Moscow's stand against the Bukharin rightists, Li Li-san got into the act by expelling Ts'ai Ho-sen from the Politburo of the CC of the CCP. On the pretext of asking the Comintern to rectify Ts'ai's error of rightist deviation, Li Li-san sent him to Moscow. In his report to the Comintern, Li Li-san chided Ts'ai Ho-sen for invariably defending the resolutions of the Sixth Congress of the CCP. Unable to see the advent of a new upsurge, Ts'ai Ho-sen allegedly neglected to mobilize the masses and coordinate them with the Workers' and Peasants' Red Army in order to take advantage of the insurrection in the cities— a clear proof that Ts'ai allegedly committed the error of rightist deviation.

This was indeed a strange antirightist phenomenon, one that the Comintern leaders regarded as downright ludicrous. In their view, Li Li-san should have borne the punishment within the CCP, not Ts'ai Ho-sen. Under the antirightist pressure, however, they apparently deemed it unpolitic to defend Ts'ai Ho-sen, so they accepted this fait accompli, which stoked up the fire of Li Li-san's blind-actionism.

Ts'ai Ho-sen arrived in Moscow in the summer of 1929. He was reticent, unwilling to express any opinion. Nor did he submit any report to the Comintern, except to request an opportunity to study in Moscow for a certain period. He simply refused to discuss internal matters of the CCP with Ch'ü Ch'iu-pai and me. He was even reluctant to meet people, closeting himself in his house and reading books diligently with the help of a dictionary. I felt duty-bound to stand up in righteousness for him, but Ts'ai Ho-sen opposed my idea, and even warned me that he would take me for a troublemaker if I defended him publicly.

Judging by his manner, Ts'ai must have felt that to be accused as a rightist under the current antirightist craze was hard luck and that there was no point in talking reasonably about it. Absolutely no kind of appeal would help. I knew that this was a negative and illogical attitude, but speaking realistically, that was the way things were. So I just dropped the matter.

Every time the presidium and secretariat of the Comintern held a meeting, they gave me a bundle of documents to read and notified me that I should attend it. I often absented myself on some pretext. Even when I attended a meeting, I never spoke my mind. After the outbreak of the Ts'ai Ho-sen case, I became more depressed than ever. Naturally people thought that my antirightism was not vigorous enough, but I couldn't care less.

Mif's administrative assistant, Eugen Varga, finally questioned me about why I seldom attended the Comintern meetings or raised my voice against rightist deviation. I admitted that I should have spoken out on the Ts'ai Ho-sen case, but that I had decided against it in order not to pollute the atmosphere of the antirightist campaign. As to other matters, Ch'ü Ch'iu-pai had spoken adequately. I figured that Varga would convey my remarks to his superior, but there was no further development.

During this period, the intra-Party struggle in Moscow took a broad-minded attitude toward foreign comrades, and a number of Comintern leaders were reluctant to label any person a rightist at will. My predicament apparently was extremely delicate, for I was well known as a person who had once been disgruntled with the Comintern and who was only lukewarm in opposing rightist deviation. However, there were also people who thought that some day the CCP would need me. Moreover, realizing that I already suffered a grievance at the hands of blind-actionism, they did not want to exert undue pressure against me, thus saving me, under such a delicate situation, from a great deal of trouble.

Ch'ü Ch'iu-pai found himself in a worse predicament. Not only was Mif against him, but the antirightism flame was also licking at his body. Though he claimed firmly that he was carrying out Comintern instructions, he was always being besmirched by gossip and sullied with such stigma as the opportunism of Ch'en Tu-hsiu, putschism, and even the current antirightist drive. All this frightened him. He apparently thought that the dispute within the CCP was not as serious or fierce as the strife in Moscow. Consequently, thanks to Borodin's good offices, the gap between Ch'ü Ch'iu-pai's viewpoint and mine was gradually reduced.

Needless to say, Mif's every movement showed the color of, and pivoted around, the occupant of the Kremlin. Since Moscow was busy opposing rightist deviation, Mif apparently thought that the CCP should not concern itself exclusively with opposing putschism; since Moscow was against the kulaks, so should the CCP be against the rich peasantry. He ignored such serious cases as that of Ts'ai Ho-sen, but instead zealously looked for the right-deviationist faults of CCP leaders. On the basis of the CCP report to the Comintern about uniting with the rich peasantry, and seeing that Ch'ü Ch'iu-pai also advocated collaboration with the rich peasants, Mif figured that these facts provided him with good material for his antirightist ideas.

Though they might have had different points of departure, Ch'ü Ch'iu-pai and Borodin both belittled Mif's behavior, and both agreed that not only could the CCP not afford to oppose the rich Chinese peasants, but that it should sometimes even implement its policy of uniting with them. Ch'ü Ch'iu-pai was of the opinion that if the CCP were to oppose the rich peasants vehemently, it would narrow the foundations for the Chinese Soviet movement, possibly even causing the danger of its own collapse.

Borodin, who was then living in Moscow under restraint as a disappointed politician, was in fact reluctant to talk about practical politics, but he allowed himself to be involved in the problem of China's rich peasantry. I was a frequent guest in his spacious drawing room. As a result of the friendship we had fostered while he was in China, we could talk freely. He was always in an effusive mood, telling Russian folk tales movingly; and sometimes he played chess with me, although he was much more skillful than I.

Borodin was familiar with the international political situation. With regard to the China problem, he still held his outlook of the Wuhan period. He revealed that he had no confidence in the Chinese policies regarding the establishment of a Soviet regime. He believed that Japan's ambition with respect to China knew no bounds. He thought that one day Stalin would want the CCP and the Nationalists in China to form an alliance again in order to repel foreign aggression. Consequently, he felt that it would be a mistake and would show ignorance of the China problem if the CCP should at this time stress its opposition to the rich peasantry.

After raising his voice against Mif, Borodin frankly pointed out that collaboration between Ch'ü Ch'iu-pai and me would be of great significance. He disagreed with Ch'ü's leftist style of work, and persuaded him to correct himself. He believed that Ch'ü would not oppose me again. It turned out subsequently that Ch'ü did "tune the strings"; although we could not patch up our great friendship of the early days, Ch'ü indeed no longer attacked me thereafter.

Once Mif convoked a meeting to discuss the China problem, and he asked Borodin to give a speech on the question of China's rich peasantry. I would not say that Borodin's speech was a brilliant one. He favored uniting with the rich peasants from the standpoint of broadening the base of the Chinese revolution. His delivery of this speech was hesitant—as if he were unwilling to divulge his disapproval of the CCP's present Soviet policies—and this made his arguments sound unconvincing.

Taking advantage of this opportunity, Mif thereupon maneuvered so as to criticize Borodin's views as backward and full of contradictions, and simultaneously he cunningly described China's rich peasantry as a semifeudalistic class. He narrowed the scope of the rich peasantry, defining an affluent peasant who hired one or two tillers as merely a well-off middle peasant who should not be opposed. He held that rich peasants were those who in addition to hiring laborers to till their farms, also leased out land to other farmers. Thus he fouled up the distinction between a landlord and a rich peasant.

Mif was riding high during the month of June, 1929, when the Comintern was discussing the problem of China's rich peasantry. Soviet Russia was then intensifying its attacks against the kulaks, so the Comintern people thought that it was only logical for the CCP to implement its anti-rich-peasantry policies also. However, Ch'ü Ch'iu-pai did not see eye to eye with Mif, maintaining that rich peasants were mainly exploiters of labor and that Mif's definition of a rich peasant was wrong on principle. Moreover, China's conditions then did not permit strong opposition to the rich peasants. They tried to talk each other down, but to no avail.

At the time I took a neutral attitude, but I did persuade Ch'ü Ch'iu-pai not to hold his ground firmly. I pointed out to him that the CCP's present policy was equal distribution of land; so it had to be against rich peasants, or else a revision of policy would be in order, and this was not feasible at the moment. As to the definition of rich peasants, this was secondary. Perhaps as a result of my persuasion, Ch'ü Ch'iu-pai somewhat reluctantly agreed to the resolutions proposed by Mif.

The controversy over the rich-peasantry problem had great repercussions. Ch'ü Ch'iu-pai was considered an advocate of the rightist line who opposed the correct Comintern views. He came under the enveloping fire of Mif and his cohorts, who accused him of collaborating with Borodin and other disgruntled Comintern elements in expressing their disloyalty to the Comintern. Mif was also furious about my noncommittal attitude. He criticized me for my past disagreement with the Comintern and for my passive opposition to the rightist deviation. Now, on the question of rich peasants, my attitude was allegedly not only unclear, but I also compromised with Ch'ü Ch'iu-pai on the sly, so evidently I was not the kind of person that the Comintern could rely upon. As a result of this controversy, the Mif faction among the Sun Yat-sen University student body became more active, and their scheme to grasp the leadership of the CCP thus became more open.

The issue of student strife in Sun Yat-sen University caused a further deterioration in our relationship with Mif, against whom we had already quarreled over the rich-peasantry problem. Ch'ü Ch'iu-pai and I were both infuriated by his behavior, sizing him up as a selfish person who thought nothing about the future of the CCP, but was merely forming cliques in the name of the Comintern. We also despised Mif, regarding him as a new bureaucrat since the October Revolution who now dared to brandish a whip to show off his color before us path-breakers of the CCP. This we had to oppose.

The events in Moscow that have been described in the preceding pages affected the CCP and caused incessant internecine conflicts, among which was the nurturing of the development of the Li Li-san line.

One who attacks other people indiscriminately may often be likened to a person who lifts up a rock only to drop it on his own feet. This was manifest during the Li Li-san incident. The Li Li-san line was bred during the antirightist movement. Because Moscow was reticent about the Ts'ai Ho-sen case, Li Li-san got the upper hand all the more. Believing that his viewpoint had already won the formal approval of Moscow, Li regarded the directive that was personally written by Stalin at the end of 1928 as a worthless scrap of paper. Furthermore, Moscow's request for intensification of the drive against the rich peasantry apparently strengthened Li Li-san's confidence in his leftist extremism.

Brandishing his fighting sword, Li Li-san attacked on all fronts. Ch'en Tu-hsiu was the next victim after Ts'ai Ho-sen. Perhaps Li thought that he was invincible in China, therefore he pointed his sword at the China-based representatives of the Comintern, first accusing the two Germans of being members of the rightist compromise faction, and then placing the shadow of his glittering sword over Mif's head. Although he harbored no objection to Mif's political views, Li regarded Ch'en Shao-yü and some other persons whom Mif placed under his wing as enemies that were veering to the Right, and he attacked them unceremoniously. Finally, unrolling his map and revealing his dagger, Li Li-san let it be known that the Comintern and Stalin were also rightist targets that he wanted to fight against.

Beginning in August, 1929, Ch'en Tu-hsiu repeatedly expressed his Trotskyite attitude before the CCP. He opposed having the CCP take any action under the slogan "Establish a Soviet Regime!" prior to the existence of conditions indicating a revolutionary high tide. For the time being, he was in favor of "convoking a national assembly and struggling onward."[9] In mid-November, Li Li-san's CC expelled Ch'en Tu-hsiu from Party membership. On December 10, Ch'en published his "Letter to All Comrades of the Party," in which he supported the views of Trotsky and opposed the Comintern and the CC of the CCP. The expulsion of Ch'en from membership was immediately approved by Moscow, which also lauded Li Li-san's work-style of defending the Comintern.

After the Sixth Congress of the CCP, Ch'en's relations with the Comintern went from bad to worse, and his dissatisfaction with Li Li-san's leadership of the CCP increased day by day. Meanwhile, Liu Jen-ching, an important member of the Trotskyite faction, returned to China from Moscow. However, since Ch'en Tu-hsiu was well known as a rightist opportunist, Liu Jen-ching thought that he should not join the Trotskyite faction—although the political opinions of Liu and Ch'en were close to each other. According to reports, Trotsky, who was then living in exile in Mexico, criticized Liu Jen-ching's attitude as naïve. Trotsky reportedly wrote to Ch'en Tu-hsiu, expressing his high esteem and inviting his cooperation in fighting Stalinism. In this way Ch'en formally joined the Trotskyite faction. Although at that time Ch'en had many followers, the Trotskyite faction was so full of leftist theorist who talked endlessly without having anything concrete to suggest and so ridden with clique-ism that even Ch'en's reputation failed to rescue the faction from its sinking position. Therefore, in the long run they achieved nothing in China.

Li Li-san was pleased with himself for having resolved "the anti-Party case of Ch'en Tu-hsiu" smoothly. This was followed by the development of his bad relationship with the China-based Comintern representatives. The representatives the Comintern sent to China in the summer of 1929 were two famous German leaders of the rightist compromise faction named August Thalheimer and Heinrich Brandler. Due to their opposition to Thälmann's leadership of the German Communist Party, they had been pronounced rightist moderates by the Comintern and were no longer permitted to take an active part in the affairs of the German Communist Party.

The Comintern, realizing that Li Li-san was still carrying out his putschist activities after the outbreak of the Ts'ai Ho-sen incident, tried to set him straight subtly by dispatching these two rightist moderates as its representatives in China with a view to curbing Li's recklessness. In doing so, perhaps the Comintern itself was in a quandary and was compelled to soothe the two comrades who were already famous in Germany and international circles and who had suffered a blow for nothing, for they had not committed any grave errors. Besides, under circumstances where people were attacked and punished indiscriminately—in fact, some comrades had already fallen as victims—the Comintern keenly felt the shortage of experts and therefore deemed it necessary to adopt a lenient and forgiving attitude.

But this method of solution indirectly created another problem. When the Comintern delegated them to China, it empowered them to find ways and means to rectify Li Li-san's deviation. At the same time, the Comintern officially informed the CC of the CCP that its two representatives were rightist moderates with regard to the German problem, but that, all the same, it hoped that the CCP would cooperate with them harmoniously. This gave Li Li-san a hint that the two delegates were not in a position to represent the Comintern fully. When Li Li-san differed with them, he would—on the basis of the Comintern advice—not respect their opinions, and sometimes he even accused them of being rightist and unqualified to represent the Comintern.

Danger lurked around the relations between the CCP and the Comintern. Apart from Li Li-san's stand, Ch'ü Ch'iu-pai and I were accused of creating schisms during the purge at Sun Yat-sen University. The Comintern pinned its hopes on Chou En-lai, and looked on Li Li-san as a mere braggart. Chou, by contrast, held real power and could influence Li Li-san's actions. For this reason, Chou was invited to come to Moscow to be handed a guideline for action.

Chou En-lai arrived in Moscow in April, 1930 (right after the conclusion of the purge at Sun Yat-sen University). The Comintern treated him with great kindness. Stalin appreciated him very much, praising his consistently fine record in handling military and intelligence work, and prizing his ability and political flair. During the latter part of June, Chou En-lai, in compliance with a request, delivered a speech before the Sixteenth Plenum of the CPSU which won enthusiastic applause from the audience. This was the first time that a member of the Chinese delegation was accorded such a special favor—even delegates of other Communist parties were rarely given such an honor.

Chou En-lai's trip to Moscow was extremely fruitful. On the one hand, he got along very well with Mif and welcomed him to go to China to guide the work of the CCP. Through Chou's effort, supporters of Mif, including Ch'en Shao-yü, were sent back to work in China. On the other hand, Chou sympathized with the grievances nursed by Ch'ü Ch'iu-pai, Teng Chung-hsia, and Yü Fei, and he assisted them in settling their problems concerning work assignments in China. At that time I was busy with my studies, and I expressed my intention to stay on in Moscow. Chou also had a fairly good opinion of me. All of this showed Chou's ability to handle problems, which won him the respect of Comintern leaders.

What the Comintern hoped to achieve through him was for Chou En-lai to subtly change Li Li-san's deviations and shoulder the responsibilities of practical leadership of the CC of the CCP. Never once did Chou show a wavering attitude, which made the Comintern trust him all the more. Who would have thought that when he returned to China, Chou would not yet be the number one leader. Perhaps this was because he was smart. As before, he continued to respect Li Li-san and Ch'ü Ch'iu-pai. Not only did he not rectify their deviations, but sometimes he even played the sycophant—much to the Comintern's chagrin.

The unsettled conditions in the KMT regime also helped to nurture the development of the "Li Li-san line." There was no end to the wars between the warlords within the KMT. After the unification of the country by the Nanking regime, a civil war broke out between Chiang Kai-shek and the Kwangsi clique in March, 1929; in September there was an anti-Nanking war launched by Chang Fa-k'uei; in October the war between Chiang Kai-shek and Feng Yü-hsiang broke out; in December, Shih Yu-shan and T'ang Sheng-chih rose up against Nanking. In the spring of 1930 the Chiang versus Feng war developed into a Chiang versus Feng Yü-hsiang and Yen Hsi-shan war. This series of civil wars in turn caused an industrial and commercial slump, increased the people's burdens, deepened the sufferings of workers and peasants, and increased hunger. The entire society was in a state of flux.

At that time the Soviet movement had already made considerable progress. At the beginning of 1930 the number of big and small Soviet bases increased to nineteen; in May, 1930, the Workers' and Peasants' Red Army increased to thirteen armies with a total strength of 62,000 men, half of whom were equipped with guns. During July, 1930, while the war between Chiang and Feng and Yen was unfolding fiercely, the Third Army Corps of the Workers' and Peasants' Red Army led by P'eng Te-huai attacked Changsha on July 27 and occupied the city for five days. These events boosted the optimism of Li Li-san, who believed that the success of the revolution was in the offing.

During the month of August, Li Li-san mapped out an overall revolutionary plan to the effect that the CC of the CCP would issue an order for the Red armies in various areas to assemble at a certain point and attack Changsha again and then, taking advantage of the situation, capture Nanchang and some other big cities. He believed that the time for the Chinese revolution was ripe, and he asked the Comintern to immediately order the Red Army in Outer Mongolia to advance in the direction of Peking and Tientsin, while the Russian Red Army would attack the Three Eastern Provinces in order to synchronize the revolutionary action of the Chinese Workers' and Peasants' Red Army. In Li Li-san's view, since the CCP had actively supported the Soviet Union during the second half of 1929 when the Russian Red Army opened fire against Chinese forces stationed in the Three Eastern Provinces in connection with the Chinese Eastern Railway Incident, it was now the Soviet Union's turn to give concrete support to the Chinese revolution.

This plan of Li Li-san's was opposed by the German representatives of the Comintern who were based in China. Li argued that the Comintern, which professed itself to be the general headquarters of the world revolution, should act in harmony with the Chinese revolution in the spirit of the Comintern's internationalism. If the Comintern refused to cooperate, Li would firmly reject its directives on the grounds that he was loyal to the Chinese revolution and therefore could no longer be loyal to the Comintern, which violated internationalism. By now, the Li Li-san line had already reached its zenith. Why, this was tantamount to giving a piece of his mind to Stalin: If you recognize socialism only for the construction of one country and belittle internationalism and do not support the Chinese revolution, then you are committing the error of rightist deviation!

From then on, Li Li-san was regarded as a semi-Trotskyite. When the Politburo of the CCP dispatched the proceedings of one of its meetings to the Comintern, the latter was astonished by the thesis introduced by Li Li-san. Comintern leaders were especially furious when they learned that Li Li-san wanted to embroil the Soviet Union in armed hostilities. Some asked, "Has Li Li-san gone mad? Is he a Japanese spy? It's simply impossible for the Soviet Union to send armies to Manchuria, or for Outer Mongolia to attack Peking and Tientsin. This would certainly be a dream come true for the Japanese militarists." Li Li-san's plan was equivalent to providing the Japanese militarists with the ideal pretext to occupy Manchuria and Mongolia and then attack the Soviet Union. Others said that Li Li-san's idea was even worse than Trotsky's, except that Li had not taken any practical step to oppose the Comintern, so at least he could be called a semi-Trotskyite.

The proceedings of the CCP meeting also clarified the stands held by Ch'ü Ch'iu-pai and Chou En-lai. In discussing Li Li-san's view, Ch'ü did not voice any objection, except for remarking that to be anti-Comintern was a serious thing and that all of the possibly serious consequences must first be studied before opposing the Comintern. Ch'ü's comment was ambiguous—either he was in agreement with Li Li-san or he was trying to dissuade him from taking any action. The Comintern leaders, ignorant of the Chinese way of expressing things, thought that Ch'ü Ch'iu-pai was adding fuel to the fire and hated him for it. Chou En-lai did not oppose Li Li-san's view either, so he was regarded by the astonished Comintern leaders as a member of the moderate faction.

Some people even remarked to the effect that the Chinese branch of the Comintern had rebelled.

As a matter of fact, there was nothing strange about Li Li-san's fallacious thesis. His insane extreme leftism was mainly caused by Stalin's arbitrary recklessness of those days. Holding aloft the Comintern banners, Stalin demanded all Comintern branches to follow him. The contradictory behavior of his disciple Li Li-san was true to logic, like using one's own dagger to pierce one's shield. But apparently the Comintern did not learn any lesson from this true-to-life incident. Although Li Li-san was consequently toppled, putschism remained the principal danger within the CCP.

The removal of Li Li-san gave Ch'en Shao-yü and other members of the Mif faction an opportunity to rear their heads. Mif, who had just arrived in China, and Ch'en Shao-yü, who had returned home from Moscow, dovetailed their actions neatly in their joint opposition to Li Li-san under the banner of supporting the correct line of the Comintern. Ch'en Shao-yü, who had nursed deep grudges against Li Li-san in the past, was only too glad to have this chance to strike back. At the same time, Li Li-san's putschism had caused too many people to lose heart. Many grumbling senior cadres throughout the country turned against Li Li-san and banded with Mif and other Comintern representatives, with Ch'en Shao-yü and other Russian returned students, and with a number of old cadres who originally supported me.

The delicate situation caused by Li Li-san's farce also prompted my homecoming. At first Ossip Piatnitski looked up Ts'ai Ho-sen and asked him to return to China immediately in order to rectify Li Li-san's error. But Ts'ai said that he did not have sufficient power to undertake this task and he was not willing to go back. Piatnitski later coaxed Ts'ai to return to China by saying that he and his cohorts always regarded Ts'ai as a very dependable comrade who not only could carry out the Comintern line, but could also rise above intra-Party conflicts. However, Piatnitski added that in contrast to Comrade Chang Kuo-t'ao, Ts'ai Ho-sen lacked the courage to shoulder responsibilities.

Despite Piatnitski's encouragement, Ts'ai Ho-sen refused to go. Instead, he suggested to Piatnitski that it would be best to delegate me to China. Piatnitski reportedly asked him whether it would be opportune to send me back home at that moment, to which Ts'ai Ho-sen replied firmly, "I guarantee that Comrade Chang Kuo-t'ao can carry out the Comintern directives and fulfill the mission of rectifying Li Li-san's error."

Ts'ai Ho-sen, whom I had not seen for a long time, looked me up to tell me about his talk with Piatnitski. He said that since the Comintern intended to send him back to China, he had been given the opportunity to read some classified papers. From these documents he had found out that Li Li-san was to come to Moscow soon. But the rectification of Li Li-san's erroneous line would require a great deal of energy. At present there were three factions within the CCP: One was the power-holders, represented by Li Li-san, Ch'ü Ch'iu-pai, and Chou En-lai, who were more or less still pursuing the erroneous policies of bygone days. Another was the Ch'en Shao-yü and Mif faction, which was scheming to seize power but possessed insufficient force to do it. The third faction was composed of Ho Meng-hsiung and other senior cadres who, though numerically superior, were regarded as rightists. The people of the last-named faction supported me and wanted the Comintern to send me back to China.

Some of what Ts'ai Ho-sen told me was new to me, and I was impressed by his words. I countered by asking Ts'ai why he refused to return to China, adding "Since the Comintern did not wish me to know about your repatriation and about the inside information concerning the CCP, would they believe your suggestion and trust me?" Ts'ai Ho-sen evaded these questions, but convinced me by saying, "The Comintern wants you to go back. I hope you won't pass up this opportunity!"

I thanked him for his good intentions, and began to consider the question of going home. I dared not place too much hope in the possibility of my repatriation. I recalled that Magyar, acting director of the China Bureau, once said to me, "The Comintern has the power to rectify Li Li-san's error by itself without asking for help from any Chinese comrade." In making this arrogant remark, perhaps he was giving me a hint that I should not entertain any idea of returning to China. After Ch'ü Ch'iu-pai's departure, I became the only Chinese representative stationed in Moscow. But this was only a nominal honor. I continued to study hard, oblivious of what was going on outside. I never vigorously defined my attitude against the Li Li-san case. And I did not express any opinion concerning the various questions brought up during my talk with Ts'ai Ho-sen.

I decided not to sacrifice my chance of going back to China. As to whether the Comintern would trust me and whether I could do anything constructive in China—I regarded these questions as secondary. Moscow's political climate indeed made me uncomfortable, and I wanted to get away from this cage into the vast motherland and do what I could. No matter what difficulties might confront me, even the danger of losing my life, I would not worry at all. If necessary, I would be prepared to pay this price for my repatriation.

The price of going home was evidently to lay down the anti-Comintern weapon. What the Comintern had all along been hoping was for me to announce openly that my past disagreement with the Comintern had been due to my own error and that I now supported the Comintern line fully. My readers should know by now that I had always avoided fulfilling this Comintern wish. With the problem coming to a head, it would be against my conscience to bow my head and plead guilty. In the past I had quietly accepted the Comintern reprimand with regard to the Sun Yat-sen University affair, for I was then under duress. But now to admit voluntarily that I had made an unacceptable mistake would be too much. I could only rationalize by recalling the words of Lenin who, in his book entitled *Leftism, An Infantile Disease*, said, "When you meet a robber, you just have to bow your head." What I wanted to be clear about at that time was: After admitting my fault publicly, what sort of political restraint would I have to perforce accept? This question I had to consider thoroughly from beginning to end.

It seemed to be necessary, and a Hobson's choice, for me to announce my loyalty to the Comintern and then to return to China and do some work. If I said that I wanted to remain in Moscow in order to complete my plan of study, this might be misconstrued as my avoiding to define my political stand. Moreover, I would be regarded as thinking selfishly about my own welfare, drained of any fighting spirit. If I were to follow in the footsteps of Ts'ai Ho-sen, the result would be unthinkable. On the other hand, if I wanted to return to China only to fight against the Li Li-san line without proclaiming my loyalty to the Comintern, I would immediately become a primary target. To get away from this bitter life in Moscow thus became the most expedient and most logical decision for me to make.

Watching China from Moscow, I was like a blind man trying to get a mental picture of an elephant by touching part of one with his hands. Books and magazines published in China were not readily available in Moscow. At the time there were no radio broadcasts and only a few travelers. What I could envisage then was that the Soviet banner had already been planted in some remote places in southern China; but to discover the true situation about this would require a close study after my return. I felt that I must not shirk the responsibility of quickly solving the internal crisis of the Party caused by the Li Li-san line and of rescuing comrades in general from their plight. Previously I had had some quarrels with the Comintern concerning the problem of KMT-CCP collaboration, but all this was a thing of the past and no longer existed. Generally speaking, I must now work hard along the policy lines set down during the Sixth Congress of the CCP. Therefore, I decided to return to China to save the Party, regardless of the personal complications to be faced.

Recalling my three visits to Moscow, I realized that the factors for my disappointment had greatly increased with the passing of time. Briefly, during my previous two short visits to the Red capital in 1921 and 1923, I, in addition to being excited about traveling, regarded the Soviet Union as the fatherland of the proletariat, and I felt a sense of belonging. Though at that period I experienced some disappointment on certain matters, I still believed that the faults and deviations were unavoidable and could be remedied. When I visited Moscow for the third time, in 1928, my outlook changed, due to my disappointments, which had increased both in number and gravity during all those years. I no longer regarded the Soviet Union as my spiritual fatherland, and in fact, as time passed, I felt like a stranger. The Comintern was no longer the general headquarters for the world revolution that I had first visualized it to be, but had become Stalin's plaything for bullying the Communists of various nations.

I arrived in Moscow in the summer of 1928. Although dogged by trouble, I regarded myself as a revolutionary with a strong determination to struggle. I wanted to make good use of my exile to steel myself, so that I could fight again after my return. I read assiduously day and night, first studying Marx's epic work, *Das Kapital,* and then observing international affairs, the situation in the Soviet Union, and recent conditions in China. I felt all confused most of the time. My life was simple, and I observed strict discipline. In my dealings with people I was humble and courteous, and many· of them sensed my enthusiasm and ambition.

The experience and lessons of the Russian Revolution could be easily used as a mirror for the Chinese revolution. I studied it from its very beginning. The materials I gathered about current conditions in the Soviet Union formed quite a special collection by itself. What a pity that after the lapse of many years, names of Russian places and people as well as events during certain periods all became blurred in my mind, making it impossible for me to present them for posterity. Consequently, this book lacks the color of a Soviet Russian travelogue. I believed that all the happenings in Russia were deeply rooted in Russian history and were full of the Russian way of life. Leninism sounded like the Russianization of Marxism. Though Stalin stressed the world significance of Leninism, he had a richer Russian flavor than Lenin.

I liked to think that I held no prejudice against Stalin. I even understood him, often putting a kind interpretation on his actions; but I did not regard him as the leader of the world Communist movement. Sometimes I admired him as a capable ruler, and at other times I hated him as a cruel, dictatorial tyrant. In my opinion, we could not condone Stalin's actions simply because the Soviet Union was a despotic government of the proletariat. Even a dictatorship should have a civilized style of work. It seemed reasonable that in Chinese political thought, traditional emperors had propagated the "royal road" (the way of right as opposed to the way of might) and disparaged tyranny. To be a statesman, the least one should do is to manage state affairs and carry out practicable policies for the welfare of the people. If one were to resort to dictatorship in order to abuse power indiscriminately and even brutally, then everything would go wrong.

Stalin supported the principle of "building of socialism in one country," that is, in the Soviet Union, and opposed Trotsky's empty talk about world revolution. No matter how you looked at it, this slogan of Stalin's was commendable. Originally, Russia was relatively weak, and suffered repeated defeats in successive wars. She rebuilt herself from the rubble following the October Revolution. Whether or not it was possible to build socialism in one country, domestic reconstruction was necessary. Therefore, the setting aside of the question of world revolution in favor of the establishment of socialism in one country, and the prevention of major wars and the rapid build-up of national power for self-defense and progress had to become urgent tasks. This had to be the conclusion of Marxian dialectical materialists.

But Stalin was boorish by nature, eager to get quick results and successes. He opposed the "way of right" propounded by Bukharin—this was Stalin's big blunder. He was morbidly afraid of external attack, and if the people were rebellious, he would teach them a lesson on the principle of "Let me turn my back on the people, not the people on me" in order to ensure his own victory, or to solve the problem of "who defeats whom" —to quote his own words. Within the CPSU, he destroyed the Trotskyite and rightist factions, opposed the compromise and double-dealing factions, and even purged the Party and liquidated his opponents. Also within the Soviet Union, he eradicated the kulaks, liquidated professional military men, and purged plotters. All this created gloom above and darkness below. It was extremely fortunate that all this did not bring destruction upon the Soviet Union.

It seems obvious that Stalin lacked general knowledge about international affairs. His ideas on the "third stage"—the period between war and revolution, the total collapse of capitalism and social fascists—were all impractical, arbitrary decisions. Under his excessive powers, such experienced, conservative personalities as Piatnitski and Kuusinen were silent, like cicadas in cold weather, and totally helpless, while little men like Mif were given important positions. Readers have only to recall how Stalin set up the Chinese Soviets and what I have said about Mif's crude performances in order to know how reckless Stalin's pronouncements and behavior had been.

My thinking changed from dissatisfaction over certain Comintern moves in China to resentment against Stalin's overall leadership—which had become quite an obsession. Since I had kept silent for a long time, was it high time for me to speak up now? I knew well that it was impossible to talk reason, so should I act in a foolhardy manner, like hitting a stone with an egg? Any outcome could only be decided by "trying my luck" in China. After expressing my loyalty toward the Comintern, I could absolutely keep my promise of not criticizing the Comintern again about problems in the past. As regards my anti-Stalin thoughts, I preferred for the time being to say nothing about them in the interests of the public welfare. However, I decided to do wholeheartedly whatever was deemed necessary on the basis of the conditions prevailing in China.

In mid-October, 1930, Piatnitski made an appointment to see me. During our meeting, he solemnly asked what my reaction would be if the Comintern should send me to China. I replied, "To return to the battlefield in China and struggle together with my friends is really my public duty, which admits of no shirking." He was delighted with my reply and said, "That's fine. We believe you are a good warrior. However, there's one thing I must tell you. It's been a long time since you showed dissatisfaction with the Comintern, but up till now you have shown no sign of a change of heart. We don't mean to find fault with your past, but we're concerned over whether or not you now support the Comintern line, whether at a crucial moment you might be anti-Comintern like Li Li-san. Therefore we do hope you will define your attitude clearly."

Of course Piatnitski's remark represented the wishes of Comintern leaders, and it was made with the permission of the big boss in the

Kremlin. Because the Third Plenum of the CCP held in Shanghai on September 28 failed to correct Li Li-san's error, and because intra-Party bickering was still rampant, they made the decision to send me to China. With a spirit of willingness to assume all consequences, I replied, "I will voice my support for the Comintern at the proper time." After hearing my words, Piatnitski clasped my hand tightly, indicating his satisfaction.

During the latter part of October, Li Li-san arrived in Moscow. This defeated hero settled down quietly, making contact with only a few people. Perhaps the Comintern leaders wanted him to do some soul-searching for a while. We met every day, and sometimes our talk would last half a day at a stretch. While in China, he had opposed me; but now I became his dear big brother. I did not blame him openly for his errors, but merely encouraged him to settle down and do some studying. Although finding himself in a strange land, Li Li-san, active and romantic, moved around with his girl friends in a relaxed way, apparently to relieve his boredom.

In the middle of November (about the third week after Li Li-san's arrival), the Comintern presidium convened a meeting to discuss the Li Li-san line. Li, who was accused of being a semi-Trotskyite, was the first to speak up. In a loud voice, he fully admitted his error and unconditionally accepted the accusation that he was anti-Comintern and a semi-Trotskyite. He hoped that his confession would help to rectify his error. However, he explained that he had never carried on any specific anti-Comintern activities, and so he had complied with the Comintern instruction to come to Moscow and accept its restraint. One can only admire his remarkable skill in adapting himself to new situations.

The second speaker was Bela Kun, sometimes known as the Lenin of Hungary. He did not believe that Li Li-san had understood his own error. Bela Kun ridiculed him by recalling that during a CCP Politburo meeting Li Li-san vigorously opposed the Comintern, but now Li transformed himself overnight into a sincere supporter of the Comintern! Taking himself as an example, Bela Kun related how it took him years of meditation before he could fairly understand his error. He asked Li Li-san to make a serious self-appraisal, and not just to admit his error verbally.

I followed up, saying that I agreed with Bela Kun. I explained that to really understand one's errors was not an easy thing. I pointed out that during the period of KMT-CCP collaboration and thereafter, I had been dissatisfied with the Comintern leadership of the Chinese revolution. This dissatisfaction was mostly my own fault, and I failed to understand this point until I had completed my year of study in Moscow. I added that I was willing to cooperate with Li Li-san, that we would encourage and restrain one another, so that I could understand my own error more thoroughly. From the standpoint of my supporting the Comintern, I would fulfill all my responsibilities.

Many people spoke up during this session, all of them examining thoroughly Li Li-san's error. But the meeting came to no conclusion whatsoever. It was during this session that I admitted my error openly for the first time. Subsequently, I revised the transcript of my speech, and after affixing my signature, I took it to the Comintern as the pronouncement expressing my error and my support. Pleased with my speech, the Comintern made its formal decision regarding the question of my repatriation.

A man's way of thinking tended to change under the pressure of a dictatorship, so my resorting to expediency meant nothing at all. I knew of many persons who supported Stalin enthusiastically in public, but who held grudges against him in private. Perhaps this was a disease naturally fostered by dictatorial policies. According to my wife, who worked in a Moscow printing plant, Communist members and workers sympathetic to communism often shouted publicly, "Long live Stalin!" However, they told my wife privately, "Our big boss is no good!" Perhaps such a situation still exists in Communist countries today.

I began to make arrangements for my return. It took my wife and me more than one month to obtain our forged passports. During this period I apparently recovered my original reputation, for I was treated with greater kindness than before by many people. The Comintern director of communications did all he could in helping to arrange my repatriation. Safarov, whom I had known for a long time, no longer avoided me but often animatedly discussed China's problem with me. Magyar, who was in charge of Chinese affairs, became friendly with me.

A few days before my departure, Magyar invited me to dinner at his house. He had a small but fine place which possessed the touch of an aristocratic home in Western Europe. He went to great lengths to make it clear that everyone in the Comintern not only did not misunderstand me, but even respected me. He hoped that I would devote all my energy to Party work in China in order to save the CCP from danger, adding that the Comintern would support me to the hilt. In this way, all my past scars from being labeled a member of the Bukharin faction, compromise faction, and Sun Yat-sen University separatist faction were wiped out at one time.

Before I left, Magyar asked me, "Do you think you will meet with difficulties and misgivings in your work in China?" I thought for a while and replied, "How do we go about indicating support for the Soviet Union?" He answered, "I think each national Communist Party should develop its own revolution within its respective country. That would be the best way of supporting the Soviet Union. On the other hand, if our national parties consider that their missions are merely and exclusively to give support to the Soviet Union, they'd be likely to be slandered as Russian fifth columnists by the capitalists." I said, "Judging from your clarification, then, there won't be any problem at all for me."

Magyar prided himself on being an extraordinary ideologue. Like a wild horse running every which way, he often voiced his opinions on random issues at the drop of a hat—which probably accounted for his downfall. According to later reports, he was eventually liquidated by Stalin. The news of his liquidation brought back many memories about the Comintern's important figures of those days, such as Piatnitski, whose later whereabouts were unknown to me. These people once supported Stalin in the name of world revolution, but eventually they were all regarded as squawking, repulsive crows.

Generally speaking, I maintained a cautious attitude before my departure, revealing nothing about my plans publicly. Behaving like a soldier, I gave one and all to understand that I could struggle onward in accordance with all the instructions of the Comintern. Perhaps as a result of this attitude I was able to bring to a successful close my two-and-one-half years of life in Moscow and to return to my motherland.

FROM THE LI LI-SAN LINE
TO THE WANG MING LINE

CHAPTER

Party Solidarity Work in "White" Areas

In January, 1931, the Fourth Plenum of the CCP blocked the Li Li-san line and at the same time delivered a heavy blow to senior cadres who opposed it. It also enabled such Mif disciples as Ch'en Shao-yü to take over control of the CCP's leading organs. Under the influence of Moscow's political climate and Mif's direct guidance, Ch'en Shao-yü (alias Wang Ming) and other Bolsheviks among the group of students who had returned from Russia first carried out their campaign of struggle on two fronts. In other words, they opposed the left-veering Li Li-san line and simultaneously rejected the anti-Li-Li-san-ist Ho Meng-hsiung and other veteran cadres whom they labeled rightists. In this manner the plotters created a situation of fragmentation within the CCP. Starting from this point, they then—on the basis of Moscow's dogmatism —grasped the reins of the CCP for nearly five years under the well-known name of the "Wang Ming line." Ten days after the adjournment of the Fourth Plenum, I arrived in Shanghai. With a view to saving the Party from this crisis, I could only earnestly appeal for intra-Party solidarity. Shortly afterward, the leadership core of the CCP scattered to various Soviet areas.

Like myself, my wife hated the strife within Sun Yat-sen University and was eager to go home. After Christmas, 1930, we moved out of the

Hotel Lux to a secret abode, bought some suitable clothing, and proceeded to plan our impersonations. Contrary to our expectations, we easily obtained two forged passports of the Republic of China. Using assumed names, we were supposed to be natives of Kiangsu, with ages similar to our own, who were returning home after studying in Germany. We carefully assumed disguises based on these particulars. Although we had never been to Berlin or Paris, we learned something about the conditions in those cities, particularly street names, the Chinatowns, and locations of the Chinese diplomatic missions in order to cope with any future interrogation. After passing a simulated test given to us by a young Russian couple who were assigned to take care of us, we started off on our homeward journey.

We were to pretend that we were returning to China from Berlin via Moscow, that we were compelled to stop over in Moscow for a few days because of my wife's sudden illness, and that now we were resuming our trip from Moscow. Arriving at the station in a horse-drawn sleigh, we acted like ordinary travelers, going through the immigration inspection, fetching our train tickets, and boarding the first-class sleeping car of the eastbound international train. At the station a Russian beggar asked us in Russian for alms. We shook our heads to indicate our ignorance of the Russian language, but gave him a few kopecks. I suspected that the beggar was placed there on orders to test whether we would inadvertently reveal our true identity.

The passengers on first- and second-class sleeping cars were mostly foreigners, mainly Japanese diplomatic personnel. When we boarded the train at Moscow, one of the Japanese passengers evinced interest in us. He tried to ferret some news from us during our conversation, but in vain. Then there was another Chinese passenger in the sleeping car who looked like an official of the Peiyang warlord regime. I think his name was Wang, but I'm not sure. I took the initiative in striking up a conversation with him, and we were often together thereafter. Apparently he was returning from Europe after having fulfilled a mission at the behest of Chang Hsueh-liang, the "King of Manchuria." So he did not want to reveal the aims and itinerary of his trip. Perhaps he figured that I was a high official of the Nanking government; therefore, he did not want to find out about the purpose of my travel, either. In this way, our contact with Mr. Wang more or less served the purpose of covering up the motive behind our journey.

As it reached the Sino-Soviet frontier, the train stopped at a Russian station for inspection. One of the inspectors was a tall Korean named Kim, whom I had known before. Softly, he asked me, "Have you come across some suspicious characters along the way? If there's any problem concerning your personal safety, I can take you off the train on the pretext of detaining you." I replied in the negative, adding that it was not necessary to take such a drastic step. After inspection, our train proceeded to the Manchouli station which was in Chinese territory.

My wife and I, as well as Mr. Wang, got off at the Manchouli railway station and transferred to another train heading for Harbin. Many Japanese were deployed at the entrance and exit of the Manchouli station. Those Japanese detectives, who were adept at disguise, wearing thick fur clothing and headgear covering even their faces, stared at us passengers. Mr. Wang, who was irritated by this sight, remarked that the railway stations in this area were crawling with Japanese spies.

As for me, I had a different thought and blurted out, "Well, at least we're back in our own country!" Mr. Wang did not understand me apparently, for he made a rejoinder, "This is our land! The national government in Nanking always groups the Three Eastern Provinces as a special area. As a matter of fact, aren't they the same as any other provinces?" He continued to explain his opposition to the special treatment of the Three Eastern Provinces and his hope for a rapprochement between Nanking and Fengtien (Mukden). His VIP identity was revealed when local military police authorities showed up to meet him and look after him. As his fellow travelers, we enjoyed his protection and were exempt from interrogation by the military police. It was indeed beyond our expectation that we could easily make use of domestic political contradictions for our benefit.

My wife and I reached Harbin without a hitch. Mr. Wang wished to play host and take care of us as best he could, but I declined his kind gesture courteously. Getting off the train at Harbin, Mr. Wang stepped out of the station amidst the plaudits of officials and the salutes of military policemen who came to welcome him back. We swaggered along close behind him, free from the inspection by military policemen and annoyance by Japanese spies, hopped into a taxi, and headed for a White Russian hotel.

From Harbin we journeyed to Dairen, where we immediately boarded a Japanese ship for Shanghai. Everything went unexpectedly smoothly. But before the boat was ready to sail, a Japanese agent gave us trouble for about two hours. For some unfathomable reason, he apparently knew a great deal about our itinerary, and expressed surprise particularly over the fact that although we had taken first class in the international train, we were now traveling deck. He deliberately told me that there were several Nanking government officials in first-class cabins aboard and suggested that we look them up. But I was carefully noncommital. Subsequently, he took our passports and looked at them closely, as if suspicious as to whether they were genuine or bogus. Finally, he said, "You're safe in Dairen and aboard a Japanese boat. Don't you worry! But when you disembark in Shanghai, do be especially careful!"

Apart from making me feel uneasy, the behavior of this Japanese detective triggered off much thought and melancholy for me. Aboard a ship sailing near the coastline on a calm sea, I dared not go up on deck for a stroll or discuss anything with my wife beside me. We closeted ourselves in the lower deck with great discomfort, but this gave me a dark secluded spot to give free rein to my imagination.

First of all, I agreed with the remark that I would be safe in Dairen and on board a Japanese vessel. I recalled that the true identities of Ch'ü Ch'iu-pai and Chou En-lai had in the past been discovered by Japanese agents while they were traveling through Dairen under assumed names, but they were eventually set free without any trouble. I presumed that the Japanese spy probably knew my real name, but that he preferred to keep quiet amidst so many staring eyes aboard a ship. The technique of the Japanese aggressors was that they were always delighted to see bickering Chinese factions killing one another off. In their opinion, it would be an interesting sight to see the detestable Chinese Communists and the incorrigible Chiang Kai-shek elements step up their mutual killings. If only the Chinese Communists could reach the capital of the opposite side like Li Tze-chen (leader of a Ming-dynasty rebellion), and if only a Wu San-kuei (Ming-dynasty general) would again burst forth within the KMT, so that the Manchus could take the opportunity to enter the Shanghaikwan pass and control China for 268 years! Disregarding the time and circumstances, perhaps the ambitious Japanese politicians thought that if the Manchus could achieve this, surely Japanese imperial forces could do it better. Alas! how sad that those Chinese who were brave about domestic disputes were so belated in their recognition of foreign aggressions.

The Japanese not only deployed spies along the South Manchurian Railway, but also in all big and small stations along the Chinese Eastern

Railway. What were they up to? I ruminated over it. In contrast with their stealthy behavior two and one-half years ago, they now carried out their activities openly along these international railway lines, daringly showing off their ambition to grab the Northeast. Lying on the bunk, I recalled Bukharin's foresight and the words of Leo Karakhan and Borodin in Moscow concerning Japan's ambition of occupying Manchuria and Mongolia and destroying China. I pondered also about how Stalin and Mif played down Japan's aggression against China. I suspected that they knew about this all along, but deliberately kept quiet either because they did not wish to offend the Japanese or because they, calculatingly, wanted to let the volcano in the Far East erupt and then see how the wind would blow afterward.

"Be especially careful when you land in Shanghai!" This warning kept churning in my head. Only then did I realize how terribly isolated from China I had been after living for two and one-half years in Moscow. I had simply become half-deaf and half-blind, feeling so undecided about everything. I somewhat regretted having headed directly for Shanghai, instead of staying for a few more days in Harbin to see the sights and get my bearings. There were many ways to get to Shanghai. What danger would I face when I landed in Shanghai? I could not think of any clue. I imagined that the Nanking guillotine was awaiting me, and this forced me back to face reality. Having shaken myself off from Moscow's cage to step into the danger-stalked "land of freedom," I could not afford to make a single mistake, for it would endanger my life. I had to concentrate my thought and observe my surroundings carefully, to discern whether anybody could see through our disguises, to be aware of the gossip of passengers about Shanghai and to improve our impersonations. All of this speculating involved a question of life or death.

Luckily, about January 20 my wife and I safely reached Shanghai, where we put ourselves up at the Oriental Hotel. A few days earlier Ho Meng-hsiung and sixteen other old cadres had been arrested in that same hotel while holding a meeting, and now we moved into it! What a coincidence! Luckily, again, it so happened that an hour after we had registered at this hotel, my wife ran into Shen Tse-min on the street, and this enabled us to get into contact quickly with the CC of the CCP and to learn of the unfortunate arrest of Ho Meng-hsiung and party. We checked out immediately and stayed temporarily at the Organization Department of the CC. There we met Chao Yün (alias K'ang Sheng), the newly elected head of the department, and Ch'en T'ieh-cheng (present name, K'ung Yüan), secretary of the department.

These comrades briefed me on how Ho Meng-hsiung and his party had been arrested. Ho was Party secretary of the Shanghai area. Together with Lin Yü-nan, who was in charge of the important propaganda work, Li Ch'iu-shih, a member of the Standing Committee of the CC of the CYC, and some others, Ho was holding a secret meeting in the hotel room to oppose Mif and Ch'en Shao-yü, when they were all rounded up. The event caused quite a furor and attracted public attention for some time. While the comrades were relating the incident to me, Shen Tse-min kept silent, not daring to say openly whether Ho Meng-hsiung and his group were rightist and anti-Party. Chao Yün and Ch'en T'ieh-cheng were distressed by the unfortunate incident that had befallen these comrades and fearful that the incident might affect the safety of all Party organs and members. They were particularly worried about the fact that a number of comrades were displeased with, and some even voiced opposition to, the CC of the Party. Lo Chang-lung, who was in charge of the All-China Federation of Trade Unions, Ch'en Yü of the Shanghai Seamen's Union, and members of the Shanghai Party Committee—Hsü Hsi-ken, Yü Fei, and Wang K'e-ch'uan—all were dissatisfied over the resolution of the Fourth Plenum of the CC. There were already some divisive moves with regard to the action opposing the Mif faction. All these events indicated that the CCP, which had gone through many trials and tribulations, was heading toward the brink of extinction.

Faced with such great changes upon my arrival in Shanghai, I could not help feeling depressed. I regretted having come too late. If I had arrived in Shanghai two weeks earlier, perhaps that tragic incident could have been averted. Ho Meng-hsiung and the others were all my comrades-in-arms, and they had supported me openly. If I had conveyed their views during the Fourth Plenum and restrained Mif and Ch'en Shao-yü, Ho and his group would not have run the risk of convening a secret meeting. But now it had got to the point where I could do nothing but try to save the situation.

I met Chou En-lai again on that very day. He knew clearly what had transpired and maintained a calm attitude. He felt extremely sad over the arrest of Ho Meng-hsiung and party. He thought that if I had been able to arrive earlier and talk things over with them, perhaps everything could have been resolved easily. He pointed out that the resolution of the Fourth Plenum was fine, and even Ho Meng-hsiung and party were agreeable to it. During the meeting, Chou himself also admitted his error of adopting a compromising attitude vis-à-vis the Li Li-san line. This admission was accepted by the participants, so he carried on with the work for the CC. He explained that Ho Meng-hsiung and his group were displeased about the fact that Ch'en Shao-yü and the other returned students from Russia brashly took over the leadership of the CC without any prior experience or training. Consequently, Ho and party objected to the Party decision concerning the selection of members of the CC during the Fourth Plenum. The arrest of Ho and party was misunderstood by Lo Chang-lung and his friends, who misconstrued it as the consequence of Ch'en Shao-yü's secret information. Chou En-lai, who was noted for his calmness and reserve, merely explained to me the main points of the event without defining his own stand. Likewise, he maintained his serenity in the midst of this serious situation, making no criticism whatever of Ho Meng-hsiung, Lo Chang-lung, Mif, or Ch'en Shao-yü. However, he could not help asking me to explain the misunderstandings to all concerned.

Chou En-lai also told me that Mif, accompanied by Ch'en Shao-yü, hurriedly returned to Moscow after the Fourth Plenum of the CC of the CCP. A Polish comrade acted as Mif's deputy in carrying on with the work. Chou offered to arrange a meeting between the Polish comrade and myself. Chou did not explain to me the reason for the sudden return of Mif and Ch'en Shao-yü, but I figured that they wanted to report to, and get the approval of, the boss in the Kremlin about the results of the Fourth Plenum. Perhaps this small-time bureaucrat Mif was most concerned about his own position in Moscow, and was not really thinking about how to make any contribution to the Chinese revolution. Within the Comintern he held the position of leader of the Chinese revolution; this was an indisputable fact. Within the CC of the CCP his close disciples already occupied strategic positions, and Mif with Ch'en Shao-yü as the CCP's representative to the Comintern formed a harmonious duo. Henceforth, as his official status rose further, he could do anything he pleased.

On the following evening Chou En-lai and I went to see the Polish comrade. I met him that one time only, and I cannot recall his name now. After identifying himself as the Comintern representative, he looked stern and said to me, "Ho Meng-hsiung and the other anti-Party elements were supporters of you. Please define your position as to whether or not you support the resolution of the Fourth Plenum of the

CCP.[1] If you don't agree, the Comintern is ready to expel you from the Politburo of the Central Committee." Chou En-lai apparently was upset by this outpouring and quickly interceded in my behalf. Controlling my anger, I turned to Chou En-lai and said, "I came home because I was prepared to struggle together with my comrades, but not to cause trouble. The Comintern has already expressed its confidence in me."

The blundering, rash Polish youth unconcernedly continued to chatter some antirightist words and even to suggest the elimination of Lo Chang-lung through assassination. Not only was he apathetic over the arrest of Ho Meng-hsiung and party, but he was also of the opinion that those anti-Party elements had surrendered themselves. He believed that Lo Chang-lung was the brains behind Ho Meng-hsiung and his group and that since Lo openly defied the Party, it was necessary to restrain and even secretly assassinate this despicable opponent. Chou En-lai was noncommittal, but pointed out, "Since there were many differing opinions within the Party, it requires separate efforts to bring about an understanding, in order not to drive dissenters to the anti-Party side. Now Comrade Chang Kuo-t'ao has returned, just in time to make a concerted effort in this matter." After hearing Chou's explanation, the Pole kept silent and our meeting was thus brought to a silent end.

My impression of that Pole was extremely bad. I deplored the fact that representatives sent by the Comintern to China were getting progressively worse as time passed. I regarded him as nothing but Mif's pawn, who only knew how to fool around with the so-called struggle on the two fronts and mop up the dissenters. The Mif faction had shifted Moscow's brutal method of struggle bag and baggage to the underground organizations of the CCP, which could herald the total destrucion of the Party. I began to suspect that the Comintern had been insincere with me, for I could not believe that the opinion expressed by the Pole was his own. Perhaps the Comintern had double-crossed me, first by expressing its confidence in repatriating me, and then by giving secret instructions to its representative in China. Perhaps at first the Comintern needed my help in connection with the rectification of the Li Li-san line, but after the conclusion of the CCP's Fourth Plenum, it felt that it no longer needed me. And now this stupid representative simply blurted out a secret directive in my presence.

This incident broke my heart, making me sleepless the whole night. I hated the Comintern, and lamented that it had completely changed color. Judging by the Pole's violent words and manners, the Comintern would do anything to achieve its goals. Perhaps it was not mere slander when some comrades accused and suspected Mif and Ch'en Shao-yü of secretly causing injury to Ho Meng-hsiung and the sixteen other old cadres. Without waiting until my arrival in China, Mif convoked the Fourth Plenum of the CCP and arbitrarily placed Ch'en Shao-yü and his close colleagues on the CC and other organs at various levels, as well as delivering a severe blow to Ho Meng-hsiung and party. Having completed these sinister jobs, Mif decamped on the eve of my arrival in Shanghai. What an ugly performance!

My analysis led me to believe that all these crimes of Mif and his party were premeditated and the natural result of dictatorship. The Communist autocratic system created a tyrant in the person of Stalin, who manipulated power, sinking idealism and righteousness to the bottom of the sea. Most of the good people could not stand on their own feet. The tyrant, riding roughshod over the people, needed a claque of hired ruffians to realize his dictatorial powers, and naturally there were mean stooges like Mif who welcomed power and abused it at will. The Comintern, which mistrusted me, and Mif, who was my foe, naturally would not leave such a righteous-minded person as myself alone. I therefore felt that my future would be thorny and that no matter how patient and humble I was, it would not be easy for me to avert danger. When I was in Moscow I had written to the Comintern expressing my loyalty and stating my decision to keep my promise. Now that the Comintern had turned its back on me, I would consider it ethical if I were to resist the international organization.

I always viewed the CCP and the Comintern through different eyes. I held an indescribable feeling toward the CCP, as if it were my own son, and I always loved it and protected it wholeheartedly. At first I thought that this boy was growing up well, but later he underwent innumerable changes and my hopes were tempered. Sometimes I felt that this son suffered so many disasters that smooth progress would be impossible. My feelings were similar to those of other fathers, in other words that good or bad the CCP was still my very own. I bitterly hated Stalin's cruel treatment of his own comrades. By contrast, I always treated my comrades-in-arms with love and broad-mindedness. Consequently, I never put Ch'en Shao-yü on the same plane with Mif. In my opinion, the 28 Bolsheviks, including Ch'en Shao-yü, committed a number of mistakes because of Mif's wrong guidance. Now, under conditions of the extremist White terror in China, they were prepared to struggle at the risk of their lives. This would give them an opportunity to reform themselves, and it was not my intention to reject them, but to exercise indulgence by letting bygones be bygones.

It was with such mixed feelings that I decided on the strategy I planned to adopt at the time. I figured that if I were to expose the crimes of the Mif faction and demand an immediate convocation of the Fifth Plenum to oust Ch'en Shao-yü and party from the CC, the situation arising therefrom might get out of hand. I might have resorted to this method if Ho Meng-hsiung and his group had not been rounded up. Now, without them, I had to seriously reconsider. I finally came out with the answer: "In throwing it at a rat, we must be careful not to break the vase." In other words, I must not allow the CCP to plunge into deeper chaos till nothing could be salvaged. I asked myself, "Can I skirt this issue and absolve myself from all responsibilities? Can I go on passively and even remove myself from the CCP battlefront?" My answer was: "Impossible! The main thing is not to allow the CCP to come to an end." My conclusion was that I should endure all sacrifice and work actively to rescue the CCP. There was no other way out. The only way to save the Party was to rely on the resolution of the Fourth Plenum, to call for solidarity within the Party, and to eradicate all disputes. I realized that one of the side effects of such a move could be to stabilize the position of the Mif faction within the CC of the Party, but at the time I subordinated this possibility to doing whatever I could to save the CCP from the crisis.

Hsiang Chung-fa had become the Party secretary general after the Sixth Congress of the CCP, but he was almost forgotten by everybody due to his incompetence. While Li Li-san was director of the Propaganda Department, Li handled many problems for the CC. But now that Li had been toppled, the Party CC was run jointly by Chou En-lai and Ch'en Shao-yü, with Chou making the final decision on important matters. When I met Hsiang Chung-fa this time, I felt that he was vacillating in everything and that he held no opinion of any kind except to support the Comintern line.

By then the Politburo elected during the Sixth Congress of the CCP had undergone a great change. Ch'ü Ch'iu-pai's qualification as a member of the Politburo was withdrawn during the Party's Fourth Plenum, but I still called on him to solicit his opinion regarding Party matters. He begged off saying much, explaining in a depressed manner that he was concentrating his efforts on writing. Li Li-san and Ts'ai Ho-sen were in Moscow, having also lost their posts in the Politburo. Hsiang Ying had already gone to the Soviet base in Kiangsi. Only Hsiang Chung-fa, Chou En-lai, and I remained. To fill a vacancy, Ch'en Shao-yü, who was not a member of the CC of the Party, had been elected a member of the Politburo during the Fourth Plenum—a move that met with much criticism. Later on, Ch'en followed Mif to Moscow. The Fourth Plenum of the CCP also reorganized a number of the organs of the CC. The Organization Department was now headed by a veteran cadre, Chao Yün. The Propaganda Department was placed in the charge of two students who had returned from Russia, Chang Wen-t'ien and Shen Tse-min. Yang Shang-k'un, another returned student from Russia, took charge of the labor movement, replacing Hsiang Ying. Ch'in Pang-hsien, also a Russian returned student, became secretary of the CC of the CYC, succeeding Jen Pi-shih, who had gone to the Soviet bases on the western Hunan-Hupeh and on the Hunan-Kiangsi borders.

Under these circumstances, I had only Chou En-lai to discuss things with, and the decisions that both of us made were decisive in character. Once I told Chou about my intention to call for intra-Party solidarity, explaining that I disagreed with the idea of struggling against comrades who had committed errors or who held opposing views. I added that we should treat them with compassion, use persuasion on them, and trust them, and that we needed to restrain only those few obstinate comrades who firmly opposed the Fourth Plenum and who obstructed our solidarity. Even so, we should not use extradisciplinary methods to deal with them. I continued by saying that the CC itself should undergo a self-readjustment, to avoid the impression among our comrades that our Party was under the control of certain people only. Chou En-lai agreed with me, adding that we should adopt concrete measures separately in order to realize our common aim.

The first time I attended a Politburo meeting was on the fifth day after my arrival in Shanghai. Among those present, apart from us three Politburo members, were Ch'in Pang-hsien, Chao Yün, Chang Wen-t'ien, and Yang Shang-k'un. (This was the first time after the Fourth Plenum of the CCP that non-Politburo members were permitted to attend and were granted equal rights with the members.) First of all, Chou En-lai proposed that in order to facilitate the convening of secret meetings, a Standing Committee of three be set up, comprising Hsiang Chung-fa, Chou himself, and me, and that this new committee be regarded as the highest policy-making body. He added that responsible persons in other departments of the CC would carry on work in accordance with decisions made by the Standing Committee and that if necessary, these heads would be permitted to attend Standing Committee meetings as observers to discuss matters affecting their departments. This proposal was passed easily. The function of this proposal was for the newly admitted leaders to make a little concession in order to weaken the anti-Mif-faction atmosphere within the Party.

Chou En-lai and I went about persuading our comrades in our own ways. I held private talks with many of them, and occasionally attended subcommittee meetings. I explained to them my policies on, and efforts toward, solidarity, saying that I would refrain from blaming those who held dissenting views, but stressing that there was no alternative for us all except to unite and struggle onward. The results of my efforts were quite good. Mutual grudges between comrades were reduced, and their mutual trust was gradually revived. For instance, Ch'en Yü, who formerly opposed the resolution of the Fourth Plenum of the CCP, now changed his mind. However, Lo Chang-lung continued to evade me, and my aim of winning him over failed dismally. As a result, he was expelled from Party membership, which made me very sad indeed.

Chou En-lai's efforts toward solidarity met with greater difficulties. Huang Ching-hun was a case in point. A student in the first class of the Whampoa Military Academy, Huang was Chou's good friend and at one time did important work in military affairs under Chou's direction. However, unable to bear the blow he received during an intra-Party struggle, Huang announced his plan to return to work with Director Chiang Kai-shek in the academy. Having failed to dissuade him, Chou En-lai finally branded Huang a rebel and eventually had him executed. Afterward, Chou told me sadly, the pessimism of this insurgent, who had been defeated during his struggle against the Li Li-san line, deteriorated into despondency, and he took the rebel's road. That was a painful case, which reflected the ferocity and cruelty of the struggle.

The case of Huang Ching-hun gave me a big shock. Seeing that I was upset, Chou En-lai explained further: Huang Ching-hun wrote a personal letter to Director Chiang, expressing his determination to repent for his past mistakes and vindicate himself. According to Chou, Huang admitted that he had written the letter and that he was determined to cross over in spite of repeated dissuasions. Chou En-lai claimed that as a result of that concrete evidence and due to the urgency of the

matter, he had had to make a snap decision of "kill first, report later."
Chou never told me how he got hold of Huang Ching-hun's letter or
how he eliminated him. Perhaps this was a secret of the intelligence
work under his direction. I assumed a stern expression and said to him,
"According to Party discipline, the most severe punishment is expulsion
from membership. We should not resort to extraordinary methods in a
rash manner like those power-holders in the CPSU." Chou said that he
had never done such a thing before and that this was the first case that
applied strictly to a rebel who endangered the existence of the Party
and not to anti-Party elements holding dissenting opinions. Lo Chang-
lung was an anti-Party element, but he was not dealt with outside the
rules of Party discipline—perhaps as a result of my remarks. However,
this situation lasted only a short time, for afterwards the hand of the
despot and the tactics of secret agents knew no bounds.

A series of grave crises arose within the CCP after the Party's
Fourth Plenum, the most conspicuous of which were the ascension to
power of Ch'en Shao-yü and company and the arrest of Ho Meng-hsiung
and party. In addition, there were other important incidents not known
to most comrades. The execution of Huang Ching-hun and the attitude
of that Pole, for instance, were known only to a very few, and were
never announced publicly. Let me relate as much as I still can recall of
what many comrades told me about the internal conditions of the CCP
of that period. At the time, most comrades' discussions pivoted around
Ho Meng-hsiung. Our readers perhaps remember that Ho Meng-hsiung
was among the first who joined the Peking branch of the SYC and of
the CCP. Although he and I seldom worked together, he was always a
close comrade-in-arms of mine. After the assassination of Li Ta-chao in
1927, Ho Meng-hsiung was transferred to work in Shanghai because he
could not get a foothold in the North. In Shanghai he was a member of
the local Party Committee and held some other important positions in
the Party. Later he became secretary of the Shanghai Party Committee,
and during his tenure he often quarreled with Li Li-san. As a result, he
acted as the spokesman for the faction of senior cadres. Whenever comrades mentioned Ho Meng-hsiung, they would invariably associate the
name with such other veteran cadres as Ts'ai Ho-sen and me in Moscow,
Mao Tse-tung and Hsiang Ying in the Kiangsi Soviet area, and Liu
Shao-ch'i in North China. When the topic of the anti-Li-Li-san line was
brought up, they would reminisce about what Ho Meng-hsiung had told

them on the matter, giving the impression that in the eyes of most essential cadres of the CCP, Ho Meng-hsiung was a genuine prototype of the CCP.

In 1928, after the Sixth Congress of the CCP, Ho Meng-hsiung, who originally opposed Ch'ü Ch'iu-pai's putschism, began to reprove Li Li-san for not abiding by the resolution of the Congress. In 1929, when Ts'ai Ho-sen was expelled from the CC of the CCP, Ho Meng-hsiung rebuked Li Li-san further for violating the resolution of the Sixth Congress of the CCP. Li's behavior was indeed a sequel to Ch'ü Ch'iu-pai's putschism. During the first half of 1930 Ho proceeded to plan for the overthrow of Li Li-san. He reprimanded Li Li-san for having caused the CCP to suffer great losses. In Ho's view, during all these years in which the KMT was in constant trouble and the wars among the warlords were raging fiercely, there were in fact plenty of chances for the CCP to rebuild itself. However, due to Li Li-san's errors, the CCP not only had missed the opportunity of self-development but also had suffered many setbacks. Ho despised Li Li-san, distrusted his leadership capability, and considered him a mere agitator, and definitely not a helmsman. Ho added that if we were to let Li carry on recklessly, the CCP would be finished.

The comrades that I came across had never mentioned that Li Li-san had requested the Soviet Union to go to war in the Northeast or Outer Mongolia to attack Peking and Tientsin in order to coordinate with his "brilliant plan" of taking Wuhan. Nobody seemed to know anything about this case which had infuriated the Comintern. Nor was there anybody discussing whether to unite with or oppose the rich peasantry, a topic which apparently became the talk of Moscow. What Ho Meng-hsiung and the other comrades knew about were those empty leftist talks by Li Li-san about the revolutionary upsurge, which they criticized on the basis of their daily experience and personal sufferings. They ridiculed Li Li-san as a "big cannon," hornblower, braggart, lover of pomp, and destructionist. They cited many concrete examples. For instance, instead of mobilizing laborers and intellectuals in the cities to oppose the KMT over this or that issue, Li Li-san would either ignore the task or subjectively bungle through it. In another instance, when workers in a certain factory agitated for a strike due to bad working conditions, Li Li-san insistently introduced demands that were too high and were unacceptable to the workers, even scaring them away. This resulted not only in the strike fizzling out, but also in a number of Party members and activist workers being arrested and dismissed from their jobs. The same thing happened in the countryside, where Li Li-san failed to give the regrouping peasants a chance to gather their strength, but ordered them, when they were unequal to the task at hand, to make attacks. In short, depressed comrades often felt this way: During the period 1925 to 1927 the CCP had already cultivated a considerable base among the worker-peasant masses and educated youths; in spite of the brutal suppression of the White terror and the KMT's anti-Communist drives, they still managed to hide and preserve their strength. Subsequently, however, due to the recklessness of Ch'ü Ch'iu-pai and Li Li-san, nearly all was lost.

Li Li-san dreamed day and night of going all-out on the strength of the Soviets and the Red Army. Though he made considerable progress, the comrades generally contended that he had missed a fine opportunity for a better-than-average result. I never heard of comrades expressing opinions that basically opposed the Soviet line (only the Trotskyite faction did so). Most comrades agreed that since the Soviet line had become a fait accompli or if they wanted to fight the KMT, they had to hoist the Soviet banner. Most of their criticisms were concentrated on Li Li-san's deviation with regard to his work-style. Sarcastically, they claimed that Li Li-san was extremely fond of issuing orders, which apparently became an obsession of his life. Li devoted his attention to empty reputation but not to practicalities, to quantity but not to quality. Sitting in that secret office of his, and acting like a commander-in-chief, he issued assignments for army units and signed commissions. For instance, if there were a few guerrillas in a certain area, he would dispatch a commander there; if another area had about one hundred men, he would give it an army unit or divisional designation. So on paper his military strength grew, and the revolutionary tide rose high. Thereupon Li Li-san would give instructions left and right, directing attacks here today and there tomorrow, or, on the basis of his subjective outlook, he would give instructions on what was or was not to be done, criticize this, and praise that—there was never a moment's quiet. As to how to implement agrarian revolution, in what manner peasants should be organized for the struggle, how to train talent, give content to the Soviets, help solve all sorts of difficulties, firmly control the Red Army and strengthen its fighting power—all these were either neglected or not diligently studied by Li Li-san.

Li Li-san was always fond of setting up action committees, as was the case when he led the 1922 labor movement at the Anyuan Coal Mine and the May Thirtieth Movement of 1925. In June and July of 1930, when he figured that the conditions for a Chinese revolution were ripe and that it was high time for an armed insurrection throughout the country to overthrow the KMT regime, Li Li-san ordered that all available CCP organs, the CYC, and the labor unions be combined together and organized into an Action Committee. The so-called Action Committee was the command post for the insurrection, comprising members handpicked by Li Li-san from the top down, and its work was directly concerned with insurrection activities. Such a work-style encountered the opposition of Ho Meng-hsiung and party and also caused the Comintern many headaches. They all contended that Li Li-san fundamentally violated the principles of Communist organization, that is, that he abolished the nuts-and-bolts operations of the CCP, the CYC, and the labor unions, such as the winning over of the masses, propaganda organization, education, training, and so forth. In a word, without these daily functions, the entire organization was as good as abandoned.

Some comrades even became disgusted with Li Li-san's work-style of issuing orders and reprimands at will. They blamed him for trampling on democracy within the Party. They recalled that while in the past Ch'ü Ch'iu-pai used to reprimand comrades quietly, Li Li-san now liked to do it in a grand manner. The way Li drove out Ts'ai Ho-sen and expelled Ch'en Tu-hsiu was colorful indeed. Although his actions caused not a few comrades to be pessimistic or to take the Trotskyite road, yet, fortunately, they did not wreck the Party's foundations. Most of the central cadres of the CCP were Li Li-san's close comrades-in-arms whom he could not possibly drive away or expel at random. True, Li continually reproved them as rightists or remnants of opportunism, but, in practice, he could not do anything more than reassign them, demote them, warn them, or place them under surveillance. Many comrades described Li as a coarse person. While engaged in the labor movement in the past, he had always been out front blasting away, leaving Liu Shao-ch'i behind him to pick up the broken pieces. Now that he occupied the seat of CCP leadership, he was still fond of "singing black (heretical) songs," while Chou En-lai rallied around him, doing the hard work. At the time, only Chou En-lai knew the real conditions of the CCP, and in his hands lay the real power. Li Li-san did not understand fully the actual operations of CCP organs in various places. Nor was he fully aware of the feeling of dissatisfaction against him that prevailed among the comrades, nor even the reason behind Ho Meng-hsiung's agitation against him. Some comrades even remarked that luckily Li Li-san was a boor, otherwise it could have been worse.

Many comrades also blamed Chou En-lai, contending that he had not tried his best to rectify Li Li-san's error and that he habitually obeyed him. Some comrades pointed out that Chou En-lai was the only person who could persuade Li Li-san, or even influence his direction. Chou also understood some of Li's mistakes, and sometimes he would quietly correct them, but he would never get involved in a direct conflict with Li. Relatively speaking, Chou understood the conditions of the CCP's organs at various levels, and he knew some of the comrades' dissatisfactions with Li. However, either Chou was playing dumb or he just could not be bothered to put in a good word or two. As time passed, the comrades stopped pinning their hopes on Chou. Some comrades said that Chou was smooth and round by nature and that in order to avoid trouble, he would not dare shoulder responsibilities that were rightfully his. Some people said that Chou and Li were birds of the same feather. After his return from France in 1924, Chou enrolled in Whampoa Military Academy to involve himself in military affairs. He did not take part in the basic work of leading the masses. He was ignorant of the art of leading the masses, except to prepare for the launching of an insurrection. That was why his thinking was close to Li Li-san's and why it was simply impossible to expect him to rectify Li Li-san's style of work concerning a military adventure.

During the first half of 1930, after the purge of students at Sun Yat-sen University in Moscow, Ch'en Shao-yü and others returned to China. Li Li-san tried to curb their activities, a move which they resisted. Mif also arrived in China during the same summer to direct the CCP's work in accordance with orders of the Comintern and in his capacity as the Comintern's delegate in China. Moreover, he was to rectify Li Li-san's error. Thus the Mif faction became actively involved in the struggle against the Li Li-san line.

Most members of the Ch'en Shao-yü clique were assigned to various organs under the jurisdiction of the Shanghai Party Committee to handle low-level work, which brought them in contact with Ho Meng-hsiung who was then working on the same Shanghai committee. During their initial talks, Ho Meng-hsiung and Ch'en Shao-yü discovered that they held similar views. Ho stressed that in order to achieve victory, the Party should draw up a document on how to strengthen and consolidate itself according to its own capabilities. Ch'en explained that it was the Comintern's view that the Party should consolidate the Soviet areas, expand and strengthen the Red Army, and adopt a policy of winning over the masses within broad areas under KMT control. He also pointed out Li Li-san's numerous violations. Ho and Ch'en collaborated well, because one was experienced in practical matters and the other was well versed in theories. After his arrival in Shanghai, Mif was able to establish rapport with Ho Meng-hsiung, thanks to Ch'en Shao-yü, who acted as his interpreter and who cemented the Mif-Ho relations as events developed. Ch'en praised Mif in front of Ho, and he also elucidated for Mif's benefit Ho's views and potential power within Party circles.

The senior comrades, however, held differing opinions with regard to the attitudes of Mif and Ch'en Shao-yü. Generally speaking, Ho Meng-hsiung felt that Mif was not entirely to blame for the way he administered Sun Yat-sen University, where he strove to train true Bolsheviks to become the leading cadres of the CCP. Ho believed that although Mif opposed Ch'ü Ch'iu-pai, he did not criticize me excessively. He also believed that Ch'en Shao-yü and party understood Marxism-Leninism and that with some further tempering, their ability could be put to good use. Therefore, Ho reasoned, senior comrades should be broadminded and should encourage new Party members, instead of discriminating against them for minor reasons. Ho maintained further that overthrowing Li Li-san's authority was the principal task and that he should back Ch'en Shao-yü and his group. Moreover, he could directly reach Mif and other Comintern representatives based in Shanghai through the good offices of Ch'en Shao-yü, thereby enhancing his own work efficiency.

At that time Lo Chang-lung strongly opposed Ho Meng-hsiung's views and behavior. Lo had gone to Moscow, where he attended the Sixth Congress of the CCP and personally experienced some of Mif's tricks. He told Ho that Mif was a snob, so how could Mif cherish the aspiration of leading the Chinese revolution? Mif only succeeded in retaining his controlling position at Sun Yat-sen University during the anti-Radek struggle there, so he was merely a schemer and not a Marxist-Leninist as he claimed himself to be. Now Mif expediently utilized his cohort to control the CCP. Ch'en Shao-yü was enticed into Mif's lair and, like a mad dog, bit people left and right, so how could he achieve anything commendable? In Lo Chang-lung's view, it was simply impossible to unite with the Mif faction in jointly opposing the Li Li-san line.

He would rather let Li Li-san control the CCP for a decade than allow the Mif faction to hold power within the Party.

The reputations of Mif and Ch'en Shao-yü were very bad. Nobody in the Party said anything good about them. Most of the students who had returned from Moscow blamed both of them for the role they played during the fratricidal strife at Sun Yat-sen University. If they now were quite forgiving and cooperative with Ch'en Shao-yü and his group, it was because most of the Party members could not endure Li Li-san's reckless pronouncements and behavior. For this reason, most of them followed in the footsteps of Ho Meng-hsiung. Consequently, Lo Chang-lung became more passive day by day and finally isolated himself from the CCP by refusing painfully to meet and discuss the matter with me anymore. This situation in turn weakened the anti-Li-Li-san movement which was led by Ho Meng-hsiung.

The Third Plenum of the CCP, which met during the month of September, 1930, was not able to rectify the error of the Li Li-san line. About the only achievement the plenary session scored was to accept nominally the political directives of the Comintern, but otherwise Li Li-san and Ch'ü Ch'iu-pai continued to control the CC of the CCP, and they even accused Ho Meng-hsiung and Ch'en Shao-yü of being rightists and anti-Party elements. Realizing the obduracy of the Li Li-san line, the Comintern deemed it necessary to interfere further, on the one hand by transferring Li Li-san to Moscow and on the other by planning to convene the next plenum in order to reorganize the Party CC.

At first Ch'en Shao-yü and party adopted a friendly attitude toward Ho Meng-hsiung by holding the senior-cadre group in high esteem. As their cooperation increased day by day, they discussed the problem of selection of candidates to succeed Li Li-san. Apparently Ho Meng-hsiung had more than once asked Ch'en Shao-yü to convey to Mif Ho's request to repatriate me. After the Third Plenum, Ho Meng-hsiung actually proposed that both Li Li-san and Ch'ü Ch'iu-pai should withdraw from the Party CC and be replaced by Ts'ai Ho-sen and me upon our arrival from Moscow. Ho also proposed that Chou En-lai continue to sit as a Politburo member only after he had rectified his mistakes. Ho Meng-hsiung told Ch'en Shao-yü that in their joint leadership of the opposition to the Li Li-san line, they should avoid any outside suspicion that they were plotting to seize power, and since neither of them was a member of the CC, they could not, according to Party regulations, become members of the Politburo. Therefore, two new persons had to be selected from the membership of the CC to fill the vacancies to be left by Li Li-san and Ch'ü Ch'iu-pai. Continuing, Ho Meng-hsiung, in the name of thirty-odd senior cadres including himself, also requested the Comintern to assign Ts'ai Ho-sen and me to China. This was the reason why Ossip Piatnitski asked Ts'ai Ho-sen to have a talk with me and why Piatnitski eventually sent me back to China.

Perhaps because Mif was peeved by the way Ho Meng-hsiung supported me, he decided to risk a "last stand." Mif made arrangements with Chou En-lai whereby after his mistakes were forgiven by the Fourth Plenum of the CCP and passed in its political resolution, Chou would—with the approval of and in the name of the Comintern—nominate Ch'en Shao-yü as a candidate for the Politburo and Chang Wen-t'ien and Ch'in Pang-hsien as appointees for important positions on the CC. Ho Meng-hsiung immediately raised an objection. Suddenly Ch'en Shao-yü bristled and reproved Ho Meng-hsiung and party as rightists, adding that after blocking the left-veering Li Li-san line, the Party should immediately turn back to oppose the dangerous rightist deviation. For good measure, he added that Ho Meng-hsiung's objection to the Comintern directives was anti-Party, pure and simple.

The Fourth Plenum of the CCP was adjourned after this quarrel. Thus, without a vote being taken, Ch'en Shao-yü and party crashed into the CC of the CCP. If the KMT had not helped Mif and Ch'en Shao-yü to defeat Ho Meng-hsiung and his followers, Ch'en Shao-yü would not have been able to sit so prettily. The situation developed to a point where what was left was merely a number of sad, grumbling cadres of the CCP. They unanimously came to realize that dictatorship was not to be underestimated. For this arbitrary power was not used only in dealing with the bourgeoisie, but was also used by certain elements to seize power within the Communist Party, as demonstrated by the performance of Mif and Ch'en Shao-yü during the Fourth Plenum of the CCP.

Although I do not have sufficient time and opportunity to go into great detail about the numerous happenings from the Li Li-san line to the Wang Ming line, the developments as outlined in the preceding pages are quite telling. Most comrades were aware of the bitter experiences that I had had in Moscow at the hands of the Mif faction. Now, thanks to my painstaking efforts to attain unity, it was naturally easy for me to achieve success for the moment. As I have already said, we had borne great losses all these years and only a little power remained, which we were not to give up easily. The loss of Ho Meng-hsiung and party was already beyond salvaging. To prevent further losses due to internecine disputes, I could only let bygones be bygones, minimize our mutual suspicions, and appeal for solidarity and continuation of the struggle! The crimes of Mif and Ch'en Shao-yü were temporarily covered up by these moving words of mine, but the bad seeds they planted caused their downfall several years later. Mao Tse-tung's rectification drive in Yenan was directed against them. If we should ruminate about the historical sources of the current deterioration of Sino-Soviet relations, the CCP leadership could not help recalling vividly the "virtuous rule" of the Mif faction.

The crisis within the CCP was not limited to Shanghai. It permeated all corners, especially in the various CCP organs in the North. These bodies, the activities of which were centralized in Peking, suffered repeated repressions after the April, 1927, assassination of Li Ta-chao; and the CC of the CCP did not possess the strength to give aid. Later on, Li Li-san invariably placed the blame for the bad situation on the bickerings of rightist elements within the Party's Northern Bureau, and this resulted in arguments on several occasions between the CC and the Northern Bureau. After easing the tension within the Party in the Shanghai area, I proposed that I go north to take a look and to convene an emergency meeting of the Northern Bureau in order to rescue the situation. This was a risky trip, but there was nobody else who could substitute for me. After my suggestion had been approved by the CC and after I had made the necessary preparations, in the middle of February I traveled directly to Tientsin by sea.

Arriving in Tientsin, I immediately looked for the CCP secret liaison post located within the precincts of the Japanese Concession. This was the only contact point I knew of, and there I met a young couple whom I did not recognize offhand. They briefed me, saying that the place was extremely unsafe and that they were actually preparing to move somewhere else. They blamed the CCP for not giving a thought to their safety. Everything in the house was austere. They knew that I was staying in a hotel inside the French Concession and that in locating the liaison post, I had passed directly through the main street of the Japanese Concession, and this worried them. For at the crossroads of that main street there was a "traitor" named Chang K'ai-yün[2] who usually stood guard there especially to hunt for CCP members.

Learning how worried the couple were, I gave them words of

encouragement. They told me that the majority of the comrades, whom I had entrusted them to invite to meet me, would be arriving from Peking and other places that same day. As to the venue of our projected conference, there was no better place than the very same liaison post. So I decided to hold the meeting there first thing the next morning, and told them that as a cover, the comrades were to come as well-wishers at a birthday party. The couple also told me that on my next visit there, I should skirt around the main street of the Japanese Concession.

The following morning, I was the first person to reach the meeting site, while the invited comrades arrived separately later. Nine persons, including myself, attended the conference. We gathered in the bedroom around a square table, on which were placed mah-jongg tiles, Chinese dominoes, and other gambling paraphernalia—just in case of a raid. The young couple, who were acting as hosts for the birthday party, stood guard downstairs.

The meeting was chaired by Ch'en Yuan-tao, secretary of the Northern Bureau of the CCP. In 1927 he had been director of the Organization Office of the CCP's Honan Committee and was once a student at Sun Yat-sen University in Moscow, where he was an important member of the anti-Mif faction. He returned to China early in 1929 to participate in Party work in the North, and was later promoted to area secretary. Most of the other participants came from Peking. Taiyuan and Kaifeng were each represented by one person. No comrade came from Tsinan or Sian. (I cannot recall their names, but perhaps among the present Peking leadership there might be some persons who took part in that makeshift conference.)

As soon as the meeting was declared open, the participants said that they felt that we should make it as brief as possible for safety's sake. I, however, thought that since it was not easy to hold such a gathering, everybody present should be given a chance to express his opinion without any time limit. I suggested that everybody take off his shoes to muffle the noise, should they walk about in the room, also that each refrain from smoking to prevent smoke from blowing out of the window, and that they speak softly to avoid attracting the attention of the neighbors. I also encouraged them to speak freely without fear so as to facilitate the clearing up of accumulated problems. They were all elated by my suggestions.

The remarks made by the participants were touching. Some of the events they recounted were new to me; with tears rolling down their cheeks, some of them told how the various CCP organs in the North suffered after Li Ta-chao had been murdered. Still others were furious about the way the Party's CC after the August 7 Emergency Conference discriminated against the Northern Bureau on the alleged grounds that it was largely influenced by opportunism. Another speaker talked about intra-Party quarrels and dissatisfaction among the comrades. For example, in 1928 Chang Chin-piao (also known as Chang Mu-t'ao), secretary of the Peking Committee of the CYC, by utilizing Trotskyite slogans, ran away with more than forty members and set up another CC of the CYC, thus creating a schism. By turn they criticized Li Li-san who, after the Sixth Congress of the CCP, issued orders at random, completely disregarding the actual conditions in North China. For example, Li ordered a Communist comrade, who had just reported for duty in the KMT armed forces as a low-ranking officer, to stage a mutiny—this was suicide. At the same time, he instructed the CCP organs in the North to sabotage communications lines in order to coordinate their activities with the insurrection plan in the South. Such tasks were not only meaningless, but also delayed the Northern Bureau's independent task of winning over the masses. The bureau's leaders had raised their voices against these directives, but their objections were overruled by the Party's CC as opportunism.

The implementation of Li Li-san's orders by the Peking Party Committee resulted in the destruction of the organization and the arrest of its members. However, Li Li-san was not able to take remedial measures, so the Northern Bureau received no help from the CC, while 90 percent of its requests were turned down. Li Li-san's bullying style of work created a centrifugal tendency among the comrades. Some became passive, others disobeyed orders, and still others refused to attend meetings. Party discipline became lax. "If the Party does not love its members, why should we obey the Party?" was a question often asked by the comrades in the North. They implored me to find ways and means to improve the work-style of the CC of the CCP, and to grant them more authority to fulfill their own tasks.

These comrades were doubtful whether or not the Fourth Plenum of the CCP had succeeded in blocking the Li Li-san line and were deeply concerned over Ch'en Shao-yü's leadership. One of them asked me whether, after the Fourth Plenum, the CC was under the complete control of the Mif faction, whether Chou En-lai had already become Mif's puppet, and whether the arrest of Ho Meng-hsiung and party was due to secret information supplied by the Mif faction. Someone also asked me, "Regarding your repatriation from Moscow, what plan have you got to rescue the Party from this crisis?"

I was greatly moved, and tears welled in my eyes. I tried my best to soothe them, and I explained my views. I begged them to forget the past, unite together, and start all over again. My remarks were seconded by Ch'en Yuan-tao, who expressed his confidence in my ability to tide the Northern Bureau of the CCP over the crisis. He asked those present to make concrete suggestions.

After hours of discussion, I made a summing-up and reached the following main conclusions:

1. All past erroneous directives of the CC of the CCP were declared null and void, while all punishments meted out to disgruntled comrades, with the exception of Chang Mu-t'ao and his cohorts, were withdrawn.

2. All work would henceforth be carried out on the basis of resolutions made during the Sixth Congress of the CCP, the Fourth Plenum of the CCP, and the present emergency meeting of the Northern Bureau of the CCP.

3. The Party's Northern Bureau and other organs under its jurisdiction were to stress collaboration with comrades and sympathizers hiding in various factories, railway lines, schools, villages, and army units; to devote their energy to organizing work secretly; to dispel the air of pessimism; to expand activities and win over the masses by taking advantage of anti-imperialist emotions and workers' demands for their immediate interests; as well as to pay attention to guiding the development of guerrilla warfare in Shensi and other areas.

4. Work procedures in the North were to be decided upon on the basis of objective conditions in the North, with the CC of the CCP respecting the opinions of the Northern Bureau, which, in turn, would also respect the views of all organs under its jurisdiction.

5. In assigning work to comrades, the CC of the CCP was to take into account the comrades' wishes and their safety and to expand democratic procedures within the Party, if and when circumstances permitted.

6. In the event that a comrade was arrested, the Party should exert

its utmost effort to come to his rescue and grant appropriate relief to his family dependents.

The comrades taking part in the meeting were highly satisfied with the conclusions. Some said they could see the light of day again; some felt that the spirit of various CCP organs in the North would be revived; while others described the gathering as a change from "whip and sword" to "warmth and love." I also explained that if the Northern bodies could do this preliminary basic work properly, it would not be difficult for them to set up a Soviet regime in the North.

Our meeting was not concluded until late at night, whereupon the participants scattered, satisfied that the practical problems they had brought up had been appropriately resolved one by one. Ch'en Yuan-tao and I were the last to leave the house. Before parting, he said that every problem had been satisfactorily thrashed out on that particular day. He asked me to return to Shanghai as soon as possible, adding that he would collate the conclusions into a written resolution to be reported to the CC of the CCP and proclaimed among all organizations under the Northern Bureau's jurisdiction. We shook hands about 10 P.M. I never met him again after that, and I did not know when he lost his life.

The next morning I took the sea route again to return to Shanghai, where I reported to the CC about my trip. A few days later, the official report of the CCP's Northern Bureau conference arrived, expressing support of the leadership of the CC and promising to implement the decisions made at the meeting. This attitude of the CCP's Northern Bureau was something unheard of during the previous two years, so the comrades of the CC were highly elated and gratified by the report, while those in other areas reacted favorably, too. Thus an atmosphere of harmony and solidarity permeated the Party.

Hsiang Chung-fa was touched by my activities in Shanghai and Tientsin. He said to me, "I used to scold you as an opportunist, now I know you've made a great contribution to the Party. I do believe you're really carrying out the correct line of the Comintern." I had no doubt that he expressed his sentiment from the heart, but I felt that while my work might understandably benefit the Party, it was not necessarily in keeping with the Comintern line. As a matter of fact, all of my efforts might be beneficial for Liu Shao-ch'i's subsequent underground work in the White areas. However, after I left the CC of the CCP in Shanghai, the doctrinaire repressions were again imposed upon the Northern

Bureau by those students who had returned from Russia, and the effect of my work was greatly diminished.

The Shift to Soviet Areas

Early in 1931 the Soviet movement of the CCP developed considerably, accompanied particularly by military successes. During January of the same year, Kiangsi's Red Army operating in the Yungfeng-Lungkang area wiped out Chang Hui-tsan's Eighteenth Division of the KMT armed forces—with Chang himself captured and more than four thousand rifles surrendered—and broke away from the KMT's first so-called bandit encirclement campaign. At the same time, the Red Army on the Hupeh-Honan border defeated a great part of Yueh Wei-chün's division in the area of Chiulikuan. Yueh was taken prisoner, and more than two thousand rifles were confiscated. As the existing Communist bases in big cities under KMT control, which traditionally had formed the pillars of the CCP, had fallen into disrepair, we were highly excited by the military victories in these border areas, which we regarded as the emergence of the Soviet light. Desirous of grasping this good opportunity, the CC of the CCP quickly decided to move its main force to the Soviet areas.

After the failure of the Nanchang Uprising, the Autumn Harvest Uprising, and the Canton Insurrection, all remnants of the army units retreated to remote mountain regions to start a guerrilla life. The Sixth Congress of the CCP watched these guerrilla operations closely and prophesied a great future for them in the Chinese Soviet movement. The political resolution of the Sixth Congress of the CCP pointed out: "The degree of consolidation of the reactionary regime in different areas is uneven; therefore, the revolution, in the general new, rising tide, may succeed first in one or more provinces."[3] However, the resolution warned that this was merely a prospect, since at present there was no possibility of realizing such successes.

During the 1929–30 period, Communist guerrillas who had scattered in various places succeeded in overcoming great difficulties and were developing further. The main reason for this development was the continual existence of civil wars among army factions within the KMT. Similarly, the formation of the Li Li-san line had this same objective circumstance as its background. Li Li-san was always boasting about this guerrilla development, especially in July, 1930, after P'eng Te-huai's brief occupation of Changsha, which encouraged Li to take further risks. In Li's opinion, the new upsurge of the Chinese revolution had arrived, and revolutionary conditions in various places were gradually moving toward an even development. Not only must the CCP attack big cities to achieve preliminary successes in one or more provinces, but it should also, with the military support of Soviet Russia, aim for a nationwide victory.

Then the KMT pacification campaigns were temporarily concluded in September, 1930. While the KMT had not succeeded in unifying the country, it was evident that Chiang Kai-shek, who represented the greatest military power, had emerged victorious; and this strengthened the KMT considerably. By contrast, the CCP's Soviet strategy, limited by its own inability to capitalize on the incessant civil wars within the KMT, had to depend on guerrilla warfare for its struggle. Although it scored some scattered successes, its real power was still insignificant. Making a dispassionate appraisal of the situation, it was easy to discover how ridiculous Li Li-san's reckless thinking was. For the consolidation of the Soviet areas as emphasized by the Comintern was simply a task that was beyond the ability of the powerless CCP to accomplish.

Investigating closely the real conditions of the Soviets and the Red Army, I could only get a general idea from incomplete materials. According to Red Army unit numbers designated by Li Li-san, there were the First Front Army led by Chu Teh and Mao Tse-tung in southeastern Kiangsi, Ho Lung's Second Army Corps operating in the Hung Lake region in the western part of Hunan and Hupeh, P'eng Te-huai's Third Army Corps in the western Kiangsi region, K'uang Chi-hsün's Fourth Army Corps operating in the Hupeh-Honan-Anhwei (Oyüwan*) border region, Huang Kung-lüeh's Fifth Army in the western Kiangsi region, Hsiao K'o's Sixth Army in the Hunan-Kiangsi border region, Li Ming-tuan's Seventh Army and Yü Tso-po's Eighth Army both operating in southwestern Kwangsi, Lo Ping-hui's Ninth Army in southern Kiangsi, Fang Chih-min's Tenth Army in eastern Kiangsi, and K'ung Ho-ch'ung's Sixteenth Army operating along the Hunan-Hupeh-Kiangsi border. Among these army units, only three were worth elaborating on: The units under Mao Tse-tung, Chu Teh, and P'eng Te-huai in Kiangsi possessed a total of fifteen thousand rifles; the Fourth Army Corps operating

---

* In ancient China the people commonly referred to Hupeh as "O," Honan as "Yü," and Anhwei as "Wan"; therefore the Soviet that was formed in the border areas of these three provinces was called the Oyüwan Soviet.

along the Hupeh-Honan-Anhwei border had ten thousand rifles; and the troops under Ho Lung in the western Hunan-Hupeh area had about seven thousand rifles.

Only in each of the above three militarily strong areas was a Soviet regime on a county and town level established, bearing the respective names of the Kiangsi Soviet area, the Oyüwan Soviet area, and the Western Hunan and Hupeh Soviet area. Strictly speaking, none of these political structures could from any viewpoint be regarded as a government. It would be more appropriate to call them guerrilla bases. These Soviet areas indeed were born from the barrel of a gun, and they depended on the gun for their survival. Operating under difficult conditions, they struggled hard to differentiate themselves from the bandits, but they still could not be said to have had any drawing power for the national or rural agrarian revolution. The guerrillas and guerrilla areas scattered in the provinces of Hunan, Hupeh, Kiangsi, Kwangtung, Kwangsi, Fukien, Chekiang, Honan, Shensi, and Szechwan were all striving hard to get more weapons, striking out in all directions, so there was no stable guerrilla base to speak of.[4]

Documents originating from these guerrilla areas revealed that the leaders there implored the CC of the CCP to give them aid in personnel and materiel. Most of them requested medicine and medical instruments, radio sets and other communications materials, ordnance materials, and even binoculars, compasses, and wrist watches. They also asked to have personnel with expertise sent there. Apparently Li Li-san never asked for aid from the Comintern on the basis of the appeals of these guerrillas; on the contrary, he retained the money secretly transported by the guerrillas to Shanghai and used it for the purposes of the CC of the CCP. It suddenly became Li Li-san's main source of revenue. Mif apparently never helped the guerrilla troops, either, for he stressed that the guerrillas should fend for themselves.

These, then, were the general conditions, from which one can see that it was not easy to consolidate the Soviet areas. In a word, this consolidation had to depend on power, especially military power. If the CCP had the power to consolidate a Soviet area, then it would be easy to achieve preliminary successes in one or more provinces, even throughout the country. The Fourth Plenum of the CCP resolved that it was the main task of the CCP to establish and consolidate Soviet areas and then, through a national congress of Soviets, to set up a powerful Soviet regime. However, there were, within the Party, varying degrees of understanding and interpretation of this resolution, and this evoked a great deal of dispute.

Mif and his followers apparently believed that a Chinese Soviet regime could be born out of the whip they held in their hands. They kept mapping out policies regarding agrarian revolution and directives concerning land distribution, which they believed to contain some mysterious, mystical power. In addition, they drew up a series of Soviet policies which they spread around, apparently convinced that the Chinese Soviets could be formed by cracking their antirightist and antileftist whips and prodding all of the CCP units to gallop forward. Such a crazy idea was indeed not much different from Li Li-san's absurdities.

At that time most of the CCP cadres, including myself, thought that we should have a goal for the struggle toward the consolidation of the Soviet areas, although this would require a protracted effort to realize. At any rate, the slogan for consolidating the Soviet areas was more realistic and practical than that for achieving initial successes in one or more provinces. As a matter of fact, there was no alternative. First of all, only these Soviet areas and the Red Army remained as the assets of the CCP. If we did not set a goal for them to fight for and did not make a concerted effort to achieve it, the whole thing would be like a boat going against the current—if it doesn't advance, it recedes. Still I believed that not all resolutions should be viewed as inflexible, but that some leeway should be given in implementing them according to existing conditions.

In early March of 1930 I read a document written by the Western Kiangsi Bureau of the CYC, charging Mao Tse-tung with continually violating the directives of the CC of the CCP, doing things arbitrarily and taking the anti-Party, antirevolutionary road. The papers said that the Party's CYC bureaus, as well as its army commanders, in southwestern Kiangsi mostly supported the leadership of the CC (that is, the Li Li-san line). On the other hand, Mao Tse-tung allegedly dared not fight against the enemy, running away with his troops instead of attacking Nanchang as ordered by the CC—which seemed to be rightist opportunism. In the winter of 1930 not only did Mao Tse-tung fail to rectify his error, but he assassinated a large group of comrades in the name of liquidating the A-B (Anti-Bolshevik) League.[5] For these reasons, the Southwestern Kiangsi Bureau of the CYC requested the CC of the CCP to punish Mao severely.

Concerning this matter, Ch'in Pang-hsien, secretary of the CC of the CYC, was invited to make a report before the Standing Committee of the CCP. According to him, (1) the contents of the document coincided with the verbal report made by an informant of the Southwestern Kiangsi Bureau of the CYC; (2) this informant was a member of the Southwestern Kiangsi Bureau of the CYC who had visited Shanghai several times—one whom the CC of the CYC regarded as reliable and who this time brought with him scores of taels of gold and some documents; (3) all the members of the Southwestern Kiangsi Bureau of the CYC agreed with the document accusing Mao Tse-tung but refrained from affixing their signatures for fear of being liquidated as members of the A-B League by Mao, should he get wind of the information against him. Under these circumstances, Ch'in Pang-hsien deduced that the document and the informant's words were genuine.

Continuing, Ch'in Pang-hsien said that there had been a difference of opinion between Mao Tse-tung on the one side and the members of the Southwestern Kiangsi CCP and CYC Bureau and some army comrades on the other.

They once suggested the slogan "Support Chu Teh, down with Mao Tse-tung!" But under Mao's manipulations, Chu Teh himself could do nothing but back Mao. P'eng Te-huai was also dissatisfied with Mao, and the cadres in his Third Army Corps who voiced dissatisfaction against Mao were also in the majority. The Southwestern Kiangsi Bureau of the CYC suspected that the youth corps had already been infiltrated by a small number of A-B League members who, in their anti-Mao struggle, fomented trouble. The reason was that the CYC members had discovered some sabotage activities committed by A-B League members, and Mao Tse-tung, unable to discern the right from the wrong, had lumped all his opponents together as A-B League members, rounded them up, and executed them. In Fut'ien hundreds of comrades were killed in that fashion, with Chief-of-Staff Ch'en Yi acting as the executioner in the Fut'ien Incident, which constituted the most serious crisis in the Kiangsi Soviet area.

Ch'in Pang-hsien believed that Mao Tse-tung indeed had committed serious mistakes. While he pointed out that Mao's resistance to Li Li-san's directives might have been justified, Mao himself was also a rightist who knew only how to preserve his own forces and to use the guerrilla tactic of dragging his enemy deeply into a fray in order to defeat him. However, Mao allegedly ignored the launching of offensives against the enemy and the significance of consolidating the Soviet areas. Again,

Mao failed to understand the importance of the main danger of rightism. Also, regarding the problems of land and the rich peasantry, the Kiangsi Soviet area committed a rightist deviation. In the Fut'ien Incident, it was unforgivable that Mao, either deliberately or accidentally, killed the comrades who opposed him.

The Standing Committee of the CCP, after hearing Ch'in's report, regarded the case as a serious one, but unable to make an on-the-spot decision, asked Ch'in to inform the courier of the Southwestern Kiangsi Bureau of the CYC to keep the whole thing secret, awaiting the disposition of the Standing Committee of the CCP. I busied myself gathering material concerning this case, believing as I did that Ch'in Pang-hsien did not possess ample proof to accuse Mao Tse-tung of rightism. I recalled that at one time Ho Meng-hsiung and his party had suffered a big blow on trumped-up charges; they were not a bunch of people who had lost their will to fight, though they had insisted that the Party should not during the critical period of opposition to the Li Li-san line direct its attention also to the antirightist stand, as a result of which they were accused of being rightist themselves. Now, pending the acquisition of adequate evidence, we should not accuse senior cadres in the Soviet area, including Mao Tse-tung, of being rightist and liquidate them; otherwise the Soviets and the Red Army would suffer serious losses.

When the issue was discussed again during a meeting of the CCP's Standing Committee, I pointed out that the liquidation of Chang Hui-tsan's division by the Kiangsi Red Army in January was proof that there was no serious crisis there. It was generally correct for Mao Tse-tung to disobey Li Li-san's instructions, for Mao was directing military operations on the basis of actual conditions, emphasizing guerrilla tactics and political discipline, which was urgent and important. Mao was being realistic and practical when he stressed the expansion of military power instead of forcing through the consolidation of a base. Mao and his comrades in the Kiangsi Soviet Base were a hard-working lot, and they could not be regarded as rightists. Even assuming that he held some rightist opinions, it was merely an error in outlook. With regard to the problem of the liquidation of counterrevolutionaries, it appeared that he had committed grave mistakes, for in handling the case, he failed to differentiate between the counterrevolutionary leaders and the coerced followers; he even regarded people who were not counterrevolutionaries as counterrevolutionaries, and liquidated them accordingly. This indeed required rectification.

After some deliberation, the CCP's Standing Committee resolved as follows: (1) The report of the CYC Bureau in southwestern Kiangsi showed youthful impetuosity and was not entirely dependable; therefore, it was not possible to pronounce Mao Tse-tung a rightist. (2) A clarification would be appended to the decision of the CC of the CCP concerning the purge of counterrevolutionaries and dispatched to the Kiangsi Soviet area to form the basis for the rectification of errors committed by Mao Tse-tung and his clique during the drive against counterrevolutionaries; moreover, Mao was to hasten to make a true account of the Fut'ien Incident. (3) As a result of the serious situation in the Kiangsi Soviet area, the CC would take concrete measures to strengthen the Soviets and Red Army leadership.

The strengthening of the Soviets and Red Army leadership constituted a most urgent problem. Before I returned to China, the CC of the CCP had sent important cadres to various Soviet areas to solve this problem. For instance, Hsiang Ying and Liu Po-ch'eng were dispatched to the Kiangsi Soviet area, while Jen Pi-shih and Hsia Hsi were sent to the Soviet areas on the western Hunan-Hupeh and Hunan-Kiangsi borders, respectively. Now, in order to strengthen further the Party leadership, was the opportune time to carry out the decision of the CC of the CCP to move en masse to the Soviet bases. In due course this measure was approved by the Comintern.

Accordingly, Chou En-lai proposed a concrete plan which was officially adopted. Essentially, the Politburo of the CC was to go to the central Soviet base in Kiangsi under the guidance of Hsiang Chung-fa, Chou En-lai, Chang Wen-t'ien, and Ch'in Pang-hsien. A Party bureau was to be set up in the Oyüwan region and another in the western Hunan-Hupeh area; the former would be headed by myself, Shen Tse-min, and Ch'en Ch'ang-hao, while the latter would be under the charge of Hsia Hsi and Kuan Hsiang-ying, both of whom had already arrived there. After it had safely moved to the Kiangsi Soviet Base, the CC of the CCP would establish a bureau in Shanghai to guide Party work in White areas, which would tentatively be under the leadership of Chao Yün and Li Chu-sheng.

This resolution constituted an important key to the CCP's subsequent decision to transfer its work center to the Soviet areas, which had a great bearing on the CCP's future development. Our ideal hope at the time was that we could have a powerful base in Kiangsi, where we could hoist the banner of the Chinese Soviet Republic; and thence we would unite with the Red Army and guerrillas operating in various Soviet zones south of the Yangtze River, struggling together toward the goal of occupying one or more provinces. The Oyüwan Soviet area would become the main nucleus for operations north of the Yangtze, whence we would develop northward and control broader regions north of the river. As to the Western Hunan-Hupeh Soviet area, this would become an important satellite to expand and protect our operations in the Kiangsi and Oyüwan areas, and to develop itself toward the southwest.

We realized that all this was an ambitious plan. Although the requisites for realizing this plan were still lacking, under the circumstances, affairs could not develop any other way. Therefore, we had to do our best to achieve our goal. On the other hand, as our main force was shifted to the Soviet areas, naturally our work in the White regions was greatly weakened. At the time there were no accurate statistics about the total membership of the CCP. It was estimated that there were about one hundred thousand members, of whom more than 97 percent were in the Soviet areas and the Red Army, and of peasant origin. This fact brought us greater aspirations about our work in the Soviet areas. Chou En-lai was the person who stoutly maintained that our power should be concentrated at the Soviet areas, for according to his experience, he was fully aware of the difficulty of the CCP in getting a foothold in the White areas and of the likelihood of its being destroyed by the KMT. He was determined to transfer the overwhelming majority of the CCP cadres to the Soviet areas. He estimated that about four hundred of the cadres could be moved from the White regions to the Soviet areas. Of this figure, he planned to station 40 percent in the Kiangsi Soviet area and 30 percent in the Oyüwan Soviet area, while sending the remainder to the other Soviet zones.

I went to the Oyüwan Soviet area by choice. At that time a goodly number of Li Li-san remnants were still operating in that region, including its responsible leader Tseng Chung-sheng, who was a well-known supporter of the Li Li-san line. My comrades felt that my assignment to rectify the error of the Li Li-san line would be a very easy job. I myself felt that I was comparatively familiar with the situation there, and I loved the Central Plains where I could find plenty of space to run about in. So I decided to go there.

I put everything in order and got ready to go to assume my new task. At the time, the Comintern's Far Eastern Department in Shanghai (that is, the office set up by Comintern delegates based in Shanghai) was watching this matter closely. That Pole, whom I hated, wanted to discuss things with me, but I turned him down. However, I was willing to have a chat with a military representative of German nationality, from whom I asked some advice concerning military problems.

Although I met the German only once, I was deeply impressed by him. I learned that during the First World War he had been a middle-echelon officer. He carried a scar on his hand, which indicated a glorious military record. He was more than fifty years of age, clear-headed, and rich in knowledge. He was ordered to pay a visit to the Kiangsi Soviet area, and he did try to go there several times disguised as a priest, but in vain, as he was foiled by KMT troops. The Comintern then had to send a younger German army man named Li T'e (alias of Otto Braun) to the Kiangsi Soviet area, where he became military adviser. Apparently Li T'e was far less experienced than the other German, and had several clashes with Mao Tse-tung. I feel that the results would have been different if the elder German had gone to Kiangsi.

During our conversation, he was sincere and humble. He asked me not to rely on Chinese translations of military books, but to handle things according to my own judgment. He especially pointed out that a commander who was on his own must first know what to do in the event that he was defeated in a battle, for such a situation often cropped up in guerrilla warfare. I felt that most of our comrades had too fanatic a fighting spirit, marching forward daringly and often ignoring the possibility of being faced with setbacks. I considered his thesis right and to the point. I also thought that he was not a dogmatist in favor of the consolidation of the Soviet areas, but a highly practical person going about his business on the basis of prevailing conditions. This quality alone put him on a higher plane than Mif and his ilk.

In carrying out our plans, we met with difficulties continually. I arrived in the Oyüwan region in April, but other members of the CC of the CCP, due to enemy harassments, did not reach the Kiangsi Soviet area to complete their mission until August.

Summing up my effort in Shanghai during this period, I felt that the grip of the Wang Ming line over the CCP organs became tighter day by day—although to some extent I succeeded in blocking the development of this line. Those doctrinaire putschists would surely make the situation worse if and when the opportunity arose, and the resultant disaster would be greater under the protective cover of the Comintern. They would blindly implement the Comintern decisions in total disregard of existing conditions. For example, on the problem of consolidation of the Soviet areas, they often ignored the comparative strengths of the enemy and ourselves as well as the possibility of our armed forces suffering losses, and they proceeded stubbornly to defend this area or that city. And if anyone should refuse to follow their orders, he would be labeled a right-veering deserter. Other decisions of the Comintern were regarded as Holy Writ that must not be changed. This was the special characteristic of the famous Wang Ming line, the results of which were the inflexibility of the Soviet movement and the invitation of extremely serious losses. If it had not been for the Japanese aggression, which caused the CCP to turn back to the anti-Japanese national-unity front, perhaps the entire CCP would have been totally buried under the Soviet movement.

THE OYUWAN SOVIET AREA

CHAPTER

On the Way to Oyüwan

I worked in Shanghai for only two months before I went to the Red Army front. Thereafter, my five years of guerrilla life started. What I personally experienced was typical of the real situation of the Red Army at various places at that time.

In mid-March, 1931, Shen Tse-min, Ch'en Ch'ang-hao, and I were ready to go to the Oyüwan Soviet area separately. Ch'en Ch'ang-hao and I planned to go to Huang-an via Hankow. Shen Tse-min and his wife, Chang Ch'in-ch'iu, planned to go to Liu-an through Ho-fei, Anhwei Province. We knew very little about the situation of the Oyüwan Soviet area at that time. All we knew was that there were two small Soviet areas. One of those was centered around Ch'i-li-p'ing, north of the Huang-an district. It included Huang-an, Ma-ch'eng, Kuang-shan, and Lo-shan, the four districts on the boundary of Hupeh and Honan, and their adjacent villages. Another one was centered around Chin-chia-chai. It included the three districts of Liu-an, Huo-shan, and Shang-ch'eng and their adjacent territories on the boundary of Honan and Anhwei. This Soviet area established lines of communication with the CC of the CCP. However, only Chou En-lai knew how they linked together. Chou En-lai asked Ku Shun-chang to arrange all details of our secret journey for us.

Ku Shun-chang was in charge of the Secret Service Department of the CC of the CCP, which was supervised by Chou En-lai. He was also

174

a very helpful assistant of Chou's. At that time, Ku Shun-chang was actually in charge of the communications network between the CC of the CCP and the Soviets at various places. Ku Shun-chang was a worker at the Nanyang Brothers Tobacco Company in Shanghai and an active member of the Ch'ing Pang. He had been a labor leader in the May Thirtieth Movement. During the three riots of Shanghai workers in 1927 he was head of the picket corps and Chou En-lai was his assistant. Later on, Chou provided Ku with leadership. I became acquainted with Ku Shun-chang during the May Thirtieth Movement, and I appreciated his ability at that time. After five years we were meeting again. His ability had become more admirable, but there was something of the Shanghai playboy in his appearance and in his mannerisms. This was probably the one flaw in his otherwise good personality. Ku Shun-chang worked hard for me. He decided to escort me personally to Hankow. His assistants took charge of the journey of Shen Tse-min. He told me that there was an unlicensed boat that ran between Shanghai and Hankow with which they had a close relationship. He wanted me to take the boat when it left for Hankow at the end of March. He himself rushed to Hankow ahead of me to choose a suitable person to escort me to Huang-an. He also explained to me every detail of the trip and every action that I would need to take. I decided to follow his plan.

The unlicensed boat was scheduled to sail on April 1. About 9 P.M. on March 31, Ku Shun-chang's assistant hired a taxi to pick me up. I said goodbye to my wife and left my secret flat to move to the New World Hotel on Nanking Road. Ku also had a close association with the hotel, which he frequently used as a base of operations. He had booked a room for me. Even the registration form of the hotel had been filled out for me. For possible questioning, it stated that I had recently come from Hong Kong. I planned to take the boat at three o'clock the next morning. Ku took the night train to Nanking and then a boat to Hankow so that he could arrive one day earlier than I.

At three o'clock on the morning of April 1, 1931, I, dressed up as an ordinary merchant, and Ku Shun-chang's assistant, who dressed up as my employee, went straight to Yang-shu-p'u wharf in the depths of the night. The taxi driver was also one of our comrades, although we didn't know each other. When we arrived at the wharf, a policeman came to check on us. My employee got out of the car and answered a few questions. We got through without further interference. When I went to the crew's cabin, Ch'en Ch'ang-hao was already there, and he had reserved a place next to him for me to sleep. Ch'en Ch'ang-hao was also dressed up as an employee, a guise he had assumed in order to take care of everything for me. Thus, we left Shanghai without any mishap.

When the morning sun dawned, our boat had already sailed out of Wu-sung-k'ou. It was a cargo boat. All of the ten or more passengers were "stowaways" permitted by the sailors. The two of us, although dressed up as merchants, were not exactly of their type. The crew and passengers guessed that we were big opium dealers. To encourage their conjecture, we played mah-jongg with them. We decided to lose some money. It was quite natural for us to lose money, because we were poor mah-jongg players. In several days we lost nearly one hundred silver dollars. Everybody was happy; they were convinced that we were big opium dealers with no concern for money.

On the afternoon of the fourth the boat was about to arrive at Hankow. Ku Shun-chang told us that the boat should land after 6 P.M., as Ku Shun-chang thought that six o'clock was about the time that the secret agents went to supper and it would not be so dangerous to land at that time. The boat really slowed down and anchored after six. Ch'en Ch'ang-hao and I picked up our simple luggage and walked off the wharf in the twilight. At the junction of the main road outside of the wharf, there was a young man who held a current newspaper and gave us a signal. This was the man that Ku Shun-chang had sent to meet us. The young man took a rickshaw. We also took rickshaws and went to the first floor of a house on a lonely street in the Japanese Concession, which was not far from the wharf. Ku Shun-chang was waiting for us there. When he found out that there had been no trouble on our journey, Ku studied with us about the action of the next step. He told us that we could not be escorted by members of the staff of the Hankow communications office, but that we would be accompanied by a guide sent from Oyüwan. It was confirmed that a reliable guide would arrive three days later, so we had to stay in Hankow for at least three days. Then he told us that a married couple was living in our quarters. The place had been very safe, but according to the latest information, the secret detectives of the Japanese Concession had become suspicious of it. Therefore, he wondered whether we should stay there. He also told me something that I had never known, that he was the famous magician Hua Kuang-ch'i, who had performed at Hankow several times and had been showered with applause. Some big merchants and rich men were his students in magic. Some of them kept in close contact with him, but no one knew that he was Ku Shun-chang. If it were not safe for us to stay in this place, we could move to the house of one of his students. It was a big merchant's house and would not be suspected. I didn't agree to Ku Shun-chang's suggestion. I told him, "If I live in a big merchant's house, I cannot hide away from the guests. Many people in Hankow know me, and many merchants know me, too. If I should meet them, there would be trouble. Although the Japanese Concession secret detectives are suspicious of this place, it is unlikely that anything will happen in these few days. Probably it would be best to hide here and not go out." The result of our discussion was that we all agreed that "to stay put is better than to move."

The second floor had only two bedrooms. The host couple lived in the rear room, and we lived in the front room. We dared not look through the window, because we had to avoid being seen by other people. All we could do was read books and newspapers in the room. In one of the current Chinese newspapers, there was an article written by a foreigner on suppressing bandits. The gist of the article was to praise General Chiang Kai-shek's effort to completely destroy the so-called Communist bandits. It also stated that the blockade policy that had been adopted several times in Chinese history to destroy bandits had been successful. Now, Chiang was also paying attention to a blockade—building pillboxes around the bandit area and clearing villages outside it so that the bandits could not expand, then gradually tightening the circle. This was a safe and effective way. After I read the paper, I thought deeply about countermeasures.

On the evening of the seventh, Ku Shun-chang let the guide who had just arrived from Oyüwan come to our flat. The young man who had come to accompany us was short and silent and looked like an experienced shopkeeper. We decided to start the next morning by taking a bus to our destination. As it was not wise for Ku Shun-chang to show up at the bus station, he sent his assistant to take care of everything there. At 8:00 A.M. on April 8, Ch'en Ch'ang-hao and I left the Japanese Concession area, following the messenger through the small streets and lanes in the Chinese area until we arrived at the bus station. We carried our bundles and umbrellas separately, walking apart as if we didn't know each other. We bought tickets at the station separately for the bus to Li-chia-chi in Ma-ch'eng via Huang-p'o. The bus stopped twice for inspection in suburban areas, but we went through without any difficulty.

The travelers on the bus were absolutely silent before the inspection; they looked as if they were afraid that something would happen. But after the inspection they chatted and laughed. Someone on the bus said that there would be a more thorough check when the bus arrived at Li-chia-chi, but that people who ran shops there would have no trouble. There were animated discussions about too many army troops and militiamen being in the streets of Li-chia-chi. Business was not as easy to manage as before. The Communist bandits frequently disturbed places around Li-chia-chi, and many people were kidnaped. The owner of a shop had been kidnaped several days before. After I heard this, I knew that our guerrillas were really active. But kidnaping would not only lose public support, it would also bring us to the level of bandits. I couldn't speak with a Hupeh accent, so all I could do was to pretend to listen without speaking to anyone.

About 4 p.m. we arrived at a small bus stop eight li outside of Li-chia-chi. We got off the bus there and followed the guide on foot to the village via small paths. After climbing over several hills we were a long way from the highway. Then our guide slowed down and said that there would probably not be any more danger. There were fifteen li between the bus stop and the small village where we plannd to go, and it would take us an hour to walk there. We should arrive at our destination after twilight, so as to avoid being seen, therefore, it would be better to walk more slowly.

Now I had an opportunity to talk to the guide about the communications system. Although he didn't know our names, he knew that we were important leaders, so he talked to us without hiding anything. He was a native of the village. Previously the Peasants' Association had been very well organized, but after the reactionaries took over, the Peasants' Association was forbidden and all activities stopped. However, the influence of the Peasants' Association was still strong. There were twenty-six families with the same surname living in the small village to which we were going, and all of them sympathized with the revolution. Two of the families had connections with us, and the other provided protection for them. The village was also considered a sympathetic area by our guerrilla forces, and in order to maintain friendly relations, we never attacked the local tyrants here.

Every time that our guide left or entered the Oyüwan area, he picked two or three small villages in the area as places to stay. He also told me that there was a communications station located in a small shop by the side of the main road close to Li-chia-chi. The central communications station at Hankow knew only this place. This time a message had been sent to the small shop by the Hankow central communications station, telling the shopkeeper to receive us. Our guide only knew one place in Hankow as a contact point, and every time that he went to Hankow, he contacted that place. He guessed that there were many communications channels around the Oyüwan area that led to the CCP's Central office, but he knew only this one.

He also told us that there was a Red secret-service team hiding in the small village where we were going which had been sent specially to receive us. We had to walk a whole night through places that were occupied by the White Army and militia corps before we could arrive in the Kao-ch'iao area at the south end of the Oyüwan Soviet area. Usually, whether he was guiding people or transporting material, he passed through silently and secretly at night. Because we were important persons, a secret-service team had been sent to receive us.

When darkness had closed in upon the scene, we entered a house in the small village through the rear door. Once we got into the house, we could see several muscular young men gathered there. The guide told them who we were. The head of the secret-service team immediately ordered that they all be armed. In an instant, those men changed from ordinary peasants into Red Army troops with pistols. The head of the team gravely told all his members that they should pay close attention to the patrols of the militia corps and possible attacks from the enemy. The three newcomers must be protected even with their lives.

The house that we went to was quite large. There were a number of rooms and many men and women who watched us with astonished, happy eyes. The women were busy preparing a meal for us. The men went outside one by one to stand watch. The head and deputy head of the secret-service team and its eight other members hid inside the house to guard the front and rear doors.

After the meal, with our consent, the head of the secret-service team ordered us to move. We were expected to reach our destination before dawn. While we were in motion the head of the team led the way and the deputy head brought up the rear. All the way we walked in the middle without talking or smoking in order to prevent being discovered by the enemy.

It was a dark night without moonlight. From the narrow path behind the small village our group walked over a hill that was covered by pine forest. In order to avoid the sentinels of the village and the enemy, we had to vary our route. Sometimes we walked along small paths on the hill; sometimes we used the twisted footpaths between fields; and sometimes there wasn't even a path where we walked, only trenches with broken stones. All along the way no lights were seen, no dog's bark heard. We concentrated on walking quickly.

On this trip I felt relaxed and happy. In contrast to the panic that I felt when I escaped to Chia-tzu-kang at night after the failure of the Nanchang Uprising, I now thought that my life would be changed in the future. I no longer needed to be nervous about being followed by secret detectives. In front of my eyes were the ten gallant guerrilla fighters who were so dynamic and strong; and when I thought that I would see more than ten thousand persons of this type the next morning and that I would fight with them, I felt very proud.

I was not used to walking at night. The further I walked, the worse my feet became. I walked quickly in the dark night—one step high, one step low. Sometimes I stepped on stones, and this was painful. Sometimes I fell down. Although I tried my hardest, I could not avoid lagging behind the team. A member of the team who walked behind me urged me to keep up. He even quietly sang a song about lagging behind the team. I remember that one part was: "The man who lags behind has no sense of shame. Ai-yao-yao! no sense of shame." I didn't want to lag behind, and I made up my mind to train myself to be as strong as they were. Although I was sweating all over and panted when I climbed up a slope, I ground my teeth and tried my best to keep up. There was only one break for rest during the whole night's walk. A jar was used to lift up some drinking water from a small spring. Ch'en Ch'ang-hao was big and tall and was in better physical shape that I was. Even so, he could just manage to keep up, and he was exhausted. The head of the team told me that he knew that walking at night was difficult; if we delayed, however, we must be prepared to fight with the militia corps. I stirred up my courage and told him not to worry about me, I would do my best to follow.

At dawn on April 9, 1931, our team slowed its pace. The head of the team chose a suitable place to rest. He told me to put down my bundle and to relax. He pointed at the mountain in front of us and said that it was Mu-lan Mountain. The Kao-ch'iao area was on the east side at the foot of the mountain. We had passed through the defense area controlled by the militia corps. In front of us there was a small hill where our sentinels were. There were still ten li to the headquarters of the Huang-an Independent Regiment. The way that we had walked the previous night was eighty li measured along the main road, but on the twisted, small paths that we had taken, it was about one hundred and twenty li.

For the last ten li, we walked very slowly. We walked for a while, then we rested for a while. The head of the team didn't push any more. The speed at which the whole team moved depended upon my steps. I moved my feet heavily and barely went forward. About eight o'clock we arrived at a small ancestral temple in a valley of the hill. This was the temporary station of the Independent Regiment.

The staff of the headquarters of the Independent Regiment gathered together to welcome us, but I had no energy left to talk with them. I hastened to take off my shoes and stockings. Looking at my feet, I was horrified, because my feet were covered with blisters and bruises made by my shoestrings. When my comrades saw this, they took care of me as a wounded soldier. They busied themselves preparing food for us and then let us rest. The only person I knew in this regiment was Political Commissar Hsü, whom I had met during the Wuhan period in 1927. After he had introduced us to Commander Wang and Head of the Political Department Hsü, he arranged for us to get several hours' rest. This was my first day in the Oyüwan Soviet area.

My First Participation in Guerrilla Warfare

I joined the guerrilla war once I walked across the boundary of the Soviet area. Even today I have a fresh memory of the first scene of guerrilla warfare that I took part in. At noon on April 9, 1931, there were twenty to thirty people chatting in the hall of the regimental head-quarters. The officers and soldiers sat down together. There was absolutely no barrier between them. They called each other comrade. When an officer was addressed, his title was used before the word "comrade." The general name used was "Red Army Fighter." People who were not working in the army called the officers and soldiers "Comrade Red Army." The dress of the officers and soldiers was the same. It was impossible to tell who was an officer and who was a soldier. The dress of the officers and soldiers of the Independent Regiment was not as tidy as that of the secret-service team. The officers and soldiers lived and ate together. Their treatment was the same. Their happy and optimistic spirit of unity grew from their life of sharing joy and sorrow together. Ch'en Ch'ang-hao got up before I did and chatted with them in the hall. They wanted to know all the news from outside the Oyüwan Soviet area. They were particularly interested in us, the two newcomers. I heard someone ask Ch'en Ch'ang-hao, "Isn't Comrade Kuo-t'ao an opportunist?" Ch'en said, "That is a thing of the past." He also told them that I was one of the highest leaders of the CC and that I was a plenipotentiary of the CC. I had come to be secretary of the subbureau of the CC in the Oyüwan area and chairman of the Military Committee. He asked them to address me as "chairman" and to follow my instructions. He also introduced himself, saying that he had just come back to the country from Soviet Russia and had been appointed a member of the CC of the CYC. He had come here to be secretary of the subbureau of the CC of the CYC in the Oyüwan area. He was not only concerned with youth affairs, but was also interested in guerrilla warfare. He was strong and had received some military training. I got out of bed, walked into the hall, and sat down between them.

All the eyes in the hall were focused on me. Commander Wang introduced each person to me and told me that the secret-service team that had escorted us was directly subordinate to the Military Committee but was under his supervision. They were now someplace resting, and new jobs had been assigned to them. I asked him to praise them for me. To all the people there, I said, "Many of the comrades here were my old companions-in-arms. I am a newcomer, and I have a lot to learn. Please tell me anything you like about the situation." My comrades didn't answer my question, but started to talk about the past with me. Political Commissar Hsü said that he had met me at Hankow in 1927. Commander Wang said that he knew that I was responsible for the Hupeh Provincial Committee when he was at Hankow in 1927, but that he hadn't met me. Two or three other comrades said that they had heard me speak in Hankow. They said that I had become fatter than I was then.

We exchanged news while we ate. After we had eaten, Commander Wang discussed a military operation. He said that the Huang-an Independent Regiment had only six companies, with about five hundred men. For the time being, three companies of the first battalion were stationed here with about three hundred men and half that number of guns. They had arrived here two days before. The task was originally to escort us to the center of the Soviet area, but now they had a very good opportunity. Somewhere about thirty li away a company of the White Army had recently been stationed. He wanted to lead the troop to destroy that company. The main problem of the Independent Regiment was a shortage of bullets. There were fewer than ten bullets for each gun. He thought that we should stay where we were that evening, and that the Independent Regiment should undertake an operation in order to get some guns and bullets.

I agreed with Commander Wang's suggestion, and I asked him to draw a sketch of the operation. Commander Wang and all the officers present felt that they were very familiar with the surroundings of the place, but they couldn't draw. I told them it was important to learn how to draw a map. If there was no sketch of the operation, I could not understand their scheme and the officer in charge could not give accurate orders. Then they followed my advice and drew a sketch. The sketch was really poor. It looked like something that they were learning to do for the first time. Officers and soldiers were chattering so much to correct mistakes that it was very difficult to finish the sketch.

First I said that since the company of the White Army had been stationed in that place for several days, they might have built up field works. It would therefore be better to send a trained reconnaissance person to investigate the surroundings of the place where the enemy was stationed. Head of the Political Department Hsü volunteered for the job. It was expected that he could be back to report in the evening. When we agreed, he went to dress himself. In a short time, Hsü, who had been in uniform, was dressed up perfectly as a farmer gathering night soil with a basket. I was very happy as I watched the back of the "night-soil picker" walk toward the opposite slope.

That afternoon, I rested for a little while, and I found out more about the development of the Independent Regiment. The regiment had developed from the Peasant Self-defense Army. There were units of this army in villages throughout the Oyüwan Soviet area. They were organized into companies, battalions, and regiments. Each village had at least one company, and some of them had as much as a battalion. Most regions had one or more regiments. The soldiers of the Self-defense Army were the young men of the villages. On ordinary days, they were farmers. If something happened, they were mobilized for action. These Self-defense Army units were under the supervision of the Regional Military Command Office of the corresponding district

Soviet government. They were also called "Local armies not separate from production." The arms taken from the enemy were used by elite members of the Self-defense Army to form an independent regiment for the area. The soldiers of these independent regiments were separated from production and were frequently in operation. They were also called "Local armies separate from production," and were temporary organizations in between the Self-defense Army and the Red Army. These independent regiments had a full quota of manpower but had only ten or twenty rifles in the beginning. Most soldiers who did not have guns used spears to fight. The increase in rifles meant that they were able to undertake guerrilla tasks independently. The Huang-an Independent Regiment was organized by six independent companies of this type.

Commander Wang of the Huang-an Independent Regiment, who had been a farmer, was the senior member of the group with regard both to his qualifications and experience. He had been a CCP member since early 1927, at which time he was in charge of a local Peasant Association. After the expulsion of the Communists from Wuhan, he became one of the very few leaders who led the peasants in carrying on guerrilla warfare in the Kao-ch'iao area. He was the only master of guerrilla warfare who had been born and bred here. All his companions respected him very much, but some criticized him for being "Number One" (that is, he considered his seniority with some self-exaltation). Political Commissar Hsü was called "Big Hsü," and Head of the Political Department Hsü was called "Little Hsü." Both of them had been students, and had worked around here for quite a long time. Their experience in guerrilla warfare, however, could not be considered very broad. The staff officers and clerks in the regimental headquarters were low-class local intellectuals (some of them were apprentices to Taoist priests; some of them had been schooled in private tutorial classes or in primary schools). Most of the heads of companies, platoons, or groups had been promoted for their good deeds in war, but some of them were soldiers in the Red Army who had been sent to these posts so that they wouldn't have to leave their native place or to recover from wounds that they had received in combat.

In the Oyüwan area, only the Fourth Red Army was relatively well organized. The local army—the Independent Regiment—was much worse with regard to organization. Unlike the formal Red Army, it had no machine guns. It had no medical unit of its own, so its wounded and sick soldiers were sent to the local Soviet government to be dealt with. It had no supply unit of its own. The officers and soldiers never received salaries, although from time to time they were supplied by the local Soviet government with pork and mutton. The mattresses, clothes, shoes, and stockings required by the whole regiment were supplied by the peasants under government direction. When they were stationed inside the Soviet area, the government supplied their food. When they went out on operations, they robbed the local tyrants to get their supplies.

In the evening our "night-soil-picking farmer" came back and told us very happily that he had found out everything. He had picked up a full basket of dung near the place where the White Army was stationed. The White Army soldiers relieved themselves everywhere, and there was a lot of dung. He had given the full basket of dung to a peasant whose house faced ours, and the peasant had thanked him profusely. He had found out that a whole company of the White Army was stationed in the temple on the side of the hill. On a height near the temple, there was a circular field work. There were no barriers. He also knew all about the location of the roads that led to the temple and the field work. The militia corps was still stationed in the same places.

Commander Wang was able to give accurate orders for the night attack in accordance with the information obtained by Head of the Political Department Hsü. At ten o'clock the first battalion of the Independent Regiment assembled at the square in front of regimental headquarters. I delivered a short speech to them, praising their courage and encouraging them to try their best to win a victory. Very soon the troop left quietly according to schedule. Ch'en Ch'ang-hao, the guide, several sick soldiers, and I stayed at regimental headquarters. Several soldiers were left to protect us.

At dawn the next morning a messenger, returned from the front, told us loudly about the victory. He said that Commander Wang would be back very soon with his soldiers. Later, Wang came back victoriously and reported to me that they had destroyed the majority of the company of the White Army. They obtained more than forty rifles and five thousand bullets, and captured fifty men. The guns and bullets had been distributed amongst all the companies. The prisoners, after a brief propaganda exposure, were released. Only a few of our men were wounded slightly, and they were sent to the Kao-ch'iao area Soviet government to be taken care of.

Commander Wang and others all greeted me by saying that this victory had been achieved because I had supervised it correctly. Political Commissar Hsü also said that there had not been any fierce fighting this time when they entered the center of the enemy camp guided by the information obtained by Head of the Political Department Hsü. Except for a few men who escaped because of darkness, all of the enemy troops had been surrounded and disarmed. In previous operations they had always set out with the troops, and when the situation was good, they attacked; when the situation was bad, they retreated, thus wasting a trip. This time the planning had been accurate. A victory such as they had never had before was won. On their way back they had talked and had been in complete agreement that they could not have had such perfect results without my instruction.

I also congratulated them. I said that the victory was the result of the brave struggle of the officers and soldiers of the whole regiment and the masses of the Soviet area. I also mentioned that in future operations attention should be paid to capturing enemy documents and to bringing back one or two captives so that information about the enemy could be obtained. All military materiel such as tools that had been abandoned by the enemy should also be brought back. They agreed with my comments and also admitted that they had become corrupted by "guerrilla habits." They had only paid attention to taking guns and bullets and had not paid attention to the other things.

On the afternoon of the tenth the victorious troops guarded us on our move to the north. There were thirty li between the place where the Independent Regiment was stationed on the edge of the Soviet area and the center of the Kao-ch'iao area where the Soviet government was located. It was our destination for the day. I began to understand the general situation of the Soviet area.

The battalion, equipped with the newly captured guns and about thirty bullets each, were all in good spirits. Since they were marching in the Soviet area, it was not necessary to take precautions and they could sing while they moved. I, the "wounded soldier" with a pair of sore feet after the long walk, sat in a sedan chair made of bamboo poles and was carried forward with the troops. The news of our victory had spread everywhere and had been greatly exaggerated. The peasants along the way rushed first to see the guns and bullets that had been recently captured by us and also to see what I looked like—the man who had come from the CC and had been given the honorary name of "Surpassing Chu Ke, the famous literary strategist."

The relationship between the local farmers and the officers and soldiers was as harmonious as a mixture of milk and water. All along the way there were numerous peasants who walked along for a distance in company with the soldiers. Cheering of the victory was heard continuously. They also talked enthusiastically to the officers and soldiers of the Independent Regiment. When they saw me sitting in the sedan chair, some of them thought that I was a captured local tyrant. They said, "Why not turn him upside down?" or "What a white fat pig! Must be worth a lot of silver dollars!" The fighters hastened to correct them, saying, "Don't talk nonsense. He is our representative from the Central Committee," When the farmers heard the words "Central Committee," they looked as if they had heard "the Emperor." They gasped and said, "Central Committee! The one who led us to victory! Terrific! I made a mistake!"

When our troops rested in villages along the road, the peasants happily offered tea and water that they had prepared for the fighters to drink. Men and women, old and young, of the village all gathered around to watch. The fighters told them very kindly that we came from the CC, and they showed off the guns and bullets that they had captured. The family atmosphere that existed between them and the peasantry could never be found in a KMT area.

All these things made Ch'en Ch'ang-hao very happy. He discovered many unexpected "miracles." He admired especially the close relationship between the soldiers and peasants; the faith that the soldiers and the people had in the CC of the CCP; the united spirit of the army and the people in carrying out guerrilla warfare; and so forth. He concentrated on studying the actual situation, and he felt that the military knowledge he had learned before was not applicable. It was necessary to start from the beginning to learn the tactics of guerrilla warfare. Later he was appointed to the important post of Political Commissar of the Fourth Red Army, and he became an agile expert on guerrilla warfare.

About 5 p.m. we arrived at a big village where the Soviet government was located and where we were to stay. The battalion dispersed to live in various civilian houses. Some of the soldiers applied for leave to join their families. The situation became chaotic. Commander Wang explained to me that it was not necessary to take precautions at the center of the Kao-ch'iao area. Everyone could take it easy. The platoons had gone to find friends to stay with, but they would live in the hall and there wouldn't be any trouble. The soldiers whose families lived nearby applied for leave to go home; however, they would return to the regiment promptly the next morning.

We and the staffs of the regimental headquarters were stationed at the headquarters of the Soviet government of the Kao-ch'iao area. At the entrance to this house, which was relatively large, there were two big signboards. One read "Kao-ch'iao Area Soviet Government," the other "Kao-ch'iao Area Committee of the Chinese Communist Party." In addition to simple offices and bedrooms, there was a store in the house that was fully stocked with cloth shoes, straw sandals, stockings, and other things that had been contributed by the peasants. The staff of the Soviet government was busy distributing those things to the soldiers. The shoes and stockings were in many different sizes. It took quite a long time for the soldiers to choose ones that fitted them. That day the government also offered three fat pigs as a reward to be distributed among the officers and soldiers. All patrolling and cooking were carried out by peasants of the village appointed by the government, so that the officers and soldiers of the whole regiment could fully enjoy an evening of rest.

Here, for the first time I met Li Hsien-nien, who is now Vice-Premier and Finance Minister of the Chinese Communist government. At that time he was secretary of the Kao-ch'iao Area Committee of the CCP and chairman of the Soviet government of that area. This tall, slim young man, who had previously been a carpenter, was a senior member of the Party and was an efficient expert on guerrilla warfare. He looked serious and spoke very carefully. He told me about how the Kao-ch'iao area was developed, what the population was, what the membership of the CCP and CYC numbered there, and in brief about the situation of the organizations of the Self-defense Army and the Youth Vanguard. I do not remember too clearly about all of this now.

He told me especially that the Kao-ch'iao area was an isolated locality at the south end of the Oyüwan Soviet area. It was necessary to carry out guerrilla attacks frequently. If the Huang-an Independent Regiment left the area, the White Army and the militia corps would seize the opportunity to attack. Everywhere in the Kao-ch'iao area there were reconnaissance units. Once the enemy attacked, they would know about it immediately. The staffs of the Soviet government and the

Party committee would then pick up the weapons, most of which were spears, and carry the document files and go to the mountains. They ran the office in the mountains and directed the fighting; they also had to provide cover for the men and women, old and young, to "run the rebellion," that is, to hide themselves in places that the enemy could not reach easily. The Self-defense Army would harass the enemy here and there and wait for the opportunity to counterattack. Therefore the enemy did not dare to split up and penetrate the area deeply to cause any serious destruction. Sometimes the guerrillas could seize some weapons from the enemy; but sometimes they failed, and then the people and livestock were captured by the enemy and the villages were burned. What Li Hsien-nien told me gave me a clear picture. I greatly appreciated his ability. Later he was reassigned as political commissar of a regiment of the Fourth Red Army. After that we always fought together, and he eventually became one of the leaders of the Fourth Red Army Corps.

On the morning of the eleventh, under the command of Wang, the battalion that was guarding us resumed its northward march. Political Commissar Hsü was in charge of the staff that was not ordered to move on and stayed in the Kao-ch'iao area to prepare the summer clothing, and so forth. Our journey for that day was eighty li. After we had traveled north for twenty-five li, we left the Kao-ch'iao area. We had to go through fifty li of "Gray-White" area before we reached a village Soviet that was on the boundary of the Ch'i-li-p'ing Soviet area where we could stay. While we were in the Kao-ch'iao area, I saw the same things that I had seen the day before. The only difference was that no one mistook me for a local tyrant. The peasants, who were well informed, expressed their warm respects to me when they walked beside my sedan chair.

Before we left the Kao-ch'iao area, Commander Wang ordered his troops to march with arms ready. He explained to me what a "Gray-White" area was. It was substantially the same as a White area, but the people in a Gray-White area did not oppose the Soviet area actively. Generally, the relationship between the Gray-White area and us was one of mutual nonaggression. It was only fifty li from the boundary of the Kao-ch'iao area to the Huang-an district. Tung Pi-wu had grown up in this district. He had run a school in town and had a good reputation in the place. During the period of the Wuhan government in 1927, the KMT branch and the Peasant Association of Huang-an District had been very leftist. Most of the gentry and intellectuals of this Gray-White area belonged to the left wing of the KMT. Later the KMT became reactionary, and some of these people who had been involved had suffered persecution from the KMT. Therefore, the people of this area were not active in "attacking Communists." Nor did the people of the Soviet area attack the local tyrants in the Gray-White area. There had been no trouble so far.

Commander Wang showed that he was very familiar with the situation in the Gray-White area. The White Army was stationed in the town of Huang-an and at important crossroads. The militia corps was split up in different areas, but it rarely went to remote places. Usually our civilians could safely pass through at night. In the daytime some of our armed troops could also pass through. It was only on the main road between Huang-an and Ho-k'ou,[1] where the transportation line of the enemy was, that we had to take special precautions when crossing over.

When we entered the Gray-White area, the situation was obviously different. We could see no civilians on the road. No people brought tea and water for us. The peasants working in the fields as usual dared not pay attention to us. When we stopped in a village to cook, the women and children in the village did not hide from us, but the men stayed away and dared not come close to us. When we wanted to borrow something or buy food and vegetables from the women, they not only did not refuse, but they were even very kind. Commander Wang explained that if the men here tried to ignore us, it was because they were afraid of being punished after we left for "communicating with bandits."

In the afternoon when our troops were going to cross the main road between Huang-an and Ho-k'ou, we discovered that a big enemy force was marching toward Ho-k'ou. Commander Wang found that it was a brigade of the Forty-fourth Division of Hsiao Chih-ch'u, who was stationed in Huang-an. They were on the way to Ho-k'ou to relieve the guard. With my consent, Commander Wang started to divide up the troops and attack the enemy. I also got out of the sedan chair to join the guerrilla attack, thus ending the only occasion on which I sat in a sedan chair in a Soviet area.

Our troops were separated into platoons, and they spread over a vast area. Ch'en Ch'ang-hao and I followed Commander Wang. There were only ten soldiers with us, and we climbed up a hill to observe the battle. I saw that our troops were very spread out, so that some groups were here and some were there. They shot once or twice here, and two or three times there, to disturb the enemy. This was the renowned "sparrow tactic." The enemy appeared to be very frightened and did not dare to counterattack. They occupied the position, alternately providing cover and advancing. They tried to assemble in a stockade located on a high hill. Our troops fired all around the enemy. The enemy used machine guns to sweep the surrounding area. The sound of gunfire became louder and louder, until it sounded like a big battle.

In the evening all of the enemy were concentrated in the stockade. The wall of the stockade was built of big stones, and the four gates of the wall were also very solid. It was said that there were quite a lot of this type of stockade in the area, most of them having been built by local people as hideouts during the Taiping Heavenly Kingdom. Inside the stockade there were some old, shabby houses and wells. The White Army was using the place as a station.

Our force had assembled on a plateau halfway up the hill outside of the stockade to rest. Commander Wang sent two small groups to approach the gates of the stockade, and they fired several shots. The enemy then ran up to the wall of the stockade. They fired and threw bombs. The sound of guns and bombs never stopped all night long. Actually, not one of our men was wounded. Our soldiers were trained to conserve bullets, so they never shot aimlessly. That night the enemy certainly wasted innumerable bullets again. Our soldiers all jeered at the cowardice of the enemy, who could not sleep all night.

Commander Wang found that the enemy had closed the gates, so he thought that nothing would happen during the night. He ordered the troops to sleep right on the spot. He didn't even post any guards. It seemed that he was trying to avoid tiring any of his soldiers unnecessarily. Before he retired, he said, "Please go to sleep. Now we can have a good night's rest." Soon, he actually fell asleep. I, who had recently joined the guerrilla war, could not sleep with the sound of guns like thunder in my ears. Also I didn't approve of sleeping right at the front.

I got up alone and walked around the place to check. It seemed that all the soldiers had fallen asleep. No one greeted me. As I walked towards the stockade, enemy bullets whizzed over my head. I didn't see any guards as I walked around slowly and imagined that I was being the guard temporarily. Commander Wang walked towards me quietly and whispered to me gently, "Are you worrying? The enemy is hiding inside the stockade and won't dare come out. We have slept at the front several times, and nothing has happened. Furthermore, we who get used to guerrilla warfare can fall asleep as soon as we lie down. We can also wake up at once when the wind blows or the grass shakes." I told him to beware of the one chance in a thousand. If we neglected to take precautions, we would be in trouble some day. Commander Wang didn't seem to agree with me, but he was pressured into sending a group of people to stand watch.

Before dawn our troops were ready to carry on with the guerrilla war. The enemy also started to move out of the stockade and in the direction of Ho-k'ou. We turned around and moved to the right side ahead of the enemy. Just as the morning sun appeared, I was on a height and heard the shouts of thousands of peasants shaking the valley. Commander Wang told me that this signaled the arrival of the Peasants' Self-defense Corps of Ch'i-li-p'ing. Sure enough, a messenger of the Fourth Company of the Second Battalion of the Independent Regiment came to report. His company knew that we were fighting here and hurried over to assist in the operation. They also led several thousand Self-defense troops. He also showed us their headquarters on the mountain in front of us. The battle, which seemed to be both real and unreal, was a truly magnificent sight. The fully armed enemy went along the main road and occupied the heights, moving slowly towards their destination. Due to our activities, the enemy sometimes was forced to stop at certain heights and dared not move forward. Other than firing, they didn't try any attack. On the other hand, the peasant troops, scattered about like stars on the sky or chessmen on a chessboard, were very active. They threatened the enemy from all directions and tried to confuse the enemy so that they could seize their weapons.

I concentrated on observing the whole situation. The enemy was passive. I felt that their intention was to avoid our attack. Our force was active. Our attacks were very quick, and we tried here and there to probe the weak points of the enemy. However, we also had a weak point, which was that we underestimated the enemy and didn't pay enough attention to concealing ourselves. I had pointed out to Commander Wang that if we would pay more attention to concealing ourselves, the enemy would be more frightened and we could avoid damage. However, the soldiers generally felt that concealing themselves indicated that they were not very brave. Furthermore, they had not had this kind of training, and I knew that this error could not be corrected in one day or one evening.

After I had observed the fighting activities of the Independent

Regiment, I wanted to have a look at the Self-defense Army. I took the risk of crossing the field that was controlled by the network of fire from the enemy's machine guns. I reached the field of the Self-defense Army on the hill opposite to us. There I met the regimental commander of the Ch'i-li-p'ing area's Peasant Self-defense Army, the company commander of the Fourth Independent Company, and other officers. The troops of the Self-defense Army were assembling in various clumps of bushes according to their companies. Each company had many red flags, which were put in places that the enemy could see. The soldiers hid in the bushes with spears. Sometimes they moved, sometimes they shouted. Some peasants carrying baskets moved along with the Self-defense Army, ready to carry all materials captured from the enemy to the Soviet area quickly. (It was a tradition that the Self-defense Army carried baskets when it attacked the local tyrants in White areas in order to take the crops.) The regimental commander of the Self-defense Army explained to me that its task was to help the Independent Regiment threaten the enemy. They would not join the fight until the enemy was in disorder. At noon Commander Wang withdrew most of his troops to the hill, quite far from the enemy, as he could not find any opportunities to attack. On behalf of the CC, I complimented the Self-defense Army and withdrew from the front to meet Wang. We decided that Commander Wang and his troops should keep the enemy under surveillance and attack again at nightfall. Ch'en Ch'ang-hao and I resumed our trek north. It was less than ten li from where we were to a village Soviet at the edge of the Ch'i-li-p'ing area, and we would only need a few soldiers to escort us. Further on, the places were all under control of the Soviet, so we could pass through alone and guards would no longer be needed. Therefore, the Independent Regiment's task of escorting us was now completed.

While Ch'en Ch'ang-hao, the guide, and I traveled from the front to the center of the Soviet area, Ch'en Ch'ang-hao talked about the many things that he had seen in the past two days that were new to him, such as the night attack on the enemy, the activities in the Kao-ch'iao area, the peasant army harassing the strong enemy, and so forth. All of these things he had known a little about when he had read reports in Shanghai, but he could not understand them well at that time. Now that he had personally taken part in the activities, he had a more thorough understanding.

Ch'en Ch'ang-hao also told me that while mixing with the soldiers, he had heard many opinions from them. They respected the CC very much and were very interested in their visitors. He told me something else he had heard. When the soldiers saw that I sat in the sedan chair, they felt that intellectuals could not endure hardship. But on the last afternoon, when I jumped down from the sedan chair to join the fight, they were pleased to say, "The chairman got off the sedan chair to fight with us." This morning when I asked them to pay attention to concealing themselves, they felt funny. When I crossed over the firing line to see the Self-defense Army, someone said, "The chairman is really taking responsibility. He is even going to observe the fighting of the Self-defense Army." Commander Wang said, "In the past, without knowing the real situation, our superiors sent senseless orders which were very difficult to carry out. Now Chairman Chang is so careful and responsible that it looks as if we are not going to have that kind of impractical order any more!" Ch'en Ch'ang-hao felt that Wang's opinion was worth noting. It was also a holdover from the Li Li-san line, which we were going to eradicate.

In less than an hour we arrived in the place where the village Soviet government was located. It was on the boundary of the Oyüwan Soviet area. What I am going to describe next is the situation in this Soviet area.

I Promote the New Policies

After I had entered the heart of the Soviet area, I investigated the actual situation there and initiated reforms. The nature of the reforms, according to the terminology of the Chinese Communists at that time, was to oppose the Li Li-san line of taking military risks and to carry out the correct policy of consolidating the Soviet areas and the Red armies. In the meantime, in the parlance of this Soviet area, it was to oppose "guerrilla habits," which meant to oppose the tendency to act like bandits and warlords. This was a difficult task; with many restrictive factors, it was not easy to realize fully. On the afternoon of April 12, led by our guide, Ch'en Ch'ang-hao and I left for Ch'i-li-p'ing. The Ch'i-li-p'ing Soviet area was the beginning of the Oyüwan Soviet area. It was located at the foot of the Ta-pieh Mountains, north of Huang-an. Since the split of the Nationalists and Communists in 1927, it had been a hideout of CCP members and cadres of Peasant Associations and the Peasant

Self-defense Army. Also it was a center of the Autumn Harvest Uprising in 1928. It became the "Chingkangshan" of the north side of the Yangtze River. Its development and history could be considered as typical.

There were fifty li between the border village Soviet where we stayed and Ch'i-li-p'ing. All villages along the road had suffered destruction. The stockades, the ancestral halls, the temples, and other relatively big buildings had become piles of rubble. They had been destroyed deliberately by the White Army in order to stop the guerrillas from using them as stations. While we were gazing at the ruins, people told us many stories of bravery in the war.

Guard posts were located everywhere. Every two or three li we walked through, we were checked by the guard posts. It appeared that the organization of guards was even stricter than that in the Kao-ch'iao area. These guard posts were manned by members of the Youth Vanguard from the villages along the road. Three or five in a group, they watched the posts, checked the travelers, and delivered the alarm signals day and night by shifts.

We had to show our road permits and answer questions when we passed through the posts. The guide always pointed to me and said, "This is Central!" and pointed to Ch'en Ch'ang-hao and said, "This is the big boss of your little ghosts' team [the Youth Vanguard, or Young Pioneers]!" Those innocent village boys, who were under sixteen, with red scarves around their necks and holding sticks in their hands, saluted sharply when they heard the word "Central." I once jokingly asked them, "What's Central!" They knew that the "Central" was the top man who led them, the man who was even superior to the commander-in-chief. I asked deliberately, "Is this man Chiang Kai-shek?" They all knew that Chiang Kai-shek was the reactionary that they wanted to overthrow. What they supported was the Chinese Communists' Central Committee. Ch'en Ch'ang-hao, as a responsible member of the CC of the CYC, paid close attention to the activities of the Youth Vanguard. He asked the boys about the Youth Vanguard in detail. The Youth Vanguard was supervised by the CYC. Its members were organized into teams that varied in size according to the size of each village. There was at least a small team of about ten to fifty boys in each village. This organization had specific responsibility for the guard posts, which were set up in the open along the main roads and were under cover in the remote mountains and fields. This work occupied almost all the time of the children of the villages.

Ch'en Ch'ang-hao felt the fact that the children in the Soviet area could undertake the tasks of the police and custom houses was really beyond his expectations. He had closely investigated their work efficiency. Those children proudly showed him how to catch a spy, how to prevent smuggling, how to deliver the warning of an attack of the White Army or militia corps. These were jobs that they frequently did, and with good results. Ch'en Ch'ang-hao knew that most of them had no education and were illiterate. He asked them how could they distinguish the true road permits from the false. All of them could remember the secret marks on the road permits and the special meanings of the signs. If they found anything peculiar, they would question carefully. Therefore they seldom missed anything. He also asked them how to deal with an armed enemy. Their answer was that they could be supported by the adults and the Self-defense Army in the village at any time. Just one shout, and many people would come over.

After we had walked half of the way, we were no longer questioned, but were welcomed. At every village that we passed through, there were always from ten to twenty-five members of the Youth Vanguard standing in a line to welcome us. When we inspected these guards of honor, the leaders of the villages often told us that all adults, male and female, were busy performing public services and private business. Only children were left at home to rest. This indicated to us that there was undoubtedly a manpower shortage in the Soviet area.

That evening we arrived at the famous Ch'i-li-p'ing. Most of the houses in this small town had been destroyed in war but were rebuilt gradually by people organized by the Soviet. The Soviet government of the Ch'i-li-p'ing area and the area committees of the CCP and the CYC were all located here. All of the better houses were occupied by these organizations. The poor peasants crowded into the few houses that were left. There was no business in town. The atmosphere was desolate.

We lived in the headquarters of the CCP District Committee. After we had eaten, the chairman of the Soviet area, the secretary of the CCP District Committee, and other leaders of the Party and the government came to chat with us. After three days' training in walking, I no longer had any feeling of discomfort and was in good spiris. I said to them, "Please tell me about all the difficulties that you have encountered." The chairman of the Soviet area replied, "The most serious problem is food. We have just transplanted young seedlings. It is three months between now and the time of summer harvest. The provisions of the whole area that are in storage can only sustain us for one month. We'll be short of food for two months. It appears that there will be a serious famine." Everyone present agreed with the chairman's opinion. They analyzed the reasons for the food shortage. There were few paddy fields and much hilly land in this area. Large quantities of peanuts were grown here. Due to the separation of the White area and the Soviet area, the peanuts could not be sold and food could not be imported. The land had been redistributed, but some of the fields were not being used because of the shortage of manpower, plowing oxen, and agricultural tools. Many young men of the Soviet area had joined the Red Army or local armed forces. The remaining villagers also had to undertake too many tasks, such as the Self-defense Army, stretcher teams, transportation teams, and so forth. The women were making socks and shoes for the Red Army. The children were at guard posts or standing watch. The old people were also busy making straw sandals. Therefore, the shortage of manpower was extremely serious, and production work was postponed. Besides, when the enemy attacked the Soviet area, they took away the plowing oxen and destroyed the agricultural tools. This was another important reason for the shortage of this kind of equipment. Although the superiors called for pushing production forward, the basic difficulties had not been solved. Furthermore, all organizations of the Oyüwan Soviet area were located here, and their staffs numbered more than five thousand people. The Red Army frequently passed through or stationed here, and this meant extra consumption of food. The Soviet areas near here were all short of food, so there was no possibility that they could help each other.

They had been relying on attacks against local tyrants in the White area to solve the food problem. Every time the Red Army undertook an operation in the White area, the farmers all took an active part. A great many Self-defense Army and transportation teams carried large, open baskets full of crops on their way back. The crops that were carried back were distributed on a percentage basis. Usually the Self-defense Army and transportation teams took half, and the other half was given to the Soviet for public use. However, there were no more local tyrants suitable to attack in the nearby areas, so it was impossible to obtain crops except by going to distant parts of the White area.

They also thought that attacking local tyrants in the White area had caused ill feeling among the people in the White area. According to the principles of attacking local tyrants, the local peasants should be aroused and should themselves rise up. The crops thus obtained should also be given to the poor local peasants, which would not cause ill feeling in the majority. But now when the people of the Soviet area made attacks, they took all the crops away. Thus, not only did attacks on local tyrants lose their significance, but also a shortage of crops and a rise in crop prices in the White area resulted when the area was attacked and the crops taken away. Furthermore, when the Self-defense Army and the peasants of the Soviet area came to the White area, how could they tell who were local tyrants and who were not? So they just "attacked" the crops, and some waste of crops was inevitable. Therefore, the people of the White area often joined the side of the militia corps in opposition to our guerrillas. The militia corps of some places near the Oyüwan Soviet area became stronger day by day, which could be considered a result of attacks on the local tyrants. Although they were aware of this, they had no alternatives to substitute.

I felt that this was a serious problem which should be settled right away. However, this was just one area, and since the problem was connected to the overall policy, there was no way to settle it here. I discussed my ideas about increasing production with them. I asked them whether there were any quick-growing agricultural plants in this area, especially ones that they could expect to harvest in a month or two. I also told them the story of the soldiers and peasants who had nothing but pumpkin to eat for several months during the time that Chingkangshan was short of crops.

My idea aroused their interest. The old peasants that were present said that they had stressed production. However, this program was of a general nature, and the emphasis was on increasing the production of rice. Actually, this area was rich in the production of vegetables. Chinese yams, corn, and beans could also be planted on some uncultivated land. Most of them matured quickly. They would not require much manpower, and the seeds were readily available. If the old and young people and the women were urged to pay attention to raising these vegetable and various cereals, it would be very helpful in getting through the period of famine, for this year's new crops would not be ripe before the supply of last year's grain was exhausted.

As a result of our discussion, concrete measures were decided upon to increase the production of quick-growing agricultural crops. We asked that everyone in this area plant five pumpkin seeds. Every family was to cultivate a piece of land on which to plant vegetables and various cereals. Members of the Youth Vanguard were also asked to try their best in this business while they were on guard duty or resting at home. Other adults, both male and female, were also asked to use their leisure moments to do this work at places near their homes. Each family should take care of the crops that it had planted. In addition, the area Soviet should pay attention to not wasting people's time and to reducing their laborious duties and should sternly encourage saving crops, and so forth.

Those who attended the meeting felt that these measures were practical and that the promotion of production was no longer an impracticable goal but a necessity. I also warned them that attacking local rascals in the White area was very wrong in principle and must be stopped. If they did not do their best both to promote production and to save food, the people would die of starvation. The people present appeared to be very clear about this problem, as a result of their past experience. Later, as the facts proved, they did all of this actively and achieved enormous results.

The Soviet government of the Oyüwan border area and the Special Committee of Chinese Communists were the organizations of highest authority in this region. They were located in a small village fifteen li north of Ch'i-li-p'ing. (The boundary between Hupeh and Honan provinces was thirty li north of Ch'i-li-p'ing. After climbing over the Ta-pieh Mountains and walking for fifteen li, one reached a town in the Kuang-shan District in Honan Province—Hsin-chi—which was later renamed the Ching-fu District by the Nationalist government. At that time the central organizations of the Oyüwan area were located in some small villages north of Ch'i-li-p'ing, but less than a month later they were removed to the newly conquered Hsin-chi, which later became famous as the capital of the Oyüwan area.) On the morning of the thirteenth, accompanied by the secretary of the Ch'i-li-p'ing District Committee of the CCP, we moved north. It was the last leg of our trip. That morning we walked about half the way and arrived at the general military hospital of the area. We saw a big village facing a small stream. There were more than one thousand sick or wounded soldiers in the village. The hospital was supervised by the Army Surgeon's Section of the Military Subcommittee. On the village square, more than a hundred sick or wounded soldiers were bathing in the warm sunlight of the spring morning and taking off their clothes to pick lice. It made me realize that the problem of hygiene was also a serious one here. Many soldiers and civilians that I saw along my route were suffering from sores, and I supposed that these were connected with the lice. It seemed that the people here could not defeat the lice, so there was a silly saying —"the more lice you have on your body, the longer you have been in the revolution." I had been there for less than five days, but I also found some lice on my clothing. This proved that these small creatures existed everywhere.

Along the stream in front of the village, about a hundred women were washing clothes for the wounded soldiers. The secretary of the Ch'i-li-p'ing District Committee told me that those laundry women were members of the Women's Comfort Team. This organization was supervised by the Oyüwan Women's Movement Committee. It was organized into large, medium, and small teams according to the size of the geographical area. The Women's Comfort Teams of the adjacent villages took turns coming to wash clothes for the sick and wounded soldiers. They also helped in mending clothes and socks, preparing meals, and washing bandages for the hospital. As bandages were very difficult to obtain, they had to be washed frequently until they were completely shredded. The Women's Comfort Teams that were not near the hospital also had many tasks to do, such as sewing shoes and socks and clothing for the Red Army. The reactionaries spread the rumor that members of the Women's Comfort Teams in the Soviet area were really prostitutes. Actually, that was not true. They worked very hard, and many of them were old women. The secretary said that he thought the hospital was his worst headache. He told me that the director of the hospital had been injured by the wounded soldiers several days before. The morale of the wounded soldiers was especially bad. The food, which was not well prepared by the cooks, and the poor service of the nurses had caused dissatisfaction among the soldiers. When he and other comrades had come here to comfort the wounded soldiers, he had also been insulted by them. Actually, there were shortages of too many things in the hospital. Doctors, nurses, medicines, and medical instruments were all insufficient. It was hard to blame the wounded soldiers for causing trouble. Especially during surgery, due to the lack of anesthetics, the soldier being operated upon would scream dreadfully. The other wounded soldiers became frightened when they heard the screams. The political department of the hospital became the target of the wounded soldiers' insults. The military subcommittee also lacked ways to solve the problems, but it advised the hospital staff to be patient and not to make the wounded soldiers angry.

We had a look around the hospital. I felt that generally those in charge of the hospital had done everything that they could do. The wounded soldiers lived in the halls or better rooms of civilian houses. Windows had been increased in number and enlarged, so that there was enough ventilation and sunshine. The sick and wounded soldiers were assigned to live in different rooms according to their diseases or wounds. About half of them were sleeping on wooden boards; the others were sleeping on straw. All wards were dry and neat. Various kinds of recreational facilities were there—as many as there could possibly be under the existing circumstances. The sick and wounded soldiers were quite interested in such things. Therefore I thought that the dissatisfaction of the sick and wounded soldiers was a problem that was beyond the ability of the hospital authorities to overcome. I could only express my sympathy to the sick and wounded soldiers and to the staff of the hospital generally, and I dared not promise anything more.

Seven or eight li further north of the hospital was the location of the Oyüwan Border District government. Before the establishment of the Oyüwan Subbureau of the CC of the CCP, the Oyüwan Special District Committee of the CCP was the highest authority. Under the Special Committee, there were departments of organization and propaganda, a subcommittee of the Military Committee, and so forth. Tseng Chung-sheng, of the fourth graduating class of Whampoa Military Academy, was secretary of the Special District Committee and the subcommittee of the Military Committee. Kuo Shu-shen was head of the Department of Organization. Hsü Li-ch'ing was head of the Propaganda Department. (Kuo and Hsü were old cadres from the intellectuals of Hupeh Province.) Although the subcommittee of the Military Committee was part of the Special Committee, it was also directly supervised by the Military Committee of the CC. It had great authority and had a huge organization. All of the Red Army, military area command offices of Soviet governments of various districts, local armed forces, Self-defense Army units, and other military organizations of this area were supervised directly or indirectly by it. Under the subcommittee were the Army Corps Command Office, the General Staff Office, the Political Department, the Administrative Division, the Army Surgeon's Division, the Quartermaster's Division, the Military School, and so forth, which were directly subordinate organizations.

At that time the Soviet government of the Oyüwan Border District had not really been well organized. The general opinion was that the government was only something supported by the army. Most of the responsible persons in the government organizations were famous old comrades of this area. Under the government committee, there were the Finance, Land, and Internal Affairs committees and the Political Defense Bureau. The chairman of the government was Wang P'ing-chang, the chief of the Finance Committee was Cheng Wei-san, the Chief of the Internal Affairs Committee and the Land Committee was Tai Chi-ying, and the Head of the Political Defense Bureau was Chou Ch'un-ch'üan.

From the hospital, we traveled north. A little while later Wang P'ing-chang, Cheng Wei-san, Tai Chi-ying, Chou Ch'un-ch'üan, Kuo Shu-shen, Hsü Li-ch'ing, and others were all waiting on the main road to welcome us. Most of these comrades had met me before. I could not remember the names of some of them. After a long separation we had a joyous reunion. They told me about some recent military successes in this area. Mainly, it was about Hsin-chi, which was thirty li north of here. Previously, it had been a stronghold of landlords and the militia corps, but we had recently attacked and occupied it. Due to this victory, it became much easier to carry on our work in the Kuang-shan and Lo-shan districts. Tseng Chung-sheng led part of the army to continue the siege on several forts west of Hsin-chi. The purpose was to establish lines of communication between Hsin-chi and Lo-shan and the Hsüan-hua-tien Soviet area and to expand the Soviet area. They had notified Tseng Chung-sheng to hurry back to meet me.

After I met with these responsible comrades, I tried to get accurate information about the local problems, especially the food problem. However, what my comrades expected me to tell them was the good news from outside this area. Every time a VIP from the CC of the CCP came here, he first had to give a very long political speech to describe the development of the revolutionary situation of the whole country and to exaggerate the victories outside of this area. It became a magic way of cheering the people, which seemed to be in the style of the Li Li-san line. I had told them some things about the real situation in various places, but they felt that this was not exciting enough. I emphasized that if we could do the jobs in front of us better, this would be a practical step in promoting the development of the revolutionary situation of the whole country.

Our discussion started with the food problem. I told them what I had found out about the food situation at Ch'i-li-p'ing and about the emergency actions which had already been taken. I asked them to tell me about the overall situation of the area with regard to the food problem.

They told me that there were two main parts of the Oyüwan Soviet area: the one whose center was at Ch'i-li-p'ing was the Hupeh-Honan, or O-Yü, Border area; the one whose center was at Chin-chia-chai[2] was the Honan-Anhwei, or Yü-Wan, Border area. The older Soviet areas within the O-Yü Border area were the Ch'i-li-p'ing area of Huang-an, the Kao-ch'iao area, the northern area of Ma-ch'eng, and the Hsüan-hua area of Lo-shan. The shortage of food in these areas was similar. Since the Kao-ch'iao area was connected with the White area, the problem there was easier to solve. In the newly developed areas such as Hsin-chi in Kuang-shan and Sha-wo, which was east of Hsin-chi, the food situation was even worse. This was the result of attacks on the local tyrants over a long period of time. Now the north side of these two areas was completely occupied by the militia corps, and the people of the Hsin-chi and Sha-wo areas had run away when threatened by the militia corps. The land was ravaged, and there was no food.

As to the Yü-Wan area, which included the Chin-chia-chai and Ma-fou area of Liu-an, the Huo-shan area, the southern area of Shang-ch'eng, and the guerrilla area north of Ying-shan, the food situation was generally better. Therefore most of the Red Army had moved there for action and for food. They also considered that the circumstances there were similar to those at Ch'i-li-p'ing. The region around Liu-an produced lots of tea leaves, hemp, bamboo poles, and so forth. However, it was difficult to send those things out of the area to sell, and also difficult to bring in the needed food and other articles of daily use. Furthermore, when the army stayed there for a long time, they attacked the local tyrants here and there, and this would further deepen the friction between the White area and the Soviet area.

Our discussion of the food problem was immediately expanded to the discussion of general financial problems and even overall policies. In addition to promoting food production, general financial problems that had to be solved included problems of commerce inside the Soviet area and between the Soviet area and the White area as well as problems of market prices. In the Soviet area at that time, the prices of articles were fixed and were very unreasonable. For example, the prices of foods were set too low, and this resulted in food being exported. My comrades told me that some food was being sent out of the Soviet area even though there was a very serious food shortage there. We felt that price restrictions had to be abolished if we wanted to solve the food problem, and that we should raise the prices of foods to stimulate the market. Then the food would flow in from outside of the Soviet area, and at the same time the food inside the Soviet area would not flow out. We would let other local products flow out, and trade them for food. Furthermore, the Soviet government should change its economic and financial policies completely, by establishing a system of taxation instead of attacking local tyrants. However, all of these changes in policy could not be accomplished immediately.

In the discussion of these problems, two different opinions appeared. A few comrades, such as Tai Chi-ying, who leaned toward the Li Li-san line, considered that a change in economic policies would not solve the present problem of food shortage. Only paying attention to military developments, continuing to attack local tyrants, and in the meantime correcting certain errors that had happened during attacks on local tyrants were reasonably effective methods. Most of the comrades, such as Cheng Wei-san and Wang P'ing-chang, felt that attacking local tyrants had caused the confrontation between the Soviet and White areas. If this policy were to be continued, not only would consolidation of the Soviet area be impossible but the very existence of the Soviet area would be endangered. Only the gradual establishment of an economic and financial system that stressed saving and production and the gradual abandonment of the current method of attacking local rascals were sufficiently radical solutions.

Less than two days later Tseng Chung-sheng hurried back from the front and told me something about the military situation at the front and the military scheme that he was executing. At that time K'uang Chi-hsün was the commander of the Fourth Red Army Corps and Yü Tu-san was its political commissar. This corps included the Tenth, Eleventh, and Twelfth divisions. The Tenth and the Eleventh divisions each had three regiments, but the Twelfth Division had only two regiments (the thirty-fifth regiment was being expanded). There were ten thousand men and more than six thousand guns. Put the guns of the local armed forces together, and there was a total of nine thousand guns in the whole Oyüwan Soviet area.

K'uang Chi-hsün led the entire Eleventh Division and two regiments of the Tenth Division to Chin-chia-chai. Their task was to wait for opportunities to attack the enemies located in small towns in the Ma-fou[3] area in order to seize enemy weapons to strengthen themselves and to expand the Soviet area. That area had relatively more food, so our forces could operate from there. However, between here and Chin-chia-chai, there were a hundred li of White area, and there was no way of finding out about their recent operations. Tseng Chung-sheng thought that the KMT government had no overall plan for attacking the Oyüwan Soviet area. Only a few White Army men were incorporated with the militia corps in harassing the border. Therefore, after occupying Hsin-chi, K'uang Chi-hsün, with Yü Tu-san and the commander of the Twelfth Division, Hsü Hsiang-ch'ien, led the Twelfth Division and the Thirtieth Regiment of the Tenth Division into action in the area along the northwest side of Hsin-chi. He intended to expand the Soviet area of Kuang-shan and Lo-shan. Unexpectedly, the landlords there held several stockades stubbornly and would not give up. When we surrounded and attacked the stockades, our dead and wounded amounted to a thousand, and we finally had to give up. K'uang felt that attacking those stockades was a very difficult job, because the local people had been forced to move inside the stockades and all of their food and other supplies had also been moved into the stockades. Our troops were facing a very severe siege and evacuation. While the battle was continuing day after day, we had no food to sustain us. We had no heavy weapons to break down the stockades, and death and injuries were unavoidable. He also admitted that the peasants turned to the landlords and the militia corps as a result of the bad influence of our policy of attacking local tyrants.

The organization of the Military Subcommittee itself was not sound. It was facing many difficulties. First, according to what Tseng Chung-sheng told me, because of the lack of cadres, staff members were sent to the troops in the field. Thus, the Military Subcommittee itself was short-staffed. The chief-of-staff, Ts'ai Shen-hsi, had previously been commander of the Tenth Division. He was appointed chief-of-staff only because he had not recovered from a wound. He was also principal of the military school, where he lectured frequently, and he could not practically do his job as chief-of-staff. In the staff office there was a young man named Li who was in charge of the office and actually assumed the responsibility. There were very few staff officers. Yü Tu-san was head of the Political Department of the Military Subcommittee, and Yü had gone to the front. The officers of the Political Department also went with him, so only a few people were left. The students of the military school numbered fewer than two hundred. They were stationed in the Sha-wo area, which was about sixty li away. Besides attending lectures, these students also undertook very heavy guard duties. On the other hand, the staffs of the Army Surgeon's and Supply divisions were quite large. There were always about two thousand sick or wounded soldiers in the hospital supervised by the Army Surgeon's Division. The Supply Division had many small subsidiary factories, such as a mechanical repair factory, a clothing and bedding factory, and so forth. It also watched over a thousand local tyrants who had been captured. They had a total of more than two thousand people. Therefore, the organizations directly under the Military Subcommittee had more than five thousand men. Each local tyrant guarded by the Supply Division was "well treated" according to his position. It was hoped that they could give us some cash, medicine, or even military supplies. However, since they had been under pressure for a long time, it was hard to obtain anything more from them. The efficiency of the work of the Supply Division gradually decreased, due to the distance between the White and Soviet areas, the blockade of the White Army and militia corps, and the fact that those local tyrants really had nothing left to offer.

Yueh Wei-chün, a captured division commander, was a very important local tyrant. The Military Subcommittee had promised to set him free if he would give two hundred thousand dollars' worth of supplies. He was glad to accept the condition, and he thought that he could manage the sum. According to what Tseng Chung-sheng told me, the headquarters of the KMT government at Wuhan knew about the deal and tried to stop it. The supplies, which were delivered later, were either counterfeit, overdue, or even dangerous. The people who delivered the supplies were secret agents sent by the Wuhan headquarters. Tseng Chung-sheng could not judge whether the KMT government did not care for Yueh Wei-chün or whether he himself had spoiled the game deliberately.

Taking these circumstances into account, I constructed my initial plan of reform. I made the following points to my comrades: The CC of the CCP had given us the task of consolidating and expanding this Soviet area base, and of establishing a strong Soviet government and a strong Red Army so that we could, in harmony with the Central Soviet area (the Kiangsi Soviet area) and other Soviet areas, fight for greater victory. It was necessary for us to criticize our work according to the policies set by the CC since the Fourth Plenum of the CC. For the errors that should be corrected, for the policies that should be changed, action must be taken immediately. I said that I had come here recently, and there were many things that I could not fully understand. Furthermore, Comrade Shen Tse-min had not yet arrived. So, I suggested that we await his arrival before carrying out the reforms and establishing the Central Subbureau and the Provincial Committee of the Oyüwan border area. Until the reform, the Special Committee should assume responsibility. I joined the Special Committee as a representative of the CC. The Special Committee should prepare to organize a general meeting of Party members and representatives of the Special District, and a general meeting of representatives of the workers, peasants, and soldiers of the Soviet area. The task of both meetings was to set up overall policies.

The following problems should be settled immediately: (1) The error of arbitrarily attacking the local tyrants should be rectified by setting free some of the unimportant local tyrants in order to improve the relationship between the White area and the Soviet area. (2) There should be a strong push to increase production and to save food in order to relieve the food shortage. The whole Soviet area should be told to carry out the methods that I had proposed at Ch'i-li-p'ing, with suitable additions. (3) New economic policies should be carried out, the most essential of which were: to cancel price restrictions; to encourage commerce and maintain an active market; to raise crop prices; to export local products; to establish a system of taxation and a Soviet bank and to issue Soviet currency. (4) There should be an immediate investigation of the advantages and disadvantages of the land policy, the Soviet system, and the soundness of Party organization, so that appropriate reforms could be carried out.

Tseng Chung-sheng was doubtful about my opinions. Obviously he underestimated the harm caused by attacks on local tyrants; he thought that some errors were unavoidable as long as the attacks on local tyrants were carried out. He also thought that my way was too long-range to meet the urgency of the situation and that it would not solve the existing problems. With his soldier's mind, he thought that the errors I had mentioned could only be overcome after overwhelming military victory had been won. He had said to me, "I have always thought that Comrade Kuo-t'ao is a man of great strategy. He must have some way to achieve astonishing military success, however he is now only paying attention to some insignificant problems which can't be solved easily." I felt that these words were a typical example of the Li Li-san line, but it was not convenient to point this out directly. Really, at that time I did not want to be arbitrarily high-handed with my comrades, so I had never applied such terms as "residue of the Li Li-san line." I emphasized that military victory could only be obtained when policies were correct. Obvious faults should be corrected, and especially the bandit's style had to be abandoned. The cause and the effect should not be reversed. It was wrong to think that we could not preserve our internal order and regulate political discipline until military victory had been achieved. The point of view of Tseng Chung-sheng was typical in this Soviet area, and it was not easy to correct. Later, a serious campaign was carried out to correct those errors. On the other hand, there were many people with profound understanding, such as Wang P'ing-chang and Cheng Wei-san, who fully supported my opinions. They thought that these were things that they had already planned to do. Chou Ch'un-ch'üan, according to his experience of working in the Political Defense Bureau, considered that serious harm had been done by attacking local tyrants, and he thought that most of the local tyrants who had been detained should be set free. Ts'ai Shen-hsi was another respected military man who supported me. He pointed out to me that guerrilla customs existed to a serious degree in the cadres of the Red Army. The leadership of K'uang Chi-hsün and Yü Tu-san was weak. Individual heroism was causing trouble in the cadres of division and regiment rank. He asked me to pay attention first to the activities of the Red Army cadres, in order to regulate their guerrilla habits.

My opinion obtained active support from the great majority of the Special Committee. Taking my reputation into consideration, the comrades who knew something about me believed that I would lead them on a safe road to victory. After listening to my explanation, they expressed their hearty approval. Tseng Chung-sheng, who had been in doubt, now expressed his full support. Subsequently, I took over the post of chairman of the Military Committee.

It seemed to me that the problems revealed in the discussions were not simple. After some investigation of the local situation, I felt that the Li Li-san line had not developed incidentally. Their point of view was that the struggle for military victory should have first priority, that we should take advantage of the facts that the Nanking government was in great confusion and all the warlords were fighting each other by expanding the Red Army rapidly and attacking Wuhan. Although this type of plan was certainly not a modern proletarian military operation, and did not have any hope of success, Li Li-san thought that it was worth the risk. Tseng Chung-sheng also had some examples and reasons to support his opinion. I believed that Mao Tse-tung mainly adopted the method of the literary character Sung Chiang, who assembled his righteous mass at Liang-shan-po, which was to give first priority to increasing his own personal power. Although this was the only way to success, he scarcely explained his actual strategy. Probably, there were many characteristics of the peasant rebellion that did not conform to the interests of the proletariat.

I pondered my basic attitude very carefully. I asked myself whether I could make a concession to the Li Li-san line and whether I could preach the gospel of revolution and emphasize the struggle for victory regardless of everything. My answer was negative. For example, in September and October, 1930, Chiang Kai-shek had won the war against Feng Yü-hsiang and Yen Hsi-shan. Chiang's forces were strengthened even though the Nanking government had many internal problems. Chiang could now concentrate more troops to fight against the Soviet area and the Red Army. The reason that members of the CC of the CCP had to be moved to separate Soviet areas was not because there was an astonishing development of the Soviet areas. The main reason was that it was not easy to stay in Shanghai and in the whole White area. At that moment, under those circumstances, wouldn't it be strange if I were to say the same thing as Li Li-san?

Could I act like Mao Tse-tung, who, appearing in a silk-kerchief headdress and with a feather fan and claiming he had received a carte blanche from heaven, pretended to be a strategist having foreknowledge of everything even without divination? Or should I tell myself to assume a peasant style since I led the peasants? I decided that I could not, and would not, do either. Communism is obviously a modern revolutionary political system. The doctrine of Liang-shan-po is a mixture of feudalism, superstition, and some rebellious thoughts of peasants. How could they be regarded in the same light? From another point of view, probably I was too far from understanding the Chinese style of communism. I myself was deeply dissatisfied with the Comintern, especially with Stalin. They did not trust me either. Could I claim that I had the complete confidence of the Comintern? I could not; and I would not threaten the "local Communists" by talking about the correct policies of the Comintern. I had never played the role of a man holding a sword granted by the emperor in order to execute those members with Li Li-san thoughts and various other kinds of people who did not obey. Five years later, Ch'en Ch'ang-hao, who had always worked with me, criticized me. He said that I was his most respected leader and that I had some special assets that he did not have, but that he had never heard me boast about the Comintern or even mention the name of the Comintern or Stalin. This displeased him. I admitted that this was true, but that there were some things about the situation that he did not know. (The foregoing generally describes the things I meant.)

Later I summarized all these opinions in an important speech, in which I explained my attitudes and working principles to all the responsible cadres of the area. I stated that I supported the policies of consolidating the Soviet area and expanding the Red Army, but that in order to realize them, we would have to investigate on our own and draft plans other than those on which we had based our decisions. My own opinion was that we should investigate while working. I explained that although the victory of the Kiangsi Red Army, which destroyed the division of Chang Hui-tsan, was encouraging, it would be a long time before there would be a complete victory of the Soviet and Red armies. To strengthen ourselves, we must emphasize not only quantity but also quality. We must do our best to fight for victory in the war and to expand the Soviet area and the Red Army. Simultaneously, we must make the Red Army become an "Army of Justice," wiping out the members of the landlord and rich-peasant classes and letting it be completely controlled by the Chinese Communists. We should strengthen its fighting ability, not attack local rascals arbitrarily, never do anything wrong in economics, and so forth. We should make the Soviet area become a model political area, make good arrangements for land reform, put political affairs in order, and make the officials free from corruption so as to distinguish ourselves from the style of the KMT government, which oppressed the people. To accomplish these heavy tasks, the first thing to do was to let all organizations under the supervision of the Special Committee be very Bolshevik.

Frequently I joined the meetings of the Special Committee to promote my new policies. First of all, we granted unconditional releases to three hundred of the thousand local tyrants who had been detained. The others were being processed, and most of them were released very quickly. Methods for increasing the production of vegetables and quick-growing crops were introduced actively in the whole Soviet area. The leaders of the Soviet were busy distributing produce to those who were seriously in need of food. Trading became more active in several major towns of the Soviet area. The regulations about finance and economics were prepared and announced. A factory was also being built to print paper currency.

The Supply Division of the Military Committee was the most conservative unit. Those in charge of the division were upset over my reforms. They thought that freeing the local tyrants would stop the main source of revenue and would make it impossible to obtain supplies for the army. For the time being, the most urgent thing was summer clothing for the army. I had to consider the problem personally. I checked the storage area of the Supply Division thoroughly and found out its defects and extravagances. I discussed with the staff in detail how to save material, how to utilize the clothing in stock, how to control the distribution, and so forth. Consequently, we found that the material they planned to use to make ten thousand uniforms could actually be used to make fifteen thousand uniforms. That meant one-half again as many. Due to my efforts, the fact that the military supply would not be seriously affected by the change in policy was proved in practice. My comrades became less worried, and objections to the changes in policy also eased.

I had been busily tied up at this center of the Soviet area for two weeks, and a new basic scheme for our work had been established. However, I had not yet made contacts with the Fourth Red Army in general. I decided to go to Chin-chia-chai to have a look at the main force of the Red Army in order to put the same policies into operation, that is, to do away with some guerrilla habits and to cultivate some revolutionary style. In the meantime, the Special Committee also planned to move its subsidiary organizations to Hsin-chi and to prepare the general meeting of the Party and the Soviet there in order to discuss the new policies that I had put into practice.

The Trip to Chin-chia-chai

At the end of April, 1931, I set out from the Ch'i-li-p'ing district for Chin-chia-chai, the center of the Soviet region on the border of Honan and Anhwei. I stayed to work in the Fourth Red Army for a short period, during which I came to a better understanding of this Soviet district and the Fourth Red Army and made further preparations for the plan of total reform to be advanced later.

Having climbed a not-too-high hill on the border between Honan and Hupeh, I came for the first time to Hsin-chi, soon to be made the capital of the region. This small market town in the form of a castle was originally a stronghold of the landlords; now it served us well. The walls surrounding the town, after years of rebuilding, were higher and stronger than those of most county seats. The pawnshops, stores, and markets in the town were housed in large buildings, while most of the residences were also well built and relatively large—a rare sight in this part of the country. Situated in the center of the Red region, this was naturally the most suitable place for us to use as our capital. By then the landlords had fled, but most of the houses remained intact. My comrades were busy with the town administrative work and with planning for the move.

Yü Tu-san, commissar of the Fourth Red Army, welcomed me in Hsin-chi with the Thirtieth Regiment of the Tenth Division. He had hurried back from the front, which was northwest of Hsin-chi. The Thirtieth Regiment was to escort me to Chin-chia-chai. Yü Tu-san was from the working class and had formerly been a trade-union leader in Hankow during the period of the Wuhan government. He had studied at Sun Yat-sen University in Moscow and was an activist of the anti-Mif clique. He was rather worried about the ascendency of the Mifists in the CC after the Fourth Plenum. He had led the Twelfth Division in the attack on Kao-shan-chai and had suffered heavy casualties, for which he blamed himself. He felt himself unable to cope with the present job. I told him to stay in Hsin-chi for a while to direct the military operations in the district and to wait for my return from Chin-chia-chai, when I would make arrangements to solve the problems.

The next morning, I continued on my eastward journey, escorted by the Thirtieth Regiment. We were to cover only sixty li that day, and there was plenty of time for leisurely sightseeing on the way. Because I had been appointed chairman of the Military Subcommittee, I was entitled to a mount during the journey; all minor affairs were taken care of by my entourage. So, on this trip I was able to concentrate on investigations of various aspects of the places we passed through, and I was not strained by walking as I was on previous trips. Wang Shu-sheng, commander of the Thirtieth Regiment, acted as my guide, telling me about the history of the region and giving me a better understanding of its development.

Commander Wang Shu-sheng was among the first to engage in guerrilla activities in this area. From the very first days he was a member of a basic backbone guerrilla unit in this place. He worked his way up from an ordinary member to commander. So, his personal experience illustrates the history of the growth of the guerrilla unit. Our commander was strong in physique, agile in action, and knew every blade of grass and every plant in the region as well as he knew the palm of his hand. His talent as an experienced master of guerrilla warfare was often manifested in his speech and his ways of handling business. Like Wang himself, the Thirtieth Regiment under him had grown up in guerrilla warfare. In the Fourth Red Army, it was a regiment of long experience and had the greatest combat strength. There were all together some eleven hundred officers and men, some eight hundred rifles, and four heavy machine guns in the regiment, which was much superior to the strength of the Huang-an Independent Regiment. All officers and men in the Thirtieth Regiment respected Commander Wang very much. The regimental commissar, who had less experience and reputation, always followed his lead.

Here are some of my recollections of Wang Shu-sheng's vivid description of the initial stage of the guerrilla unit's development. Shortly after the occupation of Wuhan by the Northern Expedition Army in October, 1926, Ma-ch'eng was also liberated and branches of the peasant association were organized. Wang Shu-sheng, a student of Ma-ch'eng Middle School and a member of the CYC, took part in the work of the Peasant Association. Soon he was promoted because of his activism in work. He became commander of the local Peasant Self-defense Corps. At that time everybody was working with great energy. Such slogans as "Down with local tyrants and evil gentry," "Down with imperialism and warlords," "Reduction of rent and interest," and so forth were shouted throughout the places. There was once a vogue of parading the local tyrants and evil gentry through the streets with dunce caps on their heads. Around April and May, 1927, the demand to redistribute the land was proposed, but before it could be put into practice, the split between the KMT and the CCP occurred.

In July of that year the Wuhan government announced its split with the CCP. The Peasant Association in Huang-an, Huang-kang, Huang-po, and Ma-ch'eng in northeastern Hupeh Province were suppressed by the reactionary forces. The cadres of the Peasant Association, members of the CCP and the CYC, and leftists of the KMT fled to the Ta-Pieh Mountains north of Huang-an and Ma-ch'eng to "run the rebellion."[4] Some of them took the peasants with them, carrying their broken rifles and iron-pointed spears. They were in small groups, going in various directions, without a unified command and without a common program for their operations. Sometimes they resisted the enemy, and sometimes they hid themselves. There was considerable chaos.

Not long afterwards the CC of the CCP sent instructions that the Autumn Harvest Uprising was to be launched under the slogans "Equal distribution of land," "Kill off all local tyrants and evil gentry," "Organize Soviets of workers and peasants," and so forth. Wang Shu-sheng and his colleagues then gathered the scattered peasant units to attack Huang-an, Ma-ch'eng, and other county seats. The peasant units were then undisciplined mobs, without any experience in fighting. As soon as they heard a gunshot, they usually fled in every direction. Heavy losses were suffered more than once. Yet, unaware of the actual situation, the CC of the CCP often encouraged them to riot, which was tantamount to indulging in child's play.

In the second half of the year 1927 and in 1928, the White terror was at its worst. The Thirteenth Division under Hsiao Tou-yin was stationed around Huang-an and Ma-ch'eng, the latter being the hometown of Hsiao Tou-yin. Most of the officers of the division were natives of the place and were familiar with conditions in the locality. In collusion with the local landlords' militia forces, they sought out those connected with the Peasant Association and killed them off, sometimes whole families of them. Houses were burned, and the mountainside was combed region by region, village by village. Members of the CCP and the CYC with relatively long years of membership, and major cadres of the Peasant Association were generally killed. Still larger numbers of innocent peasants were also killed. The White terror was one of the factors that compelled some people to follow the peasant units up the mountains.

The White terror then seemed irresistible. Most of the comrades were either scared to death or lost. They fled in large numbers. Many buried their rifles and changed their names before running away from the terrorized area; some hid themselves in the depths of the mountain forests, changing their hiding place several times a night, in order to escape the massacre. The peasant unit that Wang Shu-sheng had joined was the toughest. It hid in the depths of the mountain forest, coming out at night and lying low in the daytime. Sometimes it made a concentrated attack; sometimes it scattered to wage guerrilla skirmishes. Occasionally it gave the enemy some blows. But there were a lot of casualties and deserters, and the unit dwindled from some one hundred to about fifty, and finally to only eighteen.

Of these eighteen men in Wang Shu-sheng's unit, nine were members of the Party or the CYC, while the rest were men of the greenwood (that is, bandits). The latter, combined with the peasants in the unit, had been in the minority and generally followed in the footsteps of the majority. But now that they formed half of the unit, they allowed their former traits to get the upper hand.

One moonlit night the nine bandits sat face to face with the nine Party and CYC members and demanded a talk between the two sides. The chief of the bandits said, "You Communists are all fools. With your lives at stake, why the hell are you talking about 'land' and 'the Soviet'? What we want is 'to eat, drink, and play around.' We shall no longer go with you Communists and be fools. Give us all your rifles, bullets, and money, and let us part peacefully. Otherwise, we will have to fight it out." Seeing the seriousness of the situation, the leader of the unit said to the bandits affably, "Please let us have some time to talk about it."

With the consent of the bandits, the nine Party and CYC members went into a secret session. They came to the conclusion that if they exchanged gunshots with the bandits, the militia corps in the vicinity would be alerted and given a chance to encircle them; in that case everyone would be caught and they would all perish. Moreover, it was more or less certain defeat if they were to challenge the sharp-shooting bandits. Being in an inferior position, they had to concede. Saying some kind words to the bandits, the leader of the unit promised to hand over all the money they had, but asked to keep the rifles and ammunition for battles against the White Army. They did not want to fight it out with the bandits. After several rounds of talks, it was finally agreed that all the money plus half the bullets in the possession of the nine comrades would be handed over to the bandits. Thus a compromise was reached. When the two sides separated, they promised not to fight each other or to sabotage each other should they meet in the future.

The nine comrades were in despair after the separation. Each of them had only about ten bullets, and they had no ways to replenish the supply. Isolated and uncertain of the future, they did not know what to do. Wang Shu-sheng was then a member of the unit. He was pained at heart, and complained that the leader was incapable and too weak to control the bandits. Fortunately, there was another member in the unit who had been a veteran peasant cadre. That was Fu Ting-yi from Kwangtung Province. He told the comrades not to be depressed, as guerrilla activities were still hopeful. He pointed out that sooner or later the bandits had to leave. The peaceful separation was a fortunate thing in an unfortunate situation. Recalling his experience in guerrilla warfare while running Peasant Associations in Kwangtung Province, Fu said he could help the comrades to solve some of the difficulties in guerrilla fighting as he had become quite familiar with the local conditions after staying there nearly a year. He was well versed in distinguishing the four directions at night, and he knew the ways of the tramps. He also claimed that, if necessary, he could go to Hankow to buy rifles and ammunition. Fu Ting-yi's speech greatly boosted the morale of the comrades, who elected him deputy leader of the unit.

Wang Shu-sheng admired Fu Ting-yi very much, regarding him as an outstanding personality produced by the progressive Kwangtung peasant movement. In the initial period of great hardship, Fu Ting-yi inspired the comrades with his far-sightedness, loyalty, and courage, playing a resuscitative role in the guerrilla warfare of the region. Finally, he sacrificed his life for it. Wang Shu-sheng could not help asking at this juncture, "Chairman, did you know this man?" I said, "Yes, I knew him. He was a Kwangtung comrade who joined the Peasant Association as an office worker at first. At the time of the Wuhan government, he was transferred to the Hupeh Peasant Association as an assistant. He was short in stature, very quiet, honest, and full of drive."

Wang Shu-cheng went on to tell me that, being intellectuals, the comrades found themselves lacking in experience even after a short spell with the guerrillas. After Fu Ting-yi became deputy leader of the unit, arrangements were made in a more satisfactory manner. Fu Ting-yi also taught the comrades something in this respect. Soon, Fu Ting-yi proposed resolutely that they should try to get some money so that he might go to Hankow to buy some rifles and ammunition. So, they became bandits for a short period.

Once, Wang Shu-sheng and one of his colleagues were sent by the unit leader to commit a robbery. The two intellectuals could not find an appropriate place to fulfill their assignment. After much pondering, Wang Shu-sheng thought of a landlord's household in his home village.

The master of the house was a distant relative of his. When he was a child, he often visited the house, and he was very familiar with the paths leading to the house. The two men hid behind the woods at the back of the house and waited till nightfall. Then they covered up their faces and entered the house by the back door. They took out their revolvers and told the people in the house not to shout. Unexpectedly, an old woman in the house recognized the voice of Wang Shu-sheng, and called him by his nickname. This shamed him considerably. The old woman turned out to be Wang Shu-sheng's paternal great-aunt. She was less frightened when she learned about their intention. Turning to her son, she suggested that he give the two men what they wanted and send them on their way as soon as possible. She believed that the two young men must be in dire need and that if the pacification corps knew of their coming to the house, there would be no end of trouble. The old lady then took out a roll of silver dollars, fifty in all, and a packet of jewelry. She handed them to the two men, but Wang Shu-sheng, relenting a little, took only the silver dollars. He blurted out, "Thanks a lot!" and sneaked out through the back door with the other comrade.

Fu Ting-yi then took the money obtained from several ventures and went to Hankow to buy weapons. This was an extremely dangerous task. For a person speaking Mandarin with a Cantonese accent, it was still more worrysome. Yet Fu Ting-yi was full of confidence and promised to return in ten days' time. On the tenth day there was no news of Fu, and everyone was worried about his safety. Some supposed that Fu must have cheated them and gone away with the money, but on the evening of the eleventh day Fu Ting-yi returned with two new rifles and several hundred bullets. The whole unit was very excited.

In his journey to and from Hankow, Fu Ting-yi took to the untraveled parts of the country, avoiding both the highways and the trails. He traveled only at night, heading in the right direction according to his own judgment. Thus, he was able to avoid all checkpoints. Actually, he had not met anybody on his way. When hungry, he stole some melons or fruit for food. Often he had to go hungry, walking on without food or drink. He had to rest for several days after his arrival before recovering his strength. While in Hankow, he found his fellow Kwangtung countrymen, who introduced him to Japanese arms merchants for the deal. It was all done through his connections with the underground world.

Since they had been able to buy ammunition, their viewpoints underwent changes. They began to plan how to expand their strength and to launch new operations. The good news was spread, calling on the comrades in hiding to dig up the guns and cash they had hidden and join the ranks again. Knowing that their ammunition could be replenished and that new rifles could be bought, the comrades were glad to come out again, and the unit gradually expanded.

Fu Ting-yi then became the sole agent "to go to Hankow." He made at least two trips a month, and sometimes he took an assistant with him. For about half a year he kept making deals, and some thirty rifles and various kinds of bullets were bought. Other things such as telescopes, compasses, and medicine and first-aid equipment were also bought in considerable quantities. Moreover, thanks to him, contact with the Party in the White area was resumed, and a line of communications was set up. From then on, the unit was able to obtain instructions from the CC and the Hupeh Provincial Committee of the CCP. It was unfortunate that Fu Ting-yi could not see the completion of his plan. He did not return from his last trip to Hankow, and it was learned later that he had been killed by the KMT.

In March, 1929, war between Chiang Kai-shek and the Kwangsi militarists broke out in the Wuhan area. The troops stationed in Ch'i-li-p'ing township of Huang-an County and Chang-tien township to the north of Ma-ch'eng were withdrawn. Wang Shu-sheng's unit then began to attack the militia corps. Despite their lack of experience in guerrilla fighting, and occasional setbacks in military operation, they succeeded in compelling the militia corps to concentrate in the larger towns and to refrain from making scattered assaults. The unit was then able to occupy some villages, to organize Soviets, and to launch the peasants in attacking the local tyrants and redistributing the land.

In the summer of 1929 Wang Shu-sheng's unit expanded to a force of some three hundred men. Hsü Hsiang-ch'ien was sent by the CC of the CCP to their unit. He was a native of Shansi Province and had studied in the Whampoa Military Academy when it first started. Before coming to the unit, where he became the commander, he had taken part in the Canton Uprising and the peasant riots in Hai-feng and Lu-feng. The unit was subdivided into three squadrons, and Wang Shu-sheng became one of the squadron commanders. According to Wang Shu-sheng, he could not understand the Shansi dialect of the unit commander in the beginning, and they often had to rely on paper and pen when they talked. Hsü Hsiang-ch'ien taught Wang Shu-sheng and the others a lot about military affairs; and giving play to his military talent, he guided them in guerrilla warfare. From then on, they usually scored victories in their military operations, and the unit expanded rapidly, from several hundred to one and then two thousand. The Soviet region also expanded, and the comrades from other places gathered around them.

Meanwhile, the border region of Honan and Anhwei, with Chin-chia-chai as its center, witnessed similar hard struggles by other local comrades, who built up another guerrilla unit. After the outbreak of the war between Chiang Kai-shek and the Kwangsi militarists, this guerrilla unit also developed rapidly. The CC sent Hsü Chi-sheng, a native of Anhwei Province and also a student of the first graduating class of the Whampoa Military Academy, to the unit, and he organized it into another detachment.

In 1930 the CC ordered the Honan-Hupeh border region and the Honan-Anhwei border region to combine to form the Hupeh-Honan-Anhwei Soviet Region (or the Oyüwan area), and put it under the leadership of the CCP's Special Region Committee. A military sub-committee was also formed, and these guerrilla units combined to form the First Red Army of Workers and Peasants. Later it was changed into the Fourth Red Army, with K'uang Chi-hsün, once brigade commander in Szechwan, as army commander. The unit under Hsü Hsiang-ch'ien was reorganized as the Tenth Division, with Hsü as division commander, while Hsü Chi-sheng's unit was reorganized as the Eleventh Division, with Hsü Chi-sheng as division commander. As the expansion continued, the Twelfth Division was soon formed, and Hsü Hsiang-ch'ien was transferred to be commander of the new division, where the task of organization was heavy. Ts'ai Shen-hsi, another Whampoa Academy student of the first graduating class, was appointed commander of the Tenth Division. At that time, cadres at the divisional level and higher were usually sent from the CC. Cadres at the regimental level and below were usually veteran guerrilla cadres.

Though Wang Shu-sheng did not know much about the development of the unit under Hsü Chi-sheng, he somehow had the feeling that the difficulties it had undergone were in no way comparable to those encountered by his own unit. He was not much impressed by the contributions that Tseng Chung-sheng, K'uang Chi-hsün, and Ts'ai Shen-hsi had made to the growth of the region. He genuinely admired Fu Ting-yi, the pacesetter of the unit. According to him, Hsü Hsiang-ch'ien was the Number Two meritorious soldier of the Fourth Red Army. He was his commanding officer and his teacher—in a word, the one who led the unit to victory.

Listening to the endless heroic accounts vividly related by Wang Shu-sheng in the wee hours of the night in the camp in front of a tiny oil lamp was a fascinating experience. Unfortunately, after all these years, my record here must have omitted a lot, and the vividness of Wang's descriptions must have been missed in my account. We also touched upon many other questions, which I shall relate briefly.

Our trip took us from Hsin-chi region in the southern part of Kuang-shan County in Honan Province through the Sha-wo region and the Ching region of Shang-cheng County to the Soviet region in the southern part of Shang-cheng. Wang Shu-sheng and I rode along on horseback, escorted by the troops. After going about twenty li, we were out of the Hsin-chi region; and going on for forty li through the district of Sha-wo, we settled down for the night in camps. There were no people along the road, and the villages were deserted for the most part. Only a few old people were found in some of them. Though the houses were intact, the mud floors inside some of them looked green with sprouting grass. The fields were lying in waste. The fortresses on the tops of the hills were in ruins. The scene of devastation along the way was really shocking.

According to Wang Shu-sheng, the surrounding area was where they usually came to conduct guerrilla activities. In the beginning, they kept their bases in Hupeh, around Ma-ch'eng and Wang-an, and went north to carry out guerrilla activities. By climbing over the Ta-pieh Mountains, they would be in the territory of Honan. The peasants of Hupeh treated Honan as a foreign country and did what they liked as soon as they were in Honan, causing ill feeling among the local people. The region was now under the control of our military forces. The peasants, though discontented, wouldn't have left their home villages on their own initiative. But the landlords' militia corps threatened them in a hundred ways, saying that anyone remaining behind would be killed without mercy. As a result, with the exception of a few old people who stayed behind to look after the houses, tens of thousands of peasants fled to the White territory to the north.

Wang Shu-sheng also showed me how to distinguish whether a place had been ravaged by the White Army or the Red Army. Take the fortresses, for example, which neither side would allow to remain intact for the use of the enemy. The destruction was thorough in the case of the Red Army, while the White Army usually just made a show of compliance with the order to destroy. Again, take the ancestral halls as an example. The White Army usually destroyed them so that the Red Army could not use them as barracks; the Red Army, in deference to the clannish affection of the peasants, usually left them alone. The White Army also destroyed the temples, while the Red Army just knocked down the idols in them, in an attempt to abolish superstition. The White Army sometimes destroyed people's houses at will, while the Red Army never did so, because we no longer adopted the policy of burning and killing.

Wang Shu-sheng reported that they had asked the peasants in this part of the county who had fled to return, but no outstanding result was in sight. They had not gone very far; most of them had gathered in the area around Pai-shueh-yuan, a couple of dozen li away. The militia corps of the landlords was holding some fortresses in the northern part of the Sha-wo region, forming a line of blockade against us. In each fortress lived about one thousand peasants. The political workers of the Red Army and the cadres of the Soviet region frequently shouted to the peasants, urging them to return. Such activities usually ended in the two sides railing at each other.

Wang Shu-sheng admitted that one of the important factors giving rise to such a phenomenon was the "indiscriminate attacks on the local tyrants" in the past. I discussed the matter with him in great detail. I suggested that a widespread program of education be carried on among the personnel of the Soviet region and the Red Army cadres, to correct the work-style of indiscriminately attacking local tyrants. We should call on the peasants to return home and guaranteed their safety after their return; all of their past misdeeds would be ignored as long as they ceased taking action against the government of the Soviet and the Red Army. Wang Shu-sheng and his colleagues agreed that these were steps that ought to be taken. We later tried very hard in this respect, and about half of the peasants returned to their villages as the result of our painstaking efforts.

Each of the areas around the Soviet region had its own characteristics. The Ching region, which we were going to enter, was a peculiar region, ruled by militia forces with an inclination towards reformism. The chief of the region was a landlord by the surname of Ku who had big holdings. He was concurrently head of the region and commander of its militia corps. Our men called him "Ku Kou-tzu." Our comrades used to say, "This old dog Ku Kou-tzu is our most malicious adversary."

Wang Shu-sheng also admitted that Ku Kou-tzu was an anti-Communist masterhand. One of Ku's nephews had been a CYC member during the period of the Wuhan government, and he knew something about socialism. Returning to the Ching region, he severed relations with the CYC and acted as adviser to Ku Kou-tzu. The reformist measures that he proposed had been adopted by Ku Kou-tzu, who turned them into a pact for the region, with some twenty articles, including reduction of rent by 25 percent, interests on loans not to exceed 20 percent, the security of the region to be guaranteed, and the barring of bandits, soldiers, and officials from disturbing the peace of the place. The pact also stipulated that people in the region who took part in the activities of the guerrilla units of the Red Army would be executed without mercy.

Ku Kuo-tzu became virtually a local emperor through the implementation of the pact, which pacified the peasants on the one hand and built up his personal dictatorship on the other. Ku Kou-tzu turned a hall in his house into a law court, where major and minor affairs were decided by Ku himself in the capacity of judge. On the square outside his house was hoisted a big banner with the words "The awe-inspiring prestige of the Great General extending in all directions" on it. There was also a guillotine on which spies having connections with the bandits had their heads cut off—the heads then being put up for the public to see.

Ku Kou-tzu dealt with our guerrilla activities with his own guerrilla tactics. He destroyed all the fortresses in the region, as he did not believe in the tactics of defending fortresses. He held that such tactics could bring only losses upon himself. Instead, he fought against us in the open, taking advantage of his knowledge of the terrain. With the money he had seized, he had bought some three hundred rifles and revolvers and had organized a strong militia regiment. When only a few of the Red Army troops entered the region, he would mobilize his militiamen and the peasants to surround and attack us. If our army came in large numbers, his men would hide in the mountains and only come out to tread on our tails when there was a suitable opportunity. Or they would attack us in the night. Their abilities in guerrilla fighting were on a par with ours. That was why Wang Shu-sheng took a whole regiment along to protect me on my trip through the Ching region.

Early the next morning we entered the Ching region after covering some fifteen li. We took a rest in a tea shop on top of a hill. There was only one old man in the tea shop, who was a spy left behind by Ku Kou-tzu, for the villagers had all gone away and hidden in the forests on the mountains. The director of the political department of the Thirtieth Regiment took the old man aside and said to him, "Go quickly to tell your Big Lord Ku that we are passing through. We shall cook and use some of your drinking water at the places where we take a rest; but we shall not damage even one plant of yours. Tell him not to put obstacles in our way; otherwise he will have to look out for our revenge." He also told the old man, with exceptional frankness, "We are the well-known Thirtieth Regiment, out here in full force, with some eight hundred rifles and four heavy machine guns. Don't make a mistake when you repeat my words!" The old man, as expected, went off along the footpaths to make his report.

I was surprised by what had happened. I asked Wang Shu-sheng if they had reached an understanding with the other side so that neither would interfere with the other. Wang denied that there had been any such agreement. They had once approached Ku Kou-tzu for an agreement on noninterference, but had been refused by him. As a result, they had often had engagements with Ku Kou-tzu. By telling him now about our strength and intentions, our wish was to warn him against any reckless move on his part to hinder our advance. As expected, we passed through the Ching region without any obstruction. But just as we were leaving the region, they fired several shots at random, and we all joked about it, saying, "That's a farewell salvo for us!"

As soon as I stepped into the Ching region, I was struck by the difference between this region and the Sha-wo region which we had just passed through. Here, the fields were green and practically no land lay fallow. On the hillsides saplings had been newly planted, some big and some small. The roads were level, and the bridges were strong. It could be seen that Ku Kou-tzu had paid attention to rural construction. The farmhouses on the roadside were in quite good condition. The houses that I had entered were neat and tidy; in some the kitchen fire was burning brightly—likely the master of the house had just gone out to the mountain. I could not help feeling that this local emperor was cleverer than Chiang Kai-shek in keeping the rural areas in peace and order. If Chiang Kai-shek had learned something from Ku, we would have encountered more difficulties in establishing our rule.[5]

Conditions in the Ching region aroused my concern over the difficulties that we would face in trying to expand. I had asked Wang Shusheng about the other regions, and he had answered my questions in detail. He said that to the east of the Ching region was the East Eighth District of Ma-ch'eng, where the landlords maintained a strong fortress. Everywhere inside this district were strongholds guarded by powerful landlord forces. Since the time of the Taiping Heavenly Kingdom, the district had gone through innumerable changes, and the landlords there had consistently adhered to the policy of guarding the peace of the place and keeping the people in safety. They did not have the reformist measures of Ku Kou-tzu, but they were actually semi-independent. If we tried to go into the district, they would resist with all-out efforts; beyond paying the necessary taxes, they did not do anything else to please the government officials. Neither would they easily let the White armies enter the district and harass the people. There were no local bandits in their district, and peace and order prevailed. As a result, the people could live in peace and happily carry on their business. Our peasant movement had not been able to penetrate the district.

To the north of the Oyüwan Soviet area was the plain of the Huai River basin. About one hundred li to the north of Hsin-chi, there were mountain strongholds like a forest of masts. Further ahead, there were water strongholds, where landlords had built citadellike houses on the plain, which were protected by surrounding moats. There were drawbridges, and guardsmen were constantly on duty. Such water strongholds were a product of many years of experience in guarding the place against bandits, particularly at the time of the Taiping Heavenly Kingdom. Wang Shu-sheng felt that these water strongholds were suitable for sustained defense and were even more difficult to storm than mountain strongholds. They successfully blocked our way to the north.

To the south of the Soviet region was the Yangtze River, with Wuhan and other important cities on both banks. To the west was the Peking-Hankow Railway, also heavily guarded by KMT troops. In places bordering on the Soviet region on these two sides there were militia corps, which were generally small in numbers and far less powerful than those in the Ching region and the East Eighth District. They could only supplement the regular troops in the locality. The militia corps in Liu-an, Huo-shan, Ying-shan, and places in their vicinity were also very weak. They were the places where we might expand with less resistance.

In Kuang-shan there was a militia corps with more than one thousand men and rifles, the biggest and best-organized in the vicinity. The chief of the corps thought of himself as another Tseng Kuo-fan, the official who had trained militiamen and defeated the Taiping Heavenly Kingdom. He suggested that the militia corps on the borders of the Oyüwan Soviet area form an alliance, increase their strength, and be put under a unified command in order to shoulder the heavy task of annihilating us. Wang Shu-sheng knew there were disagreements between the KMT armies and the militia corps. Chiang Kai-shek wanted to do away with the troops under the miscellaneous commands of the warlords, so it didn't seem likely that he would allow the militia corps to expand. Neither would he allow Tseng Kuo-fan to be reborn.

These important facts from Wang Shu-sheng gave me an initial understanding of the relations between the growth of the militia and the peasant movement, and their interaction. I came to realize that the weakness of the militia force in Hunan was an important factor for the rapid expansion of the Hunan peasant movement in the period of the Wuhan government. The fact that Mao Tse-tung was able to give play to his splendid guerrilla talent in the region around Kiangsi, Hunan, and Fukien was probably due to the relative weakness of the militia force in the locality. The progressive peasant movement in Kwangtung had suffered heavy blows from the landlords' militia force and was unable to rise again for a time. The Oyüwan Soviet area, which came into being later, was encircled by powerful landlords' militia forces, which greatly affected its development.

The Ching region lay in between the Oyü Soviet area and the Yüwan Soviet area, and was a great obstacle to us. We later took great pains to destroy this barrier, but not much was achieved. I returned to the region several times to lead attacks on Ku Kuo-tzu. If we had not been experts in guerrilla tactics, we would have suffered some losses at his hands.

Coming back to that day on our trip, we finally passed through the region safely. It was about one hundred li from our campsite to the Soviet region south of Shang-cheng. We spent the night on the premises of the Soviet government in a village at the border. Our men were welcomed by the people of the Soviet region, who gave us tea and water to drink and killed pigs and sheep to feast us. They were just as enthusiastic as the people of the Kao-ch'iao region. As soon as we arrived at the Soviet region, our men were overjoyed, as if they had returned to their home villages to reunite with their families. As the task of escorting me had been completed, Regimental Commander Wang took his men to the place where the Tenth Division was stationed. I went straight on to Chin-chia-chai, accompanied by personnel of the Soviet region.

On the third day, after covering some seventy li through the southern part of Shang-ch'eng, I arrived at Chin-chia-chai, which was a market town in Liu-an County of Anhwei Province, in the neighborhood of Shang-ch'eng, of Honan Province. The southern district of Shang-ch'eng and the Chin-chia-chai district of Liu-an were relatively old Soviet regions, which took Chin-chia-chai as their center. The Regional CCP Committee of the Oyü border area was in Chin-chia-chai. Shen Tse-min and his wife, who set out from Shanghai at the same time as I did, had arrived a fortnight earlier.

Shen Tse-min told me that they had gone to Pukow from Shanghai, and taking the train on the Tientsin-Pukow line to Pengpu, had gone from there to Cheng-yang-kuan by ferry and then came to Chin-chia-chai on foot. Everything went smoothly on the way, without such risks as passing through the White region under the cover of night, which I had done. Indeed, the confrontation between the Red and the White regions was not so acute as in the Oyü border area. The fact was that the peasant movement in Anhwei was somewhat backward, and in the Soviet campaign, class struggle was not conducted in a very fierce manner. Consequently, the destruction inflicted on people's houses was not so great as in the Ch'i-li-p'ing region.

Shen Tse-min was dissatisfied with the work in this region. He held that the Party organization here was simply not like that of a Communist party. The comrades generally were ignorant of Marxism-Leninism and did not strictly implement the CC's instructions. Many landlord and rich-peasant elements had sneaked into the Party, the CYC, the Soviet government, and the Red Army. The distribution of land was done in a slipshod way, and landlords and rich peasants still had large holdings. The commanders and officers of the Red Army were arrogant, and most of them held the Party and the Soviet government in contempt. They concentrated on reorganizing local armed forces into regular units of the Red Army and neglected the development of local armed forces. Indiscriminate attacks on local tyrants was relatively widespread. Food supply, on the other hand, was not a serious problem.

Shen Tse-min wanted to launch a campaign inside the Party and to reorganize the leadership structures, starting from the fundamental thing in every aspect. I agreed with his views, but did not approve of his radical means of reform. I told him about my experiences and the steps we had taken. I persuaded him not to destroy the achievements of the comrades in the region, which had been won through hard struggles. I held that it was necessary to help the comrades with patience and that we should not criticize them too harshly. If we adopted radical measures, opposition might be formed by the local cadres and it would be difficult to carry on with our work. Shen Tse-min was soon convinced by me and decided that he would bring his opinions to a lower key and that he would not touch on the subject of reorganization for the time being.

Soon, Secretary Li of the Chin-chia-chai District Committee of the CCP asked that I meet the members of the committee without Shen Tse-min being present. I agreed, and they all told me how Shen Tse-min had criticized them for this or that mistake as soon as he arrived but had not told them what to do to correct their mistakes, which made them very uncomfortable.

The CCP District Committee consisted of young chaps of about twenty. Some had joined the Party not long before, and the others were CYC members who had just become Party members. They lacked talent and experience, and the whole committee was rather infantile. It turned out that the guerrilla activities in this area were originally launched by comrades from other places and that the local CCP organizations were newly developed. The senior Party members had gone to work in the Red Army; those who remained were unavoidably new hands. Shen Tse-min's severe criticism of them indeed went too far.

In my talk with these comrades, I encouraged them, telling them that their past efforts were actually extraordinary. I explained to them that Shen Tse-min and I came with the aim of helping them and guiding their work and would certainly not suppress them or replace them. Shen Tse-min had criticized them out of an urgent desire for improvement, not out of distrust of them. I also told them frankly that Shen Tse-min and I had come to an understanding and had worked out some concrete measures to help them in their work, and I gave them the gist of these measures.

Having heard my explanation through, these comrades of the CCP District Committee turned from grief to joy. They stated that they

would support the Oyüwan Area Subbureau of the CC and the leadership of the CCP Provincial Committee. They also pledged to get on
well with Shen Tse-min and to work together in harmony. They were
ready to learn and to correct their former mistakes. After the settlement
of this minor dispute, my attention was turned to the Red Army, while
Shen Tse-min was in charge of the work of the Party and the Soviet
government.

Though the estrangement between Shen Tse-min and the local
Chin-chia-chai cadres had been patched up, dogmatism and empiricism
were later to cause many controversies. Shen Tse-min was a veteran
comrade, fond of reading literary works. He was one of the "28 Bolsheviks" among the students who had studied in Russia, but his friendship with me was relatively close and we could work together harmoniously. Probably due to the deep influence of Moscow, he often
judged these "native Communists" of the mountainous region by the
standard of the CPSU. He was a scholar without working experience,
but he was able to repeat from memory the dogmas of Marxism-Leninism. The guerrilla heroes of the locality, on the other hand, did not
know or care much about Marxism-Leninism, and proceeded from local
conditions in dealing with everything. The contradiction between the
two had never been completely resolved.

K'uang Chi-hsün, commander of the Fourth Red Army, was stationed in Chin-chia-chai with his Army Command staff. I lived at Army
Headquarters, and came into close contact with K'uang Chi-hsün, who
allegedly was not particularly efficient in leadership work. I paid particular attention to this point when I was with him. K'uang was originally from the ranks of the Szechwan Army, having been regimental
commander for a long time and brigade commander for a short period.
He had taken part in the mutiny in Szechwan, but he lacked experience
in guerrilla warfare. This was the first time that I saw him. I felt that
he was rich in experience as a commander of the lowest rank; but as
supreme military commander, he left something to be desired. He was
often original in his views on some tactical problems, such as night operations; but on strategic problems, he was not very creative and was not
as attentive to such problems as Ts'ai Shen-hsi.

Hsü Chi-sheng, commander of the Eleventh Division, who had
made great contributions to the military picture of the Yüwan border
area and who was stationed some seventy li east of Chin-chia-chai with
his troops, had heard of my arrival and sent the director of his Political

Department, a Comrade Huang, to come to see me. Comrade Huang was rather inexperienced and only carried out orders from Hsü Chi-sheng. The three main points in Hsü's statement were as follows: (1) Hsü was discontented with Shen Tse-min. In his opinion, this district was conquered through the efforts of the Red Army, and the leaders in the Party and Soviet organs around Chin-chia-chai were all cadres promoted by the Red Army. Shen had not made contacts with the cadres of the Red Army first, but had attempted to put the Party above the Army. Moreover, he should not have adopted an attitude of attacking the members of the Chin-chia-chai District Committee of the CCP. (2) Hsü was discontented with the leadership of K'uang Chi-hsün. He was of the opinion that K'uang Chi-hsün, the latecomer, lacked ability, as a result of which the center of gravity of the leadership of the Army fell on several division commanders. (3) Hsü had ambitions of taking over K'uang Chi-hsün's position.

Comrade Huang had explained that formerly, when Tseng Chung-sheng was dealing with the military and political affairs of the district, he usually consulted the several division commanders, among whom Hsü Chi-sheng was the most capable. Therefore, it was necessary to improve the situation with K'uang Chi-hsün exercising the military leadership. Comrade Huang particularly mentioned that Hsü had always respected my leadership and wished that I would also respect his opinion.

When I found out from detailed questioning of Comrade Huang that this was really what Hsü Chi-sheng had wanted him to say, I was quite angry about it. I felt that Hsü Chi-sheng fully manifested warlordism, which had to be corrected. I asked Comrade Huang to rush back to the front right away and tell Hsü Chi-sheng that he must respect the Party leadership and the Party's political work in the army. I warned him not to speak with indiscretion, manifesting the ways of warlords, and told him that I would go shortly to the front to have a long talk with him.

After staying in Chin-chia-chai for three days, I set out for the front with K'uang Chi-hsün and the staff of Army Headquarters. Meanwhile, Shen Tse-min stayed behind in Chin-chia-chai to guide the work of the CCP District Committee, and waited for a chance to go to Hsin-chi. About ninety li to the east of Chin-chia-chai was Ma-pu, where one brigade of Ch'en Tiao-yüan's troops was stationed, the enemy force nearest to the Soviet area. Our Tenth and Eleventh divisions were hiding in places about thirty li northwest of Ma-pu, waiting for an opportunity to annihilate the enemy troops in Ma-pu. We arrived at the camp of our army after going some seventy li from Chin-chia-chai.

Wherever we went, we saw tea plantations in the undulating, hilly district, which was famous for its abundant tea production. The well-known Liu-an tea leaves were usually sent out to Su-chia-pu via Ma-pu and Tu-shan. The saying "Golden Ma-pu, Silver Tu-shan, with Su-chia-pu as the imperial court," depicts well the prosperity of the tea trade. The barns and tea plantations had not been damaged much, and trade in the various small towns and fair sites was very brisk. The currency in use in the market was silver dollars and coppers. There was no shortage of grain, some of which even found its way in from the White territories.

The scene, so different from that in Ch'i-li-p'ing, was a great delight to me. However, careful investigations showed that what Shen Tse-min had said was true. Here, land revolution had not been done in a thoroughgoing way. The arable land had been distributed roughly in accordance with the amount of labor force in each household. Small landowners and rich peasants still owned much of the land. Some peasants who had been given land by distribution secretly paid some rent to the landlords. As to tea plantations and bamboo forests in the hilly districts, no distribution had been carried out; most of the former owners still retained ownership. Most of the leaders of the village Soviets and mass organizations were from affluent peasant families, including, naturally, small landowners and rich peasants. Some of the organizations in the countryside were similar to those in Ch'i-li-p'ing, but they were far from leaning towards the CC of the CCP, as those in Ch'i-li-p'ing did. The people also came out to welcome us along the roadside, but their enthusiasm was not very evident.

Here, there was no marked opposition between the Red and the White territories. The farther away a place was from Chin-chia-chai, the paler became the tint of the Soviet. According to the local comrades, this was the result of the "benevolent administration" of Division Commander Hsü. In the beginning, those in charge of guerrilla activities were from Shou County and the nearby area; only Division Commander Hsü was from Liu-an County. He preached that "hares do not eat the grass around their own burrows" and that the Red Army guerrillas should go in for vigorous struggles against local tyrants outside the territory of Liu-an County. In the southern part of Shang-ch'eng, they had shown themselves to be very fierce, and the opposition between the

Red and the White territories was quite manifest. Yet, inside Liu-an County, Commander Hsü only allowed suppression of those wealthy men who were also unkind; so the scope of struggles against local tyrants naturally became smaller.

When we arrived at our destination, the officers of the two divisions gathered at the square to welcome us. I met Liu Ying, commander of the Tenth Division, who had been a junior officer in the cavalry of Feng Yü-hsiang and also one of the more than three hundred sent by Feng to study in the Soviet Union. He had the fine work-style of Feng Yü-hsiang's subordinates—he was adept at the management and training of troops and strictly obedient to orders. His colleague praised him for his fine physique, his military technique, and his courage and skill in battle. Liu had been deputy commander of the Tenth Division; he was promoted when Commander Ts'ai Shen-hsi was wounded. When I first met him, I was impressed by him, finding him an exemplary military comrade.

I already knew Hsü Chi-sheng, commander of the Eleventh Division, who was a talented soldier, fond of talking about politics. When we met, he talked warmly about old times. He said that he had been a platoon or company commander since the time he had studied in the first graduating class of the Whampoa Military Academy; he had seen me many times and had been deeply influenced by me. On the eve of the Nanchang Uprising, he was a regiment commander of the Northern Expedition Army and was being kept in Kiukiang after receiving some wounds on the Honan front. On my way to Nanchang, I had passed through Kiukiang, and it was I who made arrangements for him to go to Shanghai to get treatment. After that, he had hidden in Shanghai for two years, and had then been sent to Chin-chia-chai to fight as a guerrilla. That evening he prepared a sumptuous dinner to welcome us. Then we held a military meeting of the senior officers, which approved Hsü Chi-sheng's plan of operations. Seeing that our army had stayed here for a long time and our intentions had been detected by the enemy troops in Ma-pu, as shown by their rigorous defense measures, Hsü proposed that we make a detour and attack Tu-shan to annihilate the regiment of enemy troops stationed there. Ma-pu was fifty li away from Su-chia-pu, while Tu-shan was situated in between the two. A regiment was stationed there to keep open the traffic route to the rear. According to Hsü's plan, our army was to attack the enemy at Tu-shan with only a small part of our troops, while the greater part was to engage the enemy troops at Ma-pu and those who were coming as reinforcements. As to the enemy at Su-chia-pu (about one brigade), we were to keep watch on them across the Pi River. Our main aim was to lure the enemy in Ma-pu to come out for the rescue of Tu-shan, so that we could seize the opportunity to wipe them out and occupy Ma-pu.

Army Commander K'uang Chi-hsün sent out battle orders in accordance with this plan. It was decided that we would make a detour to attack Tu-shan on the third day. The Eleventh Division would use its main force to attack Tu-shan, while part of it would keep watch over the enemy in Su-chia-pu. Army Headquarters would lead the entire Tenth Division to lie in ambush along the strategic road between Tu-shan and Ma-pu. As soon as the enemy troops in Ma-pu set out to reinforce those in Tu-shan, we would annihilate them in the open and take Ma-pu.

The second day was a day to rest. I spent most of the time chatting with Hsü Chi-sheng, and he explained most of his views to me. He criticized the policy of the CC on consolidating the Soviet area, thinking that it was conservative and might easily be misunderstood by the ordinary comrades of the Soviet area, who would think that the main task of the Red Army was to protect them. Hsü wanted freedom of development for the Red Army, without the burden of "consolidating the Soviet area." He said that the Red Army should go far away to conduct guerrilla warfare, so as to achieve rapid development. He was of the opinion that the CC's appointment of K'uang Chi-hsün as commander of the Army was a mistake, because, although he had a long record as a soldier, K'uang was less experienced in guerrilla warfare than veteran regimental commanders of the Red Army. The Fourth Red Army, according to Hsü, had lost its future, by having K'uang Chi-hsün in supreme command. Hsü Chi-sheng did not attach much importance to political work, and he complained about the incompetence of Yü Tu-san, political commissar of the Army. Most of the political workers at the other levels were newcomers. Hsü, therefore, wanted the CC to grant complete power to the senior commanders with regard to directing the troops.

Hsü Chi-sheng also admitted that the Red Army had its own shortcomings, such as its attitude toward women. Even senior officers, including himself, had had some romances. But he felt that this and other shortcomings could be removed only after the Red Army had won a decisive victory.

I gave him detailed explanations, pointing out that it was not permissible to separate the Soviet area from the Red Army, or the Party from the Red Army; that it was not permissible to harbor conceptions purely from the point of view of military expansion. Wherever the Red Army went, it would need supplies from the rear; otherwise expansion was impossible. Therefore, it was necessary to consolidate the Soviet area as the rear of the Red Army in accordance with the policy of land revolution. Whether this would prove correct depended on the full display of our strength; but, in principle, we must uphold such views. Without the Party leadership, the Red Army, even if it had some very good military commanders, would go astray from the principles of communism in its actions, and would become similar to the KMT troops. The idea of letting the Red Army go afar afield to seek expansion might be misunderstood as an attempt to go to a prosperous region to find enjoyment. It might mean fighting for ruling power by relying on military force alone. That, at best, was bandit behavior.

After hearing my explanation out, Hsü Chi-sheng seemed to see the irrationality of his ideas and said that he accepted my instruction, and would no longer complain about Shen Tse-min. I also pointed out to Hsü the difference between a CCP soldier and a bandit warlord, and advised him to strive to be a modern CCP soldier who serves the people. I told him not to indulge in thinking that he was better than a KMT soldier just because he was following the path of righteousness. As to the incompetence of Comrade K'uang Chi-hsün, the question was to be solved through proper channels. It was improper to have the ambition of taking his place. I told him that political work should be attended to and carried out; one should not make light of it in view of the current situation. I said that I welcomed criticisms and suggestions from the comrades, but I wished that they would not be stubborn about their views. Hsü Chi-sheng expressed full acceptance of my opinion, but he did not act in accordance with his promises.

On the third day a small part of our troops, assisted by the local armed forces, made a sham frontal attack on the enemy in Ma-pu, while the main force secretly moved towards Tu-shan. The operation was generally well organized; but the village Soviets along the way fully revealed their weakness. Some of them did not manifest the necessary enthusiasm in taking care of the troops coming in; in others, even the leaders hid. I found out that these Soviet organizations were nothing more than signboards. Some of the leaders were afraid of the enemy, while others might even have been dealing secretly with the enemy.

In order to keep our secrets intact, we decided not to tell them the aim of the operation.

At dawn on the fourth day, we successfully wiped out a large part of the enemy troops in Tu-shan and captured some six hundred rifles. However, the enemy in Ma-pu, who had ventured out to reinforce the Tu-shan troops, turned back to guard the highland positions in the Ma-pu area, because our troops had exposed themselves too soon. They resisted us from strategic positions. In this engagement I found that K'uang Chi-hsün was not careful enough in giving orders. His first mistake was ordering the Tenth Division to come out of ambush to attack too soon. When the enemy troops of Ma-pu turned back to their battle positions, he ordered the Tenth Division to attack the enemy's strong positions. I had to suggest to K'uang that the attack be stopped for a time. The senior officers present all agreed that I had done the right thing so as to minimize casualties.

As expected, the enemy troops in Ma-pu retreated to Su-chia-pu after two days, because Tu-shan was in our hands and they were cut off from the rear. We had expected this and had arranged to attack the enemy on its path of retreat; but we came a little late, and the enemy troops were all gone. This was also the fault of K'uang Chi-hsün's direction. He thought that the enemy troops in Ma-pu would not flee so soon, and so he had not made the necessary preparations. I could not help feeling that K'uang Chi-hsün was not sharp enough and was rather stubborn because of his love of preeminence. I did not say anything to criticize him at the time, but I was sure that it was necessary to effect some improvement in the leadership of the Fourth Red Army.

As our troops assembled in Tu-shan to take a rest, I made a careful investigation of the internal condition of the various units. I found that this was really a peasant contingent led by the CCP, with quite a number of fine traditions fostered by experiences in fighting, as well as some shortcomings, including the work-style inherited from the old-fashioned armies, the ways of bandits, and other inclinations produced by guerrilla warfare.

About eighty percent of our troops were from peasant stock, mostly poor peasants. The rest was made up of village bums who had lost their jobs or who had been accustomed to the ways of hooligans. Some of them were captives from the KMT Army, while others had come over after mutinies. The worker element in the army was negligible. Making sample investigations in several companies, I found that in each case there were not more than two or three among the rank and file who were tainted with hooliganism. I was quite satisfied with such a state of affairs, feeling that our army had an excellent foundation.

Cadres at the battalion level and above were all CCP members, while a few of the cadres at the company and platoon levels were not Party members. Strictly speaking, some of these military cadres were Party members in name only. The promotion of the Red Army cadres depended on their merits in battle and their political fortitude. When a platoon commander was to be promoted to company commander, the regiment commander would assess his ability in exercising command in accordance with his merits in battle, and the regiment's political commissar would see if he was steadfast politically. Then the headquarters of the division and the Army would approve his appointment. As the Red Army was constantly fighting, there were frequent changes of cadres; but generally speaking, the appointments were appropriate.

Every Red Army company had a branch of the Party, with its membership ranging from a few to some ten or twenty. The political work of the Red Army used the company as its basic unit, the company's political commissar being responsible for guiding the work of the Party branch. In peacetime he had to give lecture on politics; in wartime he had to boost the morale of the soldiers. Sometimes he had to mobilize the officers and men of the whole company to help the peasants in the locality where the company was stationed in organizing Soviets or distributing land. The company's political commissar sometimes had to call a rally of the whole company to review the combat experiences, political work, or improvement in living conditions. On the last question, the rank and file had a larger measure of freedom in giving their views. For instance, improvements in the mess were the responsibility of the mess committee elected by the rank and file. The soldiers were allowed to level criticism at their platoon and company commanders but could not make any decisions in these matters.

The most outstanding tradition of the Red Army was its unity. The officers and men were supposed to share weal and woe: this was achieved on the whole. During battles, cooperation between the units was an unalterable principle. When a certain company was in danger during an engagement, the companies in the vicinity would surely go all out to help it, no matter how great the danger might be to themselves. The officers took good care of the rank and file; and the latter helped each other, looking after the sick and taking care of the wounded, without any thought for the difficulties or dangers involved. When a soldier got sick on a march, the platoon or company leader would always carry his rifle for him. Giving preferential treatment to new recruits was a common practice. When a new recruit came to the barracks, the veteran soldiers usually comforted him in a hundred ways to help him overcome his uneasiness in new surroundings. The duties of the recruits were usually light, and they were able to get help from the veterans. When a recruit made a mistake, he was often forgiven by special concession. All this made the Red Army quite different from the KMT Army.

The warlord and bandit inclinations were also quite manifest in the Red Army. The Red Army suffered from a lack of detailed, complete systems and regulations, and some principles had not been strictly adhered to. Some officers became arrogant after performing good deeds; others were haunted by the old conception that "a commander fighting away from the palace may ignore the emperor's orders." They held the Soviets in contempt, regarding them as something created and supported by them, which ought to work for them. Though they dared not show contempt for the Party openly, they still thought of themselves as Party members with a difference. When they went to the White area, they turned a blind eye to the indiscriminate attacks on local tyrants, particularly to "Attacking the local tyrants without turning over the gains to the public treasury."[6] They often dallied with women in the Soviet areas. Although there was no maltreatment or killing of prisoners of war under the principle of leniency, captives were frequently robbed of their wallets. When discipline was imposed at one time or another, it was according to the wish of the senior officers concerned; there were no fixed legal procedures.

Such tendencies were especially manifest in the Eleventh Division. The Tenth Division, which saw its development in the Oyü border area, had more advanced regulations, and it did not have so many military and political cadres of landlord and rich-peasant origin. The CCP members had been in the Party for a longer period of time and were able to obey the decisions of the CC. This was due to the leadership of Hsü Hsiang-ch'ien. On the other hand, the Eleventh Division, which was first developed in the Yüwan border area, was relatively backward. There were more military and political cadres who were from landlord or rich-peasant families. The Party members were usually new, and the prestige of Hsü Chi-sheng sometimes surpassed that of the Party and the Soviet. When we organized the peasants to rise and distribute the land and to form the Soviet government in Tu-shan, landlords and rich peasants often came in and out of the house of Division Commander Hsü, who often defended them openly.

The general cadres of the Fourth Red Army greatly admired the guerrilla tactic of "attacking the weak points and avoiding the strong ones" proposed by Mao Tse-tung in Chingkangshan, but they were also proud of their valor in battle. The Fourth Red Army soldiers lacked training. On the battlefield, it was the company and platoon commanders who led the units to attack together, giving rise to rather heavy casualties, particularly among the junior cadres. Vacancies from cadres wounded or killed were not easily filled. There was a saying in the Fourth Red Army at the time, which went, "What does success in revolution mean? It means sacrificing one's life on the battlefield." This might have originated as an attempt to boost the morale of the rank and file, urging them to fight bravely and not be afraid of death; yet I had the feeling that it represented the passive idea of having lost hope for the future, which was harmful. It was also a concept fostered in fierce guerrilla warfare, when taking risks and regarding death as something unimportant was a valuable trait. This had something to do with the influence of Li Li-san's ideas. I had pointed out that the concept of defeatism was bred in guerrilla warfare. We must not lightly sacrifice ourselves during the struggles, but must win victories. Later, Chu Teh also told me that the same concept was current among Red Army cadres in the Kiangsi Soviet area and that he had tried to correct it.

Having learned about all these things, I planned to effect reforms by drawing up several projects for improvement. I felt that the task was arduous. To solve these problems, it was necessary to work out plans and systems for some, and to carry out patient education for others. Still, mass struggle would be required for some in order to effect changes. I had called several meetings of military cadres to discuss the steps that might be taken immediately by the Fourth Red Army, such as strict observance of discipline, cadre training by the divisions and regiments, strengthening of political work, and holding of military meetings before and after each operation to discuss the plan of operation and to review the experience of combat, and so forth. Other questions that were connected with too many other issues had to be left for the Party Congress to discuss and solve.

My inspection in the Oyüwan Soviet area now came to an end. I had a general idea of what needed to be done. It was necessary to convene meetings of the Party and other organs at the regional level to press forward the work to a higher stage of development.

The Important Meetings in Hsin-chi

Beginning in June, 1931, we held a series of meetings in Hsin-chi, the first being the Congress of CCP members in the Oyüwan area, followed by the Soviet Congress, the CYC Congress, the Women's Congress, and other conferences concerned with specialized subjects. The purpose of these meetings was to regularize the Soviet movement; in fact, they marked the turning point of the work in the whole area.

After the ending of the Tu-shan campaign, I made certain necessary arrangements in the Yüwan border area before I moved westward along with the main body of the Red Army. We were making active preparations for holding the Party Congress, this being the first important meeting of the Party in that area.

For the purpose of holding this meeting, large-scale military actions were temporarily halted. The Tenth and Eleventh divisions of the Fourth Red Army moved from Tu-shan to the Pai-ch'üeh-yüan district north of Hsin-chi, while the Twelfth Division also moved there from the area northwest of Hsin-chi. The stationing of the Fourth Red Army in the Pai-ch'üeh-yüan district, which lay between two Soviet areas, was to facilitate its movement in the event of an emergency and to make it easier to solve the problem of supply. The principal duties of the Fourth Red Army at that time were rest, consolidation, and training. At the same time, it might take the opportunity to arouse the masses in the Pai-ch'üeh-yüan area, set up a Soviet, and open up communications between the two Soviet areas.

I returned to Hsin-chi in the latter part of May. By that time all the Party, government, and military organizations of the Oyüwan area had already moved there, while Shen Tse-min and others had also arrived. Hence, Hsin-chi became the capital of that region. Work efficiency improved as a result of the concentration of various agencies, and a new atmosphere prevailed. At that time the Oyüwan Bureau of the CC of the CCP had not yet been established, and I concerned myself mainly with the work of the branch office of the Military Committee, while Shen Tse-min was responsible for directing the work of the Special

Committee and the Soviet government, and Ch'en Ch'ang-hao devoted his time to CYC work.

It was at that time that I met Hsü Hsiang-ch'ien again after a long separation. He was not an outstanding student in the first graduating class of Whampoa Military Academy. He did not make a deep impression on me because we had few contacts with each other. When we met again this time, I had several good talks with him and discovered that he really had the qualifications to be the leader of guerrilla operations in this Soviet area. His military viewpoint was practical, and he had very rich experience in guerrilla war. He directed the operations in an extremely responsible manner, was strict but unassuming to his subordinates, and had the deportment befitting a great military commander. He was very respectful to the Party and the Soviet, was very strict in his personal life, and had no bad habits such as were to be found among the warlords. He discussed with me only matters concerning policies and practical work, unlike Hsü Chi-sheng, who criticized at random the incorrect leadership of K'uang Chi-hsün and others.

I was kept very busy with the work of the branch office of the Military Committee. Because of the shortage of personnel and the imperfect organization, I often had to spend a lot of time tackling problems of a secondary or technical nature. Although our army was still rather small, it had too many units. Daily I had to go through and put down my remarks on the military intelligence reports and deal with emergency matters that occurred in various places.

Among my colleagues Ts'ai Shen-hsi was one with the talents of a strategist. He was one of the older comrades who had worked with me in the labor unions before entering the first graduating class of Whampoa Military Academy. He was cool-headed, careful, and sagacious. When we met this time, I saw that his left hand had been disabled during the war. But he was still working energetically as commandant of the Military School. He hated the customs of warlords and local bandits and advocated regularization of the Red Army. He was perhaps not as good a military commander as Hsü Hsiang-ch'ien, but his ideas about strategy often proved to be outstanding. Unfortunately he was unable to come over to take charge of the staff officers, so I only consulted him before I made important decisions.

Before the Party Congress was held, we had already started to carry out reforms in various fields, but the results were not significant. We had, however, made some progress in the economic field; the panic of famine had subsided; there was a bumper harvest of vegetables in various places; the families that suffered from a serious shortage of food had been given appropriate relief; measures of saving materials had been put into practice everywhere;[7] trading in the marketplaces had become active; there was an adequate supply of daily necessities such as salt and cloth on the market; even certain medical supplies needed by the army were obtainable on the market; native products were being exported in quantity from the Soviet areas; the amount of Soviet currency issued was increasing gradually, and it was circulated freely in the Soviet area at a par value four percent higher than the bank notes circulated in the White areas.

These signs of an economic recovery greatly inspired the Party Congress. The comrades in general had changed their attitude about such measures being premature and had become convinced that they could be put into effect immediately without waiting until a decisive victory had been achieved in military operations. Most of them were no longer skeptical about the policies of the CC of the CCP, and felt that such policies could guide them to a bright future.

In the latter part of June, the Party Congress of the Oyüwan Soviet area opened solemnly in Hsin-chi under a temporary bamboo structure erected in an open space. About nine hundred delegates attended. They came from Party branches of each company of the Red Army and local armed forces and from Party branches of villages in various localities, representing more than seven thousand Party members and some four thousand CYC members. In addition, there were some two to three hundred who attended in the capacity of nonvoting delegates and observers. It was indeed a grand meeting.

However, this congress was in fact similar to a mass rally of peasants. Most of the delegates were illiterate or quasi-illiterate, which made the proceedings of the meeting unusually difficult. We decided, therefore, to hold a series of group discussions following each formal session. In these group discussions, those who were better educated would take the chair and explain to the illiterate ones what had been discussed in the meeting. After repeated explanations and recitations, if the majority of the delegates could memorize the main points of a motion, this was considered a great success. Those who had opinions mostly brought them up first at the group meetings, and after such opinions were digested, they would then be brought up for debate at the Congress. This was why the Congress lasted for three weeks.

"What is a Communist Party?" This question was the most difficult to answer. The peasants held different conceptions from the city workers, for most of them had no knowledge about mass production by machinery. For this reason, the CCP comrades in this Soviet area often said, "A Communist Party is a political party of the poor." "A proletarian is one who is so poor that he has nothing." "Every poor man will be distributed a piece of land; this is communism." These explanations were obviously in line with the peasants' conception, but they are not in conformity with the original definition in Marxism-Leninism. We first intended to correct some of the incorrect points; but the more we explained, the more confused they became, so we just put up with such simple explanations.

I submitted a simply written political report to the Congress, in which I enumerated the immediate tasks of this Soviet area. I explained the important points of our future work from the angles of CCP policies, the Soviet and land revolution, and consolidating the Red Army. I made a special effort to explain the difference between the Red Army and the warlords and local bandits, and brought forth the demand that our army be built into an ironclad army that would truly serve the people and be capable of undertaking revolutionary tasks under the leadership of the CCP. I insisted that members of our army rectify such guerrilla or bandit practices as lack of respect for the Party and the Soviet, attacking local tyrants indiscriminantly, mistreatment of the fair sex, and seeking after their own interests and pleasure. I urged the cadres to set an example with their own conduct.

This question of correcting wrong guerrilla practices and enforcing strict discipline became a topic of heated discussion at the Congress. Many delegates were critical of the campaign launched some two months ago against the Kao-shan stockade, which resulted in a defeat with more than one thousand casualties. Some said that when our propaganda personnel explained to the people inside the stockade that we protected the interests of the peasants and so forth, they shouted back at us that we had attacked local tyrants at random, seized food from people who were not local tyrants in such and such places, raped the womenfolk in such and such places, and that our acts belied our words. And this was followed by a volley of stones cast upon us. Some said that the officers and men of the Red Army and the personnel of the Soviet had likewise committed undisciplined acts, and that the allegations made by the people inside the stockade were not entirely rumors engineered by the reactionaries, but that some were based on facts.

The Congress witnessed its most tense moments when criticisms were leveled at Hsü Chi-sheng. Shen Tse-min, in his speech, pointed out that the bad habits of warlords and local bandits could be found in the person of Hsü Chi-sheng in many respects. His attitude toward womenfolk in particular was extremely improper; he led a dissolute life and had many common-law wives. Shen asked Hsü, "Do any of your common-law wives have husbands of their own? Did you force them to marry you also? Isn't this kind of conduct a breach of discipline? Isn't this the hedonism pursued by local bandits? Isn't this an overbearing practice of the warlords? Are you worthy of being a member of the CCP and a high-ranking officer of the Red Army?"

This was the first time that such a high-ranking army officer in the Oyüwan area was openly taken to task at a formal meeting. In the face of such sharp criticism, Hsü Chi-sheng was ill-at-ease. He could only say that he had never raped any woman, but he admitted that he was profligate. He said that he had been a member of the CCP for a relatively long time, but that he had been stained by the evil habits of local bandits during several years of guerrilla operations. He vowed to correct such mistakes in the future, and asked the Congress to punish him for his wrongdoings.

The struggle within the Congress became sharper and sharper, and the scope of involvement was broadened accordingly. Tseng Chungsheng, former chairman of the branch office of the Military Committee, and Yü Tu-san, political commissar of the Army, were also involved in the surging struggle. They were criticized for having failed to correct Hsü's mistakes in time, and were therefore held responsible for conniving in his misconduct. Besides, they had also committed mistakes of a similar nature. A hotel merchant who had just moved to Hsin-chi from Ch'i-li-p'ing was also criticized because he was an expert "matchmaker." Such matters played a positive role in strengthening army discipline, and the general opinion was that these leaders would have to behave themselves in the future.

Finally, I stepped forward to end this struggle. I proposed to the Congress that our main concern was to make the comrades understand the serious nature of such mistakes and to work out a code of discipline to be followed by everyone; it was not our business to mete out there and then punishment for the comrades who had erred but who had expressed remorse and determination to make amends. Some comrades who had committed slight mistakes would be pardoned so long as they corrected them, so they did not need to be apprehensive.

On the basis of my proposal, the Congress then dedicated its efforts to building up a code of discipline. First of all, it was stipulated that those found guilty of raping a woman would be punished according to the law of the Soviet; in serious cases, the criminal might be sentenced to death. Those who committed other unlawful acts against the fair sex would be given a legal sanction according to the nature of each individual case. Apart from legal sanction, it was also stipulated that education should be conducted on an extensive scale to encourage legal marriages between men and women. It was also decided that lovers' chambers would be set up in the places where the Red Army was stationed and the Soviet government was located to accommodate husbands and wives as well as those who were truly in love with each other.

The Congress adopted certain regulations concerning the establishment of a revolutionary court and a workers' and peasants' supervisory committee under the Soviet government of the Oyüwan area. A military court was formed under the military committee, and a supervisory committee was formed under the CCP committee of the Oyüwan area. These organizations were charged with the responsibility of enforcing the disciplinary code.

We held that strict discipline should be enforced along with education by persuasion. We opposed sending the Peasants' Self-defense Army to the White areas to attack the local tyrants in order to solve the food shortage in the Soviet areas. We held that in case of necessity, only the Red Army might make a levy of grain from the local tyrants in the White areas, but that they should mobilize the poor people in those places to act in unison. We opposed attacking local tyrants at will, keeping what was seized from them instead of surrendering it to the Soviet government, and privately searching the wallets of prisoners. All these acts we considered to be unlawful. We required the people in the Soviet areas to respect the law of the Soviet. In particular, Red Army officers and men must not violate the law of the Soviet and take a disrespectful attitude toward the Soviet. We opposed any overbearing, repressive act on the part of the Soviet functionaries against the common people. We also opposed Party cadres issuing orders to the ordinary

Party members at will and forcing them to comply with their orders. We advocated democracy within the Party.

The problem of land was another important item on the agenda of the Congress. Shen Tse-min made a report to the Congress on this question and proposed a reallocation of land. He said that land in this area had generally been redistributed, but that the distribution was not carried out well. The main reasons for this were: (1) Land was distributed on the basis of labor productivity and the size of individual plots, without regard to the fertility of the soil. Besides, in most cases farm cattle, tools, timber forests, bamboo forests, and tea plantations had not been distributed. (2) When distribution was made, the masses had not been aroused to wage a struggle against the landlords and rich peasants, so that even though the landlords and rich peasants had been deprived of their political rights, in certain places they occupied dominant economic positions and retained their hidden political powers. (3) Land that had been distributed was not clearly demarcated. The markings set up wore away after a while, causing a great deal of confusion. It was therefore necessary to reallocate the lands and issue land-utilization certificates to the peasants. (4) The system of appointing caretakers for one's land had been introduced as a preferential treatment for members of the Red Army. This system had been abused. Besides the numerous Red Army personnel in the Soviet areas, the staff of the Soviet and members of the local armed forces also took advantage of this system and had their lands worked by the people. Consequently, the shortage of productive labor became more acute, and production was thus affected. We needed to tighten the "caretaker" system and reduce its scope.

The land policy of the CC of the CCP was to confiscate all land owned by landlords and distribute it equally among the poor peasants. Surplus land or leased land owned by rich peasants was also to be confiscated and redistributed. Theoretically speaking, equal distribution of land has nothing in common with socialism. The CC of the CCP was of the opinion that such a policy should be adopted during the democratic revolution of the bourgeoisie, for it would satisfy the land needs of the peasants, on the one hand, and arouse the broad masses of peasants to join the struggle, on the other. As a matter of fact, only the nationalization of land and socialization of agricultural production would be the starting point of socialism. The distribution of an equal portion of land to each peasant household merely changes the system of ownership from that of landlords and rich peasants to diversified ownership by poor peasants. Every peasant to whom land has been distributed is just a small owner.

Carrying out the policy of equal distribution of land was a very difficult job, so its implementation in the various Soviet areas was not entirely satisfactory despite the different approaches adopted. The main reason was that in the rural areas the classes were not clearly differentiated and it was extremely difficult to distinguish classes from a subjective point of view. Generally speaking, in China's countryside there were not many big landlords, but there were relatively more medium or small landlords, as land was distributed in a very piecemeal manner. Strictly speaking, one who had a tiny piece of land to lease was still a small landlord, but his living conditions were also poor, and some even had to hire themselves out to make a living. Whether a peasant was poor or not could not be judged merely by whether or not he owned any land. It was found only too frequently that a peasant who worked his own land and leased part of it was still living in poverty, whereas a tenant-peasant, though he had no land of his own, was relatively better off and had to hire farmhands to work the large tract of land that he held on lease. Besides, there were the merchants, peddlers, and handicraftsmen in the rural areas who also engaged in farming on the side. Some of them were regarded as peasants, others as merchants or handicraftsmen. In view of these complicated economic factors, it was really not easy to divide the people into landlords, rich peasants, middle peasants, poor peasants, and hired peasants.

Traditionally, Chinese peasants wanted to own land and settle down to a peaceful, happy life. To the poor peasants, who accounted for seventy percent of the rural population, the slogan "equal distribution of land" was truly attractive. However, the peasants in the Oyüwan area, who had gone through the ordeals of the revolution, had a deeper understanding of the meaning of this attractive slogan. When I had asked a number of peasants about their impressions of this policy, the majority of them said equal distribution of land would be useless if the Soviet were not firmly established. Some of them said a piece of land would not mean much to them without any farm cattle, tools, and capital. These simple answers hit the nail on the head. Without political security and the requisite economic conditions, the livelihood of the peasants could not be improved merely by the equal distribution of land.

The dogmatists in Moscow as well as those in the CC of the CCP boasted about the magic of this "equal distribution of land" policy. They held that if this policy were implemented properly, it would lead to the birth of a Soviet regime. In fact, without the anti-imperialist–anti-Nanking-government united front, success could not have come about so easily simply by relying on the land revolution. On the other hand, those who believed in the Li Li-san line considered military victory to be the key to all problems and did not give due attention to the policy of land distribution.

In the Congress we vigorously encouraged the comrades to whip up the enthusiasm of the peasants for the distribution of land. We pointed out that equal distribution of land had a close bearing on the consolidation of the Soviet government, and vice-versa. Only if the broad masses of peasants enthusiastically supported the distribution of land could the Soviet government be consolidated; and when the Soviet government was consolidated, the peasants would have better security for the land that had been allocated to them. Moreover, only by combining the forces produced from the land revolution in the various Soviet areas with the anti-imperialist, anti-Nanking forces in all parts of China, could the Soviet government achieve victory. We achieved considerable results from such efforts. Though we were unable to extend the land-distribution movement to the point that it swept across the whole region, we did build up the courage of the peasants in this Soviet area to take part in the land-distribution movement and to stand up against the anti-Communist forces.

The Congress decided to mobilize the masses to redistribute land according to the new regulations in all areas regardless of whether land distribution had previously been carried out or not. According to the new basis of distribution, land would be allocated according to the market value of crops reaped from it. Each poor peasant would be allocated a piece of land that could produce approximately the same amount of income (farmland and ordinary land, rich soil and poor soil were distributed together). Additionally, land distribution in this area had some fine traditions, such as: poor peasants and hired peasants received good land; there was no change in the lands of middle peasants; landlords and rich peasants received poor land; merchants and handicraftsmen to whom land was distributed had to work it themselves; one portion of land was allotted to each big household, and half a portion to each small household; and so forth.[8] The Congress decided to retain these arrangements.

Then there was some land in the villages which could not be totally distributed or was not easy to distribute, such as large tracts of forests, tea plantations, bamboo groves, reservoirs and other water-conservation installations, and large plots of uncultivated land. These were managed by the village Soviets and were called public fields and public lands of the Soviet. During the period of the Li Li-san line, these public fields and lands were organized into "collective farms." We did not approve of this method and were in favor of leasing them out or putting them under the management of cooperatives, the rents to be collected by the Soviet. The general principle was that the operators would get their due compensations, and what was left belonged to the Soviet.

The Congress also decided that farm cattle and tools should be distributed; but in view of the difficulty in distributing these things, some practical arrangements were adopted. Due to the shortages of farm cattle and tools, it was not easy to allocate an equal share to each peasant household, so we advocated joint ownership and joint utilization. If several households were joint owners of a cow, they should work out their own arrangements for feeding and using it. The method of labor exchange and mutual assistance later practiced in the Red areas was in the main developed from this system of joint ownership and utilization.

The way in which land was redistributed was that the village Soviet called a rally of peasants to examine the expediencies of the previous policy of equal distribution, and the land committee of the village Soviet would then make a final appraisal. In general, no change would be made on the lands which had been properly distributed, but those which were improperly distributed would be redistributed. To cope with the resistance put up by the landlords and rich peasants against such land reforms, the rally proposed to strengthen the poor-peasant association and, through the method of struggle, to force the landlords and rich peasants to hand over the lands, houses, farm cattle, and farm tools to be confiscated. But we did not adopt any measure designed to destroy the arrogance of landlords and rich peasants.

After the land had been distributed, the village Soviet prepared a land register and issued land-utilization certificates. Many rural delegates attending the Congress suggested the issuance of land-ownership certificates to the peasants to whom land had been allocated, so as to legalize their ownership on a permanent basis. But the presidium of the Congress held that since the Chinese Communists were going to go one step further and nationalize land, the issuance of land-ownership certificates would strengthen the peasants' conception of private ownership. Finally, the Congress adopted a decision about the issuance of land-utilization certificates. It stipulated that during the democratic revolution of the bourgeoisie, the peasants had the right to utilize the lands on a permanent basis. All peasants holding land-utilization certificates were entitled to use the lands freely, but they might not lease or sell them.

The rigid regulation adopted at the Congress that land could not be leased or sold left much to be desired. Needless to say, land is the principal asset of the peasants. If they could not sell or lease their lands freely, the utilization value of the land was greatly impaired. Besides, the peasants who had acquired their lands through distribution were inclined to feel that even though they could work on their piece of land, they could not dispose of it freely. The main reason for not allowing the land to be sold or leased freely was to prevent the peasants from losing their lands again, thus creating new landlords and rich peasants. But this was the natural trend of economic development, and it could not be stopped. In fact, some of the peasants to whom land had been distributed defied this decision and leased or transferred their utilization rights through private arrangements.

On the other hand, we adopted a flexible policy on the question of stripping the landlords and rich peasants of their political rights. Generally speaking, landlords and rich peasants were targets to be aimed at. The Congress stressed that elements with landlords or rich-peasant backgrounds must not be allowed to worm their way into the Soviet and the Red Army. But we made some exceptions. Those who hailed from landlord or rich-peasant families but had rendered meritorious service in the Red Army or were members of the CCP or functionaries of the Soviet with satisfactory service records were considered as having been revolutionized and therefore were not to be discriminated against. And those who supported the Soviet and the land revolution, even though they hailed from landlord or rich-peasant families, were also entitled to the rights of an ordinary citizen.

The Congress also adopted concrete measures with regard to reducing the scope of the "caretaker" system. A peasant household whose able-bodied men had joined the Red Army, and whose ability to work the fields consequently had been lost or reduced, needed the service of other peasant households in its neighborhood to work the fields. But the current system of enlisting such services was chaotic. The Congress stipulated that this system was applicable only to Red Army soldiers who were entitled to preferential treatment, and the service enlisted under this system should, in most cases, be of a supplementary nature. In other words, the labor force of soldiers' families must also be used in working the fields; the "caretakers" only provided them assistance and did not do all the work for them. Those who needed the service and those who provided the service must determine when and where a supplementary labor force was needed through mutual negotiations, so that there be no wastage of the labor force of the latter while the requirements of the former were met. No functionary of the Soviet or member of the local armed forces (that is, those who were not separated from the production front) might enlist service under this system, but they were encouraged to seek assistance from the peasants on a reciprocal basis to solve their labor shortage.

In addition, we adopted a unified system of graduated taxation for agriculture to replace the former informal method of levying and borrowing grain from the peasants. Under this system of graduated taxation, those peasant households with an average per-capita grain output of four piculs or below would be exempted from paying the tax; those with an output exceeding this allowance by one to three piculs would be taxed at the rate of 8 percent; those with a higher output would pay a higher tax, so that those with an output forty-five piculs in excess of the allowance would pay the tax at the rate of 43 percent.[9] (For example, a family of five with an output of twenty piculs was exempted from the tax; one with an output of twenty-two piculs would pay a tax of one peck, six pints, or 0.73 percent of the total output; one with an output of forty-five piculs would pay the tax at the rate of 35 percent, or nine piculs, two pecks, and five pints—a little over 20 percent of the total output; one with an output of seventy piculs would pay twenty piculs, five pecks, or a little over 30 percent; and so forth.) Production of miscellaneous grain crops was free from tax or taxed at a reduced rate. Rich peasants had to pay a 5-percent surtax on top of the regular rates, while dependents of servicemen or martyrs were either exempted altogether or paid at reduced rates.

While the CCP Congress was being held, the various leadership organs in the Oyüwan area were undergoing reorganization. The Congress elected a provincial executive committee for the CCP Oyüwan area that consisted of more than twenty members. In addition to members of the former Special Committee who held concurrent posts as members of the Provincial Committee, about half of the industrial and agricultural cadres were elected to serve on the committee. Liu Ch'i, a worker on the Peking-Hankow Railway, and Kao Ching-t'ing, a leader of the local peasants, were among those elected. Shen Tse-min was elected secretary of the Provincial Committee; Hsü Li-ch'ing and Kuo Shu-shen took charge of propaganda and organization work; while the Standing Committee of the Provincial Executive Committee was made up of the secretary, the directors of propaganda and organization, and several responsible persons of the Soviet government, including Wang P'ing-chang, Cheng Wei-san, and Chou Ch'un-ch'üan. Under the Standing Committee were the propaganda and organization departments, the secretariat, the workers' and women's commissions, and so forth.

The Oyüwan branch of the Military Committee of the CC of the CCP was also reorganized at that time. It was renamed the Oyüwan Military Affairs Committee and was placed under the direct supervision of the Oyüwan branch of the CC of the CCP. The members of the Committee were myself, Shen Tse-min, Ts'ai Shen-hsi, Hsü Hsiang-ch'ien, Tseng Chung-sheng, Wang P'ing-chang, Cheng Wei-san, Hsü Li-ch'ing, Kuo Shu-shen, K'uang Chi-hsün, Chou Ch'un-ch'üan, Ch'en Ch'ang-hao, and so forth. I was chairman of the committee, with Ts'ai Shen-hsi as chief-of-staff and Ch'en Ch'ang-hao as director of the Political Department. The Fourth Red Army also changed command, with Hsü Hsiang-ch'ien as commander and Tseng Chung-sheng as political commissar. K'uang Chi-hsün, former commander of the Fourth Red Army, was reassigned as commander of the Seventy-third Division (originally named the Thirteenth Division, but soon changed to the Seventy-third Division). Yü Tu-san, former political commissar of the same army, was reassigned as director of the Workers' and Peasants' Supervisory Committee of the Soviet government.

The components of the Oyüwan branch of the CC of the CCP were almost the same as those of the Military Affairs Committee. It was a policy-making organization of which I was secretary. In this capacity, I assumed direct control of the Oyüwan Provincial Executive Committee and the Military Affairs Committee, and no other executive organ was set up. Originally this branch of the CC played a very extensive role. It was charged with the responsibility of developing the Party and Soviet organizations as well as the regular Red Army and guerrilla forces north of the Yangtze River. However, the fact that its operations never went beyond the jurisdiction of the Oyüwan area indicated that its operations were of little avail.

Although our organization had expanded, our organizational power was still very weak. We were extremely short of manpower and every responsible cadre had to hold several positions concurrently. Work was exceedingly heavy, while the cultural level of the Party members was very low. When our decisions were transmitted to the county-level organizations, they often got stuck there. The staffs of the Party and Soviet organizations in the rural areas sometimes could not even understand the decisions of the higher levels. Because of an extreme shortage of intellectuals, it was often necessary to implement an order by having a committee member of the superior organ go to the villages on foot, to explain it in detail to the responsible members of the subordinate organs. Hence, work efficiency was very low and decisions were often carried out at a great discount.

The Provincial Committee was anxious to solve this problem. It enlisted the services of some capable cadres to strengthen the district and county committee organizations under it. It absorbed new Party members from among the poor peasants and the hired peasants, and exerted great efforts in training and educating them. Short-term training classes, continuation classes, and classes for learning to read were set up in the Party school under the Provincial Committee. This committee also encouraged the county committees to run Party schools of lower grades. The primary schools in the Soviet areas, although they were called Lenin Primary Schools, were very backward in content. Most of the comrades had to be given lectures before they could understand such publications as "Party Life" published by the Provincial Committee.

Shen Tse-min at one time wondered how much effort and how long it would take to elevate such a primitive Party organization to the level of the Bolsheviks. He once said jokingly that this was a task similar to that undertaken by "the foolish old man who removed the mountain bushel by bushel!" In fact, those Party members and cadres who lacked a clear conception of communism and general knowledge were imbued with some old concepts, superstitions, and habits. Most of the honest Party members relayed orders blindly without thoroughly understanding them, and often resorted to coercion and authoritarianism. Some of them acted like a *ti-pao* (bailiff) and made use of their authority for their own selfish ends. For example, in distributing land, they reserved the better pieces for themselves. It was rather difficult to deal with such matters. Being either too strict or too indulgent could cause trouble.

Time was pressing for steps to be taken to deal with such important matters as adopting a guiding principle for military affairs and effecting a reshuffle of the leading cadres. We were of the opinion that it was our immediate military duty to consolidate and expand this Oyüwan Soviet area and to take appropriate actions in cooperation with the Red Army in other Soviet areas. We planned to break through the obstructions to join together the two Soviet areas in the Hupeh-Honan and Honan-Anhwei border regions; to establish a new Soviet area embracing Yingshan, Lo-t'ien, and Yi-shui, where our guerrillas had done some groundwork; and to link this new Soviet area with the other two to form a more extensive Oyüwan Soviet area. In this way we could pose a threat to the Yangtze River traffic routes from Hankow to Kiu-kiang and provide effective support for the Red Army in Kiangsi. We could also establish a relationship of interdependence with the Red Army in western Hunan and Hupeh. At that time the Red Army cadres and the comrades at large were greatly inspired by this plan.

The promotion of Hsü Hsiang-ch'ien to commander of the Fourth Red Army was another thing that inspired the cadres. The comrades were also deeply impressed by the criticism of warlord and bandit behavior among members of the Red Army that culminated in the censure of Hsü Chi-sheng, who exemplified such tendencies. They felt that it was a very proper thing for us to boldly promote to leading military positions those whose thinking and behavior were regarded as correct. On the other hand, we did not repudiate those comrades who had committed errors. For example, Tseng Chung-sheng, who was known to have taken a conciliatory attitude toward the Li Li-san line, remained as political commissar of the Red Army, while Hsü Chi-sheng, even though he was censured, retained the position of commander of the Eleventh Division. These facts indicated that we only insisted that comrades correct their mistakes, and once they had done so, no disciplinary action would be taken against them. The comrades seemed to agree that K'uang Chi-hsün was not a capable leader. His new assignment as commander of the Seventy-third Division, which was responsible for forming a new division by reorganizing the local armed forces and for further expanding it to the Twenty-fifth Army Corps, was nevertheless a very important assignment. Besides, K'uang's division was placed under the direct command of the Military Affairs Committee, so that he would not feel too embarrassed to have to take orders from his former subordinate Hsü Hsiang-ch'ien. The comrades in general felt that such an arrangement was the result of thoughtfulness and careful consideration.

I explained to some of the military cadres the significance of these measures and called upon them to follow the decisions of their superiors, strengthen Party leadership and political work in the Army, conduct training and education on a broad scale, oppose the bad habits of guerrillas, and rigorously implement the military plan so as to win victory. Such warlordish and bandit tendencies of the Red Army were gradually rectified after a prolonged and extensive struggle. Our efforts at the Congress were only a good start in that struggle.

It was a still more difficult job to establish a Soviet government. Most of the people in this area had no idea what a Soviet government was; their understanding of this question was quite amusing. A small number of people had the idea that the Soviet was a government by workers and peasants, and that "Su-wei-ai" (Soviet) was the Chinese translation of a Russian word. Some said that the Soviet government was founded by the Comintern, which had its headquarters in Moscow, and that the headquarters in China was in Kiangsi, the Soviet government of the Oyüwan area being only a branch of it. What was even more amusing was that when I discussed this question with some ordinary comrades, someone ventured to say that "the Soviet was another name for Su Chao-cheng, the chairman of the Soviet government during the Canton Uprising. That is why our government is named after him." Another one said in refutation, "Comrade Su Chao-cheng has passed away. Su Wei-ai (Soviet) is the son of Su Chao-cheng. In the past when an emperor died, his son succeeded to the throne. Now our chairman Su Chao-cheng has passed away and is succeeded by his son Su Wei-ai. That is why our government is called the Soviet government." In fact, the term "Soviet," which was transliterated from Russian, was much too difficult for the ordinary peasants to understand.

Needless to say, the name of a government could have a great influence on the people. It was regrettable that although the Soviet government had been established in this area for about three years, its meaning was still not understood by the people. We may draw an inference from this as to how strange the name of this government was in the broad countryside of China. Neither was it understood by the majority of workers in the urban areas. The people in general felt that this was a name that did not exist in the old-time Chinese vocabulary, but was imported from Russia. Since they did not understand the true meaning of this government, they had very little sympathy for it.

Before the opening of the Party Congress, we also held a Soviet Congress (other meetings such as the CYC Congress, the Women's Congress, and many conferences on specialized subjects were also held, but I will not go into detail about them here). This Congress was opened on July 1, 1931. So that people would understand it better, we called it "The Congress of Workers, Peasants, and Soldiers." Most of the delegates attending the Congress were not elected, but were nominated by the Soviet government, civic bodies, and Red Army units at various levels. The Congress also leaned heavily toward certain emergency mobilization work, such as the strengthening of the Soviet organization at various levels, the redistribution of land, ways to solve the food shortage, and implementation of certain financial and economic policies.

In this Congress, most of the delegates focused their attention on the question of food. Many delegates criticized the former policy of borrowing grain from the peasants as improper, and they brought forward facts that showed the confusion created by this policy. Some peasant families that were enthusiastic about the revolution had their grain borrowed; but when they suffered from starvation, they could not get it back. This had dampened the peasants' enthusiasm for the revolution and had affected their feelings about production. The responsible members of the Party and the Soviet admitted that they had made a serious mistake in this respect. We pointed out at the Congress that neither the method of levying grain which had been practiced here before nor the method of borrowing grain which was introduced later was desirable. This was the evil influence left over from the Li Li-san line. In the future we should change to the method of graduated taxation on agricultural production.

The Second Soviet Congress convened in Hsin-chi on November 7, 1931. It was a formal meeting attended by 397 representatives of workers, peasants, and soldiers, who were chosen in an election in which 1.7 million eligible voters in the Soviet areas participated. The workers' and peasants' organizations in places adjacent to this area also sent about two hundred representatives to attend the Congress as observers. This Congress laid the foundation for the establishment of the Soviet government in the Oyüwan area.

The Congress issued a formal declaration enumerating the tasks of this government and drafted a provisional outline of organizational principles.[10] On the basis of these principles, responsible members of the People's Council and of the various committees under it were elected. Kao Ching-t'ing, who had formerly been a peasant, was elected chairman of the Soviet government; and Wang P'ing-chang, the former chairman, was elected chairman of the People's Council. There were twelve organizations under the People's Council, namely, the Foreign Affairs, Military Affairs, Communications, Finance and Economy, Internal Affairs, Land, Food, Cultural and Educational, and Labor departments, the Revolutionary Court, the Political Security Bureau, and the Workers' and Peasants' Supervisory Committee. The Soviet organization for the counties and villages was relatively simple. Normally, a county Soviet government consisted of Land, Finance, and Economy departments, and such other departments as were necessary, in addition to the military district command.

The Soviet government of this area was only a provincial-level local government, hence there was no question of drawing up the basic laws. This government was only concerned with the question of drawing up regulations for the implementation of regional policies. Many important regulations, such as agricultural, commercial, and revenue regulations, and regulations governing land distribution, the military district system, the judicial system, and so forth, were drawn up and adopted by the Congress.

To sum up briefly, the focus of our efforts at that time was to set up a proper Soviet government and to implement policies and regulations smoothly. We called on the Army and the people to respect the authority of the government. If the people failed to comply with the laws and regulations of the government, then they would not be able to get rid of the bad habits of warlords and bandits. In particular, the senior officers of the Red Army must respect the laws and regulations of the government; they had no special privileges, and their social status was just the same as that of ordinary men. In the face of discipline, all men are equal. Only the common will of the Party could lead the Soviet government, yet the Party should not make light of the authority of the Soviet government. All political directives were issued by the government in accordance with the decisions of the Party.

The more I learned from practical experience about the affairs of the Soviet government of the Oyüwan area, the more I worried about its future. I felt that the existence of this regime depended primarily on the disunited, confused, and cruel rule of the KMT government. The path of development of this Soviet government was also full of stumbling blocks. The organizational power of the CCP was weak; the growth of the Red Army was retarded by lack of supplies; and the land revolution could not break through the antagonism between the Red and the White areas and spread to a broader area. It would require long-term efforts to overcome the many difficulties confronted by the Soviet area. Moreover, the strength of the enemy was far superior to ours, and there was no way for us to destroy it quickly.

As far as I was concerned, the CCP's land policy had its fundamental shortcomings. We could not depend on it to arouse mass struggles from the grass roots up. Moreover, the policy of developing the Red Army through guerrilla warfare also failed to bring about quick results due to various unfavorable conditions. Also, the Soviet government was built on too narrow a foundation. This regime was confined to the scope of land revolution on some small tracts of land, and it was hard to win the understanding and sympathy of the broad masses of workers and peasants. Moreover, it had little, if any, appeal to the intellectuals and petty bourgeoisie of the country, and it failed to establish proper connections with the anti-imperialist movement centering in the cities.

After we were informed of the Japanese invasion and occupation of the three northeastern provinces on September 18, I was convinced that the Soviet movement under the leadership of the CCP was drifting farther and farther away from the anti-imperialist course. The Sixth Congress of the CCP resolved that the anti-imperialist movement and the land revolution were the two paramount tasks, but the Soviet government was inclined to lay too much emphasis on the land revolution. I came to think about Stalin, and how he showed a lack of far-sightedness in his guidance. The ideas put forward by Bukharin at the Sixth Congress of the CCP—that we should take full account of the anti-imperialist movement and not destroy the role of the petty bourgeoisie in the revolution—proved to be more correct.

I imagined that changing the name of the Soviet government to "People's Government" might lead to a more hopeful future. The "People's Government" I had in mind would still be led by the CCP, with the worker and peasant forces as its mainstay; but its political platform should be broader, so that the intellectuals and petty bourgeoisie who

were opposed to the Japanese aggression could be called upon to cooperate with us. If we stayed away from the Anti-Japanese War of
Resistance, then the people would consider this an indication that we
had no concern for the future of the country and that we dedicated ourselves to the land revolution which was injurious to the national destiny.
I brought up this point with my colleague more than once, and I am
going to mention it again in subsequent chapters. However, it was
beyond my ability to make such a fundamental change. The fundamental plan for this Soviet movement was approved by Moscow and the CC
of the CCP, and it had been put into effect in various places. The
Oyüwan area was only one of the places where this plan had been put
into effect. It would be bad and virtually impossible for us to make an
arbitrary change.

History shows that the Soviet movement led by the Chinese Communists was merely a bold experiment. In this movement, the Chinese
Communists brought into play the spirit of withstanding hardships in
struggle, and they received an important lesson on how to lead the
government and the Army. But the movement itself was a failure. It
was not destroyed by the KMT, but rather we changed its course at the
beginning of the Anti-Japanese War of Resistance. The Stalin formula
of the Soviet movement, which emphasized land revolution, was the
fundamental source of the Li Li-san line and all left-deviationist
tendencies within the CCP. Because this movement itself was a deviation to the Left, it gave rise to the military adventurist ideas of Li Li-san.
Other dogmatists just went around in circles on the basis of this formula.
Because I was among the first ones to find out the basic defects of this
movement, I was later branded as a "right-deviationist" or "renegade."
But I am satisfied with my belief that my point of view at that time
came from my sincere concern for the Chinese revolution.

The Purge

The struggle against the warlord-bandit mentality at the Hsin-chi
Party Congress had aroused the overt or covert opposition of those who
were criticized on the occasion; and the snowballing of resistance finally
touched off a sweeping purge campaign. Subsequently, certain elements
that had had secret dealings with the KMT's Reorganizationist group
were purged during the campaign. The onslaught of such a political

storm and the internal and external difficulties confronting us in those days were interrelated.

During the session of the Party Congress, opinions at the leadership level were frequently at variance. Shen Tse-min's attitude obviously was of the radical type: he believed that various kinds of punishment should be meted out to deal with those comrades who had blundered. He was not adept at handling problems in the light of practical conditions, but indulged in quoting Marxism-Leninism and resolutions of the CC of the CCP in criticizing errors in the concepts and conduct of the ordinary comrades. Even during discussions on military strategy and tactics, he ventured the opinion that the Fourth Red Army was not capable of fulfilling its mission. This remark of his aroused dissatisfaction among the comrades to varying degrees; they felt that his ideas were either too radical or somewhat amateurish.

But Shen Tse-min was by no means a stubborn person, for he had openly admitted that he had not had enough experience and that he needed to learn; actually, he was already cutting down on his leftist phrasemongering. From time to time it had become necessary for me to tone down his radical point of view at meetings; sometimes we engaged in open debates, although invariably Shen Tse-min considered it advisable to withdraw or revise his ideas. Nevertheless, the ordinary comrades couldn't help forming the impression that there were differences of opinion at the leadership level.

As the Party Congress was nearing adjournment, at Tseng Chung-sheng's suggestion, I had a heart-to-heart talk with him, Ts'ai Shen-hsi, and Hsü Chi-sheng. Both Tseng Chung-sheng and Hsü Chi-sheng seized this opportunity to give free vent to their pent-up grudges.

Sadly, Hsü Chi-sheng said that he would mend his ways. Unfortunately, his errors had been mercilessly exposed at the Party Congress. The military delegates who attended the Congress would inevitably spread reports of his errors to the troops, and his prestige as a commander was bound to be affected. He thanked me for placing my trust in him, and expressed his willingness to return to the front and redeem his mistakes with good deeds. But we couldn't help worrying that Shen Tse-min would not think of his errors with an understanding heart.

Tseng Chung-sheng was the next to speak. He fully endorsed the various resolutions passed at the Congress, and pledged to carry them out faithfully. He was, however, rather critical of Shen Tse-min's ideas, which he considered impractical, and the latter's indulgence in indiscriminately putting "caps" on the heads of veterans who had operated for a long time in this area. And naturally he resented Shen Tse-min's criticism of him; he also felt that it was unfair for the latter to censure Hsü Chi-sheng at the Party Congress.

I availed myself of this opportunity to offer lengthy explanations to these two ranking cadres who were under attack, and I tried to soothe their feelings. I pointed out that in the face of a formidable enemy, we should unite ourselves and concentrate our efforts on winning victory, and we should guard against petty grudges. In principle, errors should be criticized, while lack of proper techniques in making criticism was only of secondary importance. The primary objective of the latest Party Congress was to oppose the rightist warlord-bandit mentality and the bureaucratic tendency, as well as the leftist remnants of the Li Li-san line. It was not right to switch off to another line of thought by counter-criticizing Shen Tse-min. At worst, you could only say that he lacked experience and that occasionally he could not express himself properly, but this was understandable. Meanwhile, I singled out for commendation their ready compliance with the Party resolutions, and encouraged them to work hard for their future.

The veteran comrade-in-arms Ts'ai Shen-hsi was even more resourceful in soothing the troubled minds of Tseng and Hsü. First of all, he felt that he bore the inescapable responsibility for having failed to help them correct their errors early enough. It was an excellent thing that they were earnest about mending their ways. Furthermore, rectification of accumulated wrongs required vigorous efforts, so that it was a lucky thing that they had gone through the latest relentless struggle that had made it possible to rectify their errors. They should be no means let personal pride destroy the significance of the criticism of their errors. Without the latest criticism, our future would be like a "blind alley." Criticism had, however, exposed our shortcomings. If everyone wanted to make an earnest effort to mend his ways, the future of the Party and the individuals concerned was bound to be bright. Thus, the recent Party Congress had done nothing to dishearten us, but had rescued the Party and us. Next, he said that he was fully confident that Comrade Kuo-t'ao was capable of holding steady the helm of the Party, and that Comrade Tse-min would learn from experience; all must, without hesitation, rectify our mistakes and unite ourselves for the sake of the common struggle.

Visibly moved, both Tseng and Hsü broke into smiles and unanimously pledged that they would return to the front without grudges to exert their efforts in carrying out the Party's resolution. Both Ts'ai Shen-hsi and I were very pleased with the result, believing that most of the lurking internal worries had been removed. Unfortunately, the subsequent development of events caught us by surprise.

We didn't want to let the protracted meeting delay our military action. Shortly after the conclusion of the Party Congress in mid July, Hsü Hsiang-ch'ien and Tseng Chung-sheng, newly appointed commander and political commissar of the Fourth Red Army respectively, left with their officers and men for the front. Leaving Pai-ch'üeh-yuan for Ying-shan via Chin-chia-chai, they were prepared to destroy the enemy troops operating in Ying-shan, Lo-t'ien Yi-shui, Kuang-chi, and Huang-mei, where they attempted to expand the Soviet area northward in order eventually to merge their area with the originally existing Oyüwan region. Meanwhile, K'uang Chi-hsün and his unit remained at Pai-ch'üeh-yuan to organize local armed forces into the Seventy-third Division. At that time he had one thousand or so men under his command, and he was setting up the First Regiment of the division. This unit was what remained, after the departure of the Fourth Red Army, to defend the Soviet area there.

After the departure of the Fourth Red Army, the enemy troops naturally seized the opportunity to press toward the borders of the area, and our men began to feel increasing pressure from all sides. Quite frequently, enemy troops were spotted operating only twenty to thirty li north of Hsin-chi. The militia forces of the White Army, perhaps aware of the strong local armed units in the Soviet area, dared not penetrate into our area, but they certainly left no stone unturned in carrying out peripheral harassment. They drove away farm cattle, plundered grain, murdered able-bodied men, and even raped and abducted women. This situation forced our local forces to be constantly on the alert, and much of our energy was used up in coping with the emergency.

Besides, this Soviet area of ours was still under the enemy blockade that cut the area off from all kinds of publications and news. We could not maintain contact with any other Soviet area, and our communication with the CC of the CCP in Shanghai had practically been paralyzed. The messenger who escorted me into the Soviet area never returned after his second departure for Hankow; most likely he was killed. In order to get some sort of publications, we frequently had to send a special service detachment into the White area for that purpose; and sometimes human lives were lost in such operations.

We had no idea whether the CC of the CCP was still in Shanghai or had moved to the Kiangsi Soviet area; we were very worried about the safety of our nerve center. Ku Shun-chang, who had directed me safely to Hankow, was arrested on the very day that I took a car to proceed toward the Soviet area. Ku, the Secret-Service Chief of the CCP, who controlled all secret communications between the Party's CC and all of the Soviet areas, had suddenly appeared in Hankow under the disguise of a great magician, but KMT agents had finally managed to see through his cover. It seemed that he was about to betray the CCP to save his own life; he surrendered. It was in Hankow that he divulged to the highest KMT authorities all the secrets he had learned about the CCP. It was reported that Li-chia-chi was placed under special curfew that night to facilitate their search for me and Ch'en Ch'ang-hao. Presumably they were acting on the basis of Ku Shun-chang's confession. Shortly afterwards he was brought to Nanking to be interrogated personally by Chiang Kai-shek.

The defection of Ku Shun-chang shocked the Chinese Communists in those days. The CC of the CCP in Shanghai was soon informed of the case, so that it acted early enough to avoid still greater loss. But the case was serious enough to cause great confusion in the Party's CC and all local organizations; all offices and quarters were moved to new places, and most key personnel were completely reshuffled to ward off raids by KMT agents. Yün Tai-ying, who had already been imprisoned, but whose identity was still unknown to KMT agents, was unfortunately identified and executed because of Ku Shun-chang's testimony. Quite a few others were also executed on clues provided by Ku Shun-chang. In reprisal, the CC of the CCP ordered brutal treatment of Ku Shun-chang's dependents in Shanghai, which resulted in total liquidation of the members of Ku's family.

This incident also created an adverse effect on operations in the Oyüwan Soviet area. The plan calling for transfer to this area of large numbers of cadres by the Party CC had to be dropped. Following me and Shen Tse-min to this area were a few cadres including, for instance, Ch'en Keng, who replaced Hsü Hsiang-ch'ien as commander of the Twelfth Division; Li Teh, who was appointed chief staff officer and later was promoted to chief-of-staff of the Military Affairs Committee; Fu Chung, director of the Political Department of the Military Affairs Committee; Huang Ch'ao, secretary-general of the Military Affairs Committee; Chu Kuang, chief of the Propaganda Section of the Political Department; and three radio technicians including Wang Tzu-kang—a total of less than twenty. They arrived at different times, and their journey was even tougher than ours. Some had to make use of the local CCP organizations in Hsin-yang, Honan, and Shou-hsien, Anhwei, to reach their destination through circuitous routes; while others simply tried their luck by breaking through the enemy's line.

Secondly, the incident made it impossible for us to set up a communications network between the Party CC, the various local organizations, and the Soviet areas. Establishing radio communication was a vital part of this plan. We did our very best to train radio technicians and workers, but the radio equipment and supplies that were urgently needed could not be sent to us as a result of disrupted communication lines. Our secret codes were lost in a battle involving the Hunan-Hupeh-Kiangsi Red Army. We couldn't even get a single radio receiving and transmitting set till the end of that year. Several months had elapsed before we finally worked out a new set of not very reliable secret codes with the Kiangsi Soviet area. As to land communications lines, we never could maintain smooth operations throughout that period. The Party CC kept warning us about the grave nature of Ku Shun-chang's defection, cautioning us not to rely on the remaining communications lines, not even those that had never been known to Ku Shun-chang.

The pressure on us kept increasing. We heard a rumor that Hsiang Chung-fa, secretary of the Party CC, had been arrested, but we had no idea when the arrest had taken place, whether it had anything to do with Ku Shun-chang's defection, and how many other comrades were involved. We had the impression that both Hsiang Chung-fa's reaction after his arrest and the adverse effect on the Party CC were very discouraging; we sensed that the CC was in grave danger, and we could not rule out the possibility of its being totally destroyed. We tried to encourage ourselves that we would keep up the struggle even without the leadership of the CC.

We were not able to get any reliable news about the Party CC until the spring of 1932. The news disclosed that Chou En-lai, Ch'in Pang-hsien, and Chang Wen-t'ien had managed to reach Juichin, the Red capital in the Kiangsi Soviet area in August, 1931. The Politburo of the CC of the CCP continued to function there. On November 7, 1931, the

First All-China Soviet Congress was held at Juichin, where the central government of the Chinese Soviet Republic was proclaimed. Mao Tse-tung was elected chairman, while Hsiang Ying and I were elected vice-chairmen. At that time the Central Soviet area in Kiangsi scored some military victories which resulted in our breaking through the KMT's Third Encirclement Campaign. Particularly important was the group defection of some twenty thousand men of the Twenty-sixth Kuomintang Army under Sun Lien-chung's command, which considerably strengthened the Red Army in Kiangsi.

After the Party CC moved to the Kiangsi Soviet area, the strength of the CCP began to spread into the various major Soviet areas, and our work in the wide White area was relatively weakened. This was mentioned in the CC's letter to us. It admitted that work in the White area would become more difficult for some time, especially after Ku Shun-chang's defection and the arrest of Hsiang Chung-fa. We were also cautioned in the letter not to overestimate the trustworthiness of the Shanghai branch of the CC of the CCP and the communications line under its control; we must guard against infiltration of the enemy.

Due to a temporary blackout of news, reports of the victory in the Kiangsi Soviet area took a long time to reach us. On the other hand, the enemy invariably played up any bad news about us to step up their propaganda offensive. Enemy propaganda said that the CC of the CCP had been destroyed and that Chou En-lai had already surrendered to the enemy. By taking advantage of trade between the Red and White areas, the enemy dispatched agents into the Red area to spread rumors, either saying that the KMT had amassed troops with airplanes and artillery in preparation for launching a concentrated attack at the Soviet area, or carrying out activities to weaken relations between the people and the Soviet regime, urging them to defect to the KMT. These methods, though of questionable effectiveness, proved fairly useful in undermining public confidence in the future of the highly unstable Soviet area.

Internal difficulties in the Soviet area simply defied description. Take, for instance, the problem of diseases, which had at times caused greater losses than the enemy could inflict on us. Our sanitary conditions were very bad. The area was always infested with the much-cursed four vermin, namely, the fly, mosquito, bed bug, and louse; and malaria, dysentery, and skin diseases were also prevalent. Many workers had to keep working while suffering from malaria. The long absence of medical treatment finally compelled our workers to ignore such diseases altogether. Food was generally poor and without much nourishment. We managed to survive on little more than coarse assorted grains and peanuts; we had few vegetables, and meat was hard to obtain.

In mid July, 1931, just when the Party's Soviet Congress was about to adjourn, I fell ill; and this happened to be the most protracted illness of my life. Actually I had contracted malaria while the Congress was still in session, but as soon as my temperature was back to normal, I had forced myself to work as usual. Shortly afterwards, my body's lack of resistance resulted in my suffering from dysentery, too; worse yet, I vomited anything that I swallowed, both food and medicine. Subsequently I was so debilitated that I became bedridden. Both Western doctors and Chinese herb doctors were solicited for help, and all kinds of formulas and ready prescriptions had been tried to little avail. My illness probably would have posed no technical problem in a modern city with adequate medical facilities, but it was something else in a remote and primitive rural area where medical supplies were very hard to get. In fact, I almost lost my life. I blamed myself for being so physically weak, and I worried a great deal about the heavy responsibilities on my shoulders in this state of emergency. But worries only aggravated my illness. For more than two months I struggled to survive, and eventually I was on the road to recovery.

My illness naturally had some adverse effects on our operations in this area. Those around me worried about me, and even seriously considered what they should do if I failed to pull through; and those at the front appeared greatly perturbed. Afterwards, Tseng Chung-sheng frankly admitted that when I was critically ill, he had begun to worry about whether the power of leadership in this area would eventually be taken over by Shen Tse-min, whom he abhorred, so that he even made plans to take the Fourth Red Army away from this Soviet area.

My illness had not, however, affected or disrupted the activities of the branch of the Party CC and the Military Affairs Committee in the Oyüwan area. My posts as secretary of the above-mentioned Party branch and as chairman of the Military Affairs Committee, respectively, were taken over temporarily by Shen Tse-min and Ts'ai Shen-hsi. At that time we conveyed the decisions made at the Congress to the local levels and adopted the method of carrying on the struggle, on the one hand, and the method of persuasion, on the other, to rectify our past errors; consequently, only a very small number of persons were punished. But, there had developed an undercurrent within the Party structure that opposed the leadership of the branch of the Party CC.

This undercurrent originated from Chin-chia-chai. Right after the Congress, certain leaders of the Local Committee of the Yüwan border region began to spread words that were critical of the Congress. They said, "Trifling issues were made use of at the mass meeting to victimize the veteran cadres; new cadres opposed those who had worked in this area for a long time; natives of Huang-an and Ma-ch'eng opposed natives of Anhwei Province," and so forth. They derogatorily described Shen Tse-min as a raw and inexperienced returned student from Russia who did not know better than to invoke the Party CC's name to suppress the local authorities, when it was questionable whether the CC of the CCP even existed. After they had been told of my illness, they appeared even more outspoken in showing their distrust of Shen Tse-min. The branch of the Party CC felt that these anti-Party utterances had been spread by Hsü Chi-sheng. For one thing, while passing through Chin-chia-chai, Hsü Chi-sheng never openly pledged his compliance to the decisions made at the Congress. On the contrary, he said that indulgence in women and wine was a natural characteristic of a hero, thereby dropping a broad hint that he did not like the way he had been criticized at the mass meeting.

After the Fourth Red Army moved up to the front at Ying-shan in mid July, it routed the KMT troops stationed in that area one after another, capturing altogether some two thousand rifles and men. And in the wake of victory, the Fourth Red Army occupied the two county seats of Ying-shan and Yi-shui. In early August, Tseng Chung-sheng reported from the front that the area was fertile and prosperous and that the Red Army was well fed; at the moment, the report said, our men were collecting cloth in the city of Yi-shui to solve the problem of winter uniforms. He also mentioned that according to his sources at the front, KMT troops were launching a mopping-up operation against the Red Army units in the Kiangsi Soviet area, and the situation there was very critical. The Fourth Red Army was getting ready to move into the area of Kuang-chi and Huang-mei and, if circumstances permitted, to cut off communications on the Yangtze River. If the situation developed in their favor, they also wanted to cross the Yangtze River in the vicinity of Wu-hsueh and then move directly toward the northwestern part of Kiangsi to join with the Red Army forces there to destroy the KMT mopping-up troops.

On the other hand, a report from a member of the provincial Party committee who went with the Army contained quite different information. That report said that some senior cadres in the Fourth Red Army had suggested expanding activities toward the south after crossing the Yangtze River, and it wondered if the branch of the Party CC had changed its original plan. It criticized the inefficiency of the Fourth Red Army's political work, saying that it was only interested in solving the problem of material supplies for the Army, but neglected the mission of developing a Soviet area in the region. It further pointed out that it had disapproved of any change in the original plan, and the majority of the cadres of the Fourth Red Army had agreed on this point.

When developments in this important case were considered by the branch of the Party CC and the Military Affairs Committee, critical illness prevented me from attending the meeting. Shen Tse-min and others who were worried about my illness purposely withheld the news from me. The decision was made at the meeting to authorize Shen Tse-min to draft a letter of reply that the Fourth Red Army still should develop the Soviet zone in the Ying-shan and Yi-shui region according to the original plan, and exploit the victory already won to expand the Red Army; it should under no circumstances cross the river and push southward. The letter would also explain the question of coordinating with the Red Army in Kiangsi Province. It was the major responsibility of the Fourth Red Army to coordinate with the Red Army in Kiangsi Province, but if it pulled out from the original bases and separated from the local forces, it would have to cross the river all by itself. Such an action not only would fail to give forceful support to the Red Army in Kiangsi, but would, by evacuating the Oyüwan border area, cause that area to suffer losses. This plan actually featured the ideas of military adventurism of the Li Li-san line. If, on the other hand, the original plan was to be carried out, not only could the Oyüwan border region be expanded and the fighting strength of the Fourth Red Army increased, but the latter would also be in a better position to attract and contain still more enemy forces; and this would be the best possible support the Fourth Red Army could give to the Red Army in Kiangsi Province.

This letter of reply actually contained nothing more than a reiteration of the original plan, which should not have aroused too much criticism. Unexpectedly, both Hsü Chi-sheng and Tseng Chung-sheng took a further step in showing their opposition to the idea. Tseng was reported to have said that the letter was drafted by Comrade Tse-min, and that Comrade Kuo-t'ao, who was confined to bed, knew nothing about it; that Comrade Tse-min had always regarded the Red Army as a personal tool of protection; and that such a rightist conservative point of view was detrimental to the Red Army; and so forth. Hsü Chi-sheng stressed that the leading officers of the Fourth Red Army should decide what their army was going to do for the sake of its military future, and there was no need of paying any attention to the directive from Hsin-chi.

At a meeting of leading officers of the Fourth Red Army, Tseng Chung-sheng described his plan for pushing southward after crossing the river as part of the Army's original plan. He said that the original plan contained no specific instructions about the activities of the Fourth Red Army; it didn't forbid the Army to cross the river and advance toward the south. He seemed to think that the Yangtze River was merely a narrow ditch that the Fourth Red Army could cross and recross at will, and that the naval and air forces of the KMT could do nothing to stop the river-crossing operations. Thus, he felt that the front-line officers should have the authority to decide whether or not to cross the river without securing consent from Hsin-chi. Although the majority of the leading officers headed by Hsü Hsiang-ch'ien disagreed with the idea, they nevertheless had no intention of initiating political discussion in the Army. But they did make it clear that it would be necessary to secure permission beforehand from Hsin-chi. Besides, since most junior officers and men of the Fourth Red Army were natives of this area, there was prevalent among them a feeling of attachment to the area itself. Thus, even the senior-ranking Tseng Chung-sheng could not push through his plan.

Tseng Chung-sheng finally sent out an ultimatum-type report to Hsin-chi. He exaggerated in this report the importance of crossing the Yangtze and of severing its traffic line; he further stated that "a commander fighting away from the palace may ignore the emperor's orders." He would get ready to cross the river by a certain date should he fail to receive a clear-cut instruction from the Military Affairs Committee. The report reached Hsin-chi in early September, and it shocked us all.

Although I was still confined to bed, my general condition was improving. Upon receiving the above report, the members of the branch of the Party CC and the Military Affairs Committee gathered around my bed and held an emergency meeting there. Ts'ai Shen-hsi, who spoke first, said that it would be highly risky to attempt to cross the Yangtze

River under the close guard of heavily armed KMT troops. Even if the river-crossing could be successfully carried out, a lone army would hardly find a chance to operate south of the Yangtze. And it would be even more difficult if that army wanted to return to its original base north of the river. Such action would obviously contravene the original plan. He believed that it was the influence of the Li Li-san line that had held Tseng spell-bound, otherwise he would not so persistently stick to such an erroneous idea, unless he had his own ulterior motives. He regretted having recommended keeping Tseng Chung-sheng and Hsü Chi-sheng in their important posts, which made it possible for them to commit such a serious case of disobedience. He then suggested having Ch'en Ch'ang-hao take over Tseng Chung-sheng's post as political commissar of the Fourth Red Army and rectify Tseng's errors.

We all agreed to Ts'ai Shen-hsi's suggestion. Ch'en Ch'ang-hao and other members actually had proposed that Ts'ai Shen-hsi take over the post of political commissar of the Fourth Red Army, but Ts'ai declined the offer on the grounds of poor health. However, he was most persistent in recommending Ch'en Ch'ang-hao for the post. Finally I said that I completely accepted Ts'ai Shen-hsi's idea; and I made it clear that although the Party Congress had criticized Tseng Chung-sheng and Hsü Chi-sheng, yet when they had repented, the Party had properly adopted a lenient attitude toward them and allowed them to remain at their important posts, and Ts'ai Shen-hsi had showed deep concern for the veteran comrades, as he should have done. Besides, he had repeatedly persuaded Tseng and Hsü to give up their prejudices by complying with the directive issued by Hsin-chi. This proved that Comrade Ts'ai really had done nothing that demanded his repentance. Unfortunately, these two persons have reached a stage of open defiance which showed their persistence in sticking to the wrong attitude, so that there is no alternative but to have them replaced.

At the meeting the decision was made to send Ch'en Ch'ang-hao to the front to handle this particular case as the plenipotentiary of the branch of the Party CC and the Military Affairs Committee. He must not only stop any attempt at crossing the river, but should, if necessary, have the troops withdraw to the original Soviet area. The Military Affairs Committee, meanwhile, appointed Ch'en Ch'ang-hao to replace Tseng Chung-sheng as political commissar of the Fourth Red Army, and Tseng Chung-sheng was to be recalled to Hsin-chi. As to the status of Hsü Chi-sheng, Ch'en Ch'ang-hao could, in the light of actual conditions, decide whether to dismiss him or not. In addition to these formal decisions and directives, we also jointly wrote a letter to the senior officers, encouraging them to obey the Party's correct decisions. I made it clear right then that as soon as I could leave my bed, I would rush back to the front to help Ch'en Ch'ang-hao handle all pending cases.

About one week after Ch'en Ch'ang-hao's departure, I braced myself for a trip to the front, utterly disregarding the doctor's advice on recuperation. I managed to reach the divisional headquarters of K'uang Chi-hsün's division at Pai-ch'ueh-yuan, where I told the comrades in person about the undesirable activities of Tseng and Hsü. K'uang Chi-hsün and responsible cadres under his command expressed enthusiastic support for our decision. At the same time, Shen Tse-min and Ts'ai Shen-hsi also presented the case to the various comrades at Hsin-chi to solicit their support. It was at the time of the Japanese occupation of the northeastern provinces, better known as the September Eighteenth Incident, but those of us who were in this small world of our own were busily engaged in warding off a possible internal crisis.

A few days later an urgent message reached us from Ch'en Ch'ang-hao at the front. The message informed us that everything had been smoothly carried out in accordance with the directive issued by the Military Affairs Committee. It said that the Fourth Red Army would soon be recalled to Pai-ch'ueh-yuan, for rest and training, via Ying-shan and Chin-chia-chai, so it wouldn't be necessary for me to rush to the front. Upon receipt of this message, I then decided to remain at Pai-ch'ueh-yuan to await the arrival of the Fourth Red Army.

Two or three days later, Ch'en Ch'ang-hao returned to Pai-ch'ueh-yuan with one advance detachment, escorting Tseng Chung-sheng and Hsü Chi-sheng. He told me that during his front-line tour he not only had corrected some anti-Party activities, but also had uncovered a counterrevolutionary case. He was very much excited over the case, and believed that it could have developed into a serious problem if left undiscovered for a little while longer.

Ch'en Ch'ang-hao said that he had covered seven hundred to eight hundred li in only five days and nights to reach Army Headquarters at Yi-shui. Immediately after his arrival, Ch'en Ch'ang-hao announced to the senior officers of the Fourth Red Army the decision of the branch of the CC of the CCP and the Military Affairs Committee, and the announcement obtained the full backing of the group of senior officers headed by Hsü Hsiang-ch'ien. Realizing that the general situation had turned against him, Tseng Chung-sheng had no choice but to bow to the decision. This smoothed the way for Ch'en Ch'ang-hao to take over the post of political commissar of the Fourth Red Army. In this way the Party's directive was thoroughly implemented, and the idea of crossing the river to push southward was called off. This was an indication that Party leadership remained very strong in the Fourth Red Army. Throughout this dispute, the cadres in general appeared to be conscientious and prudent, especially Hsü Hsiang-ch'ien, whose unwavering stand had been most inspiring.

After assuming the post of political commissar of the Fourth Red Army, Ch'en Ch'ang-hao immediately started an investigation, which revealed that most senior officers dismissed Tseng Chung-sheng's idea as undesirable, but believed that he was still loyal to the Party. The attitude of Hsü Chi-sheng and a few of his trusted lieutenants was rather suspicious. Someone in the Eleventh Division even speculated, "After crossing the river, the Eleventh Division will secede from the Fourth Red Army and look for a future of its own." It seemed to Hsü Hsiang-ch'ien and his close associates that most cadres of the Eleventh Division were loyal to the Party, but it was necessary thoroughly to investigate the utterances and deeds of Hsü Chi-sheng and a few of his close followers.

Acting on the proposal of some cadres, Ch'en Ch'ang-hao, with the help of a few political workers, decided to exercise his power of supervision as political commissar of the Army; the Party thus searched the headquarters of the Eleventh Division. Recalling this incident during his personal report to me, Ch'en Ch'ang-hao admitted that he was a little frightened, because Hsü Chi-sheng might have put up resistance. But since he declared upon arrival at the divisional headquarters that he was going to search the place, most personnel there showed compliance, and the Special Service Company—the only unit directly under the divisional headquarters—appeared most enthusiastic in supporting the search. This truly frightened Hsü Chi-sheng and perhaps destroyed any idea of defiance on his part.

In the Eleventh Division's headquarters there was a staff officer named Wu, whose intimate relationship with Hsü Chi-sheng was widely known. This man often accompanied Hsü Chi-sheng in pursuit of debauchery; his strange behavior had aroused people's suspicion. Perhaps because of his complete trust in the protection of his boss, Divisional Commander Hsü, this young officer never imagined that his place would be searched, so he simply did not have enough time to destroy the incriminating evidence. Among the files under Wu's care, Ch'en Ch'ang-hao discovered evidence of secret communications with the enemy, notable among which were two letters and a secret code book that had recently arrived from the White area.

Ch'en Ch'ang-hao then asked Hsü Chi-sheng to take the young staff officer to Army Headquarters for interrogation. At that time all senior officers of the Fourth Red Army were gathered there, and their appearance suggested that either a military meeting or a military court was about to take place. Officers and men thronged the spacious hall, and the atmosphere was understandably charged with tension. Staff Officer Wu hardly had a chance to acquit himself when confronted with the evidence, which included letters and secret codes. Furthermore, most of the letters were written using the same codes, so that he had to confess his treasonous activities. He admitted that he was a member of the KMT Reorganizationist group and that Hsü Chi-sheng was fully aware of what he had been doing. He confessed that his major mission was to persuade Divisional Commander Hsü to defect to the White Army. And while the Party was caught in an internal squabble, he had already managed to establish contact with some persons in the unit; they planned to defect when the Fourth Red Army sustained anticipated setbacks during the river-crossing operations.

The discovery of this startling case prodded the senior officers of the Fourth Red Army to decide at the meeting that Hsü Chi-sheng should immediately be dismissed as divisional commander and escorted to Hsin-chi for interrogation and prosecution. In the case of Tseng Chung-sheng, although he was not suspected of counterrevolutionary activities, his anti-Party utterances were obviously used by the counter-revolutionaries, so he, too, had to go to Hsin-chi, pending investigation of his case. The Fourth Red Army would immediately withdraw to Pai-ch'üeh-yuan, and all suspects in the divisions and regiments were placed under the temporary surveillance of the political departments at the corresponding levels. Suspects were to be purged as soon as they were brought to their destinations. Having thus reported the whole case to me, Ch'en Ch'ang-hao then turned over to me the letters and secret codes, requesting me to interrogate Tseng Chung-sheng and Hsü Chi-sheng to prove the soundness of his actions.

First of all I had a personal talk with Tseng Chung-sheng; I asked him to tell me the whole truth about the case without any reservations.

He told me that while the traitorous Staff Officer Wu was being inter-rogated, he had always been present and he personally had examined all the evidence. He felt that there was no doubt about the case, but he said that Wu appeared to be merely a go-between, while Hsü Chi-sheng was the ringleader. He wondered with great remorse how he as political commissar of the Army could have completely overlooked such a notorious case of counterrevolutionary intrigue. His idea of crossing the river to push southward was used by Hsü Chi-sheng and his gang, and everything almost ended up in Hsü's trap, so he asked for punishment. I also frankly pointed out to him that he had committed serious political errors, but luckily he was not an accomplice of the counterrevolution-aries. Afterwards, he returned to Hsin-chi, where he was accused of committing anti-Party acts and of helping the counterrevolutionaries develop their plot. Subsequently he was relieved of his posts as a mem-ber of the branch of the Party CC and the Military Affairs Committee, and he became a staff officer of the Military Affairs Committee in charge of training local armed forces.

Then I asked Ch'en Ch'ang-hao, Tseng Chung-sheng, and Hsü Chi-sheng to have a talk together. Hsü Chi-sheng already appeared crest-fallen. I explained to him that he had full rights in defending himself. He said that the comrades at the front treated him quite well; they didn't put him through formal interrogation, nor did they threaten him in any manner. In the face of indisputable evidence, he admitted having countenanced counterrevolutionaries, but he did not think that he him-self had yet engaged in any counterrevolutionary activities.

Hsü Chi-sheng said that after our failure in 1927 he had maintained connections with the KMT Reorganizationists while he lived in Shang-hai. When he was assigned in 1929 to join the guerrilla forces then operating on the Honan-Anhwei border, one of his friends among the KMT Reorganizationists said that it was all right for him to join the guerrilla bandits on order of the CCP. When the KMT Reorganization-ists gained superiority in the future by overthrowing Chiang Kai-shek and seizing the political power from him, Hsü could then defect with his troops and cooperate with the KMT Reorganizationists. Hsü said that he had not accepted that offer from his friend, nor did he know that this person had later defected to Chiang Kai-shek.

Hsü Chi-sheng continued to recall related past events. He said that when he entered the Soviet area to join the guerrilla operations, he had completely forgotten this case. Unexpectedly, Staff Officer Wu called on him at Chin-chia-chai through a letter of introduction from his friend with the KMT Reorganizationists. He was already making good progress in his guerrilla operations in the area, and he assigned Wu as his staff officer on the recommendation of his old friend. He and Wu happened to be birds of a feather, both loving to fool around with women, so they became close friends in no time. After the Hsin-chi Congress, Wu told him not to bow to the Party's pressure and blackmailed him on numerous occasions. He admitted that by then he was aware of the traitorous role that Wu was playing, but Wu's frequent threats prevented him from turning Wu over to the authorities. He muddled along, not knowing what to do, but he had no intention of betraying the Party.

It was during this talk that the indignant Tseng Chung-sheng kept pressing Hsü for more information; he accused Hsü of trying to confess only the part that had already been disclosed by Wu. Meanwhile, in order to clear himself, Tseng Chung-sheng stressed the question of whether Hsü had completely kept him in the dark. In response to this query, Hsü had to admit that he had kept Tseng in the dark.

Having learned the true story of the case, I immediately assigned escorts to have Hsü Chi-sheng taken to Hsin-chi together with the complete file of the case; and I also told Tseng Chung-sheng to go along to help investigate the case, so that he could clarify his own errors. In the meantime, I suggested to the authorities at Hsin-chi that in handling the Hsü case, it would be advisable for the branch of the Party CC to set up a special tribunal to ferret out any available evidence and clues to Wu's accomplices in the various departments of the Party. But we should not confuse suppression of counterrevolutionaries with intra-Party struggle; Tseng Chung-sheng and other comrades who had committed certain mistakes deserved to receive disciplinary measures of the Party only.

Following Ch'en Ch'ang-hao's steps, Hsü Hsiang-ch'ien slowly brought his Fourth Red Army back to Pai-ch'ueh-yuan. At that time the Army was absorbed with suppression of counterrevolutionary activities; more than one hundred suspects were placed under arrest while en route to Pai-ch'ueh-yuan. The sweeping purge campaign was touched off by the discovery that the Fourth Red Army had been infiltrated by KMT Reorganizationists. All over the Soviet area "suppression of counterrevolutionaries" and "purge of KMT Reorganizationists" forged ahead like a tidal wave. The scene was reminiscent of the purge of the nobility during the French Revolution. No one really could tell the difference between a KMT Reorganizationist and a counterrevolutionary. Anyone who was testified against by an individual was inevitably swept away by this tidal wave. All suspects in the regiments and divisions of the Fourth Red Army were invariably subjected to severe interrogations. Since most trials were conducted in the presence of the masses, public indignation hardly gave the accused a chance to defend themselves. Many were even subjected to tortures during the interrogations.

Being an eyewitness to the scene, I was afraid that there would be disastrous consequences, so I acted to stop such practices without delay. In the first place I issued an instruction as chairman of the Military Affairs Committee, to prohibit indiscriminate arrest and interrogation. Those already under arrest were to be turned over to the military tribunal set up by the senior political departments, and no torture would be allowed during interrogations. Thenceforth no divisional or regimental headquarters was to detain anyone without permission from Army Headquarters or senior political departments. In the meantime, steps should be taken to invite personal confessions during the purge campaign. Luckily this order checked the tidal wave, and enabled me and other leaders to assess the true situation of the problem.

Having studied the case, I called a meeting of several hundred army cadres with representatives from each company. I made a report on the question of suppression of counterrevolutionaries at the meeting. I used the simplest possible words to explain to the audience the difference between a counterrevolutionary, a KMT Reorganizationist, and an ordinary offender. As the facts showed, the comrades frequently confused counterrevolutionary activities with ordinary offenses. Later I proved to them, on the strength of available evidence and information, that only a handful of persons took part in counterrevolutionary activities, and all of them had been arrested. The others who were incriminated in one way or another were the ones who had just committed some minor offenses. Some were influenced by counterrevolutionaries, but they were not directly related to the case.

In accordance with the guideline on suppression of counterrevolutionaries within the Party, I made it clear that a line must be drawn between a principal perpetrator and an accomplice. In other words, the major culprit must be severely dealt with, while an accomplice should be treated leniently. Those who acted under duress and manifested true repentance should be acquitted. I called their attention to a case that involved a certain individual; he was regarded as a counterrevolutionary simply because of some anti-Soviet-area activities of his family elders. Another individual was treated as a counterrevolutionary on the grounds that his dependents had shown signs of wavering toward the revolution. I reminded those present that the law in the Soviet area would not act against those peasants who had shown signs of wavering, because as the strength of the Soviet area and the Red Army had not yet become very strong, wavering would have been expected on the part of the peasants. A soldier of the Red Army should not be held responsible for the offenses of his family, especially since he himself had achieved merits in the revolution. Such a person should by no means be regarded as a counterrevolutionary, nor should the peasants be who had wavered in their attitude.

Elaborating on the subject, I pointed out that while someone attending an authorized conference who failed to repudiate some anti-Party utterances at the conference naturally didn't do the right thing, it would nevertheless be inappropriate to accuse him of trying to cover up something, or to assume that he was a KMT Reorganizationist. Again, if someone in the company of a counterrevolutionary had been caught fooling around with women, it would be going too far to call him a henchman of the KMT Reorganizationist group.

On the basis of the above analysis, I emphatically pointed out that our major mission at the moment was to continue our struggle against the warlord-bandit tendency in the Army, against rich peasants, bureaucrats, the leftist tendencies of the Li Li-san line, and wavering rightist elements. Such bad influences had provided fertile ground for counterrevolutionary activities, but only a handful of persons were directly involved, and the hard core of the counterrevolutionary organization had already been destroyed. We should not, therefore, indiscriminately involve people in the case and allow ourselves to be seized with panic. With the exception of a few serious suspects under arrest, most of them should be treated with leniency or released.

This report greatly moved my comrades, and some admitted that they had been too emotional and impulsive in the frenzied suppression of counterrevolutionary activities; some felt greatly relieved on hearing my report that no one should be incriminated unnecessarily. Hsü Hsiang-ch'ien, Ch'en Ch'ang-hao, and other ranking cadres all indicated that they would continue to carry out, in accordance with my instruction, the inter-Party struggle and the suppression of counter-revolutionaries. They admitted that while the campaign was racing toward its fiery height, they, too, were overwhelmed with emotion, which resulted in indiscriminate arrests in the various divisions and regiments. They promised to mend their ways in the future.

The Hsin-chi branch of the Party CC promptly accepted my report, passed resolutions, and issued a directive calling upon the various organizations to comply with my report. In the Soviet area certain accomplices of Hsü Chi-sheng were arrested, but most of the suspects who were subsequently purged were lawbreakers who occupied more and better lands and houses by making use of their authority in the Soviet area. According to statistics compiled by the branch of the Party CC, more than six hundred were arrested during the suppression campaign, with arrested servicemen constituting about one-third of the total. More than one hundred were purged, including Hsü Chi-sheng. Of this total, thirty to forty were sentenced to death, and the rest were sentenced to varying prison terms.

Afterwards, the Party CC commended the authorities of the Oyü-wan border area for having carried out the suppression campaign in the most appropriate manner, and called upon other Soviet areas to emulate them. In the Kiangsi Soviet area, the suppression campaign that began after the Fu-t'ien Incident had been repeatedly carried to excess, and the overall situation threatened to get out of control. After Chou En-lai entered the Kiangsi Soviet area, he reportedly criticized Mao Tse-tung for committing grave errors in the suppression campaign, but since I was not directly involved, I had no detailed knowledge of the true situation.

In general, our suppression and rectification campaign in the Oyü-wan border areas was primarily aimed at eliminating warlord-bandit tendencies; but we also dealt effective blows at the remnants of the Li Li-san line, rectified certain rightist and decadent tendencies, and liquidated a counterrevolutionary plot. But certain deviations occurred during the suppression campaign, such as unfair judgment of some cases, and tortures were applied in certain interrogations. We were not able to correct each and every case, because this reflected not only the backward social circumstances of China but also the CCP's principle of preferring to be too far Left rather than too far Right.

The Ultimate Development in the Oyüwan Area

The Oyüwan Soviet area and the Fourth Red Army Corps were in a state of prosperity and expansion when Chiang Kai-shek launched a large-scale encirclement against them from November, 1931, to July, 1932. Our expansion was the result of the above-mentioned efforts. Later, we suffered setbacks under the pressure of superior enemy forces, and the cause for the setbacks seemed to lie in the inherent shortcomings of the Soviet movement.

During this period we scored many victories, some big, some small. As a result, the strength of the Fourth Red Army was enhanced considerably. In the campaign to suppress counterrevolutionaries, we rigorously rectified the Red Army, ridding it of unreliable elements and those of landlord or rich-peasant origin, and promoting many cadres who were poor peasants by birth. Our officers were, with few exceptions, CCP members, and thus our political work was greatly strengthened. Measures to fill out the Army were regarded by us as a major move.

As we were fighting along interior lines, our military strategy consisted of wiping out the encircling enemies one by one with superior forces and expanding the Soviet regime in the areas around us. Our troops fought every day, engaging in innumerable big and small battles. It is impossible to give an account of every one of them, but here are accounts of some of the major ones.

The enemy was then adopting a defensive policy towards our region, with the main force concentrating on the Kiangsi Soviet area. According to Chiang Kai-shek's principle of destroying the CCP, the Oyüwan area was not of great importance. Surrounding us were mostly miscellaneous troops of the KMT, whose commanders were generally passive in their attitude, reluctant to seek merit and content to be free from mistakes. Their equipment was inferior to that of Chiang Kai-shek's own troops, but many of them were quite strong in combat strength, such as the Northwest Army led by Chi Hung-chang and others, which was originally under Feng Yü-hsiang. It was, in fact, well known for its fighting ability. The enemy troops were all putting up defenses in the towns, with the militia corps stationed in the outlying areas. Meanwhile, pillboxes were built along the perimeter of the region, forming an encirclement of great depth around it.

We were continually looking for ways to break through the encirclement. We felt that the guerrilla tactics adopted by Mao Tse-tung in the Kiangsi Soviet area were of little use to us in this region. Such tactics as "when the enemy advances, we retreat"; "when the enemy retreats, we advance"; "when the enemy is tired out, we fight"; "when the enemy pursues, we go round and round in circles" were only suitable for irregular skirmishing, not for dealing with an enemy given to defensive tactics. We had to take the initiative in attacking the enemy, but we lacked the heavy weapons for this purpose. So we would beseige one point and wipe out the troops coming to its rescue. The way this tactic worked was to meet encirclement with encirclement.

We developed our guerrilla tactics in accordance with the special qualities of the Fourth Red Army. The two main reasons for our success in sudden raids were our extreme mobility and our secrecy. Our troops were lightly equipped and could move about easily. Our movements were usually very clandestine, and under the cover and sham attacks of the local armed forces, the enemy was unable to discover our real intentions. We often employed the tactics of night raids and night operations to give full play to the strategy of sudden attacks. We also built defense works to minimize casualties and to economize on manpower. All these seemed to be tactics that should be adopted by inferior forces fighting battles on the interior line.

We took on each military operation as a maneuver. Before the campaign we spared no efforts in our planning and in mobilizing all parties so as to show the strength of a lion fighting a hare. After the campaign we made a detailed examination of the operation, took note of our mistakes and faults, and made plans for future operations with new methods. We made progress in this way during our operations.

While the Fourth Red Army was rectifying its ranks at Pai-ch'ueh-yuan, it exerted pressure on the enemy in Huang-chuan, Shang-cheng, and Kuang-shan and succeeded in wiping out some one thousand troops of Chi Hung-chang in a small market town near Huang-chuan, which resulted in Chi Hung-chang being dismissed by Chiang Kai-shek for the crime of "not doing his best to combat the bandits." Quite infuriated, Chi Hung-chang went to Shanghai, where he made contact with underground workers of the CCP, as his impression of the Red Army, because of his personal experience, had undergone some changes. This had something to do with the surrender of Sun Lien-chung's troops to the Red Army, which took place some time later. Chi Hung-chang was killed later by Chiang Kai-shek after he had joined the United Anti-Japanese Army organized by Feng Yü-hsiang at Chang-chia-kou.

In November, 1931, our army moved south and attacked the division under Liang Kuan-ying which was stationed in the county seat of Huang-an. We attached a great deal of importance to this operation, since we felt that the old Soviet area needed to be rid of this thorn in its flesh. Our preparations were made with greater care than previously. The operation was made by order of the chairman of the Military Affairs Committee and had been discussed at a meeting of senior commanders, which drew up the plan for the whole operation. The middle- and lower-ranking officers were carefully briefed by the senior officers at another meeting, when every move in the plan was explained.

Political work also played its role in this campaign. The political commissar in the CCP Army usually had the privilege of supervising other officers at the same level, the order of an officer at the same level not being valid without the countersignature of the political commissar. If necessary, the political commissar could remove or arrest officers at the same level. But in the Fourth Red Army, all officers were comrades. We were of the opinion that the power of supervision of political commissars should be limited to officers at the same level who were not comrades. The system adopted in the Fourth Red Army was one of equality between the commanding officer and the political commissar at the same level, who were responsible for the military and political aspects, respectively.

As a result of this system of equality, in planning military operations, the Political Department of the Military Affairs Committee and the political commissars at all levels had to submit materials on the political aspect of the operation and to draw up a plan for the political work, which was mainly a plan to boost the confidence of the troops from the political angle in implementing the plan and to mobilize the local population to cooperate with the Army in the operation. There were also measures to undermine the morale of the enemy and to encourage enemy officers and men to surrender. The Political Department at any level was the executive arm of the political commissar at that level, which implemented the plan for political work. When there was no fighting, the political commissar directed the work of the Political Department; and in time of war, he took part in the fighting. Capable regimental political commissars were usually "super" regimental commanders, or at least deputy regimental commanders. The CCP organizations in the Army were under the direction of the Political Department, playing the role of pacesetters among officers and men.

In the Huang-an campaign, we decided to let the political commissars and Political Departments of the regiments be the main agents of the political work. All work that concerned boosting morale, mobilizing the masses, and undermining the morale of the enemy was done with the regiment as the basic unit. In this way the political commissar of the Army had a good start for his work. He had only to direct the regimental political commissars to have the work run smoothly at all levels. The Party organization in the Army usually regarded the Party organ of the company as the basic unit. With the regimental political commissars directing the work of the company political commissars and Party-organ secretaries, all work ran smoothly, as a hand directing the fingers.

When our troops reached the county seat of Huang-an according to plan, first of all they wiped out the outposts of Liang Kuan-ying's troops outside the city wall. The enemy troops then all withdrew inside the county seat. The main force of our Army was stationed southwest of Huang-an, while the east and north sides were guarded by local armed forces. Our aim was to cut off the grain supply to the troops inside the county seat. As soon as the enemy troops retreated because of a shortage of food, we would wipe them out on the fields outside.

The combat strength of our troops was much superior to that of Liang Kuan-ying's troops; we also outnumbered them by one hundred percent. We were usually able to divert half of our forces to put pressure on the enemy troops in Sung-pu and Li-chia-chi south of Huang-an, so that they dared not come to reinforce their friends inside the county seat. Several times the enemy troops inside had tried to seize food outside the county seat, but we foiled their attempts by clearing all fields near the city. If they ventured too far away from the city walls, they risked annihilation.

We attached much importance to improving the relations between ourselves and the masses in the Gray-White territory between Ch'i-li-p'ing district and Kao-ch'iao district in the vicinity of Huang-an. The transport teams of our troops all came from the Soviet region. We never recruited porters and litter-bearers from the Gray-White territory. Half of the food needed by our troops was transported from the Soviet region, and the rest we confiscated from the local tyrants of the Gray-White territory. Grain was the only thing that we confiscated from the local tyrants, and we only confiscated from those designated as local tyrants by the local population. Proclamations were made everywhere, prohibiting the troops from harassing the local people, who were given the right to make reports on such behavior. If our troops damaged anything of the people, they had to pay compensation for it; if they borrowed anything, they had to return it before leaving; and they had to pay for what they bought at a fair price and were not allowed to force purchases or sales. Owing to these measures, the people in the Gray-White territory soon became quite friendly to us.

Our efforts to undermine the morale of the enemy troops were also effective. We did not ban traffic to and from the county seat by the local people. Enemy troops, whether officers or men, were allowed to go back when captured. We tried to tell the enemy by every means that outside help could not be obtained and that their food supply was nearly consumed; the only way for them to survive was to surrender and give up their weapons. By doing this, they would be given preferential treatment by the Red Army: those unwilling to join the Army might go home with traveling expenses granted to them. The Red Army had all along accepted enemy troops as a source of its recruits. The men coming to surrender with their weapons or joining the Red Army after their capture increased noticeably during and after the Huang-an campaign.

After more than a month's besiegement, the enemy in Huang-an finally fled to the southwest one night, since their food supply had run out. Because of our efficient intelligence reports and rapid action in pursuit, we soon captured nearly the whole unit of the enemy. Ch'en Ch'ang-hao once more manifested his ability and alertness. He was ordered to attack the fleeing foe some forty li from Huang-an, and he succeeded in rounding up the majority of them. Only Liang Kuan-ying, the division commander, escaped.

In this campaign, our army occupied the county seat of Huang-an and captured some five thousand enemy officers and men and some three thousand rifles. Huang-an was renamed Hung-an, and this was the county seat that remained in our possession for the longest time. It became a symbol of our victory, greatly inspiring the people of the Soviet region. The Gray-White territory around the county was turned into new Soviet territory, expanding the southern part of the Oyüwan area. Kao-ch'iao district was no longer an isolated island in the south, but the center of the new Soviet region.

While we were consolidating the fruits of our victory around Huang-an, two enemy divisions pressed on us from Sung-pu and Li-chia-chi, evidently under strict orders from Chiang Kai-shek to recapture Huang-an. The two divisions (originally belonging to the Northwest Army, whose commanders' names I do not recall) exerted themselves with special efforts. They launched a sudden raid on us one night when we were billeted some forty li south of the county seat of Huang-an. After breaking through the position of one regiment, they headed directly for our army's headquarters, putting our army in great danger. Hsü Hsiang-ch'ien, Ch'en Ch'ang-hao, and I quickly rose to counter the attack, but we only had about one hundred troops at our disposal. Hsü Hsiang-ch'ien was wounded in the left shoulder by a stray bullet, but he stayed on calmly to direct the fighting until the situation took a turn for the better.

This battle served to show the spirit of cooperation among our troops. The units stationed to the left and right of us all assaulted the rear flanks of the oncoming enemy troops as the situation required, even though they had not received orders from the command headquarters of the Army. As a result, the enemy troops were forced to retreat, and we captured more than one thousand each of men and rifles in our pursuit. They soon withdrew to the vicinity of Huang-p'o.

When we reviewed this campaign, we reproached ourselves for our negligence in defense measures and praised Hsü Hsiang-ch'ien for his valor. He continued to direct the fighting despite his wound, which, though it was bandaged in first-aid treatment, evidently weakened him considerably. In the end he saved the critical situation. Such stamina and complete disregard for one's own life certainly were valuable qualities of the Red Army. Hsü went on to fulfill his duties as commander of the Army before his wound was healed, and he only rested a little when his duties were not so pressing. The commanders of the various divisions and regiments had displayed initiative and cooperation in the fighting—a spirit we should continue to foster.

Our major military victory was won in the campaign at Su-chia-pu, where our smaller force defeated an enemy of superior strength and captured abundant booty. The victory indicated not only the growth of the combat strength of the Fourth Red Army, but also the success of our entire policy.

In the beginning of 1932, our army left Huang-an, passing through Chin-chia-chai, Ma-pu, and Tu-shan, crossed the Pi River, and advanced on Su-chia-pu. After taking Huang-an and defeating the enemy reinforcements on their way to Huang-an, we estimated that the enemy would not be in a position to attack Huang-an for a time. We therefore turned to the Huai River Basin in Anhwei Province to seek expansion. The division under K'uang Chi-hsün was left in the border region between Hupeh and Honan to continue the military operations. Though the strength of this division had been increased, it was still only suitable for small-scale guerrilla fighting.

After crossing the Pi River, our Army gradually pressed on the enemy troops, until they were confined to the major towns of Su-chia-pu, Liu-an, and Huo-shan. Su-chia-pu was the nearest enemy base to the east after our capture of Ma-pu and Tu-shan. It was an important township guarded by two brigades under Ch'en Tiao-yüan. Around the township the enemy had built fortresslike permanent defense works. Our army also built fortifications on the outer perimeters of Su-chia-pu and dug communications trenches around them. The encircled area was gradually reduced by means of those trenches.

Our plan was to encircle the town so as to cut off food supplies to the enemy inside, thus compelling them to surrender. Meanwhile the enemy from Ho-fei and Liu-an might be wiped out when they tried to come to the rescue of Su-chia-pu. The forces of the landlords and militia corps in this area were rather strong. The common people were afraid to come into contact with the Red Army. Our strength was far below that of the enemy, so we had to use our influence to the fullest before we could hope to gain victory.

We did our best to win the sympathy of the local people and to cut off the influence of the landlords and the militia corps. We publicized the fact that in places occupied by the Red Army the peasants were able to live in peace and carry on their occupations contentedly. There was no need to pay rent to the landlords for the time being or to repay loans. Reduction of rent and interest rates and redistribution of land would be carried out as soon as the situation became stabilized. We announced that the Red Army would certainly not infringe upon the interests of the poor, but would confiscate some food grain from the local tyrants. We also demanded that the landlords and militia corps refrain from opposing the Red Army; otherwise we would punish them.

Owing to the implementation of these rather moderate policies, most of the local people stayed where they were instead of fleeing under the pressure and threats from the landlords and militia corps. Some peasants were even very friendly to us. They dared not set up a Soviet regime or redistribute the land, but they were willing to help the Red Army in any operation where they did not have to show their faces. The food needed by our troops was obtained from the locality, which was actually a rich grain-producing area. When we confiscated grain, we usually asked the local poor people to decide who were the genuine local tyrants and to act as guides to show us the way to the tyrants' homes. We did not confiscate their entire stores, but half or more of them. A small portion of the confiscated grain was assigned to the poor for their relief.

The local people's sympathy for us mounted day by day, and this was very convenient for us in our military operations. It was not necessary for us to send troops to confiscate grain; this was done by the political workers accompanied by a few armed men. The common people began to feel that they were better off after the arrival of the Red Army. Most importantly, there was no more arbitrary harassment by the White Army and the militia corps in the countryside. The peasants and merchants came and went in crowds, wishing that Ch'en Tiao-yüan's troops would lose and go away as soon as possible. The local people also supplied us with valuable military information.

We paid a lot of attention to economizing in the deployment of our forces. With one regiment spread over the network of communications trenches and fortifications, the siege of the town of Su-chia-pu was efficiently carried out. A few enemy planes frequently came to bomb us; but thanks to the protection afforded by the communications trenches, we did not suffer heavy damages, nor was our freedom of movement hampered. The enemy knew that the number of our troops surrounding Su-chia-pu was only one-quarter that of the defending troops. Sudden attacks were often launched against us, sometimes under the cover of airplanes. As we could move about with complete ease and speed in the communications trenches, all enemy attacks were in vain. Enemy planes often dropped food and other supplies to Su-chia-pu, though not in great quantities. As we closed in on the enemy day by day, the enemy planes had to be very careful; otherwise the supplies would drop to our side.

The Fourth Red Army had nine regiments, only one of which was assigned to the task of besieging Su-chia-pu. This meant that we could always keep eight regiments as mobile units which could disperse with their superior strength the two brigades of Ch'en Tiao-yüan, stationed in Liu-an and Hou-shan respectively, whenever they tried to reinforce the troops defending Su-chia-pu. Later, it was possible to watch over the enemy troops in these two places with only local armed forces.

The troops defending Su-chia-pu ran out of ammunition and food after being besieged for some two months. In despair, they sent out innumerable telegrams for help. The troops of Wang Chün stationed in Peng-pu were ordered to go to their rescue via Ho-fei and Liu-an. When three divisions advanced close to Su-chia-pu, our army went all out to raid the right wing of the enemy troops, wiping out the majority of them and capturing the commander-in-chief, Li Shih-ting. The troops in Su-chia-pu, in total dispair, had to come out and surrender.

Our army scored considerable success in this campaign. Some twelve thousand of Li Shih-ting's troops were captured, together with some nine thousand rifles, and the remaining troops fled back to Ho-fei. There were about five thousand troops in Su-chia-pu, who surrendered, and some thirty-five hundred rifles. Altogether we captured fifteen thousand rifles, including those obtained in a few minor engagements. This was twice the number of rifles that we had previously possessed. No one could deny that this was an unprecedented victory.

This victory also shocked the KMT authorities. Chiang Kai-shek apparently had felt that these miscellaneous troops were no good. He began to send the main body of troops directly under him to deal with us. We found out that the Second Division of T'ang En-po's troops were gathering in Huang-chuan from Hsü-ch'ang and Hsin-yang in Honan, attempting to attack Hsin-chi while we were unprepared. Meanwhile the "28th of January" anti-Japanese battle in Shanghai had just ended, and Chiang Kai-shek was clamoring for "establishment of internal peace before resistance to foreign aggression." Our military operation in Liu-an was bound to be regarded as a crime of disturbing peace and order at the rear.

Reviewing the campaign, we felt that our combat strength had been greatly enhanced. The tactic of "besieging a point in order to wipe out the troops coming to the rescue" had been successfully applied in this campaign. The political work had also displayed its great role. Our army could have occupied Liu-an, Huo-shan, and other county seats and advanced on Ho-fei; but since T'ang En-po's troops were nearing Hsin-chi and an attack on it would be a shattering blow to the foundations of the Red region, we decided to move west in order to take the initiative in the coming battle.

Our troops soon advanced to Shang-ch'eng and Huang-ch'uan from Su-chia-pu, in search of T'ang En-po's main forces for a decisive battle. When we arrived at the county seat of Shang-ch'eng, the troops put up a strong defense inside the city walls. We pretended to besiege Shang-ch'eng, but led the whole Army towards Huang-ch'uan along the Shang-Huang highway. T'ang En-po, who was then in Huang-ch'uan, had apparently received urgent calls for help from Shang-ch'eng and planned to sandwich us in between his troops and those in Shang-ch'eng. He led his Second and Third divisions out of Huang-ch'uan toward Shang-ch'eng. Our troops met with the enemy at Tou-fu-tien, where a big engagement broke out.

As soon as the scouts of the two armies encountered each other, the enemy troops spread out and took up their positions for battle. Our troops were adept at this kind of engagement. They immediately dashed at the enemy with the force of a tempest, and after a short, close battle, the enemy troops began to totter. Our troops launched one attack after another, and the enemy units broke up completely. The enemy force was twice the size of ours and was far superior to us in machine-gun fire. However, they had much less will to fight, which became evident in the battle. The majority of the enemy troops fled towards Huang-ch'uan, while some of them stayed on both sides of the highway, guarding the outposts which were protected by water on all sides. T'ang En-po, the commander-in-chief, mixed in with the fleeing troops and retreated to one of the water-protected outposts.

Hindered by the enemy troops hidden in the various water-protected outposts along the way, we were unable to launch a vigorous pursuit. Only about two thousand men and rifles were captured, while our casualties amounted to more than five hundred, a record casualty figure for us since we had started to fight in this part of the country. When the enemy troops fled, they threw away their fine foreign-made equipment into the ponds and paddies along the way, so as to be able to flee faster. After this campaign the well-known T'ang En-po division was sent away from Huang-ch'uan for reorganization and replenishment.

After this campaign Chiang Kai-shek seemed to feel that the forces of the Oyüwan region could not be treated casually. Moreover, the Soviet region was situated in an area that was important because the Fourth Red Army was able to menace Wuhan and cut off the main communications lines of the Yangtze River and the Peking-Hankow Railway. It was not surprising that Chiang Kai-shek regarded the

Fourth Red Army as a great nuisance in this crucial spot and that he turned the spearhead of his punitive force on it. In Wuhan he set up the General Headquarters for Annihilation of the Bandits and personally took over the post of commander-in-chief, with Chang Hsueh-liang as deputy commander. Thus, the Oyüwan region seemed to be at the top of Chiang Kai-shek's agenda for the campaign against the "Bandits."

It was April, 1932. Though we could not be sure of Chiang Kai-shek's intentions, we had the premonition that we would have to deal with battles on a still larger scale. We then stepped up the strengthening of our forces. K'uang Chi-hsün was working fast at organizing the Seventy-third Division, and he was praised by the comrades. At this time we enlarged the organization of our units in this region in accordance with the directive of the CC of the CCP. Our army was expanded into the Fourth Front Army, which included the original Fourth Army and the newly organized Twenty-fifth Army, with Hsü Hsiang-ch'ien as commander-in-chief of the Fourth Front Army and Ch'en Ch'ang-hao as political commissar. Both retained their original posts in the Fourth Army as well. K'uang Chi-hsün was promoted to the post of commander of the Twenty-fifth Army. He was to go to Chin-chia-chai and Su-chia-pu with the Seventy-third Division which he had organized; and making use of the weapons captured in the Su-chia-pu campaign, he was to organize the Seventy-fourth and Seventy-fifth divisions as soon as possible. The post of political commissar of the Twenty-fifth Army was given temporarily to Ts'ai Shen-hsi; but as Ts'ai Shen-hsi was preoccupied with the duties of chief-of-staff and with work of the Red Army School, the post remained only an empty title.

A great shortcoming of our army was the lack of training. We tried our best to compensate for this. In battles, our officers usually led the men, which resulted in more casualties among the cadres, and this could not be corrected for a long time. As I had mentioned before, Hsü Hsiang-ch'ien had been wounded, and so had division commanders Liu Ying and Ch'en Keng. Numerous cadres at the regimental level and below had also been wounded. It was very difficult to fill the vacancies among the cadres. Our army took time out to train soldiers for combat, so that they might disperse and fight, taking advantage of the terrain. Thus, the officers would be freed from leading the soldiers on charges, and casualties among them would be reduced.

The equipment of our army was increased by several pieces of mountain artillery, several scores of trench mortars, and hundreds of machine guns; so we had to train more artillerymen and machine gunners. The booty included wireless sets, which had to be pieced together and repaired one by one, and personnel had to be trained to operate them. Some of the captured guns were distributed among the independent regiments of the locality, but there was still a surplus of them. Our arsenal was able to repair rifles and to produce such weapons as hand grenades, and it was in operation day and night. New recruits increased as the weapons multiplied, and training became arduous and complicated.

Our military work then proceeded in two separate sectors. Hsü Hsiang-ch'ien and Ch'en Ch'ang-hao, leading the Fourth Red Army, operated around the border region between Hupeh and Honan, strengthened the local armed forces, and stepped up training. K'uang Chi-hsün with his to-be-filled-out Twenty-fifth Army carried out the same task in the border region between Honan and Anhwei with the help of the Party and government offices around Chin-chia-chai. It was a rather onerous task for K'uang Chi-hsün, who had to face the enemy single-handed while continuing to strengthen the headquarters of the Twenty-fifth Army and the Seventy-third Division. He also had to organize two new divisions and to expand and train local armed forces and direct them in battle. His ability was not up to the heavy task, but there was no other way out for the time being, and we had to let it be temporarily.

The region also made progress in other aspects besides military work. First of all, there was no longer a shortage of food. In 1931 many parts of China had suffered from floods, but our Soviet region scored bumper harvests, owing to an adequate supply of rainfall and to the efforts of the peasants. There was no worry about a food shortage, and peace and order prevailed. The work of the Soviet government lay mainly in collecting the grain levy, storing grain, making preparations for planting, and so forth.

After the redistribution of land in the old Soviet region, great improvement was achieved. Land Utilization Certificates were distributed to the peasants, who, feeling secure with a piece of land they could use for a long time, generally became more interested in production. There was considerable improvement in the "caretaker" system of tilling the land for families of men in the Red Army, which lessened the peasants' burden in labor-service to a large extent. The common people noticed that in their own villages, there were no longer raids by the militia corps of the White Army, and the grain in the border region was no longer plundered by the enemy.

The most outstanding achievements were scored in the financial and economic field. The revenues of the Soviet government gradually approached the point where they could meet the expenses. After March or April of 1932 it was possible for us to pay one silver dollar per month to each man in our army, Party, and government offices as pocket money. Despite the strict blockade by the enemy, the supply of daily necessities was generally adequate. For instance, the Soviet bank usually had a stock of more than half a million catties of salt, which came from the White region through the sale of native products of the Soviet region.

A main factor contributing to our success in breaking through the blockade was the chaos in the KMT regime. The enemy troops guarding the area of Ku-shih and San-ho-chien to the north of Chin-chia-chai were miscellaneous units not connected with Chiang Kai-shek. They did not seriously carry out the task of blockading us. Instead, their brigade commander made a deal with us in order to get money to make up for the shortage of supplies resulting from the unfair treatment meted out to them by the military authorities of the KMT. The smuggling on their part was in the form of a trade pact with us. The pact stipulated that there would be nonintervention between the two sides, and that goods passing through their area of defense were subjected to a certain amount of duty. In the beginning our commercial organs presented the brigade commander with five thousand yuan in a lump sum as compensation for the insufficient amount of duty in the initial stage. In this way the goods to and from our region went through this break in the blockade without the slightest hindrance.

Apart from this, the administrative efficiency of the various organs of the Soviet government at all levels had been gradually improved. There was a great decrease in the number of unreliable elements and illegal acts. There were fewer cases of local tyrants being arrested and pressed for fines that they had failed to pay. Peasants from the Soviet region no longer ventured out into the White region to seize grain. There were more Party and CYC members; and the Party, the CYC, and mass organizations became stronger. In the Soviet region, repair work was carried out on roads and bridges; courier stations, various small factories, and cooperatives were set up; and work to develop culture and education was in full swing.

This progress exerted a great influence. In interviews, old peasants in the old Soviet region generally admitted that the new programme and new ways of doing things of the Soviet government were evidently different from those of other revolutionary groups they had heard of or seen, such as the White Lotus Sect, the White Wolf, and the Red Spear Society; even in comparison with the Peasant Assocation campaign of 1927, some progress could be seen. Here, a flourishing atmosphere prevailed, and if it lasted, success could be expected. They were worried about the meager strength of the Soviet region, and they wondered how many more years they had to wait before there would be universal peace. The impression that the old peasants presented was a true picture of the Soviet region at that time.

Our greatest trouble was that it was not easy to expand our forces. In April, 1932, the population of the region probably exceeded two million, only one-third of which were in the relatively stable part of the old Soviet region. The rest were in the "areas to be stabilized," where the administrative organs were not yet on a sound basis, the land had not yet been redistributed, and the local armed forces were still rather weak. Our efforts were directed mainly at the basic work in these areas, but the results were slow in coming.

We could not solve problems by issuing orders. Our method was mainly to organize the masses to wage struggles. In a new Soviet region it wouldn't do just to issue an order about redistribution of land; if the peasants were not actively involved, it was useless. We usually sent some cadres to organize the local peasants, so that they would redistribute the land of their own accord. Although most of the peasants were agreeable to the redistribution of land, they were usually afraid to act. The peasants near Su-chia-pu often said, "Let's wait till Ho-fei and Liu-an are taken before we redistribute the land."

Expansion of the Red Army was an important task which we worked at constantly. We were always in need of large numbers of recruits to fill the vacancies and to organize new armies. It was not enough to rely solely on the local armed forces in the Soviet region to supply the manpower. In the new Soviet region, we often held army-civilian get-togethers to encourage the able-bodied men to join our ranks. The officers and men of the Red Army usually made friends with young people and attracted them to the Army. All these methods had brought considerable results, but our need was still not satisfied. Some young peasants were rather hesitant; they felt that it was a dangerous thing to join in the rebellion when victory was still uncertain.

All these affairs made me sad and anxious. I felt that the Soviet region had been supported mainly by military strength. I wondered what inspirational force the agrarian revolution that we were experimenting with really possessed, and what superiority and adaptability the Soviet regime could assume. We had boosted our self-confidence and had gone all out to strive for victory, to the best of our ability. As a leader, I could not help considering how to achieve decisive victory and whether it was possible to do so. I was led to meditate on the future of the Soviet campaign.

Our Soviet region was isolated from the outside world, situated as it was in remote villages. There we lost our political sensibility. It was an ailment that troubled the entire CCP and the various Soviet regions. We were almost ignorant of the events outside the Soviet region. Usually it was a month or two before we learned of events from captured newspapers or periodicals; and then there were only fragments of the whole story. We also lacked the necessary equipment to spread our voice to the outside world. We ourselves were isolated from the CC of the CCP and the other Soviet regions, and it was impossible for us to exchange views with them. It was only on very rare occasions that we exchanged intelligence reports with one another.

The Japanese atrocity of September 18, 1931, when Japan invaded northeastern China, came to our knowledge fully two months after its occurrence. Our review of the event on the basis of available materials was made in November of the same year, at a meeting of a subbureau of the CC. I had then pointed out that we must attach importance to this event, which had evoked an anti-Japanese tide throughout the country. The agrarian revolution was a step to oppose the local tyrants and landlords and to destroy the foundation of the Nanking government; but it was not easily linked with the anti-imperialist movement. Patriotic people the country over might think that the CCP ought not go in for land revolution in the countryside if the whole country was to unite to resist Japan. The Soviet regime offered no attraction to the anti-Japanese intellectuals, and the Soviet banner was no rallying point for anti-Japanese soldiers.

Though I had posed the grave question of the interrelation between agrarian revolution and the anti-imperialist movement, I did not draw a concrete conclusion from it. Bound by the set policy of the CC, my comrades were generally unable to give any new clarification. We still held that the Nanking regime was the one that had betrayed the country and ingratiated itself with foreign countries. The one that really was anti-imperialist was the Soviet regime. Overthrow of the Nanking government and Chiang Kai-shek was the prerequisite to an effective anti-Japanese campaign. Thus, we had inadvertently put ourselves outside the anti-Japanese campaign and had abandoned the struggle to strive for the sympathy of the patriotic people.

When the Shanghai war broke out on January 28, 1932, the Nineteenth Route Army stationed in Shanghai took the line of active resistance, bringing the anti-Japanese feeling throughout the country to the boiling point. It was a surprise that the KMT regime under the state policy of "establishment of internal peace before resistance to foreign aggression" could actually take up arms against a foreign country. Our army was then besieging Su-chia-pu. We generally held that the people of the whole country and a number of soldiers of the KMT were anti-Japanese, while the KMT government hampered resistance to Japan. We advocated that "Chinese people must not fight Chinese people" and that "KMT soldiers should join the Red Army to resist Japan unanimously." But these slogans continued to be propaganda material; we could not make any changes in our policy. My discontent with the Soviet policy of the CCP thus deepened.

In April of the same year the Shanghai war had ended and our army had defeated the troops of T'ang En-po. We were making preparations for resisting the Fourth Encirclement Campaign launched by Chiang Kai-shek. Accusing the Red Army of making trouble in the rear, Chiang Kai-shek was then even more emphatic about "establishment of internal peace before resistance to foreign aggression." He stepped up the training of officers in Lu-shan and proposed the policy of "70 percent politics and 30 percent military" in dealing with the CCP. Great deployment of his troops was carried out in Wuhan in preparation for battle. To counter Chiang Kai-shek's policy, we advanced the slogan "It is essential to oppose Chiang Kai-shek before resisting Japan." We sensed the acuity of Chiang Kai-shek, who had linked "resistance to Japan" with "combat against the CCP." When the CC subbureau discussed ways and means to break through the Fourth Encirclement, I hinted to my comrades that we might suffer blows temporarily; this was due to the fact that we had not yet found a proper place in the anti-Japanese campaign.

Our top-level military strategy was not openly discussed at the CC subbureau. For the sake of secrecy, it was discussed and decided by only a few chiefs—Ts'ai Shen-hsi, Shen Tse-min, Hsü Hsiang-ch'ien, Ch'en Ch'ang-hao, and me. Ts'ai Shen-hsi was entrusted to make a draft, and what he proposed usually coincided with my own views. He drafted some positive military projects for favorable conditions; but he considered the whole situation far from optimistic. He thought that the Oyüwan Soviet region was too small and confined, with no room for maneuvers under pressure from a superior enemy. It was not easy to apply the guerrilla tactic of breaking up the whole into smaller units. He advocated that, when necessary, the Fourth Red Army should move to the region west of the Peking-Hankow Railway. The move was one involving retreat, but it was a necessary step. On the eve of the Fourth Encirclement Campaign launched by Chiang Kai-shek, Ts'ai Shen-hsi was of the opinion that this was imperative.

On the optimistic side, our strategy was to annihilate the advancing enemy separately in each attack; on the pessimistic side, we were to retreat to places west of the Peking-Hankow Railway in case of defeat, taking Hsiang-fan, Yün-yang, and other northern Hupeh counties and maintaining contact with Ho Lung's troops on the borders of Hunan and Hupeh south of the Yangtze River. When we changed from fighting on the inside line to fighting on the outside line, we could not expand to the south, north, or east, because to the south was the Yangtze, to the north the Yellow River, and to the east the Tientsin-Pukow Railway, all of which were heavily guarded at strategic points by Chiang Kai-shek's troops. From the military viewpoint, the only outlet was to the west, where the KMT forces were rather weak and there was a vast area for our maneuvering.

Chief-of-Staff Ts'ai Shen-hsi had spent a lot of time investigating the conditions of places on the western side of the Peking-Hankow Railway. At that time Ho Lung's troops had retreated to Sang-chih in western Hunan after defeats around Hung Lake; it would be very difficult for us to get in touch with him. The scattered guerrilla units in Hsiao-wei, Yün-meng, and An-lu to the west of the Peking-Hankow Railway had been annihilated by the KMT troops long since. Some of them had escaped to the western section of the Ta-pieh mountain range on the border between Hunan and Hupeh provinces. Ts'ai Shen-hsi had sent personnel to try to contact these guerrillas. He had also sent people to northwestern Hupeh and southern Shensi to investigate. Considerable progress was made in this respect. But Ts'ai Shen-hsi was killed in battle during the Fourth Encirclement Campaign, which was a great loss to our army in its expedition to the west.

In July of the same year, the Oyüwan Soviet region finally succumbed to the superior numbers of Chiang Kai-shek's troops. The Fourth Red Army's main force was compelled to move west, crossing the Peking-Hankow line, passing through northern Hupeh and southern Shensi, and finally finding a foothold in the region around Pa-chung, T'ung-chiang, and Nan-chiang in northern Szechwan, where a new "Northern Szechwan Soviet Region" was set up. The Oyüwan Soviet region from then on not only stopped expanding but became a slaughtering ground for Chiang Kai-shek. The guerrillas that stayed behind in the region to carry on the struggle stubbornly suffered extremely heavy losses. Shen Tse-min and other major cadres were martyred in the region. Hsü Hai-tung, who remained there, was compelled to move on to northern Shensi with his troops. They were the predecessors of the many Red Army units that later assembled in northern Shensi. The troops of Kao Ching-t'ing, who kept on with the struggle in the Oyüwan region to the last, were later reorganized into the Second Detachment of the New Fourth Army at the time of the Anti-Japanese War of Resistance.

The above is a summary of the story of the hard struggles waged by the Fourth Red Army in the Oyüwan region. I, as a cultivator of the Oyüwan Soviet region, am steeped in nostalgia while writing these lines.

THE SOVIET REGION
IN NORTHERN SZECHWAN

CHAPTER

The Fourth Encirclement Campaign
and the Westward Plunge of Five Thousand Li

The Soviet region in northern Szechwan was set up when the Fourth Front Army, unable to withstand pressure from Nationalist forces in the Oyüwan region, broke through the Nationalist siege and dashed to northern Szechwan after passing through northern Hupeh, western Honan, and southern Shensi. It marked the first step of migration of the Soviet movement to the Northwest (of China proper). Subsequently the Red armies from various other places were drawn in succession to this region.

Chiang Kai-shek's Fourth Encirclement Campaign was one of a series of five major actions against the Soviet regions in various places. This one was directed against the Oyüwan region, while the rest were directed against the Kiangsi Soviet regions. In May, 1932, Chiang created the Bandits Suppression Command in Wuhan, drew up a war plan, and marshaled forces of about five hundred thousand men (that is, twenty times the strength of the Fourth Front Army—to besiege and annihilate us. According to his plan, about two hundred thousand men would form the defense forces which were to set up positions in key points on a ring around the Oyüwan Soviet region, to build strongholds there, and then to push steadily closer to us in cooperation with the assault forces. The assault forces were composed of columns led by

Liu Chih, Wei Li-huang, Hsü T'ing-yao, and Ch'en Chi-ch'eng, each column being more than three times the strength of the Fourth Front Army. These columns were to advance from separate directions and to converge in a massive, decisive onslaught on the Fourth Front Army. Other troops, mainly divisions under Hu Tsung-nan, Li Yen-nien, Li Mo-en, and Huang Chieh, were reserve forces.

At that time the Nanking regime was rather stable, as the Japanese invasion had exercised a stimulating effect on the internal unity of the KMT. Hence, Chiang was better able to concentrate his attention on the Chinese Communists. The forces mobilized against us were the bulk of his crack units stationed north of the Yangtze River. His vaunted strategy of a "70 percent political and 30 percent military" solution seemed still to be in a trial stage. He relied mainly on stern penalties to galvanize the unity of purpose of his forces. He adopted a mixed line of pacification and repression towards the people in the Soviet region, but there were still evidences of inconsistency in his steps.

Our slogan was "Protect the Oyüwan Soviet Region." In fact, we had mobilized all our available strength in trying to smash the imminent siege. The Fourth Red Army, which was our main strength, had more than nine thousand rifles. The newly expanded Twenty-fifth Army had about five thousand. The local armed units were, to us, merely auxiliary forces, similar to the militia in the "White area," only capable of guerrilla actions. We had eight independent regiments and some scattered independent companies with a total of about five thousand rifles.

We realized that our power was weak for the gargantuan task of defending onr Soviet region; but instead of flinching, we screwed up our courage to strive for victory. We tried our hardest to strengthen the local armed units and to mobilize the masses to help us. We warned the populace in the area that the enemy might penetrate into our region temporarily and that enemy planes might make bombing raids everywhere in the imminent attack.

We were so weak that we could hardly stand any setback which might deal a blow to our whole plan. Nevertheless, the unprecedented defeat of our Twenty-fifth Army at Ho-ch'iu was something we were totally unprepared for. The Nationalist forces under Hsü T'ing-yao started to attack Ho-ch'iu in July, apparently to take the city as an advance point for their later assaults. But the commander of the Twenty-fifth Army, K'uang Chi-hsün, in actual contravention of the Military Committee's order, adopted the erroneous tactic of defending the city with concentrated strength. The resulting loss of two-thirds of the men in the Seventy-third Division was virtually a crippling blow to us under the prevailing circumstances.

K'uang was well aware of our war plan, which stressed dissipation of the enemy on the battlefield rather than holding firm to a city, and he had agreed on this point. Probably his various victories went to his head. Since April, when he was ordered to operate with his troops in the vicinity of Su-chia-pu, he had scored numerous isolated victories, expanding the Soviet region to that area and taking the city of Ho-ch'iu. His Seventy-third Division had become a crack unit; the organization of the Seventy-fourth Division was nearly completed; and his development of local armed units had reaped impressive results. Such things might have increased his confidence so much that he imagined he might be able to make a dazzling show to redress all his previous grievances.

When Hsü T'ing-yao advanced toward Ho-ch'iu, K'uang Chi-hsün decided to use Ho-ch'iu as a base to smash the enemy, thus underestimating the strength of the enemy and disregarding the enemy's powerful forces in the rear. He had apparently been bewitched by the slogan "Protect the Soviet Region." He stressed "not yielding one inch of Soviet ground to the enemy," without seeing the danger in being besieged.

When we got wind of K'uang's decision, we immediately sent him a telegram, pointing out the hazards of a siege and its grievous consequences and calling for immediate withdrawal of his troops from the city to south of Ho-ch'iu Lake where he might stand a better chance of whittling down the enemy in the fields. He wired back that he was already engaged in battle with the enemy and would withdraw if the position became unfavorable. This reply caused me and Chief-of-Staff Ts'ai Shen-hsi considerable consternation. Ts'ai then rushed to the Ho-ch'iu front in order to take up his duties as political commissar so as to remedy matters.

Ho-ch'iu had been doomed to defeat while Ts'ai was still en route. With superior manpower, Hsü T'ing-yao had besieged Ho-ch'iu, which was surrounded by water on three sides, and had bombed the city from the air and with cannon fire from the ground, causing many breaks in the city wall. K'uang had been obliged to fight his way out of the city with his troops in the night. The Seventy-third Division suffered more than one thousand casualties, and about the same number were captured. There were also countless losses in local armed units and transport units in the city. Only about a thousand men managed to reach safety with K'uang, away from the enemy's gunfire. It was fortunate that the

Seventy-fourth Division, stationed outside the city, suffered relatively fewer losses.

Therefore, when Ts'ai reached them, the only thing for him to do was to tidy up the mess. K'uang asked to be punished for this defeat. The incident shocked the whole Soviet region and the Communist forces. In spite of numerous demands that K'uang be court-martialed, the Military Committee acceded to Ts'ai Shen-hsi's recommendation for leniency, stripping K'uang of his command of the Twenty-fifth Army. K'uang has never been in the limelight with the Fourth Front Army since that time. Owing to the severe losses, the Seventy-third and Seventy-fourth divisions were combined into the Seventy-third Division, under the direct control of Ts'ai as commander and political commissar of the Twenty-fifth Army.

Our defeat at Ho-ch'iu was a great blow. All people in the whole Yüwan border region on our eastern front were shocked. It was generally feared that our enemy would find no difficulty in pushing straight into the region. Besides, the enemy's release of more than one thousand prisoners of war taken at Ho-ch'iu gave people the impression that the Nationalists had changed their policy of completely wiping us out. This exerted no small dampening effect on the kill-or-be-killed spirit of the people in the Soviet area. Meanwhile, encouraged by this unexpected victory, the Nationalist forces soon commenced their all-out attack on us.

The Fourth Red army was deployed in action to counter the Nationalist plan of offensive after the battles of Huang-ch'uan and Tou-fu-tien. We raided enemy strongholds everywhere to sever communications between them, and we damaged the Peking-Hankow Railway here and there to disrupt the movement of enemy troops. In July our main strength was hidden in the vicinity of Ma-ch'eng. In the sweltering heat, diseases were prevalent among our forces, and we tried to curb the spread of diseases in order to be ready to repulse effectively the enemy that would penetrate this area.

By early August we had information that enemy troops were advancing in various columns towards our Soviet region. We shifted our men to Huang-an and were heading for Ho-k'ou. But the enemy had moved with exceptional speed also. Thus, we met and fought together between Huang-an and Ho-k'ou. We routed three regiments of the enemy's vanguard, dealing severe losses to them and killing their regimental commander who was in charge of the vanguard. However, enemy reinforcements took up high positions all along their route and constructed a series of defense lines, each one stronger than the last, as we advanced. In spite of the ferocity of our assaults, we were eventually pinned down by enemy gunfire.

As the battle developed, the enemy confronting us held our main strength in check. Another column of the enemy pushed from Hsuan-hua-tien of Lo-shan towards Ch'i-li-p'ing to get to our rear. The enemy troops at Sung-pu and Li-chia-chi seized the walled city of Huang-an by storm. Those at Ma-ch'eng also took Chang-tien in the north. They also sent out a large number of planes to bomb us. Our local armed units were busy making harassing raids against the attacking enemy. When I rushed to the front at night from Ch'i-li-p'ing, there was constant gunfire all around, as if the battle were raging everywhere.

The next day, when Hsü Hsiang-ch'ien and I observed the enemy from a hilltop with binoculars, we discovered that we were far outnumbered by the enemy troops directly in front of us. They were fortifying their positions on the hilltops and were moving to outflank us. We decided that it was the enemy's strategy to pin down our main strength here while other units of theirs were trying to sever our route of retreat at Ch'i-li-p'ing by attacking from three places: Hsuan-hua-tien, Huang-an, and Chang-tien. We could hardly liquidate quickly the enemy confronting us, and we were seriously menaced from the rear, so we made up our mind to withdraw to Ch'i-li-p'ing immediately.

When we had retreated east of Ch'i-li-p'ing, three Nationalist columns under Wei Li-huang, Ch'en Chi-ch'eng, and Liu Chih from Ho-k'ou, Hsuan-hua-tien, and other places had reached the area west of Ch'i-li-p'ing and were facing us across the river, while the troops under Hsiao Chih-ch'u from Huang-an had advanced to twenty li south of Ch'i-li-p'ing; the enemy troops under Hsia Tou-yin at Chang-tien remained in their positions, and other parts of Liu Chih's forces were pushing towards the northwest of Hsin-chih. As Ch'i-li-p'ing was the most favorable stronghold in the Soviet region for us to exert our power from, we decided to make a last-ditch stand against our enemy here.

Less than two days later we decided to strike out from the Liu-lin River, five li south of Ch'i-li-p'ing. It was dusk. We concentrated our men to breach the enemy line in the middle. This developed into a large-scale night battle. By midnight we had advanced fifteen li to the command headquarters of Wei Li-huang. The enemy troops were thrown into utter confusion on a wide front. Our local armed units also kept up with harassing raids against them everywhere. The battle raged almost continuously in an area of two thousand square kilometers. The enemy seemed to be unaccustomed to nocturnal combat, which was our specialty. For example, two of our guerrillas stole well into the enemy line under the cover of darkness and fired a few shots in between two enemy divisions. This caused a misunderstanding between the two divisions, which thereupon fired on each other until daybreak.

The battle of the Liu-lin River was an unprecedentedly vicious one. At least, none of the high-ranking officers of the Fourth Front Army had ever taken part in such fierce fighting before. Ch'en Keng remarked, "The battle of the Liu-lin River was more intense than any we had ever fought in the country and could be compared to the First World War."

We had thrown all we had into the battle. Take the Fourth Red Army, for example. Except for myself and a few followers who had to stay behind at the command post, all others from the general staff, from the political workers down to the cooks, had to take up guns to fight on the front. The enemy held firm when our troops stormed Wei Li-huang's command post. As dawn drew near, continuing our attacks might have rendered us vulnerable to the enemy's superior gunfire. Besides, routing this part of the enemy troops would still leave larger numbers of their reinforcements to cope with. It was well-nigh impossible to defeat the enemy completely there and then. Hence, our front-line commander, Hsü Hsiang-ch'ien, ordered a retreat. At daybreak our main strength withdrew to the east bank of the Liu-lin River.

It has been reported that our enemy was in a state of utter confusion. Ch'en Chi-ch'eng had been in favor of withdrawal, but had to give in to Wei Li-huang's strong desire to hold out until dawn. If they had retreated, it would have been a most outstanding victory for us indeed. Wei Li-huang was later highly commended by Chiang himself for holding fast to the defense in this battle. Soon afterwards, when Chinchia-chai was taken by the enemy, Chiang ordered that it be renamed Li-huang County, apparently in commemoration of Wei's meritorious contribution in the battle of the Liu-lin River.

The Fourth Army suffered more than two thousand casualties, while the local armed units suffered about three hundred casualties. Our enemy lost far more in killed and wounded, a large proportion of which resulted from mistaking the identity of their own two divisions during the night.

At the first sign of dawn, enemy planes based in Hankow began more frantic bomb raids against us, in formations of nine to twenty-seven each time, indiscriminately and without any letup. We had placed a big red cross on the ground at our hospital, but it was bombed even more relentlessly.

Under such frenzied air attacks, we actively regrouped ourselves.

Our fighters were tired out after the all-night battle and rested in the trenches. In reviewing the battle, we considered that victory eluded us mainly because of our numerical inferiority. We proceeded to prepare for further reverses. Meanwhile, we immediately mobilized more local armed units and recruited more men for our Fourth Army to make up for our losses. We evacuated the sick and wounded to villages in the woods; we ordered the Soviet organs and the local armed units in these villages to disperse or disband; and we directed the remaining people to store food, to look after the sick and wounded, and to be ready to act independently at their own discretion.

Our enemy was also regrouping its units, and refrained from any immediate counterattacks. All was relatively quiet. Some enemy units in a chaotic state on the front were withdrawn under air cover. They seemed to realize that the deployment of too much strength on the front line might result in confusion under our nocturnal raids, and so they withdrew the bulk of their forces to the second defense line, leaving only skeletal units at the front line to watch us. Although we had no fear of imminent attack from the enemy confronting us, Nationalist troops north of Hsin-chi were advancing towards Hsin-chi, obviously to threaten our rear.

After two or three days of rest and regrouping, our forces were more or less in good shape again. With the bulk of the enemy in front of us withdrawing slightly, we found it hard to make an effective attack on them. Therefore, we decided to shift the Fourth Army secretly to the north of Hsin-chi, where we might stand a better chance of defeating the attacking enemy force which was smaller in number.

The large-scale onslaught of the enemy had also upset our men emotionally. They were uneasy about the destruction of their homes and farms, the laying waste of their houses and ancestral graves, and the absence of news about the safety of their families. We did our best to console them, pointing out that our formidable enemy could not be disposed of without quite a series of battles, that the martyrdom of relatives and the destruction of homesteads should serve to strengthen our will to fight, and that we had no alternative.

The general public of the Soviet region did not seem to share precisely the same view that our men held. As the Fourth Army was secretly moving north of Hsin-chi, I gave my regards to the peasants I met while riding along. They all indicated to me that, in the battle of the Liu-lin River, the Fourth Army had tried its best to protect the Soviet region; but because the enemy was far superior to us in strength and had held virtually all the commanding heights in front of Ch'i-li-p'ing, it had wrought serious havoc on all villages in the neighborhood. They felt that such blows to the Soviet region were unavoidable, and they hoped that we could conserve our strength so that we might make it possible for them to rise again some time in the future.

In a civilian house outside Hsin-chi, I called the last conference of the CC subbureau. The face of Hsin-chi was entirely changed. Collapsed houses, rubble, and bomb craters were everywhere. My former office had been razed by bombs. Our various organs had been evacuated to nearby villages. Many responsible comrades had been away directing the fighting at various places. Present at the conference were only a minority of the CC subbureau and the Party's Provincial Committee; the majority were the cadres of various organizations who had remained behind.

The spirit of unity and the resolve to fight were strong at the conference. It was the consensus that the Soviet region had become untenable, that the Fourth Army was likely to incur more losses militarily if it persisted in remaining and resorting to guerrilla warfare against the enemy, and that therefore it might as well, if necessary, move away to the outer perimeter of defense in the Soviet region and leave the burden of defense of the region to the local armed units.

At this same conference, our decisions were these: The commander of the Thirty-sixth Regiment, Hsü Hai-tung, who was still recovering from his wounds, was to be appointed commander of the Oyüwan Soviet Region Command, directing all guerrilla activities of local armed units of the region. The Fourth Army was to seize the opportunity to break out from the enemy's siege, in order to attack the enemy from the rear. All county and district Party and political units were to direct and participate in the guerrilla warfare. The CC subbureau, the Provincial Committee of the Party, and the Soviet organs were to be reorganized, with many leading cadres assigned to various counties and districts to strengthen the leadership in the respective places.

The Fourth Army had reached the An-chia River, forty li northwest of Hsin-chi, and were in contact with the enemy. I rushed to the front and took a look from one of the hilltops. I saw that the enemy was building up its fortifications, and large numbers of enemy troops were massed along a twenty-li front. Some tents were set up, apparently because of insufficient accommodations in civilian houses. Although we were far outnumbered, the enemy dared not attack us. They were making signs on the ground to identify themselves to their planes. We followed their example, and the bombs were dropped in no man's land in the woody, hilly areas.

For a time our front-line positions seemed to have become the most peaceful haven, so we held a military conference there. It was an important meeting, attended by most cadres of the regimental level and above. Many people spoke at the meeting. We all felt that we had nothing to be ashamed of in our encounter with the enemy between Huang-an and Ho-k'ou and the subsequent night battle at the Liu-lin River. Speaking from their personal experience, they thought that we were in danger of being besieged by the enemy after failing to defeat the enemy between Huang-an and Ho'kou as a result of the enemy's preponderance of manpower. The conclusion was reached that our retreat to Ch'i-li-p'ing was a necessary step. Although the enemy had been thrown into confusion on a wide front in the night battle at the Liu-lin River, they had powerful reserves and still possessed many strongholds. In comparison, our strength had already been taxed to the utmost. On these considerations, it was quite well and proper for our front-line commander, Hsü Hsiang-ch'ien, to order withdrawal to our original position before daybreak.

We estimated that it would be no easy matter for us to try to cripple even the enemy that was directly in front of us. Even if we succeeded in a gambling stroke, our rear was likely to be cut off, and we would be trapped on a narrow front and placed in an impasse.

We decided at this meeting that we would refrain from any offensive against the enemy in front of us, while the Fourth Army would seek to open a gap at any relatively weak spot of the enemy's defense line, dash to the enemy's rear, and crack the enemy in a piecemeal manner. All the army officers indicated that, under our exigency, there was no justifiable need for any more military meetings, and that all should take orders from the chairman of the Military Committee and the front-line commander. In fact, we did not have another similar meeting until we were in northern Szechwan.

Hsü Hsiang-ch'ien, Ch'en Ch'ang-hao, and I ordered our troops to evacuate the area near the An-chia River and move eastward to Pai-ch'ueh-yuan, with Chin-chia-chai as our destination. Ts'ai Shen-hsi met with us, and he was in complete agreement with our plan for the speedy shift of the Fourth Army to the area west of the Peking-Hankow Railway. At Chin-chia-chai we made certain necessary arrangements for some people to stay put in order to proceed with the guerrilla operations of the local armed units. Then we made assertions to create the impression that our troops would be heading east or crossing the Yangtze River to make for the Kiangsi Soviet region in the south, to divert the enemy's attention.

The Seventy-third Division led by Ts'ai Shen-hsi joined our westward-pushing forces at Chin-Chia-chai. All in all, these forces comprised the Fourth Army's Tenth, Eleventh, and Twelfth divisions and the Twenty-fifth Army's Seventy-third Division, a total of sixteen thousand men. We headed south towards Ying-shang from Chin-chia-chai. Near Ying-shang we broke through an attempted interception by enemy divisions under Hao Men-lin and Shang Kuan Yun-hsiang. We swerved west from Ying-shang to reach the vicinity of Kao-ch'iao, south of Huang-an, after passing through Ch'uang-tzu-fou and other places. (Ch'uang-tzu-fou, which was also called Ch'uang-fou, is 120 li northwest of Huang-kang in Hupeh. It bordered on Wu-hu and was close to Huang-po County, and it had a highway on the east leading to Huang-an.) Thus, in our high-speed night marches, we had made a big detour round the Soviet region.

At Kao-ch'iao I met Shen Tse-min; this was my last meeting with him. He had long since learned something about our decisions, and he rendered active support to the rapid movement of our troops to the area west of the Peking-Hankow Railway. By this time the enemy had completely occupied the part of our Soviet region near Hsin-chi and Ch'i-li-p'ing, and serious guerrilla battles had flared up between our local armed units along with some of our men who remained behind there. We held a discussion, mainly about the reallocation of personnel. I had asked Shen Tse-min and other important cadres to follow us in going to the area west of the Peking-Hankow Railway. In spite of his poor health, however, he thought that he was duty-bound as secretary of the Party's Provincial Committee for the Oyüwan border area to stay put and engage in guerrilla warfare with the enemy. He eventually gave his life in one of these guerrilla engagements.

As we had information that the bulk of the enemy's troops at Ho-k'ou had advanced to Ch'i-li-p'ing and that their defense there was relatively weak, we moved to the vicinity of Ho-k'ou without loitering in the Kao-ch'iao area, cracked the enemy defenses there, and headed straight for the Peking-Hankow Railway. Ts'ai Shen-hsi, whose troops provided cover for us to stand off enemy interception, perished in combat at that time. Among our forces, he was a popularly acknowledged strategist, and his death was grievously mourned by us.

As we headed for the area northeast of Ho-k'ou in the dark of night, our pursuing enemy was catching up with us from several directions.

We had been much exhausted by the nocturnal marches for several nights in succession, yet we were obliged to take up positions and to do battle with the strong enemy that was directly menacing us. A part of the enemy quickly pierced our defenses and cut off communication between our various units. Nevertheless, being experienced in battle, we fought bravely on our own. We suffered more than one thousand casualties in the melee, but the enemy troops that penetrated our line suffered about twice as many losses and were dealt a crippling blow. Thus, we stopped further pursuit by the enemy.

At Hsia-tien, when we were not far from the Peking-Hankow Railway, we made some final arrangements regarding our work in the Oyüwan Soviet region. We notified Shen Tse-min and others of our position after we had left them. We stressed that pressure from the pursuing enemy had made it imperative for us to go far away from the Soviet region; that it was impossible to predict when we might return; that our various units were thus obliged to fight independently and to make their own decisions; that the guerrilla units in the Soviet region could not count on any relief or support from the Fourth Front Army; that, under the adverse circumstances, they might try to join us west of the Peking-Hankow Railway; and that part of the cadres might either go to other Soviet regions or join us. That was our final directive to our comrades remaining behind in the Oyüwan Soviet region.

Some time after August 20, 1932, we crossed the Peking-Hankow Railway in the vicinity of Wang-chia-tien under cover of darkness. When the enemy came in armored railway cars to intercept us, we were already twenty li west of the railway tracks. Only random shots were audible from our pursuing enemy in the rear. We had given up our Oyüwan region and were embarking on our five-thousand-li westward march.

Enemy planes had been trailing us all the time, trying to discover our campsites and our route of movement, which furnished the basis of action to our pursuing enemy as well as to enemy garrisons trying to intercept us on our route of advance. We were also constantly harassed by the militia units all along the way. The common people dared not get in touch with us, which had a telling effect on our provisions.

Although we had withdrawn under enemy pressure, we were still anxious to split the enemy forces so that we might seize an opportunity to counterattack them. We hoped to secure a new base not too far away from the Oyüwan region. This, however, could never be accomplished without liquidating our pursuing enemy. We fought our way westward

through Lo-yang-tien, south of Sui-hsien. We made arrangements
to relieve ourselves of the burden of caring for our sick and wounded
from time to time. For example, our convalescing divisional commander
Liu Ying made his way to Shanghai from Lo-yang-tien in disguise to
seek medical treatment, and we lost contact with him at that time. We
also reduced our nocturnal marches in order not to tire ourselves too
much. Since we could never escape detection by enemy planes, it was
futile to exhaust ourselves in such fatiguing marches. We regularly detailed small guerrilla units to keep the enemy engaged, to tire them, and
to distract them from making speedy effective pursuits.

When we pushed to the vicinity of Wu-chia-chi, south of Tsao-yang,
we had the biggest encounter with the enemy in our westward movement. Wu-chia-chi was about ninety li south of Tsao-yang and about
one hundred li away from the Han River and Hsiang-yang to the west.
Our enemy had chosen to close in on us from the east, south, and north
in this area, attempting to force us to the bank of the Han River and
exterminate us there.

As we camped in the vicinity of Wu-chia-chi, the enemy pressed
close to us in the night. At daybreak we began to be locked in fierce
battle. Since we did not have the initiative, we could not shake ourselves
free unless we dealt the enemy a heavy blow. After a seesaw battle of
two days and one night, we finally managed to puncture a hole in the
enemy line to the north and thus broke the siege.

At a most critical moment in the battle the enemy fought to within
fifty yards of the command post of myself and Hsü Hsiang-ch'ien. The
battle had raged over a rather wide area, and there was no well formed
line on either side as we surged back and forth at various points. The
enemy seemed to have located our command post. They mustered strong
forces to attack in that direction on the second afternoon. About three
hundred men defending the front of the command post rushed back towards the command post after suffering heavy casualties, all company,
platoon, and section commanders having perished in the combat. Hsü
Hsiang-ch'ien kept a cool head by immediately regrouping these rem-
nant units and appointing the more energetic men among them as new
company, platoon, and section commanders. I rallied together about
three hundred men from the general staff, political workers, and others
to form a new unit. When the enemy was close enough to the command
post, at a vocal command from Hsü Hsiang-ch'ien we all rushed out,
firing and throwing hand grenades at our advancing enemy, and forced
them to retreat.

The fiercest enemy offensive was thus repulsed, and the enemy line to the north was broken. A temporary lull ensued. We tried to take advantage of the darkness of night to retreat northwards. This was a most difficult retreat for us. Ch'en Ch'ang-hao, who had been fighting to the north, led his men as a vanguard ahead of us; Hsü Hsiang-ch'ien followed with the main body of our troops; and I led some men to fight as rear guards. The retreat commenced at dusk and was scheduled to be completed by 10 P.M. However, one of our regiments went astray in our withdrawal from a wide front. In trying to trace this regiment, we could not get away from the enemy until after midnight.

We walked over a footpath for more than one hundred li that night before we reached the vicinity of Pan-ch'iao-tien, twenty li west of Tsao-yang, penetrating the enemy's second defense line. I led ten-odd riders to act as the rear guard for the entire army. It was broad daylight when we reached Pan-ch'iao-tien, and our horses, which could hardly move another step due to exhaustion, were drinking from a small stream. Suddenly, the pursuing enemy from Tsao-yang took a commanding height on our right and began to pour machine-gun bullets past my sides and to exert their control over our route of advance. If our rear-guard regiment had been less prompt in rushing back to our support, the result to me might have been unthinkable.

Under cover from our rear-guard regiment, we dismounted to fight with the enemy, withdrawing to the north as we kept the enemy engaged. We made twenty li more before meeting Hsü Hsiang-ch'ien and Ch'en Ch'ang-hao on another hill. After that, I collapsed on the ground from having overexerted myself for so many days. Most other people, including Ch'en Ch'ang-hao, were also indescribably tired. Only Hsü Hsiang-ch'ien and a few others who had extremely strong physiques could still move about. Hsü immediately reported to me that further ahead of us to the north were two enemy divisions under Liu Mou-en from Honan, which formed a third defense line to block our way, that it was imperative to crush these forces of Liu Mou-en before we could safely break away from the enemy's siege, and that he proposed that he lead troops to fight a decisive battle with Liu Mou-en's men. I could hardly say a word, but indicated my assent with my hand.

Hsü Hsiang-ch'ien then led his men, who had a brief rest, ahead to fight Liu Mou-en's troops; Ch'en Ch'ang-hao followed a little later; and I brought up the rear. Fortunately, Liu's combat strength was very weak. Hungry and exhausted as our troops were, we dispatched Liu's forces without much exertion. We continued our way northward for eighty to ninety li to reach the vicinity of Tsao-yang and Hsin-yeh on the border between Honan and Hupeh. In one day and one night we had pushed ahead more than two hundred li, leaving our pursuing enemy from Wu-chia-chi far behind. Liu Mou-en's troops also could molest us no more.

We camped on the dry fields on both sides of the road. What we needed most was rest. Even our meals became secondary; in fact, our cooks were too tired to do anything. Our horses were turned loose in the fields. I and the ten-odd others on horses at the rear did not reach the camps until very late at night. After I had learned about Hsü Hsiang-ch'ien's and Ch'en Ch'ang-hao's plans for the next day, I fell asleep right on the ground.

When I suddenly woke up under the sunshine the next day, I found that our main troops were all gone; they had set off at 5 A.M. My ten-odd followers around me were still fast asleep. After awakening them, I learned from a guard on duty that he had been notified of their departure, but had gone back to sleep before he could alert us.

We hurriedly gathered up our horses, saddled them, and rushed ahead. A night's rest had given us renewed energy. We went on for about ten li before we came to the gate of a large courtyard, where more than one hundred members of the local militia had lined up with their arms. I decided that they must be getting ready to welcome the Nationalist forces who were pursuing us. We headed straight towards them. Their leader shouted a command, and they all held up their guns to salute us. We waved our hands to answer their greetings, from horseback, and sped right past them. Soon, there were gunshots behind us. Probably the militia had mistaken us for Nationalist army officers at first, but later had realized our true identities and were trying to shoot at us. However, we were already out of range.

We galloped forward for nearly ten more li before we caught up with our main forces. Hsü and Ch'en, on being informed that we were lagging far behind, had rested by the road to wait for us. We laughed boisterously in recalling our experiences of the past three days. We thought that the enemy was no longer catching up with us. In fact, our late encounter had drawn to a close. We looked for a place to rest and a good meal for all our troops.

The last battle was an unfavorable blow to us. Although the enemy had not realized its objective, we had lost nearly two thousand men, including two regimental commanders and two regimental political advisers. The enemy seemed to have lost as much as we had, including a brigade commander. However, we had always held the belief that it was a failure to lose lives without gain. Besides, we could hardly afford to sustain any loss. The leaving behind of more than one thousand wounded was a particularly painful thing to us.

I had been immensely moved when I personally attended to the care of the wounded and sick in the rear. Most of the wounded had volunteered to stay behind instead of being a burden to the main forces, yet they were very much afraid that their lives would be in jeopardy when the enemy came. Our political workers did their best to console them and advised them to protest their rights if the enemy should mistreat or kill them.

Our forsaking of our wounded was a widely discussed, sad topic among the forces. Some felt that it was definitely unfavorable to us to be fighting without a base and urged that we speedily shake off the pursuing enemy and strive for a chance of respite. Many were rather homesick and wanted to return to their homes in the Oyüwan area and die near their homes, if need be, in guerrilla activities.

We, the leaders, were obliged to revise our plans. Seeing that we could hardly defeat the enemy or maintain our stand in the Oyüwan area, we needed to push on to the distant west and to avoid any combat with the enemy under our unfavorable circumstances. We had to strive our hardest in our quick march to tire out our pursuing enemy in the race.

We explained to our men that it was impossible, for the time being, to fight our way back to the Oyüwan area, and our Hobson's choice was to press west in quest of a new base. We wanted them to discard some old weapons, ammunition-exhausted guns or cannons, wounded or sick horses, and whatever was expendable, and to carry on their persons a three-days' supply of dry food. We also released some of our wounded cadres. Ch'en Keng, who had been wounded in Ho-k'ou, left us to seek medical treatment in Shanghai at this juncture. Thus, we became more mobile than ever before, both in our movements and in combating the enemy.

We made our way through Hsin-yeh, Teng-hsien, and Che-ch'uan in southwestern Honan and headed for the border areas between Shensi and Hupeh. The influence of the militia was quite strong in these regions. Many of the villages were well fortified and manned to repel bandits. When we camped in Hsin-yeh for the first time, the local militia slammed their doors on us. After our demonstration of strength and some negotiations, we reached some sort of compromise, with concessions from the militia. We were allowed to spend one night in any village we passed through, to buy food with cash, and to repay the local inhabitants for any damages to their property; but we were never to engage in any fighting in the villages. The militia promised not to conspire with the Nationalist troops against us. Thus, we were safe from any harassment by the militia all the way through southwestern Honan.

When we reached the Ching-tzu Pass on the Honan-Shensi border after leaving Che-ch'uan, we were blocked by the enemy garrison there. We made a pretense of attacking and then turned west, heading for Man-ch'uan Pass, which is near Yun-hsi in Hupeh, 120 li southeast of Shan-yang in Shensi. This was a mountainous area which had formerly been a rendezvous of outlaws. It was sparsely populated, and the land was only suitable for maize crops. There were only small, winding paths in and out; and Man-ch'uan Pass occupied a practically invulnerable position in this border area between Hupeh and Shensi.

On reaching the vicinity of Man-ch'uan Pass, we were halted again by enemy troops who were behind fortified defenses. From our contact with them we realized that they formed part of the enemy's main strength and were crack units. We checked our advance at once to reconnoiter the area. With great difficulty we managed to round up three persons in the hilly, wooded region. A brief cross-examination proved that they were enemy spies. We treated them well and promised to cause them no harm in hopes of obtaining some information from them. During the few days preceding, one of them had been beaten dozens of times with a pole by a village elder (guard chief) privately because of arrears in the payment of taxes, and his back still bore obvious marks. He did not need much persuasion before he divulged all he knew to us.

According to this man, the enemy planned to press us into a mountain valley near Man-ch'uan Pass, blockade us on our escape route, cause us to run short of provisions, and then exterminate us with their superior firepower. Right ahead of us, in front of Man-ch'uan Pass, were units of Hu Tsung-nan's division, which had recently transferred here from Yün-yang. Close on our heels were two enemy divisions. Stationed south of the valley were two more divisions, and north of the valley were two divisions under Hsiao Chih-ch'u. Two days earlier the village elder had ordered the local inhabitants to flee from the locality with all their provisions. That was to starve us in their trap. He also revealed to us that thirty li away to the right of Man-ch'uan Pass was a tortuous mountain path leading out of the valley to Shensi Province, and that this was a relatively easy exit for us in case Hsiao Chih-ch'u's men had not yet taken up positions there.

Our direct reconnaissance proved that this information was quite reliable. I immediately ordered Ch'en Ch'ang-hao to head quickly for the mountain path on the right of Man-ch'uan Pass with a regiment of troops. In about an hour and a half, our quick-acting Ch'en Ch'ang-hao and ten-odd horsemen had gained command of this path, just a moment ahead of Hsiao Chih-ch'u's men, whose vanguards at once became easy targets below us. Hsiao's men were forced to take up hilltop positions facing the path, in order to try to exert some measure of control over this path. The rest of Ch'en's regiment soon arrived, and a battle for these commanding heights developed. Finally, we seized all the heights overlooking this path.

Thus, we had a means of escape from our enemy's noose and from an encounter that might have turned out very unfavorably for us. Although our enemy's deployment was not really close-meshed—and even if a larger-scaled battle ensued, we could probably find other ways to deal with them—slipping through this mountain pass was the most expedient way out. All our enemy's labor was to no avail, and pressure from the pursuing enemy abated considerably. Obviously, pushing through the hilly areas was tiring them out after a long march. Most of their men had lagged behind, and they were somewhat disheartened at having been outwitted by us.

Our action was not accomplished, however, without cost. As we made our way north in the night along this narrow and rugged path, we could only move in single file at very slow speed. At daybreak the bulk of our clumsy cooking utensils had not yet pulled through, and enemy machine-gun fire was already reaching the path. To avoid casualties, we had to give up on bringing the cooking utensils over and had to let our cooking staff join us quickly. Afterwards we were obliged to make use of the kitchens of local people to cook our meals, which caused us a lot of problems and was a breach of our army's discipline.

Although Hsiao Chih-ch'u's men seemed rather slow in action, presumably due to exhaustion, they still attacked our rearguard vigorously, because they were under strict orders. Since our object was to get through quickly, we had no desire to engage them in combat, and we kept only a minimum force of rear guards. All twenty-six in the platoon fighting this rear-guard action perished in the encounter, thereby enabling the rest of us to escape safely. We were all deeply moved by their sacrifice. We gave them the posthumous honor of naming them the "Heroes' Platoon." Their undaunted spirit seemed to deal a small blow to the enemy's morale.

It was already late September. The wind was getting chilly, but we were still wearing the summer clothing that we had worn since we set out from the Oyüwan region. All of us felt cold as we walked along the mountain path, so we were obliged to permit the burning of maize stalks to make fires for getting some warmth. By this time the question of uniforms became a pressing problem as we moved forward.

The mountainous terrain of the areas on the Shensi-Hupeh border favored us if we should engage the enemy, but the place was so poor that both food and cloth were scarce. So we had to turn our way towards more prosperous districts like Tan-feng, Shang-hsien, and Lo-nan in southern Shensi.

This big group of adventurers that we had become roamed this area for quite a while, sometimes playing hide-and-seek with the enemy, whose reconnaissance planes had decreased in number considerably. The enemy held all of the important cities and towns as well as the key routes for our possible advance. We darted about here and there, trying to feel out the enemy's weak spots. We also dispatched small guerrilla units to keep the enemy busy everywhere.

We were doomed to disappointment in trying to look for a foothold. Food was quite adequate, and fruit, especially persimmons, was plentiful. Not having tasted fruit for several months, our men were greatly interested in the persimmons. However, there was an acute shortage of cloth. The few weaving looms in the villages could hardly cope with local needs and had nothing at all to spare for our uniforms.

It was at this time that we reached the decision to head for northern Szechwan. We could not go eastward, where enemy forces were strong. We could not go westward or northward, because the climate was severe and textiles were difficult to obtain. Hence we decided to leave southern Shensi, climb over the Ching-ling Range and go to the plains in Kuan-chung. The enemy forces trailing behind us would all be attracted there, whereupon we could recross the Ching-ling Range, enter the Han-chung region, climb over Pa-shan, and thus reach northern Szechwan. By making such a large detour, we hoped to shake off the bulk of the pursuing forces and establish ourselves somewhere.

To draw up this plan, I had sought the advice of a one-time expert leader of the outlaws. This sixty-year-old former commander of Yang Hu-ch'eng and other heroes, now a peasant in a village north of Shang-hsien, was conversant with the topography of this extensive region and was sympathetic with rebels.

According to his assessment and analysis of existing circumstances,

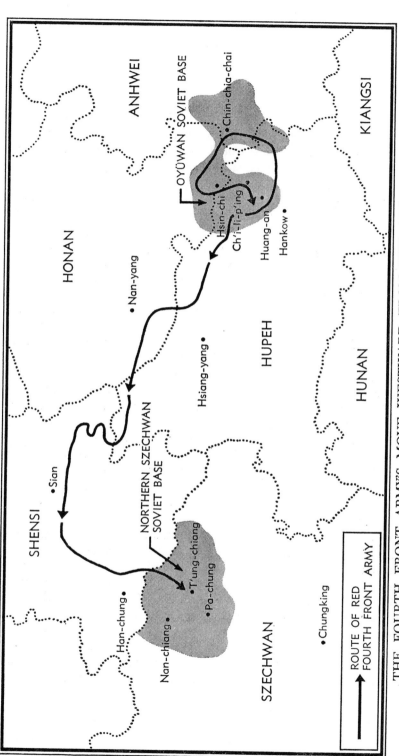

THE FOURTH FRONT ARMY'S MOVE WESTWARD FROM THE OYÜWAN SOVIET
BASE TO THE NEWLY FORMED NORTHERN SZECHWAN SOVIET BASE

it was a distinctly superior move to go via Han-chung. He thought that all the land would be wild and hazardous if we proceeded west from his vicinity to Han-chung. There would not only be difficulty in securing food supplies but also danger of setbacks in threading through enemy bastions that could easily be manned by small forces. If we were to scale the Ching-ling Range in trying to get to Han-chung, we should watch out for blockades and interceptions by the enemy in Central China from their fortified defenses. If we stayed put, the enemy, bent on encircling us, would wax in strength with growing reinforcements; and, besides, we were at our rope's end in looking for a solution to our problem of winter uniforms. His opinion strengthened our decision to head for northern Szechwan.

We pushed forward along the road from Shang-hsien to Sian. Then we made our way westward along the north side of the Ching-ling Range, south of Lin-t'ung and Sian. We had an encounter with Shensi troops at Tzu-wu-chen, and a day-and-night battle with Hu Tsung-nan's troops in the vicinity of Chou-chih. Hu Tsung-nan's men had been trailing us from Man-ch'uan Pass, regularly trying to intercept us. They had come to Chou-chih via Sian. Time and again we succeeded in withstanding enemy efforts to intercept us. Then we climbed the Ching-ling Range again from west of Chou-chih, and pushed towards Cheng-k'ou in Han-chung. The Ching-ling Range was a big, rugged mass with many peaks. It was extremely strenuous to negotiate these mountains. On both occasions we camped on the range, which was an extensive mass of utterly wild wasteland that imposed a severe test on our physical endurance and courage.

When we reached the foot of the southern slope of the Ching-ling Range, the Shensi troops in Han-chung wanted to block our exit from the mountains by holding firm to their fortified strategic points. But we pushed on with an irresistible drive, putting the enemy to flight before us. We sped forward to the vicinity of Ch'eng-k'ou. Our routed enemy could be seen everywhere in little groups; even their rifles and ammunition belts were abandoned all along the road. Such arms and ammunition were not worth anything to us now. We preferred to urge these stray soldiers of the Shensi troops to pick up their arms and ammunition and to hurry up to Nan-cheng, telling them that we had no desire to cause them trouble or to encroach on their sphere of influence in Shensi and that only the troops of Chiang Kai-shek were our enemy.

We took the opportunity, while resting near Ch'eng-k'ou, to announce to our men that northern Szechwan was our objective. We explained to them that we could hardly afford to linger in the neighborhood of Ch'eng-k'ou, as enemy reinforcements from Kuan-chung would be pouring in even though we had routed the enemy in Han-chung. We pointed out that things would be different in northern Szechwan, where warlords had firm control and had always been averse to the intrusion of troops from another province. So, when we entered northern Szechwan, our pursuers might stop short of the Szechwan border and might not be able to come to grips with us any more. Even if they should try, we could always engage them from our strategic positions in the Pa-shan area. That was why we had chosen northern Szechwan for our resting ground and possible new base.

From that time on, we no longer deserted our sick and wounded. In spite of our shortage of manpower and horses, we were still unwilling to resort to compulsory recruitment of local men. We had about one hundred wounded after the latest encounter with the enemy, and there were also some sick soldiers who could not walk. We were heavily taxed in trying to take them with us, but we gave up some of our cannons and rifles that had run short of ammunition to spare hands for carrying the sick and wounded on stretchers. Some of our valuable possessions that were carried by mules were also discarded to make it possible for more than thirty sick or wounded comrades to be borne by the mules. This exercised a galvanizing effect on our morale. All of our men realized now that when we had previously left behind our sick and wounded, it had been an absolute necessity.

It was already early November, and most of our men's hands and feet were chapped by the cold. When we waded across the Han River near Ch'eng-k'ou, the water was biting cold. However, except for the sick and wounded, none of us rode on anything to cross the river. All of our pack animals were used by the sick and wounded; Hsü Hsiang-ch'ien and I also picked our way on foot. This way of sharing pain and hardship with the common soldiers was dictated by necessity and was also our trump card for unity and loyalty under the adverse circumstances.

We trekked on towards the south of Hsi-hsiang. We were no longer harassed by pursuers from the rear or menaced by interceptors on our route of advance, and it was relatively easy to secure provisions all along. We now resumed our political work, and the soldiers all felt mentally relieved. We did our utmost to show our good will to the people in the vicinity of Ch'eng-k'ou and Hsi-hsiang, to pave the way towards maintenance of cordial relations with our prospective neighbors when we reached northern Szechwan.

After a brief stopover for two days south of Hsi-hsiang, we began to climb the Pa-shan, with T'ung-chiang as our objective. It took us two days to get over the famed Pa-shan. We spent the first night on a peak. There were only two ramshackle huts, which were hardly enough to accommodate even our sick and wounded. I personally saw that all the seriously ill and wounded were put up inside. All the rest were to sleep in the open, including myself. However, to show their warm appreciation, these seriously ill and wounded men, feeling that I was their physically and mentally overworked commander, shouted that I should be inside with them. I had to accede to their request, and I squeezed myself for the first time into their midst. That night they tried their best to swallow their moans and groans, lest I be disturbed. Today, in recalling that scene, I still feel touched by their warm love.

The next day, in the middle of November, 1932, we moved down the mountain for about one hundred li and reached Liang-ho-k'ou, a town at the northern tip of T'ung-chiang in northern Szechwan. We immediately made use of this place as headquarters for organizing our new base, a Soviet region in northern Szechwan. So far, since moving westward after crossing the Peking-Hankow Railway in late August, we had traversed more than five thousand li through Hupeh, Honan, and Shensi in the space of about eighty days to enter Szechwan, having no less than ten engagements with our pursuers or interceptors. We had lost about 40 percent of our men and arms. Originally we had a force of more than sixteen thousand men, more than twelve thousand rifles, and more than one hundred machine-guns; now we had only some nine thousand men, roughly eight thousand rifles, and only about half of the machine-guns. All of our more than thirty cannons had been abandoned.

It had been a nightmarish battle of retreat. I considered that it had been the inevitable result of a serious defect in the sovietization policy of the CC of the CCP, and that we had escaped annihilation through the Chinese Communists' formidable power of organization and the Fourth Front Army's courage and combat skill. This viewpoint of mine precipitated a grave split between me and the CC of the CCP over the fundamental policy of the sovietization campaign. I will dwell on this in greater detail later. Owing to limitations of time and materiel, I have ventured to present a mere sketch of this westward movement of the Fourth Front Army. A compilation of the numerous touching epic deeds of various comrades will depend on the efforts of the historians. I suppose that my basic viewpoint might have been shared by the comrades engaged in this westward move as well as the 25,000-li Long March from Kiangsi later on, and its validity testified to by them as well.

Our Early Days in Szechwan

Our troops had entered a completely strange land, terribly exhausted. From whatever angle you might look at it, this was a backward place. The people suffered a lot, especially from opium addiction. We had to go through a path of trial and error if we were to establish ourselves here. Our sorest need was rest; next came replenishment of our supplies; then, establishment of a base. All of these were more or less connected with the question of establishing our administration. So, how to create a popular local regime became the focal point of our discussions.

We all looked like a batch of real beggars. Except for a few comrades who had managed to get varicolored clothing on the way, all of us wore only two thin cotton uniforms on our persons, and they were already filthy rags. Most of us had neither shoes nor stockings; we just wrapped some rags around our feet. We covered ourselves with our worn army blankets day and night against the cold. We were dusty and deeply tanned, and our hands and feet had been chapped by the cold. Lice and fleas were all over us, and we had not had haircuts for three months. We looked more like ghosts than human beings, with our long, disheveled hair and unshaven beards.

I was saddened by such an unsightly state of affairs and had been trying to seek a solution all along the way. I felt that the issue at stake was political rather than military, and for me as a leader, it was more vital to comply with realistic demands than to be doctrinaire. I decided to scrap the Soviet formula, since I thought that it was at least not applicable to such backward areas in the Northwest. I was thinking about devising a new form of revolutionary and popular regime. To secure the necessary rest for our troops, I even thought of negotiating a temporary truce with the hostile forces all around us. I tried to put these ideas of mine into practice when we entered Szechwan.

At a teahouse in Liang-ho-k'ou we tried to draft a program for us in Szechwan. We found, upon inquiring, that there were only some twenty-odd shops in this little town, and most of the merchants had already fled from us. Only a few heavy opium addicts had stayed behind and were invited as our guests. All these few wore long gowns made of a single thickness of cloth. It was doubtful whether they even had under-wear. Each was carrying a little stove for greater warmth. Such was the typical picture of a local opium addict—a sickly, wan face and a mere bag of bones. It was possible that these might be spies of T'ien Sung-yao, one of the many warlords in Szechwan, whose sphere of in-fluence was in the vicinity of Liang-ho-k'ou. We did not ask about these people's backgrounds, but treated all of them to meat and wine as well as good, long puffs of opium. So, we struck up very cordial conversa-tions together.

We sat together around two very greasy square tables. I first told our guests that the Red Army was a well-disciplined force not given to indiscriminate killing or arson, and that we came not to start any war with T'ien Sung-yao but in the hope that he would leave us in peace in a small area to pass the winter. We hoped these guests of ours would spread the word so that the populace might settle down to their everyday lives and T'ien Sung-yao might be spared any misgivings about us. Then I requested them to speak freely about local affairs.

These people had quite a gift for gab, as was typical of all Sze-chwanese, whose wits must have been sharpened to cope with the in-numerable changes of warlords ruling over them. Our guests waxed eloquent after getting a full dose of opium. They did not know the status of their shabbily dressed hosts. They must have imagined that we were some subaltern officers who were less pretentious than a platoon com-mander of T'ien Sung-yao's. You see, T'ien's platoon commanders cus-tomarily rode on a sedan chair followed by ten soldiers whenever they came to the village and expected to be addressed as "Sir" by the villagers. In the eyes of our guests, our entire force must have seemed very amaz-ing. We certainly looked like routed troops, yet we were fully armed with rifles and ammunition and we were quite dignified and respectable in our spirit and conduct. Our humility, especially, was something they might never have seen before among military men. They asked many irrelevant questions, which we answered very patiently. This greatly increased their ease in speaking.

T'ien's oppression was undoubtedly highly deplored by the populace. They all said in one voice that "that God-damned bastard T'ien" had made the public suffer enough. They might have said that to ingratiate themselves with us at first, but the pathos of tone was unmistakably there and indignation gradually worked them up, especially when they talked about the multitudinous taxes and fees that he collected. They told us about the apalling burden of taxes connected with opium, such as the "lazy-man's duty" levied on nongrowers and the "opium-ban duty" on nonsmokers, besides others levied on growers and smokers. T'ien's troops were about six divisions strong, but they controlled only some ten-odd counties in northern Szechwan. The fact that such a large force of men had to be supported by people in such a limited area was probably one of the compelling reasons for his recourse to really extortionate taxation.

The method that T'ien employed to collect overdue taxes or fees was shocking. The penalty for any ordinary man involved in tax arrears of one dollar was clubbing on the buttocks one hundred times by order of the elder guard chief; this was a basic rate: arrears of three dollars would mean three hundred clubbings. After that, the arrears still had to be cleared up. The position of elder could usually be obtained through bribery. An elder had the collection of taxes and fees as his main duty, and he had the special authority to arrest or beat the common people at will. If an elder could not collect enough taxes and fees from a certain district, T'ien would dispatch a posse to press the collection. Needless to say, much chaos would then be created, and the people of the district concerned also had to bear the entire extra burden of supporting these soldiers during their period of stay there.

All the squires, army officers, usurers, and people serving in the local magistracy throughout the area under T'ien's control were as unscrupulous as T'ien. Land was practically worthless. Many people, unable to bear the burden of heavy taxation, mortgaged their estates or farms and left for Shensi or Kansu. Wealthy people saw this as an opportunity to purchase land at minimal prices. There were numerous cases of mortgaged land that was never redeemed. Land rent was in most cases a fixed rate, irrespective of what might be harvested. The interest rate on loans was even more appalling. One hundred percent per annum was considered very light, because the common practice was to charge one hundred percent per month.

As soon as we had gleaned certain information that we needed, we proceeded with the work of drafting the "Fourth Front Army's Program upon Entering Szechwan." It consisted of two portions. The first part, for immediate enforcement in any place reached by the Red Army, stressed three points: First, the Red Army would not collect or allow anyone else to collect any of the former taxes or fees. Second, land rent was to be reduced to not more than 40 percent of the harvest, and the interest rate was to be reduced to not more than 30 percent per annum. Third, the Red Army would not arrest anyone without cause, nor would it allow anyone else to do so; all clubbing or any other form of physical punishment would be dispensed with; and nobody was to be detained without charge. It was our minimum politicial program and was to take effect immediately without reservation.

The second part, called the "Sixteen-Point Program," was a statement of common aims to be strived for by the people of Szechwan and ourselves. The most outstanding characteristic was a call for the joint organization of a Szechwan Province People's Government by the people throughout Szechwan along with the Fourth Front Army, without any reference to a Soviet regime. Next came points of general policy, such as fair distribution of land, safeguard of workers' interests, complete equality of men and women, a consolidated system of taxation, promotion of culture and education, opposition to imperialism and Japanese aggression, overthrow of Chiang Kai-shek, and so forth, which were all consistent with established policies advocated by the Chinese Communists. Then came special local measures, such as relinquishment of the system of defense regions, nonintervention of various military units, and banning of opium.

Our troops advanced from Liang-ho-k'ou towards the city of T'ung-chiang along the Ta-t'ung River. When we reached K'u-ch'ao-pa, about 120 li from Liang-ho-k'ou, we held our first conference of high-level military and political cadres to make decisions about our future moves.

The consensus favored the founding of our new base here, where there was mountainous terrain all around. Very high, steep mountains rose on both sides of the Ta-t'ung River, forming precipitous cliffs of awesome height. On close inspection we found that most of the rural villages were situated in clearings in the middle of elevated land on the hills. Rice and many other subsidiary food products were grown in many of the terraced or level fields. The villagers were not afraid when they saw us coming, but went on working as usual. We decided that it was a likely place to establish our foothold.

We had the feeling that, for the time being, our enemy could not do anything to interfere with us here. The information available to us showed that in the T'ung-chiang–Nan-chiang–Pa-chung area T'ien Sung-yao's defense preparations were negligible, and the combat strength of his troops was also very weak. There was no sign that our enemy in Han-chung had followed us into Szechwan Province. We imagined that for the moment they probably would not dare to come into contact with us, tired out as they were. Liu Ch'uan-hou's force to the east of T'ung-chiang was even smaller and might not be able to withstand any blow from us. On the basis of such an analysis, we could catch our breath here for a while.

Nevertheless, we took some pains to make certain arrangements. Temporarily, we occupied only the part of T'ien Sung-yao's territory bound by T'ung-chiang, Nan-chiang, and Pa-chung to avoid making other enemies. Even against T'ien Sung-yao, we also sought to refrain from any combat with his troops so that we could have a breathing spell to replenish badly needed supplies. This was our number-one objective, for the realization of which we were willing to pay a reasonable price. We condescended to write to T'ien Sung-yao, appealing for restraint so that we might pass the winter in peace in the T'ung-chiang–Nan-chiang–Pa-chung area. We were also prepared to clarify our position to Liu Ch'uan-hou to the east and Yang Hu-ch'eng to the north, in hopes of tolerant coexistence.

We had never expected very fruitful results from our political gestures; so, in the meanwhile, we continued to prepare ourselves actively for combat. Although we were numerically much reduced, we pretended to be expanding, to put up an impressive false front. We decided to reorganize the four divisions under the Fourth Front Army into four armies under the general command of Hsü Hsiang-ch'ien and Ch'en Ch'ang-hao, in the following way:

1. The Fourth Army was formed from the Tenth Division, with Wang Hung-k'un and Chou Ch'un-ch'üan as commander and political commissar respectively.
2. The Ninth Army was formed from the Twelfth Division, with Ho Wei and Chan Ts'ai-fang as commander and political commissar.
3. The Thirtieth Army was formed from the Eleventh Division, with Ch'en Shih-ts'ai and Li Hsien-nien as commander and political commissar.
4. The Thirty-first Army was formed from the Seventy-third Division, with Wang Shu-sheng and Chang Kuang-ts'ai as commander and political commissar.

There were also many changes in personnel, mainly to draw off a batch of cadres from the troops in order to organize local Party and administrative machinery.

We also decided to let the four armies take independent action in coping with the enemy from different directions, with T'ung-chiang as their nerve center. The Fourth Army was stationed east of T'ung-chiang to deal with Liu Ch'uan-hou's troops coming from Shui-ting and Wan-

yüan. The Ninth Army would push southwest of T'ung-chiang to occupy Pa-chung. The Thirtieth Army would maneuver south of T'ung-
chiang to cope with troops of Yang Sen in Ying-shan and Ch'ü-hsien. The
Thirty-first Army advanced to the northwest to take Nan-chiang. I stayed
with the Military Committee in T'ung-chiang, temporarily, to direct the
Party, military, and political operations. The command headquarters of
the Fourth Front Army was also provisionally established in T'ung-
chiang. K'u-ch'ao-pa became the rear base for these armies.

K'u-ch'ao-pa was an important base of operations for military ventures to the north, as well as being our base in the rear. Though a small
town with some forty shops, it held a strategic position, and there were
plenty of food crops grown in the vicinity. It was an eminently tenable
place, with a big stockade on a hill in back of it. Inside the stockade
were many houses which accommodated all our sick and wounded as
well as our administrative offices. Later, we also established our mu-
nitions works and a garment and quilting factory here, since a handful
of soldiers could hold a strong attacking force at bay. North of K'u-
ch'ao-pa lay the route of our entry into Szechwan, and the extensive
Pa-shan Range provided a natural shield. We posted only a minimum
force of men at Liang-ho-k'ou to watch over the movements of our enemy
from Han-chung. That was the best we could do with our acute shortage
of manpower.

After deciding on the above military deployments, we began deliberations concerning the program we had drafted earlier at Liang-ho-
k'ou. Generally speaking, all of our comrades approved of the program
that had been drafted. They hailed the proposed immediate enforcement
of the first portion comprising three major points, which they considered
a masterpiece. As to the proposed formation of a people's government
without any reference made to a Soviet government, most agreed in
principle that this was a necessary reform under the existing circumstances, but a few found it hard to reconcile themselves with a view
rather divergent from the general line of the CC.

Under our military exigency, the pending questions did not permit
of protracted discussion. We decided, therefore, to put our draft proposals into practice immediately and to promulgate at once the "Fourth
Front Army's Program upon Entering Szechwan" in all places within the
area. We were prepared to try, upon occupying the city of T'ung-chiang,
to tentatively form the T'ung-chiang County Provisional People's Government, and, as soon as conditions in our new base became more stabilized, to call another conference of high-level cadres for more delibera-

tions on the subject and then to report to the CC. Thus, we proceeded forthwith with our planned military operations that had been decided upon in the conference right in the vicinity of K'u-ch'ao-pa.

Our command post—the Military Committee and the Fourth Front Army Command Headquarters—immediately started to move towards the city of T'ung-chiang, one hundred li away, as soon as the various armies had left. We camped first at Wa-szu-p'u. The further south we moved, the more thriving were the markets and towns. Wa-szu-p'u had more than one hundred shops, which were well stocked with native goods including dried white mushrooms and herbs. The dried white mushrooms were nationally treasured for their nutritive value and were quite cheap there, but we didn't quite know how to eat them. Our troops brought a large bucketful of this food back and boiled it until it was soft, to eat like rice gruel. As a matter of fact, white mushrooms could never fill the stomach as rice could. I had a good laugh at that time, and I also had the feeling that it would be some time before our comrades would get a clear understanding of local conditions.

Meanwhile, a fire started by T'ien Sung-yao's spies did us a great favor. The next morning, when more than a thousand of us connected with the command post were assembled at a public square outside the town, ready to set out, a big fire broke out in the town. The blaze spread rapidly because most of the houses were built of wood. We immediately rushed back to the town to do whatever we could to check the fire. Hsü Hsiang-ch'ien, Ch'en Ch'ang-hao, and I suddenly found ourselves commanders of a huge fire brigade. Our men were courageous and also quite efficient in action. As a result, almost one-half of the town's houses and large amounts of goods were saved from destruction, but quite a number of our men were wounded by the fire.

Before our arrival at this town, some of its inhabitants had fled from us in fear, and certainly not enough people had stayed behind to look after their goods. While we were fighting the fire, the refugees at first gathered on a nearby height to watch. When they saw with their own eyes how we were combating the blaze, more and more of them came back to join the battle. Soon the whole town was full of the hustle and bustle of people. After the fire we distributed the salvaged goods to their original owners and also did what we could to provide the refugees with proper shelter. The local inhabitants were intensely moved.

At this moment an innkeeper in the town publicly announced that the fire had started at his inn and that he had personally seen how it was deliberately kindled by two of his customers who had since disappeared.

He added that he could identify these two culprits as spies for T'ien Sung-yao. This created a furor. Now the people realized that the arsonists had been T'ien Sung-yao's men instead of ours and that they were trying to put the blame for the blaze on us with complete disregard for the town's inhabitants, whereas we had really been the fire fighters. This news spread far and wide, and henceforth the people of other villages no longer believed the rumor that Red Army soldiers were bloodthirsty killers and arsonists. They were not afraid of us any longer, nor did they run away from us.

On that same day we walked south for sixty li and reached T'ung-chiang. The Ninth Army had taken the city one day earlier. It was the first city taken by us on our westward trip, and we held a formal ceremony to mark our entry into the city. The city was situated in a corner of northern Szechwan, with a hill at its back and a river passing in front. Small as it was, it boasted of several paved roads and a Dr. Sun Park, which were typical examples of the Szechwan warlords' fondness for ostentation. On an elevation within the park there was also a two-story modern house. Originally the guesthouse of the local magistracy, this now became our office building, and I worked in it during most of the time that I was in northern Szechwan.

The Ninth Army pushed west towards Pa-chung after taking T'ung-chiang. After making about thirty li, they came into contact with some of T'ien Sung-yao's men at Ying-ko-tsui. Having an order not to engage T'ien's troops in combat temporarily, they halted their advance and took up defense positions there. Hearing the news of our entry into Szechwan, T'ien Sung-yao, who was based at San-t'ai, immediately dispatched his division that was stationed at Lang-chung under the command of Lo Tse-chou to hurry to T'ung-chiang to intercept us. (San-t'ai was about 480 li from T'ung-chiang, while Lang-chung was about 300 li from T'ung-chiang, in between San-t'ai and T'ung-chiang; Pa-chung was about 120 li from T'ung-chiang, in between Lang-chung and T'ung-chiang.) At that time, only some vanguards of Lo Tse-chou's troops had reached Ying-ko-tsui and were certainly in no position to start an offensive yet. For the time being, we were both watching each other.

I wrote a letter to T'ien, advising him of our intentions. I first made it clear to him that we had no wish to engage him in combat, because we were opposed to Chiang Kai-shek only and not to any of the military men in Szechwan; that we wanted merely to stop over in the T'ung-chiang–Nan-chiang–Pa-chung area, and if he would tolerate us and refrain from any attack, we planned to withdraw to Central China by the next spring. I expressed the hope that we could come to some compromise by drawing up a boundary to separate us and that each party would try not to start any conflict that might do neither party any good. To ensure that this would be received by T'ien, I handwrote several copies to be delivered to him by different couriers.

About a fortnight later, all of Lo Tse-chou's men had massed at Ying-ko-tsui. Other division of T'ien's had also been deployed in battle array at various positions. Then, T'ien showed his true colors. Lo Tse-chou arrogantly told our emissary, "The Communist bandits have fled to this place as a defeated force. I have orders to wipe them out relentlessly. Even if they try to dash away somewhere else, I will not give up the chase to finish them off." Under these circumstances, fighting soon broke out between us and T'ien.

Meanwhile, our troops had had a chance to relax and reorganize themselves. There was a considerable stock of cotton and cotton cloth in the towns in this vicinity. We had purchased much of these and had made up the greater part of the cotton-padded winter uniforms that we needed. Our shortage of cooking utensils had also been made up. We were able to pay attention to our hygiene, and there were efficacious results in the treatment of our sick and wounded and those suffering from chilblains. Reports from our various armies mostly dwelt in glowing terms on the restoration of our original fighting spirit with the dissipation of our erstwhile slovenliness.

Objective circumstances favored our optimism. There was no shortage of food, and it was quite easy to confiscate. Most of the food had been kept in the hands of the influential wealthy minority in the form of "food requisitions by the squires," whereas the majority of the people were in extreme poverty. Whenever we took action to acquire our provisions from such a source, usually hundreds, and sometimes nearly a thousand, poor people trailed behind us with baskets, making a touching sight. Every time, each of these people obtained a share of thirty to forty catties of coarse grain after our needs were met, and they could hardly hide their joy. Very often we obtained our provisions with a minimum use of force and had enough to spare towards the relief of the old and weak. Therefore, our action was enthusiastically supported by the majority of local people.

But we were not entirely without cause for pessimism when we were faced with the question of opium addiction. The overwhelming majority of the local people smoked opium. It was alleged that 90 percent of the adult males were opium addicts, and many twelve- and thirteen-year-old boys also had this bad habit; about 70 percent of the adult females were opium smokers. This situation caused us much worry.

For the first time we were confronted with the gargantuan task of getting new recruits. None of our men smoked opium. They were opposed to the habit, and we had never allowed any opium smokers to join our ranks. Now, non-opium-smoking youths were hard to find, and we were very embarrassed when many local youths volunteered to join us. Our comrades generally thought it was well-nigh impossible to expand the Red Army here since we could not take in opium addicts without lowering the quality of the Red Army. Thus, a feeling of reluctance to settle down in this area ran high among our men.

Opium was produced in the greater part of West China, and T'ung-chiang especially was a center of opium traffic. This drug had become the most valuable form of currency in business transactions in this area. Most leading merchants and wealthy people hoarded more opium than anything else. All relatively fertile land in the county was devoted to the growth of poppies. The peasants were more willing to invest their money and labor in the poppy crop than in food crops. As far as I could see, all the poppy fields were neat, well weeded, and thriving, whereas the fields with food crops obviously were in need of fertilizer, weeding, and proper attention. Opium was also a form of offering to the gods, as I could see when I found that the lips of the idols in most temples had been smeared with opium by the worshipers. The drug was also regarded as a panacea and was the first thing employed to cure any ailment.

Such an appalling state of affairs was primarily the result of warlord rule. Take the case of T'ung-chiang as an example. Tien Sung-yao had to collect $260,000 a year from this county of roughly 110,000, and the people were obliged to pay several times that amount. Anyone desirous of an appointment as a district chief for a tenure of three months had to spend at least $3,000 as palm grease. Such a district chief would not find this a lucrative proposition without gleaning several times the $3,000 he had paid out himself in addition to collecting the levies. There were ten district chiefs in the county, who spent at least $120,000 a year in palm grease and therefore had to collect at least $240,000 extra for themselves from the people. Such palm grease was necessary for all appointments from county magistrate down to village elders, tax collectors, and constables. The additional burden on the people can be imagined when each and every one of these was anxious to make a maximum profit out of his monetary investment.

T'ung-chiang was a typical center for exploiting the people. Out of about one thousand families in the city, more than two hundred ran opium dens and more than two hundred more or less depended for their living on court expenses furnished by the villagers from all over the county. It must be noted that at this time a county magistrate in Szechwan was concurrently vested with the powers of a judge who handled anything from civil and criminal cases to dunning for tax and duty payments; all conceivable issues, big and small, were taken to court and decided by the county magistrate. When we arrived at the city of T'ung-chiang, all officers of the county government had run away. More than two hundred people locked in prison were set free by us, but on the county magistrate's docket there were still more than a thousand cases not yet attended to, or, rather, seen to as a source of extra income.

The local people came to us in throngs to complain that the county magistrate had been a horrible vampire instead of a paternal official looking after the people's interests. The county magistracy had encouraged or even forced the people to seek a court verdict on everything, including petty disputes. As more and more people came to the city to appear in court, the opium dens and other trades naturally thrived and naturally yielded extra income to everybody connected with the government. The sedan-chair bearers had work to do, too. In fact, all Chinese people, including the T'ung-chiang populace, were accustomed to live amicably and were unwilling to resort to law suits, and the villagers had a fine tradition of settling their own disputes through mediators. Now, under the cruel manipulation of the warlords, they were obliged to take any trifling differences to a law court to their own detriment.

Upon our occupation of the city of T'ung-chiang, the first thing we did was to announce a ban on opium smoking. We felt extremely ill-at-ease to have entered a world of opium smokers, and we thought the ban had immense political significance, not only for the future expansion of the Red Army in this area but also for plugging the siphons of the warlords and for practicing social reform. Our revolutionary tasks were numerous and varied. Now that we had to start with a ban on opium smoking, we certainly had the feeling that our revolutionary road was indeed interminably long.

When we started our propaganda campaign concerning the ban on opium addiction, we called several public meetings about it in succession. The public response was rather cold, and only a few opium smokers attended the meetings. They all harbored the illusion that they might die if they stopped smoking opium, and they were worried that their special product might go to waste. They hoped that the ban could be postponed until some later date.

Much to our surprise, the womenfolk became the active promoters of the ban on opium addiction. At the first women's meeting, after some publicity about the necessity for the ban, the womenfolk seemed unexpectedly enthusiastic in voicing their views. Although quite a number of them were addicts themselves, they all recounted their sufferings from the bad habit. One related how she had been obliged to sell her beloved only son because her husband lacked money to buy opium. Another told how she and her husband had been reduced to such poverty that they could not afford to secure medical attention for their children and had to let them die. One said she had only one pair of trousers, which her husband had pawned to get opium, and so she was unable to leave her house for a long, long time. Another described how their debts and taxes had piled up after they began to smoke opium, how their fields were mortgaged and finally sold, and how her husband and son had disappeared after running away to Shensi and Kansu provinces. Most people at the meeting cried bitterly at the stories, and they pledged their full support of the ban.

Their enthusiasm gave us much heart. Our political department forthwith circulated an order calling more and more women's meetings in this connection. More than five thousand women participated in the first public rally of women held in the city of T'ung-chiang, some of whom came from quite remote villages. Among them were both young and old, including some with bound feet. I was moved to tears when they described their plights.

Thus, the outcry against opium addiction became louder and louder with each passing day. After a few days nobody dared to raise any objection to the ban any more. We founded rehabilitation centers for opium addicts everywhere. With the help of local herbalists, we dispensed to the addicts pills that contained decreasing daily doses of the drug. Such centers became very large and were set up by us almost everywhere in the area. The first batch of about three hundred addicts was accommodated in the centers in T'ung-chiang alone. Many of them were sent in by their mothers or their wives. This number swelled to more than one thousand in the second batch. In our public notices we stressed the fact that not a single former addict had died in any of the centers, but that most of them had actually become stronger and healthier than ever before.

We made up a set of regulations, stipulating that all men and women in their prime years were to stop smoking opium, those who were fifty and over or were suffering from illness might under extenuating circumstances give up the practice at a later date, while those joining the Red Army, the people's regime, or popular institutions had to set a good example for others by refraining from the habit. To minimize the people's losses, we did not destroy any opium or bar its exportation to other places.

After a year's efforts, it was roughly estimated that of the population in the area of T'ung-chiang, Nan-chiang, and Pa-chung, 70 percent were no longer addicts, about 20 percent were semi-addicted, and only 10 percent, mostly the aged and weak, were still smoking the drug. This may be said to have been the first major contribution of the Fourth Front Army to the people in northern Szechwan after its arrival there.

Our confidence in establishing ourselves there increased as the movement progressed. In T'ung-chiang we published a magazine entitled *Bulletin for All Cadres*. The first number appeared ten days after our occupation of T'ung-chiang. The lead article which I wrote for this issue concerned the founding of our new base in northern Szechwan. I appealed to our men to settle down here, to expand our army organization, and to dispense with feelings of nostalgia or pessimism. I explained that all obstacles were surmountable; I cited the example of the ban on opium addiction, reminding them of the anticipated promising results, cautioning them against any slighting of the local addicts, and expressing my belief that the young, able-bodied ex-addicts would be good fighters in the Red Army. I exhorted them to work hard in their various fields in accordance with our new program. This publication had the desired effect of cheering up our men. Henceforth, it served as an authoritative guide to the Fourth Front Army and continued to appear until the Fourth Front Army left northern Szechwan to join hands with the First Front Army at Mao-kung.

Meanwhile, we proceeded with the organization of county governments for T'ung-chiang and Nan-chiang. At first we held only the greater part of T'ung-chiang and a small part of Nan-chiang. In compliance with our new program, we set up provisional governments for the two counties first. Just men nominated by the local people were to participate in them. These provisional governments would then handle popular elections and the formation of permanent county governments. By this time all people connected with the old regime of T'ien Sung-yao had vanished. The new faces were from the poor people. These people helped the Red Army in requisitioning provisions here and there and in pushing the ban on opium addiction. Among them were also some respectable intellectuals. As a matter of fact, intellectuals were rather rare in T'ung-chiang. Besides, some of these intellectuals had been T'ien's parasites. So, those that were with us were indeed negligible in number.

We had considerable respect for these intellectuals, but we were rather disappointed in them. Most of them were typical pedants of the old school who had been teachers or herbalists by trade. Their good points lay in their dissatisfaction with T'ien Sung-yao's rule and their refusal to collaborate with T'ien while they led the humble, simple life of poor men in the village and did something worthwhile for their fellow villagers. Their weaknesses were their bookishness and their lack of courage in voicing their dissent to anything traditional. They had much admiration for the Red Army's fine discipline, which was distinctly superior to that of T'ien's troops, although it had already slackened after the long, exhausting march. They also gave wholehearted approval to the Red Army's ban on opium addiction as a very appropriate measure. On this account, they had entertained high hopes in us. We had received some lengthy letters from them. While they expressed their abhorrence of T'ien, they also dwelt on their versions of "The Kingly Way," "A True Son of Heaven," "Five Elements of the Universe," "Plexus Spirit," "Chuke Liang," and other outdated concepts. I met personally with these people and conversed with them, but I felt that these kind souls certainly had brains filled with backward thoughts.

Under arrangements made by our political workers, a meeting was called and a provisional T'ung-chiang County government was formed. Delegates to this meeting had been selected by the political workers as well as at public rallies in various districts and villages. The committee of the provisional government was nominated by the general political department, which was quite in line with the practice of the Red Army in letting its political department assume the powers of a local government during the early stages of liberation. There were fifteen members of the provisional government committee. Most of these were peasants, plus a handful of handicraftsmen and intellectuals. The chairman, Hsiung, had been a poor peasant. He was healthy and strong and did not smoke opium, and he had been at one time a coolie and a sedan-chair bearer. Once he had been struck by a poisoned arrow in the calf while hunting in the Pa-shan. He had plucked it out at once without hesitation, and thus managed to save his own life. His courage won the admiration of his fellow villagers. He was also noted for being public-spirited, and he had shown active revolutionary zeal and drive after the arrival of the Fourth Army.

The election caused some internal dissension among the people. The pedagogues especially were loud in expressing their dissatisfaction. These pedantic individuals thought that only scholars were fit to be government officials. They all found it inconceivable that a sedan-chair bearer should be the head of a county government. They grumbled that the Red Army, though quite nice in every other way, was grossly misinformed about local conditions. They thought that it was too great a slight to the natives of T'ung-chiang for the Red Army to put an illiterate sedan-chair man in charge of the local government. Their traditional concept of the "superiority of the gentleman" also found acceptance among the villagers at large. For a time they could hardly be convinced of its groundlessness.

As soon as the provisional county government was inaugurated, about a fortnight after our occupation of T'ung-chiang, Lo Tse-chou's men started their offensive against the city of T'ung-chiang from their positions at Ying-ko-tsui. Since they were very weak, they crumbled before us as soon as they came into contact with our men. They retreated to Ch'ing-chiang-tu, about thirty li from Ying-ko-tsui. After a few days we attacked Ch'ing-chiang-tu, and they fled before us once more. We pushed ahead to take Pa-chung, our spearheads reaching about fifty li beyond Pa-chung to confront the enemy at the En-yang River.

Pa-chung was a bigger and more prosperous county than T'ung-chiang, having more than half a million people. I went with our troops to the city and toured around it for several days. It seemed quite a likely spot for our development. There were crowds everywhere in the streets and at the shops, and trading in the market was quite brisk after the abrogation of miscellaneous taxes and duties. Public notices with our program printed on them were posted throughout the city and were read by endless streams of people. Some came from faraway villages; some read the notices aloud, explaining them to others. In their lively discussions, most people observed that peace would certainly prevail if all things said in the notices materialized. In fact, many people in Pa-chung had heard of what we had been doing in T'ung-chiang, so we had little trouble in speedily carrying out similar measures there.

For military reasons, we still had to regard Pa-chung as the front line temporarily. Although Lo Tse-chou's division had been put to rout, the bulk of T'ien Sung-yao's forces were massing and converging on this place. We could not afford to concentrate our forces at Pa-chung, since we wanted to use T'ung-chiang as our base for maneuvers. For this reason, only our Ninth Army was stationed in Pa-chung, while Hsü Hsiang-ch'ien, myself, and the majority of our other people turned back to our headquarters at T'ung-chiang to have overall control of the whole situation.

Our victory at Pa-chung gave impetus to the progress of our work in T'ung-chiang and Nan-chiang. The prestige of the new provisional county government at T'ung-chiang grew from day to day. Some additional notices were put out concerning certain things to be done or not to be done. For example, we called for a new reorganization of the local armed units and the surrender of private arms. More than one thousand rifles, mostly old and worn, were delivered to the county government from various villages and districts, far and near, in the county. This was proof that the government's order could be enforced throughout the county, a thing that the old regime under the warlords could never have expected to do.

All our measures were introduced as step-by-step implementations of our new program. These had brought about a new look in the three counties of T'ung-chiang, Nan-chiang, and Pa-chung. However, a radio-telegram was received from the CC of the CCP which expressed adamant opposition to our new program. So, our schemes had to be dropped in favor of the old road of sovietization, and henceforth northern Szechwan emerged as another Soviet region.

Dispute over the Soviet Policy

The CC of the CCP was most displeased with the fact that the Red Fourth Front Army had left the Oyüwan region and come west to northern Szechwan, regarding this as rightist escapism. When it learned of our Program upon Entering Szechwan, it sent us an ultimatum-type wire, ordering us to correct our mistakes immediately and to stick to the system of Soviet government and other policies consistently laid down by the CC.

Radio communications between ourselves and the CC were extremely rare, as we could not be absolutely sure about the secret codes we were using. As I mentioned before, our copy of the original secret code had been lost during battles in the Soviet region of Hunan and western Hupeh. After some efforts, we made do somehow, but we dared not entirely trust the reliability of the code. Finally we were obliged to draw up a new code through radio communications made by the operators on both sides, but we were not sure that the enemy had not listened in. As a result, no confidential messages were exchanged between ourselves and the CC by radio.

The CC had not been informed beforehand of our departure from the Oyüwan region for the west, and, ignorant of our situation, it was worried about our operation. In the beginning, it had informed us of some intelligence concerning the enemy. When we arrived in southwestern Honan, it had sent us a directive opposing our further retreat to the west. When we came to Kuan-chung after crossing the Ching-ling Range, it had sent us another radiotelegram, much more serious in tone, which declared, "If you continue to flee to the west, we are going to oppose you openly."

We made a careful study of the stern warning, but still we did not dare to disclose the plan of our operation in our radio reply for fear of giving away our military secrets to the enemy, and so we used such vague phrases as "looking for new bases." In fact, our movements were dictated by the situation we were in.

After we had climbed the Pa-shan and entered northern Szechwan, we informed the CC in a radio message that we were going to set up a base there. In reply, the CC told us that the secret code seemed to be quite reliable and asked us to send as much information as possible about our situation, except for confidential military intelligence. Subsequently, we did as instructed.

About ten days after our arrival at T'ung-chiang, I sent a long radio message to the CC to discuss the problem of policy. The radio message quoted the full text of the Program upon Entering Szechwan and pointed out that it had been drawn up in accordance with our experience and had proved, according to its trial implementation in northern Szechwan, to be quite suitable for the locality. We believed that it might prove applicable throughout the whole country.

While we were fighting against the division under Lo Tse-chou, we received the reply from the CC, which stated that it was not permissible to substitute abolition of oppressive duties and miscellaneous taxes and reduction of rent and interest for the policy of agrarian revolution that stipulated confiscation of the land of the landlords and its distribution among the poor peasants. It was also not permissible to give the illusion of a people's government. The message went on to denounce us, saying that our actions would fan the defeatist feeling of fleeing westwards and would eventually give rise to negativism, which was most harmful to the Soviet campaign. The CC ordered us to be bold, to hoist the banner of the Soviet and carry out land distribution. As to abolition of oppressive duties and miscellaneous taxes, opposition to the system of warlord defense areas, prohibition of opium smoking, and so forth, they could only make up the supplementary items. Finally, the message gave a stern warning that if we would correct this erroneous policy, the CC would continue to trust Comrade Chang Kuo-t'ao, as the plenipotentiary representative of the CC, with the power to give guidance on behalf of the CC for the work of the Party, the government, and the Army before the establishment of subbureaus of the CC. Otherwise, the CC would consider the step of changing the line-up of leadership.

Though it was not altogether unexpected, this order from the CC did give us a shock. We did not yet have a firm footing in northern Szechwan, and there were lots of difficulties ahead. Apart from this, the Red Fourth Front Army had had some differences of opinion since its march westward, the essence of which was connected with the CC's order. This made it all the more difficult for us to deal with the problem properly.

There was no definite plan anticipating our march into northern Szechwan when the Red Fourth Army embarked on its westward expedition. Every move was decided by a few leaders—Hsü Hsiang-ch'ien, Ch'en Ch'ang-hao, and I—on the spur of the moment in the light of the actual needs of the situation. Step by step we had moved along, and here we were. The ordinary senior cadres had neither the opportunity to participate in policy decisions nor any understanding of the background giving rise to such decisions. Most of the comrades did not agree with the idea of going too far away from the Oyüwan Soviet region, bound up as they were by the slogan "Resolutely defend the Oyüwan Soviet region." Consequently, they more or less ignored the existing difficulties and could not entirely forgive us for some actions that we had taken because of dire necessity.

When our troops crossed the Peking-Hankow Railway to go west, the slogans of the Political Department still concentrated on annihilation of the enemy bordering the Oyüwan region. Some political cadres supposed that we would circle around northern Hupeh with the target still in the direction of the Oyüwan region. They became worried when they found out that our troops were heading west. They began to debate, arguing that going west offered no future and that we would be too far away from the other Soviet regions in the country. These views coincided with those of the CC in its denunciation of us.

On the question of military strategy, there were also differences of opinion among my comrades, some of whom leaned to the Left, others to the Right. Some opposed rapid retreat towards the west, as they underestimated the strength of the enemy and their determination to attack us in pursuit. They criticized our military strategy as "fleeing" or "avoiding combat," which eventually, according to them, would lead to the total collapse of the Red Fourth Front Army. Rather than being dragged to final collapse, they preferred to wage a decisive battle against the enemy, staking everything on a single throw. Other comrades overestimated the strength and determination of the enemy, and blamed us for not taking still more rapid steps to get ourselves out of reach of the enemy. According to them, if we had genuinely adopted the strategy of rapid retreat to the west, the Tsao-yang campaign, which was unfavorable to us, could have been avoided.

Holders of these divergent views gradually joined together to form an opposition of those who were dissatisfied with the current leadership. When our troops arrived at Hsi-hsiang in Han-chung, a meeting was convened by Chang Ch'in-ch'iu and Fu Chung, cadres in charge of the Political Department. The meeting, attended by more than ten people including Tseng Chung-sheng and K'uang Chi-hsün, cadres who had been punished, and Chu Kuang, head of the Propaganda Section of the Political Department, examined the errors of the westward march. At the meeting, Chang Ch'in-ch'iu read out the two orders of the CC that opposed the westward flight. The participants expressed discontent with the existing leadership and demanded that a meeting of the Military Affairs Committee be held.

Not long afterwards Chang Ch'in-ch'iu told me about these people's opinion. She and some of the other comrades did not favor the plan to go west. She held that this opinion was compatible with the directive of the CC. These people also made various criticisms of the military strategy. She admitted that she had held several talks with these comrades who held differing views, but no opposition had been formed. There was also a lack of unanimity among these opponents. According to Chang Ch'in-ch'iu, the military viewpoints of Tseng Chung-sheng, who was a follower of the well-known Li Li-san Line, stemmed from a rightist viewpoint (the Li Li-san Line was accused in Communist phraseology of being leftist sometimes and rightist sometimes; when it was accused of being rightist, its acts were termed rightist actions under the pretense of leftism) and were not identical with hers. She did not trust the oft-erring K'uang Chi-hsün, and his views were not given much attention. She invited them to the talks simply for academic reasons—that their military knowledge might be of some help. She disclosed that their aim was not to deal blows to the existing leadership's authority nor to attempt to overthrow it; they only wanted to revive the meetings of the Military Affairs Committee and those of the senior cadres, so that more people might participate in making policy decisions.

After we had crossed the Pa-shan and started to set up a new base, the opposition of Chang Ch'in-ch'iu and the others subsided. We were all preoccupied with the development of the new situation and had no time to examine the past. Still, those political-work personnel with differing views were more or less lacking in confidence in the setting up of a new base in northern Szechwan. According to them, since northern Szechwan was a remote region, it would not be able to cooperate with the other Soviet regions in the country even if a base could be set up. Still less could it play a part in dealing blows to the vital positions of Chiang Kai-shek. This world of opium impressed them as an utterly backward place, where the expansion of the Party and the Red Army would meet with innumerable difficulties.

It was not easy to insist that all my comrades have sufficient determination and confidence in the setting up of a new base in northern Szechwan. Their worries and hesitation could not be erased entirely despite the local people's warm support for the Red Army, the zealous campaign to ban opium, and my enthusiastic appeals to them. In fact, conditions for setting up a base in northern Szechwan were inadequate. The comrades had pointed out this or that difficulty, some of which were of far-reaching consequences and insurmountable. But the core of the matter was that we had no choice, being forced into it by the situation.

One of the problems that worried us most was the supply of arms and ammunition. All along we had relied on captured enemy guns and bullets to replenish our supply. Most of the arms and ammunition of the Szechwan troops were native-made and highly inefficient. The Szechwan warlords usually bought arms from foreign countries or from places on the lower reaches of the Yangtze River with the money they had scraped up from the people, but the arms were often confiscated by Chiang Kai-shek and other warlords on the way. As a result, most of their arms and bullets were still native-made. Most of the ammunition used by our troops in battles in northern Szechwan was captured from Chiang Kai-shek's troops and was of a better quality, while that captured from the Szechwan troops was of an inferior quality. Moreover, the Szechwan warlords conducted their battles like guerrillas, swarming to attack when winning and disappearing like a wisp of smoke when losing, so it was not an easy matter to capture large quantities of weapons from them. We felt that the Red Army's operations in northern Szechwan could not solve the problem of arms replenishment, and the deterioration in its equipment might lead to a weakening of its combat strength.

Because we were concentrating on unifying the will of comrades and planning battles against T'ien Sung-yao and steps to set up the new base, the radioed order from the CC put us in a dilemma. We should have spent more of our energy on the newly occupied Pa-shan Range; instead, we had to retreat from the front to T'ung-chiang to call a meeting to discuss the basic policy problem. A number of comrades were unable to attend this important meeting of senior cadres because of the urgent military situation. Those present included Hsü Hsiang-ch'ien, Ch'en Ch'ang-hao, and me, as well as Chang Ch'in-ch'iu, Fu Chung, Liu Ch'i, Chou Ch'un-chüan, and some ten others.

First of all at the meeting I passed around the radio messages that had been sent by the CC on previous occasions, and then I made a report, a sort of defense for the policy pursued thus far. I first reviewed the reasons for and the progress of the Red Fourth Front Army's movement towards the west after its inability to find a foothold in the Oyüwan Soviet region. I pointed out that despite the best efforts of the Party, the Red Fourth Front Army was unable to gain strength rapidly in order to resist the pressure of the enemy troops which were far superior in strength. I disclosed that the plan to go west had been worked on carefully by myself and Ts'ai Shen-hsi for a long time, with a view to preserving the greatest number of our forces and acquiring time and bases in more distant areas for staging a comeback. In recounting the efforts to resist the Fourth Encirclement Campaign, I pointed out that the night battle at the Liu-lin River had been necessary and proper. If it had not been for the heavy blow to the enemy in that campaign, there would have been still more difficulties to hinder the Red Fourth Front Army in its attempt to leave the Oyüwan Soviet region. I also pointed out that the situation of our army might be still worse if it had scattered in the Oyüwan region to wage guerrilla warfare or had taken any other strategic moves. I affirmed the success of the battle at Ho-k'ou, which, despite heavy casualties, enabled us to break through the encirclement. I admitted that the battle at Wu-chia-chi in Tsao-yang could and ought to have been avoided. The two days' fierce battle had caused us two thousand casualties and had affected the future moves of our army. It must be soberly admitted that I was guilty of giving wrong military guidance in the conduct of the battle. It was the error of using the wrong person that had caused the loss. K'uang Chi-hsün's disobeying of orders ought to be investigated in accordance with the rules of discipline. Shortly before that battle I had temporarily promoted K'uang back to a position of commander because of others being wounded and had ordered him to occupy a commanding height while we were camping in Wu-chia-chi. His idea was that the place was so precipitous, how could the enemy occupy it? He did not obey the order, and the enemy occupied that height and took the initiative from us. I denied the accusation that our army had fled to the west, saying that the accusers had not adhered to the facts and had not given due recognition to the heroic struggles of the Red Fourth Front Army. I then went on to show that the best thing to do was to stay in northern Szechwan.

After making the necessary explanations in defense of past military operations, I went on to comment on the Program upon Entering Szechwan. I pointed out frankly that the foundation for the Soviet was too narrow and that the agrarian revolution did not have much attraction. Facts had shown that at present it was not the agrarian revolution that had enhanced the forces of the Red Army, but that the momentary victories that the Red Army had achieved had encouraged a small number of peasants to rise and distribute the land. The fatal shortcoming of the Soviet campaign was that it could not be linked with the anti-imperialist and anti-Japanese movements of the whole country. It was isolated in remote villages and lost touch with the intellectuals and petty bourgeoisie of the big cities. The Program upon Entering Szechwan was drawn up to correct these errors in policy. I further explained that the program was suitable for such a province as Szechwan. In fact, it was the only feasible policy, as the slogan of the "Szechwan People's Government" had great appeal, while a Soviet government would only arouse the amazement and laughter of the backward Szechwan people. I also explained that through the efforts of our Party, the Szechwan government, if it achieved anything, would belong to the Chinese Soviet government. Could it be that in the modern revolutionary movement, there could not be other names than that of the "Soviet government"? Pursuing the point further, I said that if the Szechwan People's government was actually set up and proved the correctness of the policy, then the Soviet governments throughout the country might change their names to "Revolutionary People's Government." Such an adaptation in policy was the prerequisite for victory.

The third urgent and important question was the overall strategy for battles against T'ien Sung-yao. First of all, I expressed my determination to defeat T'ien Sung-yao's troops then and there and to set up a firm base in northern Szechwan around "Tung-Nan-Pa," because our army was unwilling for the time being to wander around any more. It wanted to settle down for a long time. T'ien Sung-yao had about three times as many troops as we had, while Liu Ts'un-hou, Yang Sen, and Sun Wei-ju together also had about three times as many. Our army was to adopt the strategy of inducing the enemy to penetrate our territory and then concentrating our major forces to annihilate it at a suitable spot. Our first target was the troops of T'ien Sung-yao. I reckoned that it was necessary to deal a heavy blow to T'ien Sung-yao's troops before we could stand on our feet. In view of this central task, I gave instructions to the Party, the administration, and the Army to try to achieve this end.

This was indeed a speech of key importance. Despite the passage of time, I can still remember its general outline quite clearly. All the participants were moved and unanimously expressed their complete trust in me. They acknowledged that the Red Fourth Front Army was certainly not fleeing in its struggle to resist the Fourth Encirclement Campaign, but was actually fighting the enemy most heroically. They paid tributes to me for having been able to put a firm grip on the helm of the ship amid turbulent waves and for having turned danger into safety innumerable times. Chang Ch'in-ch'iu and the others also declared on the spot that owing to their ignorance of the situation, they had suspected the leadership of committing errors, but now, in the light of indisputable conditions and facts, they would abandon the attitude of suspicion and place complete trust in my leadership.

During the discussions some comrades praised the selection of northern Szechwan as the new base, while others testified to the great appeal of the Program upon Entering Szechwan and disapproved of making any changes in it. They also made some suggestions for its execution. Some pointed out that the present campaign to abolish oppressive duties and miscellaneous taxes would soon develop into the agrarian revolution calling for distribution of land. Most of the participants were still more enthusiastic about the specific strategy to annihilate the troops of T'ien Sung-yao. But when the differences of opinion concerning the CC were mentioned, all seemed heavy-hearted and did not want to talk much about it.

Just as I had expected, Hsü Hsiang-ch'ien, Ch'en Ch'ang-hao, and two or three other major cadres came to me for a confidential talk in the middle of the night. They all declared that they were unwilling to continue the dispute with the CC, stressing that since our army was still groping for a foothold in northern Szechwan, there were a lot of difficulties ahead, and the battle against T'ien Sung-yao's troops was getting more urgent every day. If we persisted in the Program upon Entering Szechwan and criticized the ineptitude of the Soviet campaign, the CC might send a radio message ordering a change in leadership. In that case, though they would certainly protest to the CC and might even disobey its order, disturbances would be caused in the Red Fourth Front Army. Realistically, they urged me to avoid disputes with the CC and wait till after the Red Fourth Front Army had surmounted its crucial difficulties.

After some painful deliberation and taking into consideration the overall situation, I finally decided to accept their suggestion and I made some concessions. I drafted a radio telegram, making no defense of any of the accusations leveled at us by the CC, but only declaring that the directive of the CC would be obeyed and that the Northern Szechwan Soviet government would be set up immediately. The CC seemed to sense something and, in its radioed answer, said some kind words to show its concern for us. It declared mainly that the CC trusted my leadership. This abortive suggestion of mine was later picked up by Stalin, who put an end to the erroneous Soviet policy and turned to the policy of an anti-Japanese national united front and also to the policy of KMT-CCP cooperation for resistance to Japan. There were many reasons why I was unable to change the erroneous policy of the CCP, one of which was that I was not ruthless by my character, which, I must say, was not the best character to have. I, therefore, did not regret what I had done.

After this serious dispute died down, we started to make another public declaration which amended the original Program upon Entering Szechwan. The statement explained that since the Szechwan warlords had persisted in their customary reactionary work-style and had refused to cooperate with the Red Army to work for the welfare of the Szechwanese, the Red Fourth Front Army was obliged, first of all, to overthrow the reactionary rule of the Szechwan warlords. Besides continuing with the policy of abolishing oppressive duties and miscellaneous taxes, our army called on all poor peasants to carry out the distribution of land immediately and to organize their own Soviet government of workers and peasants, which would be a part of the Chinese Soviet Republic.

In accordance with our previously decided strategy against T'ien and owing to the weakness of our army, we avoided the occupation of big cities at the moment so as not to increase our military burden. But our army still attached much importance to the rear area that we had built up in T'ung-chiang, where we could recruit new soldiers and acquire other supplies. We had to rely on our available military strength to maintain the safety of this rear area, and our strategy with regard to the troops of T'ien Sung-yao was to sap their strength gradually. We tried to lure them into the neighborhood of T'ung-chiang and then to make short work of them.

From then on, our purpose was no longer to take a short rest in Szechwan nor to form a people's government with the progressive forces of the province, but to fly high the banner of the Soviet at the southern foot of the Pa-shan Mountains, hoping that the banner would shed its light all over the surrounding land.

After the Establishment of the New Soviet Region

Generally speaking, the Northern Szechwan Soviet region was only a military base, far inferior to the Oyüwan region with regard to mass support. During the two and one-half years that we stayed in northern Szechwan, we were constantly busy fighting, first with the troops of T'ien Sung-yao, then with other warlords of Szechwan, with very little respite. The administrative setup of the Northern Szechwan Soviet region was generally modeled after that of the Oyüwan Soviet region, with some differences which were bound up with the different historical backgrounds and social conditions of the two regions. We were short of personnel in northern Szechwan, so that our work could not be done in such a thoroughgoing way as in the Oyüwan region. That was why the protracted struggle that took place in the Oyüwan region did not happen in Szechwan when the Red Fourth Front Army left at a later date.

At the end of 1932 we set up Soviet governments in all of the occupied areas from the lower to the upper levels and began to distribute the land; but these political organs, for the most part, offices catering to the armies. We needed an especially large labor force to support the armies fighting in the mountainous region. The Soviet governments at all levels were going all-out to get supplies for the armies. The people had the feeling that the Soviet government was the product of the Red Army and that its existence depended on victories in battle.

Early in 1933 the troops of T'ien Sung-yao began to attack the Northern Szechwan Soviet region. T'ien Sung-yao himself was staying at San-t'ai, but his forces were all deployed to the front, with Sun Chen, his deputy, as commander-in-chief. The troops under Sun Chen, amounting to some thirty regiments, which advanced on us from west of Nanchiang and Pa-chung, were the main force in the whole campaign. In addition, some ten regiments of Yang Sen were to our south, and nine regiments under Liao Chen, a subordinate of Liu Ts'un-hou's, were to our east, cooperating with the troops of T'ien Sung-yao to keep us in check. In the Han-chung region to our north, the division of Sun Wei-ju under Yang Hu-ch'eng was keeping a watchful eye on us. Some of Hu Tsung-nan's troops that were stationed in T'ien-shui advanced to Kuang-yüan and Chao-hua to serve as reinforcements for T'ien Sung-yao.

Our army was growing stronger with each passing day. In the two months following our entrance into Szechwan, we had recruited some five thousand new soldiers. What was lacking was the cooperation of local armed forces. We had to defend the periphery of the Soviet region with our forces quite scattered. The Fourth Army guarded the eastern border, while the Thirtieth Army guarded the southern, dealing with the troops of Liu Ts'un-hou and Yang Sen respectively. The Fourth and Thirty-first armies had to take out a part of their forces to watch over the enemy in Han-chung. The ones left to engage the troops of T'ien Sung-yao were the Ninth and Thirty-first armies, which had less than six regiments.

Our troops avoided decisive battles with those of T'ien Sung-yao, but on each defense line we always gave the enemy some setbacks before retreating slowly. Our aim was to sap the enemy's strength gradually. The longer the war lasted, the deeper the wounds to the enemy. Meanwhile, the enemy's supply line would be extended to a greater length. We were waiting for a suitable time and place to counterattack.

A few days after the battle started, we abandoned Pa-chung County. The enemy troops were elated and boasted of their victory. In fact, the loss of Pa-chung County was a great setback for us. The local people, seeing our departure, could not help wavering. Even those engaged in the work of the Soviet government were not altogether clear about the strategy of our army. They were at sixes and sevens, and some went to such lengths as to make preparations for the eventuality that the Red Army might back out of northern Szechwan.

The uncertainty among the people made it still more difficult for us to mobilize the local people to support the Red Army. Fighting in this region of high and steep mountains, we often had to transport food to the front along a hundred li of mountain path; and the wounded and the sick among the troops had to be transported back to the rear over the same paths. For this arduous task we always needed a transport team of some five thousand men, including permanent as well as temporary workers. Such an immense transport team, in itself, involved a lot of difficulties. Take, for example, medical care for the sick. We sometimes found it impossible to deal with cases adequately. In short, the personnel of the Soviet governments at all levels were all terribly busy just with the job of mobilizing transport labor, giving them sufficient rest by arranging shift work, supplying them with daily necessities, looking after their sicknesses, and so forth.

The war had become a protracted one. The enemy was pressing on us, while we were retreating and retreating. By July, 1933, our army had even forsaken the county of T'ung-chiang and was retreating towards Ku-tsao-pa. The enemy guessed that our army would retreat to Han-chung along the route we had come, through Liang-ho-k'ou. Sun Chen, the front-line commander-in-chief of T'ien Sung-yao's troops, concentrated his main force at Liang-ho-k'ou, moving them up from Pan-ch'iao in T'ung-chiang, in an attempt to attack the left wing of our army, thus cutting us off from the rear. The division of Liu Ts'un-hou's troops under Liao Chen advanced from Chu-ku-kuan in Wan-yüan County to the right flank of Liang-ho-k'ou, forming a pincer drive upon our army. Yet, the enemy's estimate was all wrong. They had forgotten that in the past six months it was they who had suffered the greater losses in battle. They were also unaware of our strategy of enticing the enemy to penetrate deeply.

On the face of it, our army was indeed retreating. In fact, the places under our control became fewer and fewer. But this was favorable to us in that we could concentrate more forces to counterattack. First of all, on the right wing we attacked Liao Chen's division, which immediately retreated into Wan-yüan County. Then we concentrated all our forces at Liang-ho-k'ou to raid Sun Chen's troops from their left rear. On the day of the attack, our troops individually rushed out from the trails among the dense forests and bamboo growths in Pa-shan, taking the heights at the left rear of Sun Chen's troops, thus controlling the main outlet to the rear. The enemy troops fled in disorder under the sweeping fire of our machine guns and were completely routed.

Pursuing the enemy on the tide of victory, our army soon recovered all the lost territories in the region of T'ung-chiang, Nan-chiang, and

Pa-chung, expanding the Soviet region considerably. On the Nan-chiang front, we chased the enemy to the vicinity of Kuang-yüan; on the Pa-chung front we went as far as the county of Lang-chung. We formed a defense line between Kuang-yüan and Lang-chung, with the Chia-ling River lying between ourselves and the enemy. T'ien Sung-yao had lost the greater part of his troops in the past six months. Our army had captured about three thousand men and weapons, but T'ien Sung-yao had lost five times that number (the loss of men was due mainly to casualties and sickness, while the weapons were mostly abandoned and thrown into deep ravines). Our army lost about one-tenth the number that T'ien lost; but replacements were obtained immediately, and we were much stronger than before.

This victory of ours greatly shocked the Szechwan warlords. They began to realize that they must go all-out to deal with the Red Army. Sun Chen, who was in command of the troops, was deeply puzzled by the cause of his defeat. Actually it was inadvisable to deploy large army corps in this strategic area. Sun Chen had concentrated nearly thirty regiments in a small space among high mountains and steep cliffs, which is something all writers on military tactics advise against. Moreover, the troops under his command were extremely weak in fighting strength. Our army was numerically small, but the men were all picked, trained soldiers. The victory was no accident of fate.

Military victory laid the foundation for the development of the Soviet region in northern Szechwan. The enemy around us no longer dared to attack us, which brought about a short truce. The local people, encouraged by the victory, became active and enthusiastic. We organized Soviets in all of the occupied territories and were making preparations for the convocation of a regional Soviet congress and the establishment of the Soviet Government of the Northern Szechwan Soviet region. (Within the framework of the Chinese Soviet Republic, this would be a Soviet at the provincial level.)

We were then unaware of the constitution and legislation of the Chinese Soviet Republic in Jui-chin, Kiangsi. Everything was done in the light of local conditions and taking as reference the experience of the Oyüwan region. Our work was of necessity wanting in nicety, as time was urgent and everything was decided and acted upon in a hurry. In a short time we established the CCP Provincial Committee and began to recruit new Party members in the locality, where branch organizations were set up. There was no subbureau of the CC in northern Szechwan, so as chairman of the Military Affairs Committee I had to command the Army, and as a representative of the CC I guided the work of the Provincial Committee. The affairs of the Party, the government, and the Army all devolved on me, making me exceedingly busy. I therefore had to delegate authority to responsible comrades of the various departments so that no time would be lost in dealing with important matters.

The Northern Szechwan region was, after all, an isolated area. Szechwan itself is situated in a remote corner of China, while the T'ung-chiang–Nan-chiang–Pa-chung area lies in a remote part of Szechwan. This was a time when Japanese aggression in China was spreading from the three northeastern provinces to North China, but the ordinary people of Szechwan were still living their peaceful lives in complete ignorance of that fact. The tide of the anti-Japanese campaign had not yet spread to this distant place. The Central Government of the Chinese Soviet Republic existing in Jui-chin, Kiangsi, was something the people had not even heard of. According to the Szechwanese, Szechwan was like a nation unto itself. Their attention centered on events in Szechwan, and these were what they talked about. The meanings of such terms as Kuomintang, Three Principles of the People, and Chiang Kai-shek were not well understood even by the local warlords, not to mention the ordinary masses.

I recall that towards the end of the year 1933, Wang Ling-chi, a "very capable" warlord of Szechwan, was appointed commander-in-chief of the Fifth Route Punitive Army against the Communists. When he led Liu Hsiang's troops to attack us, he issued a long proclamation of warning which said, in the main, that "the Three Principles of the People advocate restriction on capital and are the right way to save the country and the people, while communism advocates equal rights in land proprietorship and is a heresy like communizing property and sharing wives." He had thus made a hash of the principles of Dr. Sun Yat-sen, which stipulated both restriction on capital and equal rights to land. What was still more ludicrous was that he had put "Chang's hat on Li's head."

This state of isolation from the world also affected the CCP organizations in Szechwan. After we had completely defeated T'ien Sung-yao, Lo Shih-wen, secretary of the Szechwan Provincial Committee of the CCP, secretly came to T'ung-chiang from Ch'eng-tu. He was warmly welcomed by us everywhere. He made speeches wherever he went, emphasizing the fact that although T'ien Sung-yao had been defeated, the other more powerful Szechwan warlords were planning to encircle

and attack us with all their forces. He advised that we must make preparations for battle. He also told us that the organization of the Szechwan
Committee of the CCP was weak, with only a small membership, and
its work was still undeveloped. He did not know about the details of the
Central Government of the Chinese Soviet Republic and the attitude
of the CC towards the anti-Japanese campaign, because he had been
out of touch with the CC for a long time. He immediately became a
member of the Standing Committee of the Provincial Committee of the
CCP for the Northern Szechwan Soviet region, an important position for
making policy decisions. Yet, this shot of new blood was not able to
bring the changes outside Szechwan Province to this remote region.

In a mere matter of less than two months, the First Soviet Congress
of the Northern Szechwan Soviet Region opened in T'ung-chiang during
the last ten days of August. The delegates attending the congress numbered more than one thousand, all peasants elected from the villages. I
addressed the congress in my capacity as vice-chairman of the Central
Government of the Chinese Soviet Republic. I spent some time explaining
in very simple language the meaning of the term Soviet and other terms,
and the significant points of our policy. In order that the delegates
might understand these problems, group discussions were organized,
during which further explanations were given. It took quite an effort to
make these delegates understand the issues under discussion, as they
were all uneducated.

The countryfolk here had not been baptized by the revolution and
were totally ignorant of the terms Communist Party, Soviet, and so forth.
Unlike the peasants of the Oyüwan region, who had undergone the trials
of revolutionary storms, they knew nothing about the National Revolution of 1927, or about the Peasant Associations. Generally speaking, the
peasants of the Oyüwan region were aware of the CC of the CCP, which
was leading them in the revolution; but the peasants in northern Szechwan knew nothing about it. The former had heard about Su Chao-
cheng and could relate the Soviet to him; but the latter found the word
"Soviet" utterly alien. The names they were familiar with were those of
the few warlords of Szechwan.

Influenced by the old notions of divine power and fate, the people
in northern Szechwan could not understand why the Red Fourth Front
Army, which was totally different from the Szechwan armies, had appeared and why it had come to T'ung-chiang, Nan-chiang, and Pa-chung.
As far as they knew, troops from other provinces who came to Szechwan
always ran amuck. Why was it that the Red Fourth Front Army took up

the cudgel against injustice for the poor, quite opposite from other armies from other provinces? They did not understand such abstract terms as Communist Party and Soviet. They wanted to find a concrete person to fit in with their notions of divine power and fate. In this way, a laughable incident occurred.

The attention of the countryfolk was focused on my person as a leader. They had many ways of explaining about me, all of which were forced interpretations by some stretch of the imagination. They recalled a young peasant with the surname Chang from K'u-ch'ao-pa, who, in the beginning of the Chinese Republic (some twenty years earlier) had led an uprising in the form of taking away from the rich to aid the poor. The uprising quickly failed and Chang So-and-so disappeared. The people of K'u-ch'ao-pa and its vicinity were the first to say that the present Chang Kuo-t'ao was the same person as the leader of the uprising twenty years before in K'u-ch'ao-pa. They said that the two men were more or less the same in stature and age. They supposed that Chang So-and-so of K'u-ch'ao-pa must have received instruction from some deities while he was wandering outside Szechwan and had now returned after some fundamental transformation. They reasoned that if it were not Chang So-and-so of K'u-ch'ao-pa, how could the Red Fourth Front Army find its way to T'ung-Nan-Pa? Furthermore, the men of the Red Army regarded the place as their own hometown, showering on it their infinite love and care. All this showed that the present Chang must be the same man as the other Chang. So the rumor spread, and soon the whole northern Szechwan region was rife with it, and the common people in the countryside were quite convinced of the story; they thought that all those chantings of the Communist Party and the Soviet were but charms exercising the power of heaven.

As the rumor swept over the place, everybody in T'ung-Nan-Pa seemed to think that a genuine "song of heaven" had appeared. This was linked up with the good influences of the geomancy of T'ung-Nan-Pa and the destiny of the people. Even the wife of that leader of the peasant uprising—Chang So-and-so—came to see if I was her lost husband. Yet, we were reluctant to encourage the superstitious notions of the country-folk. My comrades and I all spared no efforts in denying all this. We energetically explained to the people about the origin of the Communist Party and the Soviet and that the Red Army was founded by the Communist Party. We told them that Chang Kuo-t'ao was a veteran member of the Communist Party and that he had not been born in Szechwan.

After a lot of explanation, people gradually understood what Communist Party and Soviet meant, and the rumor gradually subsided.

The above story shows that the ideals of communism and the old concepts of the local people were poles apart. I should not waste too much of my readers' time to unearth more of the details. In short, the local CCP organization in northern Szechwan was at best a peasant revolutionary body, although later a number of revolutionary personalities did emerge in the Northern Szechwan Soviet region.

The Soviet Congress officially founded the Northern Szechwan Soviet Government, which was similar to that of the Oyüwan Soviet region and conducted work of the same sort. In the course of its work a number of difficulties cropped up that showed the peculiarities of the locality.

The primary task of distributing the land was actively implemented in northern Szechwan. Generally speaking, the T'ung-Nan-Pa region had more land than people. After the ban on poppy planting was put into effect, more land was allocated to the planting of grain crops. There was also land on the mountain slopes which lay fallow because of a shortage of labor. Since there was more land than people, the work of distributing the land was easily done. We conducted the distribution thus: peasants who tilled their own land retained ownership of it; land that belonged to landlords but was tilled by tenant farmers was distributed to the tenant farmers concerned. Rich peasants with surplus land and tenant farmers who took over too large a tenancy of land had to give up a portion to those with less, some of whom were also given land on the mountainside. We handed out Land Utilization Certificates as before, but reserved the right to make further redistribution in the future after investigations.

Dependents of local Red Army soldiers usually got better and larger portions of land, and they were allowed to hire half- or part-time farm hands to till the land for them. There was no such problem as the one that arose in the Oyüwan region—the problem concerning the system of doing farm work for the families of Red Army soldiers. In the past, oppressive taxes and the poison of opium had reduced the number of able-bodied men in the mountainous region of northern Szechwan, so an unusual custom existed of men marrying into the families of women. Sometimes even deserters from the Red Army were taken in by the mountain women. Owing to the manpower shortage, the only way to avoid laying waste the land of dependents of Red Army soldiers was to allow them to use hired labor.

The local poor peasants nurtured a bitter hatred against the evil gentry and local tyrants. Mass rallies held in the villages were imbued with the desire for revenge. One local tyrant or evil gentry might incur the accusations of several score or even a hundred injured parties. Even a person who had been in charge of tithing was often the target of the peasants' accusations. The policy of the Soviet government was to want the peasants to distinguish between major and minor culprits, between serious and petty crimes. It did not want the peasants to regard the petty lackeys of the local tyrants and evil gentry as the real culprits. However, in the various villages the peasants sometimes took direct actions to deal with these local tyrants and evil gentry. The Soviet government had ruled that these cases were to be handed over to the Political Security Bureau of the county government or the revolutionary courts to be punished according to law.

The political-work personnel of the Red Fourth Front Army did not directly punish the local tyrants and evil gentry, and often corrected the excesses of the local peasants. It was not often that the tyrants were arrested or pressed for fines. When the political workers of our army, together with the local people, went to confiscate the grain of the local tyrants and evil gentry, they also confiscated the opium in their possession. The value of the opium was usually enough for upkeep of the troops. Confiscation of the opium was a very justifiable and natural thing to do during the upsurge of opium prohibition, and no ill feeling was aroused among the people.

The distribution of land and the beating up of local tyrants gradually evoked resistance from the local tyrants and landlords and caused further class segregation among the people. The landlords and local gentry in the beginning sang the praises of the Red Army's stipulations regarding abolition of oppressive taxes and miscellaneous duties, but they feared the revenge of the local poor people. They invited those newly emerged personalities connected with the Red Army to have meals in their homes, hoping that they would make fewer reports on them and would not seize the opportunity to avenge themselves. As they found that their efforts failed, they came to realize that the poor people and the Red Army were identical. They then changed their tactics and adopted a stand opposing the Soviet government. They conducted underhanded activities, spread rumors, and showed that there was discord between the Soviet regime and the people.

The poor people of the locality were high in revolutionary spirit, but they were weak in organizational power. This could be seen from the local armed forces. Just as in the Oyüwan region, large numbers of peasants were organized into self-defense corps and a few independent detachments. But the self-defense corps could not easily be rallied for concerted action, and the independent detachments were weak in combat strength. The crucial problem was a lack of competent cadres for the local armed forces. In the summer of 1934 a few landlords in southern Pa-chung assembled some one hundred armed troops and took Chieh-chia-chai, thus launching a riot against the Soviet government. Our local armed forces were unable to resist them, and it was the Red Army that finally put down the rebellion.

The economy of the region was self-sufficient. Except for salt, which had to be obtained from outside, all daily necessities could be produced locally. But manufactured goods, such as arsenal equipment, sewing machines, and medicine, were in short supply. The markets and commodity prices fluctuated in accordance with the state of the military situation. The local people were keen on reducing the prices of goods and usually restricted prices at will, causing a slowdown in trade.

Our economic policy did not favor price controls. It encouraged trade and prosperity in the markets and dealt blows only to speculators who raised prices inordinately, forbidding them to make trouble. We set up a bank of the Soviet region, issued currency, and collected agricultural and commercial taxes. Commercial commissioners were posted in all market towns, and these were usually the members of the economic committee of the local Soviet government. Their main tasks included supervision of standard weights and measures and abolition of malpractice in trade and exploitation by middlemen. Some results were achieved by means of these measures.

Numerous urgent tasks consumed much of the energy of the regional Soviet government. As was mentioned in the above passages, in addition to mobilizing the people to join the transport team, the Soviet government had to carry on a fight against disease. Dysentery, malaria, and influenza were all prevalent in the region, as well as cholera and venereal and eye diseases. There was a general lack of knowledge about hygiene, which greatly encouraged the spread of epidemics. As soon as it was founded, the government of the Northern Szechwan Soviet region set up hospitals in all parts of the area. This was a place with shortages of both medical personnel and medicine, and the people were used to relying on deities, fortunetellers, and opium. Following our efforts to oppose these superstitions and prejudices and to promote hygienic habits and medical treatment, the Chinese herbalists became much respected personalities, and the shops selling Chinese herb medicines in the market towns did a roaring business.

In the autumn of 1934 there was an epidemic of dysentery. The hospitals under the Soviet government were unable to accommodate all the patients. There were 2,200 in the government's General Hospital of the Northern Szechwan Soviet region, and about 500 in each of the county hospitals. Most of those in the countryside accommodated 40 or 50 each, with the largest accommodating 200. The death rate in these hospitals amounted to some 170 in one day at the peak. More than one-third of the 200 Chinese herbalists working in these hospitals contracted the disease and died. The epidemic lasted some two months, resulting in a scene of terror. According to the old peasants of the region, there had been two grave epidemics in the previous ten years. Since there had been no government to take care of the people, as the Soviet government did, the situation was much worse even than this.

The women in this region became especially active. They organized a women's federation, which not only did sewing, but also took part in transporting food and in military work of a defensive nature. Their stamina was no less than that of the men. They were in the vanguard in prohibiting the use of opium, and they took an active part in the work of the various departments of the Soviet government. In order to satisfy the demands of the women, we once organized an independent regiment of women (a number of whose members later came to Yen-an). The women swarmed to apply for membership when the regiment was set up. After some careful selection, more than one thousand were accepted. This was the first time that we had an independent women's detachment of the army. The regiment did a lot in taking care of the wounded and the sick in the Army.

The greatest difficulty we encountered in this region was a lack of cadres. Since we lacked instructors, we were unable to set up military schools or Party schools on a long-term basis. We had to let the armies and regiments train their own cadres, while the CCP Provincial Committee established some short-term training courses. The Soviet government set up schools in the various villages, but owing to a shortage of teachers, the teaching staff consisted mainly of aged pedants from the small and backward rural hamlets.

In the fine autumn weather of September, 1933, when the work of setting up the Soviet regime was more or less completed, we started to move our troops east to attack the positions of Liu Ts'un-hou's troops. Liu Ts'un-hou, an evil relic of the imperial system who had been entrenched in Sui-ting for nearly twenty years, was finally defeated by us in this campaign. Then we launched a war against all the warlords of Szechwan, who, despite repeated blows from us, continued to keep us busy because they had forces of Chiang Kai-shek's backing them up. The war persisted, and we were unable to win a decisive victory.

In July of the same year, after T'ien Sung-yao's troops had been defeated, the Szechwan warlords headed by Liu Hsiang immediately dispatched their troops to deal with us. There were disagreements among these warlords, which impeded their rapid action. In order to preserve his own strength, Liu Hsiang was reluctant to send his troops right to the front to have hard battles with us. He kept discussing with the other warlords his plan of "all going ahead together." The troops of Yang Sen, being inferior in strength, drew back to Ying-shan. After heavy blows from us, T'ien Sung-yao was depressed and was further disturbed by differences of opinion within his ranks. As the positions of his troops were in danger of being seized at any moment, T'ien Sung-yao, it was said, deeply regretted that he had not accepted our proposal to avoid fighting in the first place. Consequently, he dared not engage us. Cowed by our defeat of T'ien Sung-yao, Yang Hu-ch'eng in Han-chung secretly sent someone to contact us, and we came to an agreement of nonintervention. (The association between Yang Hu-ch'eng and the CCP on a military basis started in August, 1932.) Thus, we were in a position to deal with Liu Ts'un-hou separately.

Without much delay, we decided to take the initiative. We loathed Liu Ts'un-hou, because he not only refused all along to accept our proposal of mutual nonintervention, but also attacked Chu-ku-kuan while we were being attacked by T'ien Sung-yao. Liu Ts'un-hou had accumulated some arms in Sui-ting, but his troops were not strong enough to withstand our blows. Our aim was to seize the arms in Liu Ts'un-hou's magazines, so as to strengthen ourselves for battle against the other warlords of all Szechwan.

Using more than half of our troops, we assaulted the defense line of Liu Ts'un-hou's troops, who fled at the first encounter. In a few days we swept over a large portion of his positions, occupying the counties of Sui-ting, Hsüan-han, and Wan-yüan. The savage rule of Liu Ts'un-hou even surpassed that of T'ien Sung-yao. The local people swarmed to help the Red Army and made short work of the remnants of Liu's troops. Mass actions to destroy the old power, such as assaulting the local tyrants and distributing grain, came into full swing. Thereafter, Liu Ts'un-hou disappeared from the scene, and his remaining troops came under Liao Chen, who then became a subordinant to Liu Hsiang. This was the first major victory of the Red Fourth Front Army after its entrance into Szechwan. We captured nearly ten thousand old rifles and one million native bullets. The arsenal, the ammunition and garment factory built in the county seat of Sui-ting by Liu Ts'un-hou, and his hoards of gold, silver, and other supplies, all became our war prizes, excepting, of course, those that were damaged or lost. This was indeed the richest replenishment our army had ever obtained.

Thanks to this victory, the Red Fourth Front Army expanded rapidly. The people within Liu Ts'un-hou's defense area swarmed to join the Red Army. We lowered the standard for recruitment, accepting all and sundry so long as they were physically fit, regardless of whether or not they were opium addicts. Thus, the Red Army got more than one thousand recruits every day. In less than a fortnight the rank and file increased from twenty thousand to fifty thousand, giving each army an increase of from four thousand to about ten thousand. The standard of the troops, however, dropped immensely, due to a shortage of instructors to train the large numbers of new recruits.

Riding on the tide of victory, our troops moved from Sui-ting and Hsüan-han towards Liang-shan, the defense area of Liu Hsiang, giving a great shock to Chungking and Wan-hsien and boosting the joint action of the Szechwan warlords. Liu Hsiang then became commander-in-chief of the "Punitive Expedition Against the Bandits of Szechwan Province," with Teng Hsi-hou as commander of the First Column attacking the Soviet region from Kuang-yüan and Chao-hua; T'ien Sung-yao as commander of the Second Column advancing on us from Lang-chung; Yang Sen as commander of the Third Column and Li Chia-yu and Lo Tze-nan as commander-in-chief and deputy commander of the Fourth Column, respectively, assaulting us from the south; and Wang Ling-chi as commander of the Fifth Column, which consisted of the troops directly under Liu Hsiang, attacking us frontally from Liang-shan. This was the main force of the enemy in future battles. Moreover, Chiang Kai-shek immediately set up a provisional headquarters in Szechwan for the "Punitive Expedition Against the Bandits," with Ho Kuo-kuang as director. Chiang Kai-shek declared that he would send Hu Tsung-nan's troops in T'ien-shui and Yang Hu-ch'eng's troops in Han-chung to support the military operations of Liu Hsiang.

By October the troops of Wang Ling-chi's Fifth Column had assembled at Liang-shan and had started to launch a counteroffensive against us. The war situation took an adverse turn for us. The troops directly under Liu Hsiang were stronger than those of T'ien Sung-yao, particularly the Third Division under Wang Ling-chi (which had the strength of two ordinary divisions and was armed with equipment from abroad). In the first two engagements our troops, encumbered with an excessive number of new recruits, suffered considerable casualties. We then decided to retreat step by step in order to carry out reorganization and training.

When our troops retreated from the front line of Liang-shan to the northern bank of the Sui-ting River, Wang Ling-chi's units soon launched an all-out attack and pressed a crossing. But on the battlefield at the Tung-lin River they suffered heavy blows from us, and used up a large part of the weapons and ammunition that Wang Ling-chi had confiscated in Wan-hsien during the past years from other Szechwan warlords as they were shipped from the lower reaches of the Yangtze River to Szechwan. The price was too high for the successful crossing of the river. Thereafter, the combat strength of his troops gradually declined.

After retreating to the second defense line, which was about thirty li from the north bank of the Sui-ting River, we were aware that the combat strength of Wang Ling-chi's troops was limited; and we started to give strenuous training to our units. The work was rather complicated. The primary course was training in shooting and combat; then there were courses on military regulations and military discipline, as well as on general culture subjects and hygiene. There were also the opium addicts among the new recruits who had to be taken care of. Our method of helping the addicts was a combination of persuasion and force. The company political instructors controlled the supply of curative pills, giving gradually decreasing amounts to the smokers who were trying to abstain until they could stop smoking entirely by a set date. The training courses were under the personal supervision of Hsü Hsiang-ch'ien, Ch'en Ch'ang-hao, and me.

The great success of our training surprised the enemy. Once, when our troops held canon-firing practice near the battlefield, Wang Ling-chi mistook it for an internal disturbance within our army and was going to launch an attack against us; but he soon found that the defense works of our troops were done fast and well, and the men on the front line fought with agility. This showed that no internal disturbance had taken place, which puzzled Wang.

Under the pressure of Wang Ling-chi's continuous assaults, our troops were compelled to retreat three times, right to the area some one hundred li north of Sui-ting. The price paid by the enemy, however, mounted with each attack. During the last offensive Wang Ling-chi lost nearly three thousand men, while our losses were less than one-tenth the number of his. Wang Ling-chi's ardor was thus dampened, and he had to admit that the "Communist Bandits" had not weakened despite their retreat.

As we entered the year 1934 we had been tied up in battles with Wang Ling-chi's troops for about three months. Wang Ling-chi felt that it was impossible for him to put down the "Communist Bandits" rapidly; yet he underestimated our ability to wage a counterattack. Towards the end of the Chinese lunar year, Wang Lin-chi's wife, concubines, and other relatives all urged him by telegram to return to Wan-hsien for the Chinese New Year and to manage his private affairs. In the early part of February, Wang Ling-chi returned to Wan-hsien secretly, without notifying Liu Hsiang or his subordinates. He only told his chief-of-staff to take over the duties of commander during his absence. As we were able to decode his telegrams, we were fully informed of his every move and made active preparations to counterattack.

Early on the morning of February 14, 1934 (Chinese New Year's Day), we started our counteroffensive, attacking the right wing of Wang Ling-chi's troops. The defending brigade was soon routed under our fierce assault, and the brigade commander was killed in battle. The men on the second line of defense stampeded, and we advanced thirty li, until we reached Wang Ling-chi's headquarters, where Wang's chief-of-staff led a hasty retreat. The division and brigade commanders of Wang's troops then found out about Wang's secret departure before the Chinese New Year and created an uproar. Fortunately for Wang, the commanders on the left wing fought calmly, putting up stiff resistance in defense of their positions. This saved the units from a complete rout. As soon as Wang Ling-chi heard the news, he dashed back to the front to remedy the situation and plan counterattacks; but Liu Hsiang no longer trusted him.

Wang Ling-chi was dismissed by Liu Hsiang and kept under house arrest for a time. The two men were at variance with each other in the first place. Wang Ling-chi had had illicit dealings with Chiang Kai-shek and had expanded his own forces. Liu Hsiang felt that Wang Ling-chi harbored the ambition of taking his place if the opportunity arose. Wang Ling-chi, in order to curry favor with Chiang Kai-shek, had done his very best in the battles against us, and Liu Hsiang thought that his own strength was being wasted by Wang at will. Wang's secret departure from his post in violation of military discipline gave Liu Hsiang just the right excuse to punish him.

The period between October, 1933, and February, 1934, was the time when our army fought the fiercest battles against the Szechwan troops. Besides resisting the frontal attacks of Wang Ling-chi, our troops had to ward off assaults from Teng Hsi-hou, Yang Sen, T'ien Sung-yao, Li Chia-yu, and Lo Tze-nan, who were all pressing towards the Soviet region to support Wang Ling-chi. There had been some fierce fighting, and in order to shorten the defense line, our troops gradually retreated to the vicinity of Nan-chiang and Pa-chung. After the defeat of Wang Ling-chi's troops, the military situation temporarily remained at a stalemate.

There was an amusing episode in the campaign. Driven to the end of his tether, Liu Hsiang brought forth a Liu Shen-hsien (Liu the God), whose real name was Liu Chung-yun, a fortuneteller and "Chu-ke Liang" (braintruster) of Liu Hsiang's. The latter used to call him his teacher, and all major and minor warlords of Szechwan followed suit, making him quite an authority for a time. Liu Shen-hsien did help Liu Hsiang with negotiations between the warlords. Liu Hsiang was very concerned about the waxing and waning of the influence of the various factions among the warlords in Szechwan. He was reluctant to let his own forces suffer any losses in the event of trouble, and he was anxious to have others pick the chestnuts from the fire for him. It seemed that he brought out Liu Shen-hsien to facilitate deploying the troops of the various factions.

Immediately after Wang Ling-chi's dismissal, Liu Hsiang reshuffled the line-up of his team. He himself remained in Ch'eng-tu, while a front-line military committee was set up in Nan-chung to take charge of the war as a whole, with Liu Shen-hsien as chairman. The post of commander-in-chief of the Fifth Column, originally held by Wang Ling-chi, was given to Tang Shih-tsun, commander of the First Division and a favorite of Liu Hsiang's. The setting up of the military committee in Nan-chung was apparently to empower Liu Shen-hsien to oversee and step up attacks on our troops by the forces of Teng, T'ien, Yang, Li, and Lo.

In March, Liu Shen-hsien, the sorcerer who cast magic spells to delude the public, arrived at Nan-chung with great pomp. Imitating Chu-ke Liang, he issued a long oath-taking proclamation, and orders signed by the chairman of the Front-Line Military Committee poured into the various units, urging them to advance. Actually, Yang Sen's troops were already advancing towards the southern part of Pa-chung and Nan-chiang.

Our strategy was to thwart Liu Hsiang's plan, preventing genuine cooperation among the Szechwan warlords and concentrating on dealing blows to the Fifth Column, the unit directly under Liu Hsiang. We assembled about one-third of our forces to beat off the adventurous troops of Yang Sen, which fled back to Ying-shan. Our troops pressed on and surrounded the county seat of Ying-shan. We also made a direct assault on Nan-chung, forcing Liu Shen-hsien to flee back to Ch'eng-tu. We then proclaimed that we had no intention of taking the defense area of Yang Sen, so long as the sorcerer Liu was not allowed to wreak havoc; we declared that we only wanted to deal blows to Liu Hsiang and hoped that the other warlords of Szechwan would not allow themselves to be made into cats' paws by Liu Hsiang. To prove our word, we withdrew our troops from Yang Sen's defense area.

Liu Shen-hsien was no longer supernatural, and the Front-Line Military Committee was abolished. Liu Hsiang, the commander-in-chief of the Punitive Expedition Against the Bandits, still stayed in Ch'eng-tu and dared not take one step outside the city. Yet, he had to see to everything himself, as Liu Shen-hsien had proven himself useless as a tool.

Tang Shih-tsun, commander-in-chief of the Fifth Column, followed a work-style quite different from Wang Ling-chi's. Tang seemed to be more earnest and generous and could rally his subordinates; to Liu Hsiang, he was all obedience. All steps taken by him had to be approved by Liu Hsiang first. More troops were sent to the front, with sixty thousand men on the front line as compared to forty thousand at the time of Wang Ling-chi's command. Tang didn't try to seek glory in exercising his command; he just tried not to make mistakes. All of his battle orders were routine documents, formal and steady. The tasks were also equally distributed among the troops, as Tang dared not show any partiality.

Beginning in April, 1934, Tang Shih-tsun had organized several large-scale offensives against us. Still adhering to the strategy of inducing the enemy to penetrate deeply, we retreated step by step, so that there were no heavy casualties on either side. In May, when our troops retreated to the last line of defense, the left wing taking Wan-yüan County as its last stronghold, Liu Hsiang thought that his military plan had been successful at every turn and gave a strict order that Tang Shih-tsun seize Wan-yüan County rapidly, attempting to raid the rear of our troops to the north of T'ung-chiang from Wan-yüan. Thus started the three-month's campaign for the control of Wan-yüan County.

Wan-yüan was situated on strategic terrain, easy to defend but difficult to attack. Our troops put up strong resistance, so as to consume the strength of the enemy. By then, Liu Hsiang had built an airfield in Liang-shan, where scores of airplanes from Chiang Kai-shek were at Liu Hsiang's disposal. Tang Shih-tsun launched an attack on an average of once a week; but each time his troops suffered heavy blows, and finally he could not stand the strain any longer.

Tang Shih-tsun's routine assaults consisted mainly of the following characteristics. His troops took turns doing the main job of the attack, which was launched invariably at dawn. At about eight or nine o'clock the planes started out from Liang-shan and came to the front (usually in formations of nine), at which time the troops would dash forward and chase us up the slopes. Then our fire would check them, and they would be hemmed in, unable to move forwards or backwards. By about four in the afternoon the airplanes would stop flying over, and we would start to counterattack. In the hand-to-hand fighting, the enemy ordinarily used hand grenades as their major weapon. But their hand grenades usually took some ten seconds to explode; and our men, short of hand grenades, often took up the enemy's grenades and threw them back, just in time for them to explode on the opposite side. Thus, under the hand grenades and our machine-gun fire, the enemy troops suffered heavy casualties and had to retreat to their original battle positions. During this period the enemy lost from three hundred to more than a thousand men in each assault.

The strength of the enemy thus petered out. This was not only apparent on the battlefield. The subordinates of Tang Shih-tsun all demanded replacements and reorganization, and Tang himself also begged Liu Hsiang to stop the assault owing to tragically heavy casualties. The losses of our troops were much smaller, and our morale was high, giving us a good opportunity to counterattack.

At dawn one August day we launched a counterattack from the region between Wan-yüan and Chu-ku. In a short time we broke through the defense line of the enemy, then our main force detoured to surround them from the rear. It was a long-distance encirclement, but the enemy troops in Wan-yüan fled to the rear even before we reached them. There was a definite possibility that we would completely annihilate the enemy; unfortunately, pouring rain together with the outbreak of mountain floods hindered our pursuit. When we came to Sui-ting and Hsüan-han, the greater part of the enemy troops had crossed the Sui-ting River and controlled the means of crossing. Unable to cross the river owing to the rising torrent, our men were obliged to give the enemy a chance to rest and take a breather.

This victory brought us back all the territories that we had lost during our battles with the Szechwan warlords. Our original domain had included all of the counties of T'ung-chiang, Nan-chiang, Pa-chung, and Wan-yüan and parts of the counties of Sui-ting, Hsüan-han, Kuang-yüan, Tsang-chi, Lang-chung, and Yi-lung. When Tang Shih-tsun attacked Wan-yüan County, the enemy on the western front took the opportunity to occupy the county seats of Nan-chiang and Pa-chung. It was not until the rout of Tang Shih-tsun's Fifth Column that they retreated to the west bank of the Chia-ling River under pressure from our troops. The Northern Szechwan Soviet region now extended to Pa-shan in the north, bordering on Han-chung, to the Sui-ting River in the east and the Chia-ling River in the west, and in the south to Ying-shan and Ch'ü-hsien, bordering on the domain of Yang Sen.

As Liu Hsiang's columns retreated after successive defeats, there was an intermission in the war. Then, after some reshuffling, he appointed Wang Tsuan-hsu, commander of the Second Division, to succeed Tang Shih-tsun as commander-in-chief of the Fifth Column. Wang Tsuan-hsu took active steps to reorganize the troops, so he was unable to counterattack for the time being. Our troops also needed some reorganization and replacements after the long period of combat.

Long months of fighting in the mountainous region caused extremely heavy damage to the locality, affecting both our side and that of the enemy. But owing to inferior organizational ability, the enemy suffered more than we did. The Fifth Column of Tang Shih-tsun, relying on Liang-shan as its rear base, constantly needed about eighty thousand men to keep up normal supplies for the whole front.[1] Most of these transport troops were opium addicts who had been pressed into service, and untold numbers of them had died on the road. In the places that Tang Shih-tsun's troops had occupied, such as Sui-ting, Wan-yüan, and Hsüan-han, dead bodies as well as wounded and sick men who had been abandoned could be found everywhere. There were soldiers among them, but the majority were transport laborers. The local inhabitants had fled after harassment by the enemy, leaving nine out of ten houses empty. There was an extreme shortage of material supplies.

The territory of the Northern Szechwan Soviet region was also a scene of desolation, particularly the places ravaged by enemy troops. Farming had been impeded by the fighting, and the fields were either overrun with weeds or left untilled. The food and other supplies of the inhabitants were partly consumed by the Red Army and partly destroyed by the enemy. Epidemics were rampant, including infectious dysentry in the autumn of 1934, which was mentioned above. The market towns in the Soviet region were bleak, since there was a sharp decline in visitors and goods. The voices of the people expressed either fear of disease and death or complaints about shortages of supplies.

We tried our best to minimize the damage. Our troops pursued the enemy on the one hand and cleared the battlefield on the other. We buried the dead, took care of the wounded and the sick, and disinfected all the surroundings. The defeated enemy, as they retreated, doused the grain in the barns of Wan-yüan County with kerosene so that we could not use it. Nevertheless the starving refugees returning from the mountain forests grabbed the kerosene-soaked grain, and the number of sick people increased. As soon as combat ceased, we immediately mobilized the local people in a crash program to save and replant late autumn crops, and we distributed food rations and gave relief to heavily damaged areas. Salt became a scarce item after the campaign. We went to such lengths as digging up the dirt floors of the old salt shops, boiling the dirt down in hopes of getting come salt out of it. Publicity on the prevention of diseases was circulated on a large scale, and all-out efforts were made to stamp out dysentry. Red Army soldiers helped the people in many ways, and military doctors of the Red Army took time out to care for sick civilians, although they were already extremely busy.

While we were preoccupied with urgent relief work, news came that the Red Army in Kiangsi had left the Jui-chin base on October 16, 1934, and was moving west. This shocking information reached us a few days after the Red Army's departure. In July and August, while Tang Shih-tsun was launching an offensive on Wan-yüan County, the CC of the CCP had sent us many radio messages from Jui-chin expressing their concern over our situation. Yet no mention was made of the condition in the Kiangsi Soviet region. When we routed the enemy in August and September, the CC sent us wires expressing their delight. We read in between the lines of these telegrams that the CC's situation was far from happy.

A meeting of senior cadres was then held to discuss the problems arising from the departure of the Central Red Army (that is, the First Front Army) from the Kiangsi Soviet region. We were not informed of their operation beforehand, and from the data that we received directly, we concluded that this was a forced retreat by the Central Red Army under enemy pressure. We could not say for certain whether the Red Army could prevent the enemy from pursuing and whether it could find a foothold in the Southwest. We believed that it was a heavy blow to the Soviet campaign on the whole if the Central Red Army found it impossible to stand on its own feet in Kiangsi.

In the light of these guesses, we discussed the principles to be followed in the future by the Red Fourth Front Army. We all agreed that we should support the Central Red Army in our future operations and strive to expand to areas outside Szechwan. We noted that there was no need to defend rigidly the Northern Szechwan Soviet region, which in our eyes had become a lemon with all its juice squeezed out. It would not be easy to expand if we relied on just this one region. The basis for this view included two main points: First, the quality of our weapons and ammunition was getting worse and worse. There were about fifty thousand men in our army, but the number of rifles that could be used in battle was less than twenty thousand, more than half of which were native-made ones that we had captured from the Szechwan warlords. Moreover, it was very easy to damage the rifles in battle. The comrades were very worried about this. They thought that only by fighting with Chiang Kai-shek's own troops could they get better equipment to replenish their supply. Second, the ravages of battle had deprived the Northern Szechwan Soviet region of food and other supplies. There might be a famine the following year in the months before the crops were mature. If the Red Army remained there, it was impossible to solve the food problem for the people, and the Army might have to contend with the people for food.

No definite decisions were made at the meeting, but the supreme command was empowered to use its own discretion in handling the situation. We started to make preparations for our future operations. Encouraged by the forced departure of the Red Army in Kiangsi from its old base, the warlords of Szechwan began to launch small-scale attacks on us from every side. Our main force assembled in strategic points rather far away from the front and dealt with the enemy attacks with only a small force. Cadres at the middle level and above were withdrawn to organize a senior military training course, whose main task was to study the military situation in various parts of the country, particularly the general condition of the Northwest.

The training course was originally for cadres who were recovering from wounds. Later, cadres were continually taken out of army units to join the course. After our reunion with the Central Red Army, the course expanded into the Red Army School. The director of the training course was Ho Wei, former commander of the Ninth Army, who had been seriously wounded. He was a tailor of European suits from Hong Kong who had taken part in the Canton–Hong Kong strike of 1925. During the Soviet campaign he had joined the guerrillas on the border between Kwangsi and Vietnam, fighting the French armies in Vietnam side by side with Vietnamese revolutionaries. He was transferred in 1931 to the Oyüwan region to be a regimental commander in the Red Fourth Front Army. He had been wounded eleven times, and the wounds finally disabled him. Hence, the training school in its initial stage was a sort of sanatorium.

We actually slackened our fight against the Szechwan warlords, while our reconnaissance radio worked day and night to ascertain the progress of the Central Red Army and the operations of the enemies near it. Only a small amount of time was allotted to reconnoitering enemy activities in Szechwan. When the Central Red Army reached the border between Kwangsi and Kweichow, we began supplying it with intelligence reports. This was a very onerous task. Every day our reconnaissance radio monitored a lot of the enemy's coded messages and decoded them so that staff officers could turn them into summary reports, which were later sent to the Central Red Army after I had assessed them. Our radio station had to wait for the Central Red Army's station to come on; sometimes the wait lasted from seven in the evening till about three o'clock the following morning. Sometimes I myself sat beside the radio set, waiting to answer any questions the other side might raise.

For at least two months the Central Red Army relied entirely on our intelligence reports (particularly when it was advancing from Tsun-yi to Yunnan). Since the troops were marching day and night, their radio station could not find time to do reconnaissance work. As soon as the troops stopped for the night or for a rest, their radio station immediately communicated with us. They decided on their operations and issued orders in accordance with our reports. This activity of ours acted as the eyes and ears for the well-known Long March of 25,000 li.

When the Central Red Army had withdrawn inside the border of Kweichow Province, the news became more and more unfavorable to us day by day. The pursuing KMT troops were all boasting of their victories. Chiang Kai-shek's troops were moving west from all sides, some reaching Chungking in Szechwan, and others moving to Han-chung and

T'ien-shui via Sian. The Szechwan warlords were extremely frightened. They thought that the Central Red Army of Kiangsi would proceed from Kweichow to Szechwan and unite with the Red Fourth Front Army there. Meanwhile, large numbers of Chiang Kai-shek's troops had moved into Szechwan. The Szechwan warlords felt that it would not be easy for them to keep their domains. They clamored that they must, first of all, beat the Red Fourth Front Army, to prevent the two Red armies from supporting each other from the north and south.

Our military operations to support the Central Red Army began in December, 1934. According to a rough calculation, we thought that the Central Red Army and the Red Fourth Front Army would meet somewhere in western Szechwan. We deemed it our duty to support the Central Red Army. We reasoned that the best base for us would be the border region of Szechwan, Shensi, and Kansu. The troops of Hu Tsung-nan, defending the line between T'ien-shui and Kuang-yüan, were the biggest obstacle to the realization of our plan.

In December the main force of our army advanced to the Ning-ch'iang area in Han-chung. This was the first military operation that we waged outside of Szechwan. Yang Hu-ch'eng's troops stationed in Han-chung were very alarmed. They soon sent a delegate to ask us why we had violated the nonintervention agreement reached by the two sides some time before. We told them that it was not we, but they, who had violated the agreement. When our units were locked in battle at Wan-yüan with Liu Hsiang's troops, the Shensi troops had crossed Pa-shan and harassed the northern rear of our forces. Recently the Shensi troops had made active arrangements, implying a response to Chiang Kai-shek's call for a punitive expedition against the Communists. However, we also comforted the delegate from Yang Hu-ch'eng, explaining that our operation did not aim to occupy Han-chung, but was heading elsewhere.

Indeed, our first aim was to look for Hu Tsung-nan's troops, to whom we were determined to deal appropriate blows. However, his main force was far away in T'ien-shui, while the units stationed at Pi-k'ou on the border of Szechwan and Shensi and at Kuang-yüan in Szechwan were merely a brigade in each case. We sent a small force to make a trial attack on the troops at Pi-k'ou and Kuang-yüan, but the enemy troops did not come out right away, relying, as they were, on their fine strategic positions and their superior firepower. We were thus unable to hit Hu's troops outside of their strongholds.

Another aim of our operation was to find Hsü Hai-tung's whereabouts. In the same year Hsü Hai-tung's units had entered the Shensi region from the Oyüwan region. We got a smattering of reports about Hsü Hai-tung by monitoring enemy intelligence reports, but soon we heard no more about him. We guessed that Hsü Hai-tung was looking for us, and we wanted to send some men to support him. Our search in Han-chung was in vain. We did not know where his troops were and could not ever ascertain whether such troops existed.

In mid-January, 1935, while still in the Ning-ch'iang area, we received a radio message from the CC on the main points of the resolution of the Tsun-yi conference. The resolution affirmed that the CC's political line on the Soviet campaign was correct, but that it had made serious mistakes in the military line. Primarily, the Central Red Army had incorrectly adopted the slogan of defending the Soviet region, which reflected a conservative defensive strategy, and had abandoned the fine tradition of waging guerrilla warfare, thus causing military setbacks. The message also informed us that Mao Tse-tung had been elected as an additional member of the Politburo of the CC.

We held a meeting to discuss the radio message. From a military viewpoint, we felt that the Red First Front Army in the Kiangsi Soviet region and during its westward movement had suffered heavy losses. We, therefore, seriously criticized the error of the military line. Soon we were informed that the Red First Front Army was moving towards the northwest from Tsun-yi, heading for Ch'ih-shui on the border between Szechwan and Kweichow. We guessed that they were trying to cross the Yangtze River to meet us in northern Szechwan.

We then abandoned our plan to engage Hu Tsung-nan's troops in the triangular area on the Szechwan-Shensi-Kansu border and returned to the Northern Szechwan Soviet region. By this time the Szechwan warlords had reoccupied Sui-ting, Wan-yüan, and the neighboring area, with their main force advancing towards Yi-lung and Pa-chung from the south. In order to defend the Northern Szechwan Soviet region, we were compelled to retreat southward quickly.

In the light of conditions that existed at that time, we decided to cross the Chia-ling River from Tsang-hsi and to move west to support the Red First Front Army. Hsü Hsiang-ch'ien led the larger part of our troops to deal with the enemy to our south, while Ch'en Ch'ang-hao raced back to T'ung-chiang to deal with the enemy to our east. After we crossed the Chia-ling River it would not be easy to defend T'ung-chiang, and it was necessary to make arrangements for guerrilla activities beforehand. I myself rushed to Tsang-hsi to make preparations for the crossing.

This was a decision that affected the very existence of the Northern Szechwan Soviet region. We had explained to the general cadres and the people within the region that it was imperative for the Red Fourth Front Army to carry out the military plan of supporting the Red First Front Army, and that for a time the region might have to suffer enemy harassment. We dared not announce the news about the plight of the Red First Front Army. We only stressed that the Red First Front Army was a much more powerful unit than the Red Fourth Front Army, and that the two would join forces to seize Ch'eng-tu.

The implementation of this military plan paved the way for our reunion with the First Front Army in the Mao-kung area; it also marked the actual end of the Soviet region that had T'ung-chiang as its center.

THE MEETING OF THE ARMIES
AND THE INTERNAL STRIFE

CHAPTER

Crossing the Chia-ling River

In our view, crossing the Chia-ling River to support the First Front Army in its march into the western Szechwan area was our primary task. The First Front Army constituted the main force of the Red Army of China, with the CC of the CCP and many major cadres going along with it during the march. It was now in the grips of difficulties and was struggling to survive. If we had failed to go to its assistance in time, a tremendous loss might have been inflicted on the Chinese revolution and we might have had to bear a guilty conscience. Because of this very important duty, we braved difficulties and stepped into dangers to go to its aid, even going to the lengths of forsaking the Northern Szechwan Soviet region, which could have been defended. It was completely beyond our expectation that our actions would bring down upon us un-called-for accusations and, following that, disputes and cleavage.

I was personally in charge of the plan to cross the Chia-ling River. I kept track of the movements of the Red First Front Army, on the one hand, and made preparations for the crossing, on the other. The First Front Army was then circling around the northern parts of Kweichow and Yunnan, without any definite course. Enemy armies were setting up defenses along the Yangtze River to prevent the First Front Army from crossing by stealth. I tried to judge if the First Front Army would be able to do so, for if it couldn't, then we would naturally refrain from abandoning the Northern Szechwan Soviet region needlessly. Later, judging by their radio messages to us, we learned that they had determined to cross the Yangtze. Consequently, we decided to cross the Chia-ling River and move westward.

The Chia-ling is deep and wide, with rapid currents. On both banks overhanging cliffs and steep precipices dominate the scene. The enemy troops guarding the strategic defenses were those of Teng Hsi-hou and T'ien Sung-yao. To us, who were poorly equipped, they posed an insurmountable barrier. Scanning all the possible places for a crossing, I finally settled on the one near the county seat of Ts'ang-ch'i. There, the river was wide and the enemy on the opposite bank was formidable. My military advisers generally disagreed with this choice, but I held that it provided the best conditions. Moreover, the enemy would not dream that this would be our choice, and we could take advantage of their negligence.

Taking advantage of the fine conditions in this part of the river, we made preparations for our battle to cross the Chia-ling. The first problem to settle was the means of transport. Our enemies had kept all boats in their custody on the opposite bank. We organized an engineering battalion, composed of some three hundred men who were capable of building or manning boats and could swim very well. The battalion built one hundred boats that looked like landing craft, with sandbags piled up on the prow for defense. Each boat was capable of carrying a squad of twelve men across the river. Officers and men used these boats for training at Wang-chia-pa, a market town on the bank of the Tung-ho, a tributary of the Chia-ling River, some fifty li from Ts'ang-ch'i County. We had to build a road from Wang-chia-pa to Ts'ang-ch'i to transport these boats over the high mountains to a stream near Ts'ang-ch'i.

One April evening in 1935 everything was ready for our forced crossing under fire. Unfortunately, the enemy had got news of our crossing, and their senior commanders stayed up till midnight on the opposite bank to keep watch over the river. Seeing no activity on our side, they began to doubt the reliability of their intelligence report. Not a single boat was in sight on the opposite shore. They decided that the Red Army could not possibly cross this rapid river, more than three hundred meters in width, and they relaxed their guard.

Yet, it was during that very night that we succeeded in crossing the river at three in the morning. The hundred boats that we had transported to Ts'ang-ch'i were hidden away on a stream out of the enemy's sight.

At about 3 A.M. the boats set sail directly for the opposite bank and, without much ado, seized the enemy's beachhead. The bulk of our troops followed and took all the heights on the opposite bank one after another. Our river-crossing operation greatly shocked and amazed the enemy.

Owing to our careful preparations for the crossing, we were able to seize all the boats kept in custody by the enemy, and we built a pontoon bridge at a ford of the Chia-ling in the county seat of Ts'ang-ch'i. By the time the enemy started to bomb us about noon the next day, our pontoon bridge had already been completed. The enemy airmen didn't seem to be very accurate in their bombing; none of their several hundred bombs hit our pontoon bridge. As their rear had been attacked by surprise, the troops of Teng Hsi-hou and T'ien Sung-yao were obliged to retreat from the defenses on the Chia-ling River and to withdraw to the county seats of Chien-ko, Tzu-t'ung, and Yen-t'ing. Our army got control of about one hundred li up and down the east bank of the Chia-ling River, and we continued our pursuit of the retreating enemy.

Despite our success in crossing the Chia-ling River, enemy pressure was mounting. In January of that year Chaing Kai-shek had come to Chungking to see to military arrangements against us. Quite a number of his troops had come to Szechwan from the Yangtze and from Kweichow. Three divisions of the Nineteenth Route Army, which he reorganized, had arrived at the Shensi-Kansu region to the north of us. In a few days these enemy troops would be coming near us.

The enemy was quite aware of our goal. As soon as our army crossed the Chia-ling River, the enemy cried, "The Communist bandits are trying to meet in western Szechwan." The way to deal with us was naturally to keep us separated. The enemy's radio messages mentioned more than once, "The Red Army of Chu [Teh] and Mao [Tse-tung] is at the end of its tether and can easily be annihilated in Yunnan and Kweichow. The troops under Ho Lung and Hsiao K'o [namely, the Second and Sixth armies, collectively known as the Second Front Army], drifting about in the border regions of Szechwan, Kweichow, Hunan, and Hupeh, are the weakest. But Hsü Hsiang-ch'ien's units in northern Szechwan are the most seditious." In fact, the main attention of the enemy was focused on the Red Fourth Front Army.

As our main force crossed the Chia-ling River to move west, the Szechwan troops on our east quickly occupied T'ung-chiang and Pa-chung counties and advanced to Nan-chiang. By this time, Hsü Hsiang-ch'ien's troops had retreated from the front at Yi-lung and had crossed the Chia-ling River in Ts'ang-ch'i County. Ch'en Ch'ang-hao left some guerrillas in this area to launch activities to check the enemy, using the Pa-shan Range as their chief base. Ch'en himself led the units that were bringing up the rear to Ts'ang-ch'i in rapid retreat. In a few days we three met again somewhere near Chien-ko.

Chien-ko and Tzu-t'ung were strategic points on the Szechwan-Shensi highway, where the enemies could easily attack us from both the north and the south. It was impossible for us to stay there very long. So we continued to move westward, setting as our goal the region around Chiang-yu, Ping-wu, and Pei-ch'uan. On the other hand, the enemy might suppose that we would go south to Ch'eng-tu or north to attack Shensi and Kansu, now that we had got hold of the key points on the Szechwan-Shensi highway. We thought we might as well play along with them, and started to give wide publicity to the move while making sham guerrilla attacks towards both the north and the south. The shock made all hearts tremble in Szechwan, Shensi, and Kansu.

After making some moves to confuse the enemy, the main body of our troops headed directly for Chiang-yu from Chien-ko via Ching-hung-pa. Thirty li south of Chiang-yu was Chung-pa, which was called "Little Ch'eng-tu," where the commerce of all northern Szechwan concentrated. The seventy-li journey from Ching-hung-pa to Chiang-yu ran through flat land, which was planted with poppies in a vast stretch, presenting a spectacular sight of multicolored blossoms. This was the largest field of poppies I had seen since my arrival in Szechwan. I couldn't help being sad as I saw the fertile fields committed to the production of poison.

Our troops were assembling around Chiang-yu in successive waves. Chiang-yu and Chung-pa were both guarded by units under Teng Hsi-hou. Part of our troops went on to encircle the two key points, while the majority settled down separately in this zone of abundance, with replenishing supplies as the objective. Meanwhile, they also went north and west in two columns to take the county seats of Ping-wu and Pei-ch'uan, respectively. However, the troops of Hu Tsung-nan had arrived ahead of us and had taken Ping-wu. We encountered them in the vicinity of the county seat and kept them at bay in order to protect the rear of our army to the north. The column that went west took Pei-ch'uan, providing a stepping stone for our army in its westward advance.

Air harassment by the enemy was on the increase as the main forces of the Szechwan warlords assembled south of Chiang-yu from the east. The Szechwan troops, it seemed, could not match us in agility. The activities of enemy planes showed that Chiang Kai-shek had assembled more planes in Szechwan in an attempt to stop us from marching south. We played hide-and-seek with enemy planes in the Chiang-yu region for some time. When enemy planes made reconnaissance flights over us, we placed soldiers in openings in the forest to deceive them. As soon as the planes were gone, we went away from the openings and also asked the inhabitants in the neighborhood to evacuate them. When enemy planes came later and dropped a lot of bombs, it was only a no-man's zone that was hit in most cases.

It was now May, 1935—another critical moment for us to decide on a principle to guide our future moves. We had abandoned the Northern Szechwan Soviet region; it was still uncertain whether the Red First Front Army would be able to cross the Yangtze River. The region now in our possession around Chiang-yu, Ping-wu, and Pei-ch'uan was inhabited by people of various minority groups, in some cases, as in the villages of Pei-ch'uan, with more minority-group than Han people. Further west, it was thickly inhabited by Tibetans.

The meeting of senior cadres that was held in the neighborhood of Chiang-yu had taken all these issues into consideration. The participants all agreed that we could not continue to wait and see, but had to decide our policy in accordance with the circumstances. We decided that with the area around Pei-ch'uan as our starting point, we should extend our activities to northwestern Szechwan, southern Kansu, and Sikang in order to form a Szechwan-Kansu-Sikang base.

In accordance with this policy decision, I advanced the proposal of forming a Northwest Federation. I explained that in the newly occupied areas we could only implement such regulations as abolishing oppressive taxes and miscellaneous duties that we had laid down in the Program upon Entering Szechwan, which we had drawn up when we first arrived in that province. For the time being it was not feasible to organize Soviets and to distribute the land. A wider margin in the policy would have to be left in dealing with the minority groups. There would be no opposition to the chieftains, headmen, and lamas of the minority tribes, and help would be given them in organizing autonomous governments within their regions or tribes. Delegates of these autonomous governments would join the delegates elected by the Han people to organize the Northwest Federation.

The meeting accepted my proposal, and we started to organize the Northwest Federation, with Chou Ch'un-ch'üan, former political commissar of the Fourth Front Army, elected as chairman of the government.

The Program for the Northwest Federation was drawn up and made public everywhere. The program was discussed in greater detail than the Program upon Entering Szechwan had been. We noted that the Chinese Central Soviet government had not been able to exercise its functions since the Red First Front Army left Kiangsi. The Northwest Federation that we now organized in the light of actual needs would become part of the Chinese Central Soviet government when it was able to function again in the future.

The Program of the Northwest Federation emphasized, first of all, the importance of opposing the Japanese and opposing Chiang Kai-shek. It then went on to demonstrate that the present form of government was suitable for the Northwest with its many nationalities. The principal stipulations of the program were the abolition of oppressive taxes and miscellaneous duties, reduction of rents and interest rates, bans on indiscriminate arrests and killing, opposition to rule by warlords, opposition to discrimination against minority groups by the Hans, strict prohibition of opium, support for the Red Army, and so forth. Stipulations for the minority groups in the Northwest included autonomy for the various national groups and tribes, whose chieftains were to organize autonomous governments upon the approval of a congress of their own people. All autonomous governments were to obey the common program of the Northwest Federation, which, in its turn, would respect the customs of the autonomous governments, such as not interfering with religious freedom and the privileges of the chieftains.

We temporarily took the county seat of Pei-ch'uan County for the seat of the Northwest Federation. The county was in the northwestern corner of Szechwan Province, where Hans and minority groups, mainly Tibetans, lived side by side. Most of the Han people lived in places with communications facilities, while most of the minority groups lived in the mountainous region. Among the minorities there were both civilized and uncivilized groups. The ones in this area could speak the Szechwan dialect and were quite accustomed to the Han way of life; they were usually known as civilized minorities. Those in the Sikang region to the northwest of Pei-ch'uan were known as uncivilized minorities, as they spoke no Szechwanese and did not have much intercourse with the Han people. They kept to the dialects and customs of their own tribes.

Pei-ch'uan County was situated in a mountainous region, with the Ta-hsueh-shan (Big Snowy Mountains) of the Min-shan Range to its west. The roads in the county were hewn out of rocky cliffs and were twisting, dangerous, and steep. The rivers in the county were swift and looked like waterfalls. In some places the river beds had been widened by stonecutters. The great engineering feats of the stonecutters were amazing. The local people worshiped Ta-yu, the saint in Chinese history who had subdued the flooding rivers. Ta-yu was supposed to be a native of Pei-ch'uan County, where temples dedicated to him were found in great numbers. I imagine that this had something to do with encouraging the stonecutters to build roads and control the rivers. Rice and poppies did not grow well in the high, cold terrain of the county. Only ching-ko barley, beans, and maize were grown.

When we came here, we seemed to have arrived in an alien land. Even the majority of our soldiers from the Tung-Nan-Pa area felt the same way. We had to launch an educational campaign throughout the Army, teaching the soldiers how to get along with the minority people and to respect their religion and customs. In order to blend in with the local people, they were to learn to eat kou-pa* with their hands. Our soldiers, who were used to eating rice as their staple diet, found this very inconvenient, and Ch'en Ch'ang-hao had to demonstrate how to eat kou-pa many times to the soldiers. This, for a time, became the main item in his political work.

The Northwest Federation under Chou Ch'un-ch'üan also took active steps in its work. He got some delegates of the tribes from Pei-ch'uan and Mao-hsien to its southwest to take part in the work of the government. He explained to these delegates that the Red Army and the tribes were kith and kin of one family. The Red Army was helping them to get rid of the oppression of the warlords and would certainly not oppose their chieftains and religion. The only wish of the Red Army was that the tribes would coexist peacefully with it. He also talked about plans for the future Northwest Federation, when there would be autonomous regions for the various nationalities, such as Tibetan, Hui, and Mongolian. He wanted the delegates to convey the program of the Northwest Federation government and the wishes of the Red Army to the various tribes in the Northwest. He had, in fact, done part of the job.

About three weeks after our work in Pei-ch'uan had started (around the end of May and the beginning of June), we heard the news that the First Front Army had crossed the Chin-sha River by stealth. Immediately we embarked on our plan of giving it assistance. Our headquarters

---

* Kou-pa, the staple food of the native people, which was made from ching-ko barley powder that had been roasted and mixed with cheese, was eaten in the form of a ball kneaded together in the hands.

was moved from Pei-ch'uan to Mao-hsien; the Thirtieth Army was ordered to cross the Min River at Wen-chuan and to go directly to the Ta-tu River via Li-fan and Mao-kung, annihilating the enemy troops in this area to ensure that the First Front Army could cross the river in safety; the Ninth and Thirty-first armies were ordered to retreat to the area of Pei-ch'uan and Mao-hsien from the front lines of Chiang-yu and Ping-wu in order to deal with the enemy there; and the Fourth Army went north to Sung-fan to protect the north side of our army.

Enemy troops were in close pursuit. Wherever we retreated one step, the enemy stepped in to fill the gap. As soon as our Ninth and Thirty-first armies retreated to Pei-ch'uan and Mao-hsien, they encountered the superior force of the Szechwan troops in the southeastern part of the region, and fierce fighting ensued. In the mountainous region of thick forests and dense bamboo, enemy troops tried to drive a wedge in our army, which was intercepting them and attacking them wherever it could. When the Fourth Front Army arrived in the Sung-fan region, the troops of Hu Tsung-nan also came, and both armies engaged in fierce fighting in the vicinity of the county seat. Finally Hu Tsung-nan's troops took the county seat, while the Fourth Front Army captured the strategic points south of Sung-fan, checking the enemy in his attempt to go south to threaten Mao-hsien.

Our Thirtieth Army advanced by forced march and met the advance troops of the Red First Front Army about one hundred li south of Mao-kung. The First Front Army had been extraordinarily quick in crossing the Chin-sha River and the Ta-tu River. The Ta-tu River was a well-known natural barrier, where the troops of Shih Ta-kai, the famous general of the Taiping Heavenly Kingdom, were wiped out by the armies of the Ching dynasty as they were trying to cross the river. The comrades and I rejoiced immensely when we received the radio news in Mao-hsien that Ch'en Shih-ts'ai and Li Hsien-nien of the Thirtieth Army had met the First Front Army, which was assembling around Mao-kung. We admired the spirit of the First Front Army in carrying on a hard struggle over long periods of time and discussed how to show our solicitude for the soldiers of the First Front Army, so that they might thoroughly enjoy a good rest. I immediately sent a radio message to Mao Tse-tung and the others, extending our congratulations and informing them of my departure for Mao-kung to talk everything over with them. Thus the Red Fourth Front Army succeeded in helping the First Front Army despite many dangers and difficulties.

The Reunion at Mao-kung

When I first met Mao Tse-tung and the others at Mao-kung, I found that our two groups maintained quite different views on politics, military matters, and the relations between the two armies. Recalling the events of those bygone days, I would say that some seem ludicrous now, although they actually happened at that time. Of course, these differences of opinion were not accidental. They resulted when the Wang Ming line of the CC of the CCP ("Chinese Stalinism") and the guerrilla heroism of Mao Tse-tung collided with my pent-up discontent over the leadership of the CC (particularly with the policy of the Soviet movement), which stemmed from my realistic pragmatism. People invariably try to avoid strife in time of trouble, but actually the opposite happens. In the CCP particularly, internal strifes have not been well handled because of its lack of democratic training.

In June, 1935, I set out in excitement from Mao-hsien to Mao-kung to meet Mao Tse-tung and the other comrades whom I had not seen for a long time. Hsü Hsiang-ch'ien and Ch'en Ch'ang-hao stayed behind in Mao-hsien, and the organs of my Military Subcommittee also continued with their routine business in Mao-hsien.

Going from Mao-hsien to Mao-kung via Wen-chuan and Li-fan, I passed through areas mostly inhabited by Tibetans. The rivers there were rapid torrents spanned by bamboo-rope bridges and overhanging wooden bridges, or crossed by means of ox-hide boats or overhanging ropes. It was inevitably extremely difficult for our soldiers to march over such terrain. West of Wen-chuan was a vast primeval forest, where timber felled by the lumber companies that were run by the Szechwan warlords for the sake of gathering in profits lay crisscross on the ground, waiting to be plunged into the rivers, when the water rose, and floated down to Wen-chuan, where they would be made into rafts and transported outside the province. As a result of their indiscriminate felling, damage to the forest was very great. Moreover, owing to the large number of logs in the rivers, the roads along the banks were prone to flooding and being destroyed when the rivers rose during mountain floods. When we crossed through the forest, my entourage and I had to make big detours around dense forests and mountain trails, because the usual paths were blocked by timber, causing more difficulties in our trip.

The Tibetans of various tribes in this region seemed to be particularly docile and were believers in Lamaism. All their customs were different from those of the Han people. Their houses were usually three-story

THE RED FIRST FRONT ARMY AND THE RED FOURTH FRONT
ARMY MEET AT MAO-KUNG AND SEPARATE AT MAO-ERH-KAI

stone buildings for the deities, men, and animals. The ground floor was for the cattle and goats; it had heaps of dung, was dark and unventilated, foul-smelling and unbearably filthy. In order to keep the cattle warm and to store up the much-prized cattle dung which could be used for fuel, the Tibetans could not worry about hygienic conditions. The second floor housed the humans, who lived in rooms facing the outside. There were no windows except for very small draft holes. The foul smell from the cattle dung downstairs was almost suffocating. The third floor was Buddha's abode, and was kept scrupulously clean. In the middle of the room was the idol of Buddha, and all around were scrolls of sutras. This was the most sacred place in the whole building. In the bedrooms of the Tibetans there might be heaps of ching-ko barley, cheese, and clothing; but everything was kept in its place, and the rooms looked tidy. The only thing that was rarely seen was ironware, which, it was said, the Tibetans kept out of others' sight, as it was something very hard to get and very valuable in their eyes. The Tibetans had a very devout belief in Lamaism, and the reason for their terribly high death rate should be apparent to anyone with modern knowledge as soon as he entered their abodes.

In this remote region the influence of foreigners could also be seen. All the way from T'ung-chiang every county seat and large market town had a church with a cross as its symbol. Some of these were managed by foreign missionaries. The Japanese also came to this part of the country, some running photographic studios and others dealing directly in opium and morphine. In the neighborhood of Li-fan I visited a church of considerable size, which showed the influence of foreigners in this region.

This stone church was supposed to be an important building in the locality. There was a Western missionary staying there all of the time. When our Thirtieth Army passed through the place, the missionary went away. But the church was intact, with no loss or damage. The church ran a very large apiary, and the land around the church was planted with all kinds of crops. Inside the church compound was a large barn filled with maize and a lot of farming implements. All this showed that the missionary had employed many people to work for him on the farm; he was actually a big landlord in the locality. He was probably very fond of high living, as he had an excellent mill, which gave him very fine grain for his food. He had imported large quantities of Sunkist oranges, apples, and foreign wines and liquor, enough for his personal enjoyment for a long time.

Since I was in a hurry to get to Mao-kung, I did not have much time to observe the places on the way. Followed by Huang Ch'ao and some ten cavalrymen as guards, I climbed high mountains, traversed a dense primeval forest, and made my way through rough, rocky slopes overgrown with shrubbery and grass. After more than three days we came to Fu-pien, about ninety li north of Mao-kung, which was the temporary camping place of Mao Tse-tung, Chu Teh, and the others.

At about 5 P.M. on a day in June, Mao Tse-tung, together with the members of the Central Politburo and other high-ranking military and political cadres, stood at the roadside some three li from Fu-pien to welcome us. There were some forty or fifty people standing around. As soon as I saw them, I got down from my horse and ran towards them to embrace them and shake hands with them. Words could not describe our rejoicing at this reunion after so many years of tribulation. Mao Tse-tung stood up on a platform prepared beforehand to deliver a welcoming speech to me. Then I made a speech in reply, paying tribute to the CC of the CCP and expressing solicitude for the First Front Army which had gone through many hard struggles.

Mao Tse-tung and I and the others soon walked side by side towards Fu-pien, talking and laughing all the way, telling one another our separate adventures. They told me that they had rested in Fu-pien for four days and were anxious to have me with them to discuss future military plans. Our stroll soon took us to Fu-pien, where there were some thirty households. Comrades working in the various Central organs in Fu-pien came out to greet me as they heard us coming. I waved to them, smiling. Mao Tse-tung and the then Madame Mao (Ho Tzu-ch'en) lived in a house at the southern end of the market town. Organs of the secretariat of the CC, the Military Affairs Committee, and the General Political Headquarters were all crowded together in the center of town. I was assigned to a shop at the northern end of the place. My office was behind the counter of the shop, whose doors were always open, and in front of the counter the members of my entourage had their headquarters.

The First Front Army was resting at that time. The Third Army under P'eng Te-huai, the Fifth Army under Tung Chen-t'ang, and the Twelfth Army under Lo Ping-hui were assembled at Cho-ko-chi, north of Fu-pien, while the First Army under Lin Piao was stationed near Mao-kung. The main task of guarding security was shouldered by the Fourth Front Army: Its Thirtieth Army was south of Mao-kung, checking the flight of enemy troops from the direction of Ya-an; its Ninth and Thirty-first armies were fighting hard against the enemy on the east around

Mao-kung and Pei-ch'uan; and its Fourth Army was guarding the north in the neighborhood of Sung-fan, keeping the enemy from coming south. Most of the members of the CC of the CCP were then in Fu-pien. They were Chang Wen-t'ien, former chairman of the People's Council of the Central Soviet government, who at the Tsun-yi Conference was elected secretary of the CC, to be in charge of the CC secretariat; Mao Tse-tung, who was newly elected at the Tsun-yi Conference to be a member of the CC Politburo, while retaining his post as chairman of the Central Soviet government and of the CC Military Affairs Committee; Chu Teh and Chou En-lai, who were vice-chairmen of the Military Affairs Committee, Chu Teh being commander-in-chief of the Red Army and Chou being in charge of the routine business of the Military Affairs Committee; and Ch'in Pang-hsien, who was relieved of the post of secretary of the CC at the Tsun-yi Conference but still retained his position as a member of the Politburo and acted for the wounded Wang Chia-hsiang as director of the General Political Department. These five plus myself were the six Politburo members in Fu-pien. The other members were Hsiang Ying, who remained in the Kiangsi Soviet region; Jen Pi-shih, who was with the Second Front Army in the Szechwan-Hunan-Hupeh-Kweichow border region; Wang Ming, who was in Moscow as a representative of the CCP in the Comintern; and Wang Chia-hsiang, who was in Cho-ko-chi getting medical treatment for his wound.

We six members of the Politburo were seeing one another every day. Also staying in Fu-pien at the time were Liu Po-ch'eng, chief-of-staff of the Military Affairs Committee, and Teng Fa, head of the Political Security Bureau. Those not in Fu-pien because of various duties included K'ai Feng, head of the Propaganda Department of the CC; the major commanders Lin Piao and P'eng Te-huai; Yeh Chien-ying and Tso Ch'üan, deputy chiefs-of-staff of the Military Affairs Committee; and the older veterans Lin Po-ch'ü and Tung Pi-wu. I had not met any of these.

As the wave of warm-hearted rejoicing passed away, there came the internal strife of the Party. At dinner on the first evening the big shots did not talk about the Long March or the Tsun-yi Conference. They were not even interested in listening to my account of the Red Fourth Front Army. Mao Tse-tung, a Hunanese who was fond of chili, made chili-eating the topic of merry conversation, discoursing at length on the theme that chili-eaters were revolutionaries. He was refuted by Ch'in Pang-hsien, a native of Kiangsu Province, who did not eat chili. Such talk was fun and helped create an atmosphere of light-heartedness. Some thought it was sophistry, while I found it all very dull, despite the leisurely air it diffused.

After dinner Chu Teh accompanied me back to my quarters, where he started a long discourse as soon as he sat down. It ran on and on, like the torrent of the Yangtze River, gushing along, knowing no end. He was sometimes excited, sometimes sad, in his account of what had happened and what he had endured. Our talk lasted all night. If what we said had been recorded at the time, it would have been extremely valuable material on the history of the CCP. I can only jot down a summary of it after all these years, as I remember it now.

Giving a detailed account of the courageous struggles of the First Front Army, Chu Teh, an old comrade-in-arms of mine, sighed, "Now, the First Front Army can fight no more. It used to be a giant, but now all the muscles are gone, there is only a skeleton left." To illustrate his point, he told me that eight months before, when the First Front Army set out from Kiangsi to go west, there were about ninety thousand men. After innumerable hardships, only ten thousand of them arrived at Mao-kung. The First Corps of Lin Piao had the largest number of men, about thirty-five hundred; the Third Corps of P'eng Te-huai had about three thousand; the Fifth Corps of Tung Chen-t'ang had less than two thousand; while the Twelfth Corps of Lo Ping-hui had only a few hundred men left. These, together with the units directly under the CC, numbered about ten thousand men. Meanwhile, all the artillery had been lost and not many machine guns were left, while most of these had empty barrels. The rifles had an average of five bullets each (ranging from two and three to some ten rounds). This pitiful amount, according to him, was only enough for the maintenance of the rifles. He noted that if it were not for the help of the Fourth Front Army, the First Front Army would have come to a dead end after all those hard struggles.

Recalling the past, Chu Teh was deeply grieved. His mind went back to many past events, such as our separation at San-ho-pa[1] eight years before, during the Nanchang Uprising. The scene appeared again before our eyes in great vividness. At that time the comrades fighting the guerrilla war together became pessimistic and depressed under enemy pressure. So many had deserted that at the worst moment there were only twenty-eight men left at his side. Among these twenty-eight there were some who suspected that he might desert, and they put sentry guards to watch over him. Later, things began to take a turn for the better, and after many years of struggle the First Front Army was formed. Now, the situation was more or less like that of bygone years. But, in the past, although only twenty-eight men were left, he had been in high spirits; whereas now, despite the larger number of men available, he was sad and depressed. With the passage of time the enemy was stronger than it had been seven or eight years before. He noted that our future was uncertain; it was hard to foresee whether we would be able to fight our way out and turn danger into safety.

Chu Teh also noted that it was fortunate that the majority of the cadres of the First Front Army were safe and sound. This thought seemed to lessen his pessimism a little. When the First Front Army was pursued and attacked by the enemy in Yunnan and Kweichow, it was not easy to keep its cadres from danger. However, Chu Teh and the others adopted the principle of safeguarding cadres with great determination. Whenever a cadre, whether male or female, was wounded or ill, the soldiers had to carry him or her along on a stretcher. Sometimes troops were even taken out of combat to do this job. This had once caused grumblings among the common soldiers, whose wounded and sick comrades were left behind, while the cadres were carried along by them. The soldiers did not like to be sedan-chair coolies, carrying the big shots and their wives. Chu Teh said that they had scored some successes in saving cadres despite the grumbles of the common soldiers. Now, in the First Front Army there were plenty of cadres but few soldiers. Cadres were now used at two grades below their usual rank, a former company commander now being a squad leader. Chu Teh felt that, in this respect, the First Front Army was valuable even though only a skeleton was left.

Chu Teh also talked about the situation in the CC of the CCP. He said that after its move to Jui-chin in August, 1931, Mao paid no attention to his duties because he had been censured. Later, Mao always expressed opinions different from those of the CC. For instance, he was unhappy about opposition to the rightist line of Lo Ming. He had his own views, particularly on military matters, about how to deal with the Fukien Incident (that is, the Incident of the Fukien People's Government) and about the Fifth Counterencirclement Campaign. Since the beginning of the Long March, Mao had criticized the military strategy of the CC as being an erroneous defensive line.

Chu Teh then said that it was not necessary to attach too much significance to the Tsun-yi Conference, which elected Mao to take charge. Both the CC and the First Front Army were in a difficult and dangerous situation, and Mao, whose experience in guerrilla warfare was useful just then, had many original ideas. His election to a responsible post seemed to bring peace to the Party, as the internal disputes stopped. Chu Teh felt that the most urgent business at the moment was the problem of military strategy, that is, what military action to take after the union of the First and the Fourth Front armies. (The Second Front Army under Ho Lung, the Tenth Army under Fang Chih-min, and guerrilla troops scattered in the various Soviet regions would have to struggle for themselves.) There was no time at the moment for discussing such political issues as a review of the work of the CC, the future of the Chinese Soviet Republic, and so forth. Chu Teh was in effect hinting to me that I should not mention the political problems.

Chu Teh spoke with great excitement of his impression of the Fourth Front Army. He said that before coming into contact with the Fourth Front Army, he was not prepared to make a high valuation of it. Now that he had seen it with his own eyes, he was unable to find words to describe his feeling of joy. When he first met the Thirtieth Army on the highway south of Mao-kung, the troops were marching to T'ien-ch'üan and Lu-shan to resist the pursuing enemy. Passing through right in front of Chu Teh and the others, the Thirtieth Army soldiers looked agile and strong and full of high spirits. Each of them had about one hundred rounds of bullets on his back. They had machine guns with no missing parts, plus donkeys and horses hauling cases of machine-gun ammunition, and mortars of all sizes. Both the way that the soldiers took refuge during air raids and their battle array served to convince Chu Teh that this was a powerful force capable of strenuous combat. The soldiers were all smiles, their demeanor fully demonstrating their warm love for the CC and the First Front Army. They chatted with the soldiers of the First Front Army, and shared their provisions with them. They solemnly saluted the commander-in-chief, who was then dressed like a stoker. They cheered with fervor, praising the CC and the Red Army. Their slogans included "Welcome to the Central Red Army!" "Support the CC!" "Support the Chinese Soviet Republic!" and "Support Chairman Mao and Commander-in-Chief Chu!" Hearing such cheers, Chu Teh and the other comrades of the CC were extremely excited. It was more than they expected, and they were happy about it. They came to understand that the Fourth Front Army was indeed a basic backbone force of the CCP.

Chu Teh told me that there would be a meeting of the Military Affairs Committee at nine o'clock the following morning at Mao's house. It would be a meeting to discuss and decide military matters. Chu Teh said that I knew more than the others about the Northwest and that future fighting would have to depend on the efforts of the Fourth Front Army. As a respected and beloved leader, I was expected to make some proposals to the meeting in view of the situation of the First and Fourth Front armies and the situation at home and abroad. He believed that my proposals would be respected by the participants. He also said that the gentlemen of the CC Politburo, although they had mixed with the Red Army for a time, were still far from being knowledgable about military matters. If Mao, Chou En-lai, and I agreed to any military plan, the others would not say no. Chu Teh was sure that the members of the Politburo were anxious to go north as soon as possible and would not want to stay long in this region of minority groups. He himself also favored this view.

I had done my best to console Chu Teh during our talk. I praised the First Front Army for its bravery and perseverance. When the Fourth Front Army left Oyüwan and went to T'ung-Nan-Pa, it was in a similarly embarrassing plight. The enemy pressure exerted on the First Front Army now was much greater, and it was an amazing achievement that the First Front Army had been able to preserve even a skeletal force after spending eight months on the Long March. The Fourth Front Army was in need of cadres, while the First Front Army had an excess. Some of their cadres could be assigned to the Fourth Front Army, which could supply the First Front Army with some soldiers and ammunition. The First and Fourth Front armies were parts of the same force, and the Fourth Front Army cadres were completely willing to do this.

I also gave a detailed account of the actual strength of the Fourth Front Army, which at that time numbered about forty-five thousand men, with some twenty thousand rifles. Men outnumbered rifles because of the special situation in northern Szechwan, where it was not easy to get rifles, while there were ample resources of manpower for the Army. As a result, the Fourth Front Army had a large following in its subordinate organs, such as the engineering battalions, propaganda teams, women's teams, and so forth. The stretcher-bearer teams, cooking teams, transport teams, and others attached to the divisions and regiments of the armies were also well supplied with manpower. There was a large number of so-called miscellaneous personnel. I also told Chu Teh the various good points and shortcomings of the Fourth Front Army. The good points were bravery in combat; unanimity of officers and men; strict discipline in military and political matters; and skill in night marches and operations. Among the shortcomings were inferiority of the ammunition, 70 percent of the bullets being homemade; shortage of cadres owing to the large number of casualties; and the low cultural level of the officers and men. Summing up these advantages and disadvantages,

I pointed out frankly that the Fourth Front Army was no longer the mighty combat force that it had been in the Oyüwan era. One of the reasons for this was its having been engaged with the Szechwan armies for too long.

I also revealed my innermost thoughts to Chu Teh. I emphasized the necessity for unity and our support for the CC of the CCP. After all these years of setbacks, veteran comrades of the CC were valuable to us. Now that we had reassembled at Mao-kung, it was all the more necessary to unite as one person and not to forget our painful past experience. I and the comrades of the Fourth Front Army would certainly not keep aloof from the comrades of the CC simply because we had not worked side by side with them for so many years. I enumerated the efforts of the Fourth Front Army in giving support to the First Front Army, and explained that at the time when it was still doubtful whether or not the First and the Fourth Front armies could meet, we had made some political and military plans in the light of our situation.

It was already dawn when Chu Teh rose to leave. We had to take a short rest before attending the meeting scheduled for 9 A.M. As Chu was leaving, I suggested that we should spend some more time together and hold another meeting or two to thrash over our viewpoints. Meanwhile, the cadres of the two Front armies would have a chance to gain a better understanding of one another, which would facilitate our future dealings. I rested for less than three hours after Chu Teh's departure. At nine o'clock I went to the military meeting.

At 9 A.M., Mao Tse-tung, Chu Teh, Chou En-lai, Chang Wen-t'ien, Ch'in Pang-hsien, and I—the six of us members of the Politburo—together with Chief-of-Staff Liu Po-ch'eng, assembled at Mao Tse-tung's residence for the military meeting. First of all, Mao Tse-tung proposed the military plan of going north to Kansu and Ningsia. He explained that the Comintern had cabled instructions, telling us to go toward Outer Mongolia. In the light of our present situation, this was also the only thing that we could do. I then asked, "When did the Comintern send us these instructions?" Chang Wen-t'ien stood up and answered, "About ten months ago, before we left Jui-chin, the Comintern wired us a directive saying that the Chinese Red Army might approach Outer Mongolia in case of extreme necessity. The CC had not been able to contact the Comintern after leaving the Kiangsi Soviet region, and it was now impossible to communicate with the Comintern by wire.

Mao Tse-tung continued with his speech in a bright mood. He said, looking at the map, that it could be seen that in all the Northwest only

Ningsia was a prosperous region and that the troops of Ma Hung-k'uei who were defending that part of the country were rather weak. Though it had been a long time since Moscow had sent us that directive, he believed that Moscow would give us support from Outer Mongolia and that there was no need for us to be afraid of the vast desert separating Ningsia from Outer Mongolia.

In a rhetorical flight, Mao asked himself, "Why should we go to Ningsia?" Then he answered his own question, "Mainly because of the mighty power of Chiang Kai-shek's airplanes and guns. Now Chiang Kai-shek is elated, while we are meeting with reverses. He is trying to seek us out and attack us, brandishing his prowess, but we shall certainly not fall into his traps. We must avoid engagement with his troops, and go straight to Ningsia without fanfare. When we have our back to Outer Mongolia, Chiang Kai-shek will not be able to do anything to us." He went on to say that some comrades would not honestly admit the mighty power of airplanes and guns. Now we had to play some tricks and get some airplanes and guns from Outer Mongolia so as to return in kind what Chiang Kai-shek had done to us. Without airplanes and guns we could not say, "Down with Chiang Kai-shek" any more.

"To call a spade a spade," he continued emphatically, "there is now the danger of our being annihilated." He explained that in order to get to Ningsia, it was necessary to have the Fourth Front Army assume the responsibility of covering the CC and the majority of the cadres until they arrived safely in Ningsia. If worst came to worst and it was impossible to gain a foothold in Ningsia, the CC and a number of cadres might go to Outer Mongolia by car through the desert and thus preserve some seeds from the revolution, which would stage a comeback in the future. He declared that this was the result of his cool calculations, which might be regarded as rightist. He begged us to consider his plan very carefully.

This speech of Mao Tse-tung's, which was seasoned with interesting remarks but was extremely poignant, evoked sympathy rather than ill-feeling in me. His plan had not stressed going to Shensi, nor had it mentioned "going north to resist Japan," for at the time, being isolated as we were, we were rather vague about "resistance to Japan." He had not mentioned the possibility of uniting with the troops of Liu Tzu-tan, Kao Kang, and Hsü Hai-tung after arriving in northern Shensi, because we were then unable to tell whether Hsü Hai-tung's troops were still there, and the names of Liu Tzu-tan and Kao Kang were unknown. Naturally, it was impossible to foresee either the future cooperation between the CC of the CCP and Chang Hsueh-liang and Yang Hu-ch'eng or the Sian Incident. I actually gave very careful consideration to his plan, finding it long on some points and short on others. I was partly worried and partly delighted.

I took the floor after Mao, reporting on the situation in the Northwest as I knew it and persenting my views for the comrades to consider. I suggested that there might be three possible plans for our activities in the Northwest. First, the Szechwan-Kansu-Sikang plan, which would take as its starting point what territory we possessed at present and extend it to northern Szechwan and southern Kansu up to Han-chung, taking Sikang as its rear. Second, the plan of going north proposed by Mao Tse-tung, according to which we would launch our operations in the northern parts of Shensi and Kansu, seize Ningsia as our rear, and take Outer Mongolia as our backstop. Third, the plan to go west, according to which we would move to the Ho-hsi Corridor west of Lanchow and take Sinkiang as our rear. I then outlined the pros and cons of the three plans, and as I spoke, everyone pored over the maps.

Concerning the first plan, I pointed out that the region around the borders of Szechwan, Shensi, Kansu, and Sikang was of strategic importance. The warlords in these provinces were rather weak militarily and could not take steps unanimously. Chiang Kai-shek's own troops could not possibly be deployed in this region in very large numbers. Because of the strategic terrain, the enemies' airplanes and guns were unable to play their roles to the full. Most of the soldiers of the Fourth Front Army were natives of the T'ung-Nan-Pa area who were quite familiar with conditions in this region. Moreover, this was a rice-producing region, where the people's habits and customs were closer to those of us southerners. The First Front Army was in dire need of a good rest, and this was just the place for it. On the other hand, under unfavorable conditions, we might be forced to go to Sikang, where the inhabitants were all Tibetans. It was thinly populated, food was in short supply, and its rear was not connected with Mongolia or the Soviet Union. In a word, the plan was easy to execute, but the escape route to the rear was not to our advantage.

Then I revealed that the Fourth Front Army had drawn up a plan to set up a new base—the Szechwan-Kansu-Sikang border region. It was made in May, when the comrades of the Fourth Front Army were in the Chiang-yu area and when it was uncertain whether the First Front Army would soon be able to come north across the Chin-sha and Ta-tu rivers. Politically, the plan stipulated formation of the Northwest Federation and implementation of a program suited to the minority ethnic groups. Militarily, it would not be difficult for our armies to proceed from Mao-hsien and Pei-ch'uan to fight the Szechwan armies in the east and to reconquer the prosperous region of Chiang-yu. Towards the south, we could launch our activities around T'ien-ch'üan and Lu-shan. Although Hu Tsung-nan's troops had occupied the strategic points of Ping-wu and Sung-fan to our north, there were plenty of gaps along the enemy's defense line. It would not be difficult for us to go into southern Kansu, where there was a larger population.

Concerning the second plan, I first recalled how a year ago Hsü Hai-tung's troops had moved west from the Oyüwan region to Shensi, intending to join us in northern Szechwan. From intelligence reports we learned that he had come to the mountainous region on the borders of Shensi and Kansu via the Ching Range. Later, checked by the enemy, he crossed the Wei River and went north, and there was no more news of him. Early in the year the Fourth Front Army had entered the Ning-ch'iang area in Han-chung, in an attempt to deal blows to Hu Tsung-nan's troops and lay the foundation for the northward march of the First and Fourth Front armies. We also hoped to get news of Hsü Hai-tung and had got a detachment ready to go to northern Shensi to contact his troops. But the plan fell through because we did not know exactly where to find Hsü Hai-tung.

I went on to speak about conditions in northern Shensi and Kansu and the region around Ningsia, which we came to know when we were in Ning-ch'iang. The further north we went from here towards Ningsia, the greater the expanse of bare loess mountains in which we would be more exposed to attacks by enemy planes. Northern Shensi and Kansu were thinly populated, and the food supply there was far from abundant in comparison with that in these Szechwan-Shensi-Kansu border regions. To the south of Ningsia was the Yellow River, and to its east, west, and north was the Great Gobi Desert. We might easily be blockaded by the enemy once we got into that area. Moreover, the Yellow River offered a much more difficult barrier than the Yangtze. Owing to these factors, the Red Fourth Front Army had always kept more to the south after it left the Oyüwan region.

I then went on to point out the advantages of the second plan. If our army arrived in northern Szechwan, Shensi, Kansu, and Ningsia, we should be in a position to threaten Lanchow, Sian, and Tung-kuan to the south, or advance eastward to Shansi and Suiyüan, and in all likelihood get to the Central Plain. However, the disadvantage was that the way of retreat was unfavorable, with the vast desert to the northwest. The desert would pose no problem only if Moscow could really extend its support to us via Outer Mongolia as it had previously helped Feng Yü-hsiang's Northwest Army.

Concerning the third plan, I reported that we had learned from intelligence reports that the Soviet Union had sent airplanes and troops to help the authorities in Sinkiang put down the rebellion of Ma Chung-ying's troops.[2] This showed that the Soviet Union had considerable influence in Sinkiang and that the authorities there were probably pro-Russian. If we could move to the Ho-hsi Corridor and Sinkiang, the way of retreat there was the most favorable. In case of unfavorable conditions, a lot of cadres and troops could save themselves by going to the safe area of Sinkiang. The disadvantage was that the place was too far from the hinterlands of China proper. If Chiang Kai-shek blockaded the Ho-hsi Corridor, then we would have no choice but to fly our Soviet banner temporarily in the region of the Kun-lun and Al-tai mountains.

I also discussed the preparations to be made if we were to adopt this plan to go west. To go to the Ho-hsi Corridor from here, it would be necessary to cross the Yellow River and engage the Hui cavalrymen. I proposed that the best thing to do at first would be to implement the first plan, that is, to stay temporarily in the Szechwan-Sikang area and establish a foothold, so as to have time to put our troops in order and to train them for fighting with cavalry. If we could translate the Szechwan-Sikang plan into reality through our experiments, there would be no need to go north or west. If our experiments proved that it was impossible for us to gain a foothold in Szechwan and Sikang, then we could go north or west. Even though by then the way to the north might have been blockaded by the enemy, the way to the west would still be open, because it was not easy for the enemy to blockade that way.

These three plans I proposed included the suggestion made by Mao Tse-tung of going north, but they showed that there was more than one way to solve the problem, thus diverting attention from Mao's one-and-only plan of going towards Outer Mongolia. This probably displeased him, and he criticized my Szechwan-Sikang plan as likely to lead the First and Fourth Front armies to retreat to Sikang. According to his investigations, Sikang, with its population of two hundred thousand, would not be able to support the Red Army. If we were blockaded inside Sikang by the enemy, we would become turtles in an urn. He held that the plan to go west should be considered, as it would enable the Red Army to get supplies and reorganize in Sinkiang. The trouble was that it was too far away from China proper. He could not offer any answers to the points I had raised in my criticism of the plan to go north to Ningsia, northern Shensi, and Kansu.

Mao's speech showed that he was sensitive and that he distrusted me. He went out of his way to dwell on minor problems. He doubted my report on the Red Fourth Army's activities early in the year when it advanced northwards to Han-chung and Ning-ch'iang to explore the possibilities of going north and to try to help the troops of Hsü Hai-tung. He said, "What a pity! You had advanced to Han-chung, why didn't you continue to go north?" He went on to say that if we had actually gone north then, it would have been impossible for us to reunite now in Mao-kung, and the CC of the CCP and the First Front Army would have had to go several thousand li further to contact the Fourth Front Army. Mao was full of sarcasm when he said all this, as if he questioned my sincerity in giving support to the CC of the CCP and the First Front Army.

Mao's words made me unhappy. I felt that he had fostered a sense of suspicion during the guerrilla fighting and had not viewed my actions with good will. I didn't dwell on this, but explained that as soon as I and the comrades of the Fourth Front Army learned the news that the First Front Army would cross the Yangtze to come north, we had immediately taken it upon ourselves to give support to the First Front Army, which we regarded as our primary task. Our advance to Ning-ch'iang was aimed chiefly at dealing blows to Hu Tsung-nan's troops, which in itself was an operation to give support to the First Front Army. We had no intention of leaving the First Front Army behind and going north by ourselves. Now that we had finally reunited at Mao-kung, I and the comrades of the Fourth Front Army were all very pleased about it. Mao didn't say another word after hearing my explanation, but turned his talk to other matters.

We discussed and exchanged intelligence reports at our meeting. Our discussion concentrated on Mao's suggestion of going north. We all felt that having some guerrilla bases in northern Shensi would be a great advantage to us in executing the plan to go north. Chang Wen-t'ien and others stated that the CC of the CCP had no idea whether Hsü Hai-tung's troops still existed after going to northern Shensi from the Oyüwan region or whether there were other guerrilla units in northern Shensi. This was the first time that they had heard the news that Yang Hu-ch'eng had not taken active steps to attack the Communist troops and had made contacts with the Fourth Front Army. Moreover, nobody could say for certain that Moscow would give us support via Outer Mongolia, as it had promised to do ten months earlier. Some of us supposed that the Soviet Union and Outer Mongolia might have second thoughts on giving us support, due to the recent change in the foreign relations situation—we were dimly aware that Japan was invading Inner Mongolia and exerting pressure on Outer Mongolia.

In their speeches the participants focused their attention on avoiding combat and finding a place for a long rest. They didn't mind very much where they went, so long as they could leave this place where the staple food was kou-pa. The majority of them supported Mao's proposal, but they did not veto my suggestion of going west.

I therefore said that as our aim was to avoid combat and to find a place for a long rest, and as it was still uncertain whether the Soviet Union would give us effective help, it might be a good idea to go to Sinkiang. It was then necessary to make a detailed study of the plan to go west. In Sinkiang there was a greater likelihood of our getting help from the Soviet Union, and Chiang Kai-shek's troops would not find it as easy to go to Sinkiang. Essentially, this was the background to what the chronicles of the CCP called the dispute on whether to go west or north.

The meeting lasted some three hours, but no definite conclusion was reached. At lunchtime Mao Tse-tung declared in his capacity as chairman, "This is an important question with grave consequences. Let us take some time to deliberate on the best course." It was quite a surprise that this phrase "to deliberate on the best course" did not materialize. There was no more discussion on this question. It was taken for granted that Mao's proposal to go north had been approved by the majority, and it was implemented. This was perhaps a way of avoiding disputes, which the Chinese favor in solving a problem. But it was not the way of the CCP, which used to make definite resolutions on all important questions at meetings. This was the exception rather than the rule. Later it was proved by facts that the CC of the CCP had decided to go north even before its arrival at Fu-pien, but I had not been informed of the decision. After this make-believe discussion, it was not convenient to veto my suggestion openly.

After the meeting I returned to my quarters, where during lunch my secretary, Huang Ch'ao, handed me a copy of *Bolshevik News*, which was published by the CC of the CCP. This mimeographed journal was the first publication of the CC after its arrival at Mao-kung. The first article in the journal was one written by K'ai Feng, head of the Propaganda

Department of the CC, entitled "Lenin on Federation." It said that Lenin had opposed the European Federation; therefore, the Northwest Federation was in violation of Leninism. Furthermore, the so-called Northwest Federation was a violation of the Soviet line of the CC. To advance the formation of the Northwest Federation at this crucial moment was tantamount to a negation of the Chinese Soviet Republic.

I got very angry after reading the article. I sensed that it was no routine matter that the CC had put out *Bolshevik News* in a hurry soon after arriving at Mao-kung and had published an article that opposed my views. I deduced that the CC had held meetings to discuss the matter carefully before deciding to "oppose the opportunism of Chang Kuo-t'ao" and publishing this article signed by K'ai Feng. I felt that the article had no firm basis. Lenin did oppose the European Federation, but his opposition was not directed at the system of federation itself,[3] he only opposed the formation of the federation on the basis of capitalism, which he regarded as incorrect. The present Northwest Federation chiefly recognized the autonomous governments of minority ethnic groups in the Northwest as members of the federation. In the declaration of the Second Congress of the CCP,[4] the slogan "Chinese Federal Republic" had been introduced. It was not to be mentioned in the same breath as Lenin's opposition to the European Federation. I was sorry that the CC members who had returned from Russia had criticized me at will by rigidly mouthing the dogmas of Lenin.

Huang Ch'ao then told me that the journal was given to him secretly by a cadre of the First Front Army. The CC had published the journal two or three days earlier, but it had been circulated only among cadres of the First Front Army. It had been decided that cadres of the Fourth Front Army would not be allowed to read it. I was all the more uneasy after hearing these words from Huang Ch'ao. I disagreed with the CC's idea of having different treatment for the cadres of the First and Fourth Front armies. Usually, such an action would have been regarded as an action of "factionists" or labeled as being in violation of the principle of organization. Previously, after the Li Li-san line, the CC had been in the hands of Wang Ming and other Mif-ists (that is, the Wang Ming line). That was in the spring of 1931 in Shanghai where I had my first taste of it, and now it appeared again in Mao-kung.

At this juncture, Chang Wen-t'ien came to see me. I showed him the publication and asked, "By publishing K'ai Feng's article in the CC's organ, does the CC mean to unfold a debate on the Northwest Federation?" If so, than I intended to write something in defense of the Northwest Federation. K'ai Feng had not mentioned the minority ethnic groups in the Northwest and had not given a clear indication that the CC approved of autonomy for ethnic groups and recognized their right to form their own independent governments. Instead, he rigidly quoted Lenin to deny the right of minority groups to organize a federation together with the Han nation.

I went on to ask Chang Wen-t'ien, "Was this article written in accordance with the resolution of the CC? If so, why didn't the CC wait for my arrival at Fu-pien, so that I might have a chance to take part in the discussion before publishing it? Why didn't the CC show me a copy of the journal even after I'd been here for twenty hours? Was it permissible for the CC's organ to criticize openly the political proposal of a member of the Politburo? This form of criticism was made only when the member of the Politburo refused to obey a resolution of the majority and persisted in his own erroneous views. I had openly proposed the formation of the Northwest Federation, and the other members of the Politburo had not expressed any criticism, but the CC's organ published this article openly. Why was this so?"

Chang Wen-t'ien evaded my questions. Despite his high post as secretary of the CC, he was ambivalent in his attitude, and he looked rather embarrassed. Bound by dogmatism, he could only say that K'ai Feng's quotations from Lenin were correct. Yet, he felt that this Party matter had been handled awkwardly. He said hesitantly that it was not suitable to discuss questions that would cause disputes when it was urgent that the First and Fourth Front armies should take unanimous action. He paid lip service to the heroic struggles waged by the Fourth Front Army, but was unwilling to commend the Fourth Front Army in the name of the CC.

Before my talk with Chang Wen-t'ien was finished, Chou En-lai walked in, and Chang Wen-t'ien seized that opportunity to say good-bye. Chou En-lai avoided talking about the question of the internal dispute of the Party. He only wanted to discuss military matters with me as a practical worker of the Military Affairs Committee. He showed me the draft of a telegram that conveyed a resolution of the Central Politburo, which ruled that, besides having Mao Tse-tung as chairman of the Military Affairs Committee and Chu Teh and Chou En-lai as vice-chairmen, Comrade Chang Kuo-t'ao was to be appointed vice-chairman of the Military Affairs Committee in addition. All armies would be under the command of the Military Affairs Committee, with the former First Front Army, renamed the Left Column, under the command of P'eng Te-huai and Lin Piao as commander and deputy commander, and Nieh Jung-chen and Teng Hsiao-p'ing as commissar and deputy commissar; the Fourth Front Army, renamed the Right Column, under the command of Hsü Hsiang-ch'ien as commander and Ch'en Ch'ang-hao as commissar, as before. Chou En-lai informed me that the resolution had been made before my arrival at Fu-pien, and it would be made public to the whole army now. I approved the resolution with pleasure, considering this the most natural procedure to take after the reunion of the two armies.

That same afternoon Chou En-lai came with the draft of another telegram in his hand. It dealt with movement of the troops. The First and Third armies of the Left Column were to assemble around Mao-erh-kai, and the Fifth and Twelfth armies were to stay where they had been, around Tang-pa on the Ta-chin-chuan. The Thirtieth Army of the Right Column was to advance to the area of Cho-ko-chi from Mao-kung, leaving some troops to guard Mao-kung. The troops of Hsü Hsiang-ch'ien and Ch'en Ch'ang-hao were to retreat from Mao-hsien and Pei-ch'uan to the west of the Min River, stationing temporarily in the region east of Cho-ko-chi and Mao-erh-kai. The Fourth Army was to stay near Sung-fan, taking Mao-erh-kai as its rear. All armies were to be ready for further orders at the appointed places.

After reading the telegram, I said, "In the forenoon, when the meeting adjourned, Mao had said that it was necessary to deliberate on the best course, hadn't he? This draft says in fact that the discussion this morning has been concluded." Chou suavely explained that the draft had been carefully studied by Mao and that the other members of the Politburo, who were reluctant to stay too long in the Sikang area, agreed to it. As to the question of going north or west, it could be discussed at length when everyone arrived at Mao-erh-kai. I felt that if I opposed the telegram, I would have to insist on staying on the banks of the Min River. At the moment I was reluctant to set myself against all the other members of the Politburo. So I told Chou En-lai that since everybody else was in favor of the telegram, I would not stick to a different opinion all by myself.

After the Long March the First Front Army, needless to say, was in a sorry state. Discipline had become quite lax. Two small incidents that I witnessed personally should suffice to illustrate this. One afternoon, at about five o'clock, Chu Teh and I and some ten others were taking a stroll in the suburbs of Fu-pien. Scores of soldiers of the First Front Army were surrounding a herd of some ten cattle, trying to shoot one of them for their dinner. They fired more than ten rounds before the target was hit. The other cattle ran off in fright, while many Tibetans looked on angrily.

The incident became the topic of our conversation. Chu Teh lamented the laxness of discipline in the First Front Army. Furthermore, it was sheer wastefulness to use more than ten bullets to kill one animal. This way of killing would also arouse the ill-feeling of the local people. I added that for the Tibetans, wealth meant the possession of scores or even hundreds of cattle. A man with some ten cattle might be a poor man. The Fourth Front Army only shot the cattle of local tyrants and spared those of poor men. It was a moot question whether the animal just shot by the soldiers of the First Front Army belonged to a local tyrant, as there were only some ten cattle in the herd. Moreover, the Fourth Front Army had learned a way to kill cattle without firing a single bullet. They would entice the cattle to spread out, and then they would drag one down separately with a rope. The animal could then be killed without the use of bullets.

At dinner time another incident occurred that was connected with cattle, and evidently one that violated discipline. One of Ch'in Pang-hsien's guards came to my quarters with a piece of beef and asked my communications squad to exchange some bullets for it. As they were speaking different dialects, they could not understand each other very well, and a dispute followed. My communications troops explained to the guard that this was a violation of military discipline. According to the discipline of the Fourth Front Army, a soldier was not allowed to exchange bullets for anything with other people. The soldiers were not even allowed to trade among themselves. Ch'in Pang-hsien's guard was there, shouting away that it was a fair deal to exchange a piece of beef for bullets. He complained that their refusal meant that the Fourth Front Army soldiers were not regarding him as one of their own people, that they looked down upon the First Front Army and the CC, and so forth. Shouting thus, he went away in anger.

I was amused by their dispute, but I did not go out to interfere. Then the commander of the communications company came in to report to me on what had happened and to propose that the company present two hundred rounds of revolver bullets to the guards of the Central organs so as to avoid any misunderstanding. He was in sympathy with the First Front Army soldiers who were actually short of bullets. I felt that the company commander was very tactful and gladly approved of his proposal, which was immediately acted upon. When Ch'in Pang-hsien heard of the matter, he didn't say anything about it. Perhaps he thought it was an insignificant incident.

After dinner, Ch'in Pang-hsien came to see me to talk about political work in the army. He didn't seem very adroit, though he had been secretary of the CC for three years and had gone through censure and repudiation at the Tsun-yi Conference. What was charming about him was that he spoke his mind frankly. He was one of the younger set in the CC of the CCP who was fond of making a show of his cleverness, just like his old self as one of the "28 Bolsheviks" at Sun Yat-sen University in Moscow years before. As he spoke, he mentioned the others as Comrade This or Comrade That, emitting a flavor of Moscow. For my part, I stuck more or less to the traditional Chinese style, calling the comrades by their courtesy names, as we used to do before the Great Revolution of 1927, such as calling Mao Tse-tung "Jen-chih" and Chu Teh "Yu-chieh." Sometimes I added "younger brother" or "elder brother" to these aliases. All this was unpalatable to Ch'in Pang-hsien, who departed from the main theme of our conversation and asked me, "Are you still fond of calling other men elder and younger brothers?" He considered this customary among KMT members but incompatible with Bolshevik ideology.

I did not know whether to laugh or cry in the face of such questioning. He was actually making a mountain out of a mole hill. I had to explain to him patiently, as if talking to a primary-school pupil. I said calling other men elder and younger brothers was a traditional way of expressing friendliness among the masses of the Chinese people and had nothing whatsoever to do with KMT warlords. This way of addressing people showed equality and friendliness between the speaker and the parties concerned and was equivalent to "comrade" in meaning. In the initial period of the CCP, this form of addressing people was prevalent among Party members. The KMT warlords also used the same form, but there was not a shred of fraternal feeling between them.

After his first arrow failed to hit its target, Ch'in Pang-hsien continued with his second one. He pointed out that the CC had corrected the class concept between officers and men in the army and had substituted for it a cordial relationship between comrades. For instance, commanders of armies, divisions, and regiments were called command personnel, and cooks and grooms were called kitchen personnel and feeding personnel. Meanwhile, the Fourth Front Army retained the old titles of the warlord period, complete with "Army Commander," "Division Commander," and even "orderlies," "cooks," and "grooms." The name "orderly," for example, called to mind the feeling of a footman, and the name "groom" made men feel that they were doing some menial job. He asked me, "Don't these old names also preserve the old concepts of the warlords?"

I again explained that retaining old names did not necessarily preserve old concepts. If he investigated in detail the internal situation of the Fourth Front Army, he would find that a comradely friendliness existed between officers and men. Take a regiment, for example. The regimental commander and commissar led exactly the same kinds of lives as their orderlies and grooms. They slept in the same quarters and had their meals in the same mess. They called one another by their first names or nicknames, and chatted together and laughed without the slightest inhibition. It was impossible to find such an atmosphere among the troops of the warlords. We could certainly not accuse the Fourth Front Army of preserving the old tradition only because it had retained the titles of an old-fashioned army. Moreover, the Fourth Front Army had not yet received the CC's order on reform in this area. If we would have made up some new titles in accordance with the new concepts, they might have been at variance with those laid down by the CC. In that case, when we reunited at Mao-kung as we had done now, Director of the Political Department Ch'in Pang-hsien might have had cause to complain that the Fourth Front Army had recklessly made up new titles of their own, which was tantamount to making rebellion.

Ch'in Pang-hsien claimed to be a Bolshevik; but only he alone, and nobody else, could so claim. The Fourth Front Army had been away from the CC's leadership for a long time, and he quite naturally thought that since the men in Fourth Front Army lacked the flavor of Bolsheviks, they must therefore be warlords. Continuing with his challenge, he pointed out that the officers of the Fourth Front Army still resorted to scolding and beating soldiers, which was a symbol of warlord rule. He had personally seen a company leader of the Fourth Front Army scold a soldier under him, and he inferred that there was a lack of comradely friendliness between the officers and men of the Fourth Front Army. When an officer showed a lack of the spirit of persuasion and education in dealing with soldiers, it was a sure sign that he was practicing warlord rule.

I protested his slander of the Fourth Front Army and proclaimed that friendliness and a democratic spirit prevailed in the Fourth Front Army. The officers and men of the companies led the same kinds of lives; and the men often held meetings to discuss the company's mode of living, their opinions usually having a decisive effect. It had become a custom for the officers to cherish the rank and file. New recruits were given preferential treatment, and the wounded and the sick were given generous help. All of these things were done with infinite care. I cited an example to prove my point. A representative of Yang Hu-ch'eng, who had climbed the Pa-shan from Han-chung to T'ung-chiang, saw that our men in the outpost company wore overcoats made from fox fur or sheep skin, while the company and platoon commanders wore cotton-padded coats and trousers. He regarded this as the greatest difference between the Red Army and the armies of the warlords.

I admitted that scolding and beating still existed in the Fourth Front Army, but they were used only in individual cases and were not widely practiced. It was not permissible to infer from this that there was warlord rule in the Fourth Front Army. I told him that scolding and beating in the Red Fourth Front Army were rather rare when it was in the Oyüwan region. There were more instances after we came to northern Szechwan, which had something to do with the large number of new recruits and the ban on opium smoking. I also pointed out that isolated instances of scolding and beating existed in the First Front Army, but I certainly wouldn't accuse the First Front Army of warlord rule just because of this.

I advised Ch'in Pang-hsien not to foster such misunderstanding, which would cause unnecessary estrangement. I suggested that he make some constructive plans to strengthen the understanding between the two armies and to correct the shortcomings in both by means of setting up positive goals. I warned him emphatically that it would be unfair and harmful if he tried to dub the Fourth Front Army guilty of warlordism on the grounds of this or that incident. It was a pity that Ch'in Pang-hsien did not accept my views, for all these problems caused antagonism between the First and Fourth Front armies at a later date.

Then Chang Wen-t'ien came back to continue with our unfinished talk about Party work. I told him something about the work of the Party in the Fourth Front Army. Chang Wen-t'ien, however, was unwilling to say much about the evolution of the CC since its transfer to Jui-chin in 1931. He only said that after the Tsun-yi Conference there were no differences of opinion in the CC. From that time on, the CC had been mainly concerned with military operations, which, everyone agreed, Mao Tse-tung was to take charge of. Now the order on the military operations to be embarked on after the reunion of the two armies had been sent out, and everything seemed to have gone smoothly.

Summing up what had happened since my arrival at Fu-pien, I spoke of my views in general. First of all, I reasoned that the setbacks of the Soviet and the Red Army could not be entirely attributed to the mighty power of the enemy planes and artillery. To say so would inevitably lead to the conclusion that the CCP was doomed. I asked him why he didn't look for the reason from the political angle, such as studying whether the policy of the Soviet campaign was correct. I said that according to my own experience, the Soviet campaign and the distribution of land had failed to move the masses, while strengthening the military force of the Red Army and advocating such policies as abolition of oppressive duties and miscellaneous taxes had made a tremendous impact. I asked him for what reasons he affirmed that the Soviet policy was correct, while the policy of the Northwest Federation was wrong.

I went on to point out that, following the stiffening of our political concepts, our military concepts also became rigid. We were, in general, doggedly sticking to one formula, that is, the not-to-be-questioned infallibility of the political line of the CC and all of its actions. It was claimed that because of the mighty power of the enemy planes and artillery, we could not beat the enemy and had to avoid engagements with it, and thus had to go to Outer Mongolia or Sinkiang. But the ordinary comrades might not see things the same way. They might ask, "Since we had the opportunity to deal blows to the Szechwan armies in Pei-ch'uan and Mao-hsien, why do we have to retreat to the region west of the Min River? Where should we go after assembling at Mao-erh-kai?"

I asked Chang Wen-t'ien why we didn't try to find a solution from the political angle. Was there nothing we could do politically to strengthen our forces? I recalled that when we came to northern Szechwan in 1932, I had the feeling that we would not be able to fight any more. The way we had resolved the problem was not to avoid fighting completely, but when we entered Szechwan, to advance our program, the people's government, and other political means. Not long ago we had further proposed to strive for the setting up of a new base in the Szechwan-Kansu-Sikang region and the establishment of the Northwest Federation. I stressed that, in principle, it was even permissible and justifiable to adopt political measures that called for some concessions, as on the questions of minority ethnic groups and resistance to Japan.

The CC of the CCP was holding fast to the empty leftist carcass of the Soviet, but was actually practicing the rightist policy of military retreat. Thus, the majority of the members of the CC were led to think that what I said was superfluous. Some even thought that I was walking along the road of opportunism and that the Red Fourth Front Army was going the way of warlords. All such things as the Program upon Entering Szechwan, the Northwest Federation, and what not were extreme heresies. However, the CC had neglected some "minor questions." Wherever they might go in the Northwest, they would have to face the questions of whether the Soviet banner was suitable and how best to handle the problem of minority ethnic groups.

I said emphatically that political dissension had always existed within the Party. The Tsun-yi Conference had not found a suitable solution, while the present CC dared not touch upon political questions but concentrated on military operations instead. This was a worrisome scene. I worried that we might suffer tragic defeats both politically and militarily and that there would be no easy way to get ourselves on our feet again. This would lead to estrangement between the First and Fourth Front armies and to disputes within the Party. If we could cast off the bondage of the set formula, abandon prejudices, and boldly make investigations on the political plane in the light of existing circumstances, there would still be time for us to make amends.

Chang Wen-t'ien did not say anything definite after hearing me out. He only said that discussions on political questions would have to wait till we turned the corner in military matters. He also expressed anxiety about the occurrence of disputes within the Party. He did not criticize my views, but tried to persuade me to be patient and not to bring up questions that might lead to arguments. We talked throughout the day until midnight, but we did not come to any conclusions. Owing to the delaying tactics of Chang Wen-t'ien, the situation gradually worsened.

Early in the morning of the third day, the CC big shots in Fu-pien started for Mao-erh-kai. Mao Tse-tung set out before the others, as he was in a hurry to get to Mao-erh-kai to make plans for the advance northward. The other members of the CC followed one after another on the same day. I stayed one more day in order to settle some affairs.

Early that morning, Teng Fa called on me to talk about setting up a Political Security Bureau in the Fourth Front Army. He told me that the Bureau's tasks in the Army were to guard against spies, to censure counterrevolutionary and anti-Party words and deeds, and to maintain the discipline of the Army and the Party. The Central Political Security Bureau had an independent work chain directly under the CC in the First Front Army; from the army, division, and other high-level commands down to the company level, there were personnel of the Political Bureau working in secret. Nominally, they were subordinate to the political departments at the various levels, but actually they were directed by the Central Political Security Bureau. In addition, these personnel also took it upon themselves to keep an eye on the cadres. Even the guards of the cadres at all levels had been trained by the Political Security Bureau, and their task was to ensure the safety of the officers as well as to keep watch over their words and deeds. In case reactionary actions were perpetrated by their commanders, the guards had to take immediate action against them. Teng Fa boasted of his achievement in this work, which guaranteed the dominance of the Party over the Army. He mentioned in particular Li Ming-jui, commander of the Seventh Army, who, when trying to escape from the Kiangsi Soviet region, was shot to death by the guard at his side—the guard that he, Teng Fa, had trained and sent to the post.

I was utterly disgusted by Teng Fa's account. I believed that such actions would change the nature of the Party. In accordance with Party law, a member joins the Party of his own free will because of his belief in communism, and the CC is elected by the members. Now the CC had set up a Political Security Bureau to watch over the words and deeds of Party members. The Party, then, had become one in which Party members were ruled by the CC. All kinds of corrupt practices would result from this. Stalin was an obvious example. He made use of a secret-service system to rule the CPSU, killing hundreds of thousands of comrades, including the majority of the veterans of the revolution. With the disciples of Stalin in the CC of the CCP following in his footsteps, the future of the CCP would be too horrible to contemplate.

I told Teng Fa my views calmly. I said that the Fourth Front Army had not set up an independent link in the chain of the Political Security Bureau. When we were in the Oyüwan region, we had discussed this problem. We had held that it was not necessary to send someone to watch over the cadres, as the majority of them were Party members who could conduct ordinary political work. The political-work personnel and the Party organization in the Army would constantly attend to the political situation in the Army (a few of them also took up political-security work concurrently). The officers in general were supervised by the political commissar. It was not reasonable organizationally to send watchdogs to the military units at all levels and to assign guards to watch over the cadres at all levels. It would also cause uneasiness among those being watched.

According to Teng Fa, since this was a system laid down by the CC, it would not be appropriate for the Fourth Front Army to claim exemption from it. He asked me to introduce the personnel under him to the

Fourth Front Army so that they could immediately set up an independent work system of the Political Security Bureau and to give an order to send him the reliable guards in the Fourth Front Army who were Party members, so that he could train them. They would then go back to their former posts after they had been trained. Because of this affair, I, for the first time in Fu-pien, uttered the word "No." I told Teng Fa that I could not do this, as I was only a member of the CC and had no power to give orders.

After lunch the big shots of the CC left, one after another. I heaved a sigh of relief, because before their departure, they had taken turns talking to me, coming in and out like a revolving door, making me quite dizzy. The outcome of our talks was generally unsatisfactory. From the military point of view, we had lost the chance to go east or south to expand our influence, as we had abandoned Mao-hsien, Pei-ch'uan, and the region south of Mao-kung. As to the plan to go north, it had yet to be decided upon specifically after our arrival at Mao-erh-kai. Concerning the political problems within the Party, there had been a lot of talk but no conclusions had been reached. Hence, I felt that the Mao-kung meeting had been a failure.

It was well after midday before I could find time to speak to the cadres of the Fourth Front Army. Most of the cadres of the Thirtieth Army who had moved north from Mao-kung to Fu-pien were quite worried about the reunion of the First and Fourth Front armies. They told me that when the Thirtieth Army first met the troops of Lin Piao of the First Front Army on the road south of Mao-kung, both parties showed great cordiality. When the VIP's of the CC saw the Thirtieth Army, they had praised the Fourth Front Army from many angles. But in less than two days this friendly atmosphere underwent a change.

The cadres of the Fourth Front Army made the following points in their talk: First, the cadres of the First Front Army were always emphasizing the mighty power of the airplanes and artillery of Chiang Kai-shek, which the Fourth Front Army had not had occasion to meet. Since the First Front Army, which used to be much stronger than the Fourth Front Army, was unable to withstand the enemy, how could the Fourth Front Army expect to do so? Our colleagues were worried about the spread of defeatism which might affect the morale of the Fourth Front Army.

Second, some of the cadres of the First Front Army had slandered me, saying that I was an old opportunist, distrusted by the Comintern and the CC, and that my proposal to form the Northwest Federation was a concrete expression of my rightist tendency. This had evoked ill-feeling among the cadres of the Fourth Front Army, who, having gone through many struggles with me throughout the years, directly refuted these slanders in the light of their own experiences.

Third, the CC had sent some investigators to the Thirtieth Army to look into actual conditions in the Army. These investigators usually exaggerated the shortcomings of the Fourth Front Army. When they found a few officers scolding the soldiers, they concluded that warlord ways prevailed in the Fourth Front Army.

Fourth, finding that the ordinary cadres of the Fourth Front Army usually knew only the names of Mao Tse-tung, Chu Teh, and so forth, instead of all the names on the list of Politburo members, the investigators insisted that the Fourth Front Army did not respect the CC. They even went to such lengths as to say that this was the result of Chang So-and-so's deliberate manipulation.

A responsible comrade of the Political Department of the Thirtieth Army showed me his transcript of talks with comrades of the First Front Army. The transcript included the above-mentioned points. According to the verbatim record of the conversations of the two parties, it could be seen that the comrades of the Fourth Front Army were aware of their major obligations, and all explanations offered by them were tactful and reasonable, while the comrades of the First Front Army sounded prejudiced and fastidious. Reading the record, I felt that the fault lay neither with the First nor with the Fourth Front Army. It was the result of problems in the leadership of the CC. Since the comrades of the CC were associated with the First Front Army, comrades in the Fourth Front Army were unable to distinguish between the two, thinking that they were one and the same.

All the comrades that I talked to were more or less disappointed with the CC and the First Front Army. Most of them said that the ordinary rank and file of the Fourth Front Army had had great faith in the CC and the First Front Army; but after the reunion and actual contacts with them, they felt altogether differently. They accused the First Front Army of slackness in military discipline, of indiscriminately attacking local tyrants, and of an overbearing attitude towards the Tibetans. They had seen along the way how the personnel of the First Front Army beat and scolded the Tibetans and took things from the Tibetans secretly. Some of our cadres also expressed displeasure at having a few CC members ride in sedan chairs. They regarded this as lack of consideration on their part in relation to the rank and file. Some even said that the leadership of the CC over the First Front Army was exercised more through force than anything else.

There were also people in the First Front Army who were dissatisfied with the leadership of the CC. They usually gave vent to their feelings in front of comrades of the Fourth Front Army whom they knew very well. According to them, during the Long March the CC leadership had avoided combat all the way, giving rise to a decrease in the will to fight. They were unhappy about retreating without a definite destination. They held that wherever they went, there was the possibility that the enemy would follow. It just wouldn't do to flee blindly all the time. They wanted to let the whole army have some rest and to reorganize. They hoped that the First and Fourth Front armies would unite sincerely and would not let the prejudice of the CC affect their relationship. Out of warm love for the Party, they hoped that the cadres of the Fourth Front Army could influence the depressing attitude of the CC with their own spirit of heroic struggle.

Some of them pointed out frankly that the CC intended to get control of the Fourth Front Army as soon as possible. When the VIP's of the CC first saw the Thirtieth Army, there was general excitement. But the spirit and behavior of the Fourth Front Army soon made them uneasy. Therefore, as soon as the CC arrived at Fu-pien, a meeting of the Politburo was held, and the following decisions were made:

1. In order not to give the Fourth Front Army cause for looking down on the CC, all comrades of the CC and the First Army should refrain from talking about the unfortunate sufferings of the First Front Army and the internal disputes within the CC when speaking to cadres of the Fourth Front Army. They should only talk about the good points of the CC and the First Front Army.

2. As the Fourth Front Army had been far away from the CC and under the leadership of that opportunist Chang So-and-so, it was impossible to expect to come up to their ideal. It was decided, therefore, to publish an article in the *Bolshevik News* criticizing the proposal of setting up the Northwest Federation. It was also decided to send investigators to the Fourth Front Army to find convincing evidence that warlord ways existed there.

3. It was decided that only military matters would be talked about when meeting Chang So-and-so; there would be no talk about political questions. Chang Kuo-t'ao would be appointed deputy chairman of the Military Affairs Committee, so that the actual command of

the Fourth Front Army would go directly into the hands of the CC, and the march to the north would be embarked upon immediately.

Comparing what my comrades told me with what I had personally witnessed in the previous two days, I found that the above-mentioned points tallied, generally speaking, with the facts. I felt that the CC could only resort to tactics of gaining control as it had invited military defeats through the implementation of the erroneous Soviet policy. I also sensed that Mao Tse-tung and the other veteran guerrilla experts were teaming up with those who had returned from Russia, such as Chang Wen-t'ien, Ch'in Pang-hsien, and others, to deal with me. I believed that I had the responsibility of correcting the mistakes of those comrades and saving the CCP from defeat.

I was convinced that at this crucial moment it was inappropriate to let disputes break out within the Party. Internal unanimity was the overriding need now. There were many in the CC and the First Front Army who were clear about the major obligations, such as Chu Teh. I wanted to try to achieve reform by moderate methods.

So I told the comrades of the Fourth Front Army that the CC might have formed some wrong conceptions over a long period of hard struggle. Now that I had joined the CC in its work, it would be possible to try to bring about improvements. We should advance our suggestions on the premises of unity within the Party and close cooperation between the First and Fourth Front armies. I told the comrades that they must not be oversuspicious about the plan to rally at Mao-erh-kai and that they should prepare for the march northward. Even if it was an erroneous decision, it was better than having disputes break out within the Party. I advised them to try to keep calm and cool, so that I might have a chance to bring about improvements.

Early on the morning of the third day, I packed up everything and set out for Cho-ko-chi, too. The malignant growth that had developed throughout the years of erroneous policy and guerrilla warfare worsened with each passing day. The three-day meeting at Mao-kung and my moderate efforts thereafter proved to be a totally ineffective remedy, as was shown by ensuing events.

The Mao-erh-kai Conference

The differences of opinion within the Party soon developed into overall dissension. The comrades of the Fourth Front Army and I accused the CC of incorrect leadership, while the majority of the CC insisted that its policies were perfectly correct, and refused to concede. The purpose of the Mao-erh-kai Conference was to patch up the dissension, but owing to the excessive stubbornness of the majority of CC members, it failed to do so, causing further deterioration in the suitation within the Party.

The majority of members of the CC of the CCP, including Mao Tse-tung, wanted to go north as soon as possible; but it was not easy to do so smoothly, because we did not know about conditions in the Szechwan-Kansu border regions, and the troops of Hu Tsung-nan were in control of Sung-fan and important key points to the north of it. Our troops, therefore, had to stop at places north of Cho-ko-chi. An advance unit was ordered to reconnoiter the route to the north; and major cadres of the Fourth Front Army, including Hsü Hsiang-ch'ien and Ch'en Ch'ang-hao, were ordered to come to a meeting to settle specific questions concerning the direct command of the Fourth Front Army by the Military Affairs Committee of the CC.

When I came to the place where the CC was stationed northeast of Cho-ko-chi, I was assigned to a lodging in a village some li from where the other members of the CC were staying. Nobody from the CC called on me. It seemed that I had been demoted. But I kept a cool head, took no notice of anything, and even found pleasure in having some rest temporarily. In two days, Hsü Hsiang-ch'ien, Ch'en Ch'ang-hao, and other cadres of the Fourth Front Army arrived one after another. They all came to see me, and I had to tell them what had really happened during the talks at Fu-pien. I also told them to obey the direct commands of the Military Affairs Committee of the CC.

Due to increasing contacts between the cadres of the First and Fourth Front armies, estrangement between them continued to mount. Cadres of the First Front Army usually ignored the heroic struggles of the Fourth Front Army and leveled unnecessary criticisms at it, such as that the Fourth Front Army had deviated from the correct leadership of the CC, was not immune from ways of warlords, and so forth. Cadres of the Fourth Front Army also ignored the glorious record of the First Front Army, and similarly voiced unnecessary criticism of it, saying that the personnel had lost their will to fight, and so forth. Such criticism evoked emotional reactions, the impact of which blurred the distinction between right and wrong.

The CC of the CCP, obviously, ought to be held responsible for fermenting such a situation. Its members had not taken into full consideration the fact that the CC was now staying among the army units, where any dissension within the Party might easily turn into alienation between the two armies. In their haste to go north, they had done everything in a hurry, neglecting to foster the understanding that was needed between the two armies. They had overestimated the prestige of the CC and had forgotten about the dissatisfaction that existed among the ordinary comrades.

Among the questions put before the CC by the cadres of the Fourth Front Army were the following: Why did the CC insist on going north right away? Why should we abandon Mao-hsien, Pei-ch'uan, and other base-points for further development towards the southeast, including those south of Mao-kung? What were the grounds for the claim that if we stayed a few days longer, we would be blockaded by our enemies, like turtles in an urn? Why didn't they take time to hold some meetings to get a clear picture of all problems through discussions? Why was the leadership of the Fourth Front Army criticized before the conditions in the Army were understood? As this was the first meeting between the First and Fourth Front armies, why were the cadres of the two armies not given the chance to understand one another and learn from each other? Why did the CC spread among cadres of the First Front Army words of dissatisfaction about the cadres of the Fourth Front Army? All these questions and other similar ones were not easily explained away by the dignitaries of the CC.

As these questions were not answered adequately, the cadres of the Fourth Front Army further criticized the CC for discriminating against the Fourth Front Army and not regarding it as a unit of the Committee's own flesh and blood. They criticized the CC leaders for making mistakes, for doing things unmethodically. They called going north a flight, a way of sacrificing the Army to enable a few people to flee to Outer Mongolia. Everybody understood that "wherever you go, the enemy can go also" was a simple truth. They claimed that the criticism the CC leveled at the leadership of the Fourth Front Army was all biased. They particularly objected to the CC's discrimination against me and declared that only I could represent the majority of the comrades in the Fourth Front Army.

Taking advantage of their relationship with Ch'en Ch'ang-hao as members of the "28 Bolsheviks" in Moscow, Chang Wen-t'ien, Ch'in Pang-hsien, and others asked Ch'en Ch'ang-hao candidly, "Since Chang Kuo-t'ao is a veteran opportunist, why do the cadres of the Fourth Front Army choose to follow him rather than the CC?" Ch'en Ch'ang-hao told them that criticism against me in the past had been unfair. He said that I had exercised correct leadership in the Fourth Front Army with meritorious achievements and had been loved and respected by the general cadres. He warned that discrimination against me by the CC would arouse ill-feeling in the Fourth Front Army. The improper activities of those who had returned from Russia in attempting to alienate the cadres from me thus fell through.

Sensing the seriousness of the situation, Chu Teh and some others tried to intervene. He frankly admitted that the meeting of the two armies had not been well arranged, mainly due to the hurried decision to go north, which deprived the two armies of the opportunity to get acquainted and make friends. Moreover, there were some people in the CC who indulged in random criticism. He worried about the estrangement between the comrades, which might affect the military command and might even cause adverse consequences in future military operations. He, therefore, advanced a scheme concerning unified military command, which stipulated mainly the strengthening of the General Headquarters of the Red Army, with Chu Teh as commander-in-chief and me as chief political commissar responsible for the command of the whole army. Thereafter, decisions on strategic questions would be drawn up by General Headquarters and submitted to the Military Affairs Committee and the Politburo of the CC for approval. The scheme had not been discussed at the meetings of the Politburo of the CC, but was made public as being unanimously approved by the members of the Politburo. (The reluctance of the Politburo to hold meetings at that time stemmed, apparently, from its desire to avoid talking about political problems.) For the sake of unity, I took up my post with pleasure. Thus, the upheaval that was brewing quieted down temporarily.

The internal climate around us had changed. Unity and unanimity were overriding needs at the time. Some dignitaries of the CC had earnestly told me and cadres of the Fourth Front Army that they had come to believe that my prestige in the Fourth Front Army was the natural result of many years of struggles and was not shaped by opposition to or ignoring of the CC. They promised that thenceforth there would be mutual trust and common efforts to plan the smooth progress of our work. I had addressed cadres of the Fourth Front Army at a meeting, calling for unity. However, this atmosphere of unity could not check some people's deep-rooted prejudice. The scheme of unified command soon encountered obstacles in practice.

I started to work side by side with Commander-in-Chief Chu Teh at General Headquarters, but he only held an empty title, with no independent functions or organs of his own. He actually was a member of the Military Affairs Committee of the CC. After I joined him, I let everything proceed as usual, without making any adjustment in accordance with the scheme of unified command. The Military Affairs Committee and General Headquarters were actually one and the same organ. Liu Po-ch'eng was chief-of-staff, Yeh Chien-ying and Tso Ch'üan were deputy chiefs-of-staff, and Chang Yün-yi was head of the Bureau. No changes were made in these posts. As Ch'in Pang-hsien was unwilling to continue with his post as acting director of the Political Department, it was assigned to Li Cho-jan, a returned student from Russia. All of the personnel in the offices of my original Military Subcommittee were assigned to the headquarters of the Right Route Army as a measure to strengthen its leadership. Our General Headquarters would wait until completion of the reorganization of the Right Route Army before personnel would be transferred to us.

I was then giving most of my attention to unity between the First and Fourth Front armies. As soon as I took up the post of chief political commissar, I ordered each of the four armies of the Right Route Army to send a regiment to fill out the Left Route Army. This was also a measure to promote mutual understanding and thorough cooperation between the First and Fourth Front armies. It actually aroused excitement among the comrades. The Left Route Army was reinforced in manpower as well as in its supply of ammunition, as the four regiments that were transferred had brought with them an ample supply of ammunition. This was one of the main causes for the increased combat strength of the Left Route Army that was shown in future battles. By refraining from taking active steps to reorganize General Headquarters and to transfer personnel of the Fourth Front Army to General Headquarters, I showed my spirit of impartiality in the hope that close unity might prevail in all future work.

What I needed was a clear division of labor between General Headquarters and the Military Affairs Committee, and the establishment of proper work procedures. This involved General Headquarters in the administration of all organs originally under the Military Affairs Committee. These organs would have to deal with all work upon direct orders from the commander-in-chief and the chief political commissar, and all orders of the Military Affairs Committee would have to be conveyed to the lower levels by General Headquarters. The Military Affairs Committee of the CC was actually under the Politburo. The committee would have to direct General Headquarters, examining and approving its military plans and major personnel changes. The Military Affairs Committee would no longer issue military orders directly.

However, Mao Tse-tung spoiled the scheme of unified command. In the past, Mao Tse-tung, as chairman of the Military Affairs Committee, had decided everything arbitrarily, leaving the commander-in-chief with only an empty title. Now he continued to do so, without the slightest change. He read all documents from the military organs, whether they were intelligence reports, battle plans, administrative records of the army units, or plans for personnel changes. He also noted down the methods of dealing with these matters, and then handed them over to us for execution. In this way the commander-in-chief and the chief political commissar became his secretarial staff. He was singing solo, all by himself.

This work-style of Mao Tse-tung's was strongly opposed by Chief-of-Staff Liu Po-ch'eng, who held that modern warfare, being organized fighting, could not be dealt with by the talent and wisdom of one person alone. According to him, an initial battle plan ought to be drawn up by the chief-of-staff in close consultation with the political-work personnel and other personnel concerned, based on a draft scheme from the War Bureau, which, in turn, had taken into consideration the intelligence reports from the head of the Intelligence Bureau which had been approved by the chief-of-staff. The initial plan had to be approved by the commander-in-chief and the chief political commissar before it was given to the Military Affairs Committee for discussion or to the chairman of the committee for endorsement. Then it was the duty of General Headquarters to convey it to the lower levels for execution. I had upheld Liu Po-ch'eng's opinion, noting that if we could keep to this procedure, there would be greater efficiency in our military command, and many disputes within the Party could be avoided.

The dictatorial work-style of Mao Tse-tung's seemed to be a deep-rooted habit. On this point he was like Chiang Kai-shek. Both kept a tight grip on the decision-making power and had a penchant for giving instructions. Mao Tse-tung not only wanted his own decisions to be final; he actually deprived other comrades of the chance to make suggestions. He often gave instructions before others could make any proposals. Mao Tse-tung always boasted of his unsurpassed military talent, comparing himself to Moltke, the modern German military expert. While in the Kiangsi Soviet region, he often had involved squabbles over this with Chou En-lai, Liu Po-ch'eng, and the German military adviser Richter. After the Tsun-yi Conference, Chou En-lai became his deputy and suffered innumerable grievances at his hand.

On the other hand, Mao Tse-tung was not a brilliant dictator. He was imaginative and sensitive; his thinking sometimes became quite bizarre, and he would make mythical utterances. He lacked the ability to organize and was reluctant to make precise calculations when dealing with difficult matters. Sometimes his ideas were not clearly expressed, and he often defended his "opinions of a genius" in an emotional mood.

Mao Tse-tung was also a peculiar supporter of "military first." He admired ancient Chinese military theories but lacked modern military knowledge. He showed contempt for all that was written in contemporary military works, regarding them as outdated clichés. He wanted to give full play to his guerrilla talent without any hindrance. The military orders he drew up were usually "inspirational orders," full of passionate phrases to describe the importance of a certain task and to urge those who received the order to take immediate action. When giving instructions to the individual military organs to take up certain specific tasks, he often used loose terms, as if the respective organs were expected to act in the light of the occasion.

Generally speaking, we were all guerrilla masterhands at that time, with more or less the same temperament as Mao Tse-tung. Yet, he was the one who had displayed it in the most extravagant manner, so much so that we could not help feeling that he had gone too far astray. I had talked to him many times about this, but I found that it was not too easy to exchange views on military matters with him, still less to form an organized and unified command.

Mao Tse-tung not only ignored the scheme of unified military command but also launched a barrage of criticism against the Fourth Front Army. As a result, all efforts at reconciliation became quite futile. The Politburo of the CC suddenly issued a notice on the convening of a joint meeting of the Politburo and the Military Affairs Committee, the agenda for which I was not told beforehand. The participants included members of the two organs, Hsü Hsiang-ch'ien, Ch'en Ch'ang-hao, and the·major staff officers of the Military Affairs Committee. The meeting was chaired by Mao Tse-tung, who, after declaring the meeting open, asked Hsü Hsiang-ch'ien to report on the military situation of the Fourth Front Army. Hsü Hsiang-ch'ien immediately made a report in simple terms, giving an account of the conditions of the Fourth Front Army in the same vein as my descriptions in the above passages, and added his views on the strong and weak points of the Fourth Front Army in its tactics.

The report said nothing about the dissension within the Party. It was given candidly and impartially, fully displaying the typical character of a Communist military man.

Without making any detailed study, Mao Tse-tung immediately criticized Hsü Hsiang-ch'ien's report, accusing the Fourth Front Army of two major mistakes. One of them was that the Fourth Front Army should not have abandoned the original Northern Szechwan Soviet region, leaving the base insufficiently protected and the guerrilla troops without reinforcement. The other was that not enough armed forces had been employed to control the strategic key point of Sung-fan, greatly hindering the implementation of the plan to go north. He said nothing encouraging about the hard struggles of the Fourth Front Army and its efforts to help the First Front Army. Instead, he asked the meeting to accept his review and adopt it as a decision.

I immediately stood up to defend the Fourth Front Army. I pointed out that the Northern Szechwan Soviet region should have been protected and that Sung-fan should have been put under our control, but that this had depended on the strength of the Fourth Front Army, not on our subjective wishes. I explained that our main task at that moment was to assist the First Front Army, and as our strength was limited, it was impossible to scatter it in using it. If the CC thought that the Fourth Front Army had not made an unnecessary or erroneous move in assisting the First Front Army, it should not have made harsh accusations against the Fourth Front Army for not fulfilling additional military tasks that were beyond its strength. The Northern Szechwan Soviet region could not have been defended even if more forces had been kept there. Moreover, there had still been doubt about whether the First Front Army could successfully cross the Ta-tu River and reach Mao-kung. If the Fourth Front Army had spared no effort in order to seize Sung-fan to the north, would the CC not have criticized us for watching the fire on the opposite bank and ignoring the major obligation of caring for our brother army which was in distress?

My speech found response only in Ch'en Ch'ang-hao. Mao Tse-tung persisted in his views, as if he was criticizing for the sake of criticizing. The others present kept silent throughout the meeting, as if nobody wanted to get involved. The meeting did not come to a decision, but it fully exposed Mao's intentions.

The joint meeting once more aroused the anger of the cadres of the Fourth Front Army. Some of them held that the CC was consistently discriminating against the Fourth Front Army; others proposed launching an overall examination to review not only the Fourth Front Army, but also the First Front Army. It should review whether the leadership of the CC was correct. Still others thought that the CC had not been fair in its actions, that it had been biased and encumbered with emotion. Its sole aim was to play the trick of attacking the Fourth Front Army in order to cover up the failure of the leadership of the CC of the CCP. Some worried about the defeatism that was overwhelming the CC. There didn't seem to be any outcome other than creating disputes within the Party, and no way to a new life was in view.

So we tarried at Cho-ko-chi for more than a week. The situation was not at all optimistic. The CC continued to attack the Fourth Front Army and its leadership politically behind the smoke screen of not talking about politics. This aroused discontent among the cadres of the Fourth Front Army, and improvement in the relationship between the two armies became impossible. Military operations of the northward march also came to a halt. I had suggested that the Fourth Front Army be assigned the task of attacking Sung-fan and opening up the road to the north, but Mao Tse-tung objected. Instead, he relied on Yeh Chien-ying, who was attempting to occupy the road leading to the north with some of Lin Piao's troops; but the fatigued First Front Army was not up to the task on short notice.

The organs of the CC and the main military departments soon moved north to Mao-erh-kai. As the route to the north was not yet clear, it was necessary to wait some days. I suggested that it would be best to use this time in clearing up the dissension within the Party. The main point of my proposal was to convene a meeting of the Politburo to make an overall study of Party work and current military problems. Then a meeting of the senior cadres of the two armies was to be convened by the Politburo to form a unified plan and to select some new men to take part in the meetings of the Politburo and the work of the CC. The Politburo was thus obliged to set a date for a meeting, which was the only formal meeting of the Politburo after the meeting of the two armies. The CCP later named it the Mao-erh-kai Conference.

The conference was actually held at Sha-wo, some twenty li from Mao-erh-kai, where a Tibetan village spread out in the valley with wooded hills all around. It was in a world of its own. The organs of the CC of the CCP were stationed there. At seven on the evening of the appointed day, I rode to the conference site with Ch'en Ch'ang-hao and some ten cavalrymen from the neighborhood of Mao-erh-kai. Chang Wen-t'ien was standing just outside the mountain gap to Sha-wo to receive me. He said, "This is a confidential meeting in which Ch'en Ch'ang-hao cannot participate." I pointed out that Ch'en Ch'ang-hao was a member of the Standing Committee of the CC of the CYC and was entitled to take part as an observer. Chang Wen-t'ien, however, refused to listen to me. Ch'en Ch'ang-hao had to stay at a pavilion for cowherds outside the village and wait for me so that we could return to our place together.

I walked into the valley with Chang Wen-t'ien and one of my guards. On the way we had to pass through several sentry posts, where the sentries were using a special password. The conference site seemed to be under heavy guard. The organs of the CC had set up a Central Column Headquarters to guard the safety of the Central organs. On that evening the whole village was surrounded by guards as if a powerful enemy were approaching. I said to Chang Wen-t'ien with a smile, "General Headquarters need not worry about the safety of the Central organs now that they guard themselves so closely." Chang Wen-t'ien was obviously embarrassed by my words.

The conference took place in the outer pavilion of a Lamist temple. The participants included Mao Tse-tung, Chu Teh, Ch'in Pang-hsien, Chang Wen-t'ien and myself, all members of the Politburo. (Chou En-lai and Wang Chia-hsiang were on sick leave.) The two observers were Teng Fa and K'ai Feng, while the secretary general of the Central secretariat, Wang Shou-tao, was responsible for the minutes. As soon as the conference started, Mao Tse-tung showed me a draft copy of the resolution of the conference, which had been prepared before the conference was held.

This not-too-lengthy document declared that the political line of the CC of the CCP was correct and that great victories had been won in the Soviet campaign and the agrargian revolution, as well as in the struggle to oppose the various encirclement campaigns and punitive expeditions of the KMT. It admitted that in the past the CC had made mistakes in its military line, but that they were corrected at the Tsun-yi Conference, after which all the lines taken by the CC were correct. It called on the entire Party and the entire Army to rally around the CC and continue to strive for a Soviet China.

I passed the document on to the others who were present as soon as I had finished reading it, but I was told that they had already read through it. It seemed to me that they not only had read through it, but had also discussed it. I was the only one who was not in the know. The atmosphere at the conference seemed somewhat tense; every face looked cold and stern. When the chairman of the conference, Chang Wen-t'ien, announced that it was time for discussion, nobody spoke. The heavy guard outside and the tense expression on the faces of the comrades inside reminded me of the well-known "Hung-men feast" of Chinese history.[5]

I was the first to take the floor. In order to ease the tense atmosphere, I started on a light note. I said that the differences of opinion amongst us were nothing to be surprised about. The chaps of Liang-shan-po wouldn't have become good friends had they not gone through some tussles. It didn't matter if there had been squabbles. Because of our long years of experience with struggles, it would not be very difficult for us to come to an understanding. Moreover, our aim was fundamentally to reach an understanding and not to increase the dissension.

I regretted that we had not thoroughly aired our views on the issues during our first meeting in Fu-pien. As a result, some unnecessary estrangement was caused and some unwarranted opinions were expressed, such as that I was a warlord who wished to blackmail the CC on the strength of my military power; or that I was definitely a veteran opportunist who must be punished; or that I looked down upon all other members of the Politburo because of my seniority and wanted to destroy the whole CC under the pretext of correcting its mistakes. There were also people who quoted from Marxist classics to show that the Northwest Federation was a betrayal of the Soviet, and others who claimed that the function of the chief political commissar overruled those of the chairman of the Military Affairs Committee and the whole CC. All these rumors seemed to have painted a very poor picture of me.

At this point, Mao Tse-tung put in a word. He said, "Such rumors are quite numerous. For example, some people said that I, Mao Tse-tung, was Tsao Tsao, and that the CC had become Emperor Hsien-ti of the Han dynasty, or a mere puppet in my hands." He then added that some people believed that the political line of the CC had been wrong and that the whole Party was now ruled by militaristic and bureaucratic methods. This was the problem the conference was to solve.

Continuing with my speech, I pointed out that the political line might be wrong, owing to possible mistakes either in the directives of the Comintern or in our execution of them. This might be the result of the changing situation and times, which demanded a change in our policy. When we insisted upon examining the political line of the CC, it did not follow that we demanded the overthrow of the whole CC. I noted that we had all experienced amazingly hard struggles and had exerted ourselves for the sake of communism. The Party could not abandon us, nor could we abandon the Party. At the Sixth Congress there were people who said that comrades who had made mistakes were still the best comrades in the Party, and such comrades were decreasing in number. In discussing political problems, it was necessary, therefore, not to connect them with the question of responsibility.

Then I criticized the predrafted document and advanced my proposal. I pointed out that the conference might not be in a position to affirm or deny rashly the correctness of the political line of the CC. But it was an obvious and easily observed fact that the Soviet campaign was a failure and not a success; for all the Soviet regions had been lost, the Red Army had suffered heavy losses, and we had retreated to the Tibetan region. All these defeats were undeniable facts. As to the reasons for the setbacks in the Soviet campaign, I felt that they were mainly due to the incompatibility of the campaign with the times and the masses. It could not be said that they were due to the mighty power of enemy airplanes and guns, or to military miscalculation on our part. The Tsun-yi Conference affirmed that the political line of the CC was correct, but declared its military line incorrect. This seemed to be a case of reversing cause and effect.

I ridiculed the secrecy in which the conference was held, and I criticized the predrafted resolution for being a little too mysterious, saying that this would hamper the free exchange of opinions. I insisted that the predrafted resolution be put aside for the time being and that an unfettered study be made of the situation. I hoped that the comrades would not look at my suggestion through prejudiced eyes, but would discuss the question in a matter-of-fact manner.

I proposed that a meeting of senior cadres be held to forge a unified will within the Party. When I was in the Oyüwan region, and later in northern Szechwan, I often held such meetings of senior cadres with satisfactory results. With the currently existing alienation between the cadres of the First and Fourth armies and the discontent with the CC, it was all the more necessary to hold such enlarged meetings. There was no need for us to be afraid of such meetings, thinking that they might end in squabbles. If we came to a unanimous agreement through discussions now and put the case in front of the senior cadres' meeting for discussion, giving explanations for any misunderstanding that might have existed, extolling the two armies for their spirit of hard struggle, and promoting mutual admiration, unity would result.

I held that the CC ought to select some new men to take part in its work, so as to consolidate its leadership. Referring to the Politburo members present, I pointed out that not all of them had been elected at the Sixth Congress as members of the CC (including Chang Wen-t'ien, Ch'in Pang-hsien, Wang Chia-hsiang, and Chu Teh). It often happened that those who were not CC members attended meetings of the Politburo as observers. There would be a hundred advantages but not a single disadvantage if we selected a few cadres from the First and Fourth Front armies to attend the Politburo meetings as observers and to take part in the work of the Military Affairs Committee and other Central organs. For example, I was a member of the CC, but I was usually regarded as the spokesman of the Fourth Front Army. Why should we not let the cadres of the Fourth Front Army directly air their views at meetings of the CC?

Convening meetings of senior cadres and absorbing new men into the work of the Central organs were ways of displaying democracy within the Party and not plots to overthrow the CC. I made it clear that the functions of a meeting of senior cadres might be left for future discussion. It might take the form of an enlarged CC meeting, or it might be a meeting for making suggestions to the CC. In point of fact, the CC was at the moment isolated from other Party organizations in various places in the country. Its leadership could extend only as far as the First and Fourth Front armies, and it was only natural and legal to organize a meeting of the senior cadres of the two armies. It was something that had to be done. If some people were so sensitive as to feel that such a meeting might be overwhelmed by the greater number of cadres from the Fourth Front Army, they were really letting their fancies run wild. I could assure them that the comrades of the Fourth Front Army would not seek to be a majority in the meeting—we only hoped for a chance to express our opinions.

Lastly, I stressed that use of the democratic process in the Party would resolve differences of opinion. Take, for example, the question of military operations. If we made decisions after discussion in a meeting of senior cadres, we would show much more determination and confidence in carrying them out. Conversely, if the CC refused to convene a meeting of senior cadres, to let new blood join in the work of the CC, and to let comrades have a chance to express their opinions on important political and military issues, it would be in effect blocking the road to unity.

After I spoke, those present all expressed support for the predrafted copy of resolutions. Mao was still the most voluble among them. He first expressed the opinion that the policy of the Soviet movement was determined by the Comintern and passed by the Sixth Congress—thus there could be no question of its correctness. He twisted logic in insisting that the Soviet movement had been victorious and could not be deemed a failure. He indicated that if we were now to say that the Soviet movement had failed, it would disappoint the comrades in general. Furthermore, henceforward we should hoist the Soviet flag no matter where we went.

Mao also turned down all my proposals. He declared that the CC belonged to the entire nation, not just to the First and Fourth Front armies, since there still existed the Second Front Army and the nationwide underground Party organizations in the White areas. The political line of the CC, then, could not be examined by just the First and Fourth Front armies. He opposed convocation of a meeting of any nature by senior cadres of the First and Fourth armies, and he also refused to let any additional comrades join in the work of the CC. In his view, democracy within the Party was out of the question in the midst of military operations; everything must be carried out according to the commands issued by the CC.

Although each of us maintained his own views, we were still anxious to come to an understanding. The major shortcoming of this conference was that no one proposed a measure on the political level. Even I myself, who was opposing the political line of the CC, did not advance any positive proposal. We talked about the question of resistance to Japan, but nobody suggested that the current Soviet policy should be changed to the anti-Japanese national united-front policy. We did not think of finding our life belt in the issue of resistance to Japan. At the conference some people mentioned the CC's declaration on going north to resist Japan in 1932, which demanded that all armies in the country stop attacking the Red Army and unanimously turn their guns towards the Japanese invaders. Yet, none of us believed that Chiang Kai-shek would stop attacking us just because of the slogan "unanimous resistance to Japan."

Quite unexpectedly, while we were arguing heatedly about whether the policy of the Soviet campaign was correct, Stalin had quietly put away this magic wand and picked up a new weapon: the anti-Japanese national united front. In the summer of 1935, at the Seventh Congress of the Comintern held in Moscow, Chairman Dimitrov stressed in his political report that in colonial countries an anti-imperialist national united front was to be set up, particularly in China, where the anti-Japanese national united front was to be set up. Following this, Wang Ming, the representative of the CC of the CCP at the Comintern, issued the "August First Declaration" in the name of the CC of the CCP, proposing the formation of an all-China united national defense government and allied armies for resistance to Japan.[6]

Because Mao and others held on to dogmas and made no compromise, the meeting ended fruitlessly. In this meeting there was no discussion of military matters. I even maintained that if the political problem within the Party was properly resolved, then the dissension over military strategy would disappear. But those present did not seem to attach any importance to my words. No one mentioned the question of the Northwest Federation; apparently nobody was interested in the policy toward minority races. This meeting seemed to deal specifically with internal disputes, but the internal disputes were not settled by this meeting. However, the resolutions drafted by Mao were not voted upon either, mainly to avoid too much tension in the atmosphere.

After the meeting adjourned around 3 A.M., I walked out of the Sha-wo hills to meet Ch'en Ch'ang-hao and told him what had happened at the meeting. Ch'en was very pained; he asked me in great agitation, "Why does the CC ignore the comrades of the Fourth Front Army so stubbornly? If you were to publicize more clearly that the CC's political line is completely in error and that the CC leadership is bankrupt, what would the result be? Would doing this force the CC to concede?"

Ch'en's questions aroused many sentiments in me. I thought of the internal strife in the past in the Taiping Heavenly Kingdom and the KMT, and felt that the CC should not fall into the same trap. I bemoaned the fact that the CC had developed a deep inferiority complex through defeats and setbacks to the point of isolating itself and not daring to exchange views with the comrades in general. I did not regret the moderate stand I had adopted. If the internal dispute were to worsen in the face of great adversity, it would be tantamount to seeking our own death. Due to these psychological factors, Ch'en Ch'ang-hao and I persisted in our view of making continuous efforts to reach an understanding.

The following day, Ch'en Ch'ang-hao made an appointment with Chang Wen-t'ien for a heart-to-heart talk. He had wanted to persuade Chang Wen-t'ien to accept some of my views. It so happened that an army commander of a unit of the Fourth Front Army was present who was quite fed up with the involved arguments, and he blurted out to Chang Wen-t'ien, "The leadership of the CC has made mistakes; I, as a Party member, shall never trust the CC any more." Chang Wen-t'ien was so taken by surprise that he was tongue-tied, and his face and ears were all red. Ch'en Ch'ang-hao then explained that this was only a frank remark made by an individual Party member, and asked Chang Wen-t'ien not to pay any attention to him. Yet, later Chang Wen-t'ien charged the Fourth Front Army with forming a militaristic clique.

For my part, I visited Wang Chia-hsiang, who was convalescing, hoping that he would play the role of mediator. Wang was wounded during an air raid while in the Kiangsi Soviet region. The wound involved his large intestine, and he had to depend on a rubber tube through his abdomen for elimination. All the way north from Kiangsi, he passed his days on a stretcher, numbing the pain with opium. By then he was an addict, extremely weak and thin. Chu Teh was very worried about the futility of his own mediation, and he had urged Wang Chia-hsiang to act as a mediator. Though Wang was a returned student from Russia, he did not reek of dogmatism. During his convalescence he was able to give the problems cool consideration.

Wang Chia-hsiang told me that he was willing to do his utmost to bring about a reconciliation so as to dispel the dissension within the Party. According to him, there shouldn't have been anything barring the way to an understanding. He pointed out that the demands that I and the Fourth Front Army had put forward to the CC were all understandable and mostly reasonable. He asked me to temporarily refrain from criticizing the political line of the CC, leaving that for future study. He proposed that at the moment, efforts should be made to bring about a relatively large meeting of cadres and to absorb a few comrades of the Fourth Front Army into the work of the Central organs, in the hope that the opinions within the Party might be unified gradually and that military operations might be carried out smoothly. I encouraged him to make such efforts, but in the end nothing much happened. The reasons were, naturally, unknown to me.

The military situation soon became even worse. As we had abandoned Mao-hsien, Pei-ch'uan, and the area south of Mao-kung, our army was in an unfavorable position, even if the enemy armies had not continued their pursuit. The area around Mao-erh-kai and Cho-ko-chi was part farmland and part pasture of the Tibetans, with little population and a shortage of food. If our armies stayed too long in this area, shortages in supplies would result. Our march from Fu-pien to Mao-erh-kai via Cho-ko-chi had taken us more than three weeks, and it was already July. If we stayed on, our enemies would concentrate a greater force to blockade us, not allowing us to leave this area. The comrades were very worried about the stagnation in military operations.

In order to relieve the situation, I finally proposed that we put aside the issue of dissension within the Party and concentrate on finding a way out militarily. I proposed that the whole Red Army enter the area of Min-hsien and Lin-tan in southern Kansu as quickly as possible before we decided whether we should go north or west in accordance with the situation that developed. General Headquarters would lead the Ninth and Thirty-first armies of the original Fourth Front Army now stationed west of Mao-erh-kai and go north via Sha-chin-ssu, forming the Left Column of the Army. Hsü Hsiang-ch'ien and Ch'en Ch'ang-hao would lead the rest of the original Fourth Front Army, forming the Right Column, which would check the enemy at Sung-fan and places north of it. The troops of P'eng Te-huai and Lin Piao would form the Central Column, whose duty it was to protect the Central organs. Tung Chen-t'ang and Lo Ping-hui would lead their troops to bring up the rear. All army units would be in combat readiness, waiting for orders from General Headquarters for action.

The military plan that I had proposed obviously conformed with the situation and was impartial and considerate. Our armies could not possibly concentrate in a small area in view of the terrain, housing problems, and food supply. The Left Column directly under General Headquarters had to pass through a large tract of steppe land, where many obstacles were expected during the march. The Right Column of Hsü Hsiang-ch'ien and Ch'en Ch'ang-hao was responsible for fighting the enemy. Only the original First Front Army units were taking up relatively light duties—including those of protecting the safety of the Central organs.

Mao Tse-tung and the others gladly approved my plan, and the ordinary comrades were relieved and happy. All felt that the military plan to go north had not been hampered by the dissension within the Party. Some felt that the separate operations would automatically get rid of some chances of squabbling over right and wrong. It would be of no avail to have the big shots of the CC assembled in Mao-erh-kai, apparently of one accord but divided in spirit, none willing to yield. Chu Teh and I, together with Chief-of-Staff Liu Po-ch'eng and a few staff officers, immediately took the road to the west. Henceforth, all our attention was concentrated on military matters. The problem of the dispute within the Party, which the Mao-erh-kai Conference had not settled, was temporarily set aside.

The Split

Mao Tse-tung and the others secretly led the First and Third armies away in a separate operation, violating the supreme principle of unanimous action of the CCP and the Red Army, which eventually caused splits in both. If history were a description of facts, the verdict would be "Mao Tse-tung split the CCP and the Red Army." Yet the current chronicles of the CCP hold me responsible for the split that occurred at that time. This is a reversal of what is true and what is false.

In July, 1935, our General Headquarters headed west from Mao-erh-kai and turned north after climbing a mountain range. In about five days, we reached Sha-chin-ssu, where mountain ranges rise and fall in complicated patterns. There are numerous streams in the valleys; those flowing north join the Yellow River, and those flowing south join the Yangtze. Sha-chin-ssu stands on one of the tributaries of the Yellow River. During the last three days of our journey we passed through a vast, limitless steppe, my first such experience in years of army life.

This was only the fringe of the western steppe. Carpets of green grass all over the mountains and plains were decorated with multicolored flowers, presenting a magnificent spectacle. All the trails were paths beaten by the flocks, usually dozens of them running parallel to one another. The rivers, untouched by human labor, twisted and turned, following the pattern of the terrain, flooding the low-lying land when it rained. When crossing those marshy pools, our soldiers had to be very careful; otherwise both horses and men would bog down.

Throughout this steppe, famous Lamaist temples were found approximately every three hundred li. Around the temple were scores or even a hundred residences for the lamas. Occasionally, there were a few lodgings for laymen and some shops which formed a village. The Lamaist temple seemed to be everything at once. It was the holy place of worship for the Tibetans, and the center of all political and social activities. The wool, grain, and other commodities of the Han people and Tibetans were bartered in the village. Wooden pens for the cattle were set up on the wooded hills or in the lowlands, so that men and beasts could rest or spend the winter. Usually, the herdsmen lived in tents, set up wherever there was water and pasture land.

As they crossed the steppe, our soldiers had to fight against nature. Camping was one of the difficulties. The threat of hunger was overcome because our soldiers had always followed the rule of carrying dry provisions with them for at least three days. (The First Front Army, which did not have this habit originally, had learned this from us after our meeting.) Of course, we could always billet in the Lamaist temples, but they were usually encountered only after three or four days of marching. Our equipment for camping in the open was very inadequate, and those who fell ill had to be left behind, owing to the great difficulty in giving them help while on the move. Quite a number of the sick were being left behind, and the common soldiers were very unhappy about this.

During our stay of two or three days at Sha-chin-ssu, we took active steps to find out about the route to the north. The surrounding terrain was quite foreign to us, and the maps we had with us were often wrong. We had to make new surveys and investigations. Painstakingly, Chief-of-Staff Liu Po-ch'eng interviewed the local people and the lamas and finally made up a map for our northward march.

In accordance with the data supplied by Liu Po-ch'eng, Chu Teh and I gave orders for the whole army to move northward, setting our destination in southern Kansu around Min-hsien and Lin-tan. Each unit had a clear idea of its task and the course to take. The most important part of the maneuver was that the two armies led by Hsü Hsiang-ch'ien and Ch'en Ch'ang-hao had, first of all, to attack the troops of Hu Tsung-nan north of Sung-fan in order to open up the way to the north on the right side, and to protect the whole army's Right Column.

Our General Headquarters then moved forward to Upper and Lower Pao-tso from Sha-chin-ssu in accordance with the plan. Unexpectedly, after one day of marching, it began to rain heavily. Fearing that our way might be blocked, we braved the rain and marched forward. In the evening we put up our army blankets to form tents right on the wet ground. On the afternoon of the third day we found that our way was blocked by a tributary on the upper reaches of the Ma-chu River. It had been just a small stream, less than knee-deep; now the water had risen until it was more than ten feet deep and three hundred meters wide. It was impossible to cross the river at that time. There didn't seem to be any chance that the river would recede in a few days, no means of transport were available within a range of one hundred li from the river, and our dry provisions were more than half gone. In view of the situation, we could do nothing but return to Sha-chin-ssu.

We radioed Mao Tse-tung and the other military organs about the situation, and ordered all units to stop moving forward until General Headquarters decided on the next step after returning to Sha-chin-ssu. It took us three days to return to Sha-chin-ssu. There was no rain during those days, but the men were tired out, and sickness increased. It was imperative to rest for a day or two.

On the day when we were barred by the rising river, Hsü Hsiang-ch'ien and Ch'en Ch'ang-hao had taken a fortress occupied by Hu Tsung-nan's troops about one hundred li north of Sung-fan. The defending regiment of the enemy was almost annihilated, and the remaining troops fled to Sung-fan. Our way to the north was thus clear.

When we arrived back at Sha-chin-ssu, we received an urgent radio message from Hsü Hsiang-ch'ien and Ch'en Ch'ang-hao, reporting that the First and Third armies had secretly marched forward, in defiance of the order from General Headquarters to stop advancing temporarily. Several radio messages that came in its wake reported to the effect that Mao Tse-tung had not waited for further orders, but had directly ordered the First and Third armies to march north separately under the name of "Advance Troops of the Northern March." As the troops of Hsü and Ch'en had cleared the way and the Left Column had been barred by the flood, he did not want to wait and thus lose this good opportunity. The operation was done completely in secret, no notice having been given to Hsü and Ch'en beforehand.

In the radiotelegrams of Hsü and Ch'en, Mao was accused of taking improper actions. When the First and Third armies secretly moved away in the dark with the Central organs, they had abandoned their duty of keeping watch over the enemy, having made no arrangements with the other units, thus exposing certain camps of the Fourth Front Army to enemy attack. When Hsü and Ch'en finally found out about it, the personnel of the First and Third armies that were bringing up the rear told them that they were acting under direct orders from the CC.

The extraordinary move of Mao Tse-tung and the others caused quite a stir among us in Sha-chin-ssu. Some of us pointed out frankly that Mao Tse-tung was playing the trick of the cicada shedding its shell. Taking advantage of the occasion when the northern route was cleared by the Fourth Front Army after heavy losses, he went away quietly, without sparing a thought for the majority of his comrades and the other army units. By using the name "Advance Troops of the Northern March," but secretly taking along with him the Central organs and the important personalities, he was misleading Chiang Kai-shek into believing that the central core of the CCP was still at Mao-erh-kai, so that the spearheads of Chiang's attack would not be pointed at his detachment. The reasons for his doing so included his defeatism and his Machiavellian idea "It is better that I turn my back on others than vice versa." Under the sway of such psychological factors, all Communist principles and moral concepts were thrown overboard. Only Mao Tse-tung was capable of playing such a trick. When one looks back now, it is obvious that Mao had always been toying with Machiavellian intrigues after the meeting of the two armies. Die-hards and naive dogmatists were just his tools.

After cool consideration, some responsible comrades and I agreed that such divisive moves could not be allowed. It often happened that Red Army units carried out separate operations, with the Central organs going along with any one of the units. But it was done according to an overall plan, and was not kept secret from the comrades. This was particularly an offense when dissension existed within the Party. If Mao Tse-tung and the others had notified Hsü Hsiang-ch'ien and Ch'en Ch'ang-hao of their move to go north separately, or had discussed the matter with General Headquarters, they would certainly not have been prevented from going forward; they might even have had better ways suggested to them for the fulfillment of their plan. Now that they had secretly moved off from the defense line and gone north, it was obviously an act of selfishness that disregarded the overall situation.

Chu Teh also agreed that such a secret separate move was uncalled for. It was done in disregard for the unity of the Party, the authority of General Headquarters, and the security of the troops of Hsü and Ch'en. However, he thought that Chiang Kai-shek would still be hard on our heels, even if Mao and the others reached the Kansu area. He, therefore, hoped that the comrades would turn a big problem into a small problem and try to patch up the breach.

General Headquarters soon radioed all military organs, urging them all to be calm and pointing out that although Mao's move violated the principle of unity within the Party, it would not bring any unfavorable consequence militarily. The units were ordered to report back on the activities of the enemy as soon as possible, so as to enable General Headquarters to decide on future steps in the light of the changed situation. General Headquarters was to stay in Sha-chin-ssu for three days.

The following day we received a radio message from Hsü and Ch'en, saying that Lin Piao had radioed them reporting on his arrival at a bridge over a canyon, which was now guarded by one of his companies. As the company was going to move north immediately, Lin Piao asked Hsü and Ch'en to send a unit there the next day to take over defense of the bridge. Hsü and Ch'en had not done as they were asked, because the bridge was some two hundred li away and could not be reached in one day even at forced-march speed. Meanwhile, wires from Tung Chen-t'ang and Lo

Ping-hui at Cho-ko-chi reported that there was no change in the area south of Mao-kung, where the enemy units were massing around Ya-an. We soon received radio messages from Hsü and Ch'en, reporting that the separate operation northward by Mao had attracted the attention of the enemy in the north, and that if we followed suit, we not only might not be able to catch up with the First and Third armies, but also might meet strong enemy fire that would prevent us from advancing. The main forces of Hsü and Ch'en were resisting Hu Tsung-nan's troops around Sung-fan. There were about eight hundred wounded, for whom arrangements were urgently needed. If they were to send a large unit to control the area northwest of Sung-fan and the route to the north, the rear at Mao-erh-kai would be exposed to enemy raids. They, therefore, had ordered their troops to guard their original positions, taking Mao-erh-kai as their rear, while waiting for further orders from General Headquarters.

It was not until the third day that a radio message arrived from Mao Tse-tung. It said, in general, that owing to the urgent need to seize the initiative, the First and Third armies had gone north ahead of the others and had now reached the area south of Min-hsien. It hoped that General Headquarters would follow the same route north together with the other units. This was the first radio message that we had received from him after the split. But it had not mentioned what future moves he would take or the activities of the enemy in the area. So, we were unable to take action accordingly.

In the light of the situation as we saw it at that time, we considered that the opportunity to move north had vanished. The enemy had had ample time to send troops to guard the strategic points in southern Kansu. Some of the major bridges on the way to the north might have been destroyed by the enemy. We, therefore, made a plan to go south temporarily. We ordered the various military units to make preparations and to put up a show to mislead the enemy. General Headquarters then moved the troops in the direction of A-pa.

Going west through the steppe, we arrived at A-pa without mishap in three days. A-pa, known as the "Ch'eng-tu of the Tibetans," was a well-known town in the southern part of the western steppe and a center for the Tibetans in the area. The great Lamaist temple complex in A-pa was a magnificent sight, with fine, awe-inspiring buildings. On both sides of the main temple there were some smaller Lamaist temples, with nearly a thousand lamaseries and a hundred laymen's lodgings around it, forming a rectangle about the same size as a county seat in the hinterlands.

Nearby, the placid Ta-chin River flowed through a large tract of flat land where ching-ko barley grew on the river banks. Further afield, the vast, beautiful steppe stretched all around. When we arrived, most of the lamas had fled, leaving large quantities of food, which would be enough for our army for several months.

We continued to study the future military plan for our army. A-pa was connected with Hsia-ho in southwest Kansu by a direct route that had Lamaist temples at intervals all along the road. But the easily flooded river posed a problem. It was impossible for us to go north along this route. But since we had come here, we ought to understand something about this vast steppe in preparation for future operations.

Additional information proved that it was not favorable for us to move north at that time. The enemy had come to realize that the Advance Troop led by Mao Tse-tung was but a small part of the Red Army, and inferred that our army would continue to move north subsequently. Troops were dispatched posthaste to strategic points on the border region of Szechwan and Kansu to intercept us. The enemy was trying to cut our army in two and then annihilate each part separately. The main force, however, was concentrated on our section. Meanwhile, some of the enemy troops to our south had gone away, never guessing that we would grasp the opportunity and move south. It was now August. Autumn, with its cool weather, would pose a problem for us of getting warm clothing for our soldiers if we took the northern route.

We consequently decided to go south temporarily. Our plan was to take the enemy by surprise and turn south to the area around T'ien-ch'üan and Lu-shan to the west of Ch'eng-tu, where we could prepare winter clothing for our troops. In case of an unfavorable situation, we could retreat to the Tibetan area in Sikang for the winter. We felt that this would be preferable militarily. Moreover, such an enormous operation to camouflage our real intentions would draw the attention of the enemy to our side and lessen the pressure on the advance force going north. It would also give us a chance to go north during the coming spring and summer.

After staying in A-pa for a few days, we went south to Cho-ko-chi along the Ta-chin River. We were going to hold an important meeting of cadres to discuss the problems within the Party. Hsü Hsiang-ch'ien and Ch'en Ch'ang-hao were ordered to rally their troops around Cho-ko-chi, leaving a small number of them around Mao-erh-kai to check the enemy at Sung-fan. Some of the troops of Tung Chen-t'ang and Lo Ping-hui that had originally been stationed around Cho-ko-chi were dispatched to take the strategic points south of Mao-kung and pave the way for the southern march of our army.

Our march southward from A-pa along the Ta-chin River was quite smooth. The common soldiers were all sure that the further south they went, the better the situation would be. Morale was pretty high. We soon entered the mountainous region of the Ta-chin basin after leaving the steppe of A-pa. The river became a rapid torrent among the high mountains, and we followed the banks of the river in going south. On the flat land along the river, there were usually villages or market towns, where farm products were bought and sold. The region was often hit by hailstorms, which every year destroyed crops. We encountered a few of them while passing through the areas. This was probably one reason why the place was not easily developed.

In a few days we came to Cho-ko-chi. The other major military cadres all arrived on time. Though it was a Tibetan region, there were many Han people living there. Agriculture was better developed than in Mao-erh-kai or A-pa, making it a more suitable place for our army to stay in. The people here got along well with the Red Army, and very few people fled from us. Here I also saw large dance gatherings of the Tibetan people held in the open.

A meeting of senior cadres soon took place in Cho-ko-chi to discuss the schismatic action taken by Mao Tse-tung and the others. About thirty leading military and political comrades assembled in the sitting room of a house in the market town of Cho-ko-chi, their hearts heavy with grief and indignation. First, Ch'en Ch'ang-hao reported on what had happened at Mao-erh-kai. He made it clear that after General Headquarters had moved to Sha-chin-ssu, he and Hsü Hsiang-ch'ien had got on very well with Mao Tse-tung and the other members of the Politburo of the CC of the CCP, discussing with them questions that cropped up and having no disputes with them at all. On the day when Mao Tse-tung and the others fled to the north, they were completely in the dark. The action was abrupt, secret, and perfidious, wrecking the unity of the Party and the Red Army.

After Ch'en, comrades from the Fifth and Twelfth armies who were attending the meeting all spoke up, accusing Mao Tse-tung and the others of taking improper action. They pointed out that the two armies were subordinate to the First Army and had always been informed beforehand about important military operations in the past. However, they were not notified when Mao Tse-tung and the others secretly led the First and Third armies away to the north. They were greatly angered by this action, some pointing out frankly that as leaders of the CC, they should not have taken such a step in violation of the discipline of the Party and the Army.

At the meeting, it was decided unanimously that the schismatic action of Mao Tse-tung and the others was one that had violated the unity of the Party and the unanimity of action of the Red Army. The root of the action lay in defeatism and guerrilla habits, which had led them to degenerate to such an extent. The most indignant accusation pointed out directly that this was an intrigue, selfish, infamous, and immoral—a shameful act never before witnessed in the history of the CCP and the Red Army. The majority declared that they would no longer recognize the original CC, which had lost its credit.

Chu Teh looked depressed throughout the meeting. He regretted the uncalled-for action that had taken place. He said emphatically, "As the case stands, the comrades will not recognize the original CC any longer, but I hope that some room will be left for future negotiations."

Besides giving an account of the main events, I, in my speech, stressed the point that it was impossible for any organization to avoid making some mistakes. We must have confidence that there would be ways to correct the mistakes; the darkness that existed was but a temporary phenomenon. We should not be discouraged by the schismatic action of Mao and the others, but should raise high the banner of communism and strive with still greater confidence. The comrades of the First and Fourth armies would be still more closely united in order to win military victories. At the proper time we would hold a Party congress or an enlarged conference of the Party to reorganize the CC. Meanwhile, the comrades should support the meeting of senior cadres, trust the leadership of General Headquarters, and temporarily accept no orders from the original CC.

The meeting approved two important resolutions. One, which was passed by unanimous vote, concerned the refusal to recognize the original CC and the founding of a provisional CC, with myself as secretary. This resolution ruled that after a suitable interval, a Party congress or conference would be convened to set up a CC officially. It declared that a radio message would be sent to Mao Tse-tung and the others, informing them that although we would no longer accept orders from the original CC, we would cooperate with them in military operations. The other resolution ruled that General Headquarters would be vested with the power to command the whole army in accordance with the decision of the Provisional CC. All army units were to act on the orders of General Headquarters. Li Cho-jan, deputy director of the General Political Department, would be promoted to the post of director, and Liu Po-ch'eng, chief-of-staff, would run the Red Army School concurrently. Hsü Hsiang-ch'ien and Ch'en Ch'ang-hao would lead the troops of the original Fourth Front Army to operate around T'ien-ch'üan and Lu-shan, while Tung Chen-t'ang and Lo Ping-hui would lead their troops to guard the rear in the vicinity of Mao-kung and Cho-ko-chi. It was expected that the new Szechwan-Sikang Soviet region would be set up.

The above passage describes the main process in the split in the CCP. Melancholy recollections overwhelmed me as I recalled how the responsible comrades of the CC of the CCP met with great joy at Mao-kung after long years of separate struggles, but abruptly went their separate ways at Mao-erh-kai. I felt that the main reason for our being forced into such a corner was the die-hard ways of Moscow, plus the errors of the CC of the CCP. In fact, we Chinese Communists, whether together or separated, had always fought to back one another up. Despite our disputes, we relied on each other for our existence. The major issue at stake was life or death, and our main efforts were directed at dealing with the enemy. Under any circumstances, we would not neglect our tasks against the enemy because of internal disputes. Hence, the split was but an episode in the history of the struggle of the CCP.

FROM SPLIT TO UNIFICATION

CHAPTER

In Sikang

The agitation for a split was followed by an urgent demand for unification within the Party. Mao Tse-tung hurried north from Mao-erh-kai. The Cho-ko-chi Conference made everybody who attended it indignant. These two events reflected the climax of the Party split. We, as guerrilla heroes, were awakened by these two events. Everybody's heartfelt cry was "What we need is not a split but unification." Pressure from the enemy forced us to overcome the sorrow and patch up our differences. The Seventh Congress of the Comintern instructed the CCP to take up the campaign for a national united anti-Japanese front and remove the roots of our internal dispute. At that time the Second Front Army under Jen Pi-shih and Ho Lung arrived in the Sikang area after undergoing many hardships. Their linking up with us expedited our internal unification. In the summer of 1936 we moved northward towards Kansu and Shensi from Sikang. At Pao-an in northern Shensi, Party organs and all units of the Red Army united into one body once again.

After the Cho-ko-chi Conference, our main attention shifted to fighting the enemy. We were unwilling to argue about the problem of internal strife, so we did not strengthen the organization and functioning of the provisional CC, which seemed to be merely a name without an organization, without elected members, and without any sanctions imposed on old members. Naturally, such action was taken by the provisional CC in consideration of Chu Teh's suggestion of leaving room for negotiations.

429

Moreover, we felt that the nonrecognition of the former CC and the creation of the provisional CC were only acts of discriminating between right and wrong. The action of appealing for justice was in no way intended to split the Party. It also prevented the members from striving for personal power.

We were busy mobilizing our men to the south. Our current slogan to encourage the men was "Fight our way to T'ien-ch'üan and Lo-shan to eat rice." This slogan was very attractive to our men because we had not eaten rice for more than two months. The slogans of our southward drive were "Removal of All Excess Taxes and Miscellaneous Duties," "Reduction of Farm Rent and Interest Rates," "Equal Distribution of Land," "Cessation of Civil War in Order to Resist Japan," and "Non-aggression and Willingness of the Red Army to Share the Defensive Area with the Szechwan Army." We did not again advocate such things as the establishment of a new Soviet region in western Szechwan or the establishment of the Northwest Federation, as these would not be decided upon until we could lay a firm foundation in the areas of T'ien-ch'üan and Lo-shan.

Units under the command of General Headquarters were still the First and Fourth Front armies. (Although the Central organs and the First and Third armies moved northward, the Twelfth Army and the Fifth Army and about one hundred individuals working in General Headquarters were former members of the First Front Army.) The forthcoming struggles required that we unite. The commander-in-chief at the front, Hsü Hsiang-ch'ien, felt that internal unification was essential if we were to conquer the enemy in the future. He regretted the past split, which had created a barrier in the friendship between members of the First and Fourth Front armies. He also blamed the leaders of the CC for their incompetent guidance and hoped that they would greatly improve their leadership.

We placed Party unification as the first priority in our program of work. We blamed the CC, because in the past, after the linking up of the First and Fourth Front armies, it had only criticized the Fourth Front Army, disregarding its meritorious contributions. The unfairness with regard to reward and punishment caused a friendship barrier between our comrades which, in turn, resulted in the Party split. In the future, we would have to change our customs by praising the efforts and contributions of our comrades, pointing out the brave struggles of both the First and Fourth Front armies in the past, and removing any factional boundary between the two Front armies. We required comrades to learn from each other, to understand each other, and to make friends with each other. If there was any discussion and criticism, it must be motivated by good intentions.

I personally paid special attention to this unification. I had spoken in front of all the cadres of the Fourth Front Army, pointing out the past bravery of the First Front Army to the best of my ability. I told our cadres that the members of the First Front Army had acquired much valuable experience and knowledge and that we should learn from them and treat them as members of our army, so that we would be able to advance hand in hand in future battles. Also, I had made the same sort of speech to the cadres of the new First Front Army; and I had visited leaders of the former First Front Army, including Tung Chen-t'ang and Lo Ping-hui, asking their opinions on military problems and problems within the Party. These efforts more or less resulted in removing the barriers to friendship. For instance, Tung Chen-t'ang seriously expressed his personal view that in the past he had always been considered by the CC as a general who had defected from the KMT and that he didn't seem to be "their own man." Since he would be treated as equal to everyone else in the future, he would dare to take up the responsibility of a real commander in future operations.

Several days later we departed for the south. We set off from Cho-ko-chi, passed Mao-kung, and quickly occupied the county seat of Pao-hsing County. This small county is situated south of Mao-kung, at the exit from the Ta-hsueh Mountains. From Pao-hsing to T'ien-ch'üan and Lo-shan, the terrain is rather flat. In mountainous Szechwan, T'ien-ch'üan and Lo-shan have a vast area of alluvial soil. The land is fertile, while the climate is mild; and rice is abundant in this area.

At that time Szechwan was dominated by the favorite units of Chiang Kai-shek. The Central Army of the KMT, which followed the First Front Army into Szechwan, was distributed at all strategic points. In fighting against these well-equipped troops, we had to, of course, adopt a different attitude from that we used in fighting against the Szechwan Army when we first moved to northern Szechwan. I remembered that when we approached Pao-hsing, we first fought with the Szechwan Army. Immediately after contact, we defeated them in no time. To exploit our success we occupied most of the village areas of T'ien-ch'üan and Lo-shan, while the county seats of these two counties were still in the hands of the Szechwan Army.

During the fighting in this area, Chiang Kai-shek's air force showed itself to be very effective. At dawn, when we advanced towards T'ien-ch'üan, we destroyed all the defensive lines held by the Szechwan Army. We immediately launched a pursuit towards the county seat, following the key route along the ridge. At about nine o'clock, however, enemy airplanes made one raid after another on us, checking our offensive with all-out bombing. We held a conference after that battle, and we discovered that almost every one of our three-hundred-odd casualties resulted from enemy bombing. We also found out that in this battle the position of enemy pillboxes was more effective than it had been before. Apparently this evidence indicated that the enemy was dealing with us in accordance with the experience that he had gained in Kiangsi.

The destruction of enemy aircraft and pillboxes was, in fact, beyond our military power. When fighting with the enemy in Kiangsi, the First Front Army assumed a strategy known as "Cutting off the tortoise's head." Before the arrival of enemy aircraft, the First Front Army took swift action to annihilate those of the enemy that went outside the pillboxes. However, this strategy achieved very few results. Consequently, the Kiangsi Soviet was encircled with pillboxes, and eventually was forced to move westward. Later, Mao Tse-tung criticized this strategy as "erroneous defensive strategy."

We did not expect to commit the same mistake that we had made in the Kiangsi Soviet region; therefore, we decided that our military operations in T'ien-ch'üan and Lo-shan would be only temporary activities. So it would not be necessary for us to establish the Western Szechwan Soviet region, and our primary mission in this area would only be to settle our supply problem. In view of this, we concentrated our maximum manpower and animal power to convey the rice, which we got from the local tyrants, to the mountain area north of Pao-hsing. At the same time we purchased as much cloth and cotton as we could from the nearby markets in order to prepare winter clothing for the men. In case anything happened, we were ready to move back to Mao-kung.

The situation was becoming unfavorable to us. Later, two columns, each containing about three divisions, under Hsueh Yueh and Chou Hun-yuan, respectively, who had spent a very long time fighting the Communists in Kiangsi, assembled in front of us and advanced towards us while taking precautions at every step that they moved. We gained no advantage in fighting with them. It had been our practice to avoid fighting a battle unless we were assured of victory. Furthermore, we were unwilling to involve ourselves in a sustained war. We therefore withdrew to the mountain area north of Pao-hsing, and the enemy did not pursue us. Probably they did not dare take the risk of fighting with us in the mountain area. At the same time they thought that we could be blockaded in the mountains and that we would give up some day when we were out of food. Evidently our campaign to the south achieved no results, so we concluded it in less than one month. This seemed to prove that Mao Tse-tung's statement "Enemy aircraft and artillery are powerful" was right. At that time we held a meeting to critically examine our situation, and everybody accepted the fact that in the military field the enemy possessed an overwhelming superiority. Nevertheless, the area in which we were now located was vast, and there was no way for the enemy to blockade us. The terrain in our area was also very difficult and had no communication routes, so the enemy would never dare to pursue us. Therefore, we felt that it would be safe to stay here for the winter, and we were not afraid of being "turtles in an urn."

In September, 1935, we moved back to Mao-kung and a group of towns that were situated along the west side of the Ta-chin River. These were Tang-pa, Ch'ung-hua, Pa-t'i, and Tan-pa. Under military pressure from us, Liu Wen-hui of the Szechwan Army, formerly located in Tan-pa, fled towards Lo-ting in confusion. Our General Headquarters was located in Tang-pa, near Ch'ung-hua. The enemy east and south of us was about one hundred li away from us and would not threaten us directly.

Our problem was the inadequate supply of food, which aroused resentment from the Tibetans. There had always been a barrier to friendship between the Tibetans and the Chinese, and the Tibetans hated the Chinese intensely for their aggression. Since we had moved to the Tibetan area, there had been several conflicts between the Tibetans northeast of Mao-erh-kai and us. Because we were a foreign tribe in the eyes of the Tibetans, they not only resisted our moving in, but they were also unwilling to share their limited food supply with us. Since we were located in this area for a long time, we competed with the Tibetans for food. This situation became more serious as we continued to stay on. As a matter of fact, our policy was to avoid making trouble with the Tibetans. Therefore, we planned to leave as soon as possible, because we did not like having to consume their food.

To protect their food, the Tibetan chieftains used to assemble several hundred men to resist our "Food-searching team." When we were located in Ch'ung-hua, several conflicts of a similar nature occurred. The Tibetan troops were nothing but an undisciplined mob. While they were easy to assemble and easy to disperse, they could not manage to fight for long.

We never attacked them deliberately; we just watched them, allowing them to disperse of their own accord. We had been trying to explain to the Tibetans that our situation gave us no alternative but to take a small amount of food from them, and that we did not want to put them on the verge of starvation. Of course, this explanation achieved very little, so we took as little food from them as possible. Besides, we moved from place to place in order to minimize the food shortage for the local people.

We were particularly unyielding and resolute, since we were not afraid of any difficulties in searching for a way to survive. Our Soviet movement had failed, and there was an internal split; we were trapped in a remote corner, there was no food to eat, and the resistance of the Tibetans made us feel ashamed. We did not despair, however, but put on a brave front and carried out the training of our men aggressively in order to prepare ourselves for future action.

The Red Army School was our training center, with Ho Wei as commandant and Liu Po-ch'eng as chief instructor. Ho Wei was still convalescing, however, and actually could not attend the school, so Liu Po-ch'eng was entrusted with responsibility for the school. In this school there were around one hundred students, most of whom were company and battalion commanders of the Fourth Front Army, with a few division and corps commanders. Chang Tsung-hsün, Kuo T'ien-min, and T'ang T'ien-chi were important instructors of tactics. Our training principle was joint study for the instructors and the students, emphasizing both theory and practical application. Usually, after a lesson was over, the instructors and the students went to the units located in the vicinity for a practical exercise.

The training requirements of this school were not bad. The instructors were outstanding and appropriate textbooks were available. When we ran the Red Army School in the Oyüwan region, we had no textbooks of our own, so we had to borrow textbooks from the KMT. While it was in Jui-chin, Kiangsi, the CC of the CCP had translated and printed two textbooks published in Moscow—USSR Infantry Drill Regulations and Political Work in the Red Army. After the calamity of the Long March, though, these two books were difficult to find. Fortunately, a lower cadre of the First Front Army had tried as hard as he could to keep one copy of each in good shape. When I discovered them, I read them once and regarded them as treasures. I immediately sent them to be reprinted as textbooks for this school.

The training policy of this school emphasized standardization of the Red Army. Liu Po-ch'eng, the one-eyed general, was an experienced army officer from Szechwan. Both his military knowledge and his experience were regarded as outstanding by our comrades. He was the only cadre of the CCP who was a graduate of the USSR Army College. Since his return to China, he had been chief-of-staff of the Red Army. Therefore he had everything about the Red Army at his fingertips. He had advocated that the Red Army cadres learn the tactics of the regular army while using their guerrilla experience only in coordination with regular-army tactics. In speaking, he was fond of using ironical phrases. Criticizing guerrilla experience was a routine affair for him. There was even a touch of irony in his voice when he spoke to Mao Tse-tung.

Being a professional soldier, Liu Po-ch'eng always set up a hypothetical situation when giving lessons to the students. Assuming that two hostile groups of military units having the same number of men with equipment of the same amount and quality were drawn up in a battle, the victory always belonged to the group that possessed bravery, tenacity, and better tactical application. Actually, nobody can deny that this concept is scientific. It is also in complete accord with dialectical materialism, which is highly recommended by the Communists. However, the Red Army was always in an inferior situation when fighting with the enemy; therefore, the promotion of bravery, tenacity, coordination, and taking the enemy by surprise, in the long run, constituted a kind of "guerrilla concept." Previously, we had emphasized the outstanding function of superior men and small groups in fighting and had disregarded material power.

Eventually the tactical concept of the regular army collided with the guerrilla concept. Yu T'ien-yun, who was a student in the Red Army School, strongly inclined towards the guerrilla concept. He came from a peasant family and was clever but stubborn. Because of distinguished service in battle, he had been promoted from private to platoon, to company, and to division commander, and then to corps commander. He had been a regimental commander for several years, while he had been a division and corps commander for only a short time. Since it required more advanced military knowledge to qualify him for a division and corps commander, he had been transferred to the Red Army School for training. He was the senior cadre who argued with Liu Po-ch'eng and many other instructors on a few tactical problems. Later, the argument developed into an act of violating school discipline. As Yu T'ien-yun's former superior, Commandant Ho Wei stepped in to stop this argument. However, Yu still expressed his disobedience and was confined for a short time as punishment for his disobedience.

Immediately after this event, I went to the Red Army School and held a meeting for all of the comrades. In my speech I pointed out that the comrades should not be satisfied just to know guerrilla tactics, they should seriously learn regular tactics. I particularly commended Liu Po-ch'eng for his military knowledge, and said that most of the comrades and I had to learn from him. I was completely in favor of the speech he delivered in Shua-chin-chih, in which he said that all Red Army cadres had to receive additional military education. In my speech I also made it clear that it was possible to hold free discussion between instructors and students. This had been true in the past, and it would be true in the future. Nevertheless, the students should be humble while they were studying and should not hold fast to their own opinions, so that they would not interfere with their learning and would not violate school discipline, which they should strictly observe. Finally, I told the students that I was in favor of the punishment that the school had given to Yu T'ien-yun, but I asked all of the students to continue to respect him and to help him with his education.

Yu T'ien-yun's case in the Red Army School was considered closed. Actually, most of the instructors and students did not favor Yu's viewpoint. After this case, the students seemed to get along more smoothly with their studies. Some comrades and I tried to comfort Yu T'ien-yun. Although he was unhappy, he did not seem to show signs of dissatisfaction. Later, the Red Army School moved from Tang-pa toward Tan-pa; and on the way to Tan-pa, Yu T'ien-yun committed suicide by jumping from a cliff into the furious current of the Ta-chin River.

All of the cadres were shocked by Yu T'ien-yun's suicide. Some comrades complained about the severe punishment that the school authorities and I had given to Yu, which made him feel that he had been unbearably insulted, while some criticized him for being too stubborn and proud with his strong support of the guerrilla concept. Some comrades even took Yu's case as evidence that the Red Army cadres, especially the cadres of the Fourth Front Army, were filled with a very bad warlord habit. Frankly speaking, Yu T'ien-yun was just another Mao Tse-tung in miniature. Mao Tse-tung is stubborn and proud, has a high regard for power, and achieves his ends regardless of the means. Both insisted on the guerrilla concept, and each of them had an argument about tactical concepts with Liu Po-ch'eng on the same grounds. Both regarded themselves as talented guerrillas and felt that what is sacred cannot be violated. The only difference was that one was a rustic while the other was educated. Consequently, one turned his indignation into suicide, while the other acts in a tyrannous manner by using his deceitfulness. After this unfortunate incident, I delivered a very grave and mournful speech, requesting the comrades to learn an important lesson from this incident. First of all, I bemoaned Yu T'ien-yun's death and praised him for the contribution that he had made to the Red Army in the past. He had been wounded in action several times and had fought for victory in the revolution, regardless of personal sacrifice. Nevertheless, I pointed out that his act of suicide was not right, for Red Army cadres should be able to stand the trials of criticism and punishment. It was not desirable for Red Army cadres to regard life lightly. I repeatedly pointed out that the discipline in the Red Army should be strict and should apply impartially to senior cadres as well. Punishment was only a means of implementing education, it was not an act of insult.

We explored the thinking behind Yu T'ien-yun's suicide. I said that Communists believed that the great majority of the people could be led by a small minority in implementing a revolution, because the minority had the self-confidence to rebuild nature in accordance with nature. From this fundamental idea, many comrades overemphasized the function of the Communist Party in rebuilding nature. More or less, this idea is motivated by subjective reasoning. In the previous history of the Chinese Communists, the blunt action of Ch'ü Ch'iu-pai and the Li Li-san line were reflections of this concept; and especially during the period of guerrilla warfare, Mao Tse-tung, the chairman of the CC of the CCP, was also influenced by this subjective viewpoint. All of the comrades were also under the influence of the guerrilla concept; they thought that individual bravery and strategy could bring about results that were beyond anyone's imagination. Although Yu T'ien-yun did not have the same selfishness as the warlords, he did view himself as a guerrilla hero. Therefore, once he was under criticism, he was unsure of himself, and because of his deep indignation, he committed suicide. The comrades should not take Yu's case as an example to imitate, but as an action to avoid. Today I recall the suicide of Kao Kang in 1955, the cause of which was almost identical to that of Yu T'ien-yun's. At the time of Yu T'ien-yun's death, however, I did not think of, much less did I censure, Yu's suicide as an anti-Party act.

Our educational efforts were conducted in the face of great difficulties. What I have said about Yu T'ien-yun's suicide is quite enough to explain the depth of our problem. I had a thorough discussion with all senior cadres. We thought that we should continue to implement a rigid education, but that the method of education should be improved. In other words, we should not punish the comrades without due consideration. We should be very careful about our explanations and criticism. Also, we should not completely eliminate the guerrilla concept, but should enhance the students' tactical concepts with professional military knowledge.

At that time we thought that we should make use of this rest period to train the cadres in order to increase their knowledge and ability. But we worked too fast. As a matter of fact, the results of training could only be obtained after a longer period of training. Due to the limitations of time, the results of our efforts were, of course, not so good as we had previously expected.

At the end of October, 1935, we crossed the Eternal Snow Mountains (Ta-hseuh Mountains) and arrived in the areas of Tao-fu, Lo-ho, and Kan-tse. Earlier, our troops had been located in the areas of the Ta-chin River valley and Mao-kung for about a month and a half. We had eaten up all the food that we brought from T'ien-ch'üan and Lo-shan. Because the Red Army had been located in the Mao-kung area for about four months altogether, the local food supply was running out. Therefore, we had to move to other places for food. Tao-fu, Lo-ho, and Kan-tse are key towns along the Szechwan-Tibet highway. Population in these towns is rather large compared to other towns in the area, and we estimated that the food in this area could supply our troops all through the winter. It was the end of autumn, and if we had not moved then, we would never have made it through the snowy mountains in winter, when snow falls and blocks all the traffic in these mountains.

We chose a shortcut between Tan-pa and Tao-fu. We left Tan-pa and marched west, taking two days to cross the Ta-hsueh Mountains. At the end of the first day we stopped half-way up the mountains and had to bivouac for the night at the edge of the snowy ground. On the morning of the following day we crossed the peak, which was about seven thousand meters above sea level, and then we descended and found a place to rest in a village at the foot of the mountains. The air was thin over the peak, and while we were crossing it, we had difficulty breathing. We all brought ginger along with us as a kind of medicine for stimulating our hearts. All of the mountains were whitened by snow, and an avalanche could have happened at any moment. Fortunately, we had made full preparations before the march, and we were therefore able to pass through the mountains smoothly.

In this area, Lamaist influence is particularly prominent, especially Yellow Lamaism. In the largest Lamaist temple in Tao-fu there were more than eight hundred lamas. Everywhere on the streets you could see lamas dressed in red robes. In the lamaist temples there were iron-bar lamas (lamas with iron bars in their hands), who maintained discipline in the temples. When they saw iron-bar lamas approaching, the lamas in the streets would disperse immediately. The Lamaist temples and lamaseries are very elegant structures. As if they were in school, the lamas repeat prayers in the temples all year round. Sometimes the lamas look like organized troops. Most of them know how to use weapons, and they customarily carry on organized military activities. The lamas surpass the local populace in knowledge and ability. Agriculture, building construction, and medical care for the people depend on the lamas. The Grand Lama, like Living Buddha Hutukhtu, is both religiously and politically the head of his patriarchate.

Polyandry is prevalent in this area, and the status of women is particularly low. It is customary for the brothers in a Tibetan family to marry the same woman, who has to entertain all of the brothers and maintain a spirit of brotherhood among them. Any case of jealousy, regardless of the reason, is the responsibility of the wife. Women veil themselves when walking in the street, and some of them destroy their beauty by deliberately cutting their faces and then applying charcoal to the spot, allowing the spot to turn into a black scar. The women must stay away from the lamas when walking along the street, otherwise they are considered immoral. It is considered a sin when a young and beautiful woman dares to attract the attention of the lamas. Wives who cause jealousy among their husbands and women who arouse the sexual desire of the lamas are usually sent to a convent, as nuns. On a small hill on the outskirts of the city of Tao-fu there is a well-organized convent which is full of nuns of this type.

The relations between the Tibetans and the Han people along the Tibetan River had been very bad. From the time of the Manchu dynasty to the Chinese Republic, the rulers had traditionally despised the Tibetan tribe. At the time Liu Wen-hui, a Szechwan warlord, was the ruler of Sikang. He fished every possible coin out of the Tibetans. The Chinese who ran businesses in Sikang also made huge profits in every deceitful way. I discussed this matter with some Tibetans and the lamas. Most of them could tell the story of their removal to the mountain area, which was forced on them by the Chinese.

Tibetan culture is low. All year round, the Tibetans wear an oily, unlined fur garment made out of goatskin, which weighs almost thirty pounds. This garment has become one of their daily burdens. It is still a common practice for Tibetans to use knotted cords as a mode of reckoning and recording. Although they have their own language, their vocabulary is not sufficiently large. For example, it is impossible to express a rather complicated idea such as "organization," because there is no such word in the Tibetan language. Perhaps the closest idea to "organization" is the phrase "one heart and one mind."

Since we were living in that area, we had to get along with the local people and gain their understanding and cooperation insofar as possible. Under our supervision, the autonomous governments of the Tibetan tribe were organized in many places, although most of the autonomous governments were merely empty names. All the same, the Tibetans did not fully understand the Red Army. To them we were just a hateful tribe that came to rob them of their food, but at the same time we treated them kindly and peacefully. This surprised them, and they could not understand it. The Living Buddha of Kan-tse was the divinity for this vast area. He expressed his viewpoint to us: "If the situation of the Red Army were to improve, it would not be as bad as Liu Wen-hui. But now that the Red Army is in a state of poverty, its action in searching for food and other supplies is worse than that of Liu Wen-hui." This statement of the Living Buddha accurately depicted the true situation of the Red Army in that area.

During our stay in Sikang—from November 1, 1935, to June, 1936—there was no fighting on the front. Liu Wen-hui's unit in Sikang, which opposed us, was separated by the Che-to Mountains; so we did not interfere with each other. Our troops spread westward to the left bank of the Chin-sha River, while the smaller Tibetan forces of the Dalai Lama, a British-trained force, were located on the right bank of the river. These two forces also did not fire on each other. Chiang Kai-shek and Liu Wen-hui had used a few Tibetans to organize a guerrilla force in an attempt to harass our troops. However, these Tibetans, who were used by Chiang and Liu, were considered traitors by their own people, and it was therefore difficult for them to accomplish their mission. After we made a series of attacks, they disappeared. There were other sporadic cases of resistance on the part of the Tibetans, but we managed to settle the troubles through political channels.

We still concentrated our efforts on training our troops. Our main objective was to enable all of our men to understand the situation in the Northwest and the tactics to be used against cavalry attacks. We thought that we might stay in the Sikang area for a long time. To solve our food problems, we would have to spend more time on agricultural production. In so doing, however, we would turn our combat units into an agricultural force, and this would make us abandon our mission as leaders of the national revolution. Of course, that was not what we wanted to do. In accordance with our policy, we were supposed to advance westward and seize the corridor of Kansu west of the Yellow River and Sinkiang, thus constituting a wing of the Red Army in northern Shensi. Therefore, our training was conducted with this objective in mind.

At this time we promoted a project of "Cultural Recreation" among our units, which was mainly the contribution of the political workers of the former First Front Army. The First Front Army developed around the revolutionary center in the areas of Hunan, Kwangtung, and Kiangsi, south of the Yangtze Valley. More intellectuals joined this army, and therefore their "cultural recreation" work was also more developed.[1] By then our General Headquarters was located in a Lamaist temple in Lo-ho. There was a piece of open ground in front of headquarters. In charge of the cultural recreation project was a woman comrade named Li Po-chao, a returned student from Russia who was then Director of Cultural Recreation in the Political Department, and she often led cultural recreation teams to perform there. Chu Teh, myself, and others frequently joined the soldiers at these entertainments. The short plays, dances, and songs in their shows not only boosted the morale of the soldiers at that time, but even now they bring back fond memories as I recall the past.

The main struggle in our daily lives was still against nature. The climate here was very cold; cloth and cotton were in pitifully short supply, but abundant wool was there for the taking. Over the year shops, warehouses, and lamaseries had been piled full of wool, mostly unprocessed, which could not be sold due to transportation problems. Our soldiers kept themselves busy processing the wool, spinning it into coarse thread, and knitting it into garments and socks. During the months of November and December, 1935, our army almost turned into woolen textile factories, and not much later all our uniforms were made of woolen textiles of various colors, with white predominating. We encouraged the soldiers by sponsoring competitions and exhibitions to show off their efforts. This solved our winter clothing problem beautifully.

The problem of food took even more energy from us. The local ching-ko barley was mostly in our control; we established a ration system, encouraged thrift, and opposed waste. On most days the ching-ko barley ration was one catty per person. The butchering of cattle was under stricter control—the use of dried beef was promoted, so that one steer could supply a company for a week. Food-processing facilities were scarce, so our army took turns with the Tibetans in processing the barley, with the result that sometimes the soldiers had to boil raw barley for their meal.

This area was extremely short on vegetables. The vegetable output was not even sufficient to supply the needs of the Tibetans. While we were there, our diet usually included barley, beef, and cheese, but no vegetables. This was really a serious problem in our food supply. Fortunately, there was a kind of tuberose plant growing wild everywhere, known as the ginseng fruit (it was probably the kind of fruit that the Pig ate in the Chinese book entitled *The Westward Adventures*, or *Hsi Yu-chi*). Since it could be used for food, a competition was instituted to encourage the men to search and dig for the ginseng fruit. One man could usually dig ten catties or more of it per day. The record was fifty catties. When the ginseng fruit was mixed with ching-ko barley in a dish, it was very delicious and nutritious. But since we had a great number of men who were digging it every day, this wild plant soon became more and more scarce. We also encouraged the men to hunt and fish for food. But the Tibetans were very superstitious and usually showed signs of unhappiness when they saw us fish and hunt, destroying the animal life.

Between the spring and summer of 1936 we even organized a wild-vegetable committee. The mission of this committee was to search for edible food among the wild plants that grew all over the mountains. There were more than twenty members of this committee, with Chu Teh as chairman. Other members were experienced farmers and herbalists. Among the wild plants they discovered twenty-two kinds of wild vegetables that could be used for food. This solved our dire need for chlorophyl! On one occasion the committee judged a certain wild plant to be edible, and it was tasted by a few men before it was distributed to everyone to eat. But the men who tasted this plant became unconscious and were revived only after being given immediate medical treatment. In the twentieth century, this ancient method of finding out if a wild plant was edible by having a human mouth taste it seemed ridiculous; but the spirit behind the method was still admirable.

A backward country is liable to be threatened by diseases. The more backward the country, the more serious this situation becomes. The Tibetans were unable to protect themselves from diseases. At times, all of the people in a village would be killed by a certain kind of disease.

Imposition of a severe quarantine was the only method they used to deal with human beings and animals that were affected by a disease. Usually a patient was put in an isolation house, and even his family did not attempt to visit him. They only brought him food and water when it was time to eat. The food and water were placed in a basket that hung on one end of a long pole. The basket was extended to the patient through a little opening in the isolation house. The patient had to pick up the food by himself. Whether or not a patient was able to recover depended on his personal resistance to the disease. If he died, his family cremated him, along with the isolation house. If there was an infectious disease in a certain village, all the villagers would evacuate that village. This method of quarantine constituted a special moral code. In other words, it was considered immoral if people were unwilling to leave or forsake a patient, or if people were willing to stay on to look after the patient. Ignoring a patient was what everybody should do.

When we were in this area of the Tibetan tribe, we were seriously threatened by typhoid fever. A great number of our men were affected for a long time. From the time that the First and Fourth Front armies linked up at Mao-kung until we finally left the area of Sikang, this disease had been our faithful companion. Fortunately, we strictly observed sanitary routines and controlled the infectious rate of typhoid fever; thus we were able to avoid any large-scale epidemics. Dr. Fu Lien-chang, who had formerly been a doctor in a Christian hospital of Changchow in Fukien, contributed greatly to the prevention and cure of typhoid fever. In the plateau region, air is thin and fuel is in short supply. We were usually unable to bring water to a boil at 100° C, consequently, we could not kill the germs in the water. Dr. Fu believed that unclean drinking water was one of the main causes of typhoid and other diseases; so in accordance with his instructions, we placed a bellows by the side of the stove to increase the intensity of the fire so that water could be boiled. By so doing, we were able not only to reduce the spread of typhoid, but also to reduce other diseases.

We also lacked medicine, so we could not combat typhoid fever that way. However, Dr. Fu did cure a lot of patients by the Chinese herb method. After that, Dr. Fu, who had previously ignored the Chinese herb method, began to be interested in that method of treating patients. Later he wrote an article in a leading medical magazine in Shanghai, explaining how he had cured about 90 percent of the typhoid sufferers through the use of the Chinese herb method. At present Dr. Fu is a vice-director of the Medical Board of the Chinese Communist government, and he is specially keen about promoting the simultaneous use of the Chinese herb method and the Western method in treating patients.

Over one hundred men were victims of typhoid fever. A few of them were cadres at regimental and divisional levels. One of the victims, Comrade Tsai, was an expert at radio monitoring. An educated youth, clever and resolute, Comrade Tsai had come from the province of Fukien. From the time that we were in the Oyüwan region, he had had responsibility for radio monitoring. During his tenure of duty, he had contributed greatly to the Red Army. He was not only my colleague, but also a close personal friend. Needless to say, I was very moved by his death in the sense of losing a friend, and I felt even worse over losing an expert at radio monitoring.

The Anti-Japanese National United Front

In early 1936, Lin Yu-ying, Chinese Communist representative to the International Labor Union in Russia, returned to northern Shensi from Moscow, bringing with him the new policy of the Anti-Japanese National United Front, transmitting the main outline of the resolution passed at the Seventh Congress of the Comintern and reestablishing contact between the Comintern and the CC of the CCP.

Although our Chinese Communist leaders had wrangled over conflicting opinions, while the action of the Red Army was also divided into two parts, the relations between our two groups did not continue to deteriorate. After the Cho-ko-chi Conference, Mao Tse-tung and his generals received our radio messages informing them of the activation of a provisional CC, but Mao did not show any emotional expression. After that, we tried to avoid the use of wording that was unacceptable to each other when exchanging messages, and we refrained from mentioning any previous conflicts. The new telegraphic code, which we arranged when we met, worked out safely and reliably. Based on our new code, we exchanged information of the current situation in sincere wording, and the messages between us were transmitted smoothly. Probably, the sufferings and misfortune that had resulted from the split brought both of us closer and made us more amicable.

When Mao Tse-tung led the First and Third armies northward from Mao-erh-kai, he had a little more than ten thousand men (the First and Third armies and the organs of the Central government totaled about seventy-five hundred men, in addition to the four replacement regiments from the Fourth Front Army), but he suffered heavy losses from enemy attacks along the way. On October 20, 1936, Mao Tse-tung linked up with Hsü Hai-tung and Liu Tzu-tan, who had formerly been located in northern Shensi, in the vicinity of Wa-yao-pao. At that time there were fewer than four thousand men left in the First and Third armies.[2]

After arriving in northern Shensi, Mao Tse-tung and his generals radioed us several times, describing their current situation. Although their messages sometimes contained exaggerations and dissimulation, the difficulties, hardships, and heavy casualties that they experienced were apparent in the words. We radioed them, comforting them and congratulating them on successfully linking up with the Red Army of northern Shensi. We also told them about the sufferings and hardships that we had been encountering. Their reply also expressed their feelings of mutual understanding and encouragement.

Immediately after his arrival in northern Shensi, Lin Yu-ying sent me a radio message, which read roughly as follows:[3] "In July, 1935, Wang Ming and I participated in the Seventh Congress of the Comintern. On the China problem, the Congress passed the new policy of an Anti-Japanese National United Front. I was ordered to go by way of Mongolia to look for the Red Army, and I arrived in northern Shensi on such and such a date with a copy of a secret code, thus accomplishing my first mission. I planned to continue my journey to the Sikang area from northern Shensi in an attempt to meet you and other comrades. Because of transportation difficulties, I do not know whether or not my plan will succeed."

I was ecstatic when I received this wire. I replied immediately, expressing my appreciation for his plan, asking him to stay in northern Shensi temporarily so as to avoid the danger of being attacked by the enemy on the way, and advising him to discuss all problems through coded communications. An educated youth from Hupeh Province, Comrade Lin Yu-ying was an uncle of Lin Piao. Lin Yu-ying and his younger brother, Lin Yü-nan, had once thrown in their lot with me. When he joined the CCP in 1922, he worked with me in the labor movement. He also worked in a factory in Hankow. In 1933 he attended the international meeting of Communist labor unions in Moscow as representative of the Chinese labor union. Later he became a member of the delegation of the CC of the CCP in Moscow. For security reasons he appeared under the assumed name of Chang Hao after returning to northern Shensi.

Lin Yu-ying's messages reached me regularly, informing us of changes in the course of the Comintern's new policy and bringing up measures necessary for unification within the Party. Reporting on the change in policy by the Seventh Congress of the Comintern, Lin Yu-ying pointed out that it was necessitated by changes in the international situation, the rise of Hitler being the main reason. Therefore, the Comintern hastily changed its former policy. Now, the Comintern summoned the Communist Party and other anti-Fascist parties throughout the world and people of every nation to unite together and organize an "Anti-Fascist United Front," or a "People's Front." This People's Front would require the Communist Party in each country to institute a certain form of cooperation with the anti-Fascist capitalist class and even the anti-Fascist government in that country. Even if this cooperation were not very stable, it was urgently needed for the current struggle against the Fascists.

Furthermore, Lin Yu-ying pointed out that the Comintern considered China to be under active aggression from Japan. Therefore, the Chinese Communist should contact all of the people of China, including the anti-Japanese capitalist class, anti-Japanese troops, and the anti-Japanese political parties, to constitute a people's nationwide anti-Japanese united front. Lin explained everything connected with this to me in detail. He also informed us of the main point of the "August First Declaration" through radio messages. His main idea was to explain that the people's anti-Japanese united front was to replace the former Soviet movement. Now, our main slogans were no longer "Down with Chiang Kai-shek," "Soviet," and "Land Revolution." Our slogan was no longer even "Oppose Chiang and Resist the Japanese," but was changed to "Unite with Chiang and Resist the Japanese," "Resist Japanese Coalition Government," and "Everything for Resisting the Japanese." The main object of the People's United Front was to unite all anti-Japanese power in China so as to oppose the Japanese aggression and the traitors.

At that time Lin Yu-ying's messages gave us the impression that the whole world seemed to have changed overnight. The Comintern's directive required the Chinese Communists to effect a complete change in their policy. Lin's message mentioned that Mao Tse-tung and the comrades in northern Shensi had agreed to the new directive and that if we also agreed to the new instruction, the Chinese Communists would start their activities on the basis of this new policy.

We were very excited about this latest news, and we unanimously favored this new policy. In the development of Chinese communism, this new policy seemed to be "another new way of survival for the Chinese Communists when reduced to circumstances of extreme necessity." A few of us wondered about the policy of "Unite with Chiang and Resist the Japanese." We thought that there was very little chance that this policy would work, while most of the comrades felt that other leaders of the Fourth Front Army and I apparently had foreseen the future. The Program upon Entering Szechwan and the establishment of the Northwest Federation, which we had once suggested, and the dispute over the Soviet movement at Mao-erh-kai proved that what we thought was right. Some said that if this news of the Comintern's change in policy had reached China earlier than it did, there would have been no dispute at Mao-erh-kai. Some even felt that since northern Shensi had secured this information earlier than we had, they must have remained in contact with the Comintern, so it was better for us to forget about the past and the question of who was right and who was wrong. Unification was our urgent need at the moment.

At that time many feelings crowded in upon me. I supported this new policy from the bottom of my heart, for I felt that this new policy agreed in principle with what I had independently decided. There was no longer a future for the Soviet movement, so this change in policy was appropriate and timely. I sighed over all the misfortune that the Chinese Communists had encountered. Earlier the Chinese Communists had advocated a united front based on democracy.[4] Later, as a result of the Comintern directive, the Chinese Communists had changed their policy by uniting with the KMT. That was an illogical turn to the Right, which resulted in catastrophe. But immediately afterwards we took a sharp turn to the Left, heading towards the Soviet road and ending in another catastrophe. Now we were returned to our starting point, which was a historical irony and our bitter grief.

After careful study, we replied to Lin Yu-ying, expressing our unanimous and warm support for this new policy and asking him to inform the Comintern that plans were being prepared for carrying out the new policy. So that we could promote this new policy in coordination with our comrades in northern Shensi, we did not mention the previous dispute in our wire. Our biggest doubt about this new policy was whether or not it would be possible for us to unite with Chiang to resist the Japanese. We presumed that by this time there must be some improvement in diplomatic relations between Nanking and Moscow. Hence the statement "Unite with Chiang and Resist the Japanese." Being unwilling to show the slightest doubt about the new policy, we did not even question this point.

In view of the unanimity of political viewpoint throughout the Party, Lin Yu-ying answered us by radio, suggesting certain measures for

Party unification and pointing out that although the previous dispute at Mao-erh-kai and the subsequent idea of two Chinese CC's were unfortunate, he considered that the situation had been unavoidable until the Soviet policy was changed. Now it was not wise to argue about the past; we should take immediate steps to seek to unify the Party. The comrades in northern Shensi had agreed to his suggestion. Henceforth, neither CC would issue orders to the opposite side. Lin was temporarily a liaison official between the two sides; his mission, based on this new policy, was to coordinate the activities of both sides closely.

Lin Yu-ying also explained that it was the decision of the Seventh Congress of the Comintern not to interfere any longer in the organizational problems of Communist parties in other countries. The internal affairs of the Communist Party in each country would be settled by the CC in that country. The Comintern would only give supervision on policy making. In view of this resolution, he held that we ourselves should find the means to resolve the internal dispute of the CCP and the leadership problem of the CC. So he made the above-mentioned proposal. He sincerely hoped that both sides would make a good showing of their ability to resolve their own problems in connection with this issue.

The Party in northern Shensi, in a radio message signed by Chang Wen-t'ien, expressed agreement with Comrade Lin Yu-ying's proposal. I, too, sent an answering message, expressing my approval and saying, among other things, that as we were now forming an alliance of all forces to resist Japan, it was of paramount importance to achieve internal unity. We certainly must not talk of alliance with outsiders while concentrating on internal struggles and neglecting democracy within the Party. Lin Yu-ying sent us several wires in which he mentioned the great admiration of the Chinese and foreign comrades in Moscow for our spirit of hard struggle and his extreme delight in our ending the present internal dissension. Then, in a formal resolution, the comrades in northern Shensi and we agreed that Comrade Lin Yu-ying would be our liaison agent and that both sides would launch activities in line with the new policy. A Party congress to resolve all problems would be convened at some later date, when an appropriate occasion arose.

The most important point in Lin Yu-ying's later wires to us was Moscow's directive on our plan to advance westward. He said that our plan for the Red Army in the Szechwan and Sikang area to fight its way out to Sinkiang had been approved by Stalin, who had held that if the Chinese Red Army was able to get control of Sinkiang and the region west of the Yellow River in Kansu, the Soviet Union would give it the necessary supply of arms and would help train it and make it into a mighty force. Therefore, Lin Yu-ying expressed the view that we should take action as soon as possible. As to the advance westward, we were to decide on it in the light of the military situation.

This good news conveyed by Lin Yu-ying greatly encouraged us. In our conjecture about the motives behind Stalin's approval of this plan to advance westward, we felt that one of the most important was to avoid conflict with Chiang Kai-shek and to realize the alliance with Chiang and resistance to Japan. We also felt that it would take time to heal the wound caused by the past internal strife of the Party; if we could realize our plan to advance westward, we would, for the time being, maintain a certain distance between ourselves and the comrades in northern Shensi. Gradually time would wash away the alienation that had once existed between us. Therefore, we prepared to go west in accordance with our military plan.

In their initial implementation of the policies of resistance to Japan and formation of a national united front, the comrades in northern Shensi found their mate in the person of Chang Hsueh-liang rather than Chiang Kai-shek. As a result, there were some changes in the policy of the CCP. In other words, the original policy of "Unite with Chiang and Resist the Japanese" became one of "Unite with Chang, Oppose Chiang, and Resist the Japanese."

At that time we were in Sikang. Our attention naturally focused on the power-holders in the Southwest. Sneaking past Kang-ting by various means, we began to lobby militarists in Szechwan and Yunnan, persuading them to unite and resist the foreign aggression from Japan. However, our efforts were to no avail. They were either rendered futile or found no response. On the other hand, the Party in northern Shensi managed to find Chang Hsueh-liang, a military leader of great importance. This development in the situation placed me in an inferior position within the Party.

A wire sent to us by the comrades in northern Shensi in January, 1936, reported that in a battle with Chang Hsueh-liang's troops, they had captured Wan Yi, a regimental commander of Chang's troops, whom they treated like an honored guest, and to whom, in line with the new policy, they gave a vigorous exposition on the significance of alliance and resistance to Japan. Finally Wan Yi was impressed. He pledged that he would return to Sian and beg Young Marshal Chang to stop fighting the

Communists and, together with them, to resist Japan. Now that Wan Yi had been released and had returned to Sian, it was hoped that there might be some results.

A miracle indeed occurred. The activities of Wan Yi brought about a change in the stagnant situation which had persisted despite their various but futile efforts. After a while, another radiotelegram from northern Shensi reported that a letter had been received from Wan Yi, which said that as a result of his persistent persuasion, Chang Hsueh-liang had promised to consider the question of ceasing to fight the Communists. Wan asked the comrades in northern Shensi to send someone to Sian as soon as possible for negotiations with Chang Hsueh-liang. The northern Shensi representatives had already set out for Sian in secrecy.[5]

In our radiotelegram in reply, we approved of their actions, although we pointed out that it was necessary to maintain contacts with various sources and pay attention to the aides of Chang Hsueh-liang, among whom were many diverse elements, including those who were pro-Japanese. We also repeated information about our former relationship with Yang Hu-ch'eng, the names of go-betweens, and how reliable they were.

In subsequent radiotelegrams from northern Shensi, reports were given on negotiations with Chang Hsueh-liang. They mainly pointed out that Chang Hsueh-liang had made progress and was really sincere in his desire to resist Japan. The subordinates of Chang Hsueh-liang could be divided into two groups, the old and the new. The former were conservative and unwilling to resist Japan; there were even some who had had dealings with Japan. The new group (in the midst of which was Wan Yi) was extremely enthusiastic about resistance to Japan. Hostile towards the Japanese for having killed his father, and oppressed by Chiang Kai-shek, Chang Hsueh-liang fully trusted the new group. He very much wished to get rid of Chiang's control over him; yet he regarded contacting the CCP with fear in his heart. He was afraid that the secret might leak out. All of which showed that Chang himself was to be trusted.

The comrades in northern Shensi were of the opinion that Chang Hsueh-liang should be taken as our only contact; all contacts with other militarists should be conducted through him. This was safer and would help to allay any worries that Chang might have. As an example of Chang's concern, the radiotelegrams referred to Chang's question about whether we had made any contacts with Yang Hu-ch'eng. Our representative said that Chang was our one and only contact, and denied any contact with Yang Hu-ch'eng. Chang Hsueh-liang was very pleased when he heard this. He said that he was able to cope with everything, including making contacts with military men in Szechwan. He asked us not to contact them directly. The aim of this radiotelegram was, naturally, to tell us not to try to influence the Szechwan military men any more; for the time being we should not inform Chang of any contacts that we had made or were planning to make with Yang Hu-ch'eng.

The relationship between the northern Shensi comrades and Chang Hsueh-liang became closer and closer with each passing day. According to radiotelegrams from northern Shensi, Chang Hsueh-liang planned to confront Chiang Kai-shek, using the Northwest as a base. He held that it was impossible to "Unite with Chiang to Resist Japan," that it was necessary to create a situation in which the Northwest would single-handedly resist Japan. Only by "Opposing Chiang and Resisting Japan" could there be a promising future. He put a high value on the possibility of contacting the Soviet Union through us, expecting, in this way, to get actual aid from the Soviet Union. He did not attach much importance to the strength of the Chinese Red Army, thinking that it would not play a big role in "Opposing Chiang and Resisting Japan." He asked that the Red Army now in the Szechwan and Sikang area march to the Northwest as soon as possible, without meddling with the Szechwan military men any longer.

In May, 1936, an alliance between the northern Shensi comrades and Chang Hsueh-liang was secretly established. The northern Shensi comrades informed us by a radiotelegram that they had decided to forge a situation of resistance to Japan in the Northwest together with Chang Hsueh-liang (referring to the Northwest Anti-Japanese Coalition Government). They pointed out that Chang was tainted with heroism. He advocated equal emphasis on resistance to Japan and opposition to Chiang, intending to become the only anti-Japanese leader. The northern Shensi comrades felt that there was ample opportunity for taking advantage of Chang's ambition. They supposed that Moscow would approve of this if some achievements could be scored in the anti-Japanese situation in the Northwest. Moreover, with the CCP in the plight that it was, there was no other choice but to take this road.

We felt that this policy was tainted with opportunism. It was difficult to say whether it would lead to victory, but there was no harm in trying it so long as it was beneficial to the existence and development of the Red Army. We sent a radiotelegram in reply, expressing our approval. We also pointed out that it was necessary to have a clear-cut program that included the policies of the CCP. Secondly, it was necessary to regard the Northwest Anti-Japanese Coalition as only a force to launch resistance to Japan, avoiding, as far as possible, large-scale civil war. Besides, we should concentrate mainly on strengthening our own forces and fight our way to Sinkiang, opening up a through road there. In this way, we would be in an invincible position. The northern Shensi comrades soon answered in a radiotelegram expressing acceptance of our ideas. This was the initial step in the campaign to "Unite with Chang, Oppose Chiang, and Resist Japan."

In June, 1936, the Second Front Army of Ho Lung and the Sixth Army of Hsiao K'o joined up with us in the Sikang area. They had been isolated to the south of the Yangtze River, having lost touch with both us and the Party in northern Shensi. It was only from enemy information that they learned that the majority of the Red Army had been moving towards the Northwest. They then advanced towards northwestern Yunnan from the border regions of Hunan, Hupeh, Szechwan, and Kweichow. The circling movement they made towards the north was even bigger than that of the First Front Army. The attacks that they suffered at the hands of enemy armies and the dangers and difficulties that they encountered on the way were really amazing.

We had focused our attention all along on the movements of the troops of Ho Lung and Hsiao K'o and had tried to help them by various means, as we had done for the First Front Army. In April, 1936, we learned from enemy intelligence that they were advancing towards Ta-li in Yunnan. We inferred that they were trying to approach us along the Ya-lung River. General Headquarters, therefore, sent several forces to the border between Sikang and Yunnan to receive them. The two armies finally met in the region south of Lei-po.

The great jubilation aroused by the meeting of the Fourth and Second Front armies in Lei-po was comparable to that aroused by the meeting in Mao-kung the year before. The troops sent by General Headquarters had thwarted pursuit of the Second Front Army from the east and the south by the troops of Yunnan's Lu Han and Szechwan's Liu Wen-hui. The Second Front Army was thus enabled to advance slowly northward and to move to places around Ya-chiang and Hsin-lung for some respite. In the opinion of ordinary comrades of the Second Front Army, the Fourth Front Army had fully displayed its solicitude and concern during the time of adversity.

At that time the troops of Ho Lung and Hsiao K'o were combined under the single title of Second Front Army. The original Second Front Army had Ho Lung as commander and Hsia Hsi as political commissar.

Hsia Hsi had drowned on the way to Yunnan. The Sixth Army originally was under the command of Hsiao K'o, with Jen Pi-shih as political commissar. These two forces had about twenty thousand men to start with. When they arrived in the Sikang area, about five thousand remained. After the death of Hsia Hsi, they combined to form one army, with Ho Lung as commander-in-chief of the Second Front Army as before, Hsiao K'o as deputy commander, Jen Pi-shih as political commissar, and Kuan Hsiang-ying, originally director of the political department of the Second Front Army, concurrently as deputy political commissar. Since the number of men had decreased, the army was cut down to three divisions.

Having had a taste of the unpleasant experience in the convergence of the armies at Mao-kung, we were particularly cautious this time. We showed our mutual concern, but refrained from picking at each other's faults. Moreover, the two armies were stationed in places quite far apart from each other. There were no warm get-togethers, so naturally there were fewer chances for conflict.

The central figure in the leadership of the Second Front Army was Jen Pi-shih, who had been elected a member of the CC at the Sixth Congress of the CCP, and later had been promoted to the Politburo. He had previously been secretary of the CC of the CYC after his return from Russia. In 1927 he had been well known because of his support of the Comintern and his opposition to Ch'en Tu-hsiu. He had formerly been imbued with the spirit of youth, but now he appeared quite old after all of his trials and tribulations. He had grown a scraggly beard, and I laughingly called him "Bearded Jen," instead of "Little Brother," as I had before. There was not a trace of the bandit in Ho Lung; instead, he appeared to be a well-disciplined Communist soldier, leaving everything in the hands of Jen Pi-shih. Commander Hsiao K'o, on the other hand, looked like a scholar and inclined to frequent grumbling, but he did not hold on to his views stubbornly. Kuan Hsiang-ying was also a youngster from the CYC who had not lost much of his youthful spirit. However, he did not speak unless an important question arose.

We had a happy reunion at Lo-ho, and all of us were friendly and kind to one another. The ordinary cadres of the Second Front Army, however, harbored some misunderstanding about or even blamed the First Front Army for leaving Kiangsi. They were particularly dissatisfied with the past leadership of Hsia Hsi, who, being one the "28 Bolsheviks," had conducted the suppression of counterrevolutionaries in a big way in the Second Front Army and had killed some good comrades by mistake. Some comrades regarded this as one of the "good deeds" of the CC after it went under the control of those who had returned from Russia. The ordinary cadres of the Second Front Army were also much concerned about all that had happened after the convergence of the First and Fourth Front armies. We felt, however, that it was inadvisable to talk too much about these past events. We should make our future plans in accordance with the new policy.

Jen Pi-shih and the others were informed about the new policy the CCP had adopted—the policy of a national united front and resistance to Japan. They studied the radiotelegrams exchanged between us and the northern Shensi comrades and came to understand the current situation and the process of turning from "Unite with Chiang and Resist Japan" to "Unite with Chang, Oppose Chiang, and Resist Japan." At first Jen Pi-shih was somewhat embarrassed by these changes. He felt that he had opposed the idea advocated by Ch'en Tu-hsiu and was now going back onto the old road of the Ch'en Tu-hsiu epoch. However, he soon decided that he should accept this policy unconditionally, as it was the decision of the Comintern. As to the alliance set up by the northern Shensi comrades with Chang Hsueh-liang, he held that the CCP must take only unanimous steps. Generally speaking, the comrades of the Second Front Army joined us after the complete change in policy. Everything would be all right so long as they expressed support for the new policy.

Jen Pi-shih himself was particularly interested in the Mao-erh-kai dispute. He spent a lot of time talking to Chu Teh, Hsü Hsiang-ch'ien, Ch'en Ch'ang-hao, Liu Po-ch'eng, and me to collect relevant data and find out the cause of the dispute. I asked him jokingly if he wanted to act in the role of Pao Cheng, the Judge.[6] He did not wholly deny this. He said that as one who had not been a participant in this dispute he might be able to do something for the reconciliation of all parties concerned if he made some investigations now.

The conclusions that Jen Pi-shih drew as a result of his investigations, as he told me later, included the following points: 1. The Fourth Front Army was sincere in its plans to assist the First Front Army; it could not be said that the comrades of the Fourth Front Army had had tendencies to oppose the CC from an early date. 2. Both sides had harbored prejudices, which were first made public in the article by K'ai Feng. 3. Most of the criticisms leveled at one another by the First and Fourth Front armies were unnecessary and unfair. 4. Before the change in the political line, the Mao-erh-kai dispute was understandable. 5. It was not proper for Mao Tse-tung and the others to lead the First and Third armies to the north without notifying me, Chu Teh, and the others. However, he felt that the outbreak of the dispute was attributable to the excessive suspicion and jealousy of Mao Tse-tung and others, on the one hand, and the voices of opposition from the Fourth Front Army on the other. These voices of opposition had aggravated the suspicion and jealousy. 6. The conference at Cho-ko-chi went too far when it decided to set up a Provisional CC.

Jen Pi-shih noted that this was a serious lesson that everybody should take to heart. In the future, we should let sleeping dogs lie. He decided to be a self-appointed conciliator, trying to bring harmony to all concerned without being partial to either side. I was grateful for his enthusiasm, but I was noncommittal at that time about his opinions. Later, when we were in northern Shensi, we did not see each other, and I did not hear him express any dissatisfaction with me. Perhaps his words were deemed inappropriate by the comrades in northern Shensi and he had no opportunity to make any more attempts.

The exhausted Second Front Army had by now had a month's rest. It was urgent to implement the plan to go northwest, so we decided that all of the troops would start north. According to our plan, the Second Front Army, under Liu Po-ch'eng, Jen Pi-shih, and Ho Lung, and the army under Lo Ping-hui would follow the route to the right, going through Min-hsien and Ching-ning in southern Kansu to the region around Hai-yüan in northern Kansu. General Headquarters would lead the original Fourth Front Army and the army under Tung Chen-t'ang to seize the Ho-hsi Corridor in Kansu by taking the route to the left, passing through Min-hsien, Lung-hsi, and Tung-wei, and then turning west.

Militarily the above operational plan aimed at occupying a vast region in the Northwest, with the Red Army of northern Shensi forming the Right Column and the Fourth Front Army, after its occupation of the Ho-hsi Corridor, forming the Left Column; the Second Front Army, after its arrival in northern Kansu would be in the zone between the two columns. Politically, this would increase our assets in the alliance with Chang Hsueh-liang. The Red Army would no longer be confined to a small patch of land in northern Shensi, but would have northern and western Kansu in its hands.. This would not only provide security for Chang Hsueh-liang's rear, but would also pave the way for making a breakthrough to reach the Soviet Union.

The comrades in northern Shensi approved of this military plan of ours. They had tried to hurry us all along, as if without our forces as capital, the anti-Japanese situation in the Northwest would not materialize. The comrades of the Second and Fourth Front armies were also satisfied with the plan. As for the Second Front Army, achieving a position in the middle would enable it to act as a bridge both militarily and politically. The comrades of the Fourth Front Army, too, felt that the Ho-hsi Corridor, being a pivotal route in the communications system of the Northwest, would be just the place for us to make a good showing of ourselves. Moreover, as the troops would not be crowded into the same place as the First Front Army, any likely conflicts could be avoided.

However, as future events evolved, this plan was never translated into reality. This was a defeat for the Fourth Front Army as well as for me.

The March to the North

In July, 1936, we started to implement the above-mentioned military plan. Owing to subsequent developments in military operations, the Second Front Army and a part of the Fourth Front Army (the Fourth and Thirty-first armies) turned toward northern Shensi, while another part of the Fourth Front Army (the Ninth and Thirtieth armies), together with the Fifth Army Corps of Tung Chen-t'ang, reached the Ho-hsi Corridor in Kansu. There, however, they were defeated by the cavalry of Ma Pu-fang, and the troops that remained fled to Sinkiang.

Everything went smoothly on our march out of the region of the Tibetans from Lo-ho and Kan-tze. The Right Column, led by Liu Po-ch'eng, Ho Lung, and Jen Pi-shih, went east to Mao-erh-kai and then turned north to Min-hsien in Kansu. Since Hu Tsung-nan's troops, originally stationed in Sung-fan, had withdrawn to T'ien-shui, the Right Column advanced without any obstructions. General Headquarters, together with the Left Column, went east, passing through Sha-chin-ssu and the Upper and Lower Pao-tso, and headed for Min-hsien. The weather was fine at that time. We had no difficulty in climbing the snowy mountains and crossing the steppe land. No one lagged behind. The river that blocked our way the year before could now be forded, as the water was below our knees. "How things change!"—this was the thought in our minds as we waded across the river.

Our main slogan for this military operation was "Go North to Resist Japan." With this slogan we hoped to persuade the armies stationed along the way not to hinder us, but to join us in resisting foreign aggression, all pointing our guns toward the foreign enemy. Our propaganda was mostly theoretical. Since we were unaware of them, we could not use as propaganda such materials as the aggression of the Japanese army in North China and Inner Mongolia, the flourishing anti-Japanese movement that was prevailing in all parts of the country, and activities in countries all over the world expressing sympathy towards China. For the Red Army itself, however, slogans played the role of morale boosters.

The comrades in northern Shensi were extremely excited about our march to the north. Every day they sent us radiotelegrams of an optimistic nature, which generally included such contents as:

1. The anti-Japanese situation in the Northwest would soon materialize. Both Yang Hu-ch'eng and Chang Hsueh-liang had agreed tacitly that they would act when the time came; their troops and other units that sympathized with resistance to Japan would not actually fight against us.

2. At present there were fewer of Chiang Kai-shek's own troops in the Northwest, so it was possible for us to advance boldly without any hindrance.

3. Information about the various documents on resistance to Japan issued to the whole nation by the comrades in northern Shensi were relayed to us, implying that the formation of the Northwest Anti-Japanese Coalition government was at hand.

By August our army had come out of the mountainous region and the steppe to the southwest of Min-hsien. The whole army rejoiced at having come to the vicinity of Min-hsien, which was a relatively prosperous region in southern Kansu that had populous market towns and villages. Our men, who were tired of their daily fare of ching-ko barley and beef, were particularly happy now that flour and vegetables were available in abundance. Moreover, enemy defense in a surrounding area of several hundred li was rather poor. The units of Lu Chi-chang that were stationed in Min-hsien, not being Chiang's own troops, could only guard the city with their weak combat forces. Hu Tsung-nan's troops stationed in T'ien-shui were checked by our troops in the Right Column. As a result, some of our men began to have the idea of staying in this place.

General Headquarters was still implementing the original plan of westward advance. The advance troops led by Ch'en Ch'ang-hao had once unsuccessfully attacked Min-hsien, incurring some four hundred casualties and using large quantities of ammunition. Later, they passed through Tung-wei and occupied the county seat of Hui-ning. They also sent reconnaissance units to look for fording points around Ching-yüan to the northeast of Lanchow. The main forces under Hsü Hsiang-ch'ien were stationed at Tung-wei to keep watch on the enemy in T'ien-shui. General Headquarters was stationed in the vicinity of Min-hsien, directly commanding an army which was advancing towards Lin-t'an and the region to the north, in order to look for fording places southwest of Lanchow.

At this point Ch'en Ch'ang-hao proposed to change the whole military plan. He advocated that our army should stay in the southern Kansu region. He made a special trip from the Hui-ning front to talk over the problem with me personally at General Headquarters. Consequently, our military operations were delayed for about two weeks.

Influenced by optimistic radiotelegrams from northern Shensi, Ch'en Ch'ang-hao overestimated the anti-Japanese situation in the Northwest and underestimated Chiang Kai-shek's ability to control the Northwest and his determination to fight the Communists. Therefore, Ch'en proposed that the Fourth Front Army set up a new base in southern Kansu, occupying the opposite corner of the Northwest from the Soviet region of northern Shensi so that we could support one another. He was particularly worried about the political situation inside the Party. He pointed out that northern Shensi had the upper hand politically, since it was in touch with Moscow and was about to form the Northwest Anti-Japanese Coalition government with Chang Hsueh-liang and Yang Hu-ch'eng. He, therefore, proposed to call a conference of senior cadres to decide on the principle of having the Red Fourth Front Army set up a base in southern Kansu. He also wanted me to rush to northern Shensi for the purpose of resolving the dispute within the Party so that Moscow might not discriminate against the Fourth Front Army and a suitable position might be given to it inside the CCP and in the future Northwest Anti-Japanese Coalition government.

This was the first time that a difference of views arose between me and Ch'en Ch'ang-hao in the course of our cooperation. It was naturally a brain-racking affair, as it developed at such a critical moment. He was evidently preyed upon by conflicting emotions. On the one hand, he respected me very much and valued dearly our close cooperation over the years. On the other hand, he noticed my discontent with the Comintern, which was the one thing he had wanted to avoid. He pointed out that I might be correct in my foresight concerning the error of the Soviet policy, but from the point of view of Moscow, it inevitably meant a lack of faith in the Comintern; and this would affect the future of the Fourth Front Army. I was of the opinion that discussion of changes in the military plan would retard our operations, but I still promised to go with him to Tung-wei to convene a conference of senior cadres.

At the time when we proceeded from Min-hsien to Tung-wei for the conference, signs appeared that were not altogether optimistic for the military situation. The troops in the Right Column suffered some losses when they were attacked by Hu Tsung-nan's troops during their march north through the neighborhood of T'ien-shui. They then retreated towards the area north of Ching-ning. As a result, we were open to attack on the east. According to our intelligence reports, the enemy troops under Hu Tsung-nan, Chu Shao-liang, Kuan Lin-cheng, Mao Ping-wen, and others were moving west towards T'ien-shui and P'ing-liang under Chiang Kai-shek's strict orders that our army was to be blocked and attacked as soon as possible in order to prevent us from meeting with the Red Army in northern Shensi.

Under these circumstances, in studying the military plan, the Tung-wei Conference held that it was inadvisable to stay in the southern Kansu region. We noted that as Chiang Kai-shek could transfer ten or more divisions of his own troops to Kansu, it was doubtful if the Northwest Anti-Japanese Coalition government could materialize. If we were to stay in southern Kansu, we might be forced to retreat to Mao-erh-kai or thereabouts under unfavorable conditions. With the slogan "Resist Japan" on our lips, our morale would be affected if we retreated further south. Meanwhile, if we broke through the enemy's encirclement and advanced towards northern Shensi, our way might be blocked by the enemy and we might be attacked. Besides, if all the Red armies crowded into northern Shensi, which was already short of food, enemy troops would be tempted to concentrate their forces to beseige us. This, of course, would be still more unfavorable to us.

Confronted with such a situation, Ch'en Ch'ang-hao retracted his proposal of setting up a base in southern Kansu. He held that we should rapidly cross the river at Ching-yüan and move west, in accordance with the original plan. All participants at the conference were quite pleased with Ch'en's swift acceptance of their opinion, but the majority of the cadres were discontented with Ch'en's impulsive proposals. They criticized him for his arbitrary decision to attack Min-hsien, an action that had caused great losses to the Ninth Army—an action, moreover, that violated the original military plan. Then he had stopped his troops from advancing and demanded that a conference be held, causing delays in the crossing of the river. This incident broke the harmony among the senior cadres and laid the roots for the defeat of the troops in the Left Column.

Concerning the resolution of the dispute within the Party, the majority among us held that I must not go to northern Shensi at that time. They thought that I should concentrate my energy on the execution of the military plan to move west. There was still time to discuss the Party dispute. Regarding this, I had made a statement to the effect that by going to northern Shensi on my own initiative, I would demonstrate my sincerity about working for internal unity. Once the plan to advance west was put into effect smoothly, I was resolved to do so. In the statement I also noted that there was no longer a confrontation between the two CC's, since the Comintern had been informed that we had approved the new strategy of the anti-Japanese national united front, and it had endorsed our plan to go west. If the Fourth Front Army was able to find a footing in the Ho-hsi Corridor, Moscow would support us in accordance with the original resolution and would not regard us as elements that opposed the Comintern.

The overnight conference held at the suggestion of Ch'en Ch'ang-hao came to a relatively satisfactory conclusion, despite much discussion and explanations about many matters. We then launched a propaganda campaign throughout the Army, pointing out that it was correct and suitable and timely for it to move west. Politically, if we occupied the Ho-hsi Corridor and the Sinkiang region, the rear of the future Northwest Anti-Japanese Coalition government would be protected and the route of contact with the Soviet Union would be kept open. Militarily, it was possible to disperse the forces of Chiang Kai-shek, whose troops in Kansu would be menaced by us from three points—the Ho-hsi Corridor, northern Shensi, and Sian. Our current tasks were to cross the river as soon as possible, to study ways of dealing with cavalry tactics, and to establish a friendly relationship with the Moslem people.

Our military operation resumed. Our troops stationed in the vicinity of Min-hsien gathered in Hui-ning, while the troops originally stationed in Hui-ning moved forward to take the county seat of Ching-yüan, thus putting a section of the Yellow River bank under their control. Acting simultaneously for our benefit, P'eng Te-huai led his troops to occupy the area around T'ung-hsin-cheng and Hai-yüan in northern Kansu, while the Fifteenth Army of Hsü Hai-tung advanced to the Ta-la-ch'ih area. Only a two days' journey separated Ta-la-ch'ih and Hui-ning. Our messengers came and went frequently, to everybody's great excitement.

Ching-yüan was an excellent place for crossing the river, but we lacked the means of transport, which were boats made of ox hide, as was the custom in this part of the Yellow River. As a result, the crossing was not accomplished as rapidly as we had wished. The troops of Yu Hsueh-chung under Chang Hsueh-liang that were then stationed in Lanchow had not attacked us. There were no enemy units on the west bank of the river. However, the river was devoid of ox-hide rowboats, and timber for making boats was not to be found anywhere in or around Ching-yüan. We tore down some buildings in Hui-ning, and by man-power we took the timber thus obtained to Ching-yüan, where boats were to be made out of it.

Our crossing operation in Ching-yüan was discovered by Chiang Kai-shek, who sent airplanes to bomb the fording place and gave strict orders for his troops to march to Hui-ning and Ching-yüan as fast as possible, trying to catch our army in the midst of crossing. Handicapped by the lack of means to cross the river and the need to take precautions against enemy bombing, only about a thousand men were able to cross the river each night. At that time, the Left Column consisted of about thirty-five thousand men. In three weeks some twenty thousand managed to cross over, including the Ninth and Thirtieth armies, the Fifth Army Corps, and officers directly subordinate to General Headquarters and the Command Headquarters of Hsü Hsiang-ch'ien and Ch'en Ch'ang-hao. On the highway between Hui-ning and Ching-yüan, resisting the pursuing enemies in battle after battle, were the Fourth and Thirty-first armies, a majority of the students of the Red Army School, and some staff officers of General Headquarters, led by Chu Teh and me.

As the enemy forces increased, their attacks from various sides became more frequent. Finally, the positions that we had on the high-way between Hui-ning and Ching-yüan to cover the crossing were all taken by enemy troops. Another enemy unit occupied the town of Ching-yüan and controlled the fording place, making it completely impossible for us to cross the river. Chu Teh and I then ordered the Fourth and the Thirty-first armies to move to an area northeast of the highway, taking the Ta-la-ch'ih area where Hsü Hai-tung's troops were stationed as our rear. Thus, our plan to go west was not completely realized. Hsü Hsiang-ch'ien and Ch'en Ch'ang-hao started independent actions on the west bank of the Yellow River, leading the various units that had crossed the river.

Chu Teh, I, and others met Hsü Hai-tung at the end of September, 1936, in a castlelike building in Ta-la-ch'ih. This old comrade-in-arms, whom I had not seen for four years, was as ingenuous and charming as ever. As soon as he saw me, he embraced me in great joy, as if reuniting with his mother. Though it was the first time he had met Chu Teh, he showed great affection towards him, as if he were an old friend of many years' standing. Both Chu Teh and I were very happy. I was so moved that I did not know what to say. I simply laughed and laughed, holding his hand in mine. In a moment the comrades from Hsü Hai-tung's army headquarters and the officers and men all came and stood around us, asking about what had happened since our separation. The scene was like a joyful reunion of a big family.

In discussing the current military situation with Hsü Hai-tung, we told him that the crossing had been captured by the enemy and that the Fourth and Thirty-first armies were in urgent need of crossing the Yellow River from Tou-cheng-pao and places north of it. We asked him to send his men there as soon as possible to survey the terrain, the condition of the enemy, the means of crossing, and so forth. We also asked him to keep watch over the area facing Hui-ning and Ching-yüan, taking strict precautions against enemy attack. General Headquarters was going to stay in Ta-la-ch'ih for a while to prepare for the crossing.

The reconnaissance made by Hsü Hai-tung's men showed that it was no longer possible for us to cross the river, as Tou-cheng-pao had been occupied and enemy planes were searching along the river, which was devoid of any means of crossing. Meanwhile, an enemy unit under Hu Tsung-nan was marching towards Wu-wei from Lanchow along the Kansu-Sinkiang highway. The cavalry troops of Ma Pu-fang were also moving north from Si-ning. All these operations aimed at blocking our way to the west. Apart from this, the enemy to our south was nearing the front comprising Ta-la-ch'ih, Hai-yüan, T'ung-hsin-cheng, and Yu-wang in an attempt to annihilate our troops on the east bank of the river.

In a radiotelegram to us, Hsü Hsiang-ch'ien and Ch'en Ch'ang-hao expressed hope that we would continue with the crossing of the river. On the one hand, they dispatched the Ninth Army to cover the advance of General Headquarters' organs toward Ku-lang, while they themselves led the Thirtieth Army and the Fifth Army Corps north to occupy positions along the river in the area of I-t'iao-shan and Ching-t'ai, so as to cover us at the crossing in Shih-fu-ssu.

In view of the current situation, we told Hsü and Ch'en in a radiotelegram that it was impossible for us to cross the river. We asked them to act independently with the troops that had already crossed the river. We pointed out that because of the enemy pressing in on us and the lack of means of transport, there was indeed no time for the Fourth and Thirty-first armies to cross the river in safety. If they still lingered on the river bank, they would lose their foothold for either advance or retreat. We advised them to take rapid action and lead all the troops to occupy the area around Wu-wei and Ku-lang. They should concentrate their forces to control the Kansu-Sinkiang highway, taking suitable places west of Wu-wei as their rear. As to General Headquarters, it would hold a large part of the enemy in check with the Fourth and Thirty-first armies and the troops under P'eng Te-huai and Hsü Hai-tung, so as to ease the pressure on the troops in the West Wing (that is, the troops under Hsü Hsiang-ch'ien and Ch'en Ch'ang-hao).

Henceforth, the troops in the West Wing under Hsü and Ch'en went their separate way. Following the orders that we radioed to them, they went from Ching-t'ai along the Great Wall to Tu-men-tzu, north of Ku-lang, and headed directly for Wu-wei. We ourselves, under enemy pressure, gradually moved eastward from Ta-la-ch'ih, Hai-tung, and T'ung-hsin-cheng, approaching the Soviet region of northern Shensi.

For two weeks in Ta-la-ch'ih, we mainly resorted to guerrilla activities to check the enemy forces. Amidst busy military operations, I still found time to chat with my old friend Hsü Hai-tung and others about events of the past. According to Hsü Hai-tung, the Fifteenth Army now under him had only three regiments, which posed as three divisions. There were about five hundred or more men in each regiment, totaling less than two thousand, with about thirteen hundred guns. Among the soldiers in the entire Fifteenth Army, there were very few men from Oyüwan; the majority were replacements from Shensi and Kansu. However, most of the military cadres were old comrades-in-arms from Oyü-wan, while the political cadres were, by and large, transfers from the First Front Army. Hsü felt that his troops were now only good for guerrilla operations, which avoided strong enemies and chose to meet the weaker ones. For fighting regular battles, the Army could only be regarded as one regiment.

The story of Hsü Hai-tung's struggles was a typical heroic epic of a Red soldier. The difficulties and dangers he had experienced in his struggles from the time he started out from Oyüwan to the present moment were greater than those we had encountered. It is a pity that I cannot recall all the details of his account. He described the hard fighting that had been waged until their last breaths by many old comrades-in-arms, such as Shen Tse-min, Wang P'ing-chang, Hsü Li-ch'ing, and others, after our departure from the Oyüwan region in August, 1932. Cheng Wei-san, Kao Ching-t'ing, Kuo Shu-shen, and others, however, stayed on to wage guerrilla warfare, and it was impossible to tell whether they were still alive there. He also gave many accounts of enemy atrocities in the Oyüwan region. It was with great reluctance that he had left that enchanting base to go west.

The savagery of the enemy's killing reached its greatest height in the Oyüwan region. According to historical data that the CCP has now made public, two hundred thousand people were killed in that region, topping all other regions. This was verified in Snow's interview with Hsü Hai-tung.[7] I have heard many accounts of enemy atrocities in the Soviet regions, including those perpetrated in the Soviet region in northern Szechwan, where after our departure many "10,000-man pits" were constructed. Yet, compared with those in the Oyüwan region, they were Lilliputian beside Brobdingnagian. The KMT then in power might have thought that killing would stop further killing. In fact, those who did too many cruel deeds would finally perish themselves, as our ancients had wisely counseled.

Hsü Hai-tung said that he had been encouraged to come west by the news of our expansion in northern Szechwan. In 1933, enemy intelligence reports often mentioned the widespread activities of the Red Fourth Front Army in northern Szechwan. Hsü Hai-tung was immensely pleased with that information. He then began to have the idea of coming west with his men to look for us. In the summer of 1934 he started the westward march with some two thousand men, waving the banner of the Twenty-seventh Red Army. Having crossed the Peking-Hankow Railway, the Army dashed on westward, fighting many, many big and small battles on the way. After arriving in Shensi, it launched operations around the Ching-ling Range. By then more than half of the Army was destroyed, and its store of ammunition was practically exhausted. At times the men had to go hungry, while sleeping in the open was a common occurrence. As the road to northern Szechwan was blocked by enemy troops, the Army had no way out but to cross the Wei River to northern Shensi to seek expansion.

Before Hsü Hai-tung and the others came to northern Shensi, they had thought that it was a notorious lair of bandits, so they were surprised to find upon arrival that the Communist Party and the Red Army were there. Very soon, they met the guerrilla troops of Liu Tzu-tan, Kao Kang, and others. Since enemy pressure lessened, they stayed on in northern Shensi. The guerrilla regions in northern Shensi were rather scattered. The two main areas were one at Shen-mu and Fu-ku and one at Pao-an, Ching-pien, and An-pien. After 1927 some veteran Shensi comrades had escaped to these remote places to stir up the local bandits and to launch guerrilla warfare. They all seemed very backward, as they were ignorant of the statutes of the Soviet and the Red Army. The elements among the guerrillas there were very complicated. In addition to Communist Party members, there were bandits and non-Communist intellectuals.

The Twenty-seventh Red Army carried out the experiences of the Oyüwan region after its arrival in the guerrilla region of northern Shensi, bringing about considerable development in the Red Army and the Soviet region. Its reputation and power were enhanced immensely. Tai Chi-ying and Nieh Hung-chün,[8] seeing the diverse elements of the guerrilla troops in northern Shensi, were anxious to set up a firmer foundation. They started rectification campaigns and purges in a big way. Many comrades from northern Shensi were labeled as local bandits or counter-revolutionaries. Some were killed, others were locked up, and still others were released after trials. Hsü Hai-tung felt that Tai and Nieh were overdoing things. They were too impulsive, acting blindly without fully taking into consideration the backwardness of northern Shensi. The purges brought a sense of uneasiness to the minds of comrades of northern Shensi, who thought that veteran Red Army soldiers from the Oyü-wan region were oppressing the local people.

Hsü expressed great admiration for Mao, who corrected Tai's and Nieh's mistakes as soon as he arrived in Shensi. He said that Chairman Mao and others, after the 25,000-li Long March, were quite exhausted when they led the Northern Advance Force into Shensi; but most comrades trusted the CC deeply all along and showed great respect when Chairman Mao's name was mentioned. Chairman Mao and other high-ranking CC officials quickly corrected the errors of Tai and Nieh and released the imprisoned Kao Kang and others. An appeal was sent out for all comrades—no matter whether they were from Kiangsi, from Oyüwan, or from northern Shensi—to unite together. A new atmosphere prevailed in the northern Shensi area.

Hsü Hai-tung talked about the development of the anti-Japanese united front after the coming of Lin Yu-ying. Hsü was optimistic about solidarity within the Party. Just as he did when he was in the Oyüwan region, he affectionately called me Chairman and expressed trust in me. He vigorously refuted the rumors that I had opposed the CC because of a desire for personal power and position. However, he was particularly concerned about Party unity. He held that unity would be the way to life, while dissension would be the way to death. He sincerely wished that I would go to Pao-an to shake hands with Mao and the others and talk amicably with them. He held that such a move would greatly boost the morale of the troops at the front.

These words from Hsü Hai-tung, an artless soldier, were an expression of real emotion. They were not only honest, but were also very moving. Similarly, I felt that the purges carried out by Tai and Nieh were excessive and that it was proper for Mao Tse-tung and others to try to correct the mistakes. Besides this, I also told Hsü Hai-tung that I would exert myself concerning Party unity.

By that time the enemy from the Shensi-Kansu highway had occupied the county seat of Hai-yüan. In order to avoid being encircled by enemy troops, we retreated eastward towards the town of T'ung-hsin-cheng. Northern Kansu was thinly populated and had shortages of both food and drinking water. The river water there contained some minerals, which made it bitter and unpotable. The people stored snow in cisterns to be used as drinking water throughout the year. Our men soon used up all the water that the people had stored up. This was another reason why it was impossible for us to stay long in northern Kansu.

In a big courtyard in T'ung-hsin-cheng the troops led by Chu Teh and me again met those led by P'eng Te-huai. We stayed in the same place for two or three days. P'eng Te-huai was then commander-in-chief at the front, commanding all of the Red armies in northern Shensi. To the south of the Soviet region of northern Shensi, a state of truce existed between our troops and those of Chang Hsueh-liang and Yang Hu-ch'eng. Therefore, P'eng was able to lead all troops of the Red Army in northern Shensi to act in coordination with us for our benefit over a wide area of the province.

This was the first time that P'eng Te-huai and I worked together. I felt that he was a soldier with rich fighting experience and political aspirations. In dealing with military matters, he was bright and shrewd, manifesting stubbornness and self-confidence. He liked to talk about politics. He had great expectations for the anti-Japanese situation in the Northwest, speaking with relish about how he captured, coddled, and finally convinced Wan Yi. He seemed to imply that he had done a great deal to shape the current situation in the Northwest. Both of us apparently avoided the topic of the Mao-erh-kai incident on purpose, which kept the atmosphere of our talks from becoming genuinely friendly.

When Mao Tse-tung and the others heard of our retreat to the town of T'ung-hsin-cheng from Ta-la-ch'ih, they informed us by radiotelegram that the main body of Hu Tsung-nan's troops was advancing towards Yu-wang County from the south, attempting to attack the rear at T'ung-hsin-cheng. They advocated that our army leave T'ung-hsin-cheng and assemble around Shan-cheng-pao, Hung-te, and Ho-lian-wan, so as to annihilate the intruding enemy troops in the area east of Yu-wang. They also sent Chou En-lai to Hung-te posthaste in order to welcome us and hold consultations with us on the campaign. In an answering radiotelegram we expressed our approval of the plan and immediately moved the whole army towards the town of Hung-te.

At the junction of the main road in the market town of Ho-lian-wan, Chu Teh and I shook hands with Chou En-lai, the "welcome ambasssador" from Pao-an, and we chatted amicably. Chou En-lai was a participant in the negotiations in Yen-an with Chang Hsueh-liang on the anti-Japanese situation in the Northwest. Upon seeing him, we naturally talked about this. He made no affirmative move concerning the formation of the Northwest Anti-Japanese Coalition government, as this depended on Chang Hsueh-liang. At present Chiang Kai-shek's own troops were concentrating on the Shensi-Kansu highway and in the region of northeastern Kansu in order to deal with us. This situation was naturally unfavorable to Chang Hsueh-liang. It was doubtful whether Chang could launch anything under the circumstances.

However, Chou En-lai's analysis of Chang's enthusiasm for resistance to Japan was relatively plausible. He held that Wan Yi, acting as the go-between, only played the role of promoting contact between Chang and us. The background to Chang's determination to resist Japan was Japan's ever-increasing aggression. The Young Marshal had gone through tragic sufferings. His father, who was known for his pro-Japanese sympathy, was murdered by the Japanese, while he himself was driven away from the Northeast. Then he became the scapegoat for others, being abused as the "unresisting general." Despite his title of deputy commander for combating the "bandits," he was discriminated against by Chiang Kai-shek, who seemed to be keen on having Chang's asset—the Northeast Army—wiped out during the battles against the "bandits." All this compelled Chang Hsueh-liang to follow the road of resistance to Japan, and fanned his hatred for Chiang Kai-shek.

Chou En-lai felt that the situation in China had undergone some changes in recent years. The patriotism of the Chinese people had been aroused by the rabid aggression of Japan. Witness the Young Marshal, who, together with his father, was openly considered to be pro-Japanese, since he had carried on much treacherous and pro-Japanese monkey business against the country's interests. They were both sworn enemies of the Communists, having murdered Li Ta-chao and other comrades.

Under the manipulations of imperialism, they had always been anti-Soviet and had even launched a war against the Soviet Union. We used to think that Chang Hsueh-liang was an even more evil reactionary than Chiang Kai-shek. Now, he had been driven into a blind alley by the Japanese bandits, and he had to turn around and join the Communists and the Soviet Union. This would have been totally unimaginable in the past. The militarists in the Southwest, including Li Tsung-jen, Pai Ch'ung-hsi, and Ch'en Chi-tang, also opposed Nanking in the name of resistance to Japan. Even within the Nanking government itself there were people who were inclined to resist Japan.

Chou En-lai went on to stress that we must not look at Chang Hsueh-liang and the Northeast Army in the same light as in the past. He pointed out that Chang Hsueh-liang in the past had been an opium-smoking dandy; now he was energetic and full of promise. The people from the Northeast all wanted to fight their way back to their old home, and the Northeast Army was one that embodied this aspiration. The great majority of the young officers in the Northeast Army were enthusiastic and anti-Japanese. Young people from the Northeast, particularly students of Northeast University, had rallied in Sian, singing the song of the refugees in heart-rending tones. Chang Hsueh-liang himself had become the bugler for resistance to Japan by the Northeast Army and the North-easterners. The pro-Japanese elements in the Northeast Army had lost their influence. Veteran commanders such as Wang Yi-che were supporting the younger soldiers in resisting Japan. Even the more conservative ones such as Ho Chu-kuo and Yu Hsueh-chung followed suit.

Chou En-lai said that during his negotiations with Chang Hsueh-liang, the latter had been frank and sincere in his attitude. Chang proposed that we take as the basis of our alliance the eight words "Stop Fighting the Communists, Resist the Japanese Unanimously." As to the concept of "the anti-Japanese situation in the Northwest," the idea was rather vague, without a clear-cut program or concrete proposals. Even the name "Northwest Anti-Japanese Coalition Government" was only a proposal from our side. Chang Hsueh-liang was noncommittal about it. Chou, however, believed that Chang would be able to build up connections with the forces in Shansi, Szechwan, Kwangtung, and Kwangsi, and that he would draw up a plan in accordance with the suggestions from all sides. For instance, Chang Hsueh-liang and Yang Hu-ch'eng were in the same place at that time, which could easily lead to conflict, yet they were coping with the situation wonderfully well and were able to act in unanimity. This could serve as a remarkable example.

Since I first entered the Oyüwan region in 1931, it had already been five and one-half years, during which time I had continously been fighting guerrilla warfare in remote areas, completely cut off from the outside world. With the passing of time, I had become a rustic, isolated and uninformed. From remote Pao-an, Chou En-lai had seen sunlight through the small window of Sian. Although what he knew was scanty and what he told us was more or less abstract ideas, we could still feel that the world had really changed, and he had definitely felt the first wind of the change. I had better hurry to study, shaking off immediately the dust of guerrilla fighting to don the robe of the intellectual to cope with the needs of urban life.

At this juncture, signs of defeat in the West Wing had become apparent. While we were in T'ung-hsin-cheng we had received radio-telegrams from Hsü Hsiang-ch'ien and Ch'en Ch'ang-hao, saying that our Ninth Army had been attacked by the cavalry troops of Ma Pu-fang in Ku-lang and had suffered heavy losses, amounting to some one thousand casualties. They stated that the reason for the defeat was their commanders' lack of familiarity with the tactics of cavalry. The main force of the Ninth Army was located on the high land on both sides of Ku-lang County; the defense works on the main road were not strong enough, while the defending forces were rather weak. As a result, the enemy cavalry was able to dash into the roads of Ku-lang County, wreaking havoc upon the organs directly subordinate to the General Headquarters of the West Wing troops. Casualties among staff officers and intelligence personnel were very heavy. The radio equipment for reconnaissance and other telecommunication installations were practically all scattered and lost. Thus the West Wing troops lost their eyes, ears, and part of their nervous system, which were indispensable in fighting.

When we arrived at Ho-lian-wan, urgent radiotelegrams reporting the critical situation streamed in from the West Wing troops. They contained mainly information on repeated attacks from every side by the troops of Ma Pu-fang, who were encouraged by the victory at Ku-lang. It was practically impossible for our troops to defend themselves. The rapid mobility of the cavalry outweighed our superiority as guerrilla specialists. The brigade led by Yang Teng-wen under Hu Tsung-nan occupied the important military base of Wu-wei ahead of us, blocking our way to the west. Our West Wing troops were trying to bypass Wu-wei and proceed via footpaths along the mountain to the region west of Wu-wei in an attempt to occupy Yung-ch'ang, Shan-tan, Chang-yeh, and so forth. Hsü Hsiang-ch'ien, Ch'en Ch'ang-hao, and the others

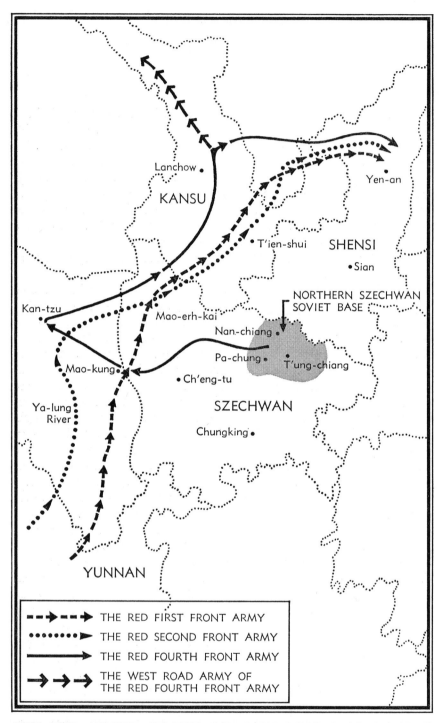

THE RED ARMIES OF THE CCP JOIN FORCES AT SHENPEI
(YEN-AN), ARRIVING AT DIFFERENT TIMES

expected us to supply them constantly with military intelligence (as they had lost their own reconnaissance radio station) and, if possible, with other military assistance.

We were very worried about the situation of the troops in the West Wing. I had discussed the matter again and again with Chu Teh and Chou En-lai, but we could not think of ways to help them effectively. Ma Pu-fang had pledged his allegiance to Chiang Kai-shek and could not be influenced by us through Chang Hsueh-liang. Militarily, we had our hands full and were unable to help the West Wing troops. All we could do was to stay on temporarily in Ho-lian-wan and supply them with the necessary intelligence by switching our communications radio station into one for reconnaissance. We also radioed to the reconnaissance radio station of the Pao-an Military Affairs Committee, asking it to supply as many intelligence reports as possible to the West Wing troops.

The military situation on our side was also very serious. When our army retreated to Shan-cheng-pao from T'ung-hsin-cheng via Yu-wang County, the main force of the First Army of Hu Tsung-nan was chasing us from behind and was now pressing on to Shan-cheng-pao. Our strategy was to strengthen our defense and hide all supplies, in the hope that the enemy would not stay long for lack of food. We guessed that the enemy was trying to occupy Shan-cheng-pao, Ho-lian-wan, Hung-te, Huan-hsien, Chu-tzu-chen, and Ch'ing-yang, which constituted the grain-producing area for the Soviet region of northern Shensi. We naturally had to stay here to check the enemy, preventing them from realizing their goal; otherwise, even Pao-an would be menaced.

The area around Ho-lian-wan, from the point of view of the Soviet region in northern Shensi, was a relatively prosperous district. Actually, it was thinly populated and its grain production was limited. It was not easy for the area to supply our large army for any length of time. Although the river water here was not bitter, the place was still part of the loess plateau. In the villages, which were few and far between, millet was the main food crop, while sheep were the chief livestock. The job of transportation was mostly done by mules. Most of our comrades noted that grain production in this place was inferior to that of the Sikang region. Some even surmised that if all of us had come to northern Shensi from Mao-erh-kai in the first place, cases of death from hunger would have resulted sooner.

We resisted Hu Tsung-nan's troops for nearly a month in the region around Ho-lian-wan and Shan-cheng-pao. The enemy finally had to retreat to Yu-wang because of the shortage of food. Taking advantage of the situation, our army attacked them while they were retreating, cutting off a section from their tail, capturing more than one thousand men and guns. The fighting at Ho-lien-wan thus came to a close. Chou En-lai told Chang Hsueh-liang about this victory in a radiotelegram, which perhaps more or less influenced the Sian Incident that broke out soon afterward.

Chou En-lai had done the most for the victory of this battle. He was well informed about local conditions and took charge of the job of strengthening the defense and hiding supplies from the enemy. He organized the transportation of food to the front for our troops, sometimes from places several hundred li away, relying on his adept manipulation of man and animal power. At the same time he organized guerrilla troops and Red Guard teams to launch activities in areas close to the enemy, shipping out all the grain available and depriving the enemy of man and animal power, thus putting the enemy into a tight position about supplies. It was chiefly due to this that the enemy was forced to retreat in the direction of Yu-wang, which, being near the main line of highway traffic, would facilitate the acquisition of supplies.

Soon after the conclusion of the current campaign, I, along with Chu Teh and Chou En-lai, held meetings to review the situation. As a result of my proposal, Chu Teh and I were to lead the students of the Red Army School to Pao-an, where we would hold talks with Mao Tse-tung and the others on future tasks. The troops at the front, including the Fourth and Thirty-first armies under us, would be temporarily put under the command of P'eng Te-huai. From then on, General Headquarters could no longer directly command the troops. Chou En-lai, however, had to go to the various counties to see to matters that would be taken care of after the campaign. Then he would proceed to Pao-an.

Henceforth, all of the Red armies were again combined into one. Concerning this, I made a report to the students of the Red Army School, answering some of the questions they had raised. In my speech, I reviewed the development of the anti-Japanese national united front and the misfortune of the West Wing troops. I also spoke about the process of establishing unity within the Party. I explained that my going to Pao-an was prompted mainly by the desire to promote unity within the Party, and to secure a supply of intelligence reports for the West Wing troops. I appealed to all comrades to discard all past prejudices and to cooperate sincerely with comrades from all other places. The problem inside the Party would have to be resolved through conferences inside the Party. The Red Army was of one identity, without any distinction to be drawn.

This is a general outline of the events from the time the Red Fourth Front Army separated with the First Front Army at Mao-erh-kai until the reunion after our march north. Here are the facts. Assessment of the rights and wrongs, gains and losses, are left to the reader's discretion.

RECONCILIATION BETWEEN THE CCP AND THE KMT

CHAPTER

The Sian Incident

The Sian Incident was the most dramatic event in modern Chinese history. It changed the overall situation in China at that time. As a result, the KMT and the Nanking government had to change the policy of "internal peace before resistance to foreign aggression" into a policy of "national solidarity and joint effort to resist the Japanese"; the CCP ended its nine-year Soviet movement and became a strange opposition party; the Red Army and the land under its occupation became, at least ostensibly, part of the Nationalist government. Even though many historical publications deal with this subject, I would like to give an account of it based upon my own experience.

On December 2, 1936,[1] Chu Teh and I, leading the directly subordinate units of General Headquarters, arrived in Pao-an. Lin Piao, commandant of the Red Army School, and the students of that school greeted us in the suburbs. Mao Tse-tung and high-ranking officials of the Central government of the CCP stood in front of the students, just as they had in Mao-kung when we first met each other. On a preconstructed rostrum we all spoke and congratulated each other. My speech emphasized solidarity and resistance to the Japanese. At that time, we discussed our future, not our past.

Pao-an was the most deserted city I had ever seen. Smaller in size than an average town on the lower reaches of the Yangtze, it had under-gone a series of calamities and famines. As most of the houses there were in ruins, we had a serious housing shortage. Chu Teh and I were each given a cave at the foot of a hill, neighboring on the caves occupied by Mao Tse-tung, Chang Wen-t'ien, Ch'in Pang-hsien, Wang Chia-hsiang, and Lin Po-ch'ü. In front of these caves there were some vegetable gardens where previously there had been a street of shops that had since been ruined. General Headquarters' personnel was grouped according to function and assigned to live in the various establishments of those corresponding functions. The students of the Red Army School that we brought with us joined the Red Army School under Lin Piao.

Pao-an was conspicuous because it was so deserted. There were hardly any educated people, and it was very hard to find a middle-school graduate in that city. As a matter of fact, most of the *hsiu-ts'ai* (graduates of the Imperial examinations) who were there during the Manchu dynasty were illiterate, since they were appointed by allocation. It was sparsely populated, and more Red Army soldiers than civilians were to be seen on the streets. It was said that a good harvest there would suffice for three years, but unfortunately that good harvest was very uncommon. Therefore, Comrade Lin Po-ch'ü, who was in charge of economic and financial affairs there, had to make every effort to solve the supply problem, just as Chou En-lai had done in Ho-lian-wan.

Historically the northern Shensi area has always been a gathering place for rebels and bandits. It is like a harbor on the coast. In Northwest China, whenever rebels would meet up with difficulties, they would either flee south to the Han-chung, Ching-ling Range, or Pa-shan areas, or escape north to northern Shensi to await opportunities, no matter what their initial objectives were. This fact can be attributed to the geographic locations of these areas.

I met Lin Yu-ying in Pao-an. He had been out of town, but when he heard about my arrival, he hurried back to see me. He was as cordial and simple as ever. His entire body came to life when he spoke, as if he wanted to reveal everything he was thinking. In order to accomplish his mission as liaison officer between the two CC's of the CCP, he expressed his hearty admiration for both Mao Tse-tung and me because of our past accomplishments. He said that we were like beads from a broken necklace before we formed the Anti-Japanese National United Front, and that he would serve as a string to connect these beads.

He told me what was going on in Moscow, mainly that the CCP's position within the Comintern had been greatly improved. When Hitler destroyed the German Communist Party, the CCP became an important branch of the Comintern, second only to the CPSU. Communists all over the world were filled with admiration for the CCP's Soviet movement and guerrilla warfare of recent years. They considered that this was a fantastic demonstration of the CCP's revolutionary spirit. The CCP's representatives in Moscow, such as Wang Ming, thus were held in greater respect by the Comintern. They were publicizing the importance of the Chinese revolution in order to win support from revolutionaries and Communists in other countries. At the Seventh Congress of the Comintern, Mao Tse-tung, Chou En-lai, Wang Ming, and I were elected to the Presidium.

I held Lin Yu-ying, the central liaison officer, in great respect. Therefore, I gave him a brief account of my past and asked about the actions he would take to bridge the gap between the Party's two CC's and thus restore a normal leadership to the CCP. He told me that in northern Shensi at that time Mao Tse-tung and Chang Wen-t'ien were still chairman of the Military Committee and secretary of the CCP respectively, while he himself was chairman of the Trade-Union Movement Committee. He also said that the most urgent task at the moment was development of the Anti-Japanese National United Front. In addition, he assured me that they were waiting for an opportunity to hold an enlarged conference of the CCP in order to solve intra-Party problems. As the central liaison officer, he thought it was his duty to convene such a meeting. He proposed that the CC membership remain unchanged, but that new hands be selected at the conference and be assigned to work with the central organization.

Except for Lin Yu-ying, the comrades did not talk about the past. It seemed that all of them were devoting their attention to the situation outside of northern Shensi. It was indeed no easy matter for people in Pao-an to keep informed of the current national situation. Their topics of conversation and speculation were usually hearsay from Sian or a bit of information from a radio newscast.

Chang Wen-t'ien thought that China had been undergoing a change over the past few years, and that remarkable progress was being made in many fields. He told me that he had read a few books from outside northern Shensi and had found many good articles written by new authors. He thought they were better works than his own. According to Chang, the popular anti-Japanese songs of recent years especially indicated the progress in literature and art. He thought that we who had been living in the mountains for these few years were a little behind the times, implying that we must study hard to catch up.

Chang Wen-t'ien especially mentioned the anti-Japanese movement launched on December 9, 1935, by Peking students.[2] In spite of his limited knowledge about that movement, he pointed out the fact that the aggression of the Japanese against North China and their attempt to set up autonomous governments there had created strong opposition among the Peking students. He thought that the December Ninth Movement was no less important than the May Fourth Movement, because it soon spread throughout the country even though the Nanking government suppressed it, and the National Vanguard Team organized by the students was stronger during the December Ninth Movement than the Students' Joint Association had been during the May Fourth Movement.

The CCP's underground organization in the White areas had been crushed by the Nationalist government and was no longer capable of leading anti-Japanese movements. After the CC of the CCP moved to the Soviet area in 1931, CCP organizations in cities such as Shanghai had repeatedly been destroyed, so that in some areas those organizations no longer existed and in other areas there were only a few individual CCP members left. Chang said that he had been trying to locate those clandestine organizations, but in vain. All he knew then was that Liu Shao-ch'i was active in Peking, and seemed to be capable of leading the CCP members there to direct the December Ninth Movement behind the scenes.

However, the political influence of the CCP was still very widespread. Many CCP members that had separated from or lost contact with the Party, as well as Communist sympathizers, became aggressive elements in anti-Japanese movements. Some of them hid themselves in rooming houses in Shanghai and acted as leftist writers. Others participated in the activities of the masses. Still others infiltrated the KMT's political and military organizations and were playing very subtle roles. Chang Wen-t'ien said that he had vaguely detected and knew that some comrades who had been regarded as opportunists or unreliable elements in the past had proved that they could fight on alone. Chang was of the opinion that the CCP should take immediate action, based upon new conditions, to reorganize the Party organization in the White areas.

Chang Wen-t'ien did not want to make any comment on our cooperation and joint efforts with Chang Hsueh-liang to resist the Japanese. He seemed not to be optimistic about the future of our cooperation. He told me that this matter was being handled by Mao Tse-tung and Chou En-lai, that Mao was the planner at home while Chou was traveling about to talk business. He said, "Old Mao knows all the tricks. Let him do it." He said this for several reasons, one of which perhaps was to hint to me not to interfere with "Old Mao."

It seemed to me that Mao Tse-tung was concentrating his attention on "national affairs" at that time. With a smile on his face, Mao once said to me that he was playing the market, implying that he was doing big business with little capital, namely, the small Red Army. According to his speculations, the Japanese aggressions against Northeast China and North China had upset the balance of power in the Far East and had very much displeased the Soviet Union, the United States, and Great Britain; while at home the anti-Japanese passion had spread deep into the Nationalist armed forces, and therefore it would be very hard for Chiang Kai-shek to persist in his nonresistance policy towards Japan.

Mao also said that the silent agreement between the Chinese Communists and Chang Hsueh-liang and Yang Hu-ch'eng was an important achievement for the Anti-Japanese National United Front and might be called a Chang-Yang-CCP Triangular Alliance. According to his speculations, Chang Hsueh-liang and Yang Hu-ch'eng would sooner or later find an opportunity to propose to the Nanking government that it "cease military operations against the Communists" and "unite to resist Japan." The Nanking government, of course, would not accept this proposal. Then an independent government would emerge in Sian. Whether this independent government could survive would depend on a clear-cut anti-Japanese policy, support from the United States, Great Britain, and the Soviet Union, as well as the support of public opinion, and also on Chang's and Yang's ability to unite with the powerholders in other provinces and their ability to cause internal dissension in the Nanking government. It seemed to me that Mao at that time did not foresee at all the Sian Incident which took place several days later.

Mao thought that Moscow would support the anti-Japanese situation in the Northwest as it supported China's resistance to Japan. He mentioned that Moscow had expressed neither support for nor opposition to Chang Hsueh-liang and Yang Hu-ch'eng. Moscow, in its telegrams to us, had pledged aid in arms and ammunition for the Red Army if it could keep a road open from Ningsia to Outer Mongolia or from the Ho-hsi Corridor in Kansu to Sinkiang. From this, we could safely say that the Soviet Union would give us more aid if we could forge an anti-Japanese situation in the Northwest on a wider basis.

The CC of the CCP at that time had not held any formal meetings, responsibility for them, apparently, having been pushed onto the shoulders of Lin Yu-ying, who, however, kept aloof from day-to-day business. Contacts with the outside world, such as radiotelegrams from and to Sian, were dealt with entirely by Mao himself. Every time Mao received a message from Sian, he would call us in to talk it over. Among these radiotelegrams were some announcing the forthcoming "bandit suppression" conference to be held in Sian by Chiang to deliver confidential instructions, and others describing the development of the anti-Japanese movement in Sian and elsewhere. We usually discussed ways to deal with the situation in the light of the contents of the radiotelegrams. Our answering radiotelegrams to Chang Hsueh-liang were all Mao Tse-tung's masterpieces, carefully worded to boost Chang's morale.

My attention at that time was focused on the situation of the West Wing troops, which were moving west and fighting hard against cavalry along the way. Despite several scattered victories, the situation was acute, as the ammunition on our side was nearly exhausted due to heavy consumption day after day. This caused me great anxiety. I studied the various conditions and tried by every means to help the West Wing troops politically and militarily in the hope of saving them from their plight.

Undoubtedly I was not in the best of humor, but the others did not take much notice of it. We gathered and talked every day in the cave that served as Mao Tse-tung's residence. Everyone avoided talking about the past. Mao Tse-tung, Chang Wen-t'ien, and others still seemed more or less unhappy about the split in the past and were not enthusiastic about helping the West Wing troops. They were inclined to hem and haw when they spoke. In order to save the troops in the West Wing, I had to talk patiently with everybody. Yet no way was found that was of any use. Miracles did not occur like a godsend.

It was nearly noon on the twelfth of December when we read the urgent radiotelegram from Chang Hsueh-liang at Mao Tse-tung's cave house. It reported mainly that he had, out of necessity, taken up arms to persuade Chiang Kai-shek to stop fighting the Communists and to unite with them to resist Japan. Previously he had made a passionate presentation of the case to Chiang, who turned a deaf ear. Now, he was keeping Chiang and his loyal favorites and retinue under custody, so as to prod him into accepting his proposals to resist Japan. He was resolved to continue the house arrest until his demands were met. Chang stated in the radiotelegram that a plane had been sent to Yen-an to take Chou

En-lai and other representatives of the CCP to Sian for consultations. He also informed us of the movements of his troops and those of Yang Hu-ch'eng towards the line between Sian and Tung-kuan, and asked the Red Army to march to Yen-an and the region south of Yen-an in unbroken columns, so as to be prepared for any eventuality.

We were very excited by this unexpected wire. Some of us said, "It serves Chiang Kai-shek right!" Others said, "Bravo, Chang Hsueh-liang!" Chu Teh, who was usually mild-tempered in his opinions and laconic in discussions, now beat the others to saying, "Kill off those blokes first! What good can be said about them?" Chou En-lai, who had returned to Pao-an a few days earlier, kept a cool head. He said, "We alone cannot decide what to do. The attitude of Chang Hsueh-liang and Yang Hu-ch'eng has to be taken into account; it is the main thing to consider." Mao Tse-tung, who was laughing like mad, then chimed in, "In this matter, we must stay behind the scenes. Let Chang and Yang fight the initial battle." I was very excited, yet I said coolly, "Let's first guess what Moscow's opinion of this event will be." Chang Wen-t'ien, Ch'in Pang-hsien, Wang Chia-hsiang, and others all wanted to telegraph Moscow for advice. So while we continued to discuss and prepare for Chou En-lai's departure for Sian, we started to draft a telegram to Moscow. As a result of our discussion, we came to the following conclusions:

1. That we would send a telegram to Chang Hsueh-liang, applauding his action and assuring him that we would follow his lead in taking future steps.
2. That Chou En-lai, Ch'in Pang-hsien, and Yeh Chien-ying would fly to Sian via Yen-an as representatives of the CCP.
3. That we would send a telegram to P'eng Te-huai and others, ordering them to direct the troops to Yen-an and the region south of Yen-an and to keep in close contact with friendly armies along the way.
4. That we would send a telegram to our liaison personnel in Sian, asking them to refrain from expressing any concrete opinions, except about the Declaration on Resistance to Japan. They must wait for the arrival of Chou En-lai and others before making further comments.
5. That while they were in Sian, Chou and the others would have to wait for the reply from the Soviet Union before making any concrete moves.

Then Chou En-lai and the others hastened to Yen-an.

Our telegram to Moscow was drafted by Mao Tse-tung. Besides giving an accurate report of the Sian Incident, it pointed out that the incident had occurred in accordance with an agreement to oppose Chiang and resist Japan that had been made by the triangular alliance of Chang Hsueh-liang, Yang Hu-ch'eng, and the CCP. It requested immediate advice from the Comintern on the proposal of the CC of the CCP to actively advise Chang and Yang to split with Chiang resolutely.

The Sian Incident gave us an occasion to stand up and cheer. It seemed that all of our problems could be resolved at the drop of a hat. We hoped that Chang Hsueh-liang would wire Ma Pu-fang, ordering him not to wreck the general plan of resisting Japan and to stop at once the battles against our West Wing troops. Chang Hsueh-liang complied with our wish, but Ma Pu-fang did not accept his order. We were worried about a food shortage for the Red Army in northern Shensi. With the movement of the troops to the south, there would be no problem in finding food and other supplies for the Army. Moreover, the KMT's anti-Communist front was now in chaos; it was just the right opportunity for us.

Radiotelegrams came from Sian in droves, mostly to report on the events of Chiang's imprisonment, Nanking's reaction, and other military matters. The most important message was the December Twelfth Declaration made by Chang, Yang, and seventeen others.[3] They advanced eight proposals:

1. Reorganize the Nanking government so as to accommodate other political parties in order to save our country together.
2. Stop all civil war.
3. Release immediately all patriotic leaders arrested in Shanghai.
4. Release political prisoners everywhere in the country.
5. Free the patriotic movement of the masses.
6. Guarantee the rights of the people to assemble and to form societies and all other political freedoms.
7. Carry out realistically Dr. Sun's legacy for our nation.
8. Convene meetings immediately to save our country.

Chang's telegrams showed hesitancy regarding what to do about Chiang Kai-shek; they also showed worry about the military pressure from Nanking. Mao drafted replies with great concentration, now calling Chang "National Leader in Resisting Japan," now extolling his "world-shaking moves." Concerning the strict security watch over Chiang, Mao's telegram said, "You, Sir, are a careful and detailed planner, and the villain will hardly slip through the net, but one dreads the chance in a million. . . ." As regards Chiang's punishment, one paragraph said, "As your telegrams have stated, Chiang is certainly a betrayer of our country and should be tried according to law. We advocate a public trial by the people. . . ."

None of us who were leaders of the CC of the CCP entertained the thought that the Sian Incident would be resolved peacefully. We all felt that to let Chiang go on living would be like nurturing trouble by leaving a cancerous spot untreated. Some of us wanted to have this anti-Communist executioner killed after a public trial by the people, so that no more trouble would remain. Others wanted to have him securely locked up, to serve as a hostage to force Nanking to resist Japan and thus to acquire military superiority for Sian.

Owing to a difference of opinion, Mao Tse-tung and Chang Wen-t'ien had an argument. It seemed that Chang Wen-t'ien criticized Mao for his less-than-resolute manner of speech in the telegram replying to Chang Hsueh-liang. While they were arguing, I happened to walk into Mao Tse-tung's cave house. Mao was railing at Chang Wen-t'ien, saying that Chang had formerly opposed Mao's advocacy of guerrilla warfare while in Kiangsi and was now opposing his attitude to Chang Hsueh-liang from a bookish standpoint. Chang Wen-t'ien went out in silence, blood rushing to his face and ears.

Mao Tse-tung then explained to me the ideas behind the phrases in his telegram. In his opinion, there was no fundamental difference between his intention and Chang Wen-t'ien's. Disagreement arose only over wording of the phrases. He explained that in the telegram to Chang Hsueh-liang, he insinuated all through the message that Chang should deal with Chiang resolutely. However, it was impossible to say so outright in so many words; otherwise evidence would be left behind for the future.

Just then Chu Teh came in. He interrupted Mao's discourse, and said loudly, "Tell Chang Hsueh-liang outright that the first thing to do is to kill Chiang." He explained that in the current situation, which was hanging on a thread, it was necessary to come to a resolute decision quickly without waiting for a directive from Moscow. We could do it now and report later. After hearing him out, Mao Tse-tung said to Chu Teh, consolingly with a smile, "There is no difference between your opinion and mine. Only our methods are different. I have given strong hints to Chang Hsueh-liang about what to do, but the word 'kill' must not come from our lips." Then he went on with an air of giving lessons,

"We mustn't be too simple and rigid in our thinking. How can you know that Chang Hsueh-liang will listen to us without the least trace of suspicion and jealousy?"

Fortunately, Moscow's answering telegram came on the evening of December 13. It consisted of one and one-half typed pages. There were three parts to it:

1. It affirmed that the Sian Incident was fabricated by Japanese intrigue. It stated that among Chang Hsueh-liang's aides and among his troops Japanese spies were hidden, who took advantage of Chang's ambition to create chaos in China, even making use of anti-Japanese slogans. If we allowed the situation to develop, China would be involved in long years of civil war and the anti-Japanese forces would perish as a result, leaving Japan to enjoy its advantage at leisure. The telegram declared that the Soviet Union would certainly not be taken in by the plot, still less would it give any support. On the contrary, the Soviet Union explicitly expressed its disapproval.

2. What China urgently needed now was a nationwide anti-Japanese national united front; therefore, the most important things were unity and cooperation, not schism and civil war. It pointed out that Chang Hsueh-liang was unable to lead the resistance against Japan. If Chiang would change his mind, he was, ironically, the sole person capable of leading the resistance.

3. The telegram instructed the CCP to strive for a peaceful solution of the Sian Incident, making use of the opportunity to hold friendly talks with Chiang Kai-shek, urging him to approve of resistance to Japan. On the favorable basis of a peaceful resolution of the Sian Incident, we should release Chiang on our own initiative.

One year later, in December, 1937, when Wang Ming returned to Yen-an from Moscow, we learned about the origin of the above telegram. He said that following the Sian Incident, the ambassadors in Moscow of Great Britain, the United States, and other countries asked the Soviet Foreign Ministry about the attitude of the Soviet government on this matter. The Soviet Foreign Ministry promptly described the incident as a Japanese intrigue, without the foreknowledge or approval of the Soviet Union. Subsequently Stalin himself drafted the telegram to the CCP. In his explanation to Wang Ming, he reasoned, in general, that Chang Hsueh-liang did not carry enough weight to be the national leader of resistance to Japan, while at the moment the CCP did not yet have the ability to lead the resistance. Although Chiang Kai-shek was an abominable enemy, he was by far the most promising single Chinese to lead the resistance to Japan. In the resistance to Japan he might become our ally.[4]

Certainly, in remote Pao-an at that time, we were unable to get information on such inside stories as Wang Ming later told us. The telegram from the Soviet Union came to us like a bolt from the blue. We all sank into deep thought. Mao Tse-tung paced the room. Some of us wondered how the Sian Incident, which clearly had been fomented by the triangular alliance of Chang, Yang, and the CCP, could be called a Japanese plot. Some agreed that long-term civil war had to be avoided. Some supposed that Chiang would deal with us ruthlessly once he was set free. Some doubted that there was any hope for the Sian Incident to succeed without the support of the Soviet Union. Mao Tse-tung said impetuously, "Everything's topsy-turvy! Heaven and earth have turned upside down! Won't Chang and Yang accuse us of capriciousness if we say the reverse of what we said a short time ago?"

In such an atmosphere, it was impossible to carry on with the meeting. Therefore, we dispersed, each to ponder more deeply or to hold individual discussions. In this way a whole evening slipped away. I did not sleep a wink all night, spending much of the time holding confidential consultations with Mao. We agreed that if we did not act in accordance with the instructions of Moscow, we would not get any support from the Soviet Union and would be encircled and attacked by various forces at home and aboard. The consequences would be serious. If we acted in accordance with the three points put forth in the Moscow directive, the triangular alliance of Chang, Yang, and the CCP might break up immediately. Even if we could avoid a split, Chiang's revenge after the peaceful solution would be inevitable. Comparing them, I thought that the first solution was clearly not feasible, while the second, though encumbered with difficulties, might offer a ray of hope.

The urgency of the situation required that we once more gather at the cave home of Mao Tse-tung in the wee hours. A meeting was held to decide on the concrete steps to be taken. We decided that we should immediately inform Chou En-lai of the telegram from Moscow, asking him to sound out Chang Hsueh-liang in light of the telegram's instructions. If he found the situation favorable, he could act in accordance with the principle set forth in the directive. If not, he should try to leave room for further maneuvers by the CCP.

After his arrival at Sian on December 13, Chou En-lai began consultations with Chang Hsueh-liang and Yang Hu-ch'eng about future measures. Chang Hsueh-liang had asked about the telegraphed instructions from Moscow and about Moscow's attitude towards the actions taken in Sian. Chou En-lai inferred from these questions of Chang's that the latter was pinning great hopes on Soviet support. Chou was also extremely surprised at Moscow's attitude when he received the telegram from us. He promised to sound Chang out secretly.

In his confidential talk with Chang Hsueh-liang on December 14, Chou En-lai said outright that the Soviet Union would probably not support Sian. The initial response of Chang Hsueh-liang was one of indignation; he seemed to feel that he had been double-crossed. In the past the CCP had constantly advertised probable Soviet support; now that he had climbed on the back of the tiger, the CCP actually skulked before the coming battle, without fulfilling its promise. All Chou En-lai could do was to give explanations in a hundred ways, patiently and modestly. He stated that this was something that the CC of the CCP had not anticipated or wanted. The Soviet Union, however, had its own problems; for instance, it could not afford to ignore pressure from foreign countries. The CCP was resolved to stand by Chang from beginning to end, shouldering all burdens with its own strength. With matters coming to a head, it was not permissible to blame each other. The only thing for them to do was to devise means together for the furtherance of the cause in accordance with the original intentions.

The two men, therefore, held secret consultations on what principles to follow. Chou En-lai told Chang Hsueh-liang that he personally thought that the best way to resolve the problem would not be to set up an independent government in Sian and impose sanctions on Chiang Kai-shek. Nanking was clamoring for punitive attacks against Sian. If we imposed sanctions on Chiang, it would give others an excuse, and Chiang's disciples would involve us in interminable struggles, which would be tantamount to long-term civil war, the outcome of which could scarcely be foretold. These arguments of Chou's finally struck a chord in Chang's heart.

Then Chou went on to say that he would like to offer for Chang's consideration a vague idea of his. He frankly stated that what we needed was a situation of total resistance to Japan throughout the country and not one confined to one corner in Sian. We, therefore, needed unity and cooperation and not division and civil war. In Nanking there were people who were unwilling to fight a civil war, as well as people who did not want to force Sian into imposing sanctions on Chiang Kai-shek. We could prepare for war on the one hand, and hold talks with Chiang on the other. If Chiang openly accepted our proposals, it would be difficult for him to go back on his word.

Chang Hsueh-liang was not averse to these ideas of Chou's. Instead, he suggested that the matter should be kept secret. Even Yang Hu-ch'eng was not to be informed for the time being. They would both discuss the concrete measures to be taken and would make an announcement to the outside world when they were quite sure of the situation. Then they went on to discuss preferential treatment for Chiang and how to speak to Chiang.

All of these events had been reported to Pao-an in detail in Chou En-lai's telegrams. Chou said that he was pleased with the proceedings and felt hopeful about a peaceful solution. We were also delighted upon receiving Chou's telegrams. We then decided that we would resolutely prod Chang and Yang onto the road of peaceful solution. Despite the decision, we were still doubtful. Chang Wen-t'ien said to me, "This is completely for the interests of the Comintern and the Soviet Union. The good of the CCP can only be sacrificed." He said that the Soviet Union was probably forced to keep aloof by pressures from foreign countries and that when Chiang was released, we would be sure to undergo great hardships.

On December 15 a conference of senior cadres was held in the cave office of Lin Po-Ch'ü to convey Moscow's instructions. We members of the Politburo all spoke, expressing our support for a peaceful solution to the Sian Incident. My statement also, naturally, expressing support for peaceful solution. However, concerning the future after the solution, I, in a similar vein, said I dared not be optimistic. I meant that Chiang might agree to our demands while in Sian; but once he got back to Nanking he might do an about face under some pretext. It was, therefore, our duty to exert greater efforts toward internal solidarity and strengthening of our forces, so as to be able to deal with any possible aggravation of the situation. Just because of these words of mine, I was later slandered by my opponents for lack of confidence in the peaceful resolution of the Sian Incident. They had ignored my proposal calling for internal solidarity in the CCP and had quoted my statement out of context. They even went so far as to say that I opposed peaceful resolution. This was indeed a case of framed indictment.

The situation at that time was rather delicate. At first there was an atmosphere of war. Then the voices of conciliation began to gain the upper hand. Nanking, like a host of dragons deprived of its leader, was in confusion for a time. It was generally thought that there was no hope that Chiang would come back alive. People with such a view wanted to launch punitive attacks on Sian. Undoubtedly there were those who rejoiced in the calamities of others. They were expecting something to happen. Among the commanders of Chang and Yang in Sian were those who felt that since Chiang had been captured by extraordinary means, the possibility of compromise was inconceivable. The situation of riding on the tiger's back made them feel like doing something drastic. Either you did not begin, or having begun, you must not give up: that was the idea in their heads.

Chang Hsueh-liang and Yang Hu-ch'eng, however, had never taken a stand in support of a complete split with Chiang. The sound of gunshots at Hua-ching Pool in Lin-t'ung had died away. Chang and Yang were waiting upon Chiang with great courtesy. The telegrams that they sent out to the whole country only dwelled on the eight points and guaranteed Chiang's safety.

The private consultations between Chang Hsueh-liang and Chou En-lai were an important factor in bringing about the peaceful resolution of the Sian Incident. Meanwhile, they had been forced to do so by the urgency of the situation. Powerful troops from Nanking had been marching to Tung-kuan, and planes had been menacing Sian from the air. The majority of the leaders in Sian could not but feel that an outbreak of war would be unfavorable to them. Powerholders in various parts of the country had maintained an attitude of reconciliation in their telegrams to Chang Hsueh-liang. Therefore, as soon as Chang Hsueh-liang's intention to seek a peaceful resolution became clear, an atmosphere of reconciliation prevailed over the smell of ammunition.

Chang Hsueh-liang insisted that Chiang must indicate his approval by signing the above-mentioned eight-point proposition. Chiang, however, resolutely refused to sign, insisting that for the sake of his and the government's prestige, it was impossible for him to make any commitments under coercion. Donald (a Westerner named Swi-la in Chinese), T. V. Soong, Soong Mei-ling, Chiang Ting-wen, and others ran to and fro between the two sides to try every means to bring about a reconciliation. The Soongs, brother and sister, even said that Chiang had agreed to the eight-point proposal. It wouldn't be a good idea to leave a scar on his mind by forcing him to put his signature to the document.

Chou En-lai, in his telegram to Pao-an, reported on his long interview with Chiang Kai-shek. First of all, Chang Hsueh-liang put in a good word for Chou before conducting him in to see Chiang. Chang Hsueh-liang said to Chiang that a former subordinate of the Generalissimo's begged for an audience, which, he hoped, the Generalissimo would grant him. Chiang remained noncommittal, whereupon Chou En-lai stepped into Chiang's room and performed a solemn salute. Adhering to the custom at Whampoa Military Academy, he addressed Chiang as "Commandant." At first, Chiang pulled a long face, taking no notice of him. Chou immediately sat down and began a spirited statement of his case. Chiang listened carefully, without uttering a word. Chou began by reiterating that the CCP by no means entertained ideas unfavorable to Chiang and the Nanking government. It was his hope that all would be resolved peacefully. The CCP was willing to support Chiang as a national leader in resisting Japan. Chou also took the opportunity to give an account of the gradual change in policy of the CCP, vigorously attesting to the necessity of removing prejudices and forging unity in order to resist foreign aggression.

Chou En-lai said in his report that his statement had soothed Chiang gradually. Chiang seemed to believe that Chou was sincere. Chou En-lai did not say a word about Chiang having to sign the eight-point proposal. Only when the tense atmosphere began to ease did Chou ask Chiang for some instructions. He then made small talk with Chiang about his family, saying that his son Chiang Ching-kuo was enjoying relatively good treatment in the Soviet Union. When Chiang imperceptibly betrayed the feeling of missing his son, Chou immediately promised that he would help to bring about a reunion of father and son.

Chou En-lai explained in his report that throughout the interview he had maintained an air of respect and submission, without a sign of coercion, in the hope that no traces of unpleasantness would be left behind to mar the chances for further interviews with Chiang. Chou also reported that Chiang had shown the proper attitude. He only mentioned his son as a private matter, but there was a hint of reconciliation between the KMT and the CCP. Chou hoped that this would be a starting point for the reconciliation of the KMT and the CCP after the ten-year war between them.

Chang Hsueh-liang, then, was overcoming numerous difficulties to give Chiang a cordial send-off on his return to Nanking. Yang Hu-ch'eng, not knowing the whole story of the peaceful reconciliation, was not entirely immune from suspicion and worry, sometimes even expressing opposition. After being persuaded by Chang Hsueh-liang, Chou En-lai, conciliator T. V. Soong, and others, Yang finally agreed to let Chiang go. On December 25, Chiang flew back to Nanking in safety.

In his telegram reporting the departure of Chiang from Sian, Chou
En-lai expressed regret that Chang Hsueh-liang had accompanied Chiang
to Nanking. He pointed out that Chang was too impulsive, never having
mentioned that he intended to accompany Chiang to Nanking; otherwise
Chou would have persuaded him not to do so. As Chiang's plane was
about to depart, Chang said to Chou, who was standing beside him
amongst the farewell crowd, "I'm going with the Generalissimo," and
stepped onto the plane. Despite Chou's restraining gesture, Chang
boarded the plane and flew away. Chou explained in his report that he
was then racked with anxiety, but being in the dense crowd, he was
unable to say anything to Chang.

Chou then went on to report that Sian was in a state of confusion
after Chang Hsueh-liang's departure. Chang had not made any arrangements beforehand, and nobody knew what to do in the future. Yang
Hu-ch'eng was planning for himself, getting ready to move his troops
to a safe area. The Northeast Army, like dragons without a leader, were
in confusion, too. The younger set among the men, in despair, shifted
the blame to the CCP, saying that the CCP had trapped their "Young
Marshal." The triangular alliance of Chang, Yang, and the CCP had
completely disintegrated. The main thing was that nobody could make
a decision; we could not find anyone with whom we could hold consultations.

Not unexpectedly, the younger set of the Northeast Army became
impatient and raised an uproar. Some fifty of their officers threatened to
kill Chou En-lai. At a meeting, they brandished their weapons and demanded that Chou tell them the whereabouts of their Young Marshal.
They argued that the CCP had incited the Sian Incident and then, after
its occurrence, had proposed a peaceful solution of the incident for its
private gains, betraying its allies and victimizing the Northeast Army by
effecting a secret compromise with Chiang's personnel. The CCP had
harped on Soviet help, which turned out to be a hoax after all. The
Young Marshal's visit to Nanking portended more of evil than of good,
and the men of the Northeast Army were certain to meet with death.
They blamed all of this on Chou En-lai, the arch-evildoer.

Faced with such a critical situation, Chou En-lai turned on all his
charismatic power and, fortunately, got away with it. He was calm in
his approach and sincere in his utterances. He explained to the officers
that Young Marshal Chang's departure for Nanking with Chiang was
totally unexpected. He did not approve of it, but he had not had time
to prevent its happening. He went on to say that the Young Marshal's

life would be endangered if we indulged in internal strife. In that case, even the Northeast Army would perish. But if we remained calm and united, Chiang would be afraid of our strength and would not dare to harm their Young Marshal. Then the triangular alliance would continue to exist and play its role. Chou swore before these angry young officers that the CCP would never betray the triangular alliance, but would stand on the same front as its partners in the alliance, never allowing any injury to be done to Young Marshal Chang and the Northeast Army. Since there was nothing else they could do, the impetuous officers were compelled to calm down for the good of all concerned.

By now the Sian Incident had come to an end. The imprisoned Chiang Kai-shek finally returned to Nanking in safety. Chang Hsueh-liang, leader of the incident, from then on had to lead a life of imprisonment, deprived of the sight of sky and sun. The CCP, one of the participants, as a partner in the anti-Chiang alliance together with Chang and Yang, became a conciliator for the peaceful solution of the Sian Incident and later started talks with Nanking to achieve a reconciliation of the KMT and the CCP. Due to internal confusion, the Chang-Yang-CCP triangular alliance no longer could make any unanimous moves. The numerous people connected with the Sian Incident were busy clearing themselves of responsibility, in order that the rod of Chiang Kai-shek's revenge might not fall on their own heads. What was more important was that the war against the Communists had stopped in effect. Taking its place was the War of Resistance Against Japan.

Yen-an's Hundred Faces

Chiang Kai-shek's deliverance from danger and his return flight to Nanking from Sian accompanied by Chang Hsueh-liang on December 25, 1936, brought immediate confusion to the Chang-Yang-CCP triangular alliance in Sian; it also caused a great jolt within the CCP, where nearly everyone felt that serious trouble was imminent. Taking advantage of the opportunity, Mao Tse-tung played speculative tricks to attain his goal, throwing overboard all moral concepts and Communist principles, employing unscrupulous means and stopping at nothing, even in the ways of evil. His aim was to prevent Chiang Kai-shek from continuing the war against the Communists or forcing their surrender after his return to Nanking and to seek ways for the CCP to continue to exist and develop. This was entwined with Mao's wily pursuit of personal dictatorship. It must be said that Mao's efforts met with considerable success. The CCP finally had a respite, and Mao himself built a foundation for his personal dictatorship.

A brief look at the situation in China at that time would show that the occurrence of the Sian Incident and its outcome and the events thereafter were no surprise at all. Japan's aggression, at that time, had caused such a grave and urgent situation that all apparently inconceivable things became possible. Among these, the major one was the CCP's sudden return to life from the brink of death. In other words, the Soviet movement had plunged the CCP into the path of death, while the resistance against Japan had not only relieved it of its plight but had given it a chance to develop in freedom.

All this is a long, long story, which, if the readers will excuse me, I will not dwell on in detail. I will only give a brief account of what I encountered personally. Generally speaking, before the Sian Incident, the CCP, hiding away in remote regions, was influenced by the anti-Japanese campaign in an indirect way. For instance, the CCP had on its own initiative contacted Chang Hsueh-liang. It was because of this contact that the CCP came to understand a lot about the anti-Japanese situation, particularly the anti-Japanese sentiment in the Northeast Army. The visits of a few American correspondents to northern Shensi also brought the VIP's of the CCP the news that foreign friends sympathized with Chinese resistance to Japan. Besides this, information, books, and periodicals on the resistance were coming to northern Shensi, which had given Chang Wen-t'ien and his colleagues an indistinct picture of the progress being made outside of northern Shensi.

After the Sian Incident, the CCP's role in the anti-Japanese campaign changed from a passive to an active one. In other words, it no longer watched the resistance from afar, but gradually infiltrated into actual anti-Japanese activities. The first landmark of this transition was the removal of the CCP capital to Yen-an, which later became the famous Red capital. As soon as the CC of the CCP learned of Chiang Kai-shek's return to Nanking accompanied by Chang Hsueh-liang on December 25, 1936, it immediately moved the Central organs originally stationed in Pao-an to Yen-an. The CC of the CCP had prepared for this long before. Just as the Sian Incident ended, it seized the opportunity to build up its foothold quietly and unobtrusively.

Yen-an, a county seat, was in the center of northern Shensi. There were enough houses and caves inside and outside the town for the use of the organs of the CC of the CCP. It was within easy reach of Sian and other places, and there was a small airfield, which had been used many times by Chou En-lai in his visits to Chang Hsueh-liang. When we, the leaders of the CCP, came to Yen-an from pitiful little Pao-an, we became quite elated. The general opinion was that Yen-an was a promising place for great events. Some said that Yen-an was a famous town historically and an important place in border defense. Others said that it was possible to recruit soldiers and buy horses there, gathering around us the brave and the gallant from the four corners of China.

The occupation of Yen-an was one important achievement that the CCP scored in the Sian Incident. After the Incident, the CCP, in response to the request of Chang Hsueh-liang, had moved the main forces of the Red Army to the front line in the vicinity of Sian, forming a continuous front with the troops of Chang Hsueh-liang and Yang Hu-ch'eng. Consequently, the Red Army advanced along the roads leading from Yen-an to Sian, with Lo-ch'uan as the site of its General Headquarters and the troops spreading out on the front south of Lo-ch'uan. Yen-an then became the main rear base for the Red Army. The counties south of Yen-an were still under the rule of the KMT provincial government in Sian. Only Yen-an, with Chang Hsueh-liang's approval, was handed over to the CCP to govern as it pleased.

Yen-an became more fluorishing each day after the CC of the CCP moved in. Its main feature was the influx of young men and women and students, who came in groups on foot. There were also some anti-Japanese, pro-Communist personalities who came from Sian in cars, which were pitifully few and far between. All of them regarded Yen-an as the holy place of the revolution and were very bitter against the KMT government in Nanking. Their chief accusation against the KMT was that it was reluctant to resist Japan and refused to permit them the opportunity to take part in the resistance against Japan. As a result, they pinned their hopes on the CCP, the inside story of which they did not quite understand. Because of all these newcomers, Yen-an began to have a housing shortage. Later, the CC of the CCP had to allocate a large number of houses for the accommodation of the Anti-Japanese Military and Political Academy.[5] The CC of the CCP also moved some of its organs to villages farther away from Yen-an and dug many new caves.

Most of my many contacts with these newcomers from the outside were through individual interviews, which, by and large, were on some concrete matters concerning the current situation. I also had occasion to enjoy cultural and artistic shows, which consisted of various performances, including the singing of anti-Japanese songs. I also watched the physical-culture activities of the young people. All in all, I felt that they were more practical and hard-working than the youths of the May Fourth period. Their zeal for the resistance against Japan brought me a very vivid appreciation of the anti-Japanese situation. I can recall even now the conjecture that I made about the anti-Japanese situation at that time. I held that Japanese aggression in China had caused discontent in the United States, Great Britain, the Soviet Union, and other countries, which had been sympathizing with and supporting China's campaign of resistance against Japan in various ways. The KMT government in Nanking had made remarkable progress, particularly in the great strides it had made in the direction of unifying China. It was capable of resisting Japan, and would soon do so. From the behavior of these young people, it could be seen that China's factions and people of different categories were capable of forming an alliance to resist Japan unanimously. I was optimistic about the resistance against Japan and was, therefore, able to bear all the torments Mao Tse-tung and the others were inflicting upon me.

Moreover, after its move to Yen-an, the CC of the CCP obtained much relief for its economic problems. The Red Army stationed in places south of the northern Shensi border region was able to feed itself with supplies from the locality. When the CCP occupied Yen-an, the area under its control was greatly enlarged, and food supply was no longer a problem. The leaders of the CCP no longer needed to busy themselves with the question of millet and vegetables every day, as they did in the days at Pao-an, when Army supplies at the front or the requirements of the rear area claimed their attention alternately. The economic-management personnel of the CCP were then able to switch their attention to other matters, such as medical and public-health supplies, mechanical equipment and spare parts, paper and stationery, and so forth, which they bought in Sian and other cities. This economic deliverance brought joy and comfort to people's hearts.

The leaders of the CCP made greatly exaggerated propaganda about these achievements, creating an optimistic atmosphere which covered up various latent troubles within the CCP and the Red Army. Moreover, they agreed among themselves that they would keep quiet about the setbacks and losses of the Red Army during the Long March of 25,000 li, its lax discipline, the internal dispute of the CC, the uncertainty over the cooperation of the CCP and the KMT for resistance against Japan, and so forth, in order not to affect the young people's anti-Japanese enthusiasm and their magnetic attraction towards the CCP.

Besides the fluorishing situation which could easily be seen by other people as mentioned above, many changes were taking place covertly inside the CC of the CCP. Owing to the dispute and the opposition between the First and Fourth Front armies, the Politburo of the CC of the CCP seemed to have ceased to exist. Meetings were no longer called in the name of the Politburo, and no one used its title. In handling the Sian Incident, the top leaders usually held consultations among themselves. The repeated discussions took some time, and this irritated Mao Tse-tung, who was the one most involved in all consultations. Although I declared that I would follow his lead, Mao was still dissatisfied, aiming, as he was, at concentrating all important power in his own hands. At this critical moment, when many urgent things waited to be dealt with and the CC of the CCP was in a state of confusion, Mao Tse-tung began fishing in troubled waters in various ways in order to attain his ambition of personal dictatorship.

First of all, Mao Tse-tung concentrated all the military power on his own person. Taking advantage of the occasion when the main force of the Red Army had to be led to the Sian front by P'eng Te-huai in the name of the commander-in-chief at the front, Mao Tse-tung issued direct commands by telegram, thus depriving General Headquarters of the power to give commands. This was done stealthily at that time. In a word, Chu Teh as commander-in-chief and I myself as chief political commissar were somehow no longer informed of the activities and conditions of the main force of the Red Army. Moreover, under the pretext of a housing shortage in Pao-an County and the need to send cadres to the Anti-Japanese Military and Political Academy for further study, the organs subordinate to General Headquarters and the personnel under the General Staff and the General Political Department were gradually absorbed into the Military Committee, which was under the direct command of Mao Tse-tung. The dissolution of the organs of General Headquarters was perpetrated on the occasion of the move from Pao-an to Yen-an. After our arrival at Yen-an, both Chu Teh and I became commanders with empty titles. Chu Teh said to me, "Old Mao is always like that, let him have his way."

What interested Mao Tse-tung most at that time was getting control of the communications systems, so that he could control all information. He himself, and he alone, took complete charge of the following:

1. All confidential messages that were telegraphed between the CC of the CCP and Moscow.

2. Liaison between the CCP and the Sian people, such as messages to and from personnel of the Nanking KMT government, Chang Hsueh-liang, Yang Hu-ch'eng, and other factions.
3. Communications between the Military Committee and Red Army troops in various places, including all orders, instructions, messages on personnel transfers, military intelligence reports, and so forth.

It could be said that Mao Tse-tung had acted upon a long-conceived, premeditated plan to accomplish this. Before the conclusion of the Sian Incident, Mao Tse-tung had stepped-up his action in this regard. With the move to Yen-an, his plan to take over control was technically fulfilled.

Taking advantage of his control of the communications system, Mao Tse-tung sent telegrams to the cadres in the Army, ordering them to study at the Anti-Japanese Academy, and large numbers of cadres responded to his publicity stunt. Mao then sent in his faithful and trusted followers to fill the vacancies and act as watchdogs. Such manipulations by Mao were aimed not only at me and the Fourth Front Army, but also at the Second Front Army's Ho Lung, Jen Pi-shih, and Hsiao K'o and at Liu Po-ch'eng, who happened to be with the Second Front Army at that time. They more or less also became commanders with empty titles.

When the CC of the CCP moved to Yen-an, Mao Tse-tung was in complete control of the power over foreign relations and military command and was spreading his personal power to the various armies. He also took advantage of his power to direct the Party affairs of the CCP. He was quite haughty in his attitude towards Chang Wen-t'ien and other Party crooks. Mao had several times said to top Party leaders smilingly, "Let me handle the various aspects of the work. The other comrades may pay more attention to more active jobs, such as winning over and influencing the young newcomers, Party affairs and the development of mass work, the improvement of local political work in the border region, and so forth." This was the protective coloring that Mao Tse-tung assumed at the start of his dictatorial regime.

At that time, most of the top people of the CCP had gone to work in various other places. Chou En-lai, Ch'in Pang-hsien, Yeh Chien-ying, and Lin Po-ch'ü had gone to Sian with large numbers of cadres. They later went to Nanking, Shanghai, and elsewhere, some conducting business with the KMT, others acting as persuasive mediators, and still others developing the work of the Party at every opportunity. P'eng Te-huai,

Liu Po-ch'eng, Jen Pi-shih, and Ho Lung were all at the front. Chang Wen-t'ien and K'ai Feng were busy with the day-to-day affairs of the CC of the CCP, while Lin Yu-ying was occupied with the trade-union movement, besides attending to intra-Party and outside business. Lin Piao and the others were concentrating their energy on the Anti-Japanese Military and Political Academy. Tung Pi-wu, who was later to be a judge, was also engaged in educational work at the academy. Chu Teh, relieved of his duties, was busy contacting the newcomers. He sometimes organized ball games and sang with the young people. As for me, I was grieved over the defeat of the West Wing troops and was trying to find means of helping them. I was then being ignored by the others. This left Mao Tse-tung, lording it over the central administration as chairman of the Military Committee of the CC of the CCP, concurrently in charge of foreign affairs. He was thus able to embrace all important power without the slightest scruple.

What gave Mao Tse-tung the greatest headache then was the revenge that Chiang Kai-shek was likely to inflict on northern Shensi after his return to Nanking. When the urgent telegram from Chou En-lai reporting the return to Nanking of Chiang Kai-shek on December 25, 1936, accompanied by Chang Hsueh-liang, arrived at Pao-an on the same evening, Mao Tse-tung appeared especially worried. He seemed absolutely certain that Chiang Kai-shek's revenge would come, revenge that would be rapid and cruel. He intermittently gave expression to the following thoughts: "What a mess! Chang Hsueh-liang followed Chiang to Nanking solely for the purpose of seeking mitigation for his crime towards Chiang. Wouldn't he put all the blame on the CCP for the same purpose? Hadn't we pushed Chang to oppose Chiang and resist Japan, saying that it would be possible to obtain Soviet aid? Hadn't we supported Chang in forming an anti-Japanese situation in the Northwest? Chang might confess all of this on his own initiative or be forced to do so. Moreover, without Chang Hsueh-liang in Sian, the Northeast Army would disintegrate and the Chang-Yang-CCP triangular alliance would no longer exist. It wouldn't take Chiang any time to pack up the forces of Chang and Yang in Sian. Then his iron fist would land on the head of the CCP, once more encircling us and attacking us from all sides. Wouldn't all these things be quite possible?"

Mao, however, also assumed a calm posture and said, "When worst comes to worst, we can fight guerrilla wars." Then he would mumble intermittently, showing his innermost thoughts, "There is, after all, some difference between the present and the past. Before, we were making rebellion, brandishing explicitly the banner of the Soviet; now, we are entering an alliance with Chiang to resist Japan and supporting him in resisting Japan. We can't possibly imitate Chang Hsueh-liang, trying to persuade him with force, can we? Then, what sort of program shall we write up? How are we to boost the morale of our soldiers?"

All the VIPs present at that time suggested investigating the actual situation carefully before making plans. Encouraged by such talk, Mao Tse-tung continually sent telegrams to Chou En-lai, demanding to know about the situation in greater detail and giving full instructions, which mainly concentrated on asking Chou to bring Chiang's trusted followers in Sian to an understanding, explaining to them that the CCP had had no part in the Sian conspiracy beforehand and that after the event it had acted as conciliator to bring about a peaceful resolution, enabling Chiang to return to Nanking in safety. What was more important still, the instructions directed Chou to sever relations with Chang and Yang ostensibly, implying in every way that the CCP did not share equal responsibility with Chang and Yang. The instructions further directed Chou to try to destroy all evidence of former intercourse with Chang and Yang, and, if possible, ask them to do the same.

Mao Tse-tung and Chou En-lai both cooperated very well, one making plans inside, and the other negotiating outside. Mao Tse-tung told Chou all his thoughts and intentions, while Chou En-lai translated them into action in the light of the actual conditions outside. Sensing Mao's anxiety, Chou had replied, saying, "Chiang, with the vainglory of a self-appointed hero, would probably not go back on his word." This telegram undoubtedly acted as a tranquilizer for Mao.

After his arrival in Yen-an at the end of December, 1936, Mao Tse-tung was still highly suspicious and lacked confidence in reconciliation between the KMT and the CCP. Prone to speculation, he would stop at nothing, even in the way of evil, to attain his end. Yet, he was adept in playing two-faced tricks. While trying to deal blows at me from all sides, he still turned a smiling face towards me when we met, just as in the good old days. However, despite our frequent encounters, he no longer informed me about confidential matters. We merely talked in general about the reconciliation between the KMT and the CCP. I can still recall our conversations at that time.

Mao Tse-tung never mentioned Chang Hsueh-liang's loyalty to his ally the CCP, which he had not once dragged in during his trial in Nanking to share the responsibility of opposition to Chiang. On the contrary,

Chang did his best to prove that the CCP had not participated in the planning of the Sian Incident and that it had from the beginning advocated the release of Chiang Kai-shek, thus acquitting the CCP of any involvement. Yet, Mao had only reproach for Chang Hsueh-liang. He either jeered at his ignorance and impulsiveness, or blamed him for putting a snakelike ending to something with a tigerlike beginning. All this in regard to Chang was tantamount to dropping stones on a man who had fallen into a well.

Tracing things to their source, it was Stalin's famous directive on the peaceful solution of the Sian Incident and subsequent telegraphed orders that hinted to Mao Tse-tung that he must forsake Chang Hsueh-liang and do all he could to seek reconciliation with Chiang Kai-shek, reproaching Chang Hsueh-liang for being made into a cat's paw by the pro-Japanese faction. Undoubtedly, whether he liked it or not, Mao Tse-tung had to act in accordance with the orders. Yet, he was reluctant to say that the Sian Incident was plotted by the pro-Japanese faction. Probably, he inferred that if this was the case, then he himself would not be immune from the charge of being pro-Japanese. Then Chiang Kai-shek could easily rephrase his slogan, from "Establishment of Internal Peace before Resistance to Foreign Aggression" to "Liquidate Traitors before Resisting Foreign Aggressors," thus launching punitive attacks against the CCP for being Japanese spies.

The most important point in Mao Tse-tung's censure of Chang Hsueh-liang was that Chang had violated the laws of the state. This was how he described the scene of the incident: "On the early morning of December 12, Chang Hsueh-liang directed his troops to attack the Hua-ching Pool, causing serious injury to Mr. Chiang, as well as many other casualties. This was something for which no explanation will do." Mao said if he had known beforehand, he would have stopped it. This was meant to curry favor with Chiang and to express support for the Nanking government's punishment of Chang. Such exalted words, however, could hardly cover up evidence that he had double-crossed an ally.

On one occasion when Mao was chatting with me, he started discoursing on the importance of law and discipline to any government or party. Then he said sarcastically, "In the KMT there are Chang Hsueh-liang and Yang Hu-ch'eng, who have violated the law; they are dubbed 'Chang-Yang.' In the CCP, there is also a 'Chang-Yang'—Chang being Comrade Chang Kuo-t'ao, and Yang being his wife, Comrade Yang Tzu-lieh; they have also somewhat violated discipline." In reprisal for Mao's words, which were uttered to harm others and profit himself, I sallied,

"Admirable, admirable! How you have exerted yourself to defend the laws of the state! Particularly the 'brilliant discourse' from the mouth of the 'hero' of Chingkangshan. Why, it's a veritable rarity! My respects, my respects!" I was actually mocking him for being unqualified to speak on law and discipline. My words embarrassed him, and from then on, his "brilliant discourse" seemed to be somewhat restrained in front of other people.

Mao Tse-tung was then resorting to every means to disassociate the CCP from any previous connection with Chang Hsueh-liang and Yang Hu-ch'eng. General Wang Yi-che, a subordinate of Chang Hsueh-liang's who was more inclined to be pro-Communist, had on several occasions sent telegrams to Yen-an to establish liaison with the CCP, in the hope of maintaining the alliance with the CCP as Chang Hsueh-liang's successor. Every time he was thwarted by Mao Tse-tung under various pretexts. Chou En-lai in Sian also adopted the same measure, refraining from having contacts with personnel of the Northeast Army. He, however, secretly sent a few young officers and men of the Northeast Army who could no longer find a foothold in Sian to obtain refuge in Yen-an. As to relations between the CCP and Yang Hu-ch'eng, they were severed even earlier. At the same time that Chiang Kai-shek left Sian, Chou En-lai had come to an agreement with Yang Hu-ch'eng on the discontinuance of open intercourse, so as not to arouse the suspicions and jealousy of Chiang Kai-shek.

At that juncture the only out for the CCP was to come to terms with Chiang Kai-shek. It was bound up with the life and death of the CCP, and Mao Tse-tung could hardly remain remiss. He hid his consistent hatred for Chiang Kai-shek and wore a hypocritical mask in dealing with everything. He tried to erase all traces of collusion with Chang Hsueh-liang and Yang Hu-ch'eng, and kept tight lips on the secret that the peaceful solution of the Sian Incident was the result of Stalin's instructions. He declared unequivocally that the CC of the CCP was acting in accordance with its policy, which was based on the anti-Japanese national united front, alliance with Chiang, and resistance to Japan, and even support for Chiang and resistance to Japan. Proceeding from such a policy, it was natural for the CCP not to take part in the secret plot of the Sian Incident and to insist on a peaceful solution. Mao Tse-tung also secretly created public sympathy, saying that it was not so easy to uphold the policy persistently in the face of internal and external obstacles; outside the Party it had been necessary to persuade Chang Hsueh-liang and Yang Hu-ch'eng at great risk, and internally Chang

Kuo-t'ao and others had opposed peaceful solution. Mao Tse-tung did this in order to exonerate himself from blame and to lay sinister traps for others, injuring others to benefit himself, dropping stones on those who had fallen into a well, and slaying others with a borrowed knife. Seeing this, I lament that such a "manly chap" would stoop to such depths when he felt cornered.

In mid-January, 1937, Chiang Kai-shek's intention was communicated to Chou En-lai through Chang Chung, the KMT representative negotiating with the CCP.[6] It purported that if the CCP and its army would sincerely obey the National government, they would be granted an opportunity to repent and start anew. Mao Tse-tung calmed down when he heard the news. He sent a telegram to Chou, ordering him to continue negotiating with Chang Chung, and then turned his attention to the struggle within the Party. From then on, there was a continuous cease-fire between the KMT and the CCP, and talks on reconciliation were actually in progress.

The defeat of the West Wing troops had considerable effect on the future development of the CCP and on the situation in the Northwest at that time. It particularly brought great blows to me, as leader of the Fourth Front Army. The spearhead of the internal strife of the CCP was pointed at me, hitting me so hard that it was impossible for me to raise my head. The strife also exposed the extreme savageness of the Mao Tse-tung type of struggle.

The West Wing troops suffered heavy losses from raids by enemy cavalry while in Ku-lang. As it struggled to move westwards, its Fifth Army was completely annihilated by the enemy at Chiu-ch'üan, and Commander Tung Chen-t'ang was killed in battle. The road to Sinkiang fell into the hands of the enemy. With the adverse turn in the fighting, and the exhaustive consumption of its ammunition, the troops were no longer able to fight pitched battles against the enemy and had to revert to guerrilla fighting at the conclusion of the Sian Incident, having turned south to the Chi-lien mountain ranges and broken up into small groups. They were then suffering from cold weather, food shortage, and enemy pressure. A small group of some four hundred men had later succeeded in fleeing to Sinkiang. There were also some very small groups of about ten men who had turned back east and crossed the Yellow River again to rejoin the main troops in northern Shensi. If it could be said that the First Front Army was only a skeleton when it completed the Long March of 25,000 li, then the Fourth Front Army's West Wing troops could be said to have actually had its spine broken by the enemy.

Laying the blame on myself, I declared that I should shoulder all responsibility for the defeat of the West Wing troops. I did not want to shirk my responsibility and lay the blame on others, and so I had not once accused anyone else, saying that directly or indirectly I was responsible for all of the mistakes. I requested that a conference of senior cadres of the CC of the CCP be convened to review the affair of the West Wing troops, but Mao Tse-tung and the others paid no attention to my request. As a result, the CC of the CCP had not reached any conclusions on the affair, and all criticisms were inevitably arbitrary.

Mao Tse-tung would naturally keep a tight grasp on all opportunities to attack me. He himself and his followers all spoke at will, without the slightest restraint. Generally speaking, their criticisms stressed the following points:

1. The military plan to advance west was fundamentally a plan to run away, or was one tainted with such intentions.
2. Chang Kuo-t'ao's leadership of the Fourth Front Army was completely bankrupt, without one good point to speak of.
3. The defeat of the West Wing troops was a shame, causing Chiang to have greater contempt for the Red Army. It would induce Chiang to attack and take revenge on the Red Army during the period of the Sian Incident, thus injuring the entire Party and the entire army.

A group of comrades, mainly cadres of the Fourth Front Army who sympathized with me and supported me, held that the defeat of the West Wing troops was the result of the incorrect leadership of Comrade Ch'en Ch'ang-hao. They held that if I had crossed the Yellow River and taken personal command of the planning and direction, there would not have been defeat, but victory. In reply to the criticism, they said principally:

1. The plan to advance west could not be called one of running away, as it had been endorsed by Moscow.
2. The Fourth Front Army, as a powerful, basic backbone force of the CCP, should not be slandered.
3. To say that the defeat would induce the KMT to encircle and attack the CCP was a ruse to bring evil upon another in malice and to shift the target from the outside to the inside. Some

comrades went so far as to rebuke Mao Tse-tung for monopoliz-
ing the Military Committee, withholding intelligence reports that
were sorely needed by the West Wing troops, and thus being
guilty of not exerting every effort to help them. There were also
a few others who accused Mao of being dangerous on the sly,
inclined to take pleasure in the calamity of others, and devoid of
brotherly affection for the Fourth Front Army. I would not say
that these accusations were fully supported by evidence at that
time, yet it testified to the fact that right and wrong remained
clear in people's minds.

Chu Teh was then quite partial to Mao Tse-tung in his stand, yet
regarding the causes of the defeat of the West Wing troops, he maintained quite fair judgment. He pointed out to me with great care that
it could not be said that the defeat of the West Wing troops stemmed
from a fundamental mistake in the plan to advance west; it should be
recognized, however, that the general command of the West Wing troops
had made tactical errors. Only half of the Fourth Front Army had
crossed the Yellow River (the Fourth and Thirty-first armies being held
back on one side of the river), and this inevitably reduced the fighting
strength of the West Wing troops. Of course, it could not be said that
the troops were doomed to defeat with only half of the forces across the
river. The Ninth and Thirtieth armies, plus the Fifth Army Corps of
Tung Chen-t'ang, should have been ample to deal with Ma Pu-fang's
troops. He criticized Ch'en Ch'ang-hao for being excessively bold but
not stable enough, while Hsü Hsiang-ch'ien was more steady, but he
respected the opinion of the political commissar in times of crisis. He
lamented that for even such a crumbling unit as the Red Army, a wrong
step by the commander, even such a minor one as consuming a few
bullets more than necessary, could lead to trouble and calamity. He believed that if I had crossed the river, there wouldn't have been the tragic
defeat at Ku-lang. Chu Teh, therefore, affirmed that the main reasons
for the defeat of the West Wing troops lay in the sudden absence of an
experienced leader to give instructions on the spot, the inappropriate
deployment of the troops, which were unable to concentrate their forces
to deal blows to the enemy, and the lack of skill in dealing with the
fighting techniques of cavalry.

Despite the absence of a conclusion as to the causes of the defeat of
the West Wing troops, Mao Tse-tung, Chang Wen-t'ien, and others made
use of the defeat to launch a campaign against me. The anti-Chang

Kuo-t'ao campaign had been carried out in secret previously. By mid-January, 1937, when the news of the possibility of reaching a reconciliation with the KMT came, it was unfolded on a large scale. Mao Tse-tung, Chang Wen-t'ien, and others were of the opinion that since the danger of a civil war had disappeared, it was a good time to rectify and purge the Party. The aim of the struggle was to restore the prestige of the original CC of the CCP after the Tsun-yi Conference, enabling it to exercise its full authority, and to expel me from the CC. In essence, the aim of the struggle was to establish the dictatorship of Mao Tse-tung.

The first step taken by Mao Tse-tung, Chang Wen-t'ien, and others was to transfer elsewhere Lin Yu-ying, who had maintained a fair-minded attitude. At the time of the Sian Incident, Lin Yu-ying was evidently being rejected by Mao Tse-tung and others. Around mid-January, 1937, Chang Wen-t'ien proposed that Lin Yu-ying be sent to take charge of the workers' movement in regions under the KMT. I opposed the move, holding that Lin, being a conciliator in the internal dispute of the Party, ought to stay in Yen-an for the time being. Chang Wen-t'ien then said that Lin Yu-ying was somewhat afflicted with mental illness and that what Lin had said previously could not be taken seriously. I questioned Chang Wen-t'ien about whether the telegram signed jointly by the members of the CC in northern Shensi, advocating that both CC's temporarily suspend their functions and let Lin Yu-ying be liaison between the two sides, could also not be taken seriously. Chang Wen-t'ien said, with a forced smile, "What else can I do if Mao said it could not be taken seriously?"

In a sincere talk with Chang Wen-t'ien, I pointed out the following main points:

1. The current dispute within the Party could be easily resolved if Lin Yu-ying, the person responsible for liaison in the CC, would convene a conference of the CC and have all the problems threshed out satisfactorily.

2. After the switch to the anti-Japanese national united-front policy by the CC of the CCP, all disputes concerning the Soviet policy had disappeared. With the considerable success gained in the course of the execution of the new policy since the Sian Incident, I would readily rescind the opposition that I had in the past and would formally propose that the Politburo elected at the Tsun-yi Conference be given back its full functions and powers.

3. I would shoulder grave responsibilities for the defeat of the West

Wing troops and would formally table a request for due punishment.

I said to Chang Wen-t'ien, with a smile, "Chang Kuo-t'ao has already been overthrown. It is not necessary to wage vigorous struggles at this critical moment. If what has been said is denied and if Comrade Lin Yu-ying is transferred elsewhere without explicit reasons, this will amount to betraying the confidence of the Party and the comrades." Chang Wen-t'ien did not utter a word at that time and did not mention this again later. Soon afterwards the campaign against me was started with a roaring bang. The proper way to deal with the case was abandoned, while the cruelty of the campaign was concentrated on the loser. Lin Yu-ying was later sent away by Chang Wen-t'ien, using his authority as secretary of the CC of the CCP. I have since heard nothing about Lin; I don't know whether he is alive or dead.

This campaign against me, claiming to have been launched from the lower to the upper levels, consisted of devious tricks in reality. First of all, K'ai Feng, head of the Propaganda Department of the CCP, held some secret meetings of eight or ten people at a time, who had all been selected beforehand and whose inclinations were generally not pro–Chang Kuo-t'ao. The participants were expected to become activists in the campaign against me. "Shorty" K'ai Feng was a well known Mif disciple, who was incompetent in both doing things and writing articles. He, however, boastfully called himself a specialist in Party struggle. Indeed, when he recited dogmas and swooped down on the target he was attacking, he usually lost his reason. In these secret group meetings against me, he often bellowed at the top of his voice, enumerating the evildoings of Chang Kuo-t'ao. He was then often requested by the comrades to cite some facts as evidence. Some of the comrades who took part in those meetings told me about them, and said outright that they had only disdain for K'ai Feng's behavior.

The Anti-Japanese Military and Political Academy was designated as headquarters for the campaign against me. By careful prearrangement, the other classes were separated from the classes of Red Army cadres, so that the internal problems of the Red Army might not be heard by outsiders. All weapons in the academy were hidden away so as to prevent acts of violence in the course of the campaign. Activists in the campaign against me were planted in the various classes for Red Army cadres. Chang Wen-t'ien and K'ai Feng, the two specialists in Party struggle, were directors of the struggle, while Lo Jui-ch'ing, deputy principal of the academy, and Mo Wen-hua, director of the political department, were the actual commanders. Mao Tse-tung did not personally take part in the campaign rallies, but he was actually the helmsman behind the scene. Lin Piao, assuming the air of principal of the academy, was also unwilling to be publicly involved in the campaign. The other top leaders of the CCP generally stayed out of the struggle.

At the start of the campaign, some senior cadres of the Fourth Front Army came to my place, some saying that such a struggle was fundamentally wrong, and others saying that the cadres of the Fourth Front Army were not entirely free from mistakes. Still others stressed the importance of study. To them I said that it was not necessary to attach much importance to such struggles. The internal struggle of the CCP should be a political struggle based on principles. It was absolutely not permissible to turn it into a struggle that was not based on principles or one for personal attacks, insults, or slander. The campaign that they were waging now was no longer pure in nature. Comrades who valued their integrity must not imitate the attackers.

In talking with the comrades who came to visit me, I said that the current internal Party struggle often got out of the usual rut. In spite of sufficient evidence, it was not easily understood and forgiven. Take my present situation, for instance. It was unfavorable because, basically, the internal Party struggle depended upon the situation and the balance of power, instead of upon truth. At the time when we were in Mao-erh-kai, I had sufficient grounds to criticize the political line of the then CC of the CCP. But now the situation was different. Mao Tse-tung and the others had first got in touch with the Comintern, and in the execution of the policy of resistance to Japan and the national united front, they had formed an alliance with Chang Hsueh-liang and Yang Hu-ch'eng. Through the Sian Incident, they had created the possibility of reconciliation with the KMT. All these achievements had changed my mind towards opposition to Mao Tse-tung. Moreover, because of the tragic defeat sustained by the West Wing troops, I was deep in self-reproach, laying the blame on myself. I was in no mood to argue with others about rights and wrongs. I, therefore, hoped that all comrades would concentrate on study, would examine their past mistakes in work, and would no longer express opposition to the CC.

Probably due to these admonitions of mine, the small number of cadres in the First Front Army who had supported me, such as Li Cho-ju and Ho Ch'ang-kung, and the majority of the cadres of the Fourth Front Army all maintained an attitude of forbearance. They expressed support for the CC of the CCP, sincerely examined the mistakes made in the course of work in the past, and no longer criticized the CC of the CCP. The struggle, however, had gotten quite out of hand. Not only did these cadres suffer a lot of uncalled-for attacks and insults, but also many incidents broke out quite unjustifiably. I will deal with these incidents in the following passages.

First of all, the leaders of the campaign set their minds to collecting evidence of my "crimes." Despite their extensive efforts, the results were disappointing. Chang Wen-t'ien, K'ai Feng, and others hinted to their aides that it would be best to get evidence of "crimes" that I had committed in opposing the anti-Japanese national united front and the peaceful solution of the Sian Incident. There were some people at the time who turned the question around and asked Chang Wen-t'ien to give a brief account of what had happened concerning the inside story of the CC of the CCP. The question embarrassed Chang Wen-t'ien, who could only say that all he wanted to know was what I had said on these two questions in private conversations. Chang Wen-t'ien hoped to get bits of notes and other things that I had written. This was evidently a case of forming a conclusion beforehand, and then looking for evidence to prove it.

After bustling around for a while, they finally got some so-called evidence, which was, ironically, mostly favorable to me and unfavorable to them. There were also some little stories that have since become laughingstock. For instance, a comrade reported that while in Sikang, Chang So-and-so had ridiculed in front of some comrades the CCP's open letter to members of the KMT, which had been radioed to Sikang from northern Shensi. Chang had said sarcastically that the letter was a parody of the ancient tune of Han Yu's "Elegy for the Crocodiles," which the comrade took as evidence of Chang So-and-so's opposition to the anti-Japanese national united front. But the open letter was written by Mao Tse-tung himself, who had on the spot admitted the parody. Chang So-and-so was right after all, while the one who accused him only showed his own ignorance of Chinese literature.

It was said that when this thing was all in a mess, no other than Mao Tse-tung himself stepped forth to put an end to it. Apparently Mao told them that he himself had more than once reported to the Comintern that I, along with other members of the CC in northern Shensi, completely approved of the anti-Japanese national united front. How was it possible to find any evidence to reverse that judgment? Mao had also pointed out that opposition to the peaceful solution of the Sian Incident could not be put forth as a subject for discussion, much less talked about in public. Mao had mocked the campaign leaders, advising them not to look for trouble. He told them to find "evidence of crimes" in other quarters.

In the eyes of the campaign leaders, my crimes, such as rightist opportunism, bankruptcy of leadership with regard to the Fourth Front Army, opposition to the Party and the CC, and so forth, were as good as settled, with the defeat of the West Wing troops as obvious evidence. Yet, when they tried to search for more "evidence of crimes" concerning the bankruptcy of my leadership among the many cadres of the Fourth Front Army, their efforts were futile. What was more, those efforts led to complicated arguments, which proved to be unfavorable to Mao Tse-tung, Chang Wen-t'ien, and the CC, which was controlled by them. As a result, they arbitrarily decided that I was "guilty" of splitting the CC, even going so far as to oppose the Party and the CC. They held that this "crime" stemmed from my "banditism" and "militarism," because only "banditism" could produce such violent opposition to the CC, and only "militarism" could lead to an attempt to usurp the authority of the CC. They thought that everything could be covered up by this simple logic.

Since the major points in my "crimes" had been settled, the emphasis in the campaign turned to winning over the cadres of the Fourth Front Army. The campaign leaders shouted at the tops of their voices that the cadres of the Fourth Front Army should return and come under the leadership of the CC of the CCP, examine their past mistakes, and not persist in their mistakes any longer under my influence. This call did not produce good results, as many cadres advocated that the examination of mistakes should be all-out and not one-sided. To put it plainly, this was a demand to examine whether the CC under Mao Tse-tung had made any mistakes.

In this way, the struggle went into a very vicious stage in which Lo Jui-ch'ing and Mo Wen-hua led a group of triggermen who launched a campaign against cadres of the Fourth Front Army individually or in small groups. They haughtily cross-examined those being attacked, their questions concentrating on the following points: "Have you killed people indiscriminately?" "Have you personally beaten up local tyrants?" "Have you raped any women?" "What have you said or done against the CC?" And so forth.

This form of struggle was extremely insulting, being no different from the KMT trials of "Communist bandits." The cadres of the Fourth Front Army were extremely disgusted. Those being attacked declared courageously and with justification that they themselves, being Red Army soldiers, were not to be insulted and would not answer any such questions. Some declared that they had gone through hundreds of battles, suffering many wounds. They had devoted their lives to the CCP from its early days, and they would certainly not admit that they were "bandits," nor would they tolerate insults. These strong protests could not awaken Mao Tse-tung and his henchmen. Finally, the students of the Anti-Japanese Academy raised an uproar. Former senior cadres of the Fourth Front Army, including Hsü Shih-yu, Wang Chien-an, and some ten others, got about four or five hundred students of the academy together under their leadership and attempted to leave the academy as their first action. Though they did not say so openly, their action was evidently tantamount to resistance to Mao Tse-tung and the CC of the CCP.

This event gave Yen-an a great shock. In order to appease the unrest, Chu Teh and Lin Piao invited me to make a speech to the academy. On the campus of the academy I solemnly addressed the entire student body. I pointed out that all students of the academy and all CCP members should refrain from actions that violated discipline, while the internal Party struggle should also be carried out in an orderly way. Every comrade, no matter from which army, must examine the errors that he might have committed in the past; he also had the right to refute, righteously and solemnly, all unjustified rebukes. If the problems could not be solved in the academy, it was not permissible to violate discipline. Every comrade had the privilege of bringing his case before the upper-level Party organization, the CC of the CCP, and even the Comintern.

This address of mine in effect appeased the unrest of the students of the academy. Yet, in the opinion of Mao Tse-tung, who regarded me as a culprit and a hostage, my words were still full of challenge. He, therefore, adopted measures of still greater pressure. Instead of keeping his promise of setting free the ten or more arrested senior cadres, including Hsü Shih-yu and Wang Chien-an, he arrested more people, bringing the total arrested to more than forty, whom he handed over to Tung Pi-wu, president of the Supreme Court, for trial.

Among those arrested was Ho Wei, former commander of the Ninth Army in the Fourth Front Army and currently deputy principal of the Red Army School. From the very beginning Ho Wei had resisted this form of struggle and had defended the leadership of the Fourth Front

Army. Ho Wei truly came from the working class, having performed outstanding deeds in battle while in the Red Army and having been wounded eleven times. Mao Tse-tung and the others could hardly do anything to him. Ho Wei had not taken part in the resistance uproar of the students of the academy, but he had protested the arrest of Hsü Shih-yu, Wang Chien-an, and others. He declared indignantly that the character of the CC of the CCP and the Anti-Japanese Academy had deteriorated until it resembled that of the government under the Pei-yang warlords. He said that he would bring the case before the Comintern, or he would leave the Communist Party. As a result, Ho Wei was secretly arrested. Later, Chang Wen-t'ien explained to me that Ho Wei had only been put under temporary custody for fear he might be despondent enough to commit suicide. He was to be accommodated and given preferential treatment, since he was disabled and had performed meritorious military deeds. He was not going to be tried in the courts. Being reluctant to aggravate the crisis in the Party, I only glared at Chang Wen-t'ien, without saying a word.

Soon afterwards, Chou En-lai met with some danger on his way from Yen-an to Sian and thence to Nanking. That was around February 20, 1937. Chou En-lai's lorry was attacked by local bandits some thirty li from Yen-an. He and his armed guards, totaling about ten people, turned back to Yen-an after the fright. This was regarded as a serious political plot by the sly, oversuspicious strongman, who was accustomed to measure a gentleman with a villain's mind. In view of the fact that Chou's guards and the units stationed at the place where the incident took place and in its vicinity were originally subordinate to the Fourth Front Army, he inferred that the danger encountered by Chou En-lai might have been masterminded by me.

On the evening of the same day, a curfew was announced in Yen-an, and the situation became very tense. My residence was guarded by a large number of troops. At midnight, when I woke up in fright from my dreams, I found that a squad of guards entrusted with the task of protecting me had manned the defense posts along the walls surrounding my residence. I immediately asked the squad leader the reason for all this. He said that they had seen the security company of the Political Security Bureau surrounding the house outside the walls, pointing their guns at the house. Meanwhile there didn't seem to be any action among the troops elsewhere. The squad leader had decided that there was a conspiracy against me. Consequently, he had ordered the whole squad to stand guard along the inside of the surrounding walls, in case anything happened. He had ordered the whole squad to take an oath, pledging to defend Chairman Chang to the death. The guards were to shoot at anyone who came near Chairman Chang's residence. They were also to notify the Guard Battalion stationed in the vicinity, which was originally subordinate to the Fourth Front Army, to come to the chairman's rescue.

I asked the squad leader why he had given such an order and why he was to agitated. He told me that the guards were already very indignant about the struggle in the Anti-Japanese Academy and were aware that someone was conspiring to harm me. The squad leader was willing to risk his life, and having done all this without requesting instructions beforehand, he was ready to shoulder all the responsibility. He had thought about all this before giving the order. I then walked along the walls surrounding my house to observe what was going on. In the moonlight I could see the security company spreading out some forty or fifty meters from my house, apparently standing at ease, with guns in their hands, waiting for orders. I told the squad leader that it seemed unlikely that the men of the company would do anything untoward. I ordered them to leave their defense posts immediately and to do as I ordered, no matter what might happen. At two o'clock in the morning, the security company finally went away.

Then, about nine o'clock, Chang Wen-t'ien came and talked to me about irrelevant things. Embarrassment was written all over his face, and he was unable to hide it. I conversed with him as usual, without once mentioning what had happened the night before. He began to regain his composure a bit, and said to me straight away, "It has been proven that the danger Comrade Chou En-lai encountered yesterday was a raid by local bandits." He also said that the troops stationed in that vicinity, originally of the Fourth Front Army, had done very well and had captured several of the bandits alive in a persistent chase. The evidence given by the captured bandits established that the raid was an ordinary robbery. They did not know that it was Chou En-lai who was passing that way. As I listened, I assumed a nonchalant air, talking and laughing freely. Thus the dense fog that had hidden the sky lightly disappeared.

The constant occurrence of such events pained me greatly. I decided to move out of the city of Yen-an, and never again to concern myself with Party matters. I toured the outskirts of Yen-an, visiting the mountains and rivers and looking for a suitable abode. Finally, on a hill to the north of Yen-an I found a dilapidated temple which had a rocky cave fit for human habitation. After some repairs had been made by my guards under my supervision, the cave took on a new look. A small square was opened up on the left of the temple, and in less than two weeks I moved into my new abode.

I felt that the CCP was moving along Stalin's road and was surpassing him rather than lagging behind him. Stalin had killed off large numbers of revolutionary veterans of great distinction; now the CCP was persecuting meritorious commanders and officers of the Fourth Front Army. Stalin had implicated his opponents falsely, making use of the murder of Kirov; now the CCP was attempting to implicate me, making use of the danger encountered by Chou En-lai. If the bandits had not been captured alive by the Fourth Front Army, imprisonment of the wrong people might have resulted. All of the protests that I had lodged against this perfidious type of struggle inside the Party had proved to be futile. It would be of no avail if I spoke up now. Communism had disappeared; all that was left was Machiavellianism and struggle, which had become unalterable principles for the maintenance of Mao Tse-tung's power. The charges against the Red Fourth Front Army and myself, such as "warlords," "bandits," and what not, were but ridiculous slanders.

Mao Tse-tung's unreasonable savageness did not always work; so he sometimes assumed a smiling face. After the incident of Chou En-lai's encounter with danger, Mao Tse-tung once said to me in a light mood that it was not important if one was criticized as a warlord or bandit. He recalled that since joining the CCP, he had been expelled from the CC three times and had received serious warnings eight times. Fortunately, he had not yet been charged with opposition to the CC. He then went on to confide that even he was not entirely immune from the ways and habits of warlords and bandits. During the period of the burning and killing policy of 1927–1928, he had given an order to kill the entire family of a landlord, including children a few years' old. These past events were embarrassing to recall; they were an expression of the ways and habits of bandits and warlords.

Evidently Mao Tse-tung said all these things in the hope that I would admit to having the "ways and habits of bandits and warlords." His hypocrisy infuriated me. I said to him, "You were a pioneer in guerrilla warfare, having experienced the period when there was a policy of burning and killing. When I went to the Oyüwan region to take over leadership work after the Fourth Plenum of the CC in 1931, the policy of burning and killing had become obsolete. I have not once given a direct order for killing people. I have opposed the CC, but my opposition can not possibly be linked with the 'ways and habits of warlords and bandits.'

Moreover, the KMT is railing against us, calling us warlords and bandits. If we inadvertently admit these charges ourselves, will it not amount to a voluntary confession?"

Lin Po-ch'ü at that time was quite fair in his attitude. Once he invited me to dinner, during which he said to me, "Each CCP leader has his strong points and shortcomings; each past event has its rights and wrongs. Now, everyone must be somewhat accommodating for the good of the whole situation." He stated that he had said this not only to me, but also to Comrade Mao Tse-tung. His main purpose was to persuade all of us to take the difficult situation into consideration and to avoid unnecessary disputes. His words did more or less influence me in my decision to accommodate myself to circumstances for the benefit of the overall situation.

Tung Pi-wu, in his handling of the trials of the arrested cadres of the Fourth Front Army, further toned down the struggle. He conducted personal interviews with the arrested cadres individually. Finally it was established that Ho Wei, Hsü Shih-yu, Wang Chien-an, and other opponents had not launched organized activities and that they had had no one to direct and manipulate them from behind the scene. They had resorted to resistance out of indignation and discontent over the campaign against the students of the Anti-Japanese Academy. Tung Pi-wu consequently released most of the comrades. A small number of them were sentenced to short terms of confinement, the longest not exceeding three months, and they were all released before their terms expired. All those who were released went back to their studies in the academy.

Though the struggle in the academy was still bent on giving vent to hatred, it was compelled to take a more moderate form, owing to the great storm it had generated. The emphasis now turned to forcing the cadres originally from the Fourth Front Army to admit their mistake of opposing the CC. Thus, a few of them, including Fu Chung and Wang Wei-chou, began to criticize errors made by the leadership of the Fourth Front Army, while the majority said that they were willing to study with enthusiasm under the leadership of the entire CC. Subsequently, the atmosphere of resistance in the Anti-Japanese Military and Political Academy gradually disappeared.

Mao Tse-tung, Chang Wen't'ien, and the others then convened a meeting to oppose me, which was called an enlarged meeting of the CC of the CCP, although most of the important leaders such as members of the Politburo of the CC, including Chou En-lai, Ch'in Pang-hsien, Wang Chia-hsiang, and Jen Pi-shih, and important persons concerned, including

Tung Pi-wu, Lin Po-ch'ü, Lin Piao, Lo Jui-ch'ing, and Mo Wen-hua, were absent. Among the more than twenty participants, the majority were students of the Anti-Japanese Academy.

The meeting started with an anti–Chang Kuo-t'ao report made by K'ai Feng. He spoke for a time on the consistent correctness of the political line of the CC of the CCP and criticized me for my error in opposing the CC. Then he answered questions from students of the academy. He said that in the academy there were some students who reproached the CC for discriminating against cadres of the Fourth Front Army and for not treating them as comrades, which was even worse than the way they treated captives. The method of struggle was contrary to Communist ethics. In replying to this sort of question, K'ai Feng quoted Stalin's words to defend the use of cruel and ruthless methods of struggle in opposing the errors of left- and right-deviationism inside the Party. This was completely beside the point. He was unable to offer any defense to the accusation of treating comrades worse than captives.

In reply to the students' statements that it was unjustifiable to ignore the heroic struggles of the Fourth Front Army and the achievements under my leadership in the Oyüwan Soviet region and the Northern Szechwan Soviet region, K'ai Feng said that the Fourth Front Army indeed had made great contributions to the CCP and the Soviet campaign, but that this could not lessen the "crimes" of Chang Kuo-t'ao. These achievements of the Fourth Front Army were attributable to the correct leadership of the Comintern and the CC of the CCP, particularly of the late Shen Tse-min, who had been able to persist in the Bolshevik principles. Chang Kuo-t'ao, however, had opposed the Comintern and the CC all along. Undoubtedly, Shen Tse-min had been able to master the correct principles due to his pure Leninist education and Bolshevik training in Moscow. Despite the many things that he had accomplished, Chang Kuo-t'ao, on the other hand, had an opportunist background. He could not become anything but a warlord and bandit and had to oppose the CC when the occasion arose.

After spending a long time answering these questions, K'ai Feng, who was in charge of the attack, turned his attention to the defeat of the West Wing troops, saying that their defeat was due mainly to the fact that the ordinary cadres of the Fourth Front Army were for the most part not sufficiently Bolshevized. Only Tung Chen-t'ang had had a bit more Bolshevik training, but he had been killed in battle. The death of Tung Chen-t'ang should be regarded as the result of Chang Kuo-t'ao's errors. It was tantamount to his being murdered by Chang Kuo-t'ao. Then he raised his voice and shouted like a lunatic, "We must make Chang Kuo-t'ao pay for the life of Comrade Tung Chen-t'ang!" Concluding his speech, K'ai Feng again shouted such phrases as "Down with warlords, bandits, and opposition to the CC."

This speech by K'ai Feng for the prosecution was far from brilliant and aroused much disgust. Displeasure was registered on the face of Mao Tse-tung, who was present. He seemed to feel that this was just an old tune of the Mif faction, quite similar in phraseology to that employed against himself in the Kiangsi Soviet region. Chang Wen-t'ien was sitting there in futile anxiety, seeing that K'ai Feng had fallen into the trap of answering questions and had lost his grip on the theme of the prosecution. The other participants remained indifferent. I, the one under attack, felt relaxed, deciding that such viciousness and mediocrity could scarcely hurt me. Indeed, after his defeat in this performance, K'ai Feng seemed to meet with difficulty in climbing higher.

In order to make up for the deficiency in K'ai Feng's prosecution, Chang Wen-t'ien immediately got up to speak. His myopic eyes deeply hidden behind the spectacles on his gloomy face, he delivered his speech, as if he were reciting notes by rote. The main idea was that my errors had developed into "anti-Party Chang Kuo-t'aoism," which was characterized first by "bandit ways," second by "warlord ways," and third by bringing about the split of the CC. All these were not only errors but crimes, which ought to be punished in accordance with Party discipline.

Mao Tse-tung, in his speech, purposely assumed a light manner, chuckling incessantly, as if to boast of his elation. The main topic in his speech could be summed up thus: "Chang Kuo-t'ao, this old friend, I understand him most clearly. He has had an inclination to oppose the CC all along and has been 'the grandfather of factionists.'" He did not mention any "charges," but went on to say that the present situation was unfavorable to Comrade Kuo-t'ao, whom all comrades were criticizing. What was to be done? He adminished with a sarcastic grin, "Confess your sins, then."

Chu Teh, evidently in a heavy-hearted mood, spoke in a solemn manner. What he said could be summed us thus: "When the Cho-ko-chi Conference set up a provisional CC, I advised against it; now everyone seems to have acknowledged it as a mistake. As far as I can see, Kuo-t'ao still smacks of the ways of Peking University, being influenced by the doctrines of science and democracy of the May Fourth Movement and the experimentalism theory preached by Hu Shih-chih and others. As a result, he like to argue about the rights and wrongs of things until what is correct and what is incorrect has been made perfectly clear, thus causing trouble for himself and others." Whether Chu Teh's mention of my smacking of Peking University seemed to indicate that he disapproved of the rebukes that I was a "warlord and bandit," or that he reproved me for my remaining bourgeois ideas, I could not say for sure.

My reply in defense of myself was quite simple. First of all, I admitted my mistake in setting up a provisional CC, pointing up that I had exaggerated the mistakes in policy committed by the CC of the CCP. Now, facts had proved that the original CC had shown enthusiasm in executing the new policy of an anti-Japanese national united front and had achieved remarkable results. We, therefore, had long since done away with the situation of having two CC's in opposition to one another. I now formally accepted the reasonable criticism of my opposition to the CC and was willing to shoulder all responsibility, as I should, for opposing the CC. Besides this, I made statements on two more points: First, it was small wonder that dissension had arisen in the Party, since the Soviet policy of the CCP had come to a dead end and the policy had not yet been changed as it should have been. How was it possible, then, to ignore the cause for my opposition to the CC and only resort to high-handed pressure? Second, I was reluctant to defend myself with regard to the reproaches I had been submitted to; but the heroic struggles of the Red Fourth Front Army were certainly not to be ignored. It should be recognized as a powerful Worker-Peasant Red Army, subordinate to the CCP, a cultured and disciplined force.

Just as I finished my speech and was going to step down from the platform, Comrade Chou Kun a veteran cadre of Chingkangshan days, stood up and shouted, "Do you call this a confession of mistakes? Let's drag him out to a public trial!" Chou Kun was an old friend of Mao Tse-tung's. Despite his age, which was less than forty, he was usually in low spirits; but that shout of his was quite uplifting. With great patience, I replied, "Well, first of all, I would like to hear your accusation. I have admitted all the mistakes that it is my duty to admit. If Comrade Chou Kun still wants to make savage attacks, I will, if you will excuse me, exercise my right to do my best to defend myself and to counterattack." Before Chou Kun could say another word, the chairman of the meeting announced that it was adjourned.

Around nine o'clock the next day, the CC of the CCP, in the name of the Politburo, held a meeting to discuss a draft resolution written by Chang Wen-t'ien in accordance with the discussions at the meeting. The main point in the draft resolution was opposition to anti-Party Chang

Kuo-t'aoism, which included traces of the thinking of warlords and bandits and had eventually caused the splitting of the CC. I arrived at the meeting on time. After reading the draft resolution, I said to Chang Wen-t'ien, with a grim smile, "It is a fact that I have opposed the CC, and punishment may be meted out at the convenience of the CC. Why is it necessary to coin the unwarranted phrase 'Chang Kuo-t'aoism'?" After waiting for a while, since Mao Tse-tung and the others failed to show up for unknown reasons, I also took my leave. I have not seen the resolution again since that time. The final draft is said to have been much milder in tone than the original. "Anti-Party Chang Kuo-t'aoism" was changed to "Chang Kuo-t'ao's anti-Party line," and there was only criticism without any mention of punishment.

The struggle seemed to have a tigerlike beginning and a snakelike ending. At the start Chang Wen-t'ien, K'ai Feng, and others were shouting "crimes," "punishment," "paying with his life," "public trial," and so forth. In fact they were prepared at least to expel me from the CC. But it finally ended with a watered-down resolution. I retained my usual posts as a member of the CC and the Politburo. According to reliable sources, the reason for this was the opposition of the Comintern, which sent a telegram saying that it was not permissible to effect organizational sanctions as Chang Kuo-t'ao was well known at home and abroad as a leader of the CCP with tangible achievements. Meanwhile, the peace talks between the KMT and the CCP had struck hidden shoals. In the event of a breakdown, it would again be necessary to have men like Chang Kuo-t'ao and cadres of the Fourth Front Army to go to the battlefield.

After the struggle, I moved to my new abode. I seemed to have undergone a great change of mood. I lived like a hermit there, alone, closing the door to visitors, even refusing to have a telephone installed. I wandered among the mountains and rivers, watching the bustling crowd down below in Yen-an, feeling calm and gratified. Thus, though an actor in name, I was really only a spectator.

Reminiscing about the past, I cannot help feeling that all was inevitably unimportant—whether I did not approve of this or that policy, or opposed this or that measure, or ran around about this or that affair. I detested struggle and power and those sorts of things, finding them to be but ridiculous games. I felt that everything in the world had its dark side. Politics incorporated evil; revolution was not necessarily sacred and pure. As to acts in violation of morals and justice that were necessary to attain some political goal, they were utterly despicable. I had not yet decided to escape from the circle I had drawn around myself, but I was sensing the threat from the dark side. I was aware that the fundamental defect of communism was too big, and that tyrannical dictatorship was extremely reactionary. It would destroy all idealism.

During my stay on the hill in the subsequent month or more, I totally disregarded the notices of meetings from the CC of the CCP and the documents of the Politburo, which kept coming to me. I did not attend the meetings, nor did I ask permission to be absent. This seemed to be my silent protest. However, an unexpected event disturbed my peace. One forenoon in the beginning of April, Mao Tse-tung visited me with all the committee members of the Politburo then in Yen-an. We shook hands and asked after one another. They were all smiles, praising my abode as Arcadia, a refuge from the bustling world. They said there was a problem on which they needed my advice. I answered courteously, thanking them for taking the tiring trip to visit me.

We sat around a square table in the courtyard outside my cave. Mao Tse-tung showed me a telegram from Chou En-lai, which said, in general, that Nanking's conditions for Communists to surrender and begin a new life were earnest repentance for past troubles, obedience to the Three Principles of the People, strict observance of State laws and military orders, and immediate reorganization of the Red Army, abolition of the Soviet government, cessation of Red propaganda, and relinquishment of class struggle.[7] It stated that after negotiations, Nanking had promised to set up a special area in the Northern Shensi Soviet region, which would be under the rule of the Shensi provincial government. The special area would be under an administrative director, who would be a person recommended by our side and appointed by the Nationalist government at the request of the Shensi provincial government. All administrative units in the special area would follow the regulations of the Nationalist government. Chou's telegram pointed out that the other side had decided not to make any more concessions, and that the only thing for us to do was to say yes or no.

As I read the document carefully, I was guessing about the intentions of the top leaders of the Politburo in honoring me with their visit. They seemed to be waiting for my views. I looked up and said coolly, "I am thinking about the time when Lenin was going to sign the Brest Peace Treaty with Germany." These words of mine pleased Mao Tse-tung. He said, "Heroes think alike." The conference then brightened up. All said that if we did not accept the conditions, we would have to consider the consequences seriously.

Everyone began to reminisce about the past and look into the future. Mao Tse-tung talked more than anybody else. His remarks could be summed up thus: First, what Chiang Kai-shek was up to was still uncertain. Some of his actions showed a tendency towards resistance to Japan, while others showed a tendency to suppress the anti-Japanese forces. In regard to the former, during the Sian Incident the faction in Nanking that favored peace (who were close to the anti-Japanese forces) seemed to have gotten the upper hand, while the faction that favored launching punitive expeditions (who were close to the pro-Japanese faction) received some blows, and such slogans as "pacification of the domestic trouble," "suppression of the bandits," and the like, were less frequently heard. The voice of resistance to Japan became louder. Moreover, Chiang himself hated Japan deeply. With regard to the latter, Chiang had dealt with people involved in the Sian Incident, attacking them one by one. At first Chang Hsueh-liang was tried and confined. Then, the troops of Chang Hsueh-liang and Yang Hu-ch'eng were forced to leave Sian and later were divided. Chiang's Central Army troops had entered Sian and were stationed there in large numbers. Chiang still called us reactionaries and had not given up the attempt to annihilate us. We would have to spend much of our energy in pushing him onto the road of resistance to Japan.

Second, the CC of the CCP had all along been pushing Chiang Kai-shek ahead onto the road of resistance. On February 10 it sent a telegram to the Third Plenum of the CC of the KMT, expressing a desire for peace and unity in the country. The KMT had generally ignored the telegram. Chou En-lai was running around outside the meeting, keeping in touch with Chang Chung all the time and contacting Chiang through Chang Chung. The KMT had decided on the principle of permitting the CCP to surrender and begin a new life, but its attitude was insufferable. Chou En-lai frequently heard such remarks as "The CCP can only surrender unconditionally, otherwise it will be annihilated." Mao Tse-tung said that the indignities that Chou En-lai suffered in the course of negotiating with the KMT far exceeded those that I had suffered in Canton after the March Twentieth Incident of 1926.

Third, Mao Tse-tung laughed at Chiang Kai-shek and the KMT for their "Ah Q" spirit (self-deceptive delusions of grandeur).[8] Obviously, the anti-Japanese elements had forced Chiang to give up suppression of the Communists, but he still assumed the nasty insolence of the Nationalist government, clamoring "Root out Red troubles" and "Make the CCP surrender," making a big fuss in both oral and written statements, but being careless and negligent when it came to enforcing them. Mao Tse-tung was of the opinion that if Chiang and the KMT wanted to be "Ah Q," then let them have the satisfaction of indulging in self-importance. What we wanted was to actually stop the civil war and to resist Japan.

Four, the CC of the CCP could send an answering telegram to Chou En-lai, accepting the so-called conditions of surrender. We approved of the Three Principles of the People as they stood in 1924, when the KMT was reorganized on the basis of these three great policies. This was quite different from the present reactionary behavior of the KMT. As to re-organization of the Red Army, abolition of the Soviets, cessation of the land revolution, and so forth, these were some of the stipulations for the anti-Japanese national united front that we had advanced earlier. In addition, we could also list some positive demands for resistance to Japan, such as resistance to Japanese aggression, guarantee of the free-dom of speech and assembly, release of political prisoners, and so forth. What we must defend resolutely was the independence of the CCP, the forces of the Red Army, and the base in northern Shensi.

Five, after agreeing to the KMT's conditions, we could still adopt the delaying policy to deal with the "Ah Q." The KMT had aimed at our utter annihilation; that was the intention behind the conditions of sur-render. We could prevent the KMT from reorganizing and dispersing our Red Army on this or that excuse. We could still ask the Nationalist government to put the northern Shensi special area under its rule, but we must strive to control the transfer of personnel by fighting for our recommendations on personnel in the special area. Land within the Soviet region that had already been distributed must not be returned to the original owners; the forces of the landlords' militia must not be allowed to rise again. So long as we could keep on with our delaying tactics, all would be resolved smoothly once the Anti-Japanese War of Resistance broke out.

Six, we felt that there would also be danger in accepting the condi-tions for surrender. In case a war of resistance against Japan did not break out for a time, Chiang Kai-shek might back out. Or in case he enforced the conditions in strong actions, sending people to count and check on the Red Army, infiltrating our forces, transferring them at will, and at the same time sending large numbers of special agents to infiltrate into the lower-level organs of the northern Shensi special area to make trouble, then there would be no time for our delaying tactics. Even if we were forced to retreat to our last battle positions, we would, nevertheless, rise up and resist. Moreover, we could thus gain time to rebuild our own strength.

Seven, we held that this was a grave and critical juncture, to be dealt with cautiously by the whole Party united as one. First of all, such statements of the KMT as that they would allow the CCP to surrender and begin a new life would cause internal disturbances when they reached the ears of the ordinary comrades. We must have the sincere cooperation of all members of the CC so as to patiently convince the comrades at all levels and, especially, to push the KMT onto the road of resistance to Japan, thus preventing it from attacking us. Steellike unity of the whole Party was all the more necessary in this case.

I expressed my approval of this way of doing things and pointed out that since we had acted for a time like the outwardly humble but inwardly vengeful Yueh Prince Kou-chien, we might as well continue in that role.[9] Mao Tse-tung applauded my words, crying, "Hear! Hear! Let Chiang Kai-shek be Ah Q while we play the role of Kou-chien!" Then we decided on the points to be covered in the answering telegram to Chou En-lai, accepting the conditions of the KMT. The meeting then concluded in an atmosphere of unity and peace. This was the only fruitful meeting that I had attended since the Sian Incident.

The meeting warmed up my cold and lonesome heart. I felt that the members of the Politburo came to my lodging to hold the meeting out of a desire to compromise, since I had not attended the meetings of the CC. It showed that my consent was regarded as important on such an important occasion. All signs at the meeting pointed to a conciliatory solicitude, which imperceptibly patched up the fissures caused by the struggles in the past. As I had given my word on shouldering the common responsibility, I had to consider whether I should attend the CC's meetings and take part in the work in the future. I finally made up my mind that I would maintain my previous attitude, not wishing to be ordered around by those schemers any longer. I decided that I would not attend any more meetings of the CC, but I would do some work.

A few days after the meeting, Ch'eng Fang-wu, dean of the Anti-Japanese Academy, invited me to teach political economics at the academy. He told me that the course was for a senior class of some forty students, all of whom were students in the economics departments of various universities, over half of them being university graduates and the ones at the lowest level being third-year students. Needless to say, they had considerable knowledge of economics. However, what they had learned was bourgeois economics. I was to teach them Marxist economics.

During the period of 1928–1930, I had studied Karl Marx's *Das Kapital* in Moscow for two years. I had had only a smattering of economics. Moreover, during recent years, I had led the life of a soldier, having thrown aside my books a long time ago. I told Ch'eng Fang-wu that a half-baked teacher like me would not be able to lecture on economics. Ch'eng insisted that I take the job, saying that if I didn't agree to do so, there would be no one else to do it. So, I had to do my best despite the difficulty.

At that time, young students from all over China were streaming to Yen-an in ever greater numbers. Like the ones before them, they rushed to Yen-an from remote corners of the country, with their rucksacks strapped to their backs, defying long treks, dangers, and difficulties. Some reached their destination only after overcoming great hardships. Some were barred from traveling further by the KMT, while others were even arrested or killed. They regarded Yen-an as the Holy Land of resistance to Japan. "Those who are for resistance to Japan go to Yen-an" had become the slogan among the young people. The KMT's policy of suppressing youths was tantamount to driving the birds to the thickets and the fish to deep waters.

The CC of the CCP allocated places in the Anti-Japanese Military and Political Academy to all of those young people coming to Yen-an. By April, there were more than one thousand students from outside, so that the academy had to be enlarged, using the site near the airfield outside the city to build new premises when the downtown campus became overcrowded. The academy was poorly equipped, lacking both teaching staff and teaching materials; but the number of students and classes increased daily. Mao Tse-tung had lectured them on philosophy and problems of strategy. The articles he published later, such as "The Problem of Strategy in the Chinese Revolutionary War," "On Contradictions," "On Practice," and so forth, were all based on lectures given at the academy. Chang Wen-t'ien and K'ai Feng had given lectures on Leninism, Party organization, and so forth, while Chu Teh lectured on guerrilla tactics and similar subjects. All the VIP's of the CC were shouldering heavy lecture schedules; I was a relative latecomer.

The course of lectures on economics that I was going to deliver would have to be completed in three months, nine hours a week, taking up three mornings. This was an onerous burden that nearly did me in. I collected all the books on economics that could be found in Yen-an, and I worked at preparing my lectures all day and until midnight every night.

My lectures were delivered in a classroom on the premises near the airfield. The students came with their own stools, sitting there in rows while listening to me lecture. There was nothing in the classroom except a blackboard. All of the students came to class on time and never missed a class except for illness. They all took notes assiduously, taking no notice of irrelevant matters. All of their questions concentrated on economics. Since they felt that they had come of their own accord to study, no inconveniences in the life of Yen-an would deter them from seeking knowledge.

Having thus exerted myself for three months, I was fortunately able to complete my task. Had it not been for the gunshots at Lu-kou-chiao (Marco Polo Bridge), which altered my life in teaching, I would have gone on teaching and perhaps become a professor of economics. My more than forty students had got on with me in perfect harmony, like the blending of water and milk. We were frank and sincere in our relationships with each other, dispensing with the usual dignified reserve that existed between teacher and students. The students found that I was the most capable of the economics professors that they had encountered. The academy authorities also regarded me as a good teacher. Though I knew that I was but a student of economics, I found all encouragements comforting.

My zeal for study made me forget my hardship, and I no longer felt the monotony of daily life. In my spare time I usually received students at my abode, and they taught me anti-Japanese songs, never getting tired of teaching me, a most stupid student in learning music. My comrades and my students sometimes came to walk and chat with me. Cadres of the Fourth Front Army also came in groups to see me. On my way down the hill to the academy, I was often surrounded by people chatting with me. My policy was that when some internal problem concerning the Party came up, I would smile and decline to answer.

The influx of progressive students from other places—mostly sympathizers with communism—brought about a change in the atmosphere of Yen-an. They had brought news from the various big cities, widening the horizon of the guerrilla heroes of Yen-an. Whether in their conversations, in cultural and entertainment activities, or in public events, the theme was no longer the monotonous story of the Long March. All topics centered on resistance to Japan. People gradually came to know about the social conditions of various places, and outside influences increased day by day. A small number of CCP members, including Liu Shao-ch'i, who had been working in the White areas, came secretly to Yen-an, directly influencing the top leaders of the CCP.

Liu Shao-ch'i came from the White area in about April and handed in a very long written report to the CC of the CCP. He described the upsurge in the anti-Japanese campaign in various places, and pointed out that the CCP was weak in its leadership of the resistance to Japan. The CCP's work in the White areas was very fragmentary, the reason for which, according to Liu Shao-ch'i, being the leftist tendency in the policy of the CCP over a prolonged period. In his opinon, the CCP's policy towards the KMT and its policy in leading the worker-peasant masses during the period of KMT-CCP cooperation tended to be more leftist than rightist. Later, in the Soviet period, the error of being leftist was even more serious, obliterating even the danger of Japan's attempt to destroy China. In view of this, he demanded that the CCP's policy be changed rapidly in the light of the existing situation.

This ten-thousand-word report by Liu Shao-ch'i made the CC of the CCP uncomfortable. The faction of students who had returned from Russia, including Chang Wen-t'ien and others, held that this was an outrageous proposal, because Liu Shao-ch'i went to such lengths as to say that the CCP had made the major mistake of being leftist during the period of the first cooperation between the KMT and the CCP. This was an outright whitewash of Ch'en Tu-hsiu's rightist opportunism. It also negated the whole Soviet campaign. They rebuked Liu Shao-ch'i's proposal as anti-Comintern and anti–CC of the CCP, and said that he was being influenced by the thinking of Chang Kuo-t'ao. There were even some people who said, "Liu Shao-ch'i is even worse than Chang Kuo-t'ao."

Liu Shao-ch'i was very cautious in his attitude, avoiding contact with me in order not to be suspected of the stain of the anti-Party Chang Kuo-t'ao line. I did not go to the town of Yen-an, nor did I attend any meetings to discuss Liu Shao-ch'i's proposal. I was reluctant to be involved in the dispute again. Mao Tse-tung seemed to be more worldly-wise than those who had returned from Russia. He was relatively more friendly to Liu Shao-ch'i, finding that Liu did not intend to oppose the CC. He, therefore, did his best to mediate between the conflicting opinions of Liu Shao-ch'i, on the one side, and Chang Wen-t'ien, on the other.

Besides this, Liu Shao-ch'i had timed his proposal at the right moment. The CC of the CCP was adopting an attitude of compromise, accepting the conditions of surrender put forward by the KMT. It was commonly felt that if the CC opposed Liu Shao-ch'i's views, it would be difficult to explain its recent move. As a result, at the meeting of the Politburo of the CCP, Liu Shao-ch'i, despite criticisms from Chang Wen-t'ien and others, was elected to membership in the Politburo, with the responsibility of directing the Party's work in the White areas. His success was due to the support of Mao Tse-tung. Thus started the cooperation between Mao and Liu in politics. Later, in 1942, they together unfolded the rectification campaign against the Mif faction.

It seemed to be the CCP's good luck that brought it through this crisis. After the CCP accepted the KMT's conditions of surrender, the KMT actually did not enforce them strictly, as the CCP had presumed it would. On the contrary, the CCP was always in the lead in the propaganda.

On May 3, 1937, Mao Tse-tung made a report on the tasks of the CCP in the period of resistance to Japan at a meeting of activists in Yen-an. In the sixth part of the report he said: "The present stage is the second stage of the new epoch. . . . Whereas the major task of the previous stage was to strive for peace, that of the current stage is to strive for democracy."[10] The phrase indicated that peace between the KMT and the CCP had been achieved, and that it was time now to struggle with the KMT for democracy.

Yen-an was then cleared of the gloomy cloud overhead. Everyone was busy working under the three slogans—peace, democracy, and resistance to Japan. The CC of the CCP was discussing how to promote democracy within the Nationalist government. I was commissioned to write an article commenting on the constitution advanced by the KMT, which advocated a greater latitude of democratic freedom. Meanwhile, Chou En-lai was shuttling between Nanking and Ku-lang, asking for CCP representation in the National Congress, to be held the coming November, that had been convoked by the KMT. All these efforts were made in an attempt to legalize the CCP as a political party.

THE ANTI-JAPANESE
WAR OF RESISTANCE

CHAPTER

The Lo-ch'uan Conference

The Sino-Japanese War broke out at Lu-kou Bridge (also called the Marco Polo Bridge) on July 7, 1937. Ten days later Chiang Kai-shek issued his famous "Talk from Lu-shan," and came out with his four points for protecting the integrity of the territory of North China, declaring that this was the "last point," from which China would budge no more.[1] On July 28 and August 1 the Japanese occupied Peking and Tientsin in succession and then closed in on Pao-ting, Tsang-chow, and Nan-kou by taking points of vantage on the Peking-Hankow, the Tientsin-Pukou, and the Peking-Suiyuan railways. The climax came on August 13, when the Japanese tried hard to attack Shanghai. These were the big events during the early stages of the eight-year War of Resistance Against Japan.

Indignant over the Lu-kou Bridge incident, the authorities of the CCP issued a circular telegram on July 8, calling for a nationwide resistance movement against Japan so that Japan would not be allowed to take even an inch of land from us. On July 15 the CCP again promulgated a statement, saying that in the interest of national salvation it was willing to collaborate with the KMT for the realization of national independence, democracy, and betterment of the people's livelihood as its sole objectives. They reaffirmed their stand by making the following four promises: 1. To strive for full implementation of Dr. Sun Yat-sen's Three Principles of the People and deem it a *sine qua non* for China today. 2. To abandon the policy of uprisings to overthrow the KMT government and communization campaigns and the policy of confiscating land. 3. To dissolve the Soviets and reorganize them as local governments. 4. To abolish the Red Army, integrating it with the National Revolutionary Army under the command of the Military Council of the Republic of China and standing by for military assignments against Japan. The statement went on to say that the Chinese Communists were ready to act immediately on their promise to dissolve the Soviets and reorganize the Red Army—these being what they had not carried out so far—so that China might be able to put up a unified front against foreign aggression.[2] These two documents are sufficient evidence of the strong desire on the part of the Chinese Communists to cooperate with the KMT for the common cause against Japan.

The emphasis in the description I am going to give here does not lie so much in portraying the actual happenings during the War of Resistance Against Japan as in analyzing the situation, particularly the formation and development of the CCP's policy on the war against Japan at that time. Around August 20, the CC of the CCP held an enlarged meeting at Lo-ch'uan to discuss problems concerning their policy against Japan. Serious arguments were aroused at the meeting. Mao Tse-tung, Chang Wen-t'ien, and their followers acted arbitrarily and also forced me, the opponent, to leave Yen-an. The piecemeal information that I am going to give here will perhaps provide the reader with some clues for understanding the development of China in the days to come.

The tempo of Japanese aggression against China was so fast and furious that the KMT and the CCP really had no choice but to stick together, burying their hatchets for the time being in order to fight Japan. Many impossible things, such as the peaceful solution of the Sian Incident and the reconciliation between the KMT and the CCP became realities. After the Lu-kou Bridge Incident the Chinese Communists found themselves provided with ample opportunities for widespread use of their guerrilla warfare. Mao Tse-tung, by taking advantage of this, ascended the throne of China and subjected her to his domination.

I can well remember that the ill-feelings that the masses of the Chinese people were harboring against Japan were mounting to a peak at the time, and those in Yen-an were certainly no exception. Capitalizing on this patriotic spirit, Mao Tse-tung shouted loudly for unification of all parties in China, stressing that all who fought against Japan were kinfolks. Meanwhile, Mao harped on the same tune within the CCP and the Red Army, saying that since we were now cooperating with the KMT and Chiang Kai-shek, we should all the more draw no distinctions among ourselves and forget past differences, we should unite so that we might exert our efforts in the resistance against Japan. These high-sounding words not only promoted public morale but also served as a far-reaching umbrella for the ambitious men to engage in sinister plots for self-advancements.

Though realizing that the only way open for China to survive was to fight, the far-sighted, cool-headed people at the time could not afford to be too optimistic about the prospects of the Anti-Japanese War that had been forced upon China. They hated to see their country lose the strength to resist or be compelled to compromise with Japan halfway under military pressure from the latter, and they hoped to receive timely aid from friendly nations. They did not want to give the pro-Japan or the appeasement elements a chance to emerge, and they believed that the defeatists could be cowed into silence by the anti-Japanese tide. All hopes focused on one point: No matter what difficulties might lie ahead and what tortures China might undergo, a bright day would dawn sooner or later so long as a unified anti-Japanese government existed.

Such utterances, which could only come from those who had nothing but the future of their country in mind, were also shared by some of the ranking intellectuals then in Yen-an. But Mao and his company turned a deaf ear to them. Like the masses, the VIP's of the CCP shouted, "Resistance will bring victory"; "Resist to the end"; "Down with weapons-superiority thinking"; "Down with those who lack confidence in resistance." A series of events that followed had, however, proved that these proclamations were a far cry from what they were plotting against the KMT government.

During that period the relationship between the KMT and the CCP was a very subtle and tricky one. While playing the same tune for national salvation and pretending to be fond of one another, these two enemies-newly-turned-partners were really nursing mutual suspicions and dreaming different dreams in the same bed. With prowess shown only in internal strife, they both lacked the gallantry for the great national cause.

When the war broke out, Mao and his followers were worried that the Nanking government would stop short of fighting, and therefore kept on giving pep talks to the Nanking authorities to carry on. Nor was Mao assured until early August that year (1937), when a large-scale battle was pitched against Japan in North China. He said openly, "At long last this torrent of misfortune, Chiang Kai-shek, is heading in the direction of the Japanese." Chang Wen-t'ien also remarked with great delight, "The War of Resistance has broken out at last. Chiang Kai-shek will be powerless to harm us." These words not only reflected the hatred and resentment that had existed for many years between the KMT and the CCP, but also showed that greater importance was attached to dealing with the domestic rival than with the foreign enemy.

Before the outbreak of the July Seventh Incident, the Nanking government had not, in general, interfered with affairs in Yen-an. After the outbreak, as contacts between the two increased, the Nanking government naturally wanted to know something about the situation in Yen-an. The Shensi provincial government, accordingly, appointed a county magistrate to Yen-an, who immediately went to take up his post. The Shensi provincial party organization of the KMT also sent someone to Yen-an to set up a county party organization. The Nanking government also asked the CCP many times to step up the reorganization of its armies and to send them to the Shansi front. It was prepared to send liaison staff officers to Yen-an. All of these events evoked great bitterness in Mao Tse-tung and others. They held that these were infiltration and troublemaking activities unfavorable to the CCP. Mao Tse-tung, Chang Wen-t'ien, and others began to make exaggerated statements, saying, "Chiang Kai-shek is still as reactionary as he used to be in his domestic policy, though on the foreign front he is engaged in the War of Resistance." They, therefore, asserted that the KMT's resistance to Japan would come to no good end; it would either meet with utter defeat or would end in compromise midway. They began to spread rumors that the armies under the CCP would not get equal treatment from the Nationalist government. If KMT commanders were allowed to direct them, the Red Army troops might be sent to the front to be sacrificed under the big guns of the Japanese Army. In that case, the KMT would take advantage of the situation and further oppress the CCP when it had been deprived of its military assets. The anti-Japanese policy of the CCP that was advanced at the subsequent Lo-ch'uan Conference by Mao Tse-tung, Chang Wen-t'ien, and others was based on these ideas.

After the outbreak of the July Seventh Incident, I stayed as usual at my hilltop abode outside the town of Yen-an, refraining from attending meetings of the CC and unwilling to be concerned with its affairs. Yet I was frequently invited to take part in the discussions of the situation that were held in the town of Yen-an. Looking back at the activities of the CCP in the preceding years—the Soviet campaign and the agrarian revolution, and now the second cooperation between the KMT and the CCP and the resistance to Japanese aggression—I found it had gone around a full cycle, with the goal of the struggle still the same— the goal of nationalism, in other words, the attempt to prevent China from becoming a colony of Japan. In painful recollection, I felt deeply the need for the CCP to do some thoroughgoing work for the resistance to Japan. The CCP had failed all along because it had indulged in empty leftist talk. If it now did not honestly carry out anti-Japanese work, it would probably become the nation's sinner.

My basic views on the War of Resistance Against Japan stemmed from the above-mentioned observations, and I had talked these over with Mao Tse-tung, Chang Wen-t'ien, and others. On the question of the KMT, I said that it was to be commended for its resolute attitude towards resistance to Japan and that it might ameliorate its internal policy somewhat, too. On the question of the relationship between the KMT and the CCP, I said, "During the first KMT-CCP cooperation, the two parties intermingled completely, giving rise to incessant quarrels. At present, there is a clear line of demarcation between the two, giving room for mutual contests rather than conflicts." As to the future of resistance to Japan, I suggested that the CCP adopt a positive policy to unite the anti-Japanese forces and to promote the progress of the KMT government, so that Japan might not easily be successful in its aggression. These preliminary talks did not, at that juncture, provoke any arguments or disputes.

In the initial period of the War of Resistance, an atmosphere of excitement prevailed everywhere. People were inspired by the anti-Japanese fervor. Yen-an became a favorite place of call for messengers from Nanking, Sian, and other places and for correspondents from Shanghai and elsewhere. One of the most important of these visitors was a military and political inspection group sent by Nanking. It consisted of more than ten senior military and government officials with a mission closely connected to KMT-CCP cooperation. I was invited, together with Mao Tse-tung, Chu Teh, and Liu Po-ch'eng, to entertain these guests with the utmost kindness in our capacity as hosts. We unanimously and emphatically voiced our support for Generalissimo Chiang in the resistance against Japan and expressed our sincere desire to fight the common enemy along with them and to carry through to the end the War of Resistance Against Japan.

Mao Tse-tung's real intentions with regard to KMT-CCP cooperation in the resistance against Japan were not yet quite clear. Yen-an presented a scene of many colors. For instance, the uniforms of the soldiers were not all alike. Some wore uniforms of the Nationalist Revolutionary Army, while others were dressed in the uniforms of the Worker-Peasant Red Army. Mao Tse-tung himself possessed two army caps, one of the type of the Nationalist Revolutionary Army, and the other his original Red Army cap with a five-pointed red star as an emblem. He put on the former when receiving guests from the outside, and the latter when he attended meetings of the CCP or when he addressed the students of the Anti-Japanese Academy. Many people at that time simply gave up wearing army caps because of the diversity that existed among them. The way Mao treated the matter was particularly eye-catching. Perhaps Mao was trying to show that what was inside him was different from what was seen on the outside.

Mao Tse-tung was then concentrating his energy on the reorganization of the Red Army. From the last ten days of July onwards, telegrams were coming and going between Nanking and Yen-an on specific details of the reorganization. Nanking was anxious to have the reorganization of the Red Army completed quickly, so that its troops could be sent to the front in the War of Resistance Against Japan. Mao Tse-tung, on the other hand, instead of seeking to send the troops to the front as soon as possible, was keen on protecting his only asset, so that it might not suffer any losses during the reorganization. Moreover, he was attempting to do a good job in manipulating this asset in preparation for his future seizure of power in the whole country. I had had no share in these undertakings, which Mao purposely concealed from me, but his intentions could be seen from many facts.

In the course of the reorganization, Mao achieved complete control over the Army, which was what he had wanted to do in the first place. The Red Army troops stationed in the vicinity of Yen-an came mainly from the First, Second, and Fourth Front armies and from local northern Shensi. These troops belonged to different organizations, came from different regions, and spoke different dialects. It was impossible to plant military cadres among them at will. In numbers, the Fourth Front Army was the largest, with the local people from northern Shensi coming second. The First and Second Front armies had the smallest number of men. Mao Tse-tung mixed up these military cadres when making appointments, so that they might supervise and control one another. He also stressed Party leadership and introduced the political-commissar system extensively. The political departments at all levels and the secret-service organizations in the Army were given great power and important functions.

What Mao Tse-tung wanted to achieve, secondarily, was to deal with the pressure from Nanking in such a way that the Red Army after reorganization might not be absorbed by the vast Nationalist Revolutionary Army, but might develop freely. Mao reported to Nanking that the total number of men in the Red Army was some 48,000. This figure actually included the rear-service personnel in Yen-an. The combat troops, in fact, consisted of a little more than 30,000 men. Yet Nanking was ready to allow only some 20,000 to be reorganized. The focal point of the dispute was, naturally, the outlay for the troops, and the categories and quantities of supplies. Mao had sent many telegrams to Chou En-lai in Nanking and to Lin Po-ch'ü in Sian, asking them to request this and that from the Military Affairs Commission in Nanking and the Provisional Headquarters in Yen-an. Mao Tse-tung did this repeatedly, disregarding the trouble it would cause, for the purpose of raising the status of the Red Army and getting more supplies for the troops. Internally, he could also boast that he was fighting for equal treatment from the Nanking government.

What Mao was willing to accept was actually reorganization in name only. He wanted to keep all regulations of the Red Army intact. Worrying that the salary system of the Nationalist Revolutionary Army might influence the Red Army cadres, he energetically advertised the superiority of the ration system used by the Red Army and the importance of having officers and men living in equality. In the Nationalist Revolutionary Army, there was actually no such thing as leadership by the KMT, and political work was not given much emphasis. Mao was afraid that the Red Army might be influenced by the KMT in these ways. He, therefore, stressed particularly that the original Party-leadership and political-work system in the Red Army was not to be altered under any circumstances.

In Mao Tse-tung's opinion, the best way to deal with Japanese aggression was to employ guerrilla tactics. In order to wage guerrilla warfare against the Japanese Army, it was, naturally, necessary to set up bases behind the enemy lines. Mao Tse-tung, of course, attached great importance to this point. He was then busy allocating large numbers of students of the Anti-Japanese Academy to the Red Army units to take part in the work of the Political Department. These students, mostly intellectuals coming to Yen-an from outside, were expected to open up bases behind the enemy lines, set up anti-Japanese democratic regimes, organize local anti-Japanese armed forces, get supplies for the troops, organize popular bodies, run branches of the Anti-Japanese Academy, and so forth, after they reached the anti-Japanese front.

There was then much work directly in connection with fighting against Japan that urgently needed attention. But Mao Tse-tung, being too busy with other matters, shelved it till a later date. I had said to Mao, face to face, "Our troops are used to fighting civil war; they are not accustomed to fighting against the Japanese Army. We should get our commanders and men acquainted with the conditions of the Japanese Army and draw their attention to what should be done when fighting a guerrilla war against it." Mao Tse-tung agreed to my proposal, but for a long time no steps were taken to put it into effect. It was Chou En-lai who, during the period of the Lo-ch'uan Conference, organized training courses for studying the Japanese language, documents of the Japanese Army, and the movements and conditions of the Japanese Army.

It was not until August 22, 1937, that the Military Affairs Commission of the Nationalist government formally published the order to reorganize the troops of the CCP into the Eighth Route Army of the Nationalist Revolutionary Army, which had already been decided on through consultations between Nanking and Yen-an as early as the last ten days of July. The order appointed Chu Teh commander-in-chief of the Eighth Route Army and P'eng Te-huai deputy commander. The Eighth Route Army consisted of three divisions—the 115th, 120th, and 129th. Lin Piao was appointed commander of the 115th Division; Ho Lung, of the 120th; and Liu Po-ch'eng and Hsü Hsiang-ch'ien, commanders of the 129th Division.[3] As the Nationalist Revolutionary Army did not have a system of political commissars, those of the Eighth Route Army remained underground commissars, without being appointed by the Nationalist government.

Early in August the Japanese Army attacked the region to the south of Peking and Tientsin, thus menacing Shansi. Nanking, in an urgent telegram, ordered the Eighth Route Army to march immediately to the Shansi front, where they would be under the command of Yen Hsi-shan and their task would be to stop the advance of the Japanese Army. Chou En-lai also sent a telegram from Nanking, asking the Eighth Route Army to set out rapidly in accordance with the order, as an expression of its enthusiasm for the resistance against Japan. Mao Tse-tung drafted for Chu Teh a telegram in reply, in which he found many excuses for dodging, saying that the supplies had not yet been filled out and that the work of reorganization had not yet been completed, and requesting that the Eighth Route Army be allowed to set out at a later date.

On August 13 the Japanese Army attacked Shanghai. The war was developing on a large scale. It didn't seem reasonable to postpone any longer the departure of the Eighth Route Army for the Shansi front. Mao Tse-tung had suggested that an enlarged meeting of the CC of the CCP be convened to decide on the overall policy of the CCP in the period of the War of Resistance Against Japan before the Eighth Route Army set out. When the decision to convene a meeting was made, Mao immediately telegraphed Chou En-lai, Ch'in Pang-hsien, and others to hurry back for the meeting. I was not informed of the decision until Mao made an appointment with me for an interview at which he formally informed me of the meeting and invited me to attend it. Without the least hesitation, I promised to go, as I thought that one must, under any circumstances, show enthusiasm for the resistance to Japan and that I ought to attend this meeting.

Around August 20, 1937, the enlarged meeting of the CC of the CCP took place in a village near the county seat of Lo-ch'uan County, about ninety kilometers south of Yen-an. The meeting was therefore called the Lo-ch'uan Conference. Lo-ch'uan was then on the border between the northern Shensi region and the KMT region. Its mayor was appointed by the KMT's Shensi provincial government. Inside the town and on the important traffic routes there were a few KMT troops, but the villages around Lo-ch'uan were where the majority of the Eighth Route Army were stationed. The enlarged meeting was held here for the convenience of the CCP commanders of the Eighth Route Army and to facilitate gathering at the meeting the various ranks of military cadres. About twenty people attended this enlarged meeting, including members of the Politburo of the CC, heads of the various departments of the CC, and important military and political cadres, including P'eng Te-huai, Ho Lung, Lin Piao, Liu Po-ch'eng, and Chu Jui.

Chang Wen-t'ien, secretary of the CC of the CCP, made the first report at the meeting, on the basic tasks of the CCP after the outbreak of the War of Resistance. He stated that the policy of the CCP in the past had been to push the KMT onto the road of resistance to Japan. Now that the War of Resistance had become a reality, it was necessary to consider the fundamental tasks of the CCP in the War of Resistance. He held that the KMT's efforts in the War of Resistance would be one-sided and would lay stress on the military aspect alone. The KMT would remain reactionary in nature. With the Nanking regime monopolized by the KMT, the War of Resistance could only strengthen the military dictatorship of Chiang Kai-shek. The KMT opposed democratization; it dared not mobilize the masses, but suppressed them in various ways. It had not yet given up its ambition of annihilating the CCP. Moreover, Chiang Kai-shek might compromise with the Japanese at any moment and turn the guns around to deal with the CCP. This was far from being a total war of resistance with the participation of all the people. It was a purely military one that sought to maintain the rule of the reactionary regime.

Chang Wen-t'ien, therefore, held that the CCP's tasks would be to fight the aggressive forces of Japan, on the one hand, and to oppose the reactionary rule of Nanking, on the other. Citing as his precedent the case of Lenin, who during the First World War adopted the strategy of working for the defeat of the Czar's government, he held that the fundamental task of the CCP during the War of Resistance would be two-fold, killing two birds with one stone—to bring defeat to Japan, Chiang Kai-shek, and all reactionary forces successively, and then to bring victory to the people, the toiling worker and peasant masses, and the CCP.

Chang Wen-t'ien was obviously aware of the defeat of the CCP in the struggle for leadership of the national revolution during the period of KMT-CCP cooperation from 1922 to 1927. If the CCP now proposed to strive for leadership in the War of Resistance, it might be accused of being equivocal and might then fall into the same old rut. He stressed that the goal of the anti-Japanese policy of the CCP would be to employ the tactics of inflicting total defeat, since it must definitely cause the defeat of Chiang Kai-shek; that is, it *must* cause the total defeat of Japan, along with Chiang Kai-shek and others. Chang Wen-t'ien also presented the draft of a resolution, the contents of which were similar to that of his speech. The resolution was entitled "The Basic Tasks of the CCP in the Resistance Against Japan," but the theme of its contents was the strategy of defeat.

Taking the floor after Chang Wen-t'ien, Mao Tse-tung, first of all, said that he supported Chang's opinions, and then he proceeded to go into the details of the actual strategy that the CCP and the Eighth Route Army should adopt. He held that the military strength of Japan far exceeded that of China, who could hardly expect to win by luck. The CCP had stressed armed resistance to Japan, but it did not think that victory could be achieved right away. Resistance to Japan was advocated because of the need to resolve domestic contradictions. Now that the War of Resistance had broken out, it was necessary to recognize coolly that the War of Resistance was arduous. The reactionary nature of the KMT would not change of its own accord. The Chinese people could have hopes of victory only if the CCP was able to adopt the right strategy during a prolonged War of Resistance.

Mao warned the participants that they must not be deceived by patriotism, nor should they go to the front to be anti-Japanese heroes. They must understand that Japanese airplanes and guns would do much more harm to us than those of Chiang Kai-shek had been able to do in the past. He proposed that the Eighth Route Army insist on guerrilla warfare, avoiding frontal conflict with the Japanese Army. They should go round the enemy to its rear to carry out guerrilla activities, avoiding the real strength of the enemy and choosing to meet it where it was weak. The major task of the Eighth Army would be to enhance its own strength and to build up anti-Japanese guerrilla bases led by the CCP at the enemy's rear.

Mao Tse-tung then went on to emphasize that the CCP and the Eighth Route Army should maintain absolute independence. He said that in the future the Eighth Route Army must continue to act in complete obedience to the instructions of the Military Committee of the CC of the CCP. Whenever it received orders from the KMT Military Affairs Commission of the Nanking government or from the commanding officers of the various battle zones, it must, first of all, report back to Yen-an for instructions. Any orders that were not in the interests of the Eighth Route Army should be bypassed under various pretexts. Despite its new name, the Eighth Route Army must keep the old system of the Red Army internally, without the slightest change. It must strictly guard against infiltration of the KMT into the Red Army. Again, everything in the anti-Japanese guerrilla bases developed by the CCP should be handled in accordance with instructions from Yen-an, forming a system of its own. In CCP organizations in cities in the KMT regions, only a few people should show their faces. They must still maintain the characteristics of an underground organization. They should spread political criticism of the KMT, particularly opposing the activities of traitors and the compromising factions, with a view to winning over the masses.

Listening to the orations of Chang Wen-t'ien and Mao Tse-tung, I was immediately aware that they had shown their hands. The policy of an anti-Japanese national united front had been trampled on, and national obligations were not being given due attention. The anti-Japanese flame had not been able to change the hearts of these two sinister, selfish schemers. I decided then and there to speak up for justice, no matter what the consequences, to be the first to criticize Chang Wen-t'ien's nonsensical theories. According to the unwritten rules of the CCP, whenever the ones in authority had advanced a policy, the opponents, or the ones regarded as opponents, were given priority in speaking, so that the positive and negative opinions would be put before the meeting for discussion.

I then stood up to speak. Countering Chang Wen-t'ien's remarks, I pointed out that the present War of Resistance Against Japan could not possibly be mentioned and discussed in the same breath as the First World War. Ours was a war of national self-defense, while the First World War was a struggle for supremacy between imperialists. During the First World War, Lenin had not joined the Czar to form a national united front against foreign aggression, and could thus afford to advance a proposal that would cause the Czar to suffer defeat. On the other hand, we had now formed the anti-Japanese national united front with the KMT and were, therefore, unable to put forward a proposal that would cause Chiang Kai-shek to suffer defeat.

I went on to say that the anti-Japanese national united front was a policy for a historical period that began and would end with the War of Resistance Against Japan. It might even be extended after the victory over Japan. I asked the participants to imagine what would happen if Chiang Kai-shek made a compromise with Japan halfway. That would be totally unfavorable to the CCP. First of all, the pressure from Japan would fall entirely on the CCP. Since the CCP had chosen to occupy the same boat as Chiang Kai-shek, it could do nothing else but push him along the road of fighting to the finish against the Japanese, and in-fluence him to make certain reforms in internal policies in order to achieve progress. In view of the present situation, defeat of Chiang Kai-shek would also mean defeat of the CCP, as the destinies of the two were linked together.

In opposition to Chang Wen-t'ien's proposal, I, therefore, proposed the strategy of striving for victory. I stated that the anti-Japanese na-tional united front aimed at bringing defeat to Japan and victory to all Chinese people, completely disregarding party affiliations. Everyone was doing his best now for the War of Resistance Against Japan and would share the fruits of victory in the future. As to which side would be in the lead in the competition, that would depend on the efforts it had made. I believed that the CCP would certainly not fall behind.

Chou En-lai spoke after me, expressing views that differed from those of Mao Tse-tung. He pointed out mainly that Chiang Kai-shek, having engaged in the resistance against Japan, would not compromise midway. Based on Chiang's personal stubbornness and the situation at home and abroad, he thought that there was no need to worry about this. He also emphasized that the CCP should take an active part in the War of Resistance, so as to elevate its political status. He particularly drew attention to what we had said before, that we had to keep our word. We had said all along that the CCP would cooperate sincerely with the KMT to win complete victory in the War of Resistance Against Japan and that the Eighth Route Army would set out for the war front to assume its duty of attacking the enemy. It wasn't good enough for our actual performance to be totally different.

He went on to say that the independence of the CCP and the Eighth Route Army could only be relative. He felt it wouldn't do to disobey openly the orders from Nanking. He stated that there were many ways to practice independence. For instance, we could tell Nan-king frankly that the battle tasks assigned to the Eighth Route Army should be those that would give full play to its guerrilla expertise. In the guerrilla bases behind the enemy lines, it was possible to carry out the orders of the Nationalist government nominally, but preserve our own spirit in fact. He disagreed with the idea that the Eighth Route Army should fight only guerrilla battles that avoided the enemy's real strength but chose to meet it where it was weak. Such actions might induce people to think that we were not doing our utmost for the War of Resistance. Under favorable conditions, the Eighth Route Army could engage in mobile warfare against the Japanese invaders on a large scale. Even if it were to suffer considerable losses during battle, it would still be worthwhile, because it would provide the people of the entire country with evidence that we were doing our best for the War of Resistance.

The other participants who made addresses after Chou begged to differ, in varying degrees, with the views of Chang Wen-t'ien and Mao Tse-tung. Some said that we should not make changes too rapidly in our implementation of the anti-Japanese national united front, which had, after all, been our idea. Others said that we should still compromise for the good of the whole situation and make an all-out effort to win victory in the War of Resistance. Still others said that it was not easy to practice absolute independence. There were also those who said that when the Eighth Route Army arrived at the front in the future, it would be impossible for it to restrict itself to guerrilla warfare.

Seeing that the situation was not at all in his favor, Mao Tse-tung proposed that the meeting adjourn for three days, to give the comrades time to make broader considerations and more consultations. This was what Mao Tse-tung was accustomed to do. When disputes arose within the Party, he didn't like to see the comrades argue until they became blue in the face. The way to round off a dispute was to adjourn the meeting. In fact, it was tantamount to stopping the discussion, as he always had his own way. Just as expected, Mao and Chang had numerous meetings with the commanders during the period of adjournment, trying to win them over to their views. These meetings were not often participated in even by Chou En-lai, not to say myself, and I had plenty of leisure and remained uninformed on many matters.

Chou En-lai, K'ai Feng, and I stayed in the village where the conference was held, while Mao Tse-tung, Chang Wen-t'ien, and the others stayed in a village near a place where Eighth Route Army troops were stationed. During the three days that the conference was adjourned, Mao Tse-tung and the others were busy holding various meetings with the military cadres. Chou En-lai, K'ai Feng, and I did not take part in these meetings. Since he had never waged campaigns against me, Chou En-lai chatted amicably with me as usual when we met. K'ai Feng was then not altogether happy about the doings of Mao and the others. He often invited me to play a game of chess or to chat with him, as if to mitigate the unceremonious treatment he had given me in the past. Chou En-lai was not often at leisure, but he still found time to play chess with us. All this pointed to the fact that both Chou En-lai and K'ai Feng were, like me, more or less excluded.

When the conference reopened after three days' adjournment, Mao Tse-tung was the first to speak. He said that now everybody's views had become more or less identical, so he had drafted some proposals for the conference to discuss. The first document that he presented was the "Ten-Point Program on Resistance to Japan and National Salvation,"[4] the contents of which clearly manifested the position and role of the CCP and the Eighth Route Army in the War of Resistance Against Japan. It also made concrete demands concerning democratization of the Nationalist government. The second document that Mao presented was the resolution on the basic tasks of the CCP, from which such terms as "making Chiang Kai-shek suffer defeat" had been deleted. It simply stressed that the CCP would do its best to strive for a total war of resistance and for victory in the war. It opposed traitors and those who sought compromise, and was against the compromise tendency of the Nanking government. There was no mention of the absolute independence of the CCP and the Eighth Route Army. It only stipulated that the CCP and the Eighth Route Army should act in accordance with the principle of independence and that the Eighth Route Army would mainly engage in guerrilla warfare; only under extremely favorable conditions would it wage large-scale mobile warfare, and so forth.

After some minor amendments, the two documents were approved unanimously. During the discussions Chou En-lai expressed approval of these two talked-over and amended documents. Although I had taken no part in the drafting of the two documents, I agreed that they had no major defects in phraseology. Chang Wen-t'ien didn't say a word, as if he wanted to express his deep displeasure at my criticism of the original draft that he had proposed, which was canceled as a result. This discussion marked the beginning of Mao Tse-tung's alliance-plus-struggle method in dealing with the KMT. To be more exact, it was a method of pretended alliance and actual struggle.

Subsequently, the conference settled many specific problems. First of all was the transfer of personnel, such as who would go to the KMT areas, who would go to the front, and who would remain in northern Shensi. Then the conference passed resolutions on the program of political work in the Eighth Route Army and the procedures for setting up anti-Japanese guerrilla bases. Many discussions were held on the steps that the Eighth Route Army would take before going to the front.

Mao Tse-tung was very much against sending three divisions to the front at the same time. He felt that if they went together, the KMT might send them to one battlefield and position warfare could not be avoided. He proposed that the three divisions go to the front along different routes and at different times, for convenience in spreading themselves out to wage guerrilla warfare. Two brigades were to remain behind in northern Shensi for defense, and this could be done under the pretext that reorganization work had not been fully completed. In this way the KMT would be denied the opportunity of sending some troops to be stationed in northern Shensi. All these problems were solved smoothly, one by one.

Finally, Mao and Chang jointly proposed that I be appointed chairman of the government in the Shensi-Kansu-Ningsia Border Region. They made successive statements, saying that the post was originally assigned to Comrade Lin Po-ch'ü, but that the application filed with the Nanking government had not been officially acknowledged and that Lin Po-ch'ü, as representative of the Eighth Route Army in Sian, was too busy carrying on liaison with the Provisional Headquarters in Sian concerning supplies for the Eighth Route Army to spend any of his time in Yen-an. They were of the opinion that it would be of great political significance both inside and outside the Party for me to assume this post.

Ch'in Pang-hsien, who had come late for a few days, was the most energetic about persuading me to accept the post. While we were in Mao-kung, he had been the first to wage a struggle against me; but now his views had undergone some changes. Perhaps he had broadened his horizons after the Sian Incident, when he was an aide to Chou En-lai in dealings with the outside world. He said that because of past disputes within the Party, the outside world had learned something about the dissensions amongst us. If I became chairman of the Border Region government now, all rumors that had been circulating outside would die away without further ado. He felt that only I was suitable for this post, because my name would easily be approved outside. He further argued that if I would accept the post on the eve of the departure of our troops, the comrades would be impressed and would feel that internal dissensions no longer existed in the Party.

I had modestly refused to accept the post on the grounds that there were limitations to my ability. Ch'in Pang-hsien further assured me that they all trusted me and had confidence in my ability to make a success of the job. Mao Tse-tung and Chang Wen-t'ien both spoke again, one after the other, saying that they completely trusted me and guaranteeing that the affairs of the Border Region government, whether internal or external, would be entirely in my hands, and that the Party would give me full support, not allowing the comrades to criticize me again for past events. They also said that the Party was in need of unity now, more than ever before, in order to deal with the anti-Japanese situation. They insisted that I should no longer refuse.

Unable to insist any longer, I proposed that Comrade Lin Po-ch'ü should still be chairman of the Border Region government, but that during his absence I would act for him. Everybody agreed to my proposal, and the conference ended in an atmosphere of harmony.

The Border Region Government

This section, obviously, will describe the events in the period between September, 1937, and the beginning of April, 1938, when I was at my post in the Border Region government. The CC of the CCP, monopolized by Mao Tse-tung and Chang Wen-t'ien, ignored the opposing views expressed at the Lo-ch'uan Conference and pushed through a policy that stressed opposition to Chiang more than opposition to the Japanese, thus disregarding the future of the resistance against Japan. The friendly posture that they assumed towards me during the Lo-ch'uan Conference was completely hypocritical. In fact, they were incessantly striking blows at me, squeezing me out, and even secretly harming me. As a result, I, as chairman of the Border Region government, was unable to do anything worthwhile. I was actually driven to a state of suffocation.

After the Lo-ch'uan Conference, I immediately moved to the headquarters of the Border Region government upon returning to Yen-an. The CCP was not keen about official ceremonies, and during the emergency period of resistance to Japan, no shirking or delay could be tolerated. No sooner said than done. The Lo-ch'uan Conference had endorsed the proposal to reorganize the Border Region government. Accordingly, the first thing I had to do was to study what steps to take to implement the resolution on reorganization.

According to the scheme of KMT-CCP reconciliation, the Nationalist government allowed the CCP to set up in northern Shensi only a Special Area Administrative Office, with its head bearing the official title of Director of the Administrative Office, which would be under the Shensi provincial government. The candidate for the post would be recommended by the CCP, while the office would be established in conformity with the rules of the Nationalist government. Before the outbreak of the July Seventh Incident, the CCP had requested the Nationalist government to put the Special Area directly under the Nationalist government itself, but the request had been turned down. After the outbreak of the War of Resistance, the CCP further requested that the organization of the Northern Shensi Special Area government be equal to that of a provincial government, but the request was again turned down by the Nationalist government. This was a very muddled case from beginning to end. I couldn't find any relevant documents to substantiate the case, despite minute investigation. Before the Lo-ch'uan Conference, the CC of the CCP had decided to organize the Shensi-Kansu-Ningsia Border Region government independently, with its establishment in complete conformity with that of a provincial government of the Nationalist government. It was said that Chiang Kai-shek would acquiesce.

As the principles for reorganization had not yet been determined, the government in northern Shensi still retained the structure of the former Central government of the Chinese Soviet Republic, only rather mutilated. There was no sign on the front door, but the official seal was the same old pattern. The original chairman, Lin Po-ch'ü, had not attended to its affairs during the past six months. Under the Border Region government were the Secretariat, the committees of Internal Affairs, Finance and Economics, and Education, and the Political-Security Bureau, five structural organs in all. In the Secretariat, only the Public Relations Section had any real work to do, and it was under the direction of Wu Hsiu-ch'üan, who was directly under the authority of the CC of the CCP. The Internal Affairs Committee was under Ts'ai Shu-fan, who had lost an arm because of wounds. That committee worked only on relief and preferential treatment for dependents of army personnel. The Finance and Economics Committee was chaired either by Lin Po-ch'ü or, in his absence, by his deputy Ts'ao Chü-ju, who became acting chairman. The monthly budget was under the direction of the Organization Department of the CC of the CCP. The Central Political Security Bureau, under the direction of Chou Hsing, was in fact directly under the CC of the CCP, and was completely out of the control of the Border Region government. Only the Education Committee under Hsü T'e-li had work to do, and it was rather busy.

Hsü T'e-li was an old educator, who was senior in years among our comrades. He was most enthusiastic about promoting the Latinization of Chinese characters, which he and Lin Po-ch'ü had advocated energetically, to facilitate the learning of the difficult and complicated Chinese logographs. The Latinization campaign had been launched in northern Shensi on a trial basis almost two years before. It was believed that northern Shensi, being a backward region culturally speaking, was an ideal place in which to launch the campaign. Hsü T'e-li had on several occasions pestered Mao Tse-tung with his Latinization campaign, and when I became chairman of the Border Region government, he turned to me as a target for his enthusiasm. He compiled teaching materials in Latinized writing, trained teachers, and supervised actual teaching with these materials in the primary schools in northern Shensi. He also found time to propagandize these materials to me with the spirit of a preacher, hoping that I would give him active support. If I said that Latinization was not quite ready to be popularized, or something to that effect, he would argue with me throughout the night.

Besides the idealism of Hsü T'e-li, the Border Region government was beset with innumerable other internal difficulties. One example should suffice to illustrate the general situation that prevailed at that time. Hsü T'e-li had an energetic aide who was a veteran Yen-an educator. He worked for the Education Committee without receiving any salary except having his meals there. He had a wife and three children, the youngest being a new-born baby at the time I went there. They were hungry at home, but the Border Region government was too poor to pay allowances for the upkeep of the families of its staff. Finally Hsü T'e-li decided to give the man a temporary allowance from the small change left over from the fund for boarding the staff of the Education Committee.

Mao-Tse-tung had said that we must make the Border Region government a model unit under the Nationalist government. Its programs should serve as a guide for anti-Japanese democratic administrations in guerrilla bases behind the enemy lines. But he did not understand the scope and contents of a government administration; he actually only wanted the Border Region government to put up a good front in some aspects. (This is probably a fundamental reason for Mao's inability to rule a nation well.) Mao and other VIP's in the CCP had many misconceptions on this question, primarily as follows:

1. They ignored many historical lessons, even Lenin's legacy, by

not treating government administration as the most important and most effective tool. In other words, they had only the ambition of grabbing governing power, but no knowledge of how to utilize government administration.

2. They overemphasized the power of the Party, but did not understand the correct relationship between the Party and the government; thus the Party interfered too much in government work.

3. They formed many crude revolutionary concepts in the course of carrying out the revolution, such as guerrilla thinking, unreasonable concepts on equality, and so on; they were unable to appreciate deeply the importance of law and constitution.

At that time the reorganization of the Border Region government could not be delayed even for a moment. In a rudimentary manner, with many important questions still unsettled, the new government was formed. In mid September, by permission of the CC of the CCP, the Border Region government was reorganized as follows: chairman, Chang Kuo-t'ao; secretary, P'an Tzu-li, a veteran Shensi cadre; director of civil affairs, Ma Ming-fang, a veteran Shensi comrade; director of finance, Ts'ao Chü-ju; director of construction, Liu Ching-fan, a brother of Liu Tzu-tan; director of education, Chou Yang, a literary writer newly arrived from the White area. From the above list it might be seen that it was more northern Shensi in coloration, while the organization was generally in accordance with Nationalist government regulations. The reorganized Border Region government immediately convened a meeting of county magistrates. The magistrates of twenty-two counties all came. My colleagues and I were all interested in the local conditions and made careful investigations. But we were confronted with a mass of generalities. There were originally only a few guerrilla areas in northern Shensi. After the arrival of Mao Tse-tung and the others, only a signboard of the "Chinese Central Soviet Government" was put up. All measures taken to get supplies for the troops were on a spur-of-the-moment basis. As a result, this ever-disturbed region was always in a mess, whether it was under the KMT or the CCP. No census had been taken; not even an approximate figure was available. No reliable rules could be found regarding government administration. We, therefore, had to concentrate on a smaller scope, such as the burdens of the ordinary people in northern Shensi. Previously, there had been various ways to tax the people—by levies, donations, and contribution in labor, such as doing farmwork for the dependents of the soldiers. In general, a person had to pay a little over 22 percent of his income. This, needless to say, was not a very exact figure. We then drafted a system of taxation that would not exact more than 22 percent of a person's income. We thought that a suitable percentage.

The first thing that the Border Region government had to do was to put its financial affairs in order and to increase revenues. In the past the main source of revenue had been opium. San-pian, in the northern part of northern Shensi, produced large quantities of opium, which were transported east to Shansi and other places by soldiers, local ruffians, and opium merchants. When Lin Po-ch'ü was in charge of finances, he had collected transit tolls and export duties from the opium peddlers. Aside from this, the opium confiscated or collected by the CCP was all exported outside northern Shensi. Duties from other commercial transactions were pitifully scarce. It was not until shortly after the Sian Incident that the CCP banned production of opium in San-pian and the surrounding area. After the outbreak of the War of Resistance, Shansi became a friendly neighbor of the CCP, and it would have been embarrassing to continue to dump opium there. As a result, the revenue of the Border Region government was greatly reduced, and it was imperative to think of ways to make up for it.

A major event in establishing a firm financial base was introduction of the national-salvation public grain levy. I drew up a draft of the regulation in accordance with the procedures practiced in northern Shensi and other Soviet regions. I could not recall the details, but the main points I remembered were as follows: Farm households whose crops barely sufficed to support the family were exempted from the levy; those households with a surplus over their minimum needs were taxed on the surplus at a progressive rate. A well-off middle peasant with an average yield of about 2,000 catties per person would have to pay about 20 percent of the surplus. Landlords and rich peasants averaging a yield of more than 4,000 catties per person had to pay about 40 percent of the surplus. The peasants were encouraged to pay in cash so as to economize on the labor to be used in transporting the grain. The staff of the county offices would be paid in kind when cash was short. All counties were to set up public granaries in accordance with the stipulation that they store grain for the Army.

The national-salvation public grain levy, imposed in the name of resistance to Japan, had very simple and flexible rules, which were easily put into effect. Under the impetus of the current slogan on resistance to

Japan—"Those who are rich donate their money, those who are strong offer their strength"—the peasants were particularly enthusiastic about paying the public grain levy, which was in fact a unified agricultural tax, basically to be paid in kind, in anticipation of the confusion and inflation of the currency as the War of Resistance dragged on. Later, in places where the Eighth Route Army was stationed and in many guerrilla bases behind enemy lines, this same levy was imposed with considerable success. The Nationalist government became interested in it, too.

The revenue of the Border Region government gradually increased, due to the public grain levy and other improvements in financial matters. In September, 1937, it was less than 70,000 yuan; in October, it increased to more than 90,000 yuan; and in November, it amounted to more than 160,000 yuan, which was sufficient for the needs of the Party and government offices in northern Shensi. With the steady increase in revenue, taxes from opium became unimportant, and resistance to the ban on opium decreased.

In addition to this, the conference of county magistrates also approved other resolutions, which primarily regulated the relationship between the county governments and the Border Region government, and set down the general rules and principles of work for county governments and the various organizations under them. Meanwhile, the functions and principles of work of the Border Region government itself and the departments subordinate to it were also fixed generally, so as to build up a new order.

Due to my situation within the Party, I did not dare to be optimistic about what I could achieve, but I still hoped that the routine work of the Border Region government would proceed smoothly. In point of fact, however, except for the public grain levy and other measures to increase revenues, which seldom met with interference, almost every other job became impracticable despite repeated efforts on the part of myself and my colleagues, who were involved in wrangling and protesting over interferences from the CC of the CCP, which had been prone to encroach upon the functions of the Border Region government. Here are a few examples to illustrate my point.

Ma Ming-fang, head of the Civil Affairs Department, was well versed about local conditions in northern Shensi. As soon as he took over the post, he was anxious to set in order the organization and work of the county governments. He was able to speak directly with Chang

Wen-t'ien and others, and was in close contact with Kuo Hung-t'ao, secretary of the Northern Shensi Special Area Committee of the CCP. He had specially asked them to attach importance to the work of the county governments, and had urged them not to transfer at will the staff members of the county governments. They had promised to comply with these requests, but what they actually did was quite another matter. The CC of the CCP and the departments subordinate to it were always handing down orders and directives to Party organizations at lower levels. The Northern Shensi Special Area Committee of the CCP, besides conveying documents of the CC to the lower levels, also issued a lot of orders of its own. These numerous documents and directives of the CCP concerned themselves with an infinite number of matters. They often included functions of the Border Region government, and a miscellaneous lot of other things. The method of executing them was usually to have the Party organs mobilize the masses, in disregard of the laws and orders of the Border Region government. As a result of these innumerable urgent militations, cadres were frequently transferred inordinately. Essential cadres in the county governments were often transferred at will by the Northern Shensi Special Area Committee of the CCP or even by the county CCP committees, without notifying Ma Ming-fang beforehand. After two or three months, Ma sighed in front of me, "I'm at the end of my tether in building up a new order in the work of civil affairs."

The Lo-ch'uan Conference had decided that the Anti-Japanese Military and Political Academy would train military and political cadres, while the Party schools would train cadres for Party work. Another institute, the Northern Shensi Public College, would be set up to train specialists in such fields as finance, economics, education, and public health, and personnel for other work needed by the Border Region government. It was decided that in the future these three types of schools would be set up gradually in places behind enemy lines. After the reorganization of the Border Region government, the signboard of the Northern Shensi Public College was put up, and it had some eight hundred students. But the Border Region government was prohibited from looking into its affairs, as it was completely under the direct administration of the CC of the CCP. The curriculum of the college was again Leninism, Party construction, and what not, turning the institute into another Party school. The Lo-ch'uan Conference had wanted to train some administrative personnel to counter those of the KMT. But the plan was no longer mentioned. The Education Department under the Border Region government was also unable to advance its educational plan and budget, the already existing primary schools and tutorial schools having to get along somehow on the subsistence that they obtained from the village and county administrations. Unfortunately, the newly appointed head of the Education Department, Chou Yang, was only keen on talking about leftist writers and literary thought and was not interested in local education, which he didn't seem to understand much about. He was deeply interested in making speeches and in writing articles. Therefore, the Latinization movement that had flourished under Hsü T'e-li's term of office as head of the Education Department began to wane after Chou Yang took over the office. Chou Yang did not advance any educational scheme; perhaps this was a realistic way of dealing with the situation which he was obliged to take over.

Ts'ao Chü-ju, head of the Finance Department, was quite excited about the increase in revenue. He planned to set up a budget for the Border Region government beginning with November of the same year. In the light of the current situation, he proposed that the sum left over from monthly revenue after deducting the expenses of the CC of the CCP be put at the disposal of the Finance Department for developing the work of the Border Region government. At the beginning of December, Ts'ao Chü-ju requested the advice of the Organization Department of the CC of the CCP on the matter, having in hand some 160,000 yuan in revenue. Unexpectedly, the head of the Organization Department totally disapproved of the plan. He ordered that the November revenue be handed over to the CC of the CCP for the development of revolutionary work. After the expenses of the Border Region were deducted, there were more than 100,000 yuan to hand over. When Ts'ao Chü-ju returned and reported to me on the matter, I was very indignant and was going to protest over it, but Ts'ao Chü-ju advised me against it, saying, "This work-style of theirs is incorrigible. Comrade Lin Po-ch'ü in the past suffered much indignity over this, but he could no nothing about it in the end. I should think it best to obey the order now."

With this viewpoint on the part of the CC of the CCP with regard to finances prevailing, it would be very difficult to set up a suitable salary system. Mao Tse-tung was very pleased about the ration system currently in force, which provided his personnel with money for meals, and then permitted the sum left over from the monthly food bill to be distributed among them as pocket money. Mao considered this the best ration system, but actually it was a breeding ground for corruption and waste. Giving of presents, for instance, was very much in vogue. Yeh Chi-chuang, who was in charge of trade with the outside world, and his assistants always brought many gifts from places outside of northern Shensi. The cigarettes, wine, medicine, tonics, and other things that Mao Tse-tung needed were in constant supply. Cadres at the level of the CC often got what they wanted through these gifts. This way of doing things, brought here from the Soviet region of Kiangsi, was evidently copied by local cadres in northern Shensi.

This work-style of increasing the burdens of the people at will was usually taken advantage of by local cadres to satisfy their personal needs. Cadres of the village and county governments of northern Shensi usually enjoyed a higher standard of living, mostly by taking advantage of their official positions. Doing farmwork for dependents of soldiers in the Red Army was a system prevalent in the various Soviet regions. When I was in the Oyüwan region, I had studied the system, and proposed to set certain limits on it in order to prevent local cadres who were not Red Army soldiers from taking advantage of the system to satisfy the needs of their families, thus increasing the burdens of the people. In northern Shensi many local cadres, and even local CCP members, had the same privilege as dependents of Red Army soldiers. In the worst individual cases, they were like landlords having a group of serfs work for them. The unreasonable system of rationing was bound to corrupt the so-called revolutionary spirit, and it bred exorbitant miscellaneous taxes and bureaucratism in a variety of forms.

The Political Security Bureau was directly under the CC of the CCP, and its work was never questioned by the Border Region government. However, because of the extensive scope of its work, it invariably came into contact with the Border Region government on many occasions, sometimes in connection with problems that were very tricky and not easy to solve. Once, when the Japanese Army was attacking T'ai-yüan, a KMT division commander stationed in the Yü-lin district to the north of the Northern Shensi Border Region sent his chief aide-de-camp to see me, to ask my permission to waive searching the luggage of some twenty to thirty families of the officers of the division who were going home to the Kuan-tung area via Yen-an and would inevitably be subjected to searches at the checkpoints under the Political Security Bureau. The chief aide-de-camp showed me passports issued by the division and other documents, saying that the group consisted solely of families of the division's officers, and that the luggage contained only personal belongings. He added that as cash was hard to come by in the Yü-lin district, each family was obliged to carry some "goods" (meaning opium). Having checked with the personnel of the Security Bureau who were accompanying the chief aide-de-camp, to make sure that the travelers were army dependents and that what they carried was a small amount of goods, I promised to let them go through without being searched. According to the laws of the Border Region government, the opium was to be confiscated. In the name of being kind to a friendly army, I let them go through. Seeing that a considerable source of private income was thus lost, the personnel of the Political Security Bureau were angered and complained privately that I was "ingratiating myself with the militarists."

The newly established Department of Construction was headed by Liu Ching-fan, who, though something of a dandy, was willing to do something useful. However, at the beginning the department had no clues to guide its work. Then a group of production cooperatives and mutual-aid groups were put under the administration of the Construction Department. After some investigation, Liu Ching-fan proposed to organize them. He therefore convened a conference of the directors of the cooperatives and groups. These cooperatives and groups were originally set up for the benefit of dependents of Red Army martyrs; some were organized by disabled veterans. As time passed, some of the members were not dependents of martyrs, and some cooperatives had a considerable number of members who were able to do productive labor. Many had their own productive undertakings. Altogether, there were more than a hundred of these cooperatives, with three to four thousand members (I do not recall the exact number), spreading over various parts of the Northern Shensi Border Region. The expenses of these cooperatives were all paid by the Border Region government under the heading "subsidy," which amounted to no small sum. The idea was to subsidize deserving personnel and disabled veterans from the coffers of the Border Region government.

Liu Ching-fan presided over the conference, and I also attended some of its sessions. It was decided at the conference that the principle of production and economy was to be implemented, and work to put the cooperatives in order was begun. Thus, some cooperatives would become genuine production cooperatives, which would be self-supporting, with the Border Region government supplying some of the raw materials. Others would be partly self-supporting, with the original subsidies reduced. Still others would need their original subsidies, or even larger ones. This would provide outlets for the production of the cooperatives, and it was, in principle, in conformity with the general principle of production and economy propounded by the CC of the CCP. It was a surprise to us that Chang Wen-t'ien vetoed the decision as secretary of the CC of the CCP, without so much as inquiring about our reasons. He argued that the subsidy system gave preferential treatment to the dependents of martyrs, and that this would not be changed under the pretext of economy. He ordered that the former system remain in force.

Among the many unreasonable interferences of the CC of the CCP in the work of the Border Region government, the most absurd was the one concerning the Construction Department. I remarked in great anger, "This is a villain's act to antagonize me, attack me, and disturb the work of the Border Region government." But I immediately regained control of myself, because I had had enough of Mao Tse-tung and Chang Wen-t'ien and their double-faced tricks, and I was extremely reluctant to continue to be a colleague of theirs. I would no longer regard them as comrades, and I would seek to release myself.

The indignities that I suffered at that time are too numerous to recount. Interference with the work of the Border Region government was nothing extraordinary, but being a person with considerable sense of responsibility, I always wanted to do something about my obligations. When even routine affairs of the Border Region government were interfered in, I naturally became quite bitter. The blows that they dealt me were even worse than those mentioned above. I will come to them in the latter part of this chapter.

Mao Tse-tung and Chang Wen-t'ien not only interfered with the administration of the Border Region government on domestic affairs, but they also throttled its activities in connection with the outside world. The Northern Shensi Border Region government was the only local regime recognized by the people outside. People who came to northern Shensi to negotiate and official documents from the outside ought to have been, in most cases, handled by the chairman, the secretary general, and the Secretariat of the Border Region government. Only a few ought to have been handled by either the CC of the CCP or the Northern Shensi office of the Eighth Route Army. But due to narrow-minded selfishness and lack of far-sightedness on the part of Mao Tse-tung and Chang Wen-t'ien, the job was in a state of confusion, which caused delays and mistakes and brought losses to both the CC of the CCP and the Border Region government.

The Public Relations Department, which was nominally under the Secretariat of the Border Region government but was actually under the direction of the CC of the CCP, was shrouded in mystery. In reality, it was a branch organ of the Political Security Bureau. Its ways of doing things were always colored by the narrow-mindedness of the secret service and were governed by the will of Mao Tse-tung and Chang Wen-t'ien. Some people from the outside who were regarded as friends of the CCP were given a warm reception. These included Liang Sou-ming, a democratic person, and Ho Chi-li, a military man with leftist tendencies. (Chiang Ch'ing, Mao's current wife, was among those received there, but she was then an artiste that did not attract much attention.) Other visitors with business to take care of often went away without having accomplished much.

Mao Tse-tung and Chang Wen-t'ien were extremely afraid that I might establish contacts with the outside world, taking advantage of my position as chairman of the Border Region government. The method that Mao Tse-tung employed to bring about my downfall was vicious and cruel, not only making it impossible for me to lift my head inside the Party, but also defaming me outside the Party, striking at me through outside influences. For instance, he spread the rumor to people outside that I had opposed the peaceful settlement of the Sian Incident. All of the bad things about the Soviet regions in the past were blamed on me, Chang Kuo-t'ao. (These rumors were spread among CCP sympathizers in particular.) Even after the July Seventh Incident, in order to delay the setting out of the Eighth Route Army for the front, he uttered falsehoods such as "Chang Kuo-t'ao's subordinates took no consideration of the whole situation of the War of Resistance and made it impossible for the Eighth Route Army to start for the front at an early date." Mao's intention was none other than to fool others into pulling out the thorn in his flesh for him. Later, making use of my speeches at the Lo-ch'uan Conference, Mao told the personnel of the Public Relations Department that they should beware of Chang Kuo-t'ao's colluding with the KMT people to harm the CCP. As a result, many people who came to the Border Region government to see me were prevented from doing so by the Public Relations Department under various pretexts. A few newspaper correspondents, whom the Public Relations Department was unable to refuse, did see me, but I was not briefed beforehand about their backgrounds or the purposes of their interviews, and thus I found it difficult to handle them properly.

Among the visitors to Yen-an were large numbers of people from nearby places, particularly from Shansi and from Yü-lin and Sui-ting to the north. They came either to observe or to do business, such as liaison in communications, the transferral of commercial and industrial enterprises and schools, the setting up of offices at the rear, the settlement of families, the handling of refugees, and so forth. Those who came on business included representatives of military and political organs and senior commanders of the Northwest. All the business negotiations were messed up by the Public Relations Department. When the personnel of the department found the situation desperate, they blamed it on the unsound organization of the Border Region government and its subordinate governments, babbling that it was impossible to meet the demands of the visitors, and thus attempting to wash their hands of the matter. Such ways of doing things indeed ran counter to the CCP's obligations with relation to the outside world in the common War of Resistance.

Ho Shao-nan, commissioner of the Sui-ting district and concurrently commander of Sui-ching, was flying from Sui-ting to Nanking upon a telegraphed order from Chiang Kai-shek. He telegraphed me, as chairman of the Border Region government, that he would arrive at Yen-an by plane on the afternoon of a certain day and would stay in Yen-an overnight, continuing his trip southward the next day. I immediately telegraphed him a reply, welcoming him. Mao Tse-tung was suspicious about Ho's stay in Yen-an, thinking that he was coming at Chiang Kai-shek's order to inquire into the situation there. He also felt that Ho's stay would have a bearing on the cooperation between the KMT and the CCP. When I went with a few important officials of the Border Region government to the airport to welcome Ho Shao-nan, Mao Tse-tung also came with a large entourage. He and other dignitaries of the CC of the CCP also attended the banquet in honor of Ho Shao-nan given by the Border Region government. Ho Shao-nan appeared supercilious, putting on the airs of a lieutenant-general and an important personality of the Nationalist government. He spoke only to the chairman of the Border Region government as his equal, and was unwilling to have anything to do with the CC of the CCP. He ignored Mao Tse-tung and the others.

After this embarrassing event, I requested the head of the Public Relations Department, Wu Hsiu-ch'üan, to make a report to Mao Tse-tung, asking for his direction. I told him to say that Ho Shao-nan's attitude was probably a bureaucrat's way of putting on airs. It might be that he was just putting on an act to gauge our internal situation. He wanted to know, first, about the recent situation in Yen-an for a report to his Generalissimo, and, second, about the question of joint defense by the Sui-ting district and the Northern Shensi Border Region in case of an invasion by the Japanese Army up the Yellow River. Mao Tse-tung did not make any reply to all these questions. However, the next day, after seeing Ho Shao-nan off, the KMT magistrate of Fu-shih County told me in private that on the previous night, about ten o'clock, Mao Tse-tung had paid a call on Ho Shao-nan at the office of the magistracy where he was staying for the night. They talked till about two the following morning, with the magistrate at their side throughout. He told me graphically how Commissioner Ho was still putting on airs in the beginning, but was unable to withstand the brilliance of Chairman Mao and finally softened. Chairman Mao had given a detailed report on the recent situation in the Northern Shensi Border Region and the Eighth Route Army, asking Ho to present it to Generalissimo Chiang. He also expressed admiration for the Generalissimo.

Had it not been for the report of the magistrate, I would have been completely in the dark. Mao at that time had no good words to say about Chiang. He was always saying that Chiang's troops could not fight and that they would eventually surrender to Japan since they could not stand to be defeated. His courtesy towards Ho Shao-nan was evidently a disguise to make use of Ho Shao-nan to deceive Chiang Kai-shek. As to his intentions in not letting me know about his activities in this connection, there seemed to be no other explanation than that, first, he wanted to monopolize relations with the outside and to prevent me from taking part in any such undertakings, and that, second, probably because the attitude of Ho Shao-nan had evoked his suspicions that I might have secretly colluded with the KMT people, he wanted to investigate this possibility for himself.

The Nationalist government then appointed Yeh T'ing commander of the New Fourth Army and made him responsible for reorganizing the CCP guerrillas scattered around Hunan, Hupeh, Anhwei, Honan, Kiangsi, Fukien, and Kwangtung who were to be sent to the front to resist Japan. Before coming to Yen-an, he had said that I was his only old friend in Yen-an. He did not know Mao Tse-tung, so he wanted me to help him and act as middleman in arranging an introduction. Mao Tse-tung and Chang Wen-t'ien, on their part, felt that the future of the New Fourth Army depended on what I said to Yeh T'ing. They hoped that I would encourage Yeh T'ing to deal with everything from the standpoint of the CCP.

When Yeh T'ing arrived at Yen-an, he first came to see me to tell me about his real intentions. Yeh T'ing was originally a CCP member, but had severed relations with the Party after the Canton Uprising. He wanted to dedicate himself to the War of Resistance, doing his utmost, and he was not sure that the CCP would still trust him. He had been appointed to his post of commander of the New Fourth Army by the Nationalist government, while the troops under his command belonged to the CCP. He came to Yen-an especially to make inquiries, and he hoped that I, as an old friend, would consider the case on his behalf, and decide whether it would be worthwhile for him to take this post.

I encouraged Yeh T'ing to assume this post, telling him that the CCP would not discriminate against him, but would regard him as a bridge between the KMT and the CCP. I suggested that he directly consult Mao Tse-tung, who was in charge of military matters, to resolve specific questions concerning the organization of the New Fourth Army. I proposed that he adopt an earnest and positive attitude during the consultations, which eventually came to a satisfactory conclusion. Yeh T'ing accepted Mao's suggestions, making Hsiang Ying political commissar of the New Fourth Army and Ch'en Yi deputy commander of the Army and commander of the First Column. The guerrillas in the areas of Hunan, Hupeh, Kiangsi, Fukien, Kwangtung, Anhwei, and Honan would be organized into six columns, each led by its original guerrilla leader. The internal organization of the Army would be patterned after that of the Eighth Route Army, while the heads of the various departments, such as the General Staff Office, the Ordnance Office, the Medical Office, and others, would be selected and appointed by Yeh T'ing himself. Negotiations with the KMT would also be conducted by him. That was the beginning of the organization of the New Fourth Army, which was the root of the evil that later spawned the military struggles between the KMT and the CCP to the north and south of the Yangtze River.

Despite the shortness of his stay in Yen-an, Yeh T'ing had heard some slanders against me, but he seemed to ignore them. Mao Tse-tung had never asked me to discuss with them the reorganization of the New Fourth Army, and I was glad to keep out of it. Before his departure from Yen-an, Yeh T'ing told me in detail about everything that had happened. He still doubted the future outcome, fearing that he might not be able to please both the KMT, whose Military Affairs Commission of the Nationalist government he would have to deal with and get funds from, and the CCP, whose troops he would have to lead. I was not in a position to say much then. I could only say casually that as he had already gone this far, the best thing to do now was to get on with it.

After the Lo-ch'uan Conference, the attitude of the CC of the CCP became quite unpredictable. For more than three months the Politburo of the CC of the CCP had not held any meetings. Among the Politburo members, only three, Mao Tse-tung, Chang Wen-t'ien, and I, were in Yen-an; the others were all away. The Secretariat of the CC of the CCP, however, held meetings regularly, which were chaired by Chang Wen-t'ien in his capacity as secretary, and these were attended by heads of departments of the CC of the CCP and the secretary general. I had attended one or two of these meetings, which invariably discussed the routine work of the departments and never touched upon the situation of the War of Resistance Against Japan. As a result, Yen-an's orientation towards the resistance to Japan could only be found in the statements made by Mao Tse-tung and Chang Wen-t'ien.

The Lo-ch'uan Conference had vetoed the policy of combining resistance against Japan with opposition to Chiang Kai-shek. Mao Tse-tung and Chang Wen-t'ien found it inappropriate to violate the decision openly, but they still resorted to two-faced tactics, doing one thing privately and another publicly. Outwardly, Yen-an was full of anti-Japanese slogans, a scene of fervent bustle. Within the CC of the CCP, however, there was a touch of gloominess, as if confidence in the future of the resistance against Japan was completely lacking. Following the unfavorable development in the military aspect of the resistance against Japan, criticism of Chiang Kai-shek increased perceptibly. Some commented on how good-for-nothing the KMT troops were; others harped about how active the Nanking advocates of compromise were and how the tendency to compromise was increasing in strength. On the eve of the imminent fall of Nanking, Chang Wen-t'ien told me that Chiang Kai-shek would soon capitulate to Japan. He wondered what those who had pinned extravagant hopes on the anti-Japanese national united front would have to say.

Chou En-lai ought to have gone to Nanking immediately after the Lo-ch'uan Conference, but he went to the Shansi front with the Eighth Route Army instead, under some pretext. Mao Tse-tung had wanted Chou En-lai to be stationed in Nanking all the time in order to get information on the situation and to handle negotiations. Besides, the Eighth Route Army had not yet received some supplies due to it, and the guerrillas of the CCP in the provinces in the south had yet to be assigned their CCP leaders, as Mao Tse-tung had demanded in the first place. The solution of these problems depended on Chou En-lai's negotiations with Nanking. Since Chou had not proceeded there, Nanking directly appointed Yeh T'ing to reorganize the CCP guerrillas under the name of the New Fourth Army. Mao Tse-tung had said that Chou En-lai, by disobeying the order to proceed quickly to Nanking, bungled important matters. How could an envoy be allowed to act at will when he received an order that he found displeasing, he commented.

This was evidently a gesture on Chou En-lai's part to show his dissatisfaction with the Lo-ch'uan Conference. He seemed to have decided that although Mao Tse-tung and Chang Wen-t'ien had made some concessions at the conference, they were actually persisting in their opinions, and if he went to Nanking straightaway, he would find himself in a very embarrassing position. Quietly he declared that he would first go to the front line in Shansi to take a look and to help the Eighth Route Army General Headquarters negotiate with the KMT. Then he would proceed directly to Nanking from Shansi. However, he stayed there for more than three months, despite Mao Tse-tung's numerous telegrams urging him to hurry to Nanking. Each time he found some excuse to delay the trip. Finally Mao Tse-tung telegraphed him an order to return to Yen-an for an interview before deciding on the next move. This order Chou En-lai obeyed, and he returned to Yen-an.

On September 29 a section of the Eighth Route Army dealt the Japanese Army a considerable blow at Ping-hsing Pass in Shansi, the first great achievement of the troops led by the CCP on the battlefield in the War of Resistance Against Japan. At every critical point the anti-Japanese troops were resisting the onslaught of the Japanese Army, which was pushing south towards T'ai-yüan after it occupied Ta-t'ung on September 13. The battle of Ping-hsing Pass, which was waged by Lin Piao's troops, who attacked the enemy from the side and the rear, caused a considerable number of casualties among the enemy troops and made them retreat a little. Lin Piao's troops also suffered more than a thousand casualties. This performance of the Eighth Route Army was essentially the result of the efforts of Chou En-lai at the front. Yen-an gave wide publicity to the victory at Ping-hsing Pass, and everybody felt that the Eighth Route Army was not only good at guerrilla warfare, but that it was also capable of achieving victory in mobile warfare. Mao Tse-tung, however, telegraphed an order to the commanders at the front, saying that fighting that involved such heavy sacrifices should be avoided in the future.

After the Lo-ch'uan Conference, parts of the Eighth Route Army were setting out for the front in Shansi continuously. Mao Tse-tung concentrated all of his attention on this operation, stressing independence and guerrilla warfare as the two guiding principles. He was rather worried that Chou En-lai might stir up trouble at the front, and his mind was not at ease when he thought that senior and junior officers might want to become anti-Japanese heroes. By November 9 of the same year, the Japanese had occupied T'ai-yüan, while most of the Eighth Route Army had reached places behind the enemy lines. The 115th Division, under Lin Piao, was in the Tai-hang Mountain Range east of the Tung-Pu Railway and north of the Cheng-Tai Railway, moving towards the Hopeh area. The 120th Division under Ho Lung was west of the Tung-Pu Railway, waging guerrilla war in northwestern Shansi. The 129th Division, led by Hsü Hsiang-ch'ien and Liu Po-ch'eng, was moving towards the Chang-yeh district in southeastern Shansi and was going to carry out guerrilla warfare behind the enemy lines in Hopeh, Honan, and Shantung. Then Mao Tse-tung began to relax a little.

Meanwhile, the KMT troops around Shanghai were forced to retreat early in November after three months of hard fighting that included many memorable battles. Shansi's Yen Hsi-shan, after the fall of T'ai-yüan, declared that he would defend every inch of the land in the War of Resistance. Mao Tse-tung never once mentioned the battles of the other armies, to say nothing of praising and encouraging their heroic feats. When the situation was in considerable confusion after the fall of Nanking and the retreat of the Nationalist Army, Mao Tse-tung elatedly gave his impression of the resistance to Japan: "If Chiang Kai-shek and the others do not capitulate to Japan, the whole of China will be occupied by the Japanese Army, but it will only be able to occupy the big cities and the main communications lines. Then the guerrillas led by the

CCP will develop on a large scale behind the enemy lines. China will rise again after long years of hard struggle. That is to say, the whole of China will be lost at the hands of Chiang Kai-shek, but the CCP will win it back from the Japanese."

I was horror-struck to hear Mao Tse-tung rant in this way. I wondered why China should become a colony of Japan, why the CCP did not actively support Chiang Kai-shek in the resistance against Japan, why it did not cooperate closely with other armies engaged in the War of Resistance. I couldn't help asking, "Will it be easy for the Chinese to rise again if the whole of China is turned into a colony of Japan?" I felt indignantly that Mao Tse-tung was actually a Chinese traitor wearing the cloak of communism. All his ideas and the deeds stemming from these ideas were actually helping Japan's aggression. He would eventually harm the CCP, the Eighth Route Army, and the whole of China.

Once more the struggle against me was whipped up following the examination of Ch'en Ch'ang-hao's responsibility in the defeat of the West Wing troops. After the defeat, Ch'en Ch'ang-hao had escaped back to his native village in Hupeh in an attempt to return to the Oyüwan Soviet region. After the outbreak of the War of Resistance, he sneaked into Yen-an in August. When he came to see me, he was full of shame and confessed that he ought to bear full responsibility for the defeat of the West Wing troops. He was waiting for the punishment of the Party. While living in the premises of the Secretariat of the CC of the CCP, waiting for reassignment, he sometimes wrote articles about the resistance against Japan.

In mid-November, the Secretariat of the CC of the CCP convened a meeting of the Yen-an activists of the CCP to examine the mistakes of Ch'en Ch'ang-hao. Mao Tse-tung and Chang Wen-t'ien chose this occasion to launch a Party struggle, as it was at the time that Shanghai and T'ai-yüan had fallen in succession and the Eighth Route Army had gone to places behind the enemy lines. The situation in the movement of resistance against Japan turned out to be just as they had expected. The struggle against me had come to an end in February of that year, but opposition to me had continued all along in private. After the fall of Shanghai and T'ai-yüan, Mao Tse-tung and Chang Wen-t'ien directly pointed out that my speeches at the Lo-ch'uan Conference showed that I had harbored rightist ideas in my views concerning the anti-Japanese national united front and in my capitulationist thinking with regard to

Chiang Kai-shek. According to them, anti-Party elements who were carrying out anti-Party activities in the new situation must be dealt heavy blows.

The meetings attacking Ch'en Ch'ang-hao lasted about one week, with an attendance of about five hundred people, most of whom were young people from outside Yen-an and CCP members among the students of the Party School, the Anti-Japanese Academy, and the Northern Shensi Public College; some were cadres of Yen-an offices of the Party and the government. Under the direct leadership of Chang Wen-t'ien, the meeting that originally aimed at criticizing Ch'en Ch'ang-hao turned its attention to me, censuring me mainly for being a bandit, a militarist, anti-Party, and what not—all the same old stuff. The students of the Party School frequently attacked and slandered at will, without basing their attacks on facts, as if all mistakes of the CCP were perpetrated by me, Ch'en Ch'ang-hao, and our gang, while the leadership of the CC of the CCP was absolutely correct.

In order to indicate my protest, I did not take part in the meetings during the first few days. I attended the session on the last day to make a general statement in my defense. I pointed out, first of all, that it was regrettable that the meeting, while examining the defeat of the West Wing troops, should involve itself again in the past events of the confrontation of the First and Fourth Front armies. I explained that the Red Army's plans to move west in those years and the defeat of the West Wing troops were parts of a complicated process. Despite his serious error, Ch'en Ch'ang-hao had made amazing contributions to the Party and the Red Army, having gone through hundreds of battles and experienced great danger to his life. In the arduous battles on the westward march, the Fourth Front Army had suffered tragic losses, and the heroic struggles of the commanders and common soldiers alike were epical. Without studying these conditions, the comrades could hardly make fair criticisms; and if they studied them, many of their speeches would become incongruous empty talk. As to opposition between the two CC's, I had already admitted that I had made errors; I also admitted having assumed more responsibility for the errors than was my due, in order to achieve unity. Moreover, all these were things of the past. If it had not been for the outbreak of the War of Resistance, I might have left my leadership post in the CCP a long time ago.

When the War of Resistance broke out, I decided to forget the past and come out to do something for the resistance to Japan. At the Lo-

ch'uan Conference the leadership cadres of the CC of the CCP, including Chang Wen-t'ien, chairman of the current meeting, begged me to
take up the post of chairman of the Border Region government and
encouraged me by saying that the attack on me had ended and would
not be mentioned again at the critical moment of the resistance against
Japan. They had expressed their trust in me, which enabled me to put
my mind at ease and do my job with composure. I did not want to say
much about the criticisms the comrades had leveled at me, but I would
like to point out a few evidently groundless accusations. I asked the
comrades to put themselves in my place and decide whether I could go
on doing the job of chairman of the Border Region government if I were
railed at like that. I also demanded to know what their motives were in
wasting a whole week to encircle and attack me loudly when they
should have spent the time on preparations for the resistance against
Japan at that critical moment in the war.

When I finished speaking, subsequent speakers stood up to accuse
me of having neither made a thorough admission of my mistakes nor put
down the weapon of resistance. Someone said that I ought to assume
more of the responsibility for the mistakes for the sake of the prestige
of the CC. Then a young chap, a newcomer to the Secretariat of the CC
whom I did not know, stood up and made personal attacks on me. He
said vaguely that gold glittered, but not all that glittered was gold.
Flies also glittered; Chang Kuo-t'ao was a fly in the CCP. Chang Wen-
t'ien, chairman of the meeting, appeared to be quite pleased with the
remark and did nothing to stop his ravings. I was so furious that I
could not hold my temper; I walked out in anger.

The day after the meeting, Mao Tse-tung asked me to come over
for an interview. Chang Wen-t'ien was already there when I arrived.
They both greeted me with smiles. They expressed regret over my
resignation and asked me to stay on. They also explained that they had
intended at the meeting only to review the defeat of the West Wing
troops, but unexpectedly the issue of the opposition of the two CC's was
brought up. They hoped that I did not mind. I deeply loathed such
hypocritical tricks of theirs, and I believed that my having accused them
of a breach of faith in my speech on the previous day had reminded
them that my case could not be disregarded and had brought them to
me to ask for my pardon once more. In fact, their plotting to oppose me
would never change. If I persisted in resigning as a sign of protest, a

split between us would result on the spot, and I did not want that to happen. So I said no more about resigning. After some exchange of commonplace remarks, the interview ended.

After the interview I met Chang Wen-t'ien two or three times, when I, as chairman of the Border Region government, had to report to him, the secretary of the CC, on the work of the government. But Chang Wen-t'ien assumed the arrogant posture of Secretary and spoke irrationally in official jargon, like a wicked mother-in-law tormenting her daughter-in-law. I was a bit upset and found in ridiculous, but I suffered patiently without saying a word in opposition. In November and December of that year it could be said that I was at the height of my suffering from these torments. The work of the Border Region government was seriously interfered with; meetings had been held for an entire week to attack me; and there were many concealed troubles. All these were masterminded by Mao Tse-tung from the wings, while Chang Wen-t'ien made the war cries on stage.

Even my wife and my son, who was not yet twelve, were discriminated against and insulted after they arrived in Yen-an one after the other in September and October, 1937. My wife and I had not seen each other for six and one-half years; and my son had been away from me for more than ten years, since our separation at the time of the Wuhan government. After experiencing so many dangers and difficulties, we were happy to see one another again; our good friends were also happy for us. Yet, the schemer who had usurped the power of the Party would not leave us alone, but dealt blows at my wife and son to aggravate my suffering.

My wife was an old Party member, and her name was listed among the leading woman cadres of the CCP. When I left Shanghai for the Oyüwan Soviet region, she stayed behind in Shanghai to carry out confidential work for the office of the CC. The CCP organs in Shanghai were destroyed several times by the enemy, but she luckily escaped being arrested or killed. Finally she lost touch with the CCP. After a great deal of trouble, she changed her name and hid in an advanced school for midwives in Shanghai to study medicine. She stayed there for nearly two years. After the outbreak of the War of Resistance, she got in touch with the Nanking office of the Eighth Route Army of the CCP. After arriving in Yen-an, she wrote home to Tsao-yang County in Hupeh Province, asking our son to join us. She then undertook training courses to educate personnel of the Border Region government and also practiced midwifery in the Border Region hospital. Her work was heavy, exceeding that of an ordinary Party member, but the Organization Department of the CC of the CCP refused to restore her membership in the CCP under the pretext that it was necessary to investigate her history after she had lost contact with the Party. Such investigation was not necessary for most Party members who returned to the Party at that time, most of whom had their Party membership restored. Those who needed to be investigated were evidently ones who were suspected and distrusted. My wife, who was a fervent and candid person, was quite upset.

At that time our son was still a primary-school pupil. As there was no suitable school for him in Yen-an at the moment, he temporarily studied in the junior class of Northern Shensi Public College. As soon as the School for Cadres' Children was set up, he was one of the first to enter it. My boy was very active; he liked singing and acting and was regarded as a child star, hard to come by in the eyes of the school's administrators. He took part in children's performances many times. There was a cultural worker in the school who had once been punished by me for his serious mistakes. He was then a lackey of Chang Wen-t'ien's, and he teased my son by asking him to play the role of the villain Chang Mu-t'ao in one of the performances. My son was dressed in the weird costume of a traitor. I was totally unaware of his role in the play beforehand, and when I arrived at the site of the performance, a group of people were ridiculing my son. Mao Tse-tung was also there, having fun. He cackled maliciously, "It fits perfectly to have Chang Kuo-t'ao's son play the role of Chang Mu-t'ao." Hearing this as I entered, I tore away the mask my son was wearing and led him away from the scene. I shouted in anger as I left, "Barbarians! Wicked people! Worse than beasts!"

It was undeniably a miracle of patience that I had not openly challenged those schemers after all of the above-mentioned events. I refused to see Mao Tse-tung, Chang Wen-t'ien, and the others after that. Around November, I purposely let the secretary general act for me with regard to my duties as chairman of the Border Region government. P'an Tzu-li, the secretary general, was an honest man who had gotten along very well with me. Witnessing conditions inside the Party and learning about my intention, he sensed the burden of his responsibility and quietly applied to the CC of the CCP for a transfer. Just then, the row of caves that the Border Region government had built outside the southern gate of Yen-an were completed, and a move was imminent. The idea was to avoid the danger of being bombed by Japanese planes. Despite my passive attitude, I continued to do what was expected of me, because the work of the government could not stop for a moment.

In December, P'an Tzu-li was transferred, and Wu Hsiu-ch'üan, the public relations officer, was promoted to secretary general. After his promotion Wu Hsiu-ch'üan fully manifested the supercilious air of a secret agent. Under some pretext he had the young assistant who cleaned and tidied up my office arrested. This was evidently a show of strength in front of me. He was probably trying to get out of the young assistant evidence of my "anti-Party behavior"; this was an open declaration that he had been sent to keep an eye on me. Yet, a few days later, Wu Hsiu-ch'üan changed his attitude somewhat. He sought my advice in everything. I could not determine why such a change had taken place. There might have been a number of reasons, one of which might have been that after studying the documents of the Border Region government, Wu Hsiu-ch'üan had found that my proposals were all well intentioned, not at all what he had expected when looking through biased eyes. He must have seen that there had not been any "anti-Party plot," while the interferences of the CC had not always been reasonable, and some had evidently been the result of prejudice.

I gradually transferred the duties of chairman of the Border Region government to Wu Hsiu-ch'üan. First, I asked him to go in my place to see Chang Wen-t'ien and other heads of departments of the CC when it was necessary to consult with someone on the work of the Border Region government. I pointed out that for him it was like driving a light cart along a familiar road, and this would benefit the smooth progress of the work. He agreed happily. For me, solving this problem was like taking a heavy burden off my back. Then I began to let him take over other duties of mine, handing them over one by one with clear explanations, and soon all the work was being done by Wu Hsiu-ch'üan instead of by me. Wu Hsiu-ch'üan worked enthusiastically. Now that he had been promoted three grades in one move and the whole Border Region government was in his hands, he was extremely gratified. For my part, I was feeling light-hearted, because this had paved the way for my future escape.

This turn in events also showed that the plotting dictators were interfering with my duties as chairman of the Border Region government. Their minds were not at ease even when I was only a coolie in the Border Region government. They wanted me to be a captive, going along with all of their manipulations under their surveillance. Even if I had been content to be an obedient puppet, I could not have escaped the danger of being purged and attacked. The malice that Mao Tse-tung harbored against dissenters combined with the madness of the anti-Trotskyite elements of Stalin to turn Yen-an into a dark, sunless dungeon.

During the last ten days of December, 1937, when Yen-an was frozen over, Wang Ming, Ch'en Yün, and Chao Yün (that is, K'ang Sheng) flew back to Yen-an from Moscow on a Soviet military transport plane. On August 21, 1937, China and the Soviet Union had signed a nonaggression pact, after which the Soviet Union supplied China with some aircraft to resist Japanese aggression, and Sinkiang became the main thoroughfare between China and the Soviet Union. The Soviet Union had personnel stationed in Lanchow and Ti-hua to assist with the management of the air-force bases. Wang Ming and the others came via the air-force bases in Ti-hua, Lanchow, and other places.

By then Nanking had been occupied, and the Nationalist government was moving to the provisional capital of Chungking. On its way, it stayed for a time in Wuhan, which became a temporary, provisional capital. In order to hurry to Wuhan, Chou En-lai had, a few days before Wang Ming's arrival, returned to Yen-an from the Shansi front. On the afternoon of the day of Wang Ming's arrival, Chou En-lai was talking to me in my office. Suddenly, we heard the droning of an aircraft. Though there had not been an air-raid alarm, we suspected that it was a Japanese plane coming to bomb us. We, therefore, walked outside to take a look. An airplane appeared on the horizon and circled around the city, flying lower and lower, as if looking for an airstrip. We both went towards the airport. I asked Chou En-lai who was coming. Chou said that we would know when we arrived at the airfield. It seemed that he had not been informed beforehand.

We arrived at the airport at the same time as Mao Tse-tung, Chang Wen-t'ien, and the others. We stood far away from the landing runway. The airport was under heavy guard, as if no one knew who was on the airplane. Probably Mao Tse-tung had received a telegram long before from Moscow, informing him that Wang Ming and the others would come, but Mao had not announced this. As to the exact date of their arrival and the means of transport, even Mao Tse-tung did not know. It was not until Wang Ming stepped out of the plane with Chen Yün and

K'ang Sheng following behind that we hurried forward and shook hands
and embraced each other. In the bliss of reunion, we talked only about
pleasant things that evening. I had not seen Wang Ming for eight
years, Chen Yün for about twelve years, and K'ang Sheng for at least six
and one-half years. There was naturally a lot to talk about when reminiscing. This was the most encouraging and joyful atmosphere that
Yen-an had ever experienced.

I do not recall who it was that asked if it would be possible to keep
traffic open between Moscow and Yen-an, so as to transport large
amounts of weapons and military supplies to Yen-an. Mao Tse-tung was
most interested in this question. Wang Ming at once explained that
according to an understanding between China and the Soviet Union, the
Soviet Air Force within Chinese territory was at the disposal of the
Nationalist government alone; that their flight here was secret and illegal. Wang Ming continued to tell us that they had waited several days
in Lanchow for the weather to clear, and it was not until that morning
that they had had good weather. The pilot of the plane had relied on a
map to find his way to Yen-an. When he saw the big signs on the gate
of Yen-an, he turned to land. Wang Ming thus pointed out that it might
not be possible to transport arms and ammunition to Yen-an by Soviet
planes. Hearing this, Mao Tse-tung sighed repeatedly and said, "If so
much can be given to Chiang Kai-shek, why can't wet get a small share?"

Because of the arrival of these people, the CC of the CCP convened
a Politburo meeting the next morning. The meeting lasted three or four
days. First of all, Wang Ming made a lengthy speech, mainly on the
new ideas of the Moscow headquarters concerning implementation of
the strategy of the anti-Japanese national united front. He pointed out,
right in the beginning, that the War of Resistance was indeed the key
to the continued existence of the Chinese nation. Since the KMT was
taking active steps to resist Japan, the CCP ought to cooperate with it
in earnest. He also said that the victory or defeat of the Chinese in the
War of Resistance had great international significance. If China could
fully employ her forces, thus giving Japan sustained and forceful resistance, Japan would not be able to attack the Soviet Union, and this would
greatly benefit the future of the international proletarian revolution.

He emphasized that the CCP, in its second period of cooperation
with the KMT during the national crisis, must not repeat the experience
of the first cooperation. The cooperation at this time must be stable and
sustained, which called for mutual understanding, mutual concessions,

and mutual help. As the CCP was taking the initiative in making up with the KMT, it must forget all the enmity between the two parties in the past. For instance, a KMT officer with armies under his command ought to be offered sincere cooperation even if in the past he had killed many CCP members, because a prolonged war of resistance could only be sustained with the support of those possessing military power.

Wang Ming again elaborated from another angle. He pointed out that the CCP should not regard itself as a proletarian Party. This was an outmoded formula that was unsuitable for the present. The CCP should boldly regard itself as a Party representing the Chinese people; it should represent the interests not only of the proletariat but of all the people of China. He explained that this did not mean that we should forsake the class concept. The new approach represented a spirit of progress, and after the Seventh Congress of the Comintern, it was the basic attitude demanded of every Communist Party in the world in its role as a member of the people's front to oppose fascism.

Wang Ming then continued to explain that the distance politically between the KMT and the CCP had been shortened in the course of the War of Resistance. Both were parties that represented the people; they differed only in their social policies, one being radical, the other conservative. As to the struggle for political power between the KMT and the CCP, this would be a problem for the distant future. The CCP ought to take the initiative in postponing this problem until after victory in the War of Resistance.

These words of Wang Ming's somewhat embarrassed Mao Tse-tung, who seemed to have received a direct blow on the head. Probably he was thinking about his past words and deeds, which turned out to be at such variance with the ideas of Moscow. Now Moscow even wanted him to form a permanent and stable alliance with the KMT.

I was of the opinion that the ideas of Moscow were far more clever than those of Mao Tse-tung. But Wang Ming had not said a word about China going the way of democratization. All plans were still based on dictatorship, with only some changes in strategy. Moscow probably did not believe that the CCP could assume leadership of the War of Resistance in a short time, and yet it was anxious to have China involve Japan in the War of Resistance; hence its demand that the CCP cooperate with the KMT.

We asked Wang Ming about the current situation in the world, with a view to assessing how much support China could get from other countries and whether Great Britain, the United States, and other powers would form an alliance to intervene in Japan's aggression against China. Wang Ming was not optimistic in this respect. He said that Japan was in collusion with Germany and Italy to form a fascist front on the international scene. The power of fascism was at its height, menacing the Soviet Union and China; it was hard to say whether Great Britain, the United States, France, and other democratic countries would lend a helping hand. Such a situation in the world made it imperative for the Soviet Union to insist that we further consolidate the anti-Japanese united front.

Wang Ming had hinted that this change in strategy was very important and that the idea came from no other than Stalin himself. He had asked Stalin point-blank, "The CCP should cooperate with the KMT to resist Japan in accordance with your instructions, but are the instructions that you and the Comintern have given in the past concerning the CCP still valid?" And Stalin had said that those were instructions of the past and that they must be set aside, without further attention being given to them. (Here he meant chiefly the advocacy of independent development of the CCP, contention with the KMT for leadership power, the waging of struggles, and so forth.)

According to Wang Ming, Stalin was of the opinion that the CCP should try to be self-reliant in the light of current conditions, without being bound by the outmoded formulae of the Comintern concerning the China problem. Stalin had said to him, "China has to swim across a wide, wide sea; you have no other choice but to rely on your own efforts." What he worried about was what would happen if we drowned midway.

Mao Tse-tung seemed quite pleased when he heard this. He was probably thinking "What shall I do now that Stalin's ideas have turned out to be different from mine? Ah! Here's a way out; he mentions the principle of self-reliance." At a future date, Mao Tse-tung criticized Wang Ming for his mistakes of rightist opportunism and for his advocacy of alliance with the KMT to the exclusion of other ideas. The correct idea according to Mao was alliance on the one hand and struggle on the other in the CCP's relations with the KMT. The struggle between Mao Tse-tung and Wang Ming started fundamentally at this discussion. Mao's weapon was emphasizing the Sinification of Marxism-Leninism, doing everything in the light of actual conditions in China, in opposition to the heresy of Wang Ming's internationalist sect.

Mao Tse-tung, Chang Wen-t'ien, and others all expressed complete approval of this political report made by Wang Ming, as if at the Lo-ch'uan Conference they had never said such things as "bring about the defeat of Chiang Kai-shek," "make the CCP independent," "enlarge the forces of the CCP to fight against the KMT," and so forth. We continued to discuss other questions, one of the most important of which was refusal to resume cooperation with Ch'en Tu-hsiu.

In October, 1937, Lo Han came to Yen-an as a representative of Ch'en Tu-hsiu and held consultations with us. Lo Han was an old comrade and a friend of mine from the days of the May Fourth Movement when we had worked together. Lo Han was also an old friend of Mao Tse-tung's. He had later left the CCP and become an important member of Ch'en Tu-hsiu's Trotskyite clique. In his interview with me he spoke about Ch'en Tu-hsiu's contribution to the CCP and Ch'en's sacrifice of his two sons for the Party. Ch'en himself had been sentenced to ten years' imprisonment and had only lately been released. Ch'en had always persisted in his socialist stand. Lo Han also pointed out that the Trotskyites were divided into many sects and cliques with different views. Ch'en Tu-hsiu and many of the important members of his clique wanted to cooperate with the CCP again. Lo Han explained that Ch'en Tu-hsiu had persistently supported the resistance against Japan and was in favor of the anti-Japanese national united-front policy of the CCP. Ch'en held that as the KMT and the CCP were able to cooperate again, old comrades of socialism ought all the more to be prepared to reunite. I said that I welcomed Ch'en's intention and asked Lo Han to talk directly to Mao Tse-tung.

Mao Tse-tung was in sympathy with this activity of Lo Han's and thought that the Trotskyites of China were not the same as those of the Soviet Union. Their behavior, as manifested by Lo Han, was quite different from the die-hard attitude of Trotsky. Mao seemed to miss the old friendship with Ch'en. He had told me that it might be possible to form a certain cooperative relationship with Ch'en Tu-hsiu, so as to rally everyone to the War of Resistance. Mao also talked about the many mistakes that had been made in suppressing counterrevolutionaries during the period of the Soviet campaign, and supposed that Stalin was making even more mistakes than we had in his current suppression of counterrevolutionaries. At present our aim was to rally all forces to resist Japan. So long as Ch'en Tu-hsiu's Trotskyites showed themselves to be repentant, we might unite with them to resist Japan.

Since Mao Tse-tung was in favor of such an attitude, Chang Wen-t'ien could do nothing but comply. After many consultations with Lo Han, an agreement consisting of nineteen articles was drawn up, which mainly stipulated that the Trotskyites were to support the resistance against Japan and the current policy of cooperation between the CCP and the KMT in the resistance and to make clear-cut expressions of this attitude in words and deeds in the near future. It was also stipulated that the Trotskyites who desired to restore their membership in the CCP must openly confess their error in having joined the Trotskyites and must break with the Trotskyite clique; those who did not so desire might cooperate with the CCP as outsiders by supporting the anti-Japanese policy of the CCP. The CC of the CCP would no longer adopt a hostile attitude toward the Trotskyite who supported resistance to Japan.

The case was discussed at this meeting of the Politburo after some delay. When Wang Ming heard about it, without asking about the reason, he very angrily expressed opposition. He pointed out that in the resistance against Japan we might cooperate with anyone except the Trotskyites. At the international level we might cooperate with politicians, warlords, or even anti-Communist executioners of the bourgeoisie, but we must not cooperate with disciples of Trotsky. In China we might cooperate with Chiang Kai-shek and the anti-Communist secret agents under him, but we must not cooperate with Ch'en Tu-hsiu. He used the most vicious terms in the dictionary, such as "traitors," "Trotskyite bandits," and "murderers," to attack the Trotskyites, and he slandered Ch'en Tu-hsiu by saying that he was a Japanese secret agent who received an allowance of three hundred yuan a month from Japan.

At the meeting we had said that Ch'en Tu-hsiu was after all different from Trotsky, and someone had said that it was surely not true that Ch'en Tu-hsiu was a Japanese spy. But Wang Ming insisted that it was inconceivable for us to keep in touch with the Trotskyites while Stalin was opposing the Trotskyites with thundering might. He pointed out that the consequences would be unthinkable should Stalin come to know of it. He elaborated, saying that in dealing with the Trotskyites, it was not permissible to have kind feelings; Ch'en Tu-hsiu must be a Japanese spy—whether he was or not. These blanket remarks of Wang Ming's silenced everyone at the meeting. Hereafter, in the propaganda of the CCP, Ch'en Tu-hsiu became "a Japanese spy receiving an allowance of three hundred yuan a month."

Wang Ming made a lengthy speech on this topic. He told us about

the experiences and lessons of the Soviet Union in suppressing Trotskyites and other anti-Party elements, and he explained that the crimes of
treason committed by well-known personalities in the CPSU had been
well substantiated. He said that according to this experience, any Party
member, no matter how deep his faith in communism and how great his
achievements had been, was capable of going to the extreme of opposing
the Party and betraying the country so long as he had any anti-Party
inclinations. He spoke of the Trotskyites and other anti-Party elements
who had made use of all sorts of opportunities to plot against the Soviet
Union and the CPSU, and to frame many good comrades by fabricating
false depositions during Party purges. Wang Ming did not say that
Stalin had killed many good comrades in his frantic purges; on the contrary, he put the blame on the Trotskyites and other anti-Party elements.
This simply horrified us.

Wang Ming said that, on principle, the CCP must not renew cooperation with the renegades. He pointed out that the politicians of the
bourgeoisie, the disciples of Chiang Kai-shek, and the Fascists were
completely unrelated to the CCP, and it was natural that they should be
anti-Communist; they could not directly influence the Party internally.
For the sake of certain political needs, we might cooperate for a time or
for a prolonged period with these people who were originally not from
the brood. The social democrats, who were relatively close to the Communists, had all along impeded the development of the Communist
movement. They were our dangerous enemies. As to the Trotskyites,
the Bukharinists, and other rightist anti-Party sects and tendencies,
which were still closer to the Communist Party and could undermine us
from the inside, they were even more dangerous enemies than the social
democrats. By purging them and purifying the Party, Stalin had further
developed Leninism, and that was the quintescence of Stalin's theory.

Wang Ming then went on to propose stepping up the struggles
against the Trotskyites and other anti-Party elements. He said that the
CPSU had large numbers of Trotskyites and anti-Party elements within
its ranks, and therefore it was unlikely that everything was all right inside the CCP, either. He was sure that there were lots of Trotskyites
and other anti-Party elements hidden inside the Party, and that they had
not been discovered only because we had not waged thorough struggles
on the two fronts. Therefore, now was not the time to renew cooperation with Ch'en Tu-hsiu, but to step up the anti-Trotskyite struggle. In
the period of the War of Resistance, there were bound to be some rene-

gades or elements who had left the Party who would seek to rejoin the Party. We must not tolerate them with magnanimity, nor should we lightly tolerate the comrades now inside the Party who had commiitted anti-Party acts or had harbored impure thoughts.

Wang Ming was like an "imperial envoy" from Moscow, holding high the emperor's double-edged sword, his manner of speech resembling that of an imperial envoy transmitting an imperial decree. Yet he was, after all, an inexperienced chap who had lofty ambitions but insufficient talent, was fond of making highfalutin remarks without actual investigations of reality, and lacked the ability and techniques to implement his ideas. His performance in the first few days caused some uneasiness among the leaders of the Party. I had the feeling that Wang Ming would fail in his struggle with Mao Tse-tung.

At the time that the question of organization was under discussion, Wang Ming, without consulting with anyone beforehand, proposed a list of sixteen members and alternate members for the Politburo of the CC. As I mentioned before, the membership of the CC had undergone many changes since the Sixth Congress was held in 1928. Many of the present members were not originally members, but had been promoted to their post as exigency required. At that time, the CC held that the time was not yet ripe for convening the Seventh Congress, but Wang Ming thought that some people ought to be included in the CC's Politburo, so he made the extraordinary move of proposing his slate.

But Mao Tse-tung seemed to feel uneasy about this independent action of Wang Ming's. His slate actually only added Chao Yün and Ch'en Yün, the two who had returned from the Soviet Union with him; all the rest were the same as before, with only some rearrangement in the order of the names. So, in principle, Mao had no objection to the list; what he was unhappy about was that Wang Ming had not asked his opinion beforehand. Mao therefore spared no effort to recommend Wang Ming as leader of the CC and excused himself from the post as not having a firm grasp on the helm in the anti-Japanese national united-front policy and in the struggle against the Trotskyites. He expressed a desire to minimize his own responsibility, and he vigorously advocated that Wang Ming be number one on the list. It was only after Wang Ming forcefully explained that he had had no intention of "seizing the commander's seal" that Mao finally said no more on the subject. The slate was adopted.

Chang Wen-t'ien, who was secretary of the CC, was demoted to seventh on Wang Ming's list. Although Wang Ming's intention seemed to be to take Chang Wen-t'ien's place, Chang Wen-t'ien said very little. Beyond expressing his approval of the political proposals that Wang Ming had brought back from Moscow, he had not made remarks on any of the practical questions, particularly on the question of electing a secretary.

At that time I was rather depressed and was unwilling to be counted among these people, so I did not enter into the dispute. On Wang Ming's list, my name was still third, after those of Mao Tse-tung and Chou En-lai. In explaining the arrangement of the names on the list, Wang Ming said that I was well known inside and outside China and that I occupied an indelible position in the CCP, but he also criticized me for having committed the error of setting up another CC. I had the feeling that Wang Ming's chief aim was to reproach me once more. As I had no desire to talk about the past again, I could only keep silent and did not answer.

Ch'en Yün and Chao Yün seemed to be a little more experienced than Wang Ming. They showed themselves to be very humble and modest in their speeches, which generally consisted of some supplementary remarks about Wang Ming's ideas. They constantly expressed admiration for us, the leaders who had persisted with the struggles inside China. Therefore, they accepted, amid applause, their important posts as head of the Organization Department and director of the Political Security Committee, respectively, while becoming members of the Politburo of the CC. Later, in Mao Tse-tung's struggle with Wang Ming, these two were not involved.

The spearhead of Wang Ming's anti-Trotskyite struggle was, unexpectedly, directed at me. Once, when I was talking with Wang Ming alone, Wang had asked me what was really the crux of the matter in the dispute at the Mao-erh-kai meeting. I had said, "In addition to criticizing the political line of the CC, it was the struggle for military leadership." And he replied, "That was not all. Another important factor was the underhanded plot of the Trotskyites." He then told me that Li Teh and Huang Ch'ao had been Trotskyites, and that they had confessed at the trials in Ti-hua chaired by Teng Fa and had been shot.

I said angrily, gritting my teeth, "Li Teh and Huang Ch'ao Trotskyites? Then anybody could be labeled a Trotskyite!" Wang Ming answered, "You yourself are not a Trotskyite, but you have been used by them." He then told me that in the great purge in Moscow, it had been proven that I had no connection with the Trotskyites; but it could not be inferred that among those in my confidence there were no Trotskyites, or that I could not have been used by the Trotskyites. He also pointed out that Yü Hsiu-sung, Chou Ta-wen, and Tung Yi-hsiang, who had been close to me, had not been exposed in the Moscow purges; but he had always been suspicious of them. When he was last in Sinkiang, he had had them arrested and tried, and they had confessed that they had been Trotskyites. So there was nothing to do but put them to death.

I pointed out to him with great patience that evidence given under duress and torture might give rise to injustice. I recalled that Hsiang Ying had carried out strict suppression of counterrevolutionaries while in the Kiangsi Soviet region, adopting the method of forcibly obtaining evidence under duress. As a result, some evidence that was given involved Hsiang Ying himself, and he then became aware that not all evidence could be trusted. I asked him why we should lose confidence in ourselves by imagining that we saw Trotskyites making trouble everywhere. Our country was then in danger of becoming a colony of Japan, and we were trying to rally all forces to resist Japan, yet we wanted to purge the Trotskyites in a big way. Wouldn't it be a help to the enemy if we purged a lot of our comrades as Trotskyites? Seeing that I was very angry and that my words were sharp, Wang Ming said, "Let's talk about this some other time!"

I was greatly hurt by what Wang Ming had told me and by his intention of following Stalin in suppressing Trotskyites. Li Teh and Huang Ch'ao had worked with me since 1931, Li being chief-of-staff and Huang secretary general. Li was a graduate of the Military and Political University of Leningrad, while Huang had taken part in the student movement in Shanghai as an activist in the student union. Before their arrival in the Oyüwan Soviet region, I had only known them superficially. They had been recommended by the CC as capable of taking on important posts. During the years that we worked together, I found out that they had done a lot for the Fourth Front Army, at the risk of their own lives. Finally, in the West Wing troops, they had led several hundred men to Sinkiang after encountering innumerable dangers and difficulties. But at Mao-erh-kai they had accused the CC of making mistakes in leadership, and this may have been the cause of their deaths.

As to Yü Hsiu-sung, Chou Ta-wen, and Tung Yi-hsiang, they were returned students from the Soviet Union with higher academic achievements than the others. All of them were old friends of mine. Yü Hsiu-sung was one of the founders of the CCP, honest and incorruptible. Chou Ta-wen, like Ch'ü Ch'iu-pai, was a graduate of the Peking Russian Language School who had attained considerable success in the study of the Russian language and Russian problems. Tung Yi-hsiang, like Shen Yen-ping, was an editor of the Commercial Press, having made some achievements in the study of literature. The three had opposed Mif while studying at Sun Yat-sen University in Moscow, and had struggled against Wang Ming and the others. After their graduation from Lenin Academy, they were assigned to posts in Sinkiang, as if to avoid having them in direct contact with the Mifists who were then in control of the CC. It was utterly unjust for Wang Ming to have framed and persecuted them, waving his "imperial double-edged sword" while passing through Sinkiang.

I was of the opinion that Wang Ming, in mimicking Stalin's work-style of carrying out frantic purges in the Party, would degrade the CCP. His proposal for close cooperation with the KMT in order to resist Japan, a proposal that he had brought back from Moscow, was close to the view that I had consistently held. But he was not proceeding from the interests of the Chinese nation; he would, in fact, fail in his struggle with Mao Tse-tung, and then it would be difficult to achieve the results that we wanted. His opposition to conciliation and renewed cooperation with Ch'en Tu-hsiu was clearly reactionary. It was an inexcusable crime for him to have killed comrades Li Teh, Huang Ch'ao, Yü Hsiu-sung, Chou Ta-wen, and Tung Yi-hsiang in Sinkiang. In 1930 Wang Ming and the other Mifists had caused the deaths of a group of veteran comrades including Ho Meng-hsiung by adopting the method of cruel attacks. Now, they had gone on to kill comrades who held views that differed from those held by people with authority in the CCP. It showed that the ghostly shadow of Stalin had followed Wang Ming to China and was getting bigger and bigger.

Because of this great provocation, I finally decided to leave the CCP after deep deliberation. I felt that by now everything had gone too far to be discussed reasonably, and there was no way to appeal. Moreover, there was no need to do so. In the critical moment of the War of Resistance Again Japan, I had no other alternative but to jump out of the circle, adopting the attitude "as long as we can agree, I'll stay; when we can't, I'll leave." Perhaps in this way I could do something in line with what I wanted to do.

At the moment, the anti-Japanese situation prevented the leadership of the CCP from doing whatever it wanted to do. After the fall of Nan-king, the rumor was rife that the Nationalist government might compro-mise with Japan. Wang Ming thought that the situation was grave and volunteered to go to Wuhan in order to keep in closer touch with the KMT and to save China from the possible crisis of compromising with Japan. A few days later, in January, 1938, Wang Ming and Chou En-lai set out for Wuhan. The differences of opinion between Wang Ming and the group that included Mao Tse-tung, Chang Wen-t'ien, and others had yet to be adjusted. My nominal office as chairman of the Border Region government was still of some use in camouflaging appearances. It seemed that the time was not yet ripe for further purging of the Trot-skyites or those used by the Trotskyites.

Between January and March of 1938, Yen-an was quiet and calm, as there were fewer activities during the cold weather when the winter gales were howling. During the period of the Lunar New Year, every-body in Yen-an, as in the rest of China, put aside his work to celebrate the Spring Festival. With Wang Ming and Chou En-lai away from Yen-an, the meeting of the Politburo of the CC was again adjourned, and nothing special happened. I had decided to leave the CCP and was looking for the earliest opportunity to leave Yen-an. This might be risky, but I felt better for my decision. I had become indifferent to everything in Yen-an; what I was thinking about all the time was how to implement my decision.

I had tasted all there was to taste in life in my eighteen years with the revolution. Without going too far back, let's take the anti-Chiang Kuo-t'ao campaign in February, 1937. That perfidious, unreasonable, and savage act made me decide never again to concern myself with the affairs of the CC of the CCP. But the outbreak of the War of Resistance Against Japan kindled my anti-Japanese fervor and drove me back into the fiery pit. I was also pushed towards the decision to leave the CCP by the plot that violated the interests of the War of Resistance and by all sorts of persecution carried on against me under a hypocritical dis-guise by Mao Tse-tung, Chang Wen-t'ien, and others after the Lo-ch'uan Conference. But because of all sorts of worries, it was not easy to make a choice immediately. From Wang Ming's words I came to realize that it was just as dark in Moscow as it was in Yen-an. The devilish claws of Stalin's purge and the malicious hand of Mao Tse-tung's plot would reach me sooner or later. Time was of the essence, hence my final decision to leave the CCP and to go away from Yen-an.

Why did Wang Ming tell me about the murders of Li Teh, Huang Ch'ao, Yü Hsiu-sung, Chou Ta-wen, and Tung Yi-hsiang in Singkiang? Why did he insist that the dispute at Mao-erh-kai was the result of Trotskyite manipulation? Why did he arbitrarily assert that I had been used by the Trotskyites? Was it due to his naïveté that he directly addressed those harsh words to me? Or was this a threat? But Wang Ming had to rush to Wuhan in an attempt to prevent the Nationalist government from compromising with Japan and to maintain the situation of resistance to Japan and promote cooperation between the KMT and the CCP—to do the things that he considered to be of paramount importance. It was due to this urgent business that the campaign against me as having been used by the Trotskyites had been postponed. Another reason for the postponement might have been that some people had advised Wang Ming not to move too rapidly, as the situation inside the CC of the CCP was more complicated than he, who had just returned from Moscow, could see. But since Wang Ming had killed five important cadres of the CCP, he would not be able to make a clean report of himself unless he waged the struggle against me for having been used by the Trotskyites.

The Politburo meeting greatly worried Mao Tse-tung and Chang Wen-t'ien, for the spearhead of Wang Ming's speeches hit them right on their sore spots. Mao Tse-tung kept a tight grip on the real power—the Army. He did not slacken one bit in his guidance of the various units of the Eighth Route Army and the sending of large numbers of personnel to the front. He did not expect much to come of Wang Ming's activities in Wuhan, but he kept silent on the issue. When he met me, he engaged in light conversation. Chang Wen-t'ien, preoccupied with the instability of his own position, had pulled in the reins somewhat. Though he did not say anything when he met me, he changed his attitude somewhat and became more respectful to me. Chao Yün and Ch'en Yün, being newcomers, usually asked others for advice and did not speak freely. My duties as chairman of the Border Region government were handled rather successfully by Wu Hsiu-ch'üan, who seldom bothered me. All this enabled me to plan for myself in peace.

Perfectly at ease, I sometimes rode to the mountains and enjoyed myself in the rural area. Sometimes I took my son or other youths on picnics in the outskirts of Yen-an and had long chats with them. My old abode on the mountain was our hangout. I often attended evening shows and ball games, mixing in well with the young chaps with great enthusiasm. I also found time to spend with my wife, who was not only busy with her own work but was also suffering from morning sickness. I shared some of her work, such as giving lessons in the training courses. My other pastimes included games of chess and dinner parties. In this way, I spent my last three months in Yen-an in relative tranquillity. During this period I reminisced a lot; some of my thoughts I will mention here briefly.

The CCP had changed, had degenerated completely. It was a million miles away from my first ideals as a founder of the Party. In its short life the CCP had gone through three major stages: the first period of KMT-CCP cooperation, the Soviet period, and the second period of cooperation between the KMT and the CCP. The leaders of the Party, including Ch'en Tu-hsiu, Ch'ü Ch'iu-pai, Li Li-san, Wang Ming, the Mifists, and Mao Tse-tung, have all been described in this book. From my descriptions the readers will see that Mao Tse-tung has been unscrupulous in his actions in order to seek personal victory; this is out-and-out reactionary, imperialist thinking, utterly incompatible with modern Communist thought. Under the cloak of Communist thinking, Mao Tse-tung has hidden his guerrilla concepts, his peasant mentality, and his strategy of the rule of might—all of which are very incompatible with communism.

Similarly, the whole Comintern had changed, had degenerated completely. It had separated itself from the workers' movement of Europe, with which it had been connected since the time of Marx, and had come under the dictatorship of Stalin, whose terrorism during the Party purges had killed millions of people, including revolutionaries. This was obviously the action of a despotic tyrant. Even the pro-Soviet Shao Li-tzu, in describing the cruelty of Stalin, had said to me, "Killing of as many people as Stalin killed has rarely been seen in this world. In the history of China there have been tyrants who killed large numbers of meritorious statesmen, but none have killed as many literati and scholars."

According to Communist principles and the constitution of the CCP, the Communist Party is an organization of faithful volunteers who hold the same beliefs. The worst punishment that the Party organization can mete out to its members is expulsion from the Party, while the members are also free to leave the Party of their own free will. In accordance with this democratic principle, there should be no such crimes as "betraying the Party" and "being renegades"; and there should be no more severe punishment than expulsion from the Party. It was only because the parties inside and outside of China had degenerated that Wang Ming was bold enough to kill the important cadres in Sinkiang; otherwise he would have been sentenced for his crime like any other murderer.

As to the War of Resistance Against Japan, it was one that every Chinese national was entitled to take part in, without any distinction between Communists and non-Communists. The CCP, as an organization, might cooperate with the KMT to resist Japan; I, as an individual, might also cooperate with the KMT and all compatriots to resist Japan. Without the bondage of the CCP, people would be able to give play to their strength in the resistance against Japan. It was completely dictatorial prejudice to say that anyone leaving the CCP was unable to resist Japan, or even to condemn him as a reactionary, a counterrevolutionary, a renegade, or a traitor. It was all misleading propaganda.

I was deeply ashamed that I had not been able to lead the CCP onto a proper path of development or to stop the CCP from degenerating. I had tried to do so in many minor ways; but all of my efforts met with setbacks, showing that I was incapable of stopping the overwhelming flood. Should I then wait for execution like Bukharin and the others, allowing Stalin to kill them as he wished? It was absolutely necessary for me to leave the CCP and go away from Yen-an. It was a just action which I should take. I had the right to act independently, to leave the Party of my own free will and never to work with those cruel and sinister dictators. But, under the circumstances, leaving the Party was a very serious thing, and I had to handle everything in a clandestine manner.

On April 4, 1938, I went to Chung-pu County to take part in the ceremony of offering sacrifices at the tomb of Emperor Huang-ti—an event presided over by a high official of the Nationalist government every year as a tribute to the ancient founder of the Chinese nation. Taking advantage of the occasion, I left Yen-an, and at that point I left the CCP for good. The ceremony was presided over that year by Chiang Ting-wen, director of the Sian Field Headquarters, as a special envoy of the Nationalist government. I went in my capacity as chairman of the Border Region government to take part in the offering. In the first year of the War of Resistance, the ceremony was definitely useful in boosting the national sentiment of the people. It was just a coincidence that I had chosen this occasion to leave the CCP, but it was full of political significance.

Setting out from Chung-pu County, I went to Hankow via Sian. This was my first trip after my departure from the CCP. While I was in Hankow, Chou En-lai, Wang Ming, Ch'in Pang-hsien, and others tried to stop me from leaving the CCP; but I was quite determined to leave, and they could do nothing about it. So they issued a document censuring me, and both the CC of the CCP and the Comintern announced that they had expelled me from the Party. There is no need to go into the details of all this. I then issued an open letter to the people of China, which I have attached to the end of this book, for the reader's reference. This document was my statement on my departure from the CCP; it marked the conclusion of my Communist career. It must be clearly understood that it was a document written during the period of the War of Resistance, reflecting the situation at that time and the circumstances under which I was living.

APPENDIX

An Open Letter to My Fellow Countrymen
from
Chang Kuo-t'ao

And a discussion with my colleagues in the CCP on the issues of the War of Resistance and the reconstruction of China

Published on May 20 of
the 27th Year of the Republic of China
(1938)

Since the outbreak of the War of Resistance Against Japan, China has been in a difficult situation. Informed circles all over the country have noted that the only way to save China from being conquered is to resist to the end, with the whole nation united as one, and that in order to attain this goal, it is necessary to give full play to the national consciousness and to increase the spirit of sacrifice a hundred-fold. After arriving at Sian from Fu-shih, this writer read the Manifest of the Provisional National Congress of the Chinese KMT and its program for the War of Resistance Against Japan and the reconstruction of the nation. It is the opinion of this writer that these documents perfectly meet the urgent needs of the nation. What moves this writer deeply is the sincerity with which the documents have been imbued in their appeal to the whole nation to strive for the common cause. This writer, therefore, left Sian for Hankow, where he hoped to have detailed discussions with the gentlemen there who are responsible for the CC of the CCP, so as to make the best efforts for the cause of the War of Resistance Against Japan and the reconstruction of the nation. Unexpectedly, before a conclusion could be reached, this writer was subjected to the disciplinary measure of expulsion from the Party by the CC of the CCP and to all sorts of slanders (for example, that this writer distrusted the anti-Japanese national united front; that he despaired of the future of the Chinese revolution; that he sabotaged the unity in resistance to Japan; and other absurd remarks). This writer

581

hereby makes a brief statement on his political views, which comprises the following four main points:

1. This writer has all along been firmly resolved to carry through to the end the War of Resistance Against Japan and has had profound confidence in its final victory, not despairing in the least over the bright outcome of the War of Resistance Against Japan and the reconstruction of the nation. Furthermore, this writer is willing to dedicate everything to the nation.

2. At this crucial moment of life or death for the nation and its people, this writer is of the opinion that the nation and its people are above everything else.

3. The "Three Principles of the People" are essential to present-day China; the Chinese KMT is the leadership core of the War of Resistance and reconstruction of the country; Mr. Chiang is the sole supreme leader in the country—these three points have not been denied by the CC of the CCP. It is a sign of progress on the part of the CC of the CCP to stand for the principle of forming the anti-Japanese national united front; and this writer agrees. But the writer feels that this is not enough. In the view of this writer, the CC of the CCP ought to make a more sincere response to the manifesto of the Provisional National Congress of the Chinese KMT and the program for the War of Resistance and the reconstruction of the nation, so as to attain further unity and to strengthen the forces for the War of Resistance and the reconstruction of the nation.

4. This writer, with an attitude of utmost sincerity, has had initial consultations with the gentlemen of the CC of the CCP on the above-mentioned proposals, but they were not accepted. It is this writer's hope that his colleagues in the CCP will make profound deliberations on the above proposals in the future.

This writer believes that the above statement is in no way incorrect in view of current political needs; yet it has come to the notice of this writer that the responsible persons of the CCP in Wuhan have, in statements and letters, continued to level slanders at this writer's views and actions. What is said in those statements and letters shows, in essence, contempt for the truth, prejudice, and even fabricated facts that reverse right and wrong. Their selfish aim is to destroy political consultation and to maintain the interests of the faction. In this case, it can be seen that the leaders of the CCP have not attached importance to the self-respect that members of a modern political party ought to have, nor have they paid much attention to political morality, all of which this writer deeply regrets.

At this crucial moment in the War of Resistance and the reconstruction of the nation, it is the firm belief of this writer that every political fighter necessarily will, in accordance with the principle of putting the nation and its people above everything else, forsake all past prejudices and set right his political tendency. It is also necessary that the entire nation, from the upper echelons to the grass roots, unite sincerely for the strengthening of the nation. In view of this, this writer wishes to explain briefly the political dissension between the CCP and this writer and the dispute that has arisen therefrom. It will be a great favor to him if his fellow countrymen, and the gentlemen of the CCP, will pay attention to it.

A comprehensive review of the political line of the CCP, being too wide in scope, cannot be dealt with in depth here. The present review will be limited to basic viewpoints on the War of Resistance and the reconstruction of the nation which the country urgently needs. This writer is firmly convinced that the origin and development of this error in the policy of the CCP are far from fortuitous, and that this error is continuing to develop. Here is where this writer has found it impossible to acquiesce without thinking.

The erroneous political line of the CCP has continually moved along an axis formed, briefly speaking, out of the following points:

1. From the beginning China has been an economically backward country under imperialistic aggression. Desultory agriculture forms the backbone of the national economy, while purely national industry occupies only a small portion of the economy. The tasks of the revolution on the home front, therefore, are to eliminate the remnants of feudalism, to set aright agrarian relations, and to realize the unification of the country, and, in its relations with foreign countries, to abolish the privileges, both economic and political, that imperialists enjoy within the territory of China, to strive for total territorial sovereignty and complete political and economic independence. This is the main content of the national revolution. The joint statement of Dr. Sun Yat-sen and Mr. Joffe has made this point clear: "Dr. Sun Yat-sen is of the opinion that the Communist organization as well as even the Soviet system is, in fact, not applicable to China, because there is no such condition in China as will make the Communist or Soviet system a success. Mr. Joffe is in full sympathy with this opinion. He also thinks that the most urgent question that confronts China is to achieve the unity of the republic and complete independence of the nation." In a word, the Chinese revolution is a national one in nature, involving all the people of the country, with the task of seeking unity at home and independence in its relations with foreign countries. As to the revolutionary forces, they include the classes of urban citizens and the rural classes of medium and small landholders and peasants tilling their own land, who form the majority and are actively against aggression from the outside, while internally they do not represent the feudal forces which impede unity. Therefore, apart from

the feudal forces with vested interests, the vast national masses are the active participants and supporters of the revolution.

The CCP is aware of these basic questions, but does not have a deep understanding of them. As a result, it often substitutes radical subjective imagination for the objective conditions of the development of Chinese society; it makes a mechanical interpretation of the forces of the democratic revolution, regarding the path of the Russian October Revolution as the only one to follow. What is still worse is that it does not understand the objective situation of the revolution, and this gives rise to erroneous policies, which have inflicted disproportionate setbacks to the vast revolutionary forces—forces which, from an objective point of view, could have taken part in the revolution. Such a situation persisted till September 18, when the national crisis became manifestly serious. Even today, there has not yet been any earnest correction in policy that has not been mere lip service.

Moreover, it is necessary to acknowledge definitely that the movement to achieve internal unity that is being led by the KMT of China is a progressive, revolutionary measure, as its aim is to oppose the feudal carving up of the country, the success of which is a prerequisite for forming an all-people's resistance to foreign aggression. Ignorant of the significance of this, the CCP has stupidly required that there be a link between the class struggle and national liberation, stressing that the more deep-seated the class struggle, the closer to success national liberation will be, thus obliterating national interests for the sake of class interests. All these basic viewpoints that are incompatible with the national revolution have been proved wrong both in theory and in practice.

2. The CCP has an extremely incorrect understanding of the Chinese KMT, which is based on its erroneous conception of the theory of national revolution. At first the CCP held that the "Three Principles of the People" constituted a reactionary ideology and that the KMT represented only the landlord and bourgeois classes. Later, it held that the KMT was a branch of fascism and that the Nationalist government was a pro-Japanese, traitorous government. But, essentially, in accordance with the essence of the "Three Principles of the People," with the components of the KMT, and with the past policy of the Nationalist government and Mr. Chiang, the CCP's opinion evidently did not tally with the facts. The Chinese KMT has, in fact, inherited the fine tradition of the history of the Chinese revolution. It has overthrown the despotic Manchurian Ching government, founded the Chinese Republic, and has been gradually completing the task of unifying China after the Northern Expedition. Even now it is shouldering the heavy tasks of waging the sacred War of Resistance Against Japan and national reconstruction. Take, for instance, the War of Resistance Against Japan; it is an unprecedented

experience in the history of China, when the entire nation, from the highest level to the grass roots, is rising as one man with great courage. Despite the sacrifice of more than half a million officers and men, fighting has continued with redoubled vigor. These manifest facts attest to the success of Mr. Chiang's leadership and are evidence of the revolutionary spirit of the KMT, which no one can deny. Furthermore, Mr. Chiang, being the supreme leader unanimously acknowledged by the whole nation, enjoys the admiration of all at home and abroad for his loyalty to the nation and for the way in which he has braced himself to shoulder the heavy responsibility concerning the rise or fall of the nation at the critical moment when the destiny of the nation is hanging by a thread. No fellow countrymen are entitled to find fault, under the pretext of some secondary questions, in order to seek their own advancement and satisfy their selfish desires. The absurd viewpoints that consider that the KMT has a dual nature, claiming that it is revolutionary at present during the War of Resistance to Japan but will no longer be so after the War, not only deny the revolutionary brilliance that will result from victory in the War of Resistance Against Japan, but will also seriously damage the great current war effort and the work of national reconstruction. This writer is quite certain about this!

3. Because of the incorrect judgment of the CCP on the Chinese revolution and because of its prejudices against the "Three Principles of the People," the KMT, and its leader, a series of errors in the general strategy and line of the CCP have resulted. The inherent shortcomings of the CCP itself and the ensuing organizational degeneration have also been revealed still more fully as a result of this erroneous line.

The concrete expression of the erroneous strategy and line of the CCP is manifested in its struggle for leadership power in disregard of the objective conditions necessary to the revolution. Since the sixteenth year of the Republic, the CCP has further proposed the slogan of the Soviet regime, adopting the policy of uprisings, seeking to encircle the cities with the countryside in order to win victory in one or several provinces first. The experiences of the past ten years have shown that the Soviet slogan runs completely counter to the national interests. With regard to its organization, the CCP has long retreated from the field of industry and has gone to remote regions, losing the mass basis that it needs and bringing about a change in its quality. It is no longer a party of the proletariat, but an aggregation of the petty bourgeoisie with peasants in the majority, continually resorting to military plots and uprisings to offer continuous obstructions to the struggle for internal unity and resistance to foreign powers.

4. Since the launching of the War of Resistance Against Japan, the urgent demand of the whole nation has been to unite as one to resist

Japan. Advocating an anti-Japanese national united front, the CCP has outwardly assumed obedience to the order of the Nationalist government, has reorganized the Red Army, abolished the Soviet regime, and stopped agrarian revolution; but inwardly it is still following its original erroneous thinking and sectarian prejudices and is rigorously defending the interests of its own small organization, thus undermining the sacred tasks of the current War of Resistance Against Japan and national reconstruction. According to the firm prejudices of the CCP, the anti-Japanese national united front is but a temporary agglomeration of two or more political bodies representing different class interests in accordance with their varying social bases. They say such things as "The KMT is a party representing the landlord and bourgeois classes; the CCP is a party representing the proletariat; and their interests are fundamentally incompatible." Here lies the root for the repetition of past history. The CCP's recent propaganda has often used such expressions as "common leadership, common responsibility, common development, common program," which are nothing but outdated thinking with regard to striving for leadership power and completely lack the far-sighted spirit of assuming responsibility for defending the national interests. Its real goal is to preserve its own strength and to maintain the special position of the Border Region government and some guerrilla regions in order to seek expansion gradually in the future. The War of Resistance Against Japan and cooperation are but propaganda means to attain such a goal. According to the CCP, the so-called national united front should exclude all those anti-Japanese elements whose opinions differ from its own and should overthrow them all. The so-called cooperation demands that it be allowed to spread erroneous and absurd propaganda in all places under the Nationalist government, while the Northern Shensi Border Region is under a news blackout even more complete than the foreign concessions. Does the CCP think that everyone can be deceived? It is the humble opinion of this writer that if the gentlemen of the CCP admit the extreme need for unity in both purpose and will for the War of Resistance and national reconstruction in the face of the current serious national crisis, they should resolutely forsake these prejudices and methods, and should sincerely lay all their cards on the table for the whole nation to see. It is never too late to mend the fold even after the sheep have gone astray.

According to the above analysis, this writer hereby makes the following suggestions on the basis of the fundamental viewpoints of the War of Resistance Against Japan and national reconstruction, and hopes that members of the CCP will give them their well-deserved consideration.

1. CCP members ought to support the campaign of resistance against Japan and national reconstruction led by Mr. Chiang, in recognition of the principle that the national interests are above everything else. They

ought to practice the "Three Principles of the People" unreservedly, keeping their actions in conformity with their words; they ought no longer to indulge in propaganda and organization in violation of this. On this basis, CCP members ought to abandon Party prejudices, eliminate differences, and advance hand in hand with KMT members under the leadership of Mr. Chiang.

2. Under whatever circumstances, there should be absolute unity of the power of the State and the Army. The Eighth Route Army, well known for its bravery in fighting the enemy, has been greatly acclaimed by our fellow countrymen. It is hoped that CCP members will radically eliminate its prejudices against the "Anti-Japanese Allied Army," and turn the Eighth Route Army into a National army. In this way, the forces of the War of Resistance Against Japan and national reconstruction will be strengthened, eliminating all unnecessary worries and anxieties, and great benefit will be achieved through exchange of experiences in the course of amalgamation. The Border Region should not be regarded as a CCP base, nor should it be turned into a special area, with its own laws, like a carved up possession of the warlords, confined in its own enclosure and rejecting all those alien to itself. In a word, there is no need for the Border Region government to exist at present. It ought to return its political power to the Nationalist government, in order to inspire the confidence of the whole world. The guerrilla regions under the leadership of the CCP should also obey the orders of the Nationalist government, to give full play to their role in the War of Resistance Against Japan.

3. The CCP should put into effect the foreign policy of the Nationalist government, proceeding from the stand of the nation.

The above constitutes what this writer considers to be the concrete content of his previous statement on "further unity of purpose and will."

This writer has been deeply involved in the history of the CCP. The experiences and lessons of the past twenty years have enabled him to understand still more profoundly the error in the CCP's policy. At a time when the nation is in mortal danger, particularly since the outbreak of the War of Resistance Against Japan, this writer has been reluctant to be part of this erroneous policy and to allow it to continue to exist. Looking back to the summer of the twenty-fourth year of the Chinese Republic [1935], this writer recalls that differences of opinion between Mao Tse-tung and this writer arose when the First Front Army, led by Mao Tse-tung, and the Fourth Front Army, led by this writer, met in western Szechwan. According to the opinion of Mao Tse-tung and his followers, the Long March had scored a victory, and they proposed to go north to Shensi to form the Szechwan-Shensi-Kansu base and to establish once more the so-called Central Government of the Chinese Soviet Republic.

According to the opinion of this writer, the Long March was a failure, and the prospect for achieving victory first in one or more provinces had become a thing of the past. This writer proposed that the first thing to do was to secure a truce with the Nationalist armies in the western Szechwan and Sikang region or in the region of northwestern Kansu and then to strive for the realization of the principle of resistance to Japan with the whole nation united as one. As a result of the differences between these two opinions, the CC of the CCP was split. The dispute gradually waned with the Comintern's decision in December of the same year concerning the principle of the anti-Japanese national united front, and eventually the First, Second, and Fourth Front armies met in northern Shensi.

This writer arrived in northern Shensi just ten days before the Sian Incident, which was the result of the CCP's propaganda on the "anti-Japanese and anti-Chiang" proposal, which was essentially a military plot in which this writer had no part beforehand. After the outbreak of the Sian Incident, it was natural for the leaders of the CCP in Yen-an to make impulsive proposals. The person who was particularly impulsive was someone other than this writer; a fact which can be verified. The principle of peaceful settlement, which was later adopted, was unanimously approved by this writer and other leaders of the CCP. Moreover, it is also a fact that the principle of an anti-Japanese national united front enabled this writer and Mao Tse-tung and his followers to come closer to each other in their views. From this it can be seen that what the documents made public by the CCP say about this writer having resolutely advocated civil war at that time is an outright rumor with ulterior motives. This writer had expressed complete approval of the policy of an anti-Japanese national united front in principle, and had held that only thorough implementation of that policy could save the nation; this writer had held that the CCP's implementation of the policy at that time was far from adequate.

The policy of a united front had brought this writer closer to Mao Tse-tung and his followers in their views; but the deeply prejudiced and ostentatious way in which Mao Tse-tung and his followers had implemented the policy greatly dissatisfied this writer. Many disputes arose between this writer and Mao Tse-tung and his followers, particularly after the launching of the War of Resistance Against Japan, over their spirit of maintaining independence and of setting up separate holdings in disregard for the interests of the nation. Hence the resolute departure from Yen-an for Wuhan. This was an honest and forthright act, based entirely on a firm belief in united action for national salvation. It should hardly have aroused the worry and anxiety of the members of the CCP. Yet, without making a thoroughgoing investigation, the leadership of the CCP wantonly attacked and unreasonably slandered this writer's positive step in participating in the War of Resistance Against Japan and national reconstruction, giving full play to its unstatesmanlike, narrow-minded, selfish, and sinister propaganda, with the aim of suppressing self-criticism inside the CCP and assuming a hostile stance towards all elements who support the Nationalist government's leadership and are eager to take part in the War of Resistance Against Japan and national reconstruction. All this can be regarded as evidence that the CCP lacks sincerity in maintaining a policy of unity for the sake of the War of Resistance Against Japan. As to the various illegitimate attempts to kidnap this writer, they were but irrational actions perpetrated by a few people, including Ch'en (Wang Ming), Chou, and Chin. Thinking people will form their just opinions on this, and no further arguments are necessary.

In a word, this writer has devoted himself to national salvation since he was twenty years old, with the sole aim of remedying the weakened state of the nation. For almost twenty years this writer has dedicated himself to the revolution. Naturally, he has to be responsible to some extent for not having been able to correct in good time the policy of the CCP. But all words and deeds throughout his career have been clearly seen and heard by his fellow countrymen, and his recent action has stemmed purely from fervent patriotism. For the sake of the members of the CCP, and of the Chinese revolution, this writer has sincerely spoken without reserve on his views. It is hoped that the Chinese people will give this statement its close attention and that the members of the CCP will awaken and correct the mistakes in the general current policy of the CCP, in a spirit of self-criticism, abandoning the nonsensical practice of concealing their faults and glossing over their mistakes, and will make their best efforts for the War of Resistance Against Japan and national reconstruction in accordance with the principle of putting the nation above all else; thus the great cause of the Chinese revolution may succeed in a short time. In that case, it will not only be a blessing for this writer as an individual, but will also benefit the entire nation.

Dated May 6, the Twenty-seventh
Year of the Chinese Republic (1938)

NOTES

Chapter 1

1. There were two opinions regarding the route for our southward movement towards Kwangtung. One favored a movement through Fu-chou and Jui-chin in eastern Kiangsi to T'ung-chiang; it was accepted by the Uprising Force. The other one, proposed by Chou I-ch'un, favored a movement via the highway along the Kan River through Chang-shu, Chi-chou, and Kan-chou. See Chou I-ch'un's report contained in "The Ashes of Defeat" by C. Martin Wilbur, in *China Quarterly* (English version), no. 2 (1964).

2. Kuo Liang and Ch'en Yin-lin were among the peasant-movement leaders in Hunan and Hupeh who made such a proposal. However, it was not recorded in documents, because their voices were not very powerful at that time.

3. According to *The Autobiography of Ts'ai T'ing-chieh* (Hong Kong: Freedom *Tenthly Magazine* Publishing Agency, 1946), I, 220, those CCP members including Fan Meng-sheng were assisted with money and sent away. However, the fact is that Fan Meng-sheng was missing from that time on. The author cannot confirm whether those men were sent away or killed.

4. The so-called A-B League was a small, clandestine anti-Communist organization of the KMT in Kiangsi. It was led by Tuan Hsi-p'eng, who was assigned to Kiangsi by Chiang Kai-shek to carry out a party reorganization there. According to those who used to be members of that organization, Tuan Hsi-p'eng inaugurated organization of the so-called A Corps and B Corps in order to unite the anti-Communist organizations in Kiangsi. The A Corps was composed of people holding high positions or prestige, while the B Corps was composed of ordinary people. Therefore, the letters A and B did not have any particular meaning. However, "A-B" was later construed as an abbreviation of "Anti-Bolshevik" by the common people because it was an anti-Communist organization. In his article "The Danger of Right-leaning in the Present Revolution," in no. 190 of *Hsiang Tao* (Guide Weekly), P'eng Shu-chih had this to say: "Tuan Hsi-p'eng has organized a small, clandestine organization with the KMT in Kiangsi. It has its own platform and regulations, and the name of 'S-M.'" The author has been unable to confirm whether "S-M" was an alias of the "A-B League" or whether it was a separate organization.

5. Hu Hua, ed., *Chung-kuo hsin min-chu chu-i ko-ming shih ch'ang k'o tzu-liao* (Reference materials on the new democratic Chinese revolution), pp. 191-223.

6. See "A Letter of the August Seventh Meeting to All CCP Members."

7. *Ibid.*

8. *Ibid.*

9. The disciplinary actions taken by this enlarged meeting were as follows: (a) T'an P'ing-shan, serving as Minister of Agricultural Affairs in the Nationalist government, acted without authorization from the Party, joined Teng Yen-ta in organizing a third party to oppose CCP Central Headquarters, asked Wang Ching-wei to grant him a leave without prior permission from CCP Central Headquarters, criticized the CCP's policy in his conversation with Wang Ching-wei's representative Ch'en Ch'un-p'u, went to Kiukiang and Nanchang to propa-

gandize for the third party in defiance of a Party order requesting him to go
to Russia, and opposed the policy of settling accounts with oppressive landlords and confiscating their land. Therefore, he should be dismissed from the
CCP. (b) Chang Kuo-t'ao, assigned by the CSC to direct the Nanchang Uprising, failed to carry out the order, even opposing it after arriving in Kiukiang,
advocated cooperation with Chang Fa-k'uei, and opposed the policy of land
confiscation after the outbreak of the Nanchang Uprising. His violation of the
policy of Central Headquarters has caused adverse effect on CCP members in
this province and also on the Revolutionary Committee. Therefore, he should
be dismissed from his positions as alternate member of the Politburo and member of the CEC. (c) The Front Committee has made a big mistake; therefore
all of its members are hereby given a warning. Hsü K'e-ying shall be placed
under surveillance for a year because he oppressed the workers, made unnecessary arrests, and killed three civilians when he was the chief of the Public
Security Bureau of Swatow. All of the members of the Kwangtung Provincial
Committee of the Southern Bureau are hereby given a warning because they
made such mistakes as failing to understand our slogans, failure to move the
people to action, and resorting only to military movements. P'eng Kung-ta, Mao
Tse-tung, Yi Li-jung, and Hsia Ming-han are dismissed from their positions as
members of the Hunan Provincial Committee. In addition, P'eng Kung-ta is
dismissed from the position of alternate member of the Politburo and is placed
under surveillance for six months. Mao Tse-tung was assigned to Hunan to
reorganize the Party organization and direct the Autumn Crop Uprising after
the August Seventh Emergency Meeting. He was actually the leader of the
Hunan Provincial Committee. Therefore, he should be held responsible for the
mistakes in Party affairs in Hunan, and should be dismissed from the position of
alternate member of the Politburo. (d) The Special Committee of Northern
Hupeh violated the order of Central Headquarters; all of its members are
hereby given a warning. Lu Shen-shih, serving as secretary of the Special
Committee, is dismissed from the CC because he failed to work for the peasant
movement and because his policy and action were based on military opportunism. (e) Fu Kuo-chih of the Southern Hupeh Action Committee shall be placed
under surveillance for six months. (f) Wang Jo-fei is given a warning because
of his wrong direction. (g) Yang P'ao-an is dismissed from the Central Control
Committee.

10. This was the first time that I heard of Neumann.
11. In September, 1927, the KMT set up in Nanking a Central Special Committee
to act for both the CEC and the Central Control Committee. Some of the CC
members of the KMT thought it a breach of the Party constitution which might
cause disorder and trouble, and so they proposed the convening of the Fourth
Plenum of the Central Executive and Central Control committees of the Second
CC. At that time, Li Chi-shen was serving as chairman of the Kwangtung
Political Branch of the Special Committee. When Chang Fa-k'uei led his force
back to Kwangtung, he said that he was protecting the Party and supporting
the proposal to convene the Fourth Plenum. At the same time he surrounded
and disarmed Li Chi-shen's troops in the Canton, Hu-men area, and deployed
his force to Chao-ch'ing, Tu-ch'eng, and Hui-chou to prevent Li Chi-shen's

counterattack. Li was compelled to leave Kwangtung. This is a brief account of the so-called Party-Protection War.

12. For detailed information concerning those foreign warships (*USS Sacramento* and *HMS Marion?*) see the article "A Brief History of the Canton Commune," in the July 1, 1951, *Southern Daily* of Canton.

13. I and other leaders of the Nanchang Uprising were wanted by the Nanking government, with a bounty of 50,000 yuan apiece.

14. See Ch'en Tu-hsiu's "A Letter to All CCP Members."

Chapter 2

1. See the political resolution of the Sixth Congress of the CCP. For the full text see Hu Hua, ed., *Chung-kuo hsin min-chu chu-i ko-ming shih ch'ang k'o tzu-liao*, pp. 224-26.

2. *Ibid.*

3. *Ibid.*

4. Karl Radek wrote *History of the Chinese Revolutionary Movement,* a translation of which was made by K'e Jen and published by the New Universe Bookstore, Shanghai, in 1929. In his book Radek made a relatively detailed analysis of the Chinese social structure. It is worth referring to.

5. See Stalin, "A Talk with Sun Yat-sen University Students," in his *Problems of the Chinese Revolution* (Shih Chih, trans.; Contemporary Publishing House, 1949), pp. 44-76.

6. Reference to the so-called 28 Bolsheviks or 28 Russian Returned Students is to the twenty-eight Chinese students at Sun Yat-sen University who supported Mif's leadership, the most famous of whom were Ch'en Shao-yü, Ch'in Pang-hsien, Chang Wen-t'ien, and Wang Chia-hsiang.

7. The Nanking government occupied Peking on June 8, 1928.

8. Before leaving for Moscow in 1927, Soong Ch'ing-ling issued a statement in Shanghai dated August 22. In Moscow, on September 6, she issued another public statement. For the texts of the two statements, see her *Struggling for New China* (1952 ed., Peking), pp. 8-11 and 14-16.

9. See Ch'en Tu-hsiu's "Letter to All Comrades of the Party," dated December 10, 1929.

Chapter 3

1. For the complete text of the resolution of the Fourth Plenum of the CCP see "A Collection of Reactionary Documents of Red Bandits," compiled by Nanchang Headquarters, II, 424-34.

2. Chang K'ai-yün was an overseas Chinese residing in Russia. After joining the Russian Communist Party, he transferred his membership to the Chinese Communist Party. He was well liked by Safarov. I knew Chang personally. He worked in the CCP's Northern Bureau for a while. After the failure of the 1927 Revolution, he became a noted anti-Communist in the North.

3. See the Political Resolution of the Sixth Congress of the CCP, *in* Hu Hua, ed., *Chung-kuo hsin min-chu chu-i ko-ming shih ch'ang k'o tzu-liao*, pp. 224-46.

4. In addition, the mobile units of Fang Chih-min in northeastern Kiangsi and Hsiao K'o on the Hunan-Kiangsi border held certain areas for short periods during their guerrilla operations.
5. This refers to the Fut'ien Incident.

Chapter 4

1. Ho-k'ou is located forty li west of Huang-an. It was an important town of Huang-p'o.
2. Chin-chia-chai is 120 li southwest of the Liu-an district of Anhwei Province. It is connected with the Shang-ch'eng district of Honan Province.
3. Ma-fou, also named Ma-fou-chen, was ninety li southwest of the Liu-an district of Anhwei Province.
4. This is a popular way of saying to escape from the fires of war and rebellion.
5. It was said that Ku Kou-tzu was later killed by Chiang Kai-shek; this was probably because Chiang had regarded Ku's principle of "safeguarding the region and insuring peace for the people" as a form of assertion of independence by occupying some part of the land.
6. This meant putting into one's private pocket the money and other effects acquired through struggling against the local tyrants.
7. Previously many peasant families had loaned their grains to the Red Army; part of this was now repaid by the Soviet government. The peasants in the Red areas all changed to two meals of congee and one meal of cooked rice a day.
8. This was calculated on the basis of labor power, and was supplementary to the method of calculation on the basis of harvest yield. In practice this method was highly flexible, the assessment being made by the village land committee according to the needs of each family and the strength of its labor force.
9. Details about the agricultural graduated taxation system adopted for the Oyüwan area were published in Circular No. 7 of the Oyüwan Area Soviet Government which is contained in *Red Flag Weekly*, No. 27, December 17, 1931.
10. I do not have with me a copy of the provisional principles of organization. Please refer to the article in No. 27 of *Red Flag Weekly* entitled "The Vigorous Development of the Soviet Movement in China," which is about this provisional outline of organizational principles.

Chapter 5

1. This figure came from a communique issued by Tang Shih-tsun, and it may be somewhat exaggerated. But even if half that figure was intended, it would be an amazing number.

Chapter 6

1. I separated from Chu Teh at the time of the Nanchang Uprising in 1927, when we were at San-ho-pa in Mei-hsien, Kwangtung Province. After that, he led some one thousand men to wage guerrilla warfare on the borders between Kwangtung and Fukien provinces. It was eight years until we met again here.

2. In December, 1933, the troops of Sheng Shih-ts'ai of Sinkiang retreated back to Ti-hua. Ma Chung-ying then issued a declaration in a telegram supporting Liu Wen-lung as chairman and demanding that Sheng Shih-ts'ai get out of Ti-hua. The war to put down the rebellion of Ma Chung-ying was launched by Sheng Shih-ts'ai. It lasted till February, 1934, when Sheng Shih-ts'ai finally defeated Ma Chung-ying with the help of the Soviet Union.

3. The Chinese edition of Lenin's "On the Slogan 'European Federation'" can be found in *Selected Works of Lenin* (1949 ed., Moscow: Foreign Languages Publishing House), I, 901-4.

4. For the declaration of the Second Congress of the CCP, see Hu Hua, ed., *Chung-kuo hsin min-chu chu-i ko-ming shih ch'ang k'o tzu-liao*, pp. 69-84.

5. When Liu Pang defeated the Ching dynasty (about 207 B.C.) and entered Hsien-yang, he was aware that his strength was far inferior to that of Hsiang Yu. He turned his troops back to wait for Hsiang Yu, who, upon hearing that Liu Pang had conquered Kuan-chung, actually came with a large army to Hsin-feng and invited Liu Pang to a feast at Hung-men. During the feast, one of his commanders, Hsiang Chuang, entertained the guests with a sword dance, intending to kill Liu Pang at the right moment. It was a scene of suspense and thrills, but Liu Pang managed to escape in the end. This is a brief account of the "Hung-men feast."

6. For the text of the "August First Declaration" see Hu Hua, ed., *Chung-kuo hsin min-chu chu-i ko-ming shih ch'ang k'o tzu-liao*, pp. 263-69.

Chapter 7

1. At that time the organization of the cultural recreation team was formed by absorbing common soldiers, but the supervisors were mostly political workers of the former First Front Army.

2. The number of men in the troops of Mao Tse-tung and others that remained after their arrival in northern Shensi was never made public officially. According to Edgar Snow's *Red Star over China* (1st rev. and enlarged ed.: New York, 1968, p. 204), the figure was "fewer than 20,000," which was evidently an exaggeration. The figure I used was reported to me by comrades when I later arrived in northern Shensi; it is closer to the true figure.

3. I do not recall the exact date of Liu's telegram, but it was during the last few days of 1935 or the first few of 1936.

4. The resolution of the Second Congress of the CCP states: "For the immediate interests of the workers and poor peasants, the CCP guides the workers to help with the democratic revolutionary movement and makes the workers and poor peasants form a democratic united front with the petty bourgeoisie. . . ." (For the full text see Hu Hua, ed., *Chung-kuo hsin min-chu chu-i ko-ming shih ch'ang k'o tzu-liao*, pp. 69-84.)

5. I do not recall clearly who the person was that went in the first place; it was probably Yeh Chien-ying. Later, Chou En-lai acted as representative.

6. Pao Cheng was an official of the Sung dynasty who was famous for his staunchness and integrity. During the reign of Emperor Jen Tsung, he was appointed subchancellor to the Imperial Council at Lung-tao-ko and later was mayor of

Kai-feng-fu for several terms. He was a person well known to every woman and child.

7. Edgar Snow, *Red Star over China* (1st rev. and enlarged ed.: New York, 1968), pp. 293-304.

8. Tai Chi-ying, who was from Hupeh, was a member of the Provincial Committee of the CCP in the Oyüwan region and political commissar of the Red Twenty-seventh Army. Nieh Hung-chun, also from Hupeh, apparently was director of the political department of the Red Twenty-seventh Army.

Chapter 8

1. In my open letter to the people of China in 1938, I mentioned that I had arrived in northern Shensi ten days before the Sian Incident; that was December 2.

2. For details of the December Ninth Movement, read "The December Ninth Movement," in *A Collection of Historical Materials on Modern Chinese History* (Peking: People's Publishing House, 1954).

3. For the text of the telegram issued by Chang Hsueh-liang, Yang Hu-ch'eng, and some ten other commanders and officers on the "Double Twelve" [Dec. 12], see "The Chiang Kai-shek I Know," by Feng Yü-hsiang (2nd ed.; Hong Kong: Cultural Supply House, 1949), pp. 49-50.

4. The diplomatic relationship between the Soviet Union and the KMT had improved somewhat before the Sian Incident. This point has been discussed by David Dallin in his book *Soviet Russia and the Far East* (New Haven, Conn.: Yale University Press, 1948), chap. 5. At the time of the Sian Incident, the attitudes of Great Britain, the United States, and the Soviet Union in their relations with the Far East had gradually been approaching one another. This could be verified from Wang Ming's words.

5. The Anti-Japanese Military and Political Academy had been called the Red Army School while it was in Pao-an. The new title was adopted officially in Yen-an. The Academy had several sections: (1) A course for Red Army cadres; (2) a training course for anti-Japanese youths from KMT regions; and (3) technical training courses, including driving, signals, engineering, public health, and so forth. In mid-January, 1937, the students in the Red Army cadres' course exceeded eight hundred, more than half of whom were cadres from the Fourth Front Army.

6. Chang Chung was a member of the CC of the KMT, a mediator between Chiang Kai-shek and Soviet Russia and the CCP, who knew Russian.

7. These conditions were the four points in the Resolution on Annihilation of Red Trouble approved by the Third Plenum of the Fifth Central Committee of the KMT (for text see *Eastern Magazine,* vol. 4, no. 6, Commercial Press, Shanghai).

8. Ah Q is the hero in Lu Hsun's famous work *Ah Q.*

9. Kou-chien was the famous Prince of Yueh in the period of the Warring States, who avenged the kingdom of Wu after suffering disgrace. The Chinese proverb about "sleeping on faggots and tasting gall" derives from his story.

10. See *Selected Works of Mao Tse-tung,* I, 246.

Chapter 9

1. For an outline of Chiang Kai-shek's speech at Lu-shan, see Chang Chi-chun, *Outline of Party History* (1st ed.; Wen-wu Kungying She, 1952), III, 1143-46.
2. For the text of the CCP's declaration on cooperation between the KMT and the CCP, see Hu Hua, ed., *Chung-kuo hsin min-chu chu-i ko-ming shih ch'ang k'o tzu-liao,* pp. 354-56.
3. After defeat of the West Wing troops, Hsü Hsiang-ch'ien had returned to Yen-an sometime before July 7, 1937, having undergone an extremely dangerous and difficult journey.
4. For text, see Hu Hua, ed., *Chung-kuo hsin min-chu chu-i ko-ming shih ch'ang k'o tzu-liao,* pp. 356-59.

LIST OF CHINESE NAMES

This list includes the names of all Chinese referred to in this volume for which the Chinese characters could be ascertained.

詹才芳	Chan Ts'ai-fang	張宗遜	Chang Tsung-hsün
張金彪	Chang Chin-piao	張聞天	Chang Wen-t'ien
張琴秋	Chang Ch'in-ch'iu	張雲逸	Chang Yün-yi
張　沖	Chang Chung	趙世炎	Chao Shih-yen
張發奎	Chang Fa-k'uei	趙　雲	Chao Yün
張學良	Chang Hsueh-liang	陳昌浩	Ch'en Ch'ang-hao
張輝讚（鑽）Chang Hui-tsan		陳繼承	Ch'en Chi-ch'eng
張開運	Chang K'ai-yün	陳濟棠	Ch'en Chi-tang
張廣才	Chang Kuang-ts'ai	陳喬年	Ch'en Ch'iao-nien
張國燾	Chang Kuo-t'ao	陳　春	Ch'en Ch'un
張慕陶	Chang Mu-t'ao	陳春圃	Ch'en Ch'un-p'u
章伯鈞	Chang Po-chun	陳　賡	Ch'en Keng
張曙時	Chang Shu-shih	陳果夫	Ch'en Ko-fu
張太雷	Chang T'ai-lei	陳銘樞	Ch'en Ming-shu
張作霖	Chang Tso-lin	陳紹禹	Ch'en Shao-yü

597

陳世才	Ch'en Shih-ts'ai	秦光遠	Ch'in Kuan-yuan
陳潭秋	Ch'en T'an-ch'iu	秦邦憲	Ch'in Pang-hsien
陳調元	Ch'en Tiao-yüan	周純全	Chou Ch'un-ch'üan
陳鐵錚 (K'ung Yuan)	Ch'en T'ieh-cheng (K'ung Yuan)	周恩來	Chou En-lai
陳獨秀	Ch'en Tu-hsiu	周　興	Chou Hsing
陳延年	Ch'en Yen-nien	周諢光	Chou Hun-yuan
陳　毅	Ch'en Yi	周逸群	Chou I-ch'un
陳蔭林	Ch'en Yin-lin	周　昆	Chou Kun
陳　郁	Ch'en Yü	周士第	Chou Shih-ti
陳原道	Ch'en Yuan-tao	周達文	Chou Ta-wen
陳　雲	Ch'en Yün	周文雄 (雍)	Chou Wen-jung
鄭位三	Cheng Wei-san	周　揚	Chou Yang
成仿吾	Ch'eng Fang-wu	朱　瑞	Chu Jui
吉鴻昌	Chi Hung-chang	朱　光	Chu Kuang
姜濟寰	Chiang Chi-huan	朱寶庭	Chu Pao-t'ing
蔣經國	Chiang Ching-kuo	朱培德	Chu P'ei-te
江　青	Chiang Ch'ing	朱紹良	Chu Shao-liang
蔣介石	Chiang Kai-shek	朱　德	Chu Teh
蔣鼎文	Chiang Ting-wen	朱務善	Chu Wu-shan
錢大鈞	Ch'ien Ta-chun	瞿秋白	Ch'ü Ch'iu-pai
秦怡君	Ch'in I-chun	屈　武	Ch'ü Wu

范孟聲	Fan Meng-sheng	何紹南	Ho Shao-nan
方志敏	Fang Chih-min	何叔衡	Ho Shu-heng
馮玉祥	Feng Yü-hsiang	賀子珍	Ho Tzu-ch'en
傅鐘	Fu Chung	何畏	Ho Wei
傅國志	Fu Kuo-chih	夏曦	Hsia Hsi
傅連璋	Fu Lien-chang	夏明漢	Hsia Ming-han
符定一	Fu Ting-yi	夏斗寅	Hsia Tou-yin
郝夢麟	Hao Men-lin	向忠發	Hsiang Chung-fa
賀昌	Ho Ch'ang	項英	Hsiang Ying
何長工	Ho Ch'ang-kung	蕭之楚	Hsiao Chih-ch'u
何基澧	Ho Chi-li	蕭克	Hsiao K'o
何家興	Ho Chia-hsing	蕭炳章	Hsiao Ping-chang
賀芝華	Ho Chih-hua	許繼盛	Hsü Chi-sheng
賀敬齋	Ho Ching-tsai	徐景唐	Hsü Ching-t'ang
何柱國	Ho Chu-kuo	徐海東	Hsü Hai-tung
何香凝	Ho Hsiang-ning	徐錫根	Hsü Hsi-ken
賀國光	Ho Kuo-kuang	徐向前	Hsü Hsiang-ch'ien
何來	Ho Lai	徐光英	Hsü Kuang-ying
賀龍	Ho Lung	徐立清	Hsü Li-ch'ing
何孟雄	Ho Meng-hsiung	許白昊	Hsü Pai-hao
何葆貞	Ho Pao-chen	許世友	Hsü Shih-yu

徐 特 立	Hsü T'e-li	關 麟 徵	Kuan Lin-cheng
徐 庭 瑤	Hsü T'ing-yao	鄺 繼 勛	K'uang Chi-hsün
薛 岳	Hsueh Yueh	龔 飲 冰	Kung Yin-ping
胡 適 之	Hu Shih-chih	孔 荷 施	K'ung Ho-ch'ung
胡 宗 南	Hu Tsung-nan	孔 原	K'ung Yuan
花 廣 奇	Hua Kuang-ch'i	郭 洪 濤	Hung-t'ao
黃 超	Huang Ch'ao	郭 亮	Kuo Liang
黃 杰	Huang Chieh	郭 沫 若	Kuo Mo-jo
黃 警 魂	Huang Ching-hun	郭 述 申	Kuo Shu-shen
黃 公 略	Huang Kung-lüeh	郭 天 民	Kuo T'ien-min
黃 紹 雄	Huang Shao-hsiung	李 濟 琛	Li Chi-shen
任 弼 時	Jen Pi-shih	李 家 鈺	Li Chia-yu
凱 豐	K'ai Feng	李 劍 如	Li Ch'ien-ju
康 生	K'ang Sheng (Ch'ao Yün)	李 求 實	Li Ch'iu-shih
高 俊 亭	Kao Ching-t'ing	李 卓 然	Li Cho-jan
高 崗	Kao Kang	李 卓 如	Li Cho-ju
高 語 罕	Kao Yu-han	李 竹 聲	Li Chu-sheng
顧 谷 宜	Ku Ku-yi	李 福 林	Li Fu-lin
顧 順 章	Ku Shun-chang	李 先 念	Li Hsien-nien
關 向 應	Kuan Hsiang-ying	李 克 農	Li K'e-nung
		李 立 三	Li Li-san

李明瑞	Li Ming-jui	劉 峙	Liu Chih
李明端	Li Ming-tuan	劉景範	Liu Ching-fan
李默庵	Li Mo-en	劉崇雲	Liu Chung-yun
李伯釗	Li Po-chao	劉 湘	Liu Hsiang
勵世鼎	Li Shih-ting	劉仁靜	Liu Jen-ching
李大釗	Li T̄ hao	劉茂恩	Liu Mou-en
李 特	Li Teh	劉伯誠	Liu Po-ch'eng
李宗仁	Li Tsung-jen	劉少奇	Liu Shao-ch'i
李維漢	Li Wei-han	劉存厚	Liu Ts'un-hou
李延年	Li Yen-nien	劉子丹	Liu Tzu-tan (Liu Chih-tan)
梁冠英	Liang Kuan-ying	劉文輝	Liu Wen-hui
梁漱溟	Liang Sou-ming	劉文龍	Liu Wen-lung
廖 震	Liao Chen	劉 英	Liu Ying
廖乾五	Liao Ch'ien-wu	羅章龍	Lo Chang-lung
廖划平	Liao Hua-p'ing	羅 山	Lo Chiao
林祖涵	Lin Chu-han	羅 覺	Lo Chueh
林 彪	Lin Piao	羅 漢	Lo Han
林伯渠	Lin Po-ch'ü	羅瑞卿	Lo Jui-ch'ing
林育南	Lin Yü-nan	羅 明	Lo Ming
林育英	Lin Yu-ying	羅炳輝	Lo Ping-hui
劉 琪	Liu Ch'i	羅世文	Lo Shih-wen

羅登賢	Lo Teng-hsien	彭述之	P'eng Shu-chih
羅澤洲	Lo Tse-chou	彭德懷	P'eng Te-huai
羅澤南	Lo Tze-nan	彭澤民	P'eng Tse-min
魯其昌	Lu Chi-chang	卜士奇	Po Shih-ch'i
盧福坦	Lu Fu-t'an	上官雲相	Shang Kuan-Yun-hsiang
盧漢	Lu Han	邵力子	Shao Li-tzu
陸沈時	Lu Shen-shih	沈澤民	Shen Tse-min
馬仲英	Ma Chung-ying	沈雁冰	Shen Yen-ping
馬鴻逵	Ma Hung-k'uei	盛世才	Sheng Shih-ts'ai
馬明芳	Ma Ming-fang	石友三	Shih Yu-shan
馬步芳	Ma Pu-fang	宋慶齡	Soong Ch'ing-ling
毛炳文	Mao Ping-wen	宋美齡	Soong Mei-ling
毛澤東	Mao Tse-tung	宋子文	T. V. Soong (Sung Tzu-wen)
莫文驊	Mo Wen-hua		
聶鴻鈞	Nieh Hung-chün	蘇兆徵	Su Chao-cheng
聶榮臻	Nieh Jung-chen	孫震	Sun Chen
白崇禧	Pai Ch'ung-hsi	孫科	Sun Fu
潘自力	P'an Tzu-li	孫連仲	Sun Lien-chung
抱扑	Pao P'u	孫蔚如	Sun Wei-ju
彭公達	P'eng Kung-ta	孫逸仙	Sun Yat-sen
彭湃	P'eng P'ai	戴繼（秀）英	Tai Chi-ying

譚 平 山	T'an P'ing-shan	段 錫 朋	Tuan Hsi-p'eng
唐 式 遵	Tang Shih-tsun	董 振 堂 (棠)	Tung Chen-t'ang
湯 恩 伯	T'ang En-po	董 必 武	Tung Pi-wu
唐 生 智	T'ang Sheng-chih	董 亦 湖	Tung Yi-hsiang
唐 天 際	T'ang T'ien-chi	萬 毅	Wan Yi
鄧 仲 夏	Teng Chung-hsia	王 稼 祥	Wang Chia-hsiang
鄧 發	Teng Fa	王 建 安	Wang Chien-an
鄧 錫 侯	Teng Hsi-hou	汪 精 衞	Wang Ching-wei
鄧 小 平	Teng Hsiao-p'ing	王 鈞	Wang Chün
鄧 演 達	Teng Yen-ta	王 仲 一	Wang Chung-yi
鄧 穎 超	Teng Ying-ch'ao	王 宏 坤	Wang Hung-k'un
田 頌 堯	T'ien Sung-yao	王 一 知	Wang I-chih
蔡 暢	Ts'ai Ch'ang	王 若 飛	Wang Jo-fei
蔡 和 森	Ts'ai Ho-sen	王 克 全	Wang K'e-ch'uan
蔡 申 熙	Ts'ai Shen-hsi	王 陵 基	Wang Ling-chi
蔡 樹 藩	Ts'ai Shu-fan	王 明	Wang Ming (Ch'en Shao-yü)
蔡 廷 鍇	Ts'ai T'ing-chieh	王 平 章	Wang P'ing-chang
曹 菊 和	Ts'ao Chü-ju	王 首 道	Wang Shou-tao
曾 鍾 聖	Tseng Chung-sheng	王 樹 聲	Wang Shu-sheng
左 權	Tso Ch'üan	汪 澤 愷	Wang Tse-k'ai
鄒 魯	Tsou Lu		

王 鑽 緒	Wang Tsuan-hsu	葉 季 壯	Yeh Chi-chuang
王 子 綱	Wang Tzu-kang	葉 劍 英	Yeh Chien-ying
王 維 周	Wang Wei-chou	葉 挺	Yeh T'ing
王 以 哲	Wang Yi-che	閻 錫 山	Yen Hsi-shan
衞 立 煌	Wei Li-huang	易 禮 容	Yi Li-jung
伍 修 權	Wu Hsiu-ch'üan	余 飛	Yü Fei
吳 鐵 城	Wu T'ieh-ch'eng	兪 秀 松	Yü Hsiu-sung
吳 玉 章	Wu Yu-chang	于 學 忠	Yu Hsueh-chung
揚 之 華	Yang Chih-hua	余 洒 度	Yu Sa-tu
揚 雲	Yang Hu	余 天 雲	Yu T'ien-yun
楊 虎 城	Yang Hu-ch'eng	兪 作 柏	Yü Tso-po
楊 匏 安	Yang P'ao-an	余 篤 三	Yü Tu-san
楊 森	Yang Sen	于 右 任	Yü Yu-jen
楊 尙 昆	Yang Shang-k'un	袁 達 時	Yuan Ta-shih
楊 騰 蛟	Yang Teng-wen	岳 維 峻	Yueh Wei-chün
揚 子 烈	Yang Tzu-lieh	惲 代 英	Yün Tai-ying
揚 殷	Yang Yin		

INDEX

Abbreviations:

C Chang Kuo-t'ao
CC Central Committee of Chinese Communist Party
CCP Chinese Communist Party
KMT Kuomintang (The Nationalist Party of China)

K •Chiu-ch'üan N I N G S I A

Chi-lien Shan A Ho-hsi SUI

Chang-yeh

Ta-hsueh Shan-tan •Corridor

Yung-ch'ang N

Ta-t'ung Tu-men-tzu •Wu-wei •I-t'iao-shan Yü-li

T S I N G H A I Ku-lang •Ching-t'ai

Ta-t'ung •Shih-fo-ssu Ching-pien•

Si-ning• T'ung-hsin-cheng •Yu-wang •An-pien

Huang Ho Ching-yüan• •Ta-la-ch'ih •Shan-cheng-pao

Ma-chu Hai-yüan• •Hung-te •Pao

•Lanchow •Huan-hsien

•Hsia-ho •Hui-ning •Chu-tzu-chen

Yangtze Ya-lung Ching-ning•

•P'ing-liang

Tung-wei

T'ien-shui S H E

Ch'ing-yang To

Chou-chih• Sian Lo

Tzu-wu-chen Shang-h

Ch'eng-ku Shan-yar

T I B E T Han Han-chung I N

Hsi-hsiang Y

n-chiang• •Pa-shan Mou

chung• Ch'ing-chiang-tu Po

§)Ts'ang-ch'i T'ung-chiang •Wan-yüar

-ang-chung •Hsüan-han

shan• Yün-yang

•Nan-ch'ung' Po

•Ch'u-hsien Wan-hsie

I N D I A -ho-k'ou Pa-t

Liang-shan

W A N H U

B •Tsun-yi

U C H O W

R

Y •Tu-shan

M

A

W A N G S I

A

INDO-CHINA